JAVA™
FOUNDATION
CLASSES

A Desktop Quick Reference

THE JAVA™ SERIES

Learning Java™

Java™ Threads

Java™ Network Programming

Database Programming with JDBC™ and Java™

Java™ Distributed Computing

Developing Java Beans™

Java™ Security

Java™ Cryptography

Java™ Swing

Java™ Servlet Programming

Java™ I/O

Java™ 2D Graphics

Enterprise JavaBeans™

Creating Effective JavaHelp™

Java™ and XML

Java™ Performance Tuning

Java™ Internationalization

JavaServer™ Pages

Java™ Native Methods

Java™ Message Service

Also from O'Reilly

Java™ in a Nutshell

Java™ Enterprise in a Nutshell

Java™ Foundation Classes in a Nutshell

Java™ Examples in a Nutshell

Jini™ in a Nutshell

Enterprise Java™ CD Bookshelf

JAVA™ FOUNDATION CLASSES

A Desktop Quick Reference

David Flanagan

O'REILLY®

Beijing • Cambridge • Farnham • Köln • Paris • Sebastopol • Taipei • Tokyo

Java™ Foundation Classes in a Nutshell

by David Flanagan

Copyright © 1999 O'Reilly & Associates, Inc. All rights reserved.

Published by O'Reilly & Associates, Inc., 101 Morris Street, Sebastopol, CA 95472.

Editor: Paula Ferguson

Production Editor: Nicole Arigo

Production Services: Nancy Crumpton

Printing History:

September 1999: First Edition.

December 2000: Java Library Set Casebound Edition.

ISBN: 1-56592-488-6 (softcover)
ISBN: 0-596-00113-4 (hardcover)
[C]

Table of Contents

Preface

This book is a desktop quick reference for Java™ programmers who are writing applications or applets that involve graphics or graphical user interfaces. The first part of the book is a fast-paced, "no fluff" introduction to the Java APIs that comprise the Java Foundation Classes, or JFC. These chapters are followed by a quick-reference section that succinctly details every class of those APIs.

This book complements the best-selling *Java in a Nutshell*. That volume introduces the Java programming language itself and provides an API quick reference for the core packages and classes of the Java platform. A third volume in the series, *Java Enterprise in a Nutshell*, covers the Java Enterprise APIs. Programmers working on server-side or enterprise applications will be interested in that book.

Contents of This Book

The first seven chapters of this book document the graphics and graphical user interface (GUI) APIs used in client-side Java programming. The chapters are:

Chapter 1: The Java Foundation Classes
Provides a quick introduction to the JFC and the APIs that comprise it.

Chapter 2: Swing and AWT Architecture
Explains the architecture used for graphical user interfaces built with the older Abstract Windowing Toolkit (AWT) and the new Swing API. The remaining chapters of the book assume an understanding of the fundamentals presented here.

Chapter 3: Swing Programming Topics
Introduces a number of the most important GUI components and application services provided by the Swing API.

Chapter 4: Graphics with AWT and Java 2D
>   Explains how to draw text and graphics. It introduces the AWT graphics API, used in Java 1.0 and Java 1.1, and the powerful new Java 2D API of Java 2.

Chapter 5: Printing
>   Covers how to draw text and graphics to a printer, using both the Java 1.1 and Java 2 printing APIs.

Chapter 6: Data Transfer
>   Explains how to enable data transfer between and within applications, using both cut-and-paste and drag-and-drop.

Chapter 7: Applets
>   Documents the Java applet API, which allows Java applets, or mini-applications, to run within web browsers.

These chapters provide enough information to get you started with each of the JFC APIs. The bulk of the book, however, is the API quick reference, Chapters 8 through 36, which is a succinct but detailed API reference formatted for optimum ease of use. Please be sure to read the *How To Use This Quick Reference* section, which appears at the beginning of the reference section. It explains how to get the most out of this book.

Related Books

O'Reilly & Associates publishes an entire series of books on Java programming. These books include *Java in a Nutshell* and *Java Enterprise in a Nutshell*, which, as mentioned earlier, are companions to this book.

A related reference work is the *Java Power Reference*. It is an electronic Java quick reference on CD-ROM that uses the *Java in a Nutshell* style. But since it is designed for viewing in a web browser, it is fully hyperlinked and includes a powerful search engine. It is wider in scope but narrower in depth than the *Java in a Nutshell* books. The *Java Power Reference* covers all the APIs of the Java 2 platform, plus the APIs of many standard extensions. But it does not include tutorial chapters on the various APIs, nor does it include descriptions of the individual classes.

You can find a complete list of Java books from O'Reilly & Associates at *http://java.oreilly.com/*. Books of particular interest to JFC programmers include the following:

Java Swing, by Robert Eckstein, Marc Loy, and Dave Wood
>   A complete guide to the Swing graphical user interface toolkit.

Java 2D Graphics, by Jonathan Knudsen
>   A comprehensive tutorial on the Java 2D API, from basic drawing techniques to advanced image processing and font handling.

Java AWT Reference, by John Zukowski
>   A complete reference manual (not a quick reference like this book) to the graphics and GUI features of the AWT. This book covers Java 1.0 and Java 1.1, and although some AWT features have been superseded by the Swing

---

and Java 2D APIs, the AWT is still the foundation for all graphics and graphical user interfaces in Java.

Exploring Java, by Pat Niemeyer and Joshua Peck
A comprehensive tutorial introduction to Java, with an emphasis on client-side Java programming.

Java Programming Resources Online

This book is a quick reference designed for speedy access to frequently needed information. It does not, and cannot, tell you everything you need to know about the Java Foundation Classes. In addition to the books listed earlier, there are several valuable (and free) electronic sources of information about Java programming.

Sun's main web site for all things related to Java is *http://java.sun.com/*. The web site specifically for Java developers is *http://developer.java.sun.com/*. Much of the content on this developer site is password protected, and access to it requires (free) registration.

Sun distributes electronic documentation for all Java classes and methods in its *javadoc* HTML format. Although this documentation is rough or outdated in places, it is still an excellent starting point when you need to know more about a particular Java package, class, method, or field. If you do not already have the *javadoc* files with your Java distribution, see *http://java.sun.com/docs/* for a link to the latest available version.

Sun also distributes its excellent *Java Tutorial* online. You can browse and download it from *http://java.sun.com/docs/books/tutorial/*. Developers who are using the Swing GUI toolkit should read "The Swing Connection," a periodically updated online newsletter devoted to Swing programming. It contains news and useful tutorial articles. You'll find it at *http://java.sun.com/products/jfc/tsc/*.

For Usenet discussion (in English) about Java, try the *comp.lang.java.programmer* and related *comp.lang.java.** newsgroups. You can find the very comprehensive *comp.lang.java.programmer* FAQ by Peter van der Linden at *http://www.afu.com/javafaq.htm*.

Finally, don't forget O'Reilly's Java web site. *http://java.oreilly.com/* contains Java news and commentary and a monthly tips-and-tricks column by O'Reilly Java author Jonathan Knudsen.

Examples Online

The examples in this book are available online and can be downloaded from the home page for the book at *http://www.oreilly.com/catalog/jfcnut*. You also may want to visit this site to see if any important notes or errata about the book have been published there.

Conventions Used in This Book

We use the following formatting conventions in this book:

Italic

> Used for emphasis and to signify the first use of a term. Italic is also used for commands, email addresses, web sites, FTP sites, file and directory names, and newsgroups.

Bold

> Occasionally used to refer to particular keys on a computer keyboard or to portions of a user interface, such as the **Back** button or the **Options** menu.

`Letter Gothic`

> Used in all Java code and generally for anything that you would type literally when programming, including keywords, data types, constants, method names, variables, class names, and interface names.

`Letter Gothic Oblique`

> Used for the names of function arguments and generally as a placeholder to indicate an item that should be replaced with an actual value in your program.

Franklin Gothic Book Condensed

> Used for the Java class synopses in the quick-reference section. This very narrow font allows us to fit a lot of information on the page without a lot of distracting line breaks. This font is also used for code entities in the descriptions in the quick-reference section.

Franklin Gothic Demi Condensed

> Used for highlighting class, method, field, property, and constructor names in the quick-reference section, which makes it easier to scan the class synopses.

Franklin Gothic Book Compressed Italic

> Used for method parameter names and comments in the quick-reference section.

Request for Comments

Please help us to improve future editions of this book by reporting any errors, inaccuracies, bugs, misleading or confusing statements, and even plain old typos that you find. Email your bug reports and comments to us at *bookquestions@oreilly.com*. Please also let us know what we can do to make this book more useful to you. We take your comments seriously and will try to incorporate reasonable suggestions into future editions.

Acknowledgments

This book is an outgrowth of the best-selling *Java in a Nutshell*. I'd like to thank all the readers who made that book a success and who wrote in with comments, suggestions, and praise.

The editor of this book, and of *Java in a Nutshell* before it, was Paula Ferguson. As usual, she's done a great job of keeping me on topic and made her best effort to keep me on schedule! Her careful and thoughtful editing has made this book a better one. Thanks, Paula.

This book had a number of high-powered technical reviewers. Jeanette Hung, of Sun Microsystems; Doug Felt and John Raley, both of IBM; and Jonathan Knudsen, author of O'Reilly's *Java 2D Graphics*, reviewed the Java 2D class descriptions. Jonathan also reviewed the Java 2D-related chapters. Marc Loy, coauthor of O'Reilly's *Java Swing* and course developer and technical trainer at Galileo Systems, LLC, reviewed all of the Swing-related material. This book is made much stronger by the valuable contributions of these reviewers. I alone must take responsibility for any errors that remain, of course.

The O'Reilly & Associates production team has done its usual fine work of creating a book out of the electronic files I submit. My thanks to them all. And a special thanks to Lenny Muellner and Chris Maden, who worked overtime to implement the new and improved format of the quick-reference section.

Finally, as always, my thanks and love to my partner Christie.

David Flanagan
http://www.davidflanagan.com
June 1999

PART I

Introducing the Java Foundation Classes

Part I is an introduction to the key APIs that comprise the Java Foundation Classes. These chapters provide enough information for you to get started using these APIs right away.

CHAPTER 1

The Java Foundation Classes

The Java Foundation Classes, or JFC, is a loose collection of standard Java APIs for client-side graphics, graphical user interfaces (GUIs), and related programming tasks. They are foundation classes in the sense that most client-side Java applications are built upon these APIs. This book covers the following APIs:

AWT

Although the most powerful and exciting features of the JFC were introduced in Version 1.2 of the Java 2 platform, the JFC also includes the graphics and GUI features of Java 1.0 and Java 1.1. These features are provided by the Abstract Windowing Toolkit (AWT). The graphics and GUI capabilities of the AWT are rudimentary, and many of them have been superseded by more advanced features in Java 1.2. Nevertheless, the AWT is the bedrock upon which more advanced JFC functionality is built.

In addition, there are certain situations in which you cannot take advantage of the new JFC functionality and must instead rely solely on the AWT. For example, common web browsers do not yet support Swing, so if you are writing applets, you have to use the AWT. Because of this, the graphics and GUI APIs of the AWT are discussed right along with the more powerful APIs introduced in Java 1.2.

Swing

Swing is an advanced GUI toolkit written in pure Java. It is built upon the AWT but provides many new GUI components and useful GUI-related application services. Swing offers a pluggable look-and-feel architecture that allows an application to be trivially configured either to display a platform-independent Java look-and-feel or to mimic the look-and-feel of the native operating system. Swing also includes an accessibility API that enables the use of assistive technologies, such as screen readers or screen magnifiers for the vision impaired. Many features of Swing are based on the pioneering design of the Netscape Internet Foundation Classes.

Swing is a core part of the Java 2 platform. It is also available, however, as an extension to Java 1.1.

Java 2D

Java 2D is the name for the state-of-the-art two-dimensional graphics API introduced in Java 1.2. Java 2D is built upon the AWT, but greatly expands on the graphics capabilities that were available in Java 1.0 and Java 1.1. Java 2D includes support for resolution independence, rotation, scaling and shearing of arbitrary graphics, antialiasing of text and graphics, alpha transparency, color compositing, and the use of the full range of fonts installed on the native system.

Printing

The ability to print text and graphics on a page is almost as important as the ability to draw text and graphics on the screen. Java 1.1 introduced simple printing capabilities as part of the AWT, and Java 1.2 includes a more powerful printing API as part of the JFC. This book describes both printing APIs.

Data transfer

An important feature of many client-side applications is the ability to allow user-directed data transfer within the application and between unrelated applications. There are two commonly used data transfer metaphors: cut-and-paste and drag-and-drop. Java 1.1 defined a basic data transfer framework and provided an API for cut-and-paste. Java 1.2 adds support for data transfer using the drag-and-drop metaphor.

Applets

The applet API allows a client-side program to run as an applet, or mini-application, within a web browser or some other form of applet viewer. Technically, the applet API is not part of the JFC, but it is a crucial piece of the client-side Java programming picture and is included in this book.

The rest of the chapters in Part I describe these APIs in far more detail. Read Chapter 2, *Swing and AWT Architecture*, first. After reading that chapter, you can read the remaining chapters in whatever order you prefer. The goal of each chapter is to introduce an API in enough detail so that you can begin to use it in your programs. While reading a chapter, you may find it helpful to refer to the quick-reference material in Part II of this book to find detailed API information on the individual classes you are reading about.

CHAPTER 2

Swing and AWT Architecture

The Abstract Windowing Toolkit (AWT) provides basic facilities for creating graphical user interfaces (GUIs), and also for drawing graphics, as we'll discuss in a later chapter. AWT has been a core part of Java since Java 1.0. The GUI features of AWT are layered on top of the native GUI system of the underlying platform. In other words, when you create a graphical push button with AWT, AWT creates a Windows push button, or a Macintosh push button, or a Motif push button, or whatever, depending on the platform on which the application is running. In Java 1.1, AWT was extended to allow the creation of "lightweight" GUI components that do not have corresponding native GUI components behind them.

Swing is a new GUI toolkit that is available as a core part of the Java 2 platform and also as an extension to Java 1.1. Swing is an extension of the AWT toolkit, not an entirely new toolkit. All of the GUI components provided by Swing are lightweight components, so they do not rely on the underlying native GUIs. The result is that Swing is more portable, making it much easier to write graphical applications that behave the same on all platforms. Swing is also larger and more comprehensive than AWT. In addition to a complete and powerful set of GUI components, Swing provides a number of utilities that make it easier to write graphical applications.

Swing offers a great step forward when compared to AWT. You should use Swing in all your Java 2 applications. You should also seriously consider using it as an extension for Java 1.1 applications. Unfortunately, at the time of this writing, common web browsers do not yet support Swing, so if you are writing applets, you should either run those applets under the Java Plug-in, or you should avoid the use of Swing and rely exclusively on the features of AWT. See Chapter 7, *Applets*, for more information on applets.

This chapter introduces the basic architecture used by both AWT and Swing. For more information on Swing and AWT, see *Java Swing*, by Robert Eckstein, Marc Loy, and Dave Wood (O'Reilly), and *Java AWT Reference*, by John Zukowski (O'Reilly), respectively.

A Simple Graphical User Interface

Example 2-1 is a simple program that uses Swing to create and display a graphical user interface. Figure 2-1 shows the GUI created by this program.

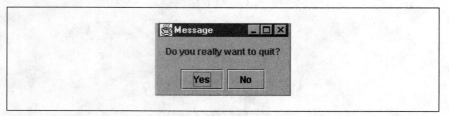

Figure 2-1: The GUI of the DisplayMessage program

The `DisplayMessage` program is designed for use in a shell script or batch file.* If you invoke the program on the command line with the text of a question, it displays the question to the user and waits for the user to click the **Yes** button or the **No** button. The program sets its exit code based on the user's response, so a shell script can examine this exit code to determine how the user responded. The program expects from one to three command-line arguments that specify the text of the question and the text for the "Yes" and "No" buttons, respectively. For example, you might invoke the program like this:

```
% java DisplayMessage "Do you really want to quit?" "Yes, Please", "No, Thanks"
```

The example illustrates step-by-step how to create a Swing GUI. Don't worry if you don't understand the details of this program yet. If you read it through once now to get the big picture, you can refer back to it as you read the sections that follow.

Example 2-1: Creating a Simple GUI with Swing

```java
import java.awt.*;               // AWT classes
import javax.swing.*;           // Swing components and classes
import javax.swing.border.*;    // Borders for Swing components
import java.awt.event.*;        // Basic event handling

public class DisplayMessage {
  public static void main(String[] args) {
    /*
     * Step 1: Create the components
     */
    JLabel msgLabel = new JLabel();        // Component to display the question
    JButton yesButton = new JButton();     // Button for an affirmative response
    JButton noButton = new JButton();      // Button for a negative response

    /*
     * Step 2: Set properties of the components
     */
    msgLabel.setText(args[0]);                          // The msg to display
```

---

* Because the Java Virtual Machine takes a long time to start up, it is not actually practical to use this program in a shell script. It is a useful example nevertheless.

Example 2-1: Creating a Simple GUI with Swing (continued)

```
    msgLabel.setBorder(new EmptyBorder(10,10,10,10));    // A 10-pixel margin
    yesButton.setText((args.length >= 2)?args[1]:"Yes"); // Text for yes button
    noButton.setText((args.length >= 3)?args[2]:"No");   // Text for no button


    /*
     * Step 3: Create containers to hold the components
     */
    JFrame win = new JFrame("Message");  // The main application window
    JPanel buttonbox = new JPanel();     // A container for the two buttons


    /*
     * Step 4: Specify LayoutManagers to arrange components in the containers
     */
    win.getContentPane().setLayout(new BorderLayout()); // Layout on borders
    buttonbox.setLayout(new FlowLayout());              // Layout left-to-right


    /*
     * Step 5: Add components to containers, with optional layout constraints
     */
    buttonbox.add(yesButton);            // Add yes button to the panel
    buttonbox.add(noButton);             // Add no button to the panel

    // add JLabel to window, telling the BorderLayout to put it in the middle
    win.getContentPane().add(msgLabel, "Center");

    // add panel to window, telling the BorderLayout to put it at the bottom
    win.getContentPane().add(buttonbox, "South");

    /*
     * Step 6: Arrange to handle events in the user interface
     */
    yesButton.addActionListener(new ActionListener() {  // Note: inner class
      // This method is called when the Yes button is clicked
      public void actionPerformed(ActionEvent e) { System.exit(0); }
    });

    noButton.addActionListener(new ActionListener() {   // Note: inner class
      // This method is called when the No button is clicked
      public void actionPerformed(ActionEvent e) { System.exit(1); }
    });

    /*
     * Step 7: Display the GUI to the user
     */
    win.pack();   // Set the size of the window based on its children's sizes
    win.show();   // Make the window visible
  }
}
```

Components

A graphical user interface is composed of individual building blocks such as push buttons, scrollbars, and pull-down menus. Some programmers know these individual building blocks as controls, while others call them widgets. In Java, they are typically called components because they all inherit from the base class java.awt.Component.

When you are describing a GUI toolkit, one of the most important characteristics is the list of components it supports. Table 2-1 lists the heavyweight components provided by AWT, where heavyweight refers to components that are layered on top of native GUI components. The components listed are all classes in the java.awt package. One of the curious features of the AWT is that pull-down and pop-up menus, and the items contained within those menus, are not technically components. Instead of inheriting from Component, they inherit from java.awt.-MenuComponent. Nevertheless, the various menu component classes are used in very much the same way that true components are, so I have included them in Table 2-1.

Table 2–1: Heavyweight AWT Components

Component Name	Description
Button	A graphical push button.
Canvas	A heavyweight component that displays a blank canvas, allowing a program to display custom graphics.
Checkbox	A toggle button that can be selected or unselected. Use the Checkbox group to enforce mutually exclusive or radio button behavior among a group of Checkbox components.
CheckboxMenuItem	A toggle button that can appear within a Menu.
Choice	An option menu or drop-down list. Displays a menu of options when clicked on and allows the user to select among this fixed set of options.
Component	The base class for all AWT and Swing components. Defines many basic methods inherited by all components.
FileDialog	Allows the user to browse the filesystem and select or enter a filename.
Label	Displays a single line of read-only text. Does not respond to user input in any way.
List	Displays a list of choices (optionally scrollable) to the user and allows the user to select one or more of them.
Menu	A single pane of a pull-down menu
MenuBar	A horizontal bar that contains pull-down menus.
MenuComponent	The base class from which all menu-related classes inherit.
MenuItem	A single item within a pull-down or pop-up menu pane.
PopUpMenu	A menu pane for a pop-up menu.
Scrollbar	A graphical scrollbar.
TextArea	Displays multiple lines of plain text and allows the user to edit the text.
TextComponent	The base class for both TextArea and TextField.
TextField	Displays a single line of plain text and allows the user to edit the text.

Table 2-2 lists the components provided by Swing. By convention, the names of these components all begin with the letter *J*. You'll notice that except for this J prefix, many Swing components have the same names as AWT components. These are designed to be replacements for the corresponding AWT components. For example, the lightweight Swing components JButton and JTextField replace the heavyweight AWT components Button and TextField. In addition, Swing defines a number of components, some quite powerful, that are simply not available in AWT.

Swing components are all part of the `javax.swing` package. Despite the `javax` package prefix, Swing is a core part of the Java 2 platform, not a standard extension. Swing can be used as an extension to Java 1.1, however. All Swing components inherit from the `javax.swing.JComponent` class. JComponent itself inherits from the `java.awt.Component` class, which means that all Swing components are also AWT components. Unlike most AWT components, however, Swing components do not have a native "peer" object and are therefore "lightweight" components, at least when compared to the AWT components they replace. Finally, note that menus and menu components are no different than any other type of component in Swing; they do not form a distinct class hierarchy as they do in AWT.

Table 2–2: GUI Components of Swing

Component Name	Description
JButton	A push button that can display text, images, or both.
JCheckBox	A toggle button for displaying choices that are not mutually exclusive.
JCheckBoxMenuItem	A checkbox designed for use in menus.
JColorChooser	A complex, customizable component that allows the user to select a color from one or more color spaces. Used in conjunction with the `javax.swing.colorchooser` package.
JComboBox	A combination of a text entry field and a drop-down list of choices. The user can type a selection or choose one from the list.
JComponent	The root of the Swing component hierarchy. Adds Swing-specific features such as tooltips and support for double-buffering.
JEditorPane	A powerful text editor, customizable via an `EditorKit` object. Predefined editor kits exist for displaying and editing HTML- and RTF-format text.
JFileChooser	A complex component that allows the user to select a file or directory. Supports filtering and optional file previews. Used in conjunction with the `javax.swing.filechooser` package.
JLabel	A simple component that displays text, an image, or both. Does not respond to input.

Table 2–2: GUI Components of Swing (continued)

Component Name	Description
JList	A component that displays a selectable list of choices. The choices are usually strings or images, but arbitrary objects may also be displayed.
JMenu	A pull-down menu in a JMenuBar or a submenu within another menu.
JMenuBar	A component that displays a set of pull-down menus.
JMenuItem	A selectable item within a menu.
JOptionPane	A complex component suitable for displaying simple dialog boxes. Defines useful static methods for displaying common dialog types.
JPasswordField	A text input field for sensitive data, such as passwords. For security, does not display the text as it is typed.
JPopupMenu	A window that pops up to display a menu. Used by JMenu and for standalone pop-up menus.
JProgressBar	A component that displays the progress of a time-consuming operation.
JRadioButton	A toggle button for displaying mutually exclusive choices.
JRadioButtonMenuItem	A radio button for use in menus.
JScrollBar	A horizontal or vertical scrollbar.
JSeparator	A simple component that draws a horizontal or vertical line. Used to visually divide complex interfaces into sections.
JSlider	A component that simulates a slider control like those found on stereo equalizers. Allows the user to select a numeric value by dragging a knob. Can display tick marks and labels.
JTable	A complex and powerful component for displaying tables and editing their contents. Typically used to display strings but may be customized to display any type of data. Used in conjunction with the javax.swing.table package.
JTextArea	A component for displaying and editing multiple lines of plain text. Based on JTextComponent.
JTextComponent	The root component of a powerful and highly customizable text display and editing system. Part of the javax.swing.text package.
JTextField	A component for the display, input, and editing of a single line of plain text. Based on JTextComponent.

Table 2-2: *GUI Components of Swing (continued)*

Component Name	Description
JTextPane	A subclass of JEditorPane for displaying and editing formatted text that is not in HTML or RTF format. Suitable for adding simple word processing functionality to an application.
JToggleButton	The parent component of both JCheckBox and JRadioButton.
JToolBar	A component that displays a set of user-selectable tools or actions.
JToolTip	A lightweight pop-up window that displays simple documentation or tips when the mouse pointer lingers over a component.
JTree	A powerful component for the display of tree-structured data. Data values are typically strings, but the component can be customized to display any kind of data. Used in conjunction with the javax.swing.tree package.

Properties

Every AWT and Swing component can have its appearance and behavior customized by specifying values for its *properties*. In Example 2-1, we set the text property of the JButton components by calling the setText() method and the border property of the JLabel by calling setBorder().

The properties of a component are not a formal part of a Java class, in the way that the fields and methods of a class are. Instead, the notion of properties is merely a naming convention adopted from the JavaBeans component framework. When a component defines a pair of public accessor methods whose names begin with "set" and "get", this pair of methods defines a property. For example, the methods setFont() and getFont() define the font property of a component. When a property is of type boolean, the "get" accessor method is often replaced with one that begins with "is". For example, the setVisible() and isVisible() methods define the visible property.

Although any given component may define only a few properties of its own, every component inherits the properties of its superclasses. If you refer to the reference pages for JComponent, Component, and MenuComponent, you'll see that there are quite a few of these inherited properties.

Thinking about GUI components in terms of the properties they define and the properties they inherit is useful because it conveniently sums up the customizable state of the component. Looking at a list of component properties tells you a lot about what you can do with the component. This is so useful, in fact, that the reference section of this book groups property accessor methods separately from other methods.

Containers and Containment

Table 2-1 and Table 2-2 listed the GUI components available in the AWT and Swing toolkits. In order to create a graphical user interface, however, these individual components must be arranged within some kind of container. A *container* is a component that can contain other components. All containers inherit from the java.awt.Container base class, which itself inherits from java.awt.Component.

Main application windows and dialog boxes are commonly used containers. Each provides a window within which GUI components can be arranged to create a user interface. A graphical application does not usually arrange all its components directly within a window or dialog box, however. Instead, an application typically uses containers nested within other containers. For example, a dialog box that contains two columns of text input fields above a row of push buttons might use three separate containers, one for each column of text fields and one for the row of push buttons. Then the dialog box container contains only these three containers, instead of the full set of text fields and push buttons.

Some kinds of containers display their children in very specific ways, while others have restrictions on the number or type of components they can display. Some other containers are generic, so they can contain any number of children, arranged in any way. A generic container uses a layout manager to specify how its children should be arranged (as we'll discuss in the next section).

Table 2-3 lists the containers provided by AWT (in the java.awt package), and Table 2-4 lists the additional containers provided by Swing (in javax.swing). Menus and menu bars, such as javax.swing.JMenuBar and javax.swing.JPopup-Menu, are containers. Because of their highly specialized use, however, I have listed them in the earlier tables of components. Also, the JComponent class extends java.awt.Container, which means that all Swing components are actually containers. In practice, however, they are not used this way; only the Swing classes listed in Table 2-4 are typically used as containers.

Table 2-3: AWT Containers

Container	Description
Applet	This subclass of Panel is actually part of the java.applet package. It is the base class for all applets. (See Chapter 7.)
Container	The base class from which all containers inherit.
Dialog	A window suitable for dialog boxes.
Frame	A window suitable for use as the main window of an application. In AWT, Frame is the only container that can contain a MenuBar and related menu components.
Panel	A generic container used to create nested layouts.

Table 2-3: *AWT Containers (continued)*

Container	Description
ScrollPane	A container that contains a single child and allows that child to be scrolled vertically and horizontally.
Window	A heavyweight window with no titlebar or other decoration, suitable for pop-up menus and similar uses.

Table 2-4: *Swing Containers*

Container	Description
Box	A general-purpose container that arranges children using the BoxLayout layout manager.
JApplet	A java.applet.Applet subclass that contains a JRootPane to add Swing features, such as support for menu bars to applets. Applets are discussed in Chapter 7.
JDesktopPane	A container for JInternalFrame components; simulates the operation of a desktop within a single window. Supports MDI (multiple document interface) application styles.
JDialog	The container used to display dialog boxes in Swing.
JFrame	The container used for top-level windows in Swing.
JInternalFrame	A lightweight nested window container. Behaves like a JFrame and displays a titlebar and resize handles but is not an independent window and is constrained to appear within the bounds of its parent container. Often used with JDesktopPane.
JLayeredPane	A container that allows its children to overlap and manages the stacking order of those children.
JPanel	A generic container for grouping Swing components. Typically used with an appropriate LayoutManager.
JRootPane	A complex container used internally by JApplet, JDialog, JFrame, JInternalFrame, and JWindow. Provides a number of important Swing capabilities to these top-level containers.
JScrollPane	A container that allows a single child component to be scrolled horizontally or vertically. Supports scrolling and non-scrolling header regions at the top and left of the scrolling region.
JSplitPane	A container that displays two children by splitting itself horizontally or vertically. Allows the user to adjust the amount of space allocated to each child.
JTabbedPane	A container that displays one child at a time, allowing the user to select the currently displayed child by clicking on tabs like those found on manila file folders.

Table 2-4: *Swing Containers (continued)*

Container	Description
JViewport	A fixed-size container that displays a portion of a single larger child. Typically used as part of a JScrollPane.
JWindow	A top-level Swing window that does not display a titlebar, resize handles, or any other decorations.

When building a graphical user interface, you must create your components, create the containers that will hold those components, and then add the components to the containers. You do this with one of the add() methods defined by java.awt.Container. In its simplest form, this process looks like this:

```
JButton b = new JButton("Push Me");
JPanel p = new JPanel();
p.add(b);
```

There are other versions of the add() method as well. In addition to specifying the component to add, you may also specify a string or an object as a constraint. The container may use this constraint object as a hint that tells it how the component should be arranged in the container. In practice, containers do not use the constraint directly, but pass it on to a layout manager, as we'll discuss shortly.

In Swing, the top-level containers JFrame, JDialog, JInternalFrame, JWindow, and JApplet are used slightly differently than containers such as JPanel, JSplitPane, and JTabbedPane.

I've said that all Swing components extend JComponent. JFrame, JInternalFrame, JDialog, JWindow, and JApplet are actually exceptions to this rule. These top-level Swing containers extend their corresponding AWT containers: Frame, Dialog, Window, and java.applet.Applet. Because these container classes do not extend JComponent, they do not inherit the Swing-specific features of JComponent.

Instead, when you create a JFrame, JInternalFrame, JDialog, JWindow, or JApplet container, the container automatically creates a single child for itself. The child is a JRootPane container. JRootPane does extend JComponent, and it is this automatically created JRootPane that will hold all of the components that are placed in the container. You cannot add children directly to the top-level container. Instead, you add them to the content pane of the JRootPane. All Swing containers that use a JRootPane implement the RootPaneContainer interface. This interface defines the getContentPane() method, which returns the container that you should use. This is not as confusing as it sounds. In practice, your code looks like this:

```
JButton b = new JButton("Press Me");        // Create a button
JFrame f = new JFrame("Test Application");   // Create a window to display it
f.getContentPane().add(b);                    // Add the button to the window
```

By default, getContentPane() returns a JPanel container, but you can override this default by creating a container of your own and passing it to setContentPane().

The JRootPane container is a complex one; it contains a number of children in addition to the content pane container. These children support features such as pop-up menus and are primarily for internal use by Swing. One notable and commonly used feature of JRootPane, however, is that it displays a JMenuBar passed to its setJMenuBar() method. (In AWT, you specify a MenuBar for a Frame by calling the setMenuBar() method of Frame.)

Layout Management

Some containers, such as JTabbedPane and JSplitPane, define a particular arrangement for their children. Other containers such as JPanel (and JFrame, JDialog, and other top-level containers that use JPanel as their default content pane) do not define any particular arrangement. When working with containers of this type, you must specify a LayoutManager object to arrange the children within the container.

AWT and Swing include various implementations of the java.awt.LayoutManager interface. Each arranges components in a different way. Table 2-5 lists the layout managers defined by AWT. Swing applications often rely on these AWT layout managers, but Swing also defines some of its own, which are listed in Table 2-6. Figure 2-2 shows how some of these layout managers arrange their children.

Table 2–5: AWT Layout Managers

Layout Manager	Description
BorderLayout	Lays out a maximum of five components: one along each of the four borders of the container and one in the center. When using this layout manager, you must add components to the container using a two-argument version of the add() method. The constraint argument should be one of the strings "North", "East", "South", "West", or "Center". Despite the simplicity of this layout system, this layout manager is used quite often.
CardLayout	Makes each component as large as the container and displays only one at a time. Various methods change the currently displayed component.
FlowLayout	Arranges components like words on a page: from left to right in rows and then top to bottom as each row fills up. Rows may be left, center, or right justified.
GridBagLayout	A flexible layout manager that arranges components in a grid with variable-sized cells. Allows explicit control over the way each component is resized when the container changes size. Requires a complex constraints set specified with the GridBagConstraints object.
GridLayout	Makes all components the same size and arranges them in a grid of specified dimensions.

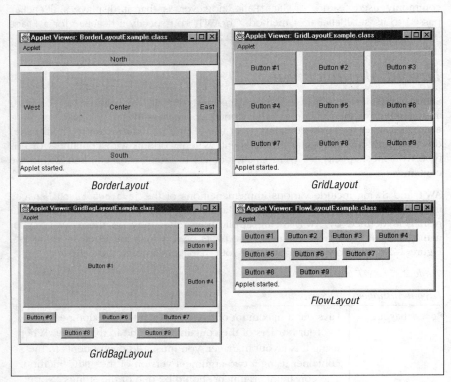

Figure 2–2: Layout managers

Table 2–6: Swing Layout Managers

Layout Manager	Description
BoxLayout	The layout manager used by the Box container. It arranges its children into either a row or a column. It uses the glue and strut components returned by static Box methods to display stretchy and rigid spaces between the children.
OverlayLayout	An obscure and infrequently used layout manager that overlaps its children based on the children's alignment values specified with the setAlignmentX() and setAlignmentY() methods inherited from JComponent. Used by AbstractButton.
ScrollPaneLayout	A specialized layout manager used by JScrollPane. Not typically useful for general-purpose layouts.
ViewportLayout	A specialized layout manager used by JViewport. Not useful for general-purpose layouts.

Some layout managers require additional information about the components they are to arrange. This information takes the form of a constraint string or constraint object passed to the add() method when the component is added to its container. java.awt.BorderLayout is the most commonly used of these layout managers: its constraint object is a string that specifies where the child should be positioned within the container. Example 2-1 showed a typical use of BorderLayout.

Every AWT and Swing container has a default layout manager. If you explicitly set the layout manager to null, however, you can arrange your components using hardcoded sizes and positions. Set the size and position with methods such as setSize() and setLocation(). However, hardcoding the layout of your components makes your GUI less portable, harder to customize, and harder to translate into other languages.

Event Handling

Using a layout manager to arrange components within a container may result in a GUI that looks good, but in order to make it do anything, you have to handle events. An event typically signifies an action by the user, such as striking a key or clicking the mouse over a JButton component. But it can also refer to any other action performed by the user or the program. An event can be generated when the value of component's property changes or when a specified amount of time elapses, for example.

The event model used in Java changed between Java 1.0 and Java 1.1. The Java 1.1 event model is used by AWT and Swing in Java 1.1 and Java 1.2. The Java 1.0 event model is largely obsolete; we'll discuss it in Chapter 7, *Applets*, however, since some web browsers still only support Java 1.0.

Event Objects

Different types of events are represented by different Java classes. The base class, from which all events inherit, is java.util.EventObject. AWT defines its own base class for GUI events, java.awt.AWTEvent, which is subclassed from EventObject. AWT then defines a number of subclasses of AWTEvent in the package java.awt.event. Swing uses many of these event types and also defines more of its own in the javax.swing.event package. Some Swing events subclass AWT events, but many subclass java.util.EventObject directly. There is one other kind of event used by Swing components: the java.beans.PropertyChangeEvent, which is part of the JavaBeans component model.

The base EventObject class defines a getSource() method that returns the object that generated or triggered the event. AWTEvent defines the getID() method; the value returned by this method is used to distinguish the various types of events that are represented by the same event class. For example, FocusEvent has two possible types: FocusEvent.FOCUS_GAINED and FocusEvent.FOCUS_LOST.

In addition to these getSource() and getID() methods, the various event subclasses define methods to return whatever data values are pertinent to the particular event type. For example, MouseEvent has getX(), getY(), and getClickCount()

methods; it also inherits the getModifiers() and getWhen() methods, among others, from its superclass InputEvent. Thus, when the user clicks the mouse, you receive a MouseEvent that specifies where, when, and how many times the user clicked, along with other information, such as the set of keyboard modifier keys that were held down at the time.

Event Listeners

An object that would like to be notified of and respond to an event is an *event listener*. An object that generates a particular kind of event, called an *event source*, maintains a list of listeners that are interested in being notified when that kind of event occurs. The event source provides methods that allow listeners to add and remove themselves from this list of interested objects. When the event source generates an event (or when a user input event such as a mouse click or a key press occurs on the event source object), the event source notifies all the listener objects that the event has occurred.

All AWT and Swing components are event sources, and all of them define (or inherit) methods for adding and removing event listeners. By convention, these methods have names that begin with "add" or "remove" and end with "Listener". So, for example, the JButton class inherits the addActionListener() and removeActionListener() methods. In the reference section of this book, you'll notice that the event registration methods of a component are grouped separately, just as the property accessor methods are. This is because one of the most important things you need to know about a component is the list of event types that it can generate.

Each type of event object typically has a corresponding event listener type. The ActionEvent event type has an ActionListener listener type, for example. Event listeners, such as ActionListener, are interfaces that extend java.util.EventListener. EventListener doesn't define any methods; it is merely a marker interface that gives all event listeners a common type. An event listener interface defines one or more methods that an event source may invoke when a particular type of event occurs. Such a method always takes an event object as its single argument. For example, the ActionListener interface defines a single method, actionPerformed(). When the user clicks on a JButton component, an ActionEvent representing that click is created and passed to the actionPerformed() method of each ActionListener object that was registered on the JButton with the addActionListener() method.

An event listener interface may define more than one method. For example, MouseListener defines several methods that correspond to different types of mouse events, including button press events and button release events. This is because MouseEvent represents several different types of mouse events. By convention, each method of an event listener is passed a single argument that is an event object of the type that corresponds to the listener. Thus, a MouseEvent object is always created when a mouse event occurs, but the object is passed to a different listener method depending on the type of mouse event that occurred.

Event Adapters

When an event listener interface defines more than one method, it is often accompanied by an event adapter class that provides empty implementations for each of the methods. For example, the `MouseListener` interface defines five different methods. If your program is interested only in the `mouseClicked()` method, it may be easier for you to subclass the `MouseAdapter` class and override `mouseClicked()` than to implement all five methods of the `MouseListener` interface directly.

Event Handling with Inner Classes

An important point to notice about the Java event handling model is that, in order to receive an event notification, you must implement an appropriate event listener interface. Sometimes you do this directly in your main application class. For example, an object interested in action and focus events might simply implement `ActionListener` and `FocusListener` directly.

However, it is also quite common to create special classes for the sole purpose of handling events. This is usually done with inner classes, as we saw in Example 2-1. With this event-handling paradigm, you create a simple inner class to handle each event type that you are interested in for a particular event source. Your code might look like this:

```
JFrame window = new JFrame("test application");
window.addFocusListener(new FocusListener() {
  public void focusGained(FocusEvent e) { /* gain focus code here */ }
  public void focusLost(FocusEvent e) {   /* lose focus code here */ }
});
```

You can also use this approach with an event adapter class, instead of an event listener interface. For example:

```
Panel panel = new Panel();
panel.addMouseListener(new MouseAdapter() {
  public void mouseClicked(MouseEvent e) { /* mouse click code here */ }
});
```

Handling Input Events Directly

Certain types of events occur as a direct result of user input. When the user types a key or moves the mouse, for example, a `KeyEvent` or `MouseEvent` is generated. Similarly, when the user resizes a window or transfers keyboard focus to a new component, a `FocusEvent` or `ComponentEvent` is generated. These types of events represent event notifications generated by the underlying native windowing system or operating system. Other types of events, such as `ActionEvent` and `PopupMenuEvent`, do not originate in the native windowing system. Instead, these events are generated directly by AWT and Swing components.

The distinction between these types of events becomes more clear when you implement a component yourself. Consider the `JButton` component, for example. It receives `MouseEvent` events and generates `ActionEvent` events in response to them. For a component like this, it is not particularly appropriate or efficient to use a `MouseListener` object to receive mouse events.

The Java event model provides a low-level way to handle input events that originate in the underlying windowing system. When such an event occurs, it is passed to the processEvent() method of the Component on which it occurs. This method examines the type of event and invokes an appropriate method to handle the event. These methods are: processMouseEvent(), processMouseMotionEvent(), processKeyEvent(), processFocusEvent(), processComponentEvent(), and processInputMethodEvent(). By default, each method simply invokes the appropriate methods on the appropriate event listeners. When you subclass a component, however, you can override any of these protected methods to perform any other type of event handling you desire. When you override one of these methods, you should usually remember to invoke the superclass method as well, so that the appropriate event listeners are notified.

There is one additional requirement to make this low-level Java 1.1 event model work. In order to receive events of a particular type for a particular component, you must tell the component that it is interested in receiving that type of event. If you do not, events of that type are simply not delivered to the component, at least on some operating systems. With event listeners, the act of registering a listener is sufficient to tell the component what kinds of events it should request. However, when you are using the processXXXEvent() methods directly, you must first call another protected method, enableEvents(), and pass in a bit mask that specifies the types of events you are interested in. The bit mask is formed by ORing together various EVENT_MASK constants that are defined by java.awt.AWTEvent. For example:

```
this.enableEvents(AWTEvent.MOUSE_EVENT_MASK | AWTEvent.KEY_EVENT_MASK);
```

Event Reference

AWT and Swing define quite a few event objects, event listeners, and event adapters in the java.awt.event and javax.swing.event packages. Fortunately, all these classes and interfaces follow the same basic naming conventions. For an event X, the event object is named XEvent, the listener interface is XListener, and the adapter, if one is defined is XAdapter. The event listener interface defines methods that vary by event type, but every event listener method returns void and accepts the corresponding event object as its single argument. The only significant variation from these rules is that the java.awt.MouseListener and java.awt.-MouseMotionListener listeners both work with MouseEvent events—there is no separate MouseMotionEvent.

You can find a list of the events generated by any given component by turning to its reference page and looking at the event listener registration methods for that component. Remember, too, that the component may also inherit events. Table 2-7 and Table 2-8 work in the opposite direction. For a given event listener type, these tables list the components that can generate events of that type. (Note, however, that they do not list classes that inherit events of that type.) These tables also list the names of the methods defined by each event listener interface. You can learn a lot about the intended usage of an event simply by looking at the list of listener methods to which it can be passed.

Table 2-7 shows the event listeners defined by AWT. These event types are not restricted to AWT components; Swing components use them too, as do some other Swing classes that are not components. Table 2-8 displays the event listeners defined by Swing. Note that I have also added two event listeners defined in the java.beans package, but used by Swing components, to this table.

Table 2–7: AWT Event Listeners and the Components That Use Them

Event Listener	Listener Methods	Registered on
ActionListener	actionPerformed()	AbstractButton, Button, ButtonModel, ComboBoxEditor, JComboBox, JFileChooser, JTextField, List, MenuItem, TextField, Timer
AdjustmentListener	adjustmentValue- Changed()	Adjustable, JScrollBar, Scrollbar
ComponentListener	componentHidden(), componentMoved(), componentResized(), componentShown()	Component
ContainerListener	componentAdded(), componentRemoved()	Container
FocusListener	focusGained(), focusLost()	Component
ItemListener	itemStateChanged()	AbstractButton, ButtonModel, Checkbox, CheckboxMenuItem, Choice, ItemSelectable, JComboBox, List
KeyListener	keyPressed(), keyReleased(), keyTyped()	Component
MouseListener	mouseClicked(), mouseEntered(), mouseExited(), mousePressed(), mouseReleased()	Component
MouseMotionListener	mouseDragged(), mouseMoved()	Component
TextListener	textValueChanged()	TextComponent

Table 2-7: AWT Event Listeners and the Components That Use Them *(continued)*

Event Listener	Listener Methods	Registered on
WindowListener	windowActivated(), windowClosed(), windowClosing(), windowDeactivated(), windowDeiconified(), windowIconified(), windowOpened()	Window

Table 2-8: Swing Event Listeners and the Components That Use Them

Event Listener	Listener Methods	Registered on
AncestorListener	ancestorAdded(), ancestorMoved(), ancestorRemoved()	Action, JComponent
CaretListener	caretUpdate()	JTextComponent
CellEditorListener	editingCanceled(), editingStopped()	CellEditor,
ChangeListener	stateChanged()	AbstractButton, BoundedRangeModel, ButtonModel, JProgressBar, JSlider, JTabbedPane, JViewport, MenuSelectionManager, SingleSelectionModel
HyperlinkListener	hyperlinkUpdate()	JEditorPane
InternalFrameListener	internalFrameActivated (), internalFrameClosed(), internalFrameClosing() internalFrameDeactivated(), internalFrameDeiconified(), internalFrameIconified() internalFrameOpened()	
ListDataListener	contentsChanged(), intervalAdded(), intervalRemoved()	AbstractListModel, ListModel

Event Listener	Listener Methods	Registered on
ListSelectionListener	valueChanged()	JList, ListSelectionModel
MenuDragMouseListener	menuDragMouseDragged(), menuDragMouseEntered(), menuDragMouseExited(), menuDragMouseReleased()	JMenuItem
MenuKeyListener	menuKeyPressed(), menuKeyReleased(), menuKeyTyped()	JMenuItem
MenuListener	menuCanceled(), menuDeselected(), menuSelected()	JMenu
PopupMenuListener	popupMenuCanceled(), popupMenuWillBecome-Invisible(), popupMenuWillBecome-Visible()	JPopupMenu
TreeExpansionListener	treeCollapsed(), treeExpanded()	JTree
TreeSelectionListener	valueChanged()	JTree
TreeWillExpandListener	treeWillCollapse(), treeWillExpand()	JTree
java.beans.-PropertyChangeListener	propertyChange()	Action, JComponent, UIDefaults, UIManager
java.beans.-VetoableChangeListener	vetoableChange()	JComponent

Swing Component Architecture

So far, we have treated components as single, self-contained GUI building blocks. And indeed, components can be written to be entirely self-contained. However, neither AWT nor Swing components are actually self-contained. As I mentioned earlier, each AWT component is simply a frontend for an underlying native user-interface object. AWT delegates all the display and event processing—that is, the look-and-feel—to these native GUI elements.

Swing components are not self-contained either. Most Swing components rely on two other objects: a user-interface (UI) delegate object and a model object. Swing supports a pluggable look-and-feel architecture, which means that a Swing application can control the appearance and behavior of its user-interface. Thus, a Swing application can be displayed in a platform-independent way or in a way that mimics the native look-and-feel of the underlying platform, for example. In order to implement the pluggable look-and-feel architecture, every Swing component must delegate its display and event-handling functions to a separate object: the UI delegate. Fortunately, you can use Swing without ever thinking about the pluggable look-and-feel. That's because, when you create a Swing component, an appropriate UI delegate object is automatically created for it.

The model object for a Swing component is responsible for storing the state of the component. For example, the JToggleButton uses an implementation of the ButtonModel interface as its model. This ButtonModel object remembers whether the button is currently selected. As another example, the JScrollBar, JSlider, and JProgressBar components use a BoundedRangeModel object to keep track of their state. This state includes minimum, maximum, and current values.

Most Swing components automatically create the model objects they rely on, so you can use these components without ever worrying about model objects. When working with more complicated components, however, models become more important. For example, the JTree component uses a javax.swing.tree.TreeModel object to represent the data it is to display. The JTree component can be used to display many kinds of hierarchically structured data. JTree does not require you to convert your data into some predefined data format, however. Instead, you implement the TreeModel interface in a way that allows JTree to understand the data. For example, to use a JTree component to display files in the filesystem, you might define a FileTreeModel class that implements the TreeModel interface on top of the capabilities of the java.io.File class. Or, if you want to use JTree to display the structure of an XML document, you might create an implementation of TreeModel that works with the parse tree returned by an XML parsing class.

The JTable component is another for which the use of a separate model object is particularly important. JTable can be used to display a tabular view of data, even when that data is not tabular by nature. To do so, you implement the javax.-swing.table.TableModel interface to provide a neat, tabular view of the data.

One advantage of this model object approach, where the actual data is separated from the component's view of that data, is that you can define multiple views of the same data. For example, if you have a large set of tabular data that implements the TableModel interface, you can have two or more JTable components that display different portions of that data at the same time. When you are writing an application that manipulates complex data structures, you should consider designing these structures so that they implement appropriate Swing model interfaces. If you do this, you'll be able to trivially display your data using Swing components. See Chapter 3, *Swing Programming Topics*, for more information about implementing TreeModel and TableModel.

CHAPTER 3

Swing Programming Topics

The last chapter provided an architectural overview of AWT and Swing; it explained how to create a graphical user interface by placing components inside containers, arranging them with layout managers, and handling the events that they generate. This chapter builds on that architectural foundation and introduces many other important features of Swing. Most of the topics discussed herein are independent of one another, so you can think of each section as a short essay on a particular topic, where the sections can be read in any order.

This chapter introduces many of the new components and features of Swing, but it cannot cover them in full detail. For more information on the topics covered herein, see *Java Swing*, by Robert Eckstein, Marc Loy, and Dave Wood (O'Reilly).

Versions of Swing

Swing is a core part of the Java 2 platform, so many developers will simply obtain the Swing libraries when they download the Java 2 SDK. Swing is also available as a separate download for use as an extension to Java 1.1. When you download Swing independently of the SDK, you must pay attention to the Swing version number. Swing 1.0.3 is an early version of Swing that was released before Version 1.2 of Java 2. It is now outdated and is not documented in this book. Swing 1.1 is the version of Swing that is being bundled with Java 1.2. You can download a version of it for use with Java 1.1 from *http://java.sun.com/products/jfc/*.

As this book goes to press, the most recent version of Swing is Swing 1.1.1. This version of Swing is bundled with Java 1.2.2 and is also available for use with Java 1.1 from the web site mentioned in the previous paragraph. Swing 1.1.1 fixes *many* bugs in the initial release of Swing 1.1 but does not change the Swing 1.1 API in any way. Its use is strongly recommended. Swing 1.1.1 is the last release of Swing that will be available for use with Java 1.1.

Development of Swing continues, and Java 1.3 will ship with a new version that includes a number of minor changes and improvements to the Swing API. This future release will focus on improving the existing APIs and should not add many new APIs.

Labels and HTML

In the initial releases of Swing 1.1 and Java 1.2, the JLabel, JButton, and related classes that display textual labels can display only a single line of text using a single font. In Swing 1.1.1 and Java 1.2.2, however, components like these can display multiline, multifont text using simple HTML formatting. To display formatted text, simply specify a string of HTML text that begins with an <HTML> tag. You can use this feature to present text using multiple fonts, font styles, and colors. Just as important, however, the introduction of HTML allows you to specify multiline labels.

This new formatted text display feature is available in Java 1.2.2 for the JLabel, JButton, MenuItem, JMenu, JCheckBoxMenuItem, JRadioButtonMenuItem, JTabbed-Pane, and JToolTip classes. It is not supported (at least in Java 1.2.2) by JCheckBox or JRadioButton, however. Formatted text display is particularly useful with JOptionPane dialog boxes (described later in this chapter), as they display text using internal JLabel objects.

Actions

A GUI application often allows a user to invoke an operation in a number of different ways. For example, the user may be able to save a file by either selecting an item from a menu or clicking on a button in a toolbar. The resulting operation is exactly the same; it is simply presented to the user through two different interfaces.

Swing defines a simple but powerful javax.swing.Action interface that encapsulates information about such an operation. The Action interface extends the ActionListener interface, so it contains the actionPerformed() method. It is this method that you implement to actually perform the desired action. Each Action object also has an arbitrary set of name/value pairs that provide additional information about the action. The values typically include: a short string of text that names the operation, an image that can be used to represent the action graphically, and a longer string of text suitable for use in a tooltip for the action. In addition, each Action object has an enabled property and a setEnabled() method that allows it to be enabled and disabled. (If there is no text selected in a text editor, for example, the "Cut" action is usually disabled.)

You can add an Action object directly to a JMenu or JToolBar component. When you do this, the component automatically creates a JMenuItem or JButton to represent the action, making the action's operation available to the user and displaying the action's textual description and graphical image as appropriate. When an action is disabled, the JMenuItem or JButton component that represents the action displays it in a grayed-out style and does not allow it to be selected or invoked.

One shortcoming of working with actions is that there is no way to tell a JMenuBar or JToolBar to display just text or just icons for actions. Although you might like an action's name to be displayed in a menu and its icon to be displayed in a toolbar, both JMenuBar and JToolBar display an action's textual name and its icon.

The Action interface helps you implement a clean separation between GUI code and application logic. Remember, however, that you cannot just instantiate Action objects directly. Since Action is a kind of ActionListener, you must define an individual subclass of Action that implements the actionPerformed() method for each of your desired actions. The AbstractAction class is helpful here; it implements everything except the actionPerformed() method.

Tooltips

A Swing component can display context-sensitive help to the user in the form of a *tooltip*: a small window that pops up when the user lets the mouse rest over the component. You can display text in this window that explains the purpose or function of the component. Specify this text with the setToolTipText() method. This toolTipText property is inherited from JComponent, so it is shared by all Swing components.

While it is a good idea to provide tooltips for the benefit of your novice users, your experienced users may find them annoying, so it is nice to provide a way to turn them off. You can do this programatically by setting the enabled property of the ToolTipManager object. The code looks like this:

```
ToolTipManager.sharedInstance().setEnabled(false);
```

Timers

The javax.swing.Timer object generates single or multiple ActionEvent events at time intervals that you specify. Thus, a Timer is useful for performing a repeated operation like an animation. They are also useful for triggering operations that must occur at some point in the future. For example, an application might display a message in a status line and then set up a Timer object that erases the message after 5,000 milliseconds. These operations can also be performed with threads, of course, but since Swing is not designed for thread safety, it is usually more convenient to use a Timer.

You use Timer objects just like regular components. A Timer has property accessor methods and an addActionListener() method that you can use to add event listeners. The initialDelay property specifies how many milliseconds the Timer waits before firing its first ActionEvent. If the repeats property is true, the Timer generates a new ActionEvent each time delay milliseconds passes. When an application (or the system in general) is very busy or when the delay property is very small, the timer may fire events faster than the application can process them. If the coalesce property is true, the Timer combines multiple pending events into a single ActionEvent, rather than letting a queue of unprocessed events build up.

The Event Dispatch Thread

For efficiency reasons, Swing components are not designed to be thread safe. This means that Swing components should be manipulated by a single thread at a time. The easiest way to ensure this is to do all your GUI manipulations from the event dispatch thread. Every GUI application has an event dispatch thread: it is the thread that waits for events to occur and then dispatches those events to the appropriate event handlers. All of your event listener methods are invoked by the event dispatch thread, so any GUI manipulations you perform from an event listener are safe.

There are times, however, when you need to update your UI in response to some kind of external event, such as a response from a server that arrives in a separate thread. To accommodate these situations, Swing provides two utility methods that allow you ask the event dispatch thread to run arbitrary code. The methods are SwingUtilities.invokeLater() and SwingUtilities.invokeAndWait(). You pass a Runnable object to each method, and the run() method of this object is invoked from the event thread. invokeLater() returns right away, regardless of when the run() method is invoked, while invokeAndWait() does not return until the run() method has completed.

The invokeLater() and invokeAndWait() methods do not run your Runnable object right away. Instead, each method encapsulates the Runnable object within a special event object and places the event on the event queue. Then, when all pending events have been handled, the Runnable object is extracted from the event queue and the event dispatch thread calls its run() method. This means that invokeLater() provides a useful way to defer the execution of some chunk of code until after all pending events have been processed. There are times when you may even want to do this with code that is already running within the event dispatch thread.

Client Properties

In addition to its normal set of properties, JComponent includes a hashtable in which it can store arbitrary name/value pairs. These name/value pairs are called client properties, and they can be set and queried with the putClientProperty() and getClientProperty() methods. Since these are JComponent methods, they are inherited by all Swing components. Although both the name and value of a client property can be arbitrary objects, the name is usually a String object.

Client properties allow arbitrary data to be associated with any Swing component. This can be useful in a number of situations. For example, suppose you've created a JMenu that contains 10 JMenuItem components. Each component notifies the same ActionListener object when it is invoked. This action listener has to decide which of the 10 menu items invoked it and then perform whatever action is appropriate for that menu item. One way the action listener can distinguish among the menu items is by looking at the text that each displays. But this approach doesn't work well if you plan to translate your menu system into other languages. A better approach is to use the setActionCommand() method (inherited from AbstractButton) to associate a string with each of the JMenuItem components.

Then the action listener can use this string to distinguish among the various menu items. But what if the action listener needs to check some kind of object other than a `String` in order to decide how to process the action event? Client properties are the solution: they allow you to associate an arbitrary object (or multiple objects) with each `JMenuItem`.

Client properties are used within Swing to set properties that are specific to a single look-and-feel implementation. For example, the default Java look-and-feel examines the client properties of a few components to obtain additional information about how it should display the components. Here are some details on these particular client properties:

'JInternalFrame.isPalette'
> When a `JInternalFrame` is being used as a floating palette, set this client property to `Boolean.TRUE` to change the look of the border.

'JScrollBar.isFreeStanding'
> `JScrollPane` sets this client property to `Boolean.FALSE` on the `JScrollBar` components it creates.

'JSlider.isFilled'
> Setting this client property of a `JSlider` to `Boolean.TRUE` causes the slider to display a different background color on either side of the slider thumb.

"JToolBar.isRollover"
> Setting this client property to `Boolean.TRUE` on a `JToolBar` causes the component to highlight the border of whatever child component the mouse is currently over.

"JTree.lineStyle"
> This client property specifies how the `JTree` component draws the branches of its tree. The default value is the string "Horizontal"; other possible values are "Angled" and "None".

Keyboard Shortcuts

A full-featured user interface does not require the user to use the mouse all the time. Instead, it provides keyboard shortcuts that allow the user to operate the application primarily or entirely with the keyboard. Swing has a number of features that support keyboard shortcuts. Every Swing component is designed to respond to keyboard events and support keyboard operation automatically. For example, a `JButton` is activated when it receives a `KeyEvent` that tells it that the user pressed the **Spacebar** or the **Enter** key. Similarly, `JMenu` and `JList` respond to the arrow keys.

Focus Management

In order for a Swing component to receive keyboard events, it must first have the keyboard focus. In the old days, before graphical interfaces, when you typed on the keyboard, the characters always appeared on the screen. There was only one "window," so there was only one place to send key events. This changes with the introduction of windowing systems and GUIs, however, as there are now lots of places that keyboard events can be directed to. When there is more than one window open on the screen, one window is singled out as the current window (or the focused window). Most windowing systems highlight this window somehow. When you type at the keyboard, it is understood that your keystrokes are directed at the current window.

Just as a screen may contain many application windows, a single application window usually contains many GUI components. An application window must redirect the keyboard events it receives to only one of these components, called the focused component. Like most GUI toolkits, Swing highlights the component that has the keyboard focus, to let the user know where keyboard events are being directed. The details of the highlight depend on the look-and-feel that is currently in effect, but focus is often indicated by drawing a bold border around a component.

A Swing component can be operated from the keyboard when it has the focus. The user can usually direct keyboard focus to a given component by clicking on that component with the mouse, but this defeats the whole point of not using the mouse. The missing piece of the picture is focus traversal, otherwise known as keyboard navigation, which allows the user to use the keyboard to change focus from one component to the next.

Swing uses the **Tab** key to implement focus traversal. When the user presses **Tab**, Swing moves the keyboard focus from the current component to the next component that can accept the focus. (Some components, such as JLabel objects, do not respond to keyboard events and are therefore never given the focus.) When the user types **Shift-Tab**, Swing moves keyboard focus backward to the previous focusable component. By default, keyboard focus moves from left to right and top to bottom within a container. You can override this, however, by setting the nextFocusableComponent property of your components, chaining them together in whatever order you desire.

When a container is given focus through this mechanism, it passes that focus on to its first focusable child. When the focus reaches the last focusable child, some containers relinquish the focus and allow it to move on, while other containers retain the focus and give it back to the first focusable child. You can determine the behavior of a container by calling isFocusCycleRoot(). If this method returns true, the container defines a focus cycle and retains the focus. The user must type **Ctrl-Tab** to traverse to the next focus cycle or **Ctrl-Shift-Tab** to traverse to the previous focus cycle. There is no setFocusCycleRoot() method: the only way you can change this behavior is by subclassing a container and overriding the isFocusCycleRoot() method. Also note that multiline text components such as JTextArea and JEditorPane use the **Tab** key for their own purposes. These components behave like focus cycles, so the user must type **Ctrl-Tab** to move the focus away from such a component.

An application sometimes needs to set the keyboard focus to a particular component explicitly. You can do this by calling the requestFocus() method of that component. Components typically call requestFocus() themselves under certain circumstances, such as when they are clicked on. If you do not want a component to respond to requestFocus() calls, set its requestFocusEnabled property to false. For example, you might set this property on a JButton so that the user can click on it without taking keyboard focus away from whatever component currently has it.

Swing focus management is handled by the currently installed javax.swing.FocusManager object. You can obtain this object with FocusManager.getCurrentFocusManager(). If you implement your own manager, you can install it with FocusManager.setCurrentFocusManager().

Menu Mnemonics and Accelerators

Although Swing components can all be operated automatically from the keyboard, doing so is often cumbersome. The solution is to provide additional explicit keyboard shortcuts for common actions, as is commonly done with items on pull-down menus. Swing pull-down menus support two traditional types of keyboard shortcuts: mnemonics and accelerators. Figure 3-1 shows both types of menu shortcuts.

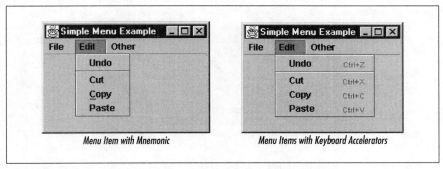

Figure 3-1: Swing menu mnemonics and accelerators

A *menu mnemonic* is a single-letter abbreviation for a menu command. When the menu has already been pulled down, the user can type this single key to invoke that menu item. The mnemonic for a menu item is typically indicated by underlining the letter of the shortcut in the menu item name, which means that you must select a shortcut letter that appears in the menu item label. Mnemonics must be unique within a menu, of course, but multiple menu panes can reuse mnemonics. Items in a menu bar may also have mnemonics. You specify a mnemonic for a menu or a menu item with the setMnemonic() method (inherited from AbstractButton):

```
JMenu file = new JMenu("File");
file.setMnemonic('F');
JMenuItem save = new JMenuItem("Save");
save.setMnemonic('S');          // Always use a capital letter
file.add(save);
```

A *menu accelerator* is a unique keyboard command that can be used to invoke a menu item even when the menu is not displayed. An accelerator is represented by a javax.swing.KeyStroke object and usually includes a keyboard modifier such as

Ctrl or **Alt**. Unlike mnemonics, accelerators can be applied only to menu items, not to menus in a menu bar. You can create an accelerator for a menu item by calling setAccelerator(). To obtain an appropriate KeyStroke object, call the static KeyStroke.getKeyStroke() method with the keycode and modifier mask for the keyboard command you want to use:

```
JMenuItem save = new JMenuItem("Save");
save.setAccelerator(KeyStroke.getKeyStroke(java.awt.event.KeyEvent.VK_S,
                                    java.awt.Event.CTRL_MASK));
```

Keyboard Actions

Sometimes even the keyboard shortcuts supported by menus are not enough. An application may need to define keyboard shortcuts for actions that are not available through the menu system. For example, an application that uses a JScroll-Pane to display a large drawing might want to allow the user to scroll the drawing with the arrow keys and the **PageUp** and **PageDown** keys.

Fortunately, every Swing component maintains a table of KeyStroke-to-ActionLis-tener bindings. When a particular keystroke is bound to an ActionListener, the component will perform the action (i.e., invoke the actionPerformed() method) when the user types the keystroke. You can register a keyboard shortcut for a component with registerKeyboardAction(). For instance:

```
Action scroll;   // This action object is initialized elsewhere
JPanel panel;    // The application's main container; initialized elsewhere

KeyStroke up = KeyStroke.getKeyStroke(java.awt.event.KeyEvent.VK_UP);
KeyStroke down = KeyStroke.getKeyStroke(java.awt.event.KeyEvent.VK_DOWN);
KeyStroke pgup = KeyStroke.getKeyStroke(java.awt.event.KeyEvent.VK_PAGE_UP);
KeyStroke pgdown=KeyStroke.getKeyStroke(java.awt.event.KeyEvent.VK_PAGE_DOWN);

panel.registerKeyboardAction(scroll, "lineup", up,
                        JComponent.WHEN_ANCESTOR_OF_FOCUSED_WINDOW);
panel.registerKeyboardAction(scroll, "linedown", down,
                        JComponent.WHEN_ANCESTOR_OF_FOCUSED_WINDOW);
panel.registerKeyboardAction(scroll, "pageup", pgup,
                        JComponent.WHEN_ANCESTOR_OF_FOCUSED_WINDOW);
panel.registerKeyboardAction(scroll, "pagedown", pgdown,
                        JComponent.WHEN_ANCESTOR_OF_FOCUSED_WINDOW);
```

This code registers four keystrokes that all invoke the scroll action. When the user types one of these keystrokes, the actionPerformed() method is passed an ActionEvent object. The getActionCommand() method of this ActionEvent returns one of the strings "lineup", "linedown", "pageup", or "pagedown". The hypothetical scroll action we are using here would examine this string to determine what kind of scrolling to perform.

The fourth argument to registerKeyboardAction() is a constant that defines under what circumstances the keyboard action should be available to the user. The value used here, WHEN_ANCESTOR_OF_FOCUSED_WINDOW, specifies that the keyboard binding should be in effect whenever the panel or any of its descendants has the focus. You can also specify a value of WHEN_IN_FOCUSED_WINDOW, which means that the keyboard action is available whenever the window containing the component has the focus. This is useful for shortcuts registered on default buttons within dialog boxes. The final allowable value for this argument is WHEN_FOCUSED, which specifies that the key binding is in effect only when the component itself has the focus. This is useful when you are adding key bindings to an individual component like a JTree.

Keymaps

Swing supports a general, yet powerful text-editing subsystem. The javax.swing.text.JTextComponent is the base component in this system; it is the superclass of JTextField, JTextEditor, and JEditorPane, among others.

Because text editing typically involves many keyboard shortcuts, Swing defines the javax.swing.text.Keymap interface, which represents a set of KeyStroke-to-Action bindings. As you might expect, when a text component has the keyboard focus and the user types a keystroke that is bound to an action, the text component invokes that action. A Keymap can have a parent Keymap from which it inherits bindings, making it easy to override a few bindings of an existing keymap without redefining all the bindings from scratch. When you are working with a large number of keyboard shortcuts, it is easier to use a Keymap than to register each one individually with registerKeyboardAction().

JTextComponent defines getKeymap() and setKeymap() methods you can use to query and set the current keymap of a text component. There are no public implementations of the Keymap interface, so you cannot instantiate one directly. Instead, create a new Keymap by calling the static JTextComponent.acdKeymap() method. This method allows you to specify a name and parent for the new Keymap. Both arguments are optional, however, so you may pass in null.

Serialization

The AWT Component class implements the java.io.Serializable marker interface, and JComponent reimplements this interface. This means that all AWT and Swing components are *serializable*, or, in other words, the state of an AWT or Swing component can be stored as a stream of bytes that can be written to a file. Components serialized to a file can be restored to their original state at a later date. When a component is serialized, all the components it contains are also automatically serialized as part of the same stream.

You serialize a component (or any serializable object) with the java.io.ObjectOutputStream class and reconstruct a serialized component with the java.io.ObjectInputStream. See *Java in a Nutshell* for more information about these classes. Because the byte stream format used in serialization changed between Java 1.1 and Java 1.2, Swing components serialized by a Java 1.2 application cannot be deserialized by a Java 1.1 application.

The serializability of Swing and AWT components is a powerful feature that is exploited by some GUI design tools. Thus, an application may create its graphical interface simply by reading and deserializing an already-built interface from a file. This is usually much simpler than creating the components of the GUI individually.

Borders

Every Swing component inherits a `border` property from `JComponent`, so you can call `setBorder()` to specify a `Border` object for a Swing component. This `Border` object displays some kind of decoration around the outside of the component. The `javax.swing.border` package contains this `Border` interface and a number of useful implementations of it. Table 3-1 lists the available border styles, and Figure 3-2 illustrates them.

Table 3-1: Swing Border Styles

Border	Description
BevelBorder	Gives the component a beveled edge that makes it appear raised or lowered.
CompoundBorder	Combines two other `Border` types to create a compound border.
EmptyBorder	A border with no appearance. This is a useful way to place an empty margin around a component.
EtchedBorder	Draws a line around the component, using a 3D effect that makes the line appear etched into or raised out of the surrounding container.
LineBorder	Draws a line, with a color and thickness you specify, around the component.
MatteBorder	Draws the border using a solid color or a tiled image. You specify the border dimensions for all four sides.
SoftBevelBorder	Like `BevelBorder`, but with somewhat more complex graphics that give the bevel a softer edge.
TitledBorder	A border that combines text with an `EtchedBorder` or any other border you specify.

The `Border` implementations defined in `javax.swing.border` cover just about every possible border you are likely to want to display. But if you ever find yourself needing a specialized border, simply implement the `Border` interface yourself.

Most of the `Border` implementations in `javax.swing.border` are immutable objects, designed to be shared. If two components have the same style of border, they can use the same `Border` immutable object. The `javax.swing.BorderFactory` class contains static methods that return various commonly used `Border` objects suitable for sharing.

Icons

All buttons, labels, and menu items in Swing can display both text and graphic elements. If you are familiar with the AWT, you might expect Swing to use the `java.awt.Image` class to represent these graphic elements. Instead, however, it uses `javax.swing.Icon`. This interface represents a graphic element more gener-

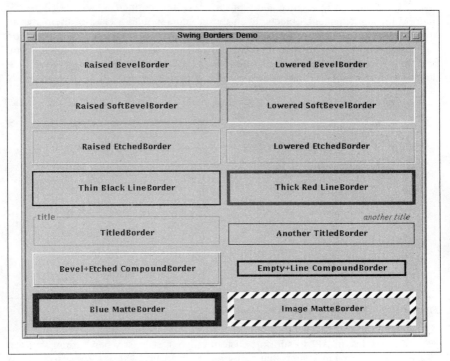

Figure 3–2: Swing border styles

ally. Its `paintIcon()` method is called to display the graphic, and this method can do anything necessary to display it.

Swing includes an `Icon` implementation called `ImageIcon`. This commonly used class is an `Image`-based implementation of `Icon`. `ImageIcon` also simplifies the process of reading images from external files. One of the constructors for `ImageIcon` simply takes the name of the desired image file.

A related utility function is the static method `GrayFilter.createDisabledImage()`. This version produces a grayed-out version of a given `Image`, which can be used to create an `ImageIcon` that represents a disabled action or capability.

Cursors

The cursor, or mouse pointer, is the graphic that appears on the screen and tracks the position of the mouse. Java support for cursors has evolved in each Java release. Java 1.0 and 1.1 included 14 predefined cursors but did not support custom cursors. In Java 1.0, the predefined cursors were represented by constants defined by `java.awt.Frame` and they could be specified only for these top-level `Frame` components. These `Frame` constants and the corresponding `setCursor()` method of `Frame` are now deprecated.

Java 1.1 included a new java.awt.Cursor class and defined a new setCursor() method for all Component objects. Even though cursors had a class of their own in Java 1.1, the Cursor() constructor and the Cursor.getPredefinedCursor() method could still return only the same 14 predefined cursors. Despite their limited number, these predefined cursors are often useful. Figure 3-3 shows what they look like on a Unix machine running the X Window System.

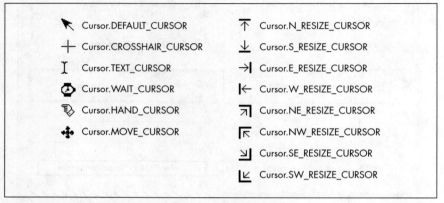

Figure 3-3: The standard Java cursors, on a Unix platform

Java 1.2 includes an API to support custom cursors, at least when running on top of a native windowing system that supports them. In Java 1.2, the Cursor class has a new getSystemCustomCursor() method that returns a named cursor defined by a system administrator in a systemwide *cursors.properties* file. Since there is no way to query the list of system-specific custom cursors, however, this method is rarely used. Instead, an application may create its own custom cursors by calling the createCustomCursor() method of the Toolkit object. First, however, the application should check whether custom cursors are supported, by calling the getBestCursorSize() method of the Toolkit. If this method indicates a width or height of 0, custom cursors are not supported (by either the Java implementation or the underlying windowing system).

To create a custom cursor, you might use code like this:

```
Cursor c;
Toolkit tk = Toolkit.getDefaultToolkit();
Dimension bestsize = tk.getBestCursorSize(24,24);
if (bestsize.width != 0)
  c = tk.createCustomCursor(cursorImage, cursorHotSpot, cursorName);
else
  c = Cursor.getDefaultCursor();
```

Double-Buffering

Double-buffering is the process of drawing graphics into an off-screen image buffer and then copying the contents of the buffer to the screen all at once. For complex graphics, using double-buffering can reduce flickering. Swing automatically supports double-buffering for all of its components. To enable it, simply call the setDoubleBuffered() method (inherited from JComponent) to set the double-Buffered property to true for any components that should use double-buffered drawing.

Remember that double-buffering is memory intensive. Its use is typically only justified for components that are repainted very frequently or have particularly complex graphics to display. Note, however, that if a container uses double-buffering, any double-buffered children it has share the off-screen buffer of the container, so the required off-screen buffer is never larger than the on-screen size of the application.

The Box Container

Chapter 2, *Swing and AWT Architecture*, discussed the general task of arranging components within containers and listed the layout managers provided by AWT and Swing. This section describes a commonly used Swing layout management technique in detail. The easiest way to create complex arrangements of Swing components is often with the javax.swing.Box container.* Box arranges its components into a single row or a single column. You can then use nested Box containers to create a two-dimensional arrangement of components.

The Box container uses the BoxLayout layout manager, but this layout manager is automatically assigned, so you never need to work with it explicitly. The easiest way to create a Box is with the static Box.createHorizontalBox() or Box.createVerticalBox() method. Once you have created a Box, simply add children to it. They will be arranged from left to right or from top to bottom.

The unique power of the Box actually comes from an inner class called Box.Filler. This class is a simple component that has no appearance; it exists simply to insert blank space in a layout and to affect the resize behavior of the layout. You do not create Box.Filler objects directly. Instead, you create them using the following static methods of Box:

```
Box.createHorizontalStrut(int width)
Box.createVerticalStrut(int height)
Box.createHorizontalGlue()
Box.createVerticalGlue()
```

If you are arranging a row of components, you can call createHorizontalStrut() to insert a fixed number of pixels of blank horizontal space. For a column of components, use createVerticalStrut() to insert a blank vertical space.

---

* For some reason, Box does not begin with the letter J as other Swing components and containers do. Nevertheless, it is a very useful and commonly used container.

The glue methods are different. They insert stretchy horizontal or vertical space into a row or column. By default, the space is zero pixels wide or zero pixels high. But, if the row or column is stretched so that it becomes wider or higher than its default size, these glue components stretch to take up that extra space. For example, say you fill a row with some horizontal glue, a JButton component, and some more horizontal glue. Now, no matter how wide the row becomes, the JButton is always centered in it. This is because the two glue components (and possibly the JButton) grow equally to take up the extra space. On the other hand, if the row consists of only one glue component followed by a JButton, the JButton always appears right justified in the row, since the glue component grows to take up all the space to the left of the button.

As another example, consider a Box used in a dialog to hold a row of **OK**, **Cancel**, and **Help** buttons. Without any glue, the buttons are resized to fill up the entire row, with no extra space between them. If we intersperse the three buttons with four glue components, however, the buttons are always nicely spaced out and the buttons and the spaces between them grow proportionally as the dialog box becomes wider.

Minimum, Preferred, and Maximum Sizes

In order to fully understand the behavior of the Box container and its glue, it is important to understand that Swing components can have a minimum size, a preferred size, and a maximum size. Many components have a natural size. For example, with a JButton, the natural size is the space required to accommodate the button text and/or Icon, plus the space required for the button border. By default, a JButton reports its natural size as its minimum size and as its preferred size. When asked for its maximum size, a JButton returns very large integers, indicating that it can grow to become arbitrarily wide and arbitrarily tall.

Swing components (but not AWT components) allow you to specify their minimum, preferred, and maximum sizes. For example, if you do not want to allow a JButton to become arbitrarily large as its container grows larger, you can set a maximum size for it by calling setMaximumSize(). Setting a preferred size for a JButton is an uncommon thing to do, as JButton has a perfectly good natural size. But some components, such as JScrollPane objects, do not have a natural size. For components like these, it is usually important that you establish a default size with setPreferredSize(). If you want to prevent a JScrollPane or similar component from becoming arbitrarily small or arbitrarily large, you should also call setMinimumSize() and setMaximumSize().

Now that you understand the concepts of minimum, preferred, and maximum sizes, we can return to the Box container and its struts and glue. Both struts and glue are instances of the Box.Filler component. When you create a Box.Filler, you are actually specifying minimum, preferred, and maximum sizes for the component. A horizontal strut is simply a Box.Filler with its minimum, preferred, and maximum width set to the number of pixels you specify. A vertical strut has a fixed minimum, preferred, and maximum height.

Horizontal glue has a minimum and preferred width of zero, but a very large maximum width. This means that the glue takes up no space by default but grows as necessary to fill up extra space. Vertical glue does the same thing in the other dimension. In order to understand glue, it is also important to understand how the Box container distributes excess space to its children. If a horizontal Box becomes wider, the extra width is allocated among the children based on their maximum widths. Children with larger maximums are given a proportionally larger amount of the extra space. When you intersperse JButton objects with glue, all the components have effectively infinite maximum widths, so all grow by equal amounts. Suppose, instead, that you restricted the sizes of your buttons like this:

```
okayButton.setMaximumSize(okayButton.getPreferredSize());
cancelButton.setMaximumSize(cancelButton.getPreferredSize());
helpButton.setMaximumSize(helpButton.getPreferredSize());
```

In this case, the buttons are already at their maximum sizes, so no extra space is allocated to them. Now the glue between the buttons gets all the extra space.

I just said that glue components have a preferred size of zero. With regard to the example of three buttons interspersed with four glue components, this means that when the row of buttons is displayed at its default size, the buttons bump into one another and appear awkwardly crowded. To remedy this, you might place horizontal struts *and* horizontal glue between the buttons. In this case, the struts provide the default and minimum spacing, while the glue components make the spacing grow. There is a more efficient way to do this, however. You can explicitly create Box.Filler components that combine the nonzero default size of a strut with the infinite maximum size of a glue object. You can create such a filler object as follows:

```
Dimension fixedwidth = new Dimension(15, 0);
Dimension infinitewidth = new Dimension(Short.MAX_VALUE, 0);
Box.Filler filler = new Box.Filler(fixedwidth, fixedwidth, infinitewidth);
```

The Other Dimension

So far, our discussion of the Box container has covered only how components are arranged horizontally in a horizontal box or vertically in a vertical box. What does Box do in the other dimension? When laying out components in a row, the Box makes the row as tall as the tallest component and then attempts to make all the components as tall as the row. Similarly, when it lays out components in a column, Box tries to make all components as wide as the widest component.

As we've discussed, however, components can have a maximum size. If a row becomes taller than a component's maximum height or a column becomes wider than a component's maximum width, the Box must decide how to position the component with respect to the others in the row or column. For a column, the component can be left, center, or right justified or positioned anywhere in between. A component in a row can be aligned along the top or bottom of the row or placed somewhere in between.

A Box positions such a component based on its alignmentX or alignmentY property. Each is a float property that should have a value between 0.0 and 1.0. The default for both is 0.5. When a component needs to be positioned horizontally in a column, the Box uses the alignmentX property. A value of 0.0 means the component is left justified, 1.0 means the component is right justified, and 0.5 means the component is centered. Other values position the component appropriately between these positions. When a Box needs to position a component vertically in a row, it uses the component's alignmentY property to place the component in the vertical plane in an analogous way.

Simple Dialogs

GUIs often use dialog boxes to handle simple interactions with the user. javax.swing.JOptionPane is a Swing component that is designed to serve as a highly configurable body of a dialog box. Instead of using the JOptionPane directly, however, most Swing programs use one or more of the many static methods defined by JOptionPane. These methods make it quite easy to implement simple dialog-based interactions.

If you take a look at the API for JOptionPane, you'll see that the class defines a group of static methods whose names begin with show and another whose names begin with showInternal. The show methods display simple dialog boxes within JDialog windows, while the showInternal methods display the same dialog boxes inside JInternalFrame windows. These static methods are further broken down by the type of dialog they display. There are several versions of showMessageDialog(), showConfirmDialog(), and showInputDialog(), as well as showInternal versions of the same methods. We'll consider these three types of dialogs—message, confirm, and input—in the sections that follow.

Message Dialogs

Message dialogs are used to display important information to users in a way that is difficult or impossible for them to miss. For example, you might use a message dialog to tell the user that a requested file was not found. To display this message with a JOptionPane, you can use code like this:

```
JOptionPane.showMessageDialog(mainpanel, "The file you requested, " +
                           filename + ", was not found. Please try again");
```

This code produces the dialog shown in Figure 3-4. The dialog remains visible until the user dismisses it by clicking **OK**.

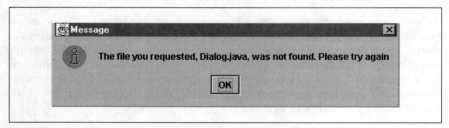

Figure 3-4: A JOptionPane message dialog

The first argument to showMessageDialog() is the component over which the dialog is to appear. You typically specify the main window or panel of your application. If you specify `null`, then the dialog will simply be centered on the screen. The second argument is obviously the message to be displayed. If you look at the API again, however, you'll notice that the *message* argument to this and other `JOptionPane` methods is defined as an `Object`, not a `String`. This means that you are not limited to textual messages. If you pass a `Component` or an `Icon`, the `JOptionPane` displays it as the message. If you pass some other kind of object, `JOptionPane` attempts to convert it to a string by calling its `toString()` method. You can even pass an array of objects as the *message* argument. When you pass more than one object, the objects are displayed top to bottom in the resulting dialog. So, to display a multiline message, for example, you can just pass in an array of `String` objects, instead of a single long `String`.

The `showMessageDialog()` function has variants that take more arguments. The *title* argument specifies the text to appear in the titlebar of the dialog. The *messageType* argument specifies the general type of the message. Legal values are the `JOptionPane` constants that end with `_MESSAGE`. The values you are most likely to use are `INFORMATION_MESSAGE`, `WARNING_MESSAGE`, and `ERROR_MESSAGE`. Specifying a message type implicitly specifies the icon that appears in the dialog box. If you don't like the default icons, however, there is a version of `showMessageDialog()` that lets you specify your own *icon* to display.

Confirm Dialogs

You can use `JOptionPane.showConfirmDialog()` or `JOptionPane.showInternal-ConfirmDialog()` when you want to ask the user a simple question that requires a **Yes** or **No** (or perhaps **Cancel**) answer. For example, you can use one of these methods to present the dialog shown in Figure 3-5.

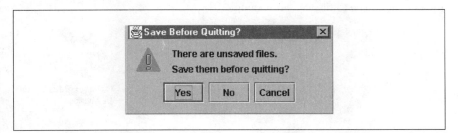

Figure 3–5: A JOptionPane confirm dialog

The arguments to `showConfirmDialog()` are much like the arguments to `showMessageDialog()`, with the addition of the *optionType* argument. This argument specifies the set of buttons that appears at the bottom of the dialog. Legal values are `OK_CANCEL_OPTION`, `YES_NO_OPTION`, and `YES_NO_CANCEL_OPTION`.

A confirm dialog asks the user a question. The return value of `showOptionDialog()` or `showInternalOptionDialog()` is an integer that represents the user's answer in terms of the button the user clicked to dismiss the dialog. The possible values are `OK_OPTION`, `YES_OPTION`, `NO_OPTION`, `CANCEL_OPTION`, and `CLOSED_OPTION`. This last value is returned if the user did not click any of the dialog buttons but instead dismissed the dialog by closing the window. Here is some simple code that asks a question with a confirm dialog (note the use of a string array for the *message* argument):

```
int response = JOptionPane.showConfirmDialog(mainpanel, new String[] {
        /* first line of the message */    "There are unsaved files.",
        /* second line of message   */    "Save them before quitting?"},
        /* dialog title             */    "Save Before Quitting?",
        /* what buttons to display   */    JOptionPane.YES_NO_CANCEL_OPTICN,
        /* icon type to display      */    JOptionPane.WARNING_MESSAGE);
switch(response) {
  case JOptionPane.YES_OPTION:        saveAndQuit();
  case JOptionPane.NO_OPTION:         quitWithoutSaving();
  case JOptionPane.CANCEL_OPTION:
  case JOptionPane.CLOSED_OPTION:     break;   // Don't quit!
}
```

Input Dialogs

The showInputDialog() and showInternalInputDialog() methods are designed to ask for input that is more complex than a yes-or-no answer. The simple versions of showInputDialog() support asking a question like "What is your name?" and letting the user type a response in a text input area:

```
String name = JOptionPane.showInputDialog(frame, "What is your name?");
```

The more complex version of this method allows the user to select an object from a list or pull-down menu of predefined options.

The arguments to showInputDialog() are quite similar to those passed to showMessageDialog() and showConfirmDialog(). To display a list of options to the user, use the seven-argument version of the method and pass in an array of choices and the default choice to display. For example:

```
String response = (String) JOptionPane.showInputDialog(
                    contentpane,                              // parent
                    "Who is your favorite chipmunk?",        // message
                    "Pick a Chipmunk",                        // dialog title
                    JOptionPane.QUESTION_MESSAGE,            // icon type
                    null,                                     // no explicit icon
                    new String[] {                            // choices
                        "Alvin", "Simon", "Theodore"
                    },
                    "Alvin");                                 // default choice
```

JFileChooser

javax.swing.JFileChooser is a specialized component that allows the user to browse the filesystem and select a file. The easiest way to use it is with the showOpenDialog() and showSaveDialog() methods. These methods differ only in the text that appears in the "Okay" button. You can also call the showDialog() method and specify your own text for that button. Each of these methods returns an integer status code that specifies how the user dismissed the dialog. If the return value is APPROVE_OPTION, the user actually selected a file, which you can obtain with the getSelectedFile() method. For example:

```
public void saveAs() {
  JFileChooser chooser = new JFileChooser();
  int result = chooser.showSaveDialog(mainpane);
  if (result == JFileChooser.APPROVE_OPTION)

save(chooser.getSelectedFile());
}
```

Note that `showSaveDialog()` and `showOpenDialog()` are instance methods, not static methods like those used with `JOptionPane`. This means that you can customize the dialog by setting properties on your `JFileChooser` object. You may be interested in setting the `currentDirectory` and `fileSelectionMode` properties before you display a `JFileChooser`. `fileSelectionMode` can be set to `FILES_ONLY`, `DIRECTORIES_ONLY`, or `FILES_AND_DIRECTORIES`. Once you create a `JFileChooser` for an application, you may want to reuse it, rather than creating a new one each time you need one. If you do so, the `JFileChooser` automatically remembers the `currentDirectory` most recently selected by the user.

Using File Filters

The `javax.swing.filechooser` package defines auxiliary classes that are used by `JFileChooser`. One of the most important of these is `FileFilter`. The abstract `javax.swing.filechooser.FileFilter` class is much like the `java.io.FileFilter` interface. Each defines an `accept()` method that is passed `File` objects and returns true for each file that should be displayed. The `FileFilter` class used by `JFileChooser` has an additional `getDescription()` method that returns a string that names the types of files accepted by the filter. For example, you might define a `FileFilter` subclass that accepts files with names ending in *.htm* or *.html* and returns a description of "HTML Files."

When you create a `JFileChooser`, you can specify the `FileFilter` it is to use with `setFileFilter()`. Alternately, you can specify an array of `FileFilter` objects with `setChoosableFileFilters()`. In this case, `JFileChooser` displays the descriptions of the filters and allows the user to choose one.

Customizing JFileChooser

The behavior of a `JFileChooser` can be customized by providing your own implementation of `FileView` and `FileSystemView`. Both of these abstract classes are defined in the `javax.swing.filechooser` class. `FileView` defines methods that affect the way individual files are displayed by the `JFileChooser`, while `FileSystemView` defines methods that enable the `JFileChooser` to handle operating-system dependencies in the filesystem. `FileSystemView` understands the notion of hidden files, and it can return a complete list of filesystem roots, a capability that was lacking from the basic `java.io.File` class prior to Java 1.2. The default `FileView` and `FileSystemView` classes provided by `JFileChooser` are perfectly adequate for most purposes, so you typically don't have to implement these classes yourself.

It is also possible to customize a `JFileChooser` by providing an accessory component. If you pass a `JComponent` to the `setAccessory()` method of `JFileChooser`, the Swing component you specify is displayed in the file chooser dialog box. A common use of a file chooser accessory is as a file preview component. In order to provide a preview of the currently selected file, the accessory must know what the currently selected file is. It can get this information by implementing the PropertyChangeListener interface and listening for changes to the selectedFile property. In order for this to work, you have to pass the accessory object to the addPropertyChangeListener() method of the JFileChooser, of course.

JColorChooser

Just as JFileChooser allows the user to choose a file, javax.swing.JColorChooser allows the user to choose a color. Figure 3-6 shows a JColorChooser dialog. You can embed a JColorChooser component directly in your application or in a custom dialog box, but the most common way to use it is to simply call the static showDialog() method:

```
Color c = JColorChooser.showDialog(contentpane,   // Dialog appears over this
                                   "Pick a Color", // Dialog title
                                   Color.white);   // Default color selection
```

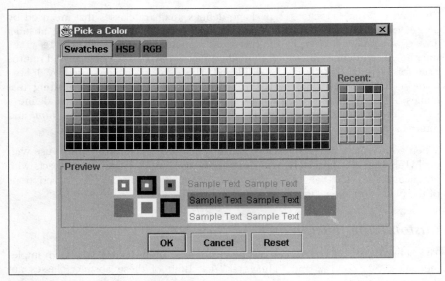

Figure 3-6: A JColorChooser dialog

As you can see from Figure 3-6, JColorChooser displays a color selection pane and a color preview pane. The selection pane is actually a JTabbedPane that allows colors to be selected in three different ways. The **Swatches** pane lets the user select a color from a palette of color swatches. With the **RGB** pane, the user picks a color by specifying the red, green, and blue components of the color, while with the **HSV** pane, the user specifies the hue, saturation, and value components of the color.

Instead of displaying a generic JColorChooser with the static showDialog() method, you can create your own instance of the JColorChooser class. You can then set properties on the color chooser object and display it in any way you want. The static JColorChooser.createDialog() method is useful here. It creates a dialog box to hold your JColorChooser pane and allows you to specify two ActionListener objects that are invoked in response to the **OK** and **Cancel** buttons in the dialog box.

You can customize a JColorChooser by adding a new color selection panel or a new color preview panel. To add a new color selection panel (for example, a panel that allows the user to select a grayscale color or a CMYK color), implement a subclass of AbstractColorChooserPanel (from the javax.swing.colorchooser package) and pass it to the addChooserPanel() method of your JColorChooser. Your custom panel contains a ColorSelectionModel that serves as the interface between your pane and the JColorChooser. All your pane needs to do is update the selected color of its ColorSelectionModel (ColorSelectionModel is also part of the javax.swing.colorchooser package).

You can use any JComponent as a custom preview panel for your JColorChooser. Simply pass the component to setPreviewPanel(). The preview component has to track the currently selected color by listening for ChangeEvent events generated by the ColorSelectionModel of the JColorChooser.

Menus

In Swing, menu bars, menu panes, and menu items are components, just like all other Swing components. JMenuBar is a container designed to hold JMenu objects. JMenu is a container designed to hold JMenuItem objects and other JMenu objects (as submenus). Working with menus is not exactly the same as working with other types of components, however, and Example 3-1 shows a simple example of creating pull-down and pop-up menus.

Example 3-1: Creating Pull-Down and Pop-Up Menus in Swing

```
import java.awt.*;
import java.awt.event.*;
import javax.swing.*;

public class MenuDemo {
  public static void main(String[] args) {
    // Create a window for this demo
    JFrame frame = new JFrame("Menu Demo");
    JPanel panel = new JPanel();
    frame.getContentPane().add(panel, "Center");

    // Create an action listener for the menu items we will create
    // The MenuItemActionListener class is defined below
    ActionListener listener = new MenuItemActionListener(panel);

    // Create some menu panes, and fill them with menu items
    // The menuItem() method is important.  It is defined below.
    JMenu file = new JMenu("File");
    file.setMnemonic('F');
    file.add(menuItem("New", listener, "new", 'N', KeyEvent.VK_N));
```

Example 3–1: Creating Pull-Down and Pop-Up Menus in Swing (continued)

```java
        file.add(menuItem("Open...", listener, "open", 'O', KeyEvent.VK_O));
        file.add(menuItem("Save", listener, "save", 'S', KeyEvent.VK_S));
        file.add(menuItem("Save As...", listener, "saveas", 'A', KeyEvent.VK_A));

        JMenu edit = new JMenu("Edit");
        edit.setMnemonic('E');
        edit.add(menuItem("Cut", listener, "cut", 0, KeyEvent.VK_X));
        edit.add(menuItem("Copy", listener, "copy", 'C', KeyEvent.VK_C));
        edit.add(menuItem("Paste", listener, "paste", 0, KeyEvent.VK_V));

        // Create a menu bar and add these panes to it.
        JMenuBar menubar = new JMenuBar();
        menubar.add(file);
        menubar.add(edit);

        // Add menu bar to the main window.  Note special method to add menu bars.
        frame.setJMenuBar(menubar);

        // Now create a popup menu and add the some stuff to it
        final JPopupMenu popup = new JPopupMenu();
        popup.add(menuItem("Open...", listener, "open", 0, 0));
        popup.addSeparator();                  // Add a separator between items
        JMenu colors = new JMenu("Colors");  // Create a submenu
        popup.add(colors);                     // and add it to the popup menu
        // Now fill the submenu with mutually exclusive radio buttons
        ButtonGroup colorgroup = new ButtonGroup();
        colors.add(radioItem("Red", listener, "color(red)", colorgroup));
        colors.add(radioItem("Green", listener, "color(green)", colorgroup));
        colors.add(radioItem("Blue", listener, "color(blue)", colorgroup));

        // Arrange to display the popup menu when the user clicks in the window
        panel.addMouseListener(new MouseAdapter() {
          public void mousePressed(MouseEvent e) {
            // Check whether this is the right type of event to pop up a popup
            // menu on this platform.  Usually checks for right button down.
            if (e.isPopupTrigger())
              popup.show((Component)e.getSource(), e.getX(), e.getY());
          }
        });

        // Finally, make our main window appear
        frame.setSize(450, 300);
        frame.setVisible(true);
    }


    // A convenience method for creating menu items
    public static JMenuItem menuItem(String label,
                                     ActionListener listener, String command,
                                     int mnemonic, int acceleratorKey) {
      JMenuItem item = new JMenuItem(label);
      item.addActionListener(listener);
      item.setActionCommand(command);
      if (mnemonic != 0) item.setMnemonic((char) mnemonic);
      if (acceleratorKey != 0)
        item.setAccelerator(KeyStroke.getKeyStroke(acceleratorKey,
                                                java.awt.Event.CTRL_MASK));
      return item;
    }
```

Example 3-1: Creating Pull-Down and Pop-Up Menus in Swing (continued)

```
// A convenience method for creating radio button menu items
public static JMenuItem radioItem(String label, ActionListener listener,
                                  String command, ButtonGroup mutExGroup) {
  JMenuItem item = new JRadioButtonMenuItem(label);
  item.addActionListener(listener);
  item.setActionCommand(command);
  mutExGroup.add(item);
  return item;
}

// An event listener class used with the menu items created above
// For this demo, it just displays a dialog box when an item is selected
public static class MenuItemActionListener implements ActionListener {
  Component parent;
  public MenuItemActionListener(Component parent) { this.parent = parent; }
  public void actionPerformed(ActionEvent e) {
    JMenuItem item = (JMenuItem) e.getSource();
    String cmd = item.getActionCommand();
    JOptionPane.showMessageDialog(parent, cmd + " was selected.");
  }
 }
}
```

Swing Prog. Topics

JTree and TreeModel

The javax.swing.JTree class is a powerful Swing component for displaying tree-structured data. Like all Swing components, JTree relies on a separate model object to hold and represent the data that it displays. Most Swing components create this model object automatically, and you never need to work with it explicitly. The JTree component, however, displays data that is much more complex than a typical Swing component. When you are working with a JTree, you must create a model object that implements the javax.swing.tree.TreeModel interface.

One approach is to use the DefaultTreeModel class, which implements the TreeModel interface using the TreeNode and MutableTreeNode interfaces (all defined in javax.swing.tree). To use DefaultTreeModel, you must implement your hierarchical data structures so that each element of the tree implements the TreeNode or MutableTreeNode interface. Now you can create a DefaultTreeModel object simply by passing the root TreeNode of your tree to a DefaultTreeModel constructor. Then you create a JTree component to display your tree simply by passing the DefaultTreeModel to the setModel() method of the JTree.

Sometimes, however, you do not have the luxury of designing the data structures used to represent your tree, so implementing the TreeNode interface is simply not an option. In this case, you can implement the TreeModel interface directly. The resulting TreeModel object serves as the interface between your data and the JTree component that displays the data. Your TreeModel implementation provides the methods that allow the JTree component to traverse the nodes of your tree, regardless of the actual representation of the tree data.

Example 3-2 shows a program that implements the TreeModel interface to represent the hierarchical structure of the filesystem, thereby allowing the file and directory tree to be displayed in a JTree component. Notice how a relatively simple implementation of `TreeModel` enables the powerful tree- browsing capabilities shown in Figure 3-7.

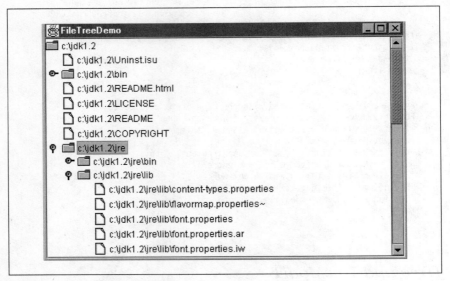

Figure 3-7: The JTree component

Example 3-2: Using JTree and TreeModel

```java
import javax.swing.*;
import javax.swing.event.*;
import javax.swing.tree.*;
import java.io.File;

public class FileTreeDemo {
  public static void main(String[] args) {
    // Figure out where in the filesystem to start displaying
    File root;
    if (args.length > 0) root = new File(args[0]);
    else root = new File(System.getProperty("user.home"));

    // Create a TreeModel object to represent our tree of files
    FileTreeModel model = new FileTreeModel(root);

    // Create a JTree and tell it to display our model
    JTree tree = new JTree();
    tree.setModel(model);

    // The JTree can get big, so allow it to scroll
    JScrollPane scrollpane = new JScrollPane(tree);

    // Display it all in a window and make the window appear
    JFrame frame = new JFrame("FileTreeDemo");
    frame.getContentPane().add(scrollpane, "Center");
    frame.setSize(400,600);
    frame.setVisible(true);
  }
}
```

Example 3-2: Using JTree and TreeModel (continued)

```java
/**
 * The methods in this class allow the JTree component to traverse
 * the file system tree and display the files and directories.
 **/
class FileTreeModel implements TreeModel {
  // We specify the root directory when we create the model.
  protected File root;
  public FileTreeModel(File root) { this.root = root; }

  // The model knows how to return the root object of the tree
  public Object getRoot() { return root; }

  // Tell JTree whether an object in the tree is a leaf
  public boolean isLeaf(Object node) {  return ((File)node).isFile(); }

  // Tell JTree how many children a node has
  public int getChildCount(Object parent) {
    String[] children = ((File)parent).list();
    if (children == null) return 0;
    return children.length;
  }

  // Fetch any numbered child of a node for the JTree.
  // Our model returns File objects for all nodes in the tree.  The
  // JTree displays these by calling the File.toString() method.
  public Object getChild(Object parent, int index) {
    String[] children = ((File)parent).list();
    if ((children == null) || (index >= children.length)) return null;
    return new File((File) parent, children[index]);
  }

  // Figure out a child's position in its parent node.
  public int getIndexOfChild(Object parent, Object child) {
    String[] children = ((File)parent).list();
    if (children == null) return -1;
    String childname = ((File)child).getName();
    for(int i = 0; i < children.length; i++) {
      if (childname.equals(children[i])) return i;
    }
    return -1;
  }

  // This method is invoked by the JTree only for editable trees.
  // This TreeModel does not allow editing, so we do not implement
  // this method.  The JTree editable property is false by default.
  public void valueForPathChanged(TreePath path, Object newvalue) {}

  // Since this is not an editable tree model, we never fire any events,
  // so we don't actually have to keep track of interested listeners
  public void addTreeModelListener(TreeModelListener l) {}
  public void removeTreeModelListener(TreeModelListener l) {}
}
```

JTable and TableModel

`javax.swing.JTable` is another powerful Swing component for displaying complex data structures. Like `JTree`, `JTable` relies on a separate model object to hold and represent the data it displays and has its own package of helper classes, `javax.swing.table`. This package contains the `TableModel` interface and its default implementations, `AbstractTableModel` and `DefaultTableModel`.

If your table data is tidily organized, it is easy to use `JTable` without worrying about the `TableModel`. If your data is an array of rows, where each row is an array of objects, you can just pass this `Object[][]` directly to the `JTable` constructor. If you want, you can also specify an optional array of column names. This is all you need to do: the `JTable` does the rest. This technique also works if your data is stored in a `Vector` of rows, where each row is itself a `Vector`.

Often, however, your data is not as regular as that. When you want to display a tabular view of data that is not, by nature, tabular, you must implement the `Table-Model` interface (or, more likely, subclass the `AbstractTableModel` class). The job of this `TableModel` implementation is to serve as the interface between your data, which is not neatly organized into a table, and the `JTable` object, which wants to display a table. In other words, your `TableModel` presents a neat tabular view of your data, regardless of how the data is organized underneath.

Example 3-3 shows how this can be done. Given a `File` object that represents a directory in the filesystem, this example displays the contents of that directory in tabular form, as shown in Figure 3-8. Once again, notice how a relatively simple `TableModel` implementation enables the use of the powerful table-display capabilities of the `JTable` component.

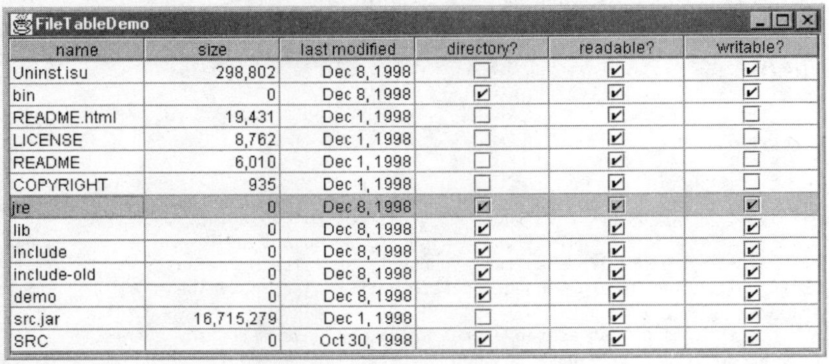

name	size	last modified	directory?	readable?	writable?
Uninst.isu	298,802	Dec 8, 1998	☐	☑	☑
bin	0	Dec 8, 1998	☑	☑	☑
README.html	19,431	Dec 1, 1998	☐	☑	☐
LICENSE	8,762	Dec 1, 1998	☐	☑	☐
README	6,010	Dec 1, 1998	☐	☑	☐
COPYRIGHT	935	Dec 1, 1998	☐	☑	☐
jre	0	Dec 8, 1998	☑	☑	☑
lib	0	Dec 8, 1998	☑	☑	☑
include	0	Dec 8, 1998	☑	☑	☑
include-old	0	Dec 8, 1998	☑	☑	☑
demo	0	Dec 8, 1998	☑	☑	☑
src.jar	16,715,279	Dec 1, 1998	☐	☑	☑
SRC	0	Oct 30, 1998	☑	☑	☑

Figure 3-8: The JTable component

Example 3-3: Using JTable and TableModel

```
import javax.swing.*;
import javax.swing.table.*;
import java.io.File;
import java.util.Date;
```

Example 3-3: Using JTable and TableModel (continued)

```
public class FileTableDemo {
  public static void main(String[] args) {
    // Figure out what directory to display
    File dir;
    if (args.length > 0) dir = new File(args[0]);
    else dir = new File(System.getProperty("user.home"));

    // Create a TableModel object to represent the contents of the directory
    FileTableModel model = new FileTableModel(dir);

    // Create a JTable and tell it to display our model
    JTable table = new JTable(model);

    // Display it all in a scrolling window and make the window appear
    JFrame frame = new JFrame("FileTableDemo");
    frame.getContentPane().add(new JScrollPane(table), "Center");
    frame.setSize(600, 400);
    frame.setVisible(true);
  }
}


/**
 * The methods in this class allow the JTable component to get
 * and display data about the files in a specified directory.
 * It represents a table with six columns: filename, size, modif:cation date,
 * plus three columns for flags: directory, readable, writable.
 **/
class FileTableModel extends AbstractTableModel {
  protected File dir;
  protected String[] filenames;

  protected String[] columnNames = new String[] {
    "name", "size", "last modified", "directory?", "readable?", 'writable?"
  };

  protected Class[] columnClasses = new Class[] {
    String.class, Long.class, Date.class,
      Boolean.class, Boolean.class, Boolean.class
  };

  // This table model works for any one given directory
  public FileTableModel(File dir) {
    this.dir = dir;
    this.filenames = dir.list();  // Store a list of files in the directory
  }

  // These are easy methods
  public int getColumnCount() { return 6; }  // A constant for this model
  public int getRowCount() { return filenames.length; }  // # of files in dir

  // Information about each column
  public String getColumnName(int col) { return columnNames[col]; }
  public Class getColumnClass(int col) { return columnClasses[col]; }

  // The method that must actually return the value of each cell
  public Object getValueAt(int row, int col) {
    File f = new File(dir, filenames[row]);
    switch(col) {
```

Example 3-3: Using JTable and TableModel (continued)

```
    case 0: return filenames[row];
    case 1: return new Long(f.length());
    case 2: return new Date(f.lastModified());
    case 3: return f.isDirectory() ? Boolean.TRUE : Boolean.FALSE;
    case 4: return f.canRead() ? Boolean.TRUE : Boolean.FALSE;
    case 5: return f.canWrite() ? Boolean.TRUE : Boolean.FALSE;
    default: return null;
    }
  }
}
```

JTextComponent and HTML Text Display

The most complex component in all of Swing is the JTextComponent, which is a powerful editor. It is part of the javax.swing.text package and generally is not used directly. Instead, you typically use one of its subclasses, such as JTextField, JPasswordField, JTextArea, or JEditorPane. The first three of these components are straightforward. They are for the entry of a single line of text, secret text such as a password, and simple, unformatted, multiline text, respectively.

It is the JEditorPane component that really makes use of the full power of JTextComponent. JEditorPane supports the display and editing of complex formatted text. In conjunction with the classes in the javax.swing.text.html and javax.swing.text.rtf packages, JEditorPane can display and edit HTML and RTF documents. The ability to display formatted text so easily is a very powerful feature. For example, the ability to display HTML documents makes it simple for a Swing application to add online help based on an HTML version of the application's user manual. Furthermore, formatted text is a professional-looking way for an application to display its output to the user.

Because HTML has become so ubiquitous, we'll focus on the display of HTML documents with JEditorPane, There are several different ways to get a JEditorPane to display an HTML document. If the desired document is available on the network, the easiest way to display it is simply to pass an appropriate java.net.URL object to the setPage() method of JEditorPane. setPage() determines the data type of the document and, assuming it is an HTML document, loads it and displays it as such. For example:

```
editor.setPage(new java.net.URL("http://www.my.com/product/help.htm"));
```

If the document you want to display is in a local file or is available from some kind of InputStream, you can display it by passing the appropriate stream to the read() method of JEditorPane. The second argument to this method should be null. For example:

```
InputStream in = new FileInputStream("help.htm");
editor.read(in, null);
```

Yet another way to display text in a JEditorPane is to pass the text to the set-Text() method. Before you do this, however, you must tell the editor what type of text to expect:

```
editor.setContentType("text/html");
editor.setText("<H1>Hello World!</H1>");
```

Calling setText() can be particularly useful when your application generates HTML text on the fly and wants to use a JEditorPane to display nicely formatted output to the user.

Example 3-4 shows one such use of the JEditorPane. This example is an alternative to Example 3-3: it displays the contents of a directory in tabular form but uses an HTML table instead of the JTable component. As a bonus, this example uses HTML hyperlinks to allow the user to browse from one directory to the next. (If you download and run the two examples, however, you'll probably notice that the JTable example is significantly faster, since it does not have to encode the directory contents into HTML and then parse that HTML into a table.) Figure 3-9 shows sample output from this example.

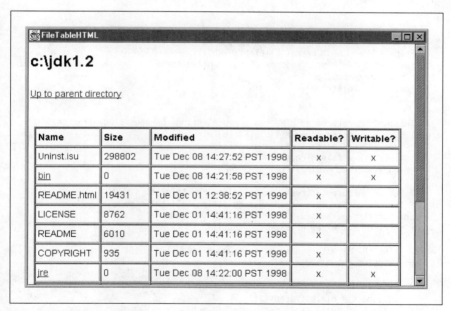

Figure 3-9: The JEditorPane component displaying an HTML table

Example 3-4: Dynamically Generated HTML in JEditorPane

```java
import javax.swing.*;
import javax.swing.event.*;
import java.io.*;
import java.util.Date;

/**
 * This class implements a simple directory browser using the HTML
 * display capabilities of the JEditorPane component
```

Example 3-4: Dynamically Generated HTML in JEditorPane (continued)

```
**/
public class FileTableHTML {
  public static void main(String[] args) throws IOException {
    // Get the name of the directory to display
    String dirname = (args.length>0)?args[0]:System.getProperty("user.home");

    // Create something to display it in
    final JEditorPane editor = new JEditorPane();
    editor.setEditable(false);                  // we're browsing not editing
    editor.setContentType("text/html");         // must specify HTML text
    editor.setText(makeHTMLTable(dirname));     // specify the text to display

    // Set up the JEditorPane to handle clicks on hyperlinks
    editor.addHyperlinkListener(new HyperlinkListener() {
      public void hyperlinkUpdate(HyperlinkEvent e) {
        // Handle clicks; ignore mouseovers and other link-related events
        if (e.getEventType() == HyperlinkEvent.EventType.ACTIVATED) {
          // Get the HREF of the link and display it.
          editor.setText(makeHTMLTable(e.getDescription()));
        }
      }
    });

    // Put the JEditorPane in a scrolling window and display it
    JFrame frame = new JFrame("FileTableHTML");
    frame.getContentPane().add(new JScrollPane(editor));
    frame.setSize(650, 500);
    frame.setVisible(true);
  }

  // This method returns an HTML table representing the specified directory
  public static String makeHTMLTable(String dirname) {
    // Look up the contents of the directory
    File dir = new File(dirname);
    String[] entries = dir.list();

    // Set up an output stream we can print the table to.
    // This is easier than concatenating strings all the time.
    StringWriter sout = new StringWriter();
    PrintWriter out = new PrintWriter(sout);

    // Print the directory name as the page title
    out.println("<H1>" + dirname + "</H1>");

    // Print an "up" link, unless we're already at the root
    String parent = dir.getParent();
    if ((parent != null) && (parent.length() > 0))
      out.println("<A HREF=\"" + parent + "\">Up to parent directory</A><P>");

    // Print out the table
    out.print("<TABLE BORDER=2 WIDTH=600><TR>");
    out.print("<TH>Name</TH><TH>Size</TH><TH>Modified</TH>");
    out.println("<TH>Readable?</TH><TH>Writable?</TH></TR>");
    for(int i=0; i < entries.length; i++) {
      File f = new File(dir, entries[i]);
      out.println("<TR><TD>" +
                  (f.isDirectory() ?
                     "<a href=\""+f+"\">" + entries[i] + "</a>" :
```

Example 3-4: Dynamically Generated HTML in JEditorPane (continued)

```
                        entries[i]) +
                "</TD><TD>" + f.length() +
                "</TD><TD>" + new Date(f.lastModified()) +
                "</TD><TD align=center>" + (f.canRead()?"x":" ") +
                "</TD><TD align=center>" + (f.canWrite()?"x":" ") +
                "</TD></TR>");
    }
    out.println("</TABLE>");
    out.close();

    // Get the string of HTML from the StringWriter and return it.
    return sout.toString();
  }
}
```

Pluggable Look-and-Feel

One of the unique features of Swing is its pluggable look-and-feel (PLAF) architecture, which allows a Swing application to change its entire appearance with one or two lines of code. The most common use of this feature is to give applications a choice between the native platform look-and-feel and a new platform-independent Java look-and-feel (also known as the Metal look-and-feel). Swing is distributed with three look-and-feels: Metal and two look-and-feels that mimic the appearance and behavior of the Windows and Motif (Unix/X) component toolkits. A look-and-feel that mimics the Macintosh platform is available as a separate download. While the Metal and Motif look-and-feels can be freely used, the Windows look-and-feel is restricted for use only on Windows platform—for copyright reasons, it does not run on any other operating system.

When a Swing application starts up, it reads the system property `swing.default-laf` to determine the classname of the default look-and-feel. In most Java installations, this property is set to the default Java look-and-feel, implemented by the class `javax.swing.plaf.metal.MetalLookAndFeel`. The end user can override this default by using the -D switch on the command line when invoking the Java interpreter. For example, to run a Swing application using the Motif look-and-feel, a user can type:

```
% java -Dswing.defaultlaf=com.sun.java.swing.plaf.motif.MotifLookAndFeel app
```

If the user is using a Windows operating system, he can start the application using the Windows look-and-feel like this:

```
% java -Dswing.defaultlaf=com.sun.java.swing.plaf.windows.WindowsLookAndFeel app
```

When you write a Swing application, you can explicitly set the look-and-feel that the application uses. To do this, simply call the static `setLookAndFeel()` method of the `UIManager` class and specify the classname of the desired look-and-feel implementation. To make this even easier, `UIManager` defines a static method that returns the classname of the default cross-platform look-and-feel (i.e., Metal) and another that returns the classname of the look-and-feel that mimics the native look-and-feel of the current platform. So, if you want your application to always look like a native application, you can simply include this line of code in your application, before it begins to create any GUI components:

```
UIManager.setLookAndFeel(UIManager.getSystemLookAndFeelClassName());
```

Or, if you want to force the application to use the cross-platform look-and-feel, regardless of installation defaults and user preferences, you can use this line of code:

```
UIManager.setLookAndFeel(UIManager.getCrossPlatformLookAndFeelClassName());
```

Note that calling setLookAndFeel() like this overrides the value of the swing.defaultlaf property, if the end user has set one. Of course, the command-line syntax for setting that property is quite awkward and may be beyond the capabilities of many end users. An alternative is to implement command-line options in your own application that give the user a choice of look-and-feels. You might set a native look-and-feel if the user specifies a -nativelook flag on the command line, for example.

The easiest time to call the setLookAndFeel() method is at application start-up, before any Swing components have been created. It is also possible to change the look-and-feel of a running application, however. This means that you can allow the user to change the current look-and-feel through a preferences dialog box, if you are so inclined. When the user selects a new look-and-feel, you first call set-LookAndFeel() to install the new look-and-feel, and then you have to notify all of the Swing components that a new look-and-feel is in effect and ask them to use it. Fortunately, there is a convenience method to do this. Your code might look like this:

```
// Set the new look-and-feel
UIManager.setLookAndFeel(UIManager.getSystemLookAndFeelClassName);
// Tell all components from main JFrame on down that LAF has changed
SwingUtilities.updateComponentTreeUI(myframe);
```

A dialog that allows the user to change the currently installed look-and-feel of a running application should probably let the user choose among all the look-and-feels that are installed on the system. An application can find out the classnames and human-readable names of all the installed look-and-feels on a given system by calling the static getInstalledLookAndFeels() method of UIManager. In the implementation from Sun, this method returns either a default list of installed look-and-feels or a list obtained from the swing.properties file of the installation.

Using Themes with the Metal Look-and-Feel

You can customize the colors and fonts of the default Java look-and-feel by sub-classing the DefaultMetalTheme class that appears in the javax.swing.plaf.metal package. When you create a custom subclass, you can specify the six different fonts and six different colors used by the Metal look-and-feel. For example, you might implement a large font theme for users who have difficulty reading the default fonts used by Metal.

If you are feeling brave and want to second-guess the skilled designers who put the Metal look-and-feel together, you can subclass the abstract MetalTheme class directly. This class defines many methods that return colors and fonts. All of these methods, however, are implemented in terms of the six basic font methods and six basic color methods of the DefaultMetalTheme class.

If you look at the DefaultMetalTheme API, you'll notice that the font and color methods do not return java.awt.Font and java.awt.Color objects as you would expect. Instead, they return FontUIResource and ColorUIResource objects. Both of these classes are part of the javax.swing.plaf package and are trivial subclasses of the more familiar Font and Color classes. The only thing these subclasses do is implement the UIResource interface. But UIResource is a marker interface, with no methods of its own. Thus, a FontUIResource is a Font object that also happens to implement UIResource. Similarly, a ColorUIResource is both a Color object and a UIResource object.

The currently installed look-and-feel assigns default values for many properties of Swing components. A look-and-feel implementation needs to be able to distinguish between default values it has specified and programmer-supplied property values. For this reason, all look-and-feel defaults, such as colors and fonts, must implement the UIResource marker interface. For our purposes here, you can subclass DefaultMetalTheme and use the FontUIResource and ColorUIResource classes exactly as you would use normal Font and Color resources.

Once you have created your own theme by subclassing MetalTheme or Default-MetalTheme, you can install it with code like this:

```
MetalLookAndFeel.setCurrentTheme(new MyCustomTheme());
```

If you are changing the current theme after having already created Swing components, you also have to reinstall the MetalLookAndFeel and notify all the components of the change:

```
UIManager.setLookAndFeel(new MetalLookAndFeel());
SwingUtilities.updateComponentTreeUI(myRootFrame);
```

Auxiliary Look-and-Feels

If you've browsed the list of Swing packages, you've probably noticed javax.swing.plaf.multi. This is the multiplexing look-and-feel. It allows one or more auxiliary look-and-feels to be used in conjunction with a single primary look-and-feel. The multiplexing look-and-feel is automatically used by a Swing application if an auxiliary look-and-feel has been requested. An application can request an auxiliary look-and-feel by calling the static UIManager method addAuxiliaryLookAndFeel(), while an end user can do this by setting the swing.auxiliarylaf property on a Java command line.

The primary purpose of auxiliary look-and-feels is for accessibility. For example, a person with impaired vision might start up a Java application using the -Dswing.auxiliarylaf= option to specify that the application should load a screen-reader look-and-feel. Auxiliary look-and-feels can be used for other purposes as well, of course. You might use an auxiliary look-and-feel to add audio feedback to a user interface. Such a look-and-feel might produce an audible click when the user clicks on a JButton, for example.

Swing is not shipped with any predefined auxiliary look-and-feels. You can implement your own, of course, although explaining how to do so is beyond the scope of this book.

Accessibility

The term *accessibility* refers to the architectural features of Swing that allow Swing applications to interact with assistive technologies, such as a visual macro recorder that allows users to automate repetitive point-and-click tasks or a screen reader.

To enable accessibility, every Swing component implements the `Accessible` interface, which, like all accessibility-related classes, is part of the `javax.accessibility` package. This interface defines a single `getAccessibleContext()` method that returns an `AccessibleContext` object for the component. The methods of `AccessibleContext` export salient information about the component, such as a list of its accessible children and its name, purpose, and description. An assistive technology can use the tree of `AccessibleContext` objects to gather information about a GUI and assist the user in interacting with that GUI.

A number of the `AccessibleContext` methods return objects that implement specialized interfaces to return specific types of accessibility information. For example, if an accessible component represents a numeric value of some sort (say a `JSlider`), the `getAccessibleValue()` method of its `AccessibleContext` object returns an `AccessibleValue` object that provides more information about that value and allows the assistive technology to query and set the value.

The interfaces and classes of the `javax.accessibility` package provide methods that allow an assistive technology to "read" a GUI. Many of the methods defined by these interfaces duplicate functionality already provided by Swing components. The point, however, is that `java.accessibility` defines a standard API for interaction between any assistive technology and any accessible application. In other words, the accessibility API is not Swing specific. You can write JavaBeans and other custom components so that they support accessibility. If you do, these components automatically work with assistive technologies.

The details of the `javax.accessibility` package are of interest to programmers who are creating assistive technologies and developing accessible components or JavaBeans. Unfortunately, the details of these tasks are beyond the scope of this book.

Most of us are not developing assistive technologies and only rarely do we have to create accessible components. What we all want to do, however, is create accessible applications. Since all Swing components support accessibility, it is quite simple to create an accessible application with Swing. The key to supporting accessibility is providing the necessary information that allows an assistive technology to interpret your GUI for a user. The most commonly used example of an assistive technology is a screen reader for the vision impaired. A screen reader needs to be able to verbally describe a GUI to a user who cannot see it. In order to do this, it needs to have names and descriptions for all the critical components in your GUI.

The easiest way to assign a description to a component is to give it a tooltip. This way, your accessibility information also serves as context-sensitive help for novice users:

```
continue.setToolTipText("Click here to continue");
```

If, for some reason, you want to assign an accessible description to a component without giving it a tooltip, you can use code like this:

```
continue.getAccessibleContext().setAccessibleDescription("Ccntinue button");
```

It is also helpful to assistive technologies if you provide names for your various components. A name should be a short human-readable string that uniquely identifies the component, at least within the current window or dialog box. Buttons, labels, menu items, and other components that display labels simply use those labels as their accessible names. Other components need to have names assigned. Here is one way to do that:

```
JTextField zipcode = new JTextField();
zipcode.getAccessibleContext().setAccessibleName("zipcode");
```

In a GUI, important components that do not display their own labels are often associated with JLabel components that serve to identify them. When this is the case, you can use the setLabelFor() method of JLabel to set the accessible name of the other component. The code might look like this:

```
JLabel zipcodeLabel = new JLabel("Zipcode");
JTextField zipcode = new JTextField();
zipcodeLabel.setLabelFor(zipcode);
```

By taking the simple step of assigning names and descriptions to your GUI components, you ensure that your application can be interpreted by assistive technologies and successfully used by all users.

Custom Components

We'll conclude this survey of Swing features with a quick look at what it takes to write a custom Swing component. Creating a custom component is a matter of subclassing an existing component and adding the new functionality you desire. Sometimes this is a simple job of adding a minor new feature to an existing component. At other times, you may want to create an entirely new component from scratch. In this case, you'll probably be subclassing JComponent, which is a bit more complicated. The following sections briefly explain the various things you'll need to consider when creating such a custom component. The best way to learn to write your own Swing-style components is to study the source code of Swing components, and since Sun makes this source code freely available, I encourage you to examine it.

Properties

You need to decide what properties you want your component to export and define accessor methods that allow them to be set and queried. If your component represents or displays some kind of nontrivial data structure, consider representing the data in a separate model object. Define an interface for the model and a default implementation of the interface.

If you think that other objects may be interested in property changes on your component, have the set methods for those properties generate the events PropertyChangeEvent or ChangeEvent and include appropriate event listener registration methods in your component. This kind of notification is often important if you follow the Swing architecture and divide the functionality of your component among a component object, a model object, and a UI delegate object.

When a property is set on your component, the component may need to be redrawn or resized as a result. You must keep this in mind when you write the property accessor methods for your component. For example, if you define a setColor() method, this method should call repaint() to request that the component be repainted. (Painting the component is a separate topic that is discussed later.) If you define a setFont() method and a change in font size causes the component to require more (or less) space on the screen, you should call revalidate() to request a relayout of the GUI. Note that the repaint() and revalidate() methods add a repaint or relayout request to a queue and return right away. Therefore, you may call these methods freely without fear of inefficiency.

Events

You need to decide what kind of events your component generates. You can reuse existing event and listener classes, if they suit your purposes, or you can define your own. Add event listener registration and deregistration methods in your component. You need to keep track of the registered listeners, and you may find the javax.swing.event.EventListenerList helpful for this task. For each event listener registration method, it is common practice to define a protected method to generate and fire an appropriate event to all registered listeners. For example, if your component has a public addActionListener() method, you may find it useful to define a protected fireActionEvent() method as well. This method calls the actionPerformed() method of every registered ActionListener object.

Constructors

It is customary to provide a no-argument constructor for a component. This is helpful if you want your component to work with GUI builder tools, for example. In addition, think about how you expect programmers to use your component. If there are a few properties that are likely to be set in most cases, you should define a constructor that takes values for these properties as arguments, to make the component easier to use.

Drawing the Component

Almost every component has some visual appearance. When you define a custom component, you have to write the code that draws the component on the screen. There are several ways you can do this. If you are creating an AWT component, override the paint() method and use the Graphics object that is passed to it to do whatever drawing you need to do.

For Swing components, the paint() method is also responsible for drawing the border and the children of your component, so you should not override it directly. Instead, override the paintComponent() method. This method is passed a Graphics object, just as the paint() method is, and you use this Graphics object to do any drawing you want. As we'll see in Chapter 4, *Graphics with AWT and Java 2D*, you can cast this Graphics object to a Graphics2D object if you want to use Java 2D features when drawing your component. Keep in mind, however, that a Swing component can be assigned an arbitrary border. Your paintComponent() method should check the size of the border and take this value into account when drawing.

When you define a custom component, you typically have only one look-and-feel in mind, so you can hardcode this look-and-feel as part of the component class itself. If you want your component to support the Swing pluggable look-and-feel architecture, however, you need to separate the drawing and event-handling tasks out into a separate javax.swing.plaf.ComponentUI object. If you do this, you should not override your component's paintComponent() method. Instead, put the painting functionality in the paint() method of the ComponentUI implementation. In order to make this work, you have to override the getUIClassID(), getUI(), setUI(), and updateUI() methods of JComponent.

Handling Events

Most components have some kind of interactive behavior and respond to user-input events such as mouse clicks and drags and key presses. When you are creating a custom component, you must write the code that handles these events. The Swing event-handling model was discussed in Chapter 2. Recall that the high-level way to handle input events is to register appropriate event listeners, such as MouseListener, MouseMotionListener, KeyListener, and FocusListener on your component. If you are using a separate UI delegate object, this object should implement the appropriate listener interfaces, and it should register itself with the appropriate event registration methods on the component when its installUI() method is called.

If you are not using a UI delegate, your component class can handle events at the lower level discussed in Chapter 2. To do this, you override methods such as processMouseEvent(), processMouseMotionEvent(), processKeyEvent(), and processFocusEvent(). In this case, be sure to register your interest in receiving events of the appropriate type by calling enableEvents() in your component's initialization code.

Component Size

Most components have a natural or preferred size that often depends on the settings of various component properties. Many components also have a minimum size below which they cannot adequately display themselves. And some components have a maximum size they wish to enforce. You must write the methods that compute and return these sizes.

If you are using a UI delegate object, you should implement the getMinimum-Size(), getPreferredSize(), and getMaximumSize() methods in the delegate. The default JComponent methods call the delegate methods to determine these sizes if the programmer using the component has not overridden the minimum, preferred, or maximum sizes with her own specifications.

If you are not using a UI delegate object, you should override these three methods in the component itself. Ideally, your methods should respect any sizes passed to setMinimumSize(), setPreferredSize() and setMaximumSize(). Unfortunately, the values set by these methods are stored in private fields of JComponent, so you typically have to override both the get and the set methods.

Accessibility

It is a good idea to make your component accessible. In order to do this, your component must implement the javax.accessibility.Accessible interface and its getAccessibleContext() method. This method must return an AccessibleContext object that is customized for your component. You typically implement AccessibleContext as an inner class of the component by extending JComponent.AccessibleJComponent or some subclass of that class. Depending on your component, you may need to implement various other accessibility interfaces on this inner class as well. Studying the accessibility code in existing Swing components can be very helpful in learning how to write your own accessible components. You might start, for example, with the source code for AbstractButton.AccessibleAbstractButton.

Miscellaneous Methods

JComponent defines a number of other methods that you can optionally override to change aspects of a component's behavior. If you take a look at the list of properties defined by the JComponent API, you'll notice that a number of these are read-only properties (i.e., they do not define set methods). The only way to set the value returned by one of these methods is to subclass the method. In general, when you see a read-only property, you should consider it a candidate for subclassing. Here are a few methods of particular interest:

isOpaque()
> If the component always fills its entire background, this method should return true. If a component can guarantee that it completely paints itself, Swing can perform some drawing optimizations. JComponent actually does define a setOpaque() method for this property, but your custom component may choose to ignore setOpaque() and override isOpaque().

isOptimizedDrawingEnabled()
> If your component has children and allows those children to overlap, it should override this method to return false. Otherwise, leave it as is.

isFocusTraversable()
> If your component wants to be included in focus traversal, it should override this method to return true. If your component does not want to be included in the keyboard navigation system, this method should return false.

`isFocusCycleRoot()`

If your component has children and wants to cycle focus among them, override this method to return `true`.

`isManagingFocus()`

If your component needs to receive the **Tab** and **Shift-Tab** key events that are normally handled by the focus manager, override this method to return `true`. If you do, the focus manager uses **Ctrl-Tab** instead.

CHAPTER 4

Graphics with AWT and Java 2D

Java 1.0 and Java 1.1 included basic graphics capabilities as part of the AWT (Abstract Windowing Toolkit). In the Java 2 platform, these capabilities have been greatly enhanced with the introduction of Java 2D. While Java 2D is part of the JFC (the Java Foundation Classes), the Java 2D API is implemented in the same `java.awt` package as the original Java graphics classes.

This chapter begins by documenting the original Java graphics model, which is still required for Java 1.1 applications, applets, and Personal Java applications. The chapter then moves on to detail the enhanced features provided by Java 2D. This chapter can provide only an introduction to the various features of Java 2D; for more complete information, see *Java 2D Graphics*, by Jonathan Knucsen (O'Reilly).

Graphics Before Java 2D

All graphics operations in Java are performed using a `java.awt.Graphics` object. The `Graphics` object serves three purposes:

- It represents the drawing surface. A `Graphics` object is used to draw into a `java.awt.Component` on the screen, to draw into an off-screen `java.awt.-Image`, or to send graphics to a printer.

- It maintains the current state of graphics attributes, such as the current drawing color, font, and clipping region.

- It defines methods that perform various graphics operations, such as drawing lines, rendering strings of text, and copying the content of `Image` objects onto the drawing surface.

The graphics capabilities of Java before Java 2D can be neatly summarized by listing the graphics attributes and operations supported by the `Graphics` object. Table 4-1 lists the attributes, and Table 4-2 lists the operations.

Table 4-1: Attributes of the Graphics Class

Attribute	Type	Description
Color	`Color`	Set with `setColor()`.
Font	`Font`	Set with `setFont()`. Only a small number of standard fonts are available.
Clipping region	`Rectangle`	In Java 1.1, set with `setClip()`. Use `clipRect()` to set to the intersection of the current clipping region and a rectangle. `setClip()` takes a `Shape` object, but prior to Java 1.2, the clipping region is, in practice, restricted to rectangles.
Origin	`Point`	Use `translate()` to move the origin. The default origin is in the upper-left corner of the drawing region, with X coordinates increasing to the right and Y coordinates increasing down.
Paint mode	`boolean`	`setXORMode()` puts the `Graphics` object into the infrequently used XOR mode, while `setPaintMode()` restores the default drawing mode.
Background color	`Color`	This attribute is used only by the `clearRect()` method, and its value cannot be set. When drawing into a `Component`, the background color is the value of the `background` attribute of the component. The value is undefined when drawing into off-screen images.

Table 4-2: Operations of the Graphics Class

Operation	Methods	Attributes Used
Line drawing	`drawLine()`, `drawPolyline()`	color, origin, clip, paint mode
Shape drawing	`drawArc()`, `drawOval()`, `drawPolygon()`, `drawRect()`, `drawRoundRect()`, `draw3DRect()`	color, origin, clip, paint mode

Table 4–2: Operations of the Graphics Class (continued)

Operation	Methods	Attributes Used
Shape filling	`fillArc()`, `fillOval()`, `fillPolygon()`, `fillRect()`, `fillRoundRect()`, `fill3DRect()`	color, origin, clip, paint mode
Text drawing	`drawBytes()`, `drawChars()`, `drawString()`	color, font, origin, clip, paint mode
Image drawing (blitting)	`drawImage()` (various versions)	origin, clip, paint mode
Clearing	`clearRect()`	origin, clip, background color

Line Drawing

An important point to notice in Table 4-1 is that there is no attribute for line width. Prior to Java 2D, Java can only draw lines that are a single pixel wide. This is perhaps the single largest limitation of the Java 1.0 and Java 1.1 graphics environments.

Colors

Colors are represented by the `java.awt.Color` class. In Java 1.0 and Java 1.1, this class represents colors in the RGB color space. It has constructors that allow you to specify red, green, and blue color coordinates as integers or as floating-point values. The class defines a static method that allows you to create a `Color` using coordinates from the HSB (hue, saturation, brightness) color space. It also defines a number of constants that represent colors by their common names, such as `Color.black` and `Color.white`.

`java.awt.SystemColor` is a subclass of `Color` introduced in Java 1.1. The class has no public constructor but defines a number of `SystemColor` constants that represent colors used on the system desktop (for systems that support a system desktop color palette). For example, `SystemColor.textHighlight` represents the color used for highlighted text

Fonts

Fonts are represented with the `java.awt.Font` class. A `Font` object is created by specifying the name, style, and point size of the desired font. In an attempt to promote platform independence, Java 1.0 supports only a handful of standard font names. Java 1.1 supports the same fonts but provides new preferred symbolic names for them. The fonts supported prior to Java 2D are listed in Table 4-3.

Table 4–3: Font Names in Java 1.0 and Java 1.1

Java 1.0 Name	Preferred Name in Java 1.1
TimesRoman	Serif
Helvetica	SansSerif
Courier	Monospaced
Symbol	Symbol
Dialog	Dialog
DialogInput	DialogInput

Fonts can be displayed in any of four possible font styles, which are represented by the symbolic constants listed in Table 4-4.

Table 4–4: Java Font Styles

Style	Java Constant
plain	`Font.PLAIN`
italic	`Font.ITALIC`
bold	`Font.BOLD`
bolditalic	`Font.BOLD + Font.ITALIC`

Font sizes are specified in points. The `Font()` constructor accepts an integer argument, so fractional point sizes are not supported in Java 1.0 and 1.1. If the native platform does not support scalable fonts, the returned font may have a different size than what you requested.

Font Metrics

If you need to figure out how big a piece of text will be, you can call the `getFontMetrics()` methods of a `Graphics` object and pass in the desired font. This returns a `FontMetrics` object. The `getHeight()` method returns the line height for the font, which can be further broken down into the font ascent and descent, returned by `getAscent()` and `getDescent()`, respectively. To measure the horizontal dimension of text, use `charWidth()` and `stringWidth()`.

Images

Images are represented by the `java.awt.Image` class. Working with images in Java 1.0 and Java 1.1 is a little tricky because the image processing model of those releases is based on streaming image data being loaded across a network. This treatment of images allows images to be partially displayed before they are fully loaded, but makes working with images somewhat more difficult.

All of the drawImage() methods of the Graphics objects require an java.awt.-image.ImageObserver object. This is the object that handles things if you try to draw an image that is not fully loaded. Fortunately, java.awt.Component implements ImageObserver, so you can use any Component or Applet object for this method argument.

If are writing an applet and want to load a predefined image from a URL, you can use the getImage() method defined by the java.applet.Applet class. This method begins downloading the specified image and returns an Image object to you immediately.

If you are writing a standalone application and want to load a predefined image from a file or URL, use one of the getImage() or createImage() methods of the java.awt.Toolkit class:

```
Toolkit.getDefaultToolkit().getImage("myimage.gif");
```

Like the getImage() method of Applet, these Toolkit methods start loading the image and immediately return an Image object. The image formats supported by these Applet and Toolkit methods are implementation dependent. Most implementations support common formats, such as GIF (including transparent GIF), JPEG, and XBM.

To ensure that an Image object is fully loaded before you use it, you can create a java.awt.MediaTracker object, pass your Image to its addImage() method, then call the waitForAll() method.

To create an empty off-screen image that you can draw into and copy pixels out of, call the createImage() method of the Component with which you plan to use the image and pass in the desired width and height of the image. To draw into the image, you have to obtain a Graphics object by calling the getGraphics() method of the image. Images created in this way are often used for double-buffering, to produce smoother animations or graphical updates.

The java.awt.image package contains classes that support rudimentary image processing and filtering. Java 2D implements more powerful image-processing techniques, so the Java 1.0 model is not described here.

Java 2D Graphics Attributes and Operations

Java 2D dramatically expands the graphics capabilities of Java. It does this through the java.awt.Graphics2D subclass of java.awt.Graphics. In Java 2, you can simply cast any Graphics object you are given to a Graphics2D object, and then you can use the new features of Java 2D.

Table 4-5 and Table 4-6 summarize the new features of Java 2D by listing the graphics attributes and graphics operations supported by the Graphics2D class.

Table 4–5: Graphics Attributes of Java 2D

Attribute	Type	Description
Foreground color	Color	Inherited from Graphics but superseded by the fill style attribute and the Paint interface.
Background color	Color	Inherited from Graphics but can now be set and queried with setBackground() and getBackground(). This attribute is still used only by clearRect().
Font	Font	Inherited from Graphics. All of the system fonts are now available to Java.
Clipping region	Shape	Inherited from Graphics. In Java 2D, however, arbitrary Shape objects may be used; the clipping region is no longer restricted to only rectangular shapes. A new method, which is called clip(), sets the clipping region to the intersection of the current region and a specified Shape.
Line style	Stroke	A Stroke object specifies how lines are drawn. The BasicStroke implementation supports line width, dash pattern, and other attributes, described in more detail later in the chapter. Set the current line style with setStroke().
Fill style	Paint	A Paint object specifies how an area is filled. Color implements this interface and fills with a solid color, java.awt.TexturePaint fills with a tiled image, and java.awt.GradientPaint fills with a color gradient. Set the current fill style with setPaint().

Graphics/
Java 2D

Table 4–5: Graphics Attributes of Java 2D (continued)

Attribute	Type	Description
Compositing	`Composite`	A `Composite` object controls how the color of a pixel is combined, or composited, with the color of the pixel on top of which it is drawn. The default compositing operation combines translucent pixels with the pixels they overlay, letting the overlaid colors "show through." The `AlphaComposite` class is an implementation of `Composite`; it performs various types of compositing, based on the alpha-transparency of the pixels involved.
Transform	`java.awt.geom.-` `AffineTransform`	Controls the translation, scaling, rotation, and shearing of the coordinate system. Set this attribute with `setTransform()`, or modify the current transform with `translate()`, `scale()`, `rotate()`, `shear()`, or `transform()`.
Hints	`RenderingHints`	A `RenderingHints` object allows a program to express preferences about various speed versus quality trade-offs made by Java 2D. Most notably, `RenderingHints` controls whether Java 2D performs antialiasing. Set with `setRenderingHints()`, `setRendering-` `Hint()`, or `addRenderingHints()`.

Table 4–6: Graphics Operations of Java 2D

Operation	Methods	Description
Drawing	`draw()`, inherited methods	`draw()` outlines an arbitrary `Shape`. Uses the clip, transform, stroke, paint, and composite attributes.
Filling	`fill()`, inherited methods	`fill()` fills an arbitrary `Shape`. Uses the clip, transform, paint, and composite attributes.

Table 4–6: Graphics Operations of Java 2D (continued)

Operation	Methods	Description
Hit detection	`hit()`	Tests whether a given rectangle (in device coordinates) intersects the interior or outline of an arbitrary `Shape`. Uses the clip, transform, and stroke attributes when testing the outline of a `Shape`.
Text drawing	`drawString()`, `drawGlyphVector()`, inherited methods	Java 2D defines text-drawing methods that take `String`, `java.text.AttributedCharacter-Iterator`, and `java.awt.font.-GlyphVector` arguments. Text drawing uses the clip, transform, font, paint, and composite attributes. Note, however, that `AttributedCharacterIterator` objects supply their own fonts.
Image drawing	`drawImage()`, `drawRenderableImage()`, `drawRenderedImage()`, inherited methods	Java 2D defines new image-drawing methods that draw special types of images. `java.awt.image.BufferedImage` is the most important new type. These methods use the clip, transform, and composite attributes.

*Graphics/
Java 2D*

The Coordinate System

By default, Java 2D uses the same coordinate system as AWT. The origin is in the upper-left corner of the drawing surface. X coordinate values increase to the right, and Y coordinate values increase as they go down. When drawing to a screen or an off-screen image, X and Y coordinates are measured in pixels. When drawing to a printer or other high-resolution device, however, X and Y coordinates are measured in points instead of pixels (and there are 72 points in one inch).

It is instructive to consider in more detail how Java 2D draws to a high-resolution device like a printer. The Java 2D drawing commands you issue express coordinates on the printer paper in units of points. This coordinate system is referred to as "user space." However, different printers print at different resolutions and support different coordinate systems, so when drawing to a device like this, Java 2D must convert your user-space coordinates into printer-specific, device-space coordinates.

On a high-resolution printer, one point in user space may translate into 10 or more pixels in the printer's device space. In order to take full advantage of all this resolution, you need to be able to use coordinates like 75.3 in user space. This brings us to one of the big differences between the Java 2D coordinate system and the AWT system: Java 2D allows coordinates to be expressed as floating-point numbers, instead of restricting them to integers. Throughout the Java 2D API, you'll see methods that accept float values instead of int values.

The distinction between user space and device space is valid even when we are just drawing to the relatively low resolution screen. By default, when drawing to a screen or image, user space is the same as device space. However, the Graphics2D class defines methods that allow you to trivially modify the default coordinate system. For example, you can move the origin of the coordinate system with the translate() method. The following code draws two identical lines at identical positions. The first line is drawn in the default coordinate system, while the second is drawn after calling translate():

```
Graphics2D g;                    // Assume this is already initialized
g.drawLine(100, 100, 200, 200);  // Draw in the default coordinate system
g.translate(100.0, 100.0);       // Move the origin down and to the right
g.drawLine(0, 0, 100, 100);      // Draw the same line relative to new origin
```

The translate() method is not all that interesting, and, in fact, a version of it existed even before Java 2D. The Graphics2D class also defines scale(), rotate(), and shear() methods that perform more powerful transformations of the coordinate system.

By default, when drawing to the screen, one unit in user space corresponds to one pixel in device space. The scale() method changes this. If you scale the coordinate system by a factor of 10, one unit of user space corresponds to 10 pixels in device space. Note that you can scale by different amounts in the X and Y dimensions. The following code draws the same simple line from 100, 100 to 200, 200 (using the default origin):

```
g.scale(2.0, 2.0);
g.drawLine(50, 50, 100, 100);
```

You can combine transformations. For example, suppose you are drawing into a 500-pixel-by-500-pixel window and you want to have the origin at the bottom left of the window, with Y coordinates increasing as they go up, rather than as they go down. You can achieve this with two simple method calls:

```
g.translate(0.0, 500.0);  // Move the origin to the lower left
g.scale(1.0, -1.0);       // Flip the sign of the coordinate system
```

rotate() is another powerful coordinate system transformation method. You specify an angle in radians, and the method rotates the coordinate system by that amount. The direction of rotation is such that points on the positive X axis are rotated in the direction of the positive Y axis. Although you typically do not want to leave your coordinate system in a permanently rotated state, the rotate() method is useful for drawing rotated text or other rotated graphics. For example:

```
g.rotate(Math.PI/4);                      // Rotate 45 degrees
g.drawString("Hello world", 300, 300)     // Draw text in this rotated position
g.rotate(-Math.PI/4);                     // Rotate back to normal
```

Note that these calls to rotate() rotate the coordinate system about the origin. There is also a three-argument version of the method that rotates about a specified point, which can often be more useful.

The final transformation method defined by Graphics2D is shear(). The effects of this method are not as intuitive as the methods we've already discussed. After a call to shear(), any rectangles you draw appear skewed, as parallelograms.

Any calls you make to translate(), scale(), rotate(), and shear() have a cumulative effect on the mapping from user space to device space. This mapping is encapsulated in a java.awt.geom.AffineTransform object and is one of the graphics attributes maintained by a Graphics2D object. You can obtain a copy of the current transform with getTransform(), and you can set a transform directly with setTransform(). setTransform() is not cumulative. It simply replaces the current user-to-device-space mapping with a new mapping:

```
AffineTransform t = g.getTransform();  // Save the current transform
g.rotate(theta);                       // Change the transform
g.drawRect(100, 100, 200, 200);        // Draw something
g.setTransform(t);                     // Restore the transform to its old state
```

AffineTransform is used in a number of places in the Java 2D API; we'll discuss it in more detail later in this chapter. Once you understand the details and some of the math behind this class, you can define AffineTransform objects of your own and pass them to setTransform().

Another use of AffineTransform objects is with the transform() method of Graphics2D. This method modifies the current coordinate system, just as translate(), scale(), rotate(), and shear() do. transform() is much more general, however. The AffineTransform object you pass to it can represent any arbitrary combination of translation, scaling, rotation, and shearing.

Shapes

One of the most fundamental abstractions in Java 2D is the java.awt.Shape. This interface describes a shape, obviously. But note that the Java 2D definition of a shape does not require the shape to enclose an area—a Shape object may represent an open curve such as a line or parabola just as easily as it represents a closed curve such as a rectangle or circle. If an open curve is passed to a graphics operation (such as fill()) that requires a closed curve, the curve is implicitly closed by adding a straight-line segment between its end points. A Java 2D shape is sometimes referred to as a "path," because it describes the path a pen would follow to draw the shape.

The Java 2D Graphics2D class defines some very fundamental operations on Shape objects: draw() draws a Shape; fill() fills a Shape; clip() restricts the current drawing region to the specified Shape; hit() tests whether a given rectangle falls in or on a given shape. In addition, the AffineTransform class has methods that allow Shape objects to be arbitrarily scaled, rotated, translated, and sheared. Because the Shape interface is used throughout Java 2D, these fundamental operations on shapes are quite powerful. For example, the individual glyphs of a font can be represented as Shape objects, meaning they can be individually scaled, rotated, drawn, filled, and so on.

Java 2D contains a number of predefined Shape implementations, many of which are part of the java.awt.geom package. Note that some basic geometric shapes have multiple Shape implementations, where each implementation uses a different data type to store coordinates. Table 4-7 lists these predefined Shape implementations.

Table 4-7: Java 2D Shape Implementations

Shape	Implementations
Rectangle	java.awt.Rectangle,
	java.awt.geom.Rectangle2D.Float,
	java.awt.geom.Rectangle2D.Double
Rounded rectangle	java.awt.geom.RoundRectangle2D.Float,
	java.awt.geom.RoundRectangle2D.Double
Ellipse (and circle)	java.awt.geom.Ellipse2D.Float,
	java.awt.geom.Ellipse2D.Double
Polygon	java.awt.Polygon
Line segment	java.awt.geom.Line2D.Float,
	java.awt.geom.Line2D.Double
Arc (ellipse segment)	java.awt.geom.Arc2D.Float,
	java.awt.geom.Arc2D.Double
Bezier curve (quadratic)	java.awt.geom.QuadCurve2D.Float,
	java.awt.geom.QuadCurve2D.Double
Bezier curve (cubic)	java.awt.geom.CubicCurve2D.Float,
	java.awt.geom.CubicCurve2D.Double

To draw a circle inside a square, for example, you can use code like this:

```
Graphics2D g;                          // Initialized elsewhere
Shape square = new Rectangle2D.Float(100.0f, 100.0f, 100.0f, 100.0f);
Shape circle = new Ellipse2D.Float(100.0f, 100.0f, 100.0f, 100.0f);
g.draw(square);
g.draw(circle);
```

In addition to these basic predefined shapes, the java.awt.geom package also contains two powerful classes for defining complex shapes. The Area class allows you to define a shape that is the union or intersection of other shapes. It also allows you to subtract one shape from another or define a shape that is the exclusive OR of two shapes. For example, the following code allows you to fill the shape that results from subtracting a circle from a square:

```
Graphics2D g;                          // Initialized elsewhere
Shape square = new Rectangle2D.Float(100.0f, 100.0f, 100.0f, 100.0f);
Shape circle = new Ellipse2D.Float(100.0f, 100.0f, 100.0f, 100.0f);
Area difference = new Area(square);
difference.subtract(circle);
g.fill(difference);
```

The `GeneralPath` class allows you to describe a `Shape` as a sequence of line segments and Bezier curve segments. You create such a general shape by calling the `moveTo()`, `lineTo()`, `quadTo()`, and `curveTo()` methods of `GeneralPath`. `GeneralPath` also allows you to append entire `Shape` objects to the path you are defining.

Bezier Curves

A Bezier curve is a smooth curve between two end points, with a shape described by one or more control points. Java 2D makes extensive low-level use of quadratic and cubic Bezier curves. A quadratic Bezier curve uses one control point, while a cubic Bezier curve uses two control points. There is some moderately complex mathematics behind Bezier curves, but for most Java 2D programmers, an intuitive understanding of these curves is sufficient. Figure 4-1 shows three quadratic and three cubic Bezier curves and illustrates how the position of the control points affects the shape of the curve.

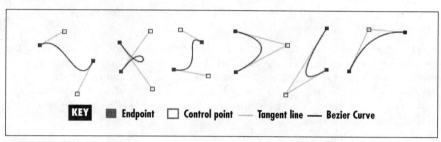

Figure 4–1: Bezier curves

How Shapes Are Implemented

Java 2D can perform some very general operations on arbitrary `Shape` objects. In order to make this possible, the `Shape` interface exposes a quite general description of the desired shape. For example, the `getBounds()` and `getBounds2D()` methods return a bounding box for the shape. The various `contains()` methods test whether a given point or rectangle is enclosed by the shape. The `intersects()` methods test whether a given rectangle touches or overlaps the shape. These methods enable clipping, hit detection, and similar operations.

The `getBounds()`, `contains()`, and `intersects()` methods are important, but they do not say anything about how to draw the shape. This is the job of `getPathIterator()`, which returns a `java.awt.geom.PathIterator` object that breaks a `Shape` down into a sequence of individual line and curve segments that Java 2D can handle at a primitive level. The `PathIterator` interface is basically the opposite of `GeneralPath`. While `GeneralPath` allows a `Shape` to be built of line and curve segments, `PathIterator` breaks a `Shape` down into its component line and curve segments.

`Shape` defines two `getPathIterator()` methods. The two-argument version of this method returns a `PathIterator` that describes the shape in terms of line segments only (i.e., it cannot use curves). This method is usually implemented with a `java.awt.geom.FlatteningPathIterator`, an implementation of `PathIterator` that approximates the curved segments in a given path with multiple line segments. The *flatness* argument to `getPathIterator()` is a measure of how closely these line segments must approximate the original curve segments, where smaller values of *flatness* imply a better approximation.

Stroking Lines

One of the new graphic attributes defined by Java 2D is the `java.awt.Stroke`; it is set with the `setStroke()` method of a `Graphics2D` object. The `Stroke` attribute is used by Java 2D whenever it draws a line. Conceptually, the `Stroke` describes the pen or brush that is used to draw the line: it controls all line-drawing attributes, such as line width and dash pattern. Java 2D defines a single implementation of the `Stroke` interface, `java.awt.BasicStroke`, that is suitable for almost all line drawing needs.

BasicStroke

A `BasicStroke` object encapsulates several different line drawing attributes: the line width, the dash pattern, the end cap style for the line, and the join style for the line. You specify values for these attributes when you call the `BasicStroke()` constructor. `BasicStroke` objects are immutable, so that they can be safely cached and shared. This means, however, that they don't have `set()` methods that allow you to change the attribute values.

The line-width attribute specifies (obviously) the width of the line. This line width is measured in units of user space. If you are using the default coordinate system, then user space equals device space, and line widths are measured in pixels. For backward compatibility, the default line width is 1.0. Suppose you want to draw the outline of a circle of radius 100, using a line that is 10 units wide. You can code it like this:

```
Graphics2D g;                                      // Initialized elsewhere
Shape circle = new Ellipse2D.Float(100.0f, 100.0f, // Upper-left corner
                               300.0f, 300.0f);    // Width and height
g.setStroke(new BasicStroke(10.0f));               // Set line width
g.draw(circle);                                    // Now draw it
```

The end-cap attribute specifies how the ends of lines are drawn, or, more specifically, what type of end caps are placed at the end of lines. There is no analogous line attribute in AWT prior to Java 2D, as end caps are necessary only for lines that are more than one-pixel wide. If you are not familiar with end caps, look at Figure 4-2, as they are best explained visually. This figure shows what lines look like when drawn with each of the three possible end cap styles.

The `BasicStroke.CAP_BUTT` constant specifies that the line should have no end cap. The `CAP_SQUARE` constant specifies a rectangular end cap that projects beyond the end point of the line by a distance equal to half of the line width; this is the default value for the end-cap attribute. `CAP_ROUND` specifies a semicircular end cap, with a radius equal to half of the line width.

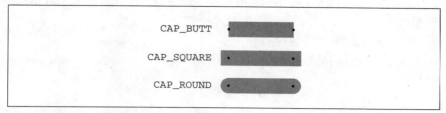

Figure 4–2: BasicStroke end-cap styles

The join-style attribute is similar to the end-cap attribute, except that it applies to the vertex where two lines join, rather than to the end of a line. Like the end-cap attribute, the join-style attribute is necessary only with wide lines and is best understood visually. Figure 4-3 illustrates this BasicStroke attribute. Note that the join style attribute is used only when drawing a shape that includes multiple line segments, not when two intersecting lines are drawn as separate shapes.

Figure 4–3: BasicStroke join styles

The default join style is a mitered join, represented by the Basic-Stroke.JOIN_MITER constant. This value specifies that lines are joined by extending their outer edges until they meet. The JOIN_BEVEL constant specifies that lines are joined by drawing a straight line between the outside corners of the two lines, while JOIN_ROUND specifies that the vertex formed by the two lines should be rounded, with a radius of half the line width. To use cap style and join style, you can use code like this:

```
g.setStroke(new BasicStroke(5.0f,                    // Line width
                    BasicStroke.CAP_ROUND,   // End-cap style
                    BasicStroke.JOIN_ROUND)); // Vertex join style
```

When you use the JOIN_MITER style to join two lines that have a small angle between them, the miter can become quite long. To avoid this situation, Basic-Stroke includes another attribute known as the miter limit. If the miter would be longer than this value times half of the line width, it is truncated. The default miter limit is 10.0.

The dash pattern of a line is actually controlled by two attributes: the dash array and the dash phase. The dash array is a float[] that specifies the number of units to be drawn followed by the number of units to be skipped. For example, to draw a dashed line in which both the dashes and spaces are 25 units long, you use an array like:

```
new float[] { 25.0f, 25.0f }
```

To draw a dot-dash pattern consisting of 21 on, 9 off, 3 on, and 9 off, you use this array:

```
new float[] { 21.0f, 9.0f, 3.0f, 9.0f }
```

Figure 4-4 illustrates these dashed-line examples. The end-cap style you specify is applied to each dash that is drawn.

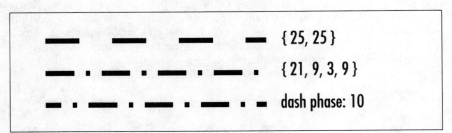

Figure 4–4: BasicStroke dash patterns

If, for some reason, you want to draw a dashed line but do not want your line to begin at the beginning of the dash pattern, you can specify the dash-phase attribute. The value of this attribute specifies how far into the dash pattern the line should begin. Note, however, that this value is not an integer index into the dash pattern array. Instead, it is a floating-point value that specifies a linear distance.

To draw a dashed line, you must use the most complicated BasicStroke() constructor and specify values for all attributes. For example:

```
Stroke s = new BasicStroke(4.0f,                   // Width
                   BasicStroke.CAP_SQUARE,         // End cap
                   BasicStroke.JOIN_MITER,         // Join style
                   10.0f,                          // Miter limit
                   new float[] {16.0f,20.0f},      // Dash pattern
                   0.0f);                          // Dash phase
```

How a Stroke Works

The BasicStroke class is sufficient for most drawing needs, so it is unlikely that you will ever need to implement the Stroke interface yourself. Nevertheless, the Stroke interface defines only a single createStrokedShape() method, and it is instructive to understand what this method does.

In Java 2D, filling an area is a more fundamental operation than drawing (or stroking) the outline of a shape. The Stroke object is the link between the two operations; it makes it possible to implement the draw() method using the fill() method.

Recall the code that we just used to draw the outline of a circle. The draw() method has to draw the outline of the circle using only the fill() method. If it simply calls fill() on the circle, it ends up creating a solid disk, not the outline of a circle. So instead, draw() first passes the circle to the createStrokedShape() method of the BasicStroke object we've specified. createStrokedShape() returns a new shape: a circle of radius 105, minus a concentric circle of radius 95. The interior of this shape is the area between the two circles, a region that always has a width of 10 units. Now draw() can call fill() on this stroked shape to draw the 10-unit-wide outline of the original circle. (We'll discuss the fill() operation and the graphics attributes that it uses in the next section.)

Paint

As we've just seen, the Java 2D Stroke attribute turns the task of drawing a line into the task of filling an area. Prior to Java 2D, an area could be filled only with a solid color, specified by passing a Color object to the setColor(·) method of a Graphics object. In Java 2D, this color attribute has been generalized to a paint attribute: you pass a Paint object to the setPaint() method of a Graphics2D object. The specified Paint object is used to generate the pixel values used to fill areas.

The most common way to fill an area, however, is still to use a solid color. So another change in Java 2D is that the java.awt.Color class now implements the java.awt.Paint interface. All Color objects are perfectly legal Paint objects and can be used to draw lines and fill areas with a solid color.

Java 2D also defines two more complex Paint implementations. The java.awt.-TexturePaint class uses a tiled image for its filling operations. The image is specified as a java.awt.image.BufferedImage. This is a Java 2D simplification of the java.awt.Image class; we'll discuss it in more detail later in the chapter. When you create a TexturePaint object, you must also specify a java.awt.geom.Rectangle2D object (java.awt.Rectangle is a kind of Rectangle2D). The purpose of this rectangle is to specify an initial position and horizontal and vertical repetition intervals for the tiled image. Typically, you can just specify a rectangle based at 0,0 with the same width and height as the image. If you are not using the default coordinate system, things are a little trickier, since image dimensions are always measured in pixels, but you must specify your rectangle dimensions in user-space coordinates.

The java.awt.GradientPaint class fills an area with a color gradient. The fill color varies linearly between a color C1 and a color C2, along the line between point P1 and point P2. You may also specify whether the gradient is cyclic or acyclic. If the gradient is cyclic, the line between P1 and P2 is extended infinitely in both directions, and the color cycles smoothly along this line from C1 to C2 and back to C1 again. If the gradient is defined to be acyclic, however, the color remains fixed at C1 beyond P1 and at C2 beyond P2.

Here's an example of creating and using a GradientPaint:

```
Graphics2D g;          // Initialized elsewhere
Paint p = new GradientPaint(0, 0, Color.red, 100, 100, Color.pink, true);
g.setPaint(p);
g.fillRect(0, 0, 300, 300);
```

Both TexturePaint and GradientPaint objects are immutable: they have no set() methods that allow their attributes to be changed. This is important because it means that a Graphics2D object can use a Paint object without worrying about its attributes being changed concurrently (i.e., the Graphics2D object does not have to make a private copy of its Paint attribute).

Blending Colors with AlphaComposite

Although a Paint object is used to generate the colors used when drawing and filling with Java 2D, these colors are not always the final colors that end up displayed on the screen. Another Java 2D attribute, the Composite object, controls the way in which the colors being drawn combine with the colors that are already visible on the drawing surface.

A compositing operation combines the pixels of your drawing (the source pixels) with the pixels of the drawing surface (the destination pixels) to produce a new, composite set of pixels. Prior to Java 2D, you could use the setXORMode() method of a Graphics object to produce a simple and very specialized kind of compositing operation. Java 2D supports generalized compositing through the java.awt.Composite interface and its implementation, java.awt.AlphaComposite.

AlphaComposite performs compositing based on alpha-transparency, letting you paint with partially transparent colors that allow some of the background color to show through. It also supports various Porter-Duff compositing rules, as we'll discuss shortly.

Transparent Colors and the Alpha Channel

Before we can discuss the AlphaComposite class, you need to understand a bit about the notion of transparent colors. With most low-end graphics systems, such as the AWT before Java 2D, colors and images are opaque. When a line is drawn, a shape is filled, or an image is rendered, that item totally obscures whatever pixels it is drawn on top of. An image is always represented as a rectangular array of pixels. Sometimes, however, we want to use an image to display a nonrectangular graphic. To allow this, some image formats support the notion of a transparent color. When the image is drawn, the background shows through whatever pixels are marked as transparent. Transparency is indicated with a bit mask: for each pixel in the image, the graphics system uses one extra bit of information to specify whether the pixel is transparent or opaque.

Bit mask transparency is an on-or-off thing: a pixel is either fully transparent or fully opaque. The notion of transparency can be generalized, however, to include translucent pixels. Instead of simply associating 1 extra bit of data with each pixel, the graphics system can associate 4, 8, 16, or some other number of bits with each pixel. This leads to 16, 256, or 65,536 possible levels of translucency, ranging from fully transparent (0) to fully opaque (16, 256, or 65536). When you think about it, these transparency bits are really no different than the bits we use to represent the red, green, and blue components of each pixel. The transparency bits are called the alpha channel, while the color bits are called the red, green, and blue channels. When you are working with pixels represented by red, green, and blue components, you are said to be using the RGB color space.

Transparent and translucent pixels do not actually exist. Inside a monitor, there are red, green, and blue electron guns (or red, green, and blue LCD elements), but there is no electron gun for the alpha channel. At the hardware level, a pixel is on or it is off; it cannot be partially on. In order to give the appearance of transparency, the graphics system (Java 2D, in this case) has to blend (or composite) transparent pixels with the pixels that are beneath them. When a source color Cs that has a transparency of α is painted over a destination color Cd, the two colors are combined to produce a new destination color Cd' with an equation like the following:

```
Cd' = Cs*α + Cd*(1 - α)
```

For the purposes of this computation, the alpha value and the values of the red, green, and blue channels are treated as floating-point numbers between 0.0 and 1.0, rather than 8- or 16-bit integers. The equation is shorthand: the computation is actually performed independently on each of the red, green, and blue channels. If Cs is fully opaque, α is 1 and Cd' is simply Cs. On the other hand, if Cs is fully transparent, α is 0 and Cd' is simply Cd. If α is somewhere between fully opaque and fully transparent, the resulting color Cd' is a combination of the source and destination colors. The remarkable fact about combining colors with this simple mathematical formula is that the resulting blended color is actually a visually convincing simulation of translucent colors.

Drawing with Translucent Colors

You create an AlphaComposite object by calling its static getInstance() factory method. (A factory method is provided instead of a constructor so that the AlphaComposite class can cache and share immutable AlphaComposite objects.) getInstance() takes two arguments: a compositing mode and a float value between 0.0 and 1.0 that specifies an alpha-transparency value. The default Composite object used by a Graphics2D object is an AlphaComposite created like this:

```
AlphaComposite.getInstance(AlphaComposite.SRC_OVER, 1.0f);
```

The AlphaComposite.SrcOver constant also refers to this default AlphaComposite object.

The SRC_OVER compositing rule places the source color over the destination color and blends them based on the transparency of the source, using the formula shown in the previous section. I'll explain this rule and the others supported by AlphaComposite in more detail shortly. For now, you just need to know that SRC_OVER is the most commonly used compositing rule and has the most intuitive behavior.

If you use the default AlphaComposite attribute of a Graphics2D object, you can achieve color-blending effects by drawing with a translucent color. In Java 2D, the Color class includes new constructors that allow you to create translucent colors by including an alpha channel. For example, you can create and use a 50% transparent red color with code like the following:

```
Graphics2D g;                              // Initialized elsewhere
Color c = new Color(1.0f, 0.0f, 0.0f, 0.5f); // Red with alpha = 0.5
g.setPaint(c);                             // Use this translucent color
g.fillRect(100, 100, 100, 100);            // Draw something with it
```

This code draws a translucent red rectangle over whatever background previously existed on the drawing surface represented by the Graphics2D object. As an aside, it is worth noting that you can achieve interesting effects by using the Gradient-Paint class to define color gradients between colors with different levels of transparency.

Now suppose that you want to draw a complex, multicolor figure, and you want to make it translucent. While you could allocate a bunch of translucent colors and draw with them, there is an easier way. As we already discussed, when you create an AlphaComposite object, you specify an alpha value for it. The alpha value of any source pixel is multiplied by the alpha value associated with the AlphaComposite currently in effect. Since the default AlphaComposite object has an alpha value of 1.0, this object does not affect the transparency of colors. However, by setting the alpha value of an AlphaComposite object, we can draw using opaque colors and opaque images and still achieve the effect of translucency. For example, here's another way to draw a translucent red rectangle:

```
Graphics2D g;                              // Initialized elsewhere
Color c = new Color(1.0f, 0.0f, 0.0f);     // Opaque red; alpha = 1.0
g.setPaint(c);                             // Use this opaque color

// Get and install an AlphaComposite to do transparent drawing
g.setComposite(AlphaComposite.getInstance(AlphaComposite.SRC_OVER, 0.5f));

g.fillRect(100, 100, 100, 100);            // Start drawing with it
```

The AlphaComposite Compositing Rules

The SRC_OVER compositing rule draws a possibly translucent source color over the destination color. This is what we typically want to happen when we perform a graphics operation. But the AlphaComposite object actually allows colors to be combined according to seven other rules as well.

Before we consider the compositing rules in detail, there is an important point you need to understand. Colors displayed on the screen never have an alpha channel. If you can see a color, it is an opaque color. The precise color value may have been chosen based on a transparency calculation, but, once that color is chosen, the color resides in the memory of a video card somewhere and does not have an alpha value associated with it. In other words, with on-screen drawing, destination pixels always have alpha values of 1.0.

The situation is different when you are drawing into an off-screen image, however. As you'll see when we consider the Java 2D BufferedImage class later in this chapter, you can specify the desired color representation when you create an off-screen image. By default, a `BufferedImage` object represents an image as an array of RGB colors, but you can also create an image that is an array of ARGB colors. Such an image has alpha values associated with it, and when you draw into the images, the alpha values remain associated with the pixels you draw.

This distinction between on-screen and off-screen drawing is important because some of the compositing rules perform compositing based on the alpha values of the destination pixels, rather than the alpha values of the source pixels. With on-screen drawing, the destination pixels are always opaque (with alpha values of 1.0), but with off-screen drawing, this need not be the case. Thus, some of the compositing rules only are useful when you are drawing into off-screen images that have an alpha channel.

To overgeneralize a bit, we can say that when you are drawing on-screen, you typically stick with the default `SRC_OVER` compositing rule, use opaque colors, and vary the alpha value used by the `AlphaComposite` object. When working with off-screen images that have alpha channels, however, you can make use of other compositing rules. In this case, you typically use translucent colors and translucent images and an `AlphaComposite` object with an alpha value of 1.0.

The compositing rules supported by `AlphaComposite` are a subset of the classic Porter-Duff compositing rules.* Each of the rules describes a way of creating a new destination color `Cd'` by combining a source color `Cs` with the existing destination color `Cd`. The colors are combined according to a general formula, which is applied independently to each of the red, green, and blue values of the color:

```
Cd' = Cs*Fs + Cd*Fd
```

In this formula, `Fs` and `Fd` are the fractions of the source and destination colors used in the compositing operation, respectively. Each of the eight compositing rules uses a different pair of values for `Fs` and `Fd`, which is what makes each rule unique.

As I already noted, with certain off-screen images, destination pixels can have alpha values. The new alpha value of a destination pixel is computed in the same way as the new color value of that pixel (i.e., using the same fractions). If `Ad` is the destination alpha value and `As` is the source alpha value, the resulting alpha value is computed like this:

```
Ad' = As*Fs + Ad*Fd
```

Table 4-8 lists the compositing rules supported by `AlphaComposite`, using the names defined by that class. Don't take the names of these constants at face value; they can be misleading. The rule names that include the words `IN` and `OUT` make the most sense if you consider the case of a 1-bit alpha channel. In this case, the alpha channel is simply a bit mask, and an image has an inside where it is fully opaque and an outside where it is fully transparent. In the more general case, with a multibit alpha channel, these compositing operations behave more generally

---

* These rules were described originally in the paper "Compositing Digital Images," by Porter and Duff, published in SIGGRAPH, vol. 84.

than their names imply. These rules also make the most sense when copying one image into another; they typically are not useful for drawing lines, text, and so on.

Table 4-8 includes the Fs and Fd values, used in the preceding formulas that define each of the compositing rules. These values are specified in terms of As, the alpha value of the source pixel, and Ad, the alpha value of the destination pixel. Note that the values of Fs and Fd listed here are for illustrative purposes, to help you understand the compositing operations. The actual formulas for computing composited colors depends on whether the source and destination color values have been premultiplied by their alpha values.

Table 4–8: AlphaComposite Compositing Rules

Rule	Fs	Fd	Description
SRC_OVER	As	1-As	By far the most commonly used compositing rule. It draws the source on top of the destination. The source and destination are combined based on the transparency of the source. Where the source is opaque, it replaces the destination. Where the source is transparent, the destination is unchanged. Where the source is translucent, the source and destination colors are combined so that some of the destination color shows through the translucent source.
DST_OVER	1-Ad	Ad	This rule draws the source based on the transparency of the destination, so that the source appears to be underneath the destination. Where the destination is opaque, it is left unchanged. Where the destination is fully transparent, the source is drawn. Where the destination is translucent, the source and destination colors are combined so that some of the source color shows through the translucent destination.
SRC	1.0	0.0	The source replaces the destination color and its alpha channel with the source color and its alpha channel. In other words, the rule does a simple replacement, ignoring the destination and doing no color blending at all.
CLEAR	0.0	0.0	This rule ignores both the source and the destination. It clears the destination by setting it to a fully transparent black.

Table 4–8: AlphaComposite Compositing Rules (continued)

Rule	Fs	Fd	Description
SRC_IN	Ad	0	This rule draws the source color using the transparency of the destination. Where the destination is fully opaque, it is replaced with an opaque version of the source. Where the destination is fully transparent, it remains fully transparent. Where the destination is translucent, it is replaced with an equally translucent version of the source. The color of the destination is never blended with the color of the source.
SRC_OUT	1-Ad	0	This is the inverse of the SRC_IN rule. It draws the source color using the inverse of the destination transparency. Where the destination is opaque, it becomes transparent. Where the destination is transparent, it is replaced with an opaque version of the source. Where the destination is translucent, it is replaced with an inversely translucent version of the source.
DST_IN	0	As	This rule ignores the color of the source, but modifies the destination based on the transparency of the source. Where the source is transparent, the destination becomes transparent. Where the source is opaque, the destination is unmodified. Where the source is translucent, the destination becomes correspondingly translucent.
DST_OUT	0	1-As	This rule is the inverse of the DST_IN rule. It ignores the source color but modifies the destination based on the inverse of the source transparency. Where the source is opaque, the destination becomes transparent. Where the source is transparent, the destination is left unmodified. Where the source is translucent, the destination is given the inverse translucency.

Finally, note that AlphaComposite also predefines constant AlphaComposite objects that use each of these rules along with a built-in alpha value of 1.0. For example, the AlphaComposite.DstOver object uses the AlphaComposite.DST_OVER compositing rule with an alpha value of 1.0. This object is the same as the object created by:

```
AlphaComposite.getInstance(AlphaComposite.DST_OVER, 1.0f)
```

Remember that if you use an AlphaComposite object with an alpha value other than the default 1.0, that alpha value is used to make the source colors more transparent before the rest of the compositing operation occurs.

Rendering Hints

Another graphics attribute used by the Graphics2D class is java.awt.Rendering-Hints. This class is a mapping (a java.util.Map) from a set of rendering hint names to a set of rendering hint values. Unlike with other attributes, Graphics2D defines more than one method to set the rendering hints attribute. setRendering-Hints() specifies a new set of hints that replaces the old set of hints, while addRenderingHints() adds a set of hints to the existing set and setRendering-Hint() sets the value for a single hint in the current set of hints.

Rendering hints are suggestions to Java 2D about how it should perform its rendering. The RenderingHints class defines a number of constants whose names begin with KEY_. These constants represent the kind of hints you can give. The class also defines a number of constants whose names begin with VALUE_. These are the legal values for the various hints. The names of the VALUE constants make it clear with which hint KEY constant each value is associated.

The purpose of the hints is to allow you to request that Java 2D turn a particular feature, such as antialiasing, on or off. In addition, the hints allow you to suggest what kind of speed versus quality trade-offs Java 2D should make. Remember that these are hints and suggestions to Java 2D, not commands. Not all Java 2D implementations support all the hints, and different implementations have different default values for the hints. Furthermore, the meanings of the hints are not precisely defined, so different implementations may interpret the hints differently.

Suppose that you are writing an application that draws complex graphics. For slow systems, you might want to support a draft mode that draws graphics quickly at the expense of high-quality output. Your code might look like this:

```java
public void paint(Graphics graphics) {
  Graphics2D g = (Graphics2D)graphics;
  if (draftmode) {
    g.setRenderingHint(RenderingHints.KEY_RENDERING,
                       RenderingHints.VALUE_RENDER_SPEED);
    g.setRenderingHint(RenderingHints.KEY_ANTIALIASING,
                       RenderingHints.VALUE_ANTIALIAS_OFF);
    g.setRenderingHint(RenderingHints.KEY_TEXT_ANTIALIASING,
                       RenderingHints.VALUE_TEXT_ANTIALIAS_OFF);
    g.setRenderingHint(RenderingHints.KEY_FRACTIONALMETRICS,
                       RenderingHints.VALUE_FRACTIONALMETRICS_OFF);
    g.setRenderingHint(RenderingHints.KEY_COLOR_RENDERING,
                       RenderingHints.VALUE_COLOR_RENDER_SPEED);
    g.setRenderingHint(RenderingHints.KEY_DITHERING,
                       RenderingHints.VALUE_DITHER_DISABLE);
  }
}
```

Fonts and Text

As we've seen, fonts are represented in AWT by the java.awt.Font class. While you can continue to use fonts in Java 1.2 exactly as you did in Java 1.1, Java 2D has added a number of powerful new features related to fonts and text rendering that you may want to take advantage of.

Available Fonts

Java 1.0 and Java 1.1 support only a small set of fonts, specified by logical font names. Although these logical fonts are guaranteed to be available on every platform, they are not guaranteed to look the same on every platform. In addition, the lack of variety severely limits the design choices available to developers. The fonts and their logical names were listed earlier in Table 4-3.

Java 1.2 allows an application to use any font installed on the native system and refer to that font by its physical font name, instead of a logical font name. A physical font name is the actual name of a font, such as "Century Gothic" or "Lucida Sans Bold." To request a specific font, simply pass its physical name to the Font() constructor. The Font() constructor always returns a valid Font object, even if the font you have requested does not exist. If you need to check whether you got the font you requested, call the getFontName() method of the returned font.

If you want to be sure that a font exists on the host system before attempting to use it, you should first query the system to find out what fonts are installed. You can do this with methods of the java.awt.GraphicsEnvironment object. The code looks like this:

```
GraphicsEnvironment env = GraphicsEnvironment.getLocalGraphicsEnvironment();
Font[] allfonts = env.getAllFonts();
```

The getAllFonts() method returns an array of Font objects that represents all of the fonts installed on the system. Each Font object in this array represents a font that is one point high, so you have to scale the font (using deriveFont() as explained shortly) before using it. Also, in the initial release of Java 1.2 at least, the getAllFonts() method can take prohibitively long to return (65 seconds on my Windows 95 system).

Another GraphicsEnvironment method, getAvailableFontFamilyNames(), returns an array of font family names instead of an array of Font objects:

```
GraphicsEnvironment env = GraphicsEnvironment.getLocalGraphicsEnvironment();
String[] familynames = env.getAvailableFontFamilyNames();
```

This method returns relatively quickly and is therefore safer to call than getAll-Fonts(). Note that this method returns font family names (e.g., "Lucida Sans"), not actual font face names (e.g., "Lucida Sans Oblique"). The good news is that you can get away with specifying a font family name instead of a font face name when you call the Font() constructor.*

Font Attributes

In Java 1.2, the Font class has a new constructor that is passed a java.util.Map object that contains a set of font attributes. These attributes specify the desired characteristics of the font; the Font() constructor tries to return a Font that matches the attributes. Typically, you use a java.util.Hashtable or java.util.Hashmap to hold your attribute values. The attribute names or keys are

---

* A bug in Java 1.2, 1.2d, and 1.2.2 prevents the Font() constructor from working with any nonlogical font name unless you have previously queried the list of available fonts or font family names.

constants defined in java.awt.font.TextAttribute. The important constants are FAMILY, SIZE, WEIGHT, and POSTURE. The TextAttribute class also defines commonly used values for the WEIGHT and POSTURE attributes.

Transforming Fonts

The Font class defines several deriveFont() methods that allow you to use a Font object to create related Font objects. deriveFont() is typically used to return a new Font object that represents an existing font at a different size or in a different style. For example:

```
GraphicsEnvironment env = GraphicsEnvironment.getLocalGraphicsEnvironment();
String[] familynames = env.getAvailableFontFamilyNames();
Font regularFont = new Font("Century Schoolbook", Font.PLAIN, 12);
Font bigFont = regularFont.deriveFont(18.0f);
Font boldFont = regularFont.deriveFont(Font.BOLD);
Font bigBoldFont = regularFont.deriveFont(Font.BOLD, 24.0f);
```

When you are passing a point size to deriveFont(), be sure to explicitly specify a float value, such as the 18.0f constant in the preceding code, so that you do not inadvertently call the version of deriveFont() that takes an integer-style constant.

You can also derive a transformed version of a Font object by passing in an arbitrary java.awt.geom.AffineTransform object. This technique allows you to arbitrarily rotate or skew any font, as we'll discuss later in the chapter.

Text-Rendering Hints

The java.awt.RenderingHints class defines two hints that apply particularly to text drawing. The first controls antialiasing. Antialiasing is a technique used to make the jagged edges of shapes, such as the glyphs of a font, look smoother. It is implemented using translucent colors and compositing: when the edge of a shape only partially covers a pixel, the color used to draw that pixel is given an alpha-transparency value that corresponds to the amount of coverage. If a fully covered pixel is drawn with an opaque color, a pixel that is only one-quarter covered is drawn with an alpha value of .25. As you can imagine, antialiasing can be computationally intensive. However, the smoothing effect it achieves is significant and is particularly useful when drawing small amounts of text at large point sizes.

The first text-related rendering hint simply requests antialiasing for text. If you want text to be antialiased, set the KEY_TEXT_ANTIALIASING hint to VALUE_TEXT_ANTIALIAS_ON. There is also a more general hint, KEY_ANTIALIASING. Java 2D defines a separate hint for text so that you can choose independently whether to request antialiasing for text and other graphics.

The second text-related rendering hint controls the low-level positioning of characters of text. When Java 2D renders the shape of an individual font glyph, it caches the rendered pixels for reuse. This technique dramatically speeds up text display. However, the cached rendering is useful only if the glyph is always drawn at an integral pixel position. By default, therefore, most implementations of Java 2D adjust character spacing so that the origin of each character falls evenly on an integer-pixel coordinate. If you want to be able to position text at arbitrary floating-point positions, without forcing each character to the nearest device pixel, set the KEY_FRACTIONALMETRICS hint to VALUE_FRACTIONALMETRICS_ON. Note, however, that the visual effect of setting this hint is rarely worth the computational overhead it requires.

Measuring Text and Fonts

Sometimes you need to obtain measurement information about a font or measure text before you can draw text. For example, to horizontally center a string of text, you must be able to figure out how wide it is. To correctly draw multiple lines of text, you need to be able to query the baseline position and the interline spacing for the font. In Java 1.0 and Java 1.1, you obtained this information with the Font-Metrics class (as described near the beginning of the chapter).

Java 2D provides another way to measure the width of a string of text. The Font class defines several getStringBounds() methods that return the width and height of a specified string as a Rectangle2D object. These methods allow widths to be returned as floating-point numbers instead of integers and are therefore more accurate than the stringWidth() method of FontMetrics. Each variant of get-StringBounds() allows you to specify a string of text in a different way. What these methods have in common, however, is that they must all be passed a FontRenderContext object. This object contains information needed to accurately measure text. It includes information about whether antialiasing and fractional metrics are being used, for example. You can obtain an appropriate FontRender-Context by calling the getFontRenderContext() method of a Graphics2D object.

The Java 1.2 Font class also defines a set of getLineMetrics() methods that are similar to the getStringBounds() methods. Each method takes a FontRenderContext object and returns a java.awt.font.LineMetrics object that contains various vertical metrics for the font. LineMetrics is similar to the older FontMetrics, except that it returns precise float values instead of approximate int values. get-Height() returns the line height of the font. This value is the sum of the values returned by getAscent(), getDescent(), and getLeading(). Ascent is the amount of space above the baseline, descent is the space below the baseline, and leading space is the empty interline spacing for the font. Other LineMetrics methods return values that allow you to correctly underline and strike through text.

The following code shows how you can obtain important metrics for a string of text, so that you can center it in a box:

```
Graphics2D g;                            // Initialized elsewhere
Font f;                                  // Initialized elsewhere
String message = "Hello World!";         // The text to measure and display
Rectangle2D box;                         // The display box: initialized elsewhere

// Measure the font and the message
FontRenderContext frc = g.getFontRenderContext();
Rectangle2D bounds = f.getStringBounds(message, frc);
LineMetrics metrics = f.getLineMetrics(message, frc);
float width = (float) bounds.getWidth();     // The width of our text
float lineheight = metrics.getHeight();      // Total line height
float ascent = metrics.getAscent();          // Top of text to baseline
```

```
// Now display the message centered horizontally and vertically in box
float x0 = (float) (box.getX() + (box.getWidth() - width)/2);
float y0 = (float) (box.getY() + (box.getHeight() - lineheight)/2 + ascent);
g.setFont(f);
g.drawString(message, x0, y0);
```

The getLineMetrics() methods all require a string to be specified, just as the get-
StringBounds() methods do. This is because a single font may have different font
metrics for glyphs in different writing systems. If you pass a string of Latin text,
you may get a different LineMetrics object than you would if you supplied a
string of Chinese text, for example. If you pass in a string that mixes text from several distinct writing systems, you get line metrics for only a prefix of that string.
The LineMetrics.getNumChars() method returns the length of this prefix.

Advanced Text Drawing

The easiest way to display text in an application is to use a Swing component such
as a JLabel, JTextField, JTextArea, or JEditorPane. Sometimes, however, you
have to draw text explicitly, such as when you are implementing a custom Swing
component.

The easiest way to draw text is with the drawString() method of Graphics or
Graphics2D. drawString() is actually a more complex method than you might
think. It works by first taking the characters of a string and converting them to a
list of glyphs in a font. There is not always a one-to-one correspondence between
characters and glyphs, however, and font encodings usually do not match the Unicode encoding used for characters. Next, the method must obtain the measurements of each glyph in the list of glyphs and position it individually. Only after
these steps can the method actually perform the requested string drawing
operation.

If you are drawing a string repeatedly, you can optimize this process by first converting the string of characters into a java.awt.font.GlyphVector.* This converts
characters to glyphs and calculates the appropriate position for each glyph. Then,
to draw the string, you simply pass the resulting glyph vector to the drawGlyph-
Vector() method of a Graphics2D object. Your code might look like this:

```
Graphics2D g;
Font f;
GlyphVector msg = f.createGlyphVector(g.getFontRenderContext(), "Hello");
g.drawGlyphVector(msg, 100.0f, 100.0f);
```

This technique is useful only if you expect to be drawing the same string repeatedly. The optimization occurs because the string is converted to glyphs only once,
instead of being converted each time you call drawString().

The GlyphVector class has a number of methods that are useful for other purposes. Once you have created a GlyphVector, you can call getOutline() to obtain
a Shape that represents the original string or getGlyphOutline() to get the Shape

---

* The drawString() method is typically already highly optimized for drawing basic ASCII or Latin-1 text
  without antialiasing. Using a GlyphVector may actually slow down the drawing process.

of a single glyph. You can also call `getGlyphMetrics()` to obtain a `GlyphMetrics` object that contains detailed metrics for an individual glyph.

Two other methods, `setGlyphPosition()` and `setGlyphTransform()`, are designed to let you set the position and transform for individual glyphs. For example, you might use `setGlyphPosition()` to increase the interletter spacing of a glyph in a `GlyphVector` in order to implement fill-justification. In the initial release of Java 1.2, however, these methods are not implemented. If you want to handle the low-level layout of glyphs, one approach is to implement your own subclass of the abstract `GlyphVector` class.

A `GlyphVector` object can represent only glyphs from a single font; the default implementation represents only glyphs that appear on a single line of text. If you want to represent a single line of multifont text, you can use a `java.awt.-font.TextLayout` object. And if you want to work with multiline text, you can use `java.awt.font.LineBreakMeasurer` to break a paragraph of multifont text into multiple `TextLayout` objects, each representing a single line of text.

`TextLayout` is a powerful class for displaying multifont text. It supports bidirectional text layout, such as when left-to-right English text is mixed with right-to-left Hebrew or Arabic text or when right-to-left Hebrew letters are mixed with left-to-right Hebrew numbers. Once you've created a `TextLayout` object, you can draw the text it represents by calling its `draw()` method, specifying a `Graphics2D` object and a position.

The `TextLayout` object does more than simply draw text. Once the text is drawn, it also provides methods that applications can use to allow a user to interact with the text. If the user clicks on the text, the `TextLayout` has a method that allows you to determine which character was clicked on. If you want to highlight portions of the text, you can tell the `TextLayout` the first and last characters to be highlighted, and it returns a `Shape` that represents the region to be highlighted. Similarly, if you want to display an insertion cursor within the text, you can specify the character position, and the `TextLayout` returns a `Shape` that you can draw to display the cursor. Although these methods may seem trivial, they in fact handle all the nontrivial complexities of multifont and bidirectional text, making `TextLayout` a powerful class for certain applications.

You can create a `TextLayout` object by specifying a `String`, a `Font`, and a `FontRenderContext`. However, a `TextLayout` created in this way can represent only single-font text. To display multifont text, you must use a `java.text.Attributed-CharacterIterator` to represent the text. The attributes associated with the text should be `java.awt.font.TextAttribute` constants, such as `TextAttribute.FONT`. The easiest way to create an `AttributedCharacterIterator` is to create a `java.text.AttributedString`, specify attributes with its `addAttribute()` method, and then get an iterator for it with its `getIterator()` method. The `java.text` API is covered in *Java in a Nutshell*, not in this book.

Text Art with Font Glyphs

As I mentioned earlier, the `GlyphVector` class allows you to obtain a `Shape` object that represents the outline of a single glyph or a string of glyphs. This is a powerful feature of Java 2D that allows you to produce sophisticated text art. The `Shape` object returned by the getOutline() or getGlyphOutline() method of Glyph-Vector can be used in the same way that you use any other Shape object. Use the draw() method of Graphics2D to draw the outline of the glyph or glyphs. Use fill() to fill the glyphs with an arbitrary Paint. You can transform the glyph shapes by scaling, rotating, and skewing them and you can even use them to perform clipping and hit detection.

Buffered Images

Java 2D introduces a new java.awt.Image subclass, java.awt.image.BufferedImage. BufferedImage represents image data that is present in memory, unlike Image, which typically represents streaming image data being transferred over a network. Java 2D also provides powerful image-processing classes that operate on BufferedImage objects and are much simpler to use than the ImageFilter class of Java 1.0.

As we discussed at the beginning of the chapter, Java knows how to read images in commonly used formats from files and URLs. You can use the getImage() method of either Applet() or Toolkit to retrieve an Image, but the image data may not have been fully read when the method returns. If you want to ensure that the image is fully loaded, you have to use a java.awt.MediaTracker. Note also that both of these methods return read-only Image objects, rather than read/write BufferedImage objects.

If you are writing a Swing application, an easy way to load an image is with the javax.swing.ImageIcon class. This class automatically waits until the image is fully loaded. For example:

```
Image myimage = new javax.swing.ImageIcon("myimage.gif").getImage();
```

As useful as ImageIcon is, its getImage() method still returns an Image object, not a BufferedImage object.

Obtaining a BufferedImage

To create an empty BufferedImage object, call the createImage() method of a Component. This method was first introduced in Java 1.0; it returns an Image object. In Java 1.2, however, the returned Image object is always an instance of BufferedImage, so you can safely cast it. After you have created an empty BufferedImage, you can call its createGraphics() method to obtain a Graphics2D object. Then use this Graphics2D object to draw image data from an Image object into your BufferedImage object. For example:

```
javax.swing.JFrame f;                    // Initialized elsewhere

// Create an image, and wait for it to load
Image i = javax.swing.ImageIcon("myimage.gif").getImage();

// Create a BufferedImage of the same size as the Image
BufferedImage bi = (BufferedImage)f.createImage(i.getWidth(f),i.getHeight(f));
```

```
Graphics2D g = bi.createGraphics();    // Get a Graphics2D object
g.drawImage(i, 0, 0, f);    // Draw the Image data into the BufferedImage
```

Note that we must pass an ImageObserver object to the getWidth(), getHeight() and drawImage() methods in this code. All AWT components implement ImageObserver, so we use our JFrame for this purpose. Although we could have gotten away with passing null, this is exactly the sort of complexity that the BufferedImage API allows us to avoid.

Sun's implementation of Java 1.2 ships with a package named com.sun.image.codec.jpeg that contains classes for reading JPEG image data directly into BufferedImage objects and for encoding BufferedImage image data using the JPEG image format. Although this package is not part of the core Java 2 platform, most Java implementations will probably contain these classes. You can use this package to read JPEG files with code like this:

```
import java.io.*;
import com.sun.image.codec.jpeg.*;

FileInputStream in = new FileInputStream("myimage.jpeg");
JPEGImageDecoder decoder = JPEGCodec.createJPEGDecoder(in);
BufferedImage image = decoder.decodeAsBufferedImage();
in.close();
```

Drawing a BufferedImage

A BufferedImage is a kind of Image, so you can do anything with a BufferedImage that you can do with an Image. For instance, the Graphics class defines a number of methods for drawing Image objects. Some of these methods take only an X and a Y coordinate at which to draw the image and simply draw the image at its original size. Other drawImage() methods also take a width and a height and scale the image as appropriate.

Java 1.1 introduced more sophisticated drawImage() methods that take coordinates that specify a destination rectangle on the drawing surface and a source rectangle within the image. These methods map an arbitrary subimage onto an arbitrary rectangle of the drawing surface, scaling and flipping as necessary. Each of these drawImage() methods comes in two versions, one that takes a background color argument and one that does not. The background Color is used if the Image contains transparent pixels.

Since all the drawImage() methods of the Graphics object operate on Image objects instead of BufferedImage objects, they all require a Component or other ImageObserver object to be specified.

In Java 2D, the Graphics2D object defines two more drawImage() methods. One of these methods draws an Image object as modified by an arbitrary AffineTransform object. As we'll see a bit later, an AffineTransform object can specify a position, scaling factor, rotation, and shear.

The other drawImage() method of Graphics2D actually operates on a BufferedImage object. This method processes the specified BufferedImage as specified by a BufferedImageOp object and then draws the processed image at the specified position. We'll talk about image processing with BufferedImageOp objects in more detail shortly. Since this drawImage() method operates on a BufferedImage object instead of an Image object, it does not require an ImageObserver argument.

Finally, the Graphics2D class defines a drawRenderedImage() method. Buffered-Image implements the RenderedImage interface, so you can pass a BufferedImage to this method, along with an arbitrary AffineTransform that specifies where and how to draw it.

Drawing into a BufferedImage

As I mentioned earlier, the createGraphics() method of a BufferedImage returns a Graphics2D object that you can use to draw into a BufferedImage. Anything you can draw on the screen, you can draw into a BufferedImage. One common reason to draw into a BufferedImage object is to implement double-buffering. When performing animations or other repetitive drawing tasks, the erase/redraw cycle can cause flickering. To avoid this, do your drawing into an off-screen BufferedImage and then copy the contents of the image to the screen all at once. Although this requires extra memory, it can dramatically improve the appearance of your programs.*

Manipulating Pixels of a BufferedImage

The Image class defines very few methods, so about all you can do with an Image object is query its width and height. The BufferedImage class, by contrast, defines quite a few methods. Most of these are required by interfaces that BufferedImage implements. A few important ones, however, allow pixel-level manipulation of images.

For example, getRGB() returns the image pixel at the specified X and Y coordinates, while setRGB() sets the pixel at the specified coordinates. Both of these methods represent the pixel value as an int that contains 8-bit red, green, and blue color values. Other versions of getRGB() and setRGB() read and write rectangular arrays of pixels into int arrays. getSubimage() is a related method that returns a rectangular region of the image as a BufferedImage.

Inside a BufferedImage

Most applications can use the BufferedImage class without ever caring what is inside a BufferedImage. However, if you are writing a program that performs low-level image-data manipulation, such as reading or writing image data from a file, you need to know more. The complete details of the image architecture are beyond the scope of this book; this section explains the basics in case you want to explore on your own.

---

* Recall that Swing components, and custom components subclassed from Swing components, automatically support double-buffering.

The image data of a BufferedImage is stored in a java.awt.image.Raster object, which can be obtained with the getData() method of BufferedImage. The Raster itself contains two parts: a java.awt.image.DataBuffer that holds the raw image data and a java.awt.image.SampleModel object that knows how to extract individual pixel values out of the DataBuffer. DataBuffer supports a wide variety of formats for image data, which is why a Raster object also needs a SampleModel.

The Raster object of a BufferedImage stores the pixel values of an image. These pixel values may or may not correspond directly to the red, green, and blue color values to be displayed on the screen. Therefore, a BufferedImage object also contains a java.awt.image.ColorModel object that knows how to convert pixel values from the Raster into Color objects. A ColorModel object typically contains a java.awt.color.ColorSpace object that specifies the representation of color components.

Processing a BufferedImage

The java.awt.image package defines five powerful implementations of the BufferedImageOp interface that perform various types of image-processing operations on BufferedImage objects. The five implementations are described briefly in Table 4-9.

Table 4-9: Java 1.2 Image-Processing Classes

Class	Description
AffineTransformOp	Performs an arbitrary geometric transformation—specified by an AffineTransform—on an image. The transform can include scaling, rotation, translation, and shearing in any combination. This operator interpolates pixel values when needed, using either a fast, nearest-neighbor algorithm or a slower, higher-quality bilinear interpolation algorithm. This class cannot process images in place.
ColorConvertOp	Converts an image to a new java.awt.color.ColorSpace. It can process an image in place.
ConvolveOp	Performs a powerful and flexible type of image processing called *convolution*, which is used for blurring or sharpening images and performing edge detection, among other things. ConvolveOp uses a java.awt.image.Kernel object to hold the matrix of numbers that specify exactly what convolution operation is performed. Convolution operations cannot be performed in place.

Table 4-9: Java 1.2 Image-Processing Classes (continued)

Class	Description
LookupOp	Processes the color channels of an image using a lookup table, which is an array that maps color values in the source image to color values in the new image. The use of lookup tables makes LookupOp a very flexible image-processing class. For example, you can use it to brighten or darken an image, to invert the colors of an image, or to reduce the number of distinct color levels in an image. LookupOp can use either a single lookup table to operate on all color channels in an image or a separate lookup table for each channel. LookupOp can be used to process images in place. You typically use LookupOp in conjunction with java.awt.image.ByteLookupTable.
RescaleOp	Like LookupOp, RescaleOp is used to modify the values of the individual color components of an image. Instead of using a lookup table, however, RescaleOp uses a simple linear equation. The color values of the destination are obtained by multiplying the source values by a constant and then adding another constant. You can specify either a single pair of constants for use on all color channels or individual pairs of constants for each of the channels in the image. RescaleOp can process images in place.

To use a BufferedImageOp, simply call its filter() method. This method processes or filters a source image and stores the results in a destination image. If no destination image is supplied, filter() creates one. In either case, the method returns a BufferedImage that contains the processed image. As noted in Table 4-9, some implementations of BufferedImageOp can process an image "in place." These implementations allow you to specify the same BufferedImage object as both the source and destination arguments to the filter() method.

To convert a color image to grayscale, you can use ColorConvertOp as follows:

```
import java.awt.image.*;
import java.awt.color.*;

ColorConvertOp op = new ColorConvertOp(ColorSpace.getInstance(CS_GRAY), null);
BufferedImage grayImage = op.filter(sourceImage, null);
```

To invert the colors in an image (producing a photographic negative effect), you might use a RescaleOp as follows:

```
RescaleOp op = new RescaleOp(-1.0f, 255f, null);
BufferedImage negative = op.filter(sourceImage, null);
```

To brighten an image, you can use a RescaleOp to linearly increase the intensity of each color value. More realistic brightening effects require a nonlinear transform, however. For example, you can use a LookupOp to handle brightening based on the square-root function, which boosts midrange colors more than colors that are dark or bright:

```
byte[] data = new byte[256];
for(int i = 0; i < 256; i++)
   data[i] = (byte)(Math.sqrt((float)i/255.0) * 255);
ByteLookupTable table = new ByteLookupTable(0, data);
LookupOp op = new LookupOp(table, null);
BufferedImage brighterImage = op.filter(sourceImage, null);
```

You can blur an image using a `ConvolveOp`. When processing an image by convolution, a pixel value in the destination image is computed from the corresponding pixel value in the source image and the pixels that surround that pixel. A matrix of numbers known as the *kernel* is used to specify the contribution of each source pixel to the destination pixel. To perform a simple blurring operation, you might use a kernel like this to specify that the destination pixel is the average of the source pixel and the eight pixels that surround that source pixel:

```
0.1111   0.1111   0.1111
0.1111   0.1111   0.1111
0.1111   0.1111   0.1111
```

Note that the sum of the values in this kernel is 1.0, which means that the destination image has the same brightness as the source image. To perform a simple blur, use code like this:

```
Kernel k = new Kernel(3, 3, new float[] { .1111f, .1111f, .1111f,
                                          .1111f, .1111f, .1111f,
                                          .1111f, .1111f, .1111f });
ConvolveOp op = new ConvolveOp(k);
BufferedImage blurry = op.filter(sourceImage, null);
```

Transformations with AffineTransform

As we discussed earlier when we considered the Java 2D coordinate system, the `java.awt.geom.AffineTransform` class represents a general mapping from one coordinate system to another. `AffineTransform` defines a general coordinate-system transformation that can include translation, scaling, rotation, and shearing.

Setting Up an AffineTransform

One of the easiest ways to obtain an `AffineTransform` object is to use one of the static methods defined by `AffineTransform`. For example, `getScaleInstance()` returns an instance of `AffineTransform` that represents a simple scaling transformation.

Another way to get an `AffineTransform` is with the `AffineTransform()` constructor, of course. The no-argument version of the constructor returns an `Affine-Transform` that represents the identity transform—that is, no transform at all. You can modify this empty transform with a number of methods. Note that `Affine-Transform` defines several other constructors, but we have to wait to discuss them until after we've discussed the mathematics that underlie `AffineTransform`.

Once you have obtained an `AffineTransform` object, you can modify it with methods just like the methods defined by `Graphics2D`. Each of the `translate()`, `scale()`, `rotate()`, and `shear()` methods modifies an `AffineTransform` by adding the specified transformation to it. Note that there are two versions of `rotate()`. One rotates around the origin and the other rotates around a specified point; both use angles specified in radians. Remember that calls to these four methods are cumulative: you can build up a complex transformation as a combination of translation, scaling, rotation, and shearing.

`AffineTransform` also defines noncumulative methods. `setToTranslation()`, `setToScale()`, `setToRotation()`, and `setToShear()` set an `AffineTransform` to a single transform, replacing whatever transform was previously contained by the `AffineTransform`.

Performing Transformations

Once you have created and initialized an `AffineTransform` object, you can use it to transform points and shapes. `AffineTransform` defines a number of `transform()` methods that transform points represented by either `java.awt.geom.Point2D` objects or arrays of numbers. `deltaTransform()` is a variant of `transform()` that performs a transformation disregarding any translation component. It is designed for transforming distances or position-independent vectors, instead of actual points. `inverseTransform()` is the inverse of `transform()`—it converts points expressed in the new coordinate system back to the corresponding points in the original coordinate system.

The `transform()`, `deltaTransform()`, and `inverseTransform()` methods are fairly low-level and typically are not used directly by Java 2D programs. Instead, a program typically uses the `createTransformedShape()` method, which provides a powerful, high-level transformation capability. Given an arbitrary `Shape` object, this method returns a new `Shape` that has been transformed as specified by the `AffineTransform` object.

The Mathematics of AffineTransform

The coordinate system transformations described by `AffineTransform` have two very important properties:

- Straight lines remain straight

- Parallel lines remain parallel

An `AffineTransform` is a linear transform, so the transformation can be expressed in the matrix notation of linear algebra. An arbitrary `AffineTransform` can be mathematically expressed by six numbers arranged in a matrix like this:

$$\begin{bmatrix} sx & shx & tx \\ shy & sy & ty \end{bmatrix}$$

In this matrix, `tx` and `ty` are the translation amounts, `sx` and `sy` are the scaling factors, and `shx` and `shy` are the shearing factors, all in the X and Y dimensions, respectively. As we'll see in a moment, rotation is a combination of scaling and shearing, so there are not separate rx and ry numbers.

To transform a point from one coordinate system to another using an Affine-Transform, we multiply the point by this matrix. Using matrix notation (and adding a few dummy matrix elements), the equation looks like this:

$$\begin{bmatrix} x' \\ y' \\ 1 \end{bmatrix} = \begin{bmatrix} sx & shx & 0 \\ shy & sy & 0 \\ 0 & 0 & 1 \end{bmatrix} \begin{bmatrix} x \\ y \\ 1 \end{bmatrix}$$

This matrix equation is simply shorthand for the following system of equations:

```
x' = sx*x + shx*y + tx
y' = shy*x + sy*y + ty
```

The identity transform does not perform any transformation at all. It looks like this:

$$\begin{bmatrix} x' \\ y' \\ 1 \end{bmatrix} = \begin{bmatrix} 1 & 0 & 0 \\ 0 & 1 & 0 \\ 0 & 1 & 1 \end{bmatrix} \begin{bmatrix} x \\ y \\ 1 \end{bmatrix} = \begin{bmatrix} x * 1 \\ y * 1 \\ 1 \end{bmatrix}$$

Mathematically, rotation is a combination of scaling and shearing. The rotation of an angle theta around the origin is expressed with a matrix like this:

$$\begin{bmatrix} \cos(\theta) & -\sin(\theta) & 0 \\ \sin(\theta) & \cos(\theta) & 0 \end{bmatrix}$$

You don't need to understand how this rotation matrix works. If you remember basic trigonometry, however, you can use it and the preceding equations to verify that this matrix works for the base cases of 90-degree and 180-degree rotations.

As we've seen, it is possible to make cumulative changes to an AffineTransform. This is done by multiplying the current transformation matrix by the new transformation matrix. For example, suppose we perform a translation by 100 units in both the X and Y dimensions and follow this by scaling both the X and Y dimensions by a factor of 2. The resulting AffineTransform matrix is the product of the two individual matrices:

$$\begin{bmatrix} 1 & 0 & 100 \\ 0 & 1 & 100 \\ 0 & 0 & 1 \end{bmatrix} * \begin{bmatrix} 2 & 0 & 0 \\ 0 & 2 & 0 \\ 0 & 0 & 1 \end{bmatrix} = \begin{bmatrix} 2 & 0 & 100 \\ 0 & 2 & 100 \\ 0 & 0 & 1 \end{bmatrix}$$

Note that matrix multiplication is not commutative. If we perform the scaling operation first and then do the translation, we obtain a different result:

$$\begin{bmatrix} 2 & 0 & 0 \\ 0 & 2 & 0 \\ 0 & 0 & 1 \end{bmatrix} * \begin{bmatrix} 1 & 0 & 100 \\ 0 & 1 & 100 \\ 0 & 0 & 1 \end{bmatrix} = \begin{bmatrix} 2 & 0 & 200 \\ 0 & 2 & 200 \\ 0 & 0 & 1 \end{bmatrix}$$

Most applications do not have to work with matrices explicitly in order to perform coordinate-system transformations. As we've seen, it typically is easier to use the translate(), scale(), rotate(), and shear() methods of either AffineTransform or Graphics2D. It is useful to understand the mathematics underlying Affine-Transform, however.

You may, on occasion, have the need to create a custom AffineTransform object from a set of six numbers. A number of AffineTransform constructors and methods take matrix elements as arguments. These matrix elements are either passed in explicitly or specified in an array. Note that the matrix-element naming system used by the AffineTransform class is different than the system I've used here. The parameter names for AffineTransform methods are based on the following matrix:

$$\begin{bmatrix} m00 & m01 & m02 \\ m10 & m11 & m12 \end{bmatrix}$$

This is nothing more that a different naming scheme for the elements we are already familiar with:

$$\begin{bmatrix} sx & shx & tx \\ shy & sy & ty \end{bmatrix}$$

When matrix elements are passed to or returned by an AffineTransform in an array of float or double values, they are stored in this order:

$$\begin{bmatrix} m00, m10, m01, m11, m01, m12 \end{bmatrix}$$

This corresponds to the following order using our mnemonic names:

$$\begin{bmatrix} sx, shy, sy, tx, ty \end{bmatrix}$$

Color Spaces

The java.awt.Color class represents a color in Java. As we discussed earlier, Java 2D has added several new constructors to the Color class, to support the creation of translucent colors. Another important change to the Color class is support for arbitrary color spaces. A color space is a system for representing a color using some characteristic set of axes.

Java 2D introduces the java.awt.color package for working with color spaces. The most important piece of this package is the abstract ColorSpace class, which represents a color space and defines a number of constants for commonly used spaces. By default, Java colors are represented in the standard, device-independent sRGB color space, in which colors are represented by idealized red, green, and blue components. There are other ways of representing colors, however. One commonly used standard is the CIEXYZ space, which represents colors in terms of three abstract components named X, Y, and Z. Applications that represent colors to be displayed on a printed page often use the CMYK color space, which represents the cyan, magenta, yellow, and black inks used in the four-color printing process. Another familiar color space is the grayscale color space, which represents shades of gray as individual values between 0.0 (black) and 1.0 (white).

An application that cares about accurate color reproduction often uses a device-independent color space to ensure that the colors it displays look the same on different monitors, printers, and other devices. To make device-independent color representation work, each monitor, printer, scanner, or other device needs to be calibrated, so that device-independent colors can be correctly and accurately converted to appropriate device-dependent colors for that device. The result of a device calibration is called a "profile." The International Color Consortium (ICC) has defined a standard file format for profiles, and the `java.awt.color` package defines classes that implement color spaces in terms of these profiles. Sun's implementation of the Java 1.2 runtime environment includes five sample profiles for five different color spaces, stored in the *jre/lib/cmm* directory of the Java installation. A more sophisticated implementation would obtain profiles from the color management system of the native OS.

CHAPTER 5

Printing

The previous chapters of this book have described how to draw graphics and display graphical user interfaces on a computer screen. This chapter explains how to transfer those graphics to hardcopy. Printing was not supported in Java 1.0. Java 1.1 added a simple printing API that was easy to use but was not tightly integrated with the printing capabilities of the underlying operating system. The Java 2 platform introduces an entirely new printing API that addresses the shortcomings of the Java 1.1 API. This chapter explains both the Java 1.1 and the Java 1.2 APIs.

Printing in Java 1.1

In Java 1.1, you use a `Graphics` object to draw to the screen or into an off-screen `Image`. To produce hardcopy, you do exactly the same thing: obtain a `Graphics` object that represents your printer and use the methods of that object to draw to the printer. The only tricky thing you need to know is how to obtain an appropriate `Graphics` object. You do this with a `java.awt.PrintJob` object, which you can obtain from the `Toolkit` object.

The basic Java 1.1 printing algorithm has the following steps:

1. First, you must begin the print job. You do this by calling the `getPrintJob()` method of the `Toolkit` object. This method displays a dialog box to the user to request information about the print job, such as the name of the printer it should be sent to. `getPrintJob()` returns a `PrintJob` object.

2. To begin printing a page, you call the `getGraphics()` method of the `PrintJob` object. This returns a `Graphics` object that implements the `PrintGraphics` interface, to distinguish it from an on-screen `Graphics` object.

3. Now you can use the various methods of the `Graphics` object to draw your desired output on the page. If you are printing an applet or a custom AWT component, you can simply pass your `Graphics` object to the `paint()` method

of the applet or component. Note, however, that built-in AWT components are drawn by the native GUI system, rather than a paint() method, and may not print correctly.

4. When you are done drawing the page, you call the dispose() method of the Graphics object to send that page description to the printer. If you need to print another page, you can call the getGraphics() method of the PrintJob again to obtain a new Graphics object for the next page and repeat the process of drawing and calling dispose().

5. When you have printed all of your pages, you end the print job itself by calling the end() method of the PrintJob object.

With the Java 1.1 printing API, the coordinate system of the printer is very much like the coordinate system used when drawing on-screen. The origin is at the top left, X coordinates run from left to right, and Y coordinates run from the top to the bottom of the page. The coordinate system uses a resolution of 72 points per inch, which is a typical resolution for monitors as well. Most printers support much higher resolutions than this, however, and they use that extra resolution when printing text, for example. However, because the Java 1.1 Graphics object does not allow floating-point coordinates, all graphics must be positioned exactly at integer positions.

Printing in Java 1.2

Java 1.2 introduces a more complete printing API. As in Java 1.1, printing is done by calling methods of a special Graphics object that represents the printer device. The printer coordinate system and base resolution of 72 points per inch are the same in both Java 1.1 and Java 1.2. Beyond these similarities, however, the Java 1.2 API flips the Java 1.1 API upside down. Instead of asking a PrintJob object for the Graphics object to draw to, Java 1.2 uses a callback model. You tell the Java 1.2 printing API the object you'd like to print, and it calls the print() method of that object, passing in the appropriate Graphics object to draw to. In Java 1.1, your printing code is in charge of the print job, while in Java 1.2, the print job is in charge of your printing code.

The Java 1.2 printing API is contained in the java.awt.print package. Key classes and interfaces in this package are Printable, which represents a printable object, Pageable, which represents a multipage printable document, and PrinterJob, which coordinates the print job and serves as an intermediary between the Java API and the native printing system. Do not confuse java.awt.print.PrinterJob with the java.awt.PrintJob class used by the Java 1.1 printing API! Another important class is PageFormat, which represents the size of the paper being printed on, its margins, and the printing orientation (i.e., portrait mode or landscape mode).

The basic Java 1.2 printing algorithm includes the following steps:

1. First, obtain a PrinterJob object to coordinate the printing. Do this by calling the static method PrinterJob.getPrinterJob().

2. Obtain a `PageFormat` object that describes the size, margins, and orientation of the page or pages to be printed. The `PrinterJob` object has methods that allow you to obtain a default `PageFormat` object and display a dialog asking the user to specify paper, margin, and orientation information. (You might display this dialog box in response to a **Print Setup** ... menu item, for example.)

3. Next, tell the `PrinterJob` object what it is that you want to print. The item to print is an object that implements either the `Printable` interface or the `Pageable` interface (we'll discuss each of these in more detail shortly). You pass this object to either the `setPrintable()` or the `setPageable()` method of the `PrinterJob`.

4. Unless you want the printing to occur silently, without any user interaction, your next call is to the `printDialog()` method of the `PrinterJob` object. This method displays a dialog box, giving the user the opportunity to specify the printer to use and the number of copies to print. If you are printing a multipage `Pageable` object, this dialog box allows the user to select a subset of pages to print, rather than printing the entire `Pageable` document. The dialog box also gives the user the opportunity to cancel the print job. If the `printDialog()` method returns `false`, the user has asked to cancel printing and you should not proceed.

5. Finally, you call the `print()` method of the `PrinterJob`. This tells the `PrinterJob` to begin the printing process.

6. The `PrinterJob` is now in control of printing. As we'll discuss later, `PrinterJob` invokes methods of the `Printable` or `Pageable` object you specified, providing the opportunity for your object to print itself to an appropriate `Graphics` object.

Printing Single-Page Objects

When the object, figure, or document you want to print fits on a single printed page, you typically represent it using the `Printable` interface. This interface defines a single method, `print()`, that the `PrinterJob` calls to print the page. The `print()` method has three arguments. The first is the `Graphics` object that represents the printer. `print()` should do all of its drawing using this object. This `Graphics` object may be cast to a `Graphics2D` object, enabling all the features of Java 2D, including the use of floating-point coordinates to position graphics elements with more precision than is possible with integer coordinates.

The second argument to `print()` is a `PageFormat` object. Your `print()` method should call the `getImageableX()`, `getImageableY()`, `getImageableWidth()`, and `getImageableHeight()` methods of `PageFormat` to determine the size and position of the area that it should draw in. Note that these methods are poorly named. The values they return represent the page and margin sizes requested by the user,not the size of the paper actually available in the printer or the imageable area of the printer (i.e., the region of the page that a specific type of printer can actually print to).

The third argument is a page number. Although the `Printable` interface is most useful for single-page documents, it can be used for multipage documents. The

PrinterJob has no way to determine how many pages a Printable object requires. Indeed, a Printable object may be implemented in such a way that it does not know how many pages it requires either (e.g., a PrintableStream object that prints a stream of text as it arrives). Because the page count is not known in advance, the PrinterJob calls the print() method repeatedly, incrementing the page number after printing each page.

One important responsibility of the print() method is to notify the PrinterJob when all pages are printed. Your method does this by returning the constant Printable.NO_SUCH_PAGE when the PrinterJob asks it to print a page that is past the end of the document.

It is also important to implement the print() method so that it can be called more than once for each page. As of this writing, Sun's Java 1.2 printing implementation calls the print() method at least twice for each page (we'll see why at the end of this chapter).

Example 5-1 shows a PrintableComponent class that can be used to print the contents of a Swing component, applet, or custom AWT component. This class is a wrapper around a Component and implements the Printable interface. Note that it defines two print() methods. One is the three-argument Printable method I already described. The other print() method takes no arguments and implements the general Java 1.2 printing algorithm. It creates a PrinterJob, displays some dialogs to the user, and initiates the printing process. To print a component, create a PrintableComponent for that component, then call its print() method with no arguments.

Example 5-1: PrintableComponent.java

```
import java.awt.*;
import java.awt.print.*;

/**
 * This wrapper class encapsulates a Component and allows it to be printed
 * using the Java 1.2 printing API
 */
public class PrintableComponent implements Printable {
  // The component to be printed
  Component c;

  /** Create a PrintableComponent wrapper around a Component */
  public PrintableComponent(Component c) { this.c = c; }

  /**
   * This method is not part of the Printable interface.  It is a method
   * that sets up the PrinterJob and initiates the printing.
   */
  public void print() throws PrinterException {
    // Get the PrinterJob object
    PrinterJob job = PrinterJob.getPrinterJob();
    // Get the default page format, then allow the user to modify it
    PageFormat format = job.pageDialog(job.defaultPage());
    // Tell the PrinterJob what to print
    job.setPrintable(this, format);
    // Ask the user to confirm, and then begin the printing process
    if (job.printDialog())
      job.print();
```

Example 5-1: PrintableComponent.java (continued)

```
}

/**
 * This is the "callback" method that the PrinterJob will invoke.
 * This method is defined by the Printable interface.
 */
public int print(Graphics g, PageFormat format, int pagenum) {
  // The PrinterJob will keep trying to print pages until we return
  // this value to tell it that it has reached the end
  if (pagenum > 0)
    return Printable.NO_SUCH_PAGE;

  // We're passed a Graphics object, but it can always be cast to Graphics2D
  Graphics2D g2 = (Graphics2D) g;

  // Use the top and left margins specified in the PageFormat Note
  // that the PageFormat methods are poorly named.  They specify
  // margins, not the actual imageable area of the printer.
  g2.translate(format.getImageableX(), format.getImageableY());

  // Tell the Component to draw itself to the printer by passing in
  // the Graphics2D object.  This will not work well if the Component
  // has double-buffering enabled.
  c.paint(g2);

  // Return this constant to tell the PrinterJob that we printed the page
  return Printable.PAGE_EXISTS;
}
}
```

There are a few important points to note about this `PrintableComponent` example. First, it is not designed to work with native AWT components, since those components do not do their own drawing. Second, it does not work well for components that use double-buffering because double-buffering locks the component drawing into the relatively low resolution of an off-screen image, rather than taking advantage of the high resolution available on the printer. Finally, `PrintableComponent` prints only the visible portion of a component, not the complete contents of the component. For example, the Swing `JEditorPane` class can display long HTML documents. If you use `PrintableComponent` to print a `JEditorPane`, however, it prints only the currently visible text, not the complete HTML document. The ability to print complete documents is a feature that is sorely missing in the current implementation of Swing.

Printing Multipage Documents

As we just discussed, the `Printable` interface can be used to print multipage documents. However, the `PrinterJob` has no way of determining in advance how many pages are required. This means that the user cannot request that only a subset of pages be printed, for example. When you know the complete contents of the document to be printed and can break it into pages before printing begins, it is better to use the `Pageable` interface than the `Printable` interface.

`Pageable` defines a `getNumberOfPages()` method that returns the number of pages to be printed. It also defines two methods that take a page number and return

PageFormat and Printable objects for that page. To print a Pageable object, the PrinterJob asks for a PageFormat and a Printable object for each page to be printed and then uses the print() method of each Printable object to print that page.

Example 5-2 shows a class that implements the Pageable and Printable interfaces in order to print a string, file, or stream of text. This is a rudimentary example of text printing. It prints only text files, using a single font, and does not even expand tabs or wrap long lines. The Java 1.2 printing API allows the use of Java 2D graphics through the Graphics2D class. This example does not use the Java 2D version of the drawString() method, however. Although that method allows text to be positioned more precisely using floating-point coordinates, there is a bug in the current implementation that prevents this method from printing correctly.

Example 5-2: PageableText.java

```java
import java.awt.*;
import java.awt.print.*;
import java.io.*;
import java.util.Vector;

public class PageableText implements Pageable, Printable {
  // Constants for font name, size, style and line spacing
  public static String FONTFAMILY = "Monospaced";
  public static int FONTSIZE = 10;
  public static int FONTSTYLE = Font.PLAIN;
  public static float LINESPACEFACTOR = 1.1f;

  PageFormat format;   // The page size, margins, and orientation
  Vector lines;        // The text to be printed, broken into lines
  Font font;           // The font to print with
  int linespacing;     // How much space between lines
  int linesPerPage;    // How many lines fit on a page
  int numPages;        // How many pages required to print all lines
  int baseline = -1;   // The baseline position of the font

  /** Create a PageableText object for a string of text */
  public PageableText(String text, PageFormat format) throws IOException {
    this(new StringReader(text), format);
  }

  /** Create a PageableText object for a file of text */
  public PageableText(File file, PageFormat format) throws IOException {
    this(new FileReader(file), format);
  }

  /** Create a PageableText object for a stream of text */
  public PageableText(Reader stream, PageFormat format) throws IOException {
    this.format = format;

    // First, read all the text, breaking it into lines.
    // This code ignores tabs and does not wrap long lines.
    BufferedReader in = new BufferedReader(stream);
    lines = new Vector();
    String line;
    while((line = in.readLine()) != null)
      lines.addElement(line);
```

Example 5-2: PageableText.java (continued)

```
    // Create the font we will use, and compute spacing between lines
    font = new Font(FONTFAMILY, FONTSTYLE, FONTSIZE);
    linespacing = (int) (FONTSIZE * LINESPACEFACTOR);

    // Figure out how many lines per page and how many pages
    linesPerPage = (int)Math.floor(format.getImageableHeight()/linespacing);
    numPages = (lines.size()-1)/linesPerPage + 1;
}

// These are the methods of the Pageable interface.
// Note that the getPrintable() method returns this object, which means
// that this class must also implement the Printable interface.
public int getNumberOfPages() { return numPages; }
public PageFormat getPageFormat(int pagenum) { return format; }
public Printable getPrintable(int pagenum) { return this; }

/**
 * This is the print() method of the Printable interface.
 * It does most of the printing work.
 */
public int print(Graphics g, PageFormat format, int pagenum) {
    // Tell the PrinterJob if the page number is not a legal one
    if ((pagenum < 0) | (pagenum >= numPages))
      return NO_SUCH_PAGE;

    // First time we're called, figure out the baseline for our font.
    // We couldn't do this earlier because we needed a Graphics object.
    if (baseline == -1) {
      FontMetrics fm = g.getFontMetrics(font);
      baseline = fm.getAscent();
    }

    // Clear the background to white.  This shouldn't be necessary but is
    // required on some systems to work around an implementation bug.
    g.setColor(Color.white);
    g.fillRect((int)format.getImageableX(), (int)format.getImageableY(),
               (int)format.getImageableWidth(),
               (int)format.getImageableHeight());

    // Set the font and the color we will be drawing with.
    // Note that you cannot assume that black is the default color!
    g.setFont(font);
    g.setColor(Color.black);

    // Figure out which lines of text we will print on this page
    int startLine = pagenum * linesPerPage;
    int endLine = startLine + linesPerPage - 1;
    if (endLine >= lines.size())
      endLine = lines.size()-1;

    // Compute the position on the page of the first line
    int x0 = (int) format.getImageableX();
    int y0 = (int) format.getImageableY() + baseline;

    // Loop through the lines, drawing them all to the page
    for(int i=startLine; i <= endLine; i++) {
      // Get the line
      String line = (String)lines.elementAt(i);
```

Example 5–2: PageableText.java (continued)

```
        // Draw the line.
        // We use the integer version of drawString(), not the Java 2D
        // version that uses floating-point coordinates. A bug in early
        // Java 1.2 implementations prevents the Java 2D version from working.
        if (line.length() > 0)
          g.drawString(line, x0, y0);

        // Move down the page for the next line
        y0 += linespacing;
    }

    // Tell the PrinterJob that we successfully printed the page
    return PAGE_EXISTS;
}

/**
 * This is a test program that demonstrates the use of PageableText
 */
public static void main(String[] args) throws IOException, PrinterException {
    // Get the PrinterJob object that coordinates everything
    PrinterJob job = PrinterJob.getPrinterJob();

    // Get the default page format, then ask the user to customize it
    PageFormat format = job.pageDialog(job.defaultPage());

    // Create our PageableText object, and tell the PrinterJob about it
    job.setPageable(new PageableText(new File(args[0]), format));

    // Ask the user to select a printer, etc., and if not canceled, print!
    if (job.printDialog())
      job.print();
}
}
```

Efficiency Issues in the Java 1.2 Printing API

Although the Java 1.2 printing API offers important design improvements over the Java 1.1 API, there are serious efficiency problems with Sun's implementation of the 1.2 API in versions of Java up to at least Java 1.2.2. All printers are good at printing text, but not all are equally good at drawing arbitrary graphics. Thus, when a page contains anything but text or very simple graphics, Java 1.2 converts the entire page to a very large image and prints it in graphics mode.

As I mentioned earlier, the current implementation of `PrinterJob` calls the `print()` method of a `Printable` object at least twice. The first call uses a dummy `Graphics` object whose sole purpose is to determine what kind of graphics the page contains. If the page contains only text, as is the case in Example 5-2, the `PrinterJob` can print the page efficiently in text mode.

However, if the page contains any other type of graphics, the `PrinterJob` uses a large, high-resolution image to capture the graphics on the page and then transmits this image to the printer for printing in graphics mode. Because such a high-resolution image is memory intensive, the `PrinterJob` typically breaks the page up into several smaller bands and calls the `print()` method several times (using a different clipping region each time). In this way, the `PrinterJob` is able to spool a large image to the printer without using a large amount of memory (a classic time versus space trade-off).

Unfortunately, the implementation is not well optimized, and printing performance is unacceptable on some systems. Printing even a simple graphic, such as one produced with the `PrintableComponent` class shown in Example 5-1, can take several minutes and can produce a printer spool file of more than 50 megabytes.

Printing with the Java 1.1 API works better in Java 1.1 than it does in current implementations of Java 1.2. The Java 1.1 API works in Java 1.2, but it suffers the same efficiency problems as the Java 1.2 API. Furthermore, the Java 1.1 API does not perform the first pass to determine what type of graphics a page contains, so even a Java 1.1 program that prints only text is inefficient when run under Java 1.2.

CHAPTER 6

Data Transfer

Data transfer refers to the ability of an application to transfer selected data in a variety of ways. For example, an application can use data transfer to support moving data between its own subparts. An application can also use data transfer to exchange data with other Java applications that are running in the same Java VM or in another Java VM or with native applications that are not running in a VM at all. There are two commonly used metaphors for data transfer: cut-and-paste and drag-and-drop. Java 1.1 included a basic data transfer architecture and supported cut-and-paste. The Java 2 platform extends the architecture in minor ways and adds support for drag-and-drop.

The Data Transfer Framework

Both the cut-and-paste and drag-and-drop metaphors rely on the same underlying data transfer architecture. This architecture was defined in Java 1.1 in the `java.awt.datatransfer` package. It consists of the `DataFlavor` class, which describes data types and data formats, and the `Transferable` interface, which defines methods that must be implemented if data is to be transferred.

The DataFlavor Class

A data transfer mechanism requires a precise and portable way to specify the type of data to be transferred. This is necessary so that both parties to the transfer—the data source and the data sink—can agree on exactly what is being transferred. Since the data source and the data sink may be entirely different applications, the mechanism for describing a data type must be general and flexible.

In Java, the type of data being transferred is described by a `java.awt.datatransfer.DataFlavor` object. The `DataFlavor` class describes data types using MIME types. MIME defines standard types like "text/html" and "image/jpeg". Because Java programs often transfer data within the same Java VM or between VMs, the

DataFlavor class also supports describing data types with Java class names. For example, to transfer a java.awt.Point object from one Java VM to another, the data transfer mechanism can simply serialize the Point object and send the resulting stream of bytes to the other Java VM, where the Point object can be deserialized. When doing data transfer between Java VMs in this way, the transfer of objects becomes totally transparent.

The DataFlavor class defines constants for several commonly used data flavors, including DataFlavor.stringFlavor, DataFlavor.plainTextFlavor, and (in Java 1.2) DataFlavor.javaFileListFlavor. To transfer another types of data, you must create a custom DataFlavor by specifying the MIME type or Java class of the data and a human-readable name for the data type. For example:

```
DataFlavor jpegFlavor = new DataFlavor("image/jpeg", "JPEG Image Data");
DataFlavor pointFlavor = new DataFlavor(java.awt.Point.class,
                                        "Java Point Object");
```

The Transferable Interface

DataFlavor objects describe data types, but they contain no data themselves. Data to be transferred using cut-and-paste or drag-and-drop must be encapsulated in an object that implements the Transferable interface.

Data transfer occurs in a heterogeneous environment. When you design the data transfer capabilities of your application, you cannot know the other applications with which the user may eventually want to exchange data. Thus, for maximum flexibility, an application that exports data—a data source—typically offers its data in multiple formats. An application that exports text might offer to transfer that data in the form of a Java String object or as a stream of Unicode characters, for example. If the receiving application is a Java program, it may choose to request the data as a Java String, while a non-Java application would choose the stream of characters instead.

The Transferable interface defines three methods. getTransferDataFlavors(), returns an array of DataFlavor objects that represent the data formats in which the data may be transferred, while isDataFlavorSupported() asks whether a particular data flavor is supported. The third method, getTransferData(), performs the actual transfer. This method takes an argument that specifies the desired data flavor and returns an Object that represents the data in the specified format. If the specified data flavor is not supported, getTransferData() throws an Unsupported-FlavorException.

The return value for getTransferData() needs a little more explanation. The type of this object depends on the DataFlavor that was requested. For any DataFlavor, the getRepresentationClass() method returns a Java Class object that represents the type of object that will be returned by getTransferData(). When a DataFlavor represents data that is transferred as a serialized Java object, the return value of getTransferData() is simply a Java object of whatever type was transferred (e.g., a String or java.awt.Point object). When a DataFlavor represents a MIME type, the data is actually transferred between applications as a stream of bytes. In this case, getTransferData() returns a java.io.InputStream object from which you can read and parse these bytes.

Because text is the most frequently transferred data type, the java.awt.datatransfer package defines a StringSelection class that implements the Transferable interface for strings. This Transferable class supports two data flavors, the predefined DataFlavor.stringFlavor and DataFlavor.plainTextFlavor constants. Unfortunately, however, there is a problem with StringSelection. When the string is requested in plain text format, the getTransferData() method returns a java.io.Reader object instead of a java.io.InputStream. Because StringSelection is widely used, applications receiving DataFlavor.plainTextFlavor data may want to use instanceof to determine whether the return value is an InputStream (a byte stream) or a Reader (a Unicode character stream). Despite the problems with StringSelection, there is a long-standing bug in Sun's Java 1.1 and Java 1.2 implementations for Windows platforms that makes it indispensable. On those platforms, StringSelection is the only Transferable class that can successfully transfer text between a Java application and a native application.

Applications that display strings in JTextField, JTextArea, and related components already support textual data transfer, as these components have cut-and-paste support built in. In other words, you typically don't have to implement textual data transfer yourself. When you do need to implement data transfer, it is probably because you are transferring some specialized type of data. Example 6-1 shows how we can implement the Transferable interface to transfer java.awt.Color objects between Java applications.

Example 6-1: TransferableColor.java

```
import java.awt.Color;
import java.awt.datatransfer.*;
import java.io.*;

/**
 * This class is used to transfer a Color object via cut-and-paste or
 * drag-and-drop.  It allows a color to be transferred as a Color object
 * or as a string. Due to a long-standing bug in Java 1.1 and Java 1.2,
 * transferring a color as a string to native Windows applications will
 * not work.
 */
public class TransferableColor implements Transferable {
  // This DataFlavor object is used when we transfer Color objects directly
  protected static DataFlavor colorFlavor =
    new DataFlavor(Color.class, "Java Color Object");

  // These are the data flavors we support
  protected static DataFlavor[] supportedFlavors = {
    colorFlavor,                  // Transfer as a Color object
    DataFlavor.stringFlavor,      // Transfer as a String object
    DataFlavor.plainTextFlavor,   // Transfer as a stream of Unicode text
  };

  Color color;                    // The color we encapsulate and transfer

  /** Create a new TransferableColor that encapsulates the specified color */
  public TransferableColor(Color color) { this.color = color; }

  /** Return a list of DataFlavors we can support */
  public DataFlavor[] getTransferDataFlavors() { return supportedFlavors; }
```

Example 6–1: TransferableColor.java (continued)

```
/** Check whether a specified DataFlavor is available */
public boolean isDataFlavorSupported(DataFlavor flavor) {
  if (flavor.equals(colorFlavor) ||
      flavor.equals(DataFlavor.stringFlavor) ||
      flavor.equals(DataFlavor.plainTextFlavor)) return true;
  return false;
}

/**
 * Transfer the data.  Given a specified DataFlavor, return an Object
 * appropriate for that flavor.  Throw UnsupportedFlavorException if we
 * don't support the requested flavor.
 */
public Object getTransferData(DataFlavor flavor)
      throws UnsupportedFlavorException, IOException
{
  if (flavor.equals(colorFlavor)) return color;
  else if (flavor.equals(DataFlavor.stringFlavor)) return color.toString();
  else if (flavor.equals(DataFlavor.plainTextFlavor))
    return new ByteArrayInputStream(color.toString().getBytes("Unicode"));
  else throw new UnsupportedFlavorException(flavor);
}
}
```

Cut-and-Paste

In addition to the data transfer framework classes, the `java.awt.datatransfer` package also defines the `Clipboard` class and the `ClipboardOwner` interface, which implement data transfer with the cut-and-paste metaphor.

A typical cut-and-paste transfer works as follows:

- In the initiating application, the user types **Ctrl-C** or **Ctrl-X** or in some other way tells the application that he wants to copy or cut some data.

- The application takes the selected data and encapsulates it in an appropriate `Transferable` object. The next step is to call the `getSystemClipboard()` method of the `Toolkit` object, to get a `Clipboard` object. The application then calls the `setContents()` method of the `Clipboard`, passing the `Transferable` object as the new clipboard contents.

- If the user issued a cut command, the initiating application typically deletes the data after transferring it to the clipboard. If the user issued a copy command, however, the application typically just highlights the data to make it clear to the user what data is available for pasting. Often this data should remain highlighted for as long as the initiating application owns the clipboard. When an application calls `setContents()`, it becomes the clipboard owner and remains such until some other application transfers data to the clipboard. The application must, in fact, pass a object that implements `ClipboardOwner` to the `setContents()` method. This object is used to notify the application when it ceases to be the clipboard owner. Until that happens, however, the application must maintain the `Transferable` object and be willing to provide the data when it is requested.

- At some point, the user moves his attention to some other application and issues a paste command in that application. This receiving first application calls Toolkit.getSystemClipboard() to obtain a Clipboard object. Then it calls getContents() to obtain a Transferable object that represents the data available on the clipboard. The application uses getTransferDataFlavors() or isDataFlavorSupported() to see if the clipboard data is available in a format it is willing to accept. If there is such a format, the application calls getTransferData() to transfer the data.

- At some point after this cut-and-paste operation, the user cuts or copies a new piece of data in an application. At this point, the original application ceases to be the clipboard owner and no longer has to make its data available for pasting. The lostOwnership() method of the originating application's ClipboardOwner object is called to notify the application of this occurrence.

Drag-and-Drop

Java 1.2 adds drag-and-drop support to Java. Drag-and-drop requires quite a bit more infrastructure than cut-and-paste, and this infrastructure is added in a package of its own, java.awt.dnd. Despite the complexity of the infrastructure, drag-and-drop is built upon the same data transfer architecture as cut-and-paste. The key classes are still DataFlavor and Transferable.

Here's the general outline of a drag-and-drop transaction from the standpoint of the initiating or dragging application or component:

- If a component within an application wants to allow data to be dragged from it, it first obtains a DragSource object and then uses this DragSource to create a DragGestureRecognizer. This DragGestureRecognizer pays attention to mouse events that occur over the component, looking for the platform-dependent gesture that indicates that the user wants to drag something.

- When the DragGestureRecognizer sees a drag gesture, it invokes the dragGestureRecognized() of a specified DragGestureListener object.

- The dragGestureRecognized() method determines if there is data available for dragging, and, if so, it encapsulates the data in a Transferable object. dragGestureRecognized is passed a DragGestureEvent object. Unlike most other event objects, many of the event objects in the java.awt.dnd package define important methods that are used during a drag-and-drop transaction. In this case, the dragGestureRecognized() method activates the native drag-and-drop system by calling the startDrag() method of its DragGestureEvent object and passing it the Transferable object. In the call to startDrag(), you also specify a cursor that is displayed during the drag and a DragSourceListener object that keeps the data source notified about how the drag is progressing. You can also specify an optional Image that is dragged along with the cursor, on systems that support it. (Call the static DragSource.isDragImageSupported() to see if image dragging is supported on the system.)

- As the user drags the data, various methods of the DragSourceListener are invoked to notify the initiating application of the status of the drag. These methods can be used to update the cursor being displayed or the image being dragged along with the cursor. The methods provide a way to implement specialized drag-over animation effects, for example. The native drag-and-drop system typically supplies basic drag-over effects, by changing the cursor when it is over a receptive drop target.

- The most commonly used DragSourceListener method is dragDropEnd(). This method is invoked when the user drops the data. The initiating application can use this method to determine whether the drop was successful. If the user were moving data instead of copying data, the initiating application should delete its copy of the data once it has been successfully transferred to the recipient. dragDropEnd() is passed a DragSourceDropEvent object. The getDropSuccess() and getDropAction() methods of this event help the initiating application decide on the appropriate action to take.

A drag-and-drop transaction looks somewhat different from the standpoint of a receiving application or component:

- A component that wants to allow data to be dropped on it must create a DropTarget object to act as an intermediary between itself and the native drag-and-drop system. When creating a DropTarget, you must specify the component on which data can be dropped and also a DropTargetListener object that can be notified when data is dragged over the component.

- When the user drags data over the component, the dragEnter() method of the DropTargetListener is invoked. This method is passed a DropTarget-DragEvent that it can query to determine the supported data flavors of the data being dragged. If the component is willing to accept a drop of that type of data, it should call the acceptDrop() method of the event object to signal its willingness. This in turn causes the dragEnter() method of the DragSourceListener in the initiating application to be invoked. The dragEnter() method of the DropTargetListener may also want to display some visual cue to the user of its willingness to accept a drop. For example, it might change colors or change its border. This kind of visual change is known as a "drag-under effect."

- The dragOver() method is called repeatedly as the user continues to drag the data over the component. If the user drags the data out of the component, the dragExit() method is called. If dragEnter() displayed a visual cue, drag-Exit() should undo it.

- If the user drops the data while over the component, the drop() method of the DropTargetListener is invoked. It is this method that performs the actual data transfer. drop() is passed a DropTargetDropEvent. The getTransfer-able() method of this event returns the Transferable object that was dropped. If the Transferable object supports a DataFlavor that the component can accept, the component calls the acceptDrop() method of the event to tell the native drag-and-drop system that the drop is valid. If it cannot work with any of the available data flavors, it should call rejectDrop(). After accepting the drop, the receiving component uses the getTransferData()

method of the Transferable object to actually transfer the data. This phase of the data transfer is done exactly as it is in cut-and-paste. Finally, the component calls the dropComplete() method of the DropTargetDropEvent, passing true if the transfer was successful or false if something went wrong and the transfer did not succeed.

A Data Source

Example 6-2 shows the ColorSource class. This is a simple JComponent subclass that displays a small block of a solid color and makes that color available for transfer via both cut-and-paste and drag-and-drop. The copy() method copies the color to the clipboard, making it available for pasting, while the dragGestureRecognized() method initiates a drag operation. This example relies upon the TransferableColor class of Example 6-1, of course. For simplicity, the copy() method is invoked when the user clicks on the component—there is no **Ctrl-C** keyboard binding or **Edit** menu command.

Example 6-2: ColorSource.java

```
import java.awt.*;
import java.awt.event.*;
import java.awt.datatransfer.*;
import java.awt.dnd.*;
import javax.swing.*;
import javax.swing.border.*;
import java.io.*;


/**
 * This simple component displays a solid color and allows that color
 * to be dragged. Also, it copies the color to the clipboard when the
 * user clicks on it.
 */
public class ColorSource extends JComponent
        implements ClipboardOwner, DragGestureListener, DragSourceListener
{
    Color color;                   // The color to display
    TransferableColor tcolor;      // The color, encapsulated for data transfer
    DragSource dragSource;         // We need this object for drag-and-drop

    /** A ColorSource normally displays itself with this border */
    protected static Border defaultBorder = new BevelBorder(BevelBorder.LOWERED);
    /** When we are the clipboard owner, uses this border */
    protected static Border highlightBorder =
        new CompoundBorder(defaultBorder, new LineBorder(Color.black, 2));

    /** Create a new ColorSource object that displays the specified color */
    public ColorSource(Color color) {
        // Save the color.  Encapsulate it in a Transferable object so that
        // it can be used with cut-and-paste and drag-and-drop.
        this.color = color;
        this.tcolor = new TransferableColor(color);

        // Set our default border
        this.setBorder(defaultBorder);

        // Listen for mouse clicks, and copy the color to the clipboard
```

Example 6-2: ColorSource.java (continued)

```
    this.addMouseListener(new MouseAdapter() {
      public void mouseClicked(MouseEvent e) { copy(); }
    });

    // Set up a DragGestureRecognizer that will detect when the user
    // begins a drag.  When it detects one, it will notify us by calling
    // the dragGestureRecognized() method of the DragGestureListener
    // interface we implement below
    this.dragSource = DragSource.getDefaultDragSource();
    dragSource.createDefaultDragGestureRecognizer(this, // Look for drags on us
                DnDConstants.ACTION_COPY_OR_MOVE,  // Recognize these types
                this);                              // Tell us when recognized
  }

  // These are component methods that make this class work as a component.
  // They specify how big the component is, and what it it looks like.
  protected static Dimension mysize = new Dimension(25, 25);
  public Dimension getMinimumSize() { return mysize; }
  public Dimension getPreferredSize() { return mysize; }
  public void paintComponent(Graphics g) {
    g.setColor(color);
    Dimension s = this.getSize();
    Insets i = this.getInsets();
    g.fillRect(i.left, i.top,
                s.width-i.left-i.right, s.height-i.top-i.bottom);
  }

  // The methods below support cut-and-paste

  /** This method copies the color to the clipboard */
  public void copy() {
    // Get system clipboard
    Clipboard c = this.getToolkit().getSystemClipboard();

    // Put our TransferableColor object on the clipboard.
    // Also, we'll get notification when we no longer own the clipboard.
    c.setContents(tcolor, this);

    // Set a special border on ourselves that indicates that we're the
    // current color available for pasting
    this.setBorder(highlightBorder);
  }

  // This ClipboardOwner method is called when something else is
  // placed on the clipboard.  It means that our color is no longer
  // available for pasting, and we should not display the highlight border.
  public void lostOwnership(Clipboard clipboard, Transferable contents) {
    this.setBorder(defaultBorder);
  }

  // The methods below support drag-and-drop

  // This DragGestureListener method is called when the DragGestureRecognizer
  // detects that the user has dragged the mouse.  It is responsible
  // for beginning the drag-and-drop process.
  public void dragGestureRecognized(DragGestureEvent e) {
    // Create an image we can drag along with us.
    // Not all systems support this, but it doesn't hurt to try.
```

Example 6-2: ColorSource.java (continued)

```
    Image colorblock = this.createImage(25,25);
    Graphics g = colorblock.getGraphics();
    g.setColor(color);
    g.fillRect(0,0,25,25);

    // Start dragging our transferable color object
    e.startDrag(DragSource.DefaultMoveDrop,      // The initial drag cursor
                colorblock, new Point(0,0),      // The image to drag
                tcolor,                          // The data being dragged
                this);                           // Who to notify during drag
  }

  // These methods implement DragSourceListener.
  // Since we passed this object to startDrag, these methods will be
  // called at interesting points during the drag.  We could use them,
  // for example, to implement custom cursors or other "drag-over" effects.
  public void dragEnter(DragSourceDragEvent e) {}
  public void dragExit(DragSourceEvent e) {}
  public void dragDropEnd(DragSourceDropEvent e) {}
  public void dragOver(DragSourceDragEvent e) {}
  public void dropActionChanged(DragSourceDragEvent e) {}
}
```

A Data Sink

Example 6-3 shows the ColorSink class, which is a simple subclass of the Swing JTextArea class. ColorSink allows color objects to be pasted or dropped on it. When either event occurs, ColorSink sets its background color to the transferred color object. In addition, the class allows the pasting of textual data, which it inserts at the current cursor position. Finally, ColorSink accepts drops of the DataFlavor.javaFileListFlavor type. This data flavor is used when the user drags and drops a file icon. When a ColorSink receives a drop of this type, it opens the specified file (which it assumes to be a text file) and reads and displays its contents.

The pastecolor() method does the work of transferring a color through cut-and-paste. Again, for simplicity, the pastecolor() method is invoked when the user double-clicks on the ColorSink. The drag-and-drop transfer is implemented primarily in the drop() method. Note, however, that dragEnter() and dragExit() perform a simple drag-under effect by highlighting the ColorSink border.

The ColorSink class also includes a simple main() method that shows how it can be combined with the ColorSource class to create a simple demonstration of cut-and-paste and drag-and-drop.

Example 6-3: ColorSink.java

```
import java.awt.*;
import java.awt.event.*;
import java.awt.datatransfer.*;
import java.awt.dnd.*;
import javax.swing.*;
import javax.swing.border.*;
import java.io.*;
```

Example 6–3: ColorSink.java (continued)

```java
import java.util.List;

/**
 * This simple JTextArea subclass allows TransferableColor objects to
 * be pasted or dropped into it.  It also supports the pasting of
 * text and the dropping of File objects.
 */
public class ColorSink extends JTextArea implements DropTargetListener {
  /** Create a new ColorSink object */
  public ColorSink() {
    // Listen for double-clicks.  Use them to trigger a paste action.
    addMouseListener(new MouseAdapter() {
      public void mouseClicked(MouseEvent e) {
        if (e.getClickCount() == 2) { pastecolor(); e.consume(); }
      }
    });

    // We have to create a DropTarget object to support drag-and-drop.
    // It will listen for drops on top of us and notify our DropTargetListener
    // methods when drag-and-drop-related events occur.
    setDropTarget(new DropTarget(this, this));
  }

  // This method is invoked when the user double-clicks on us.  It attempts
  // to paste a color or text.  Note that the JTextArea we extend
  // already supports cut-and-paste of text through the Ctrl-V keystroke.
  // This adds a different kind of cut-and-paste for demonstration purposes.
  public void pastecolor() {
    // Get the clipboard, and read its contents
    Clipboard c = this.getToolkit().getSystemClipboard();
    Transferable t = c.getContents(this);
    if (t == null) {                  // If nothing to paste
      this.getToolkit().beep();       // then beep and do nothing
      return;
    }
    try {
      // If the clipboard contained a color, use it as the background color
      if (t.isDataFlavorSupported(TransferableColor.colorFlavor)) {
        Color color = (Color) t.getTransferData(TransferableColor.colorFlavor);
        this.setBackground(color);
      }
      // If the clipboard contained text, insert it.
      else if (t.isDataFlavorSupported(DataFlavor.stringFlavor)) {
        String s = (String) t.getTransferData(DataFlavor.stringFlavor);
        this.replaceSelection(s);
      }
      // Otherwise, we don't know how to paste the data, so just beep
      else this.getToolkit().beep();
    }
    catch (UnsupportedFlavorException ex) { this.getToolkit().beep(); }
    catch (IOException ex) { this.getToolkit().beep(); }
  }

  // The methods below are the methods of DropTargetListener.
  // They are invoked at various times when something is being
  // dragged over us, and allow us an opportunity to respond to the drag.

  // This is the border we display when the user is dragging over us.
```

Example 6–3: ColorSink.java (continued)

```java
protected static Border dropBorder = new BevelBorder(BevelBorder.LOWERED);

// Something is being dragged over us.  If we can support this data type.
// tell the drag-and-drop system that we are interested, and display
// a special border to tell the user that we're interested.
public void dragEnter(DropTargetDragEvent e) {
  if (e.isDataFlavorSupported(TransferableColor.colorFlavor) ||
      e.isDataFlavorSupported(DataFlavor.javaFileListFlavor)) {
    e.acceptDrag(DnDConstants.ACTION_COPY_OR_MOVE);
    this.setBorder(dropBorder);
  }
}

/** The user is no longer dragging over us, so restore the default border */
public void dragExit(DropTargetEvent e) { this.setBorder(null); }


/** This method is invoked when the user drops something on us */
public void drop(DropTargetDropEvent e){
  this.setBorder(null);                      // Restore the default border
  Transferable t = e.getTransferable();  // Get the data that was dropped

  // Check for types of data that we support
  if (t.isDataFlavorSupported(TransferableColor.colorFlavor)) {
    // If it was a color, accept it, and use it as the background color
    e.acceptDrop(DnDConstants.ACTION_COPY_OR_MOVE);
    try {
      Color c = (Color) t.getTransferData(TransferableColor.colorFlavor);
      this.setBackground(c);
      e.dropComplete(true);
    }
    catch (Exception ex) { e.dropComplete(false); }
  }
  else if (t.isDataFlavorSupported(DataFlavor.javaFileListFlavor)) {
    // If it was a file list, accept it, read the first file in the list
    // and display the file contents
    e.acceptDrop(DnDConstants.ACTION_COPY_OR_MOVE);
    try {
      List files = (List) t.getTransferData(DataFlavor.javaFileListFlavor);
      File f = (File) files.get(0);
      BufferedReader in = new BufferedReader(new FileReader(f));
      String s;
      this.setText("");
      while((s = in.readLine()) != null) this.append(s);
      e.dropComplete(true);
    }
    catch (Exception ex) { e.dropComplete(false); }
  }
  else {  // If it wasn't a color or a file list, reject it
    e.rejectDrop();
    return;
  }
}

// These are unused DropTargetListener methods
public void dragOver(DropTargetDragEvent e) {}
public void dropActionChanged(DropTargetDragEvent e) {}
```

Data Transfer

Example 6-3: ColorSink.java (continued)

```java
/** This is a simple test program for ColorSource and ColorSink */
public static void main(String[] args) {
  // Create a window
  JFrame f = new JFrame("ColorSourceTest");
  f.getContentPane().setLayout(new BorderLayout());

  // Add some ColorSources
  JPanel panel = new JPanel();
  f.getContentPane().add(panel, BorderLayout.NORTH);
  panel.add(new ColorSource(Color.yellow));
  panel.add(new ColorSource(Color.pink));
  panel.add(new ColorSource(Color.white));
  panel.add(new ColorSource(Color.gray));

  // Add a ColorSink
  ColorSink sink = new ColorSink();
  f.getContentPane().add(sink, BorderLayout.CENTER);

  // Pop it all up
  f.setSize(400, 300);
  f.show();
  }
}
```

CHAPTER 7

Applets

An applet, as the name implies, is a kind of mini-application, designed to be downloaded over a network from a possibly untrusted source and run in a web browser or in the context of some other applet viewer application. Because of the ubiquity of web browsers, applets are a useful and powerful way of delivering Java programs to end users. In fact, it was the power of applets that popularized Java in the first place. Applets differ from regular applications in several important ways:

- An applet doesn't have a main() method like a standalone Java application does. Writing an applet is a lot more like subclassing an AWT or Swing component than writing a standalone application.

- An applet is not invoked using the command line, as a Java application is. Instead, an applet is embedded within an HTML file with an <APPLET> tag. And, instead of reading command-line arguments as an application does, an applet gets its arguments from <PARAM> tags in the HTML file.

- An applet is usually subject to a number of strict security restrictions that prevent untrusted, and possibly malicious, applet code from damaging the host system.

This chapter briefly explains how applets are written and how they are embedded in HTML pages. It also explains the security restrictions to which applets are subject.

Writing Applets

From a programmer's standpoint, one of the biggest differences between an applet and an application is that an applet does not have a main() method or any other single entry point from which the program starts running. Instead, to write an applet, you subclass the java.applet.Applet class (which is itself a subclass of java.awt.Panel and thus a descendant of java.awt.Component) and override a number of standard methods. At appropriate times, under well-defined circumstances, the web browser or applet viewer invokes the methods you have defined. The applet is not in control of the thread of execution; it simply responds when the browser or viewer tells it to. For this reason, the methods you write must take the necessary action and return promptly—they are not allowed to enter time-consuming (or infinite) loops. In order to perform a time-consuming or repetitive task, such as animation, an applet may create its own Thread, over which it does have complete control.

The task of writing an applet, then, comes down to defining the appropriate methods. A number of these methods are defined by the Applet class:

init()
> Called when the applet is first loaded into the browser or viewer. It is typically used to perform applet initialization, in preference to a constructor method. (If you define a constructor for your Applet, it must be a no-argument constructor, as that is what the web browser expects.) If your applet displays GUI components, they are typically created here. (Remember that the applet itself is a java.awt.Panel, so you can create components and add() them directly to the applet.)

destroy()
> Called when the applet is about to be unloaded from the browser or viewer. The method should free any resources, other than memory, that the applet has allocated. The destroy() method is much less commonly used than init().

start()
> Called when the applet becomes visible and should start doing whatever it is that it does. An applet that performs animation or does some other action only when it is visible needs to implement this method.

stop()
> Called when the applet becomes temporarily invisible (e.g., when the user has scrolled it off the screen). Tells the applet to stop performing an animation or other task.

getAppletInfo()
> Called to get information about the applet (e.g., its name and author). This method should return a string suitable for display in a dialog box.

getParameterInfo()
> Called to obtain information about the parameters to which the applet responds. Returns a String[ ][ ] that describes the parameters.

In addition to these Applet methods, there are a variety of Component methods that an applet may want to override. The most obvious of these methods is paint(), which the browser or viewer invokes to ask the applet to draw itself on the screen.

Applets handle events in the same way that AWT and Swing applications and components do. However, for maximum portability to old web browsers such as

Netscape Navigator 3 and early versions of Navigator 4, many applets use the deprecated Java 1.0 event model and override methods such as mouseDown(), mouse-Drag(), keyDown(), and action().

In addition to all these methods that you override when writing an applet, the Applet class also defines some methods that you may find useful to invoke from your applet:

getImage()
> Loads an image file from the network and returns an Image object.

getAudioClip()
> Loads a sound clip from the network and returns an AudioClip object.

getParameter()
> Looks up and returns the value of a named parameter, specified with a <PARAM> tag in the HTML file that contains the applet.

getCodeBase()
> Returns the base URL from which the applet class file was loaded.

getDocumentBase()
> Returns the base URL of the HTML file that refers to the applet.

showStatus()
> Displays a message in the status line of the browser or applet viewer.

getAppletContext()
> Returns the AppletContext object for the applet. AppletContext defines the useful showDocument() method that asks the browser to load and display a new web page.

A Simple Applet

Example 7-1 is a simple applet. The applet has a simple init() method but consists primarily of the paint() method that produces the applet display shown in Figure 7-1. The example also demonstrates the use of the getParameter() method to obtain the string of text that it displays.

This applet can be placed within an HTML file using the following HTML tags:

```
<APPLET code="MessageApplet.class" width=350 height=125>
  <PARAM name="message" value="Hello World">
</APPLET>
```

To run and display the applet, simply load the HTML file into a Java-enabled web browser. Alternatively, you can use the *appletviewer* program included with Sun's Java implementation to view the applet:

```
% appletviewer MessageApplet.html
```

When invoking *appletviewer*, you must specify the name of the HTML file that includes the applet, not the Java class file that implements the applet. We'll discuss how applets are embedded in HTML files in full detail later in this chapter.

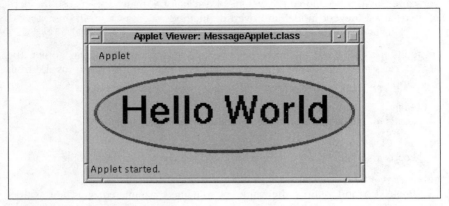

Figure 7-1: A simple applet

Example 7-1: MessageApplet.java

```java
import java.applet.*;
import java.awt.*;

public class MessageApplet extends Applet {
  protected String message;    // The text to display
  protected Font font;         // The font to display it in

  // One-time initialization for the applet
  public void init() {
    message = this.getParameter("message");
    font = new Font("Helvetica", Font.BOLD, 48);
  }

  // Draw the applet whenever necessary
  public void paint(Graphics g) {
    // The pink oval
    g.setColor(Color.pink);
    g.fillOval(10, 10, 330, 100);

    // The red outline. The browser may not support Java 2D, so we
    // try to simulate a four-pixel-wide line by drawing four ovals.
    g.setColor(Color.red);
    g.drawOval(10,10, 330, 100);
    g.drawOval(9, 9, 332, 102);
    g.drawOval(8, 8, 334, 104);
    g.drawOval(7, 7, 336, 106);

    // The text
    g.setColor(Color.black);
    g.setFont(font);
    g.drawString(message, 40, 75);
  }
}
```

Applets and the Java 1.0 Event Model

The AWT event model changed dramatically between Java 1.0 and Java 1.1. Chapter 2, *Swing and AWT Architecture*, described the Java 1.1 event-handling model exclusively, since the Java 1.0 event model is now deprecated. However, because there is still a large installed base of web browsers that support only the Java 1.0 event model, applets are sometimes still written using this model.

In Java 1.0, all events are represented by the Event class. This class has a number of instance variables that describe the event. One of these variables, id, specifies the type of the event. Event defines a number of constants that are the possible values for the id field. The target field specifies the object (typically a Component) that generated the event or on which the event occurred (i.e., the source of the event). The other fields may or may not be used, depending on the type of the event. For example, the x and y fields are defined when id specifies a BUTTON_EVENT but not when it specifies an ACTION_EVENT. The arg field can provide additional type-dependent data.

A Java 1.0 event is dispatched first to the handleEvent() method of the Component on which it occurred. The default implementation of this method checks the id field of the Event object and dispatches the most commonly used types of events to various type-specific methods, listed in Table 7-1.

Table 7–1: Java 1.0 Event Processing Methods of Component

action()	keyUp()	mouseDrag()	mouseMove()
gotFocus()	lostFocus()	mouseEnter()	mouseUp()
keyDown()	mouseDown()	mouseExit()	

The methods listed in Table 7-1 are defined by the Component class. One of the primary characteristics of the Java 1.0 event model is that you must override these methods in order to process events. This means that you must create a subclass to define custom event-handling behavior, which is exactly what we do when we write an applet, for example. However, not all of the event types are dispatched by handleEvent() to more specific methods. If you are interested in LIST_SELECT or WINDOW_ICONIFY events, for example, you have to override handleEvent() itself, rather than one of the more specific methods. If you do this, you usually want to invoke super.handleEvent() to continue dispatching events of other types in the default way.

handleEvent() and all of the type-specific methods return boolean values. If an event-handling method returns false, as they all do by default, it means that the event was not handled, so it should be passed to the container of the current component to see if that container is interested in processing it. If a method returns true, on the other hand, it is a signal that the event *has* been handled and no further processing is needed.

The fact that unhandled events are passed up the containment hierarchy is important. It means that we can override the action() method in an applet in order to handle ACTION_EVENT events that are generated by the buttons within the applet. If they were not propagated up as they are, we would have to create a custom subclass of Button for every button we wanted to add to an interface!

In the Java 1.0 model, there is no de facto way to know what types of events are generated by what GUI components nor to know what fields of the Event object are filled in for what types of events. You simply have to look this information up in the documentation of individual AWT components.

Many event types use the modifiers field of the Event object to report which keyboard modifier keys were pressed when the event occurred. This field contains a bitmask of the SHIFT_MASK, CTRL_MASK, META_MASK, and ALT_MASK constants defined by the Event class. The shiftDown(), controlDown(), and metaDown() methods can be used to test for the various modifiers.

The Event class does not have a special field to indicate which mouse button was pressed when a mouse event occurs. Instead, Event uses the keyboard modifier constants for this purpose, which allows systems that use a one-button mouse to simulate other mouse buttons by using keyboard modifiers. If the left mouse button is in use, no keyboard modifiers are reported. If the right button is used, the META_MASK bit is set in the modifiers field. And if the middle button is down, the ALT_MASK bit is set.

When a keyboard event occurs, you should check the id field of the Event object to determine what kind of key was pressed. If the event type is KEY_PRESS or KEY_RELEASE, the keyboard key has an ASCII or Unicode representation, and the key fields of the event object contain the encoding of the key. On the other hand, if id is KEY_ACTION or KEY_ACTION_RELEASE, the key is a function key of some sort, and the key field contains one of the keyboard constants defined by the Event class, such as Event.F1 or Event.LEFT.

Example 7-2 shows a simple applet that allows the user to produce drawings by scribbling with the mouse. It also allows the user to erase those drawings by clicking on a button or pressing the E key. The applet overrides methods to handle mouse events, keyboard events, and action events generated by the Button component. Unlike the applet in Example 7-1, this applet does not define a paint() method. For simplicity, it does its drawing directly in response to the events it receives and does not store the coordinates. This means that it cannot regenerate the user's drawing if it is scrolled off the screen and then scrolled back on.

Example 7-2: An Applet That Uses the Java 1.0 Event Model

```
import java.applet.*;
import java.awt.*;

/** A simple applet using the Java 1.0 event-handling model */
public class Scribble extends Applet {
  private int lastx, lasty;      // Remember last mouse coordinates
  Button erase_button;           // The Erase button
  Graphics g;                    // A Graphics object for drawing

  /** Initialize the button and the Graphics object */
  public void init() {
    erase_button = new Button("Erase");
    this.add(erase_button);
    g = this.getGraphics();
```

Example 7–2: An Applet That Uses the Java 1.0 Event Model (continued)

```
    this.requestFocus();  // Ask for keyboard focus so we get key events
  }
  /** Respond to mouse clicks */
  public boolean mouseDown(Event e, int x, int y) {
    lastx = x; lasty = y;              // Remember where the click was
    return true;
  }
  /** Respond to mouse drags */
  public boolean mouseDrag(Event e, int x, int y) {
    g.setColor(Color.black);
    g.drawLine(lastx, lasty, x, y);   // Draw from last position to here
    lastx = x; lasty = y;             // And remember new last position
    return true;
  }
  /** Respond to key presses: erase drawing when user types 'e' */
  public boolean keyDown(Event e, int key) {
    if ((e.id == Event.KEY_PRESS) && (key == 'e')) {
      g.setColor(this.getBackground());
      g.fillRect(0, 0, bounds().width, bounds().height);
      return true;
    }
    else return false;
  }
  /** Respond to button clicks: erase drawing when user clicks button */
  public boolean action(Event e, Object arg) {
    if (e.target == erase_button) {
      g.setColor(this.getBackground());
      g.fillRect(0, 0, bounds().width, bounds().height);
      return true;
    }
    else return false;
  }
}
```

Including Applets in HTML Files

Applets are typically embedded in HTML files using the <APPLET> tag. Another alternative relies on a Java Plug-in and uses the <EMBED> and <OBJECT> tags. Multiple applet files can be combined into a single JAR (Java Archive) file that a web browser can read as a single, compressed file, substantially reducing download time for some applets.

The <APPLET> Tag

A Java applet is included in a web page with the <APPLET> tag, which has the following syntax (items in brackets ([ ]) are optional):

```
<APPLET
    CODE = applet-filename
    WIDTH = pixel-width
    HEIGHT = pixel-height
    [OBJECT = serialized-applet-filename]
    [ARCHIVE = jar-file-list]
    [CODEBASE = applet-url]
```

Applets

```
        [ALT = alternate-text]
        [NAME = applet-name]
        [ALIGN = alignment]
        [VSPACE = vertical-pixel-space]
        [HSPACE = horizontal-pixel-space]
    >
  [<PARAM NAME = parameter VALUE = value>]
  [<PARAM NAME = parameter VALUE = value>]
      ...
  [alternate-text]
  </APPLET>
```

<APPLET>

The <APPLET> tag specifies an applet to be run within a web document. A web browser that does not support Java and does not understand the <APPLET> tag ignores this tag and any related <PARAM> tags and simply displays any *alternate-text* that appears between <APPLET> and </APPLET>. A browser that does support Java runs the specified applet and does *not* display the *alternate-text*.

CODE

This required attribute specifies the file that contains the compiled Java code for the applet. It must be relative to the CODEBASE, if that attribute is specified or relative to the current document's URL, by default. It must not be an absolute URL. As of Java 1.1, this attribute can be replaced with an OBJECT attribute.

WIDTH

This attribute specifies the initial width, in pixels, that the applet needs in the browser's window. It is required.

HEIGHT

This attribute specifies the initial height, in pixels, that the applet needs in the browser's window. It is required.

OBJECT

As of Java 1.1, this attribute specifies the name of a file that contains a serialized applet that is to be created by deserialization. An applet specified in this way does not have its init() method invoked but does have its start() method invoked. Thus, before an applet is saved through serialization, it should be initialized but should not be started, or, if started, it should be stopped. An applet must have either the CODE or OBJECT attribute specified, but not both.

ARCHIVE

As of Java 1.1, this attribute specifies a comma-separated list of JAR files that are preloaded by the web browser or applet viewer. These archive files may contain Java class files, images, sounds, properties, or any other resources required by the applet. The web browser or applet viewer searches for required files in the archives before attempting to load them over the network.

CODEBASE

This optional attribute specifies the base URL (absolute or relative) of the applet to be displayed. This should be a directory, not the applet file itself. If this attribute is unspecified, the URL of the current document is used.

ALT This optional attribute specifies text that should be displayed by browsers that understand the <APPLET> tag but do not support Java.

NAME

This optional attribute gives a name to the applet instance. Applets that are running at the same time can look one another up by name and communicate with one another.

ALIGN

This optional attribute specifies the applet's alignment on the page. It behaves just like the ALIGN attribute of the <IMG> tag. Its allowed values are: left, right, top, texttop, middle, absmiddle, baseline, bottom, and absbottom.

VSPACE

This optional attribute specifies the margin, in pixels, that the browser should put above and below the applet. It behaves just like the VSPACE attribute of the <IMG> tag.

HSPACE

This optional attribute specifies the margin, in pixels, that the browser should put on either side of the applet. It behaves just like the HSPACE attribute of the <IMG> tag.

<PARAM>

The <PARAM> tag, with its NAME and VALUE attributes, specifies a named parameter and its corresponding string value that are passed to the applet. These applet parameters function like system properties or command-line arguments do for a regular application. Any number of <PARAM> tags may appear between <APPLET> and </APPLET>. An applet can look up the value of a parameter specified in a <PARAM> tag with the getParameter() method of Applet.

Using Applet JAR Files

The <APPLET> tag supports an ARCHIVE attribute that identifies a JAR file containing the files required by an applet. The JAR, or Java Archive, format is simply a ZIP file with the addition of an optional manifest file. When an applet implementation involves more than one class file or when an applet relies on external image or sound files, it can be quite useful to combine all these files into a single, compressed JAR file and allow the web browser to download them all at once.

Starting with Java 1.1, Sun's Java SDK contains a *jar* command that allows you to create a JAR file. You might invoke it like this to create a JAR file named *myapplet.jar* that contains all class files, GIF images, and AU format sound files in the current directory:

```
% jar cf myapplet.jar *.class *.gif *.au
```

Having created a JAR file like this, you can tell a web browser about it with the following HTML tags:

```
<APPLET ARCHIVE="myapplet.jar" CODE="myapplet.class" WIDTH=400 HEIGHT=200>
</APPLET>
```

The ARCHIVE attribute does not replace the CODE attribute. ARCHIVE specifies where to look for files, but CODE is still required to tell the browser which of the files in the archive is the applet class file to be executed. The ARCHIVE attribute may actually specify a comma-separated list of JAR files. The web browser or applet viewer searches these archives for any files the applet requires. If a file is not found in an archive, however, the browser falls back upon its old behavior and attempts to load the file from the web server using a new HTTP request.

Web browsers introduced support for the ARCHIVE attribute at about the same time that Java 1.1 was introduced. Some Java 1.0 browsers do not recognize ARCHIVE and therefore ignore it. If you want to maintain compatibility with these browsers, be sure to make your applet files available in an unarchived form, in addition to the more efficient archived form.

Using Applets with the Java Plug-in

When a Java-enabled web browser encounters an <APPLET> tag, it starts up its embedded Java VM, downloads the class files that implement the applet, and starts running them. This approach has run into difficulties because web browser releases are not synchronized with releases of new versions of Java. It was quite a while after the release of Java 1.1 before commonly used browsers supported this version of the language, and there are still quite a few browsers in use that support only Java 1.0. It is not at all clear when, or even if, browsers will include support for the Java 2 platform. Furthermore, because of the lawsuit between Sun and Microsoft, the future of integrated Java support in the popular Internet Explorer web browser is questionable.

For these reasons, Sun has produced a product called the Java Plug-in. This product is a Java VM that acts as a Netscape Navigator plug-in and as an Internet Explorer ActiveX control. It adds Java 1.2 support to these browsers for the Windows and Solaris platforms. In many ways, Java support makes the most sense as a plug-in; using the Java Plug-in may be the preferred method for distributing Java applets in the future.

There is a catch, however. To run an applet under the Java Plug-in, you cannot use the <APPLET> tag. <APPLET> invokes the built-in Java VM, not the Java Plug-in. Instead, you must invoke the Java Plug-in just as you would invoke any other Navigator plug-in or Internet Explorer ActiveX control. Unfortunately, Netscape and Microsoft have defined different HTML tags for these purposes. Netscape uses the <EMBED> tag, and Microsoft uses the <OBJECT> tag. The details of using these tags and combining them in a portable way are messy and confusing. To help applet developers, Sun distributes a special HTML converter program that you can run over your HTML files. It scans for <APPLET> tags and converts them to equivalent <EMBED> and <OBJECT> tags.

Consider the simple HTML file we used for the first applet example in this chapter:

```
<APPLET code="MessageApplet.class" width=350 height=125>
  <PARAM name="message" value="Hello World">
</APPLET>
```

When run through the HTML converter, this tag becomes something like this:

```
<OBJECT classid="clsid:8AD9C840-044E-11D1-B3E9-00805F499D93"
codebase=
"http://java.sun.com/products/plugin/1.2/jinstall-12-win32.cab#Version=1,2,0,0"
        WIDTH=350 HEIGHT=125>
  <PARAM NAME=CODE VALUE="MessageApplet.class" >
  <PARAM NAME="type" VALUE="application/x-java-applet;version=1.2">
  <PARAM NAME="message" VALUE="Hello World">

  <COMMENT>
    <EMBED type="application/x-java-applet;version=1.2"
           pluginspage=
             "http://java.sun.com/products/plugin/1.2/plugin-install.html"
           java_CODE="MessageApplet.class"
           WIDTH=350 HEIGHT=125 message="Hello World">
    </EMBED>
  </COMMENT>
</OBJECT>
```

When Navigator reads this HTML file, it ignores the <OBJECT> and <COMMENT> tags that it does not support and reads only the <EMBED> tag. When Internet Explorer reads the file, however, it handles the <OBJECT> tag and ignores the <EMBED> tag that is hidden within the <COMMENT> tag. Note that both the <OBJECT> and <EMBED> tags specify all the attributes and parameters specified in the original file. In addition, however, they identify the plug-in or ActiveX control to be used and tell the browser from where it can download the Java Plug-in, if it has not already downloaded it.

You can learn more about the Java Plug-in and download the HTML converter utility from *http://java.sun.com/products/plugin*.

Applet Security

One of the most important features of Java is its security model. It allows untrusted code, such as applets downloaded from arbitrary web sites, to be run in a restricted environment that prevents that code from doing anything malicious, like deleting files or sending fake email. The Java security model has evolved considerably between Java 1.0 and Java 1.2 and is covered in detail in *Java in a Nutshell*.

To write applets, you don't need to understand the entire Java security model. What you do need to know is that when your applet is run as untrusted code, it is subject to quite a few security restrictions that limit the kinds of things it can do. This section describes those security restrictions and also describes how you can attach a digital signature to applets, so that users can treat them as trusted code and run them in a less restrictive environment.

The following list details the security restrictions that are typically imposed on untrusted applet code. Different web browsers and applet viewers may impose slightly different security restrictions and may allow the end user to customize or selectively relax the restrictions. In general, however, you should assume that your untrusted applet are restricted in the following ways:

- Untrusted code cannot read from or write to the local filesystem. This means that untrusted code cannot:

  - Read files
  - List directories
  - Check for the existence of files
  - Obtain the size or modification date of files
  - Obtain the read and write permissions of a file
  - Test whether a filename is a file or directory
  - Write files
  - Delete files
  - Create directories
  - Rename files
  - Read or write from FileDescriptor objects

- Untrusted code cannot perform networking operations, except in certain restricted ways. Untrusted code cannot:

  - Create a network connection to any computer other than the one from which the code was itself loaded
  - Listen for network connections on any of the privileged ports with numbers less than or equal to 1,024
  - Accept network connections on ports less than or equal to 1,024 or from any host other than the one from which the code itself was loaded
  - Use multicast sockets
  - Create or register a SocketImplFactory, URLStreamHandlerFactory, or ContentHandlerFactory

- Untrusted code cannot make use of certain system facilities. It cannot:

  - Exit the Java interpreter by calling System.exit() or Runtime.exit()
  - Spawn new processes by calling any of the Runtime.exec() methods
  - Dynamically load native code libraries with the load() or loadLibrary() methods of Runtime or System

- Untrusted code cannot make use of certain AWT facilities. One major restriction is that all windows created by untrusted code display a prominent visual indication that they have been created by untrusted code and are "insecure."

This is to prevent untrusted code from spoofing the on-screen appearance of trusted code. Additionally, untrusted code cannot:

- Initiate a print job

- Access the system clipboard

- Access the system event queue

- Untrusted code has restricted access to system properties. It cannot call System.getProperties(), so it cannot modify or insert properties into the system properties list. It can call System.getProperty() to read individual properties but can read only system properties to which it has been explicitly granted access. By default, *appletviewer* grants access to only the following 10 properties. Note that user.home and user.dir are excluded:

  - java.version

  - java.class.version

  - java.vendor

  - java.vendor.url

  - os.name

  - os.version

  - os.arch

  - file.separator

  - path.separator

  - line.separator

- Untrusted code cannot create or access threads or thread groups outside of the thread group in which the untrusted code is running.

- Untrusted code has restrictions on the classes it can load and define. It cannot:

  - Explicitly load classes from the sun.* packages

  - Define classes in any of the java.* or sun.* packages

  - Create a ClassLoader object or call any ClassLoader methods

- Untrusted code cannot use the java.lang.Class reflection methods to obtain information about nonpublic members of a class, unless the class was loaded from the same host as the untrusted code.

- Untrusted code has restrictions on its use of the `java.security` package. It cannot:

  - Manipulate security identities in any way

  - Set or read security properties

  - List, look up, insert, or remove security providers

  - Finally, to prevent untrusted code from circumventing all of these restrictions, it is not allowed to create or register a `SecurityManager` object.

Local Applets

When an applet is loaded from the local filesystem, instead of through a network protocol, web browsers and applet viewers may relax some, or even many, of the preceding restrictions. The reason for this is that local applets are assumed to be more trustworthy than anonymous applets from the network.

Intermediate applet security policies are also possible. For example, an applet viewer can be written so that it places fewer restrictions on applets loaded from an internal corporate network than on those loaded from the Internet.

Signed Applets

Java 1.1 added the ability to attach a digital signature to a JAR file that contains an applet. This signature securely identifies the author or origin of an applet. If you trust the author or originating organization, you can configure your web browser or applet viewer to run applets bearing that signature as trusted code, rather than as untrusted code. Such an applet runs without the onerous security restrictions placed on untrusted applets. Java 1.2 platform actually allows the security policy to be customized based on the origin of an applet. This means that an end user or system administrator may define multiple levels of trust, allowing fully trusted applets to run with all the privileges of a standalone application, while partially trusted applets run with a reduced list of security restrictions.

The process of attaching a digital signature to an applet's JAR file is platform dependent. In Java 1.1, you use the *javakey* program. In Java 1.2, this program has been superseded by *jarsigner*. Netscape and Microsoft also provide their own digital signature programs that are customized for use with their browsers.

The process of telling your web browser or applet viewer which digital signatures to trust is also vendor dependent, of course. In Java 1.1, you use *javakey* to specify which signatures are trusted. In Java 1.2, you use a different tool, *policytool*, to specify trusted signatures and the security policies associated with them. See *java in a Nutshell* for further details.

PART II

API Quick Reference

Part II is the real heart of this book: quick-reference material for the APIs that comprise the Java Foundation Classes. Please read the following section, *How To Use This Quick Reference,* to learn how to get the most out of this material.

How To Use This
Quick Reference

The quick-reference section that follows packs a lot of information into a small space. This introduction explains how to get the most out of that information. It describes how the quick reference is organized and how to read the individual quick-ref entries.

Finding a Quick Reference Entry

The quick reference is organized into chapters, one per package. Each chapter begins with an overview of the package and includes a hierarchy diagram for the classes and interfaces in the package. Following this overview are quick reference entries for all of the classes and interfaces in the package.

Entries are organized alphabetically by class *and* package name, so that related classes are grouped near each other. Thus, in order to look up a quick reference entry for a particular class, you must also know the name of the package that contains that class. Usually, the package name is obvious from the context, and you should have no trouble looking up the quick-reference entry you want. Use the tabs on the outside edge of the book and the "dictionary-style" headers on the upper outside corner of each page to help you find the package and class you are looking for.

Occasionally, you may need to look up a class for which you do not already know the package. In this case, refer to Chapter 1, *Class Index*. This index allows you to look up a class by class name and find out what package it is part of.

Reading a Quick Reference Entry

Each quick-reference entry contains quite a bit of information. The sections that follow describe the structure of a quick-reference entry, explaining what information is available, where it is found, and what it means. While reading the descriptions that follow, you will find it helpful to flip through the reference section itself to find examples of the features being described.

Class Name, Package Name, Availability, and Flags

Each quick-reference entry begins with a four-part title that specifies the name, package, and availability of the class, and may also specify various additional flags that describe the class. The class name appears in bold at the upper-left of the title. The package name appears, in smaller print, in the lower-left, below the class name.

The upper-right portion the title indicates the availability of the class; it specifies the earliest release that contained the class. If a class was introduced in Java 1.1, for example, this portion of the title reads "Java 1.1". If a class was introduced in Version 1.2 of the Java 2 platform, the availability reads "Java 1.2", for simplicity's sake. The availability section of the title is also used to indicate whether a class has been deprecated, and, if so, in what release. For example, it might read "Java 1.1; Deprecated in Java 1.2".

In the lower-right corner of the title you may find a list of flags that describe the class. The possible flags and their meanings are as follows:

accessible
> The class, or a superclass, implements javax.accessibility.Accessible. This flag may be followed by a parenthesized list that specifies the specific types of accessibility supported by this class. The possible accessibility types are *action, selection, value, text,* and *hypertext.* When present, a type indicates that the javax.accessibility.AccessibleContext for this class can return an accessiblity object of that type. For example, a class that is *accessible(action,selection)* has an AccessibleContext whose getAccessibleAction() and getAccessibleSelection() methods return non-null javax.accessibility.AccessibleAction and javax.accessibility.AccessibleSelection objects, respectively. The AccessibleContext for an accessible component has a getAccessibleComponent() method that returns an AccessibleComponent object. Because this is true for all components, however, it is not specially flagged here.
>
> AccessibleContext classes are typically implemented as protected inner classes of the accessible class itself. This book does not contain reference entries for these classes because all the necessary information about them is contained in the *accessible* class flag of the accessible class, in the single-line inner class synopsis that appears in the containing accessible class, and in Chapter 22, *The javax.accessibility Package.*

AWT component
> The class extends java.awt.Component, but does not extend javax.swing.JComponent.

bean container
> The class may contain JavaBeans components.

checked
> The class is a checked exception, which means that it extends java.lang.Exception, but not java.lang.RuntimeException. In other words, it must be declared in the throws clause of any method that may throw it.

cloneable

The class, or a superclass, implements java.lang.Cloneable.

collection

The class, or a superclass, implements java.util.Collection or java.util.Map.

comparable

The class, or a superclass, implements java.lang.Comparable.

error

The class extends java.lang.Error.

event

The class extends java.util.EventObject.

event adapter

The class, or a superclass, implements java.util.EventListener, and the class name ends with "Adapter".

event listener

The class, or a superclass, implements java.util.EventListener.

layout manager

The class, or a superclass, implements java.awt.LayoutManager.

model

The class is Swing class whose name ends with "Model".

PJ1.1

The class or interface is part of the Personal Java 1.1 platform.

PJ1.1(mod)

The class or interface is supported, in modified form, by the Personal Java 1.1 platform.

PJ1.1(opt)

The class or interface is an optional part of the Personal Java 1.1 platform. Support for the class is implementation-dependent.

remote

The class, or a superclass, implements java.rmi.Remote.

runnable

The class, or a superclass, implements java.lang.Runnable.

serializable

The class, or a superclass, implements java.io.Serializable and may be serialized.

shape

The class, or a superclass, implements java.awt.Shape.

swing component

The class extends javax.swing.JComponent.

unchecked

The class is an unchecked exception, which means it extends java.lang.RuntimeException and therefore does not need to be declared in the throws clause of a method that may throw it.

Description

The title of each quick-reference entry is followed by a short description of the most important features of the class or interface. This description may be anywhere from a couple of sentences to several paragraphs long.

Synopsis

The most important part of every quick-reference entry is the class synopsis, which follows the title and description. The synopsis for a class looks a lot like the source code for the class, except that the method bodies are omitted and some additional annotations are added. If you know Java syntax, you know how to read the class synopsis.

The first line of the synopsis contains information about the class itself. It begins with a list of class modifiers, such as public, abstract, and final. These modifiers are followed by the class or interface keyword and then by the name of the class. The class name may be followed by an extends clause that specifies the superclass and an implements clause that specifies any interfaces the class implements.

The class definition line is followed by a list of the fields and methods that the class defines. Once again, if you understand basic Java syntax, you should have no trouble making sense of these lines. The listing for each member includes the modifiers, type, and name of the member. For methods, the synopsis also includes the type and name of each method parameter and an optional throws clause that lists the exceptions the method can throw. The member names are in boldface, so that it is easy to scan the list of members looking for the one you want. The names of method parameters are in italics to indicate that they are not to be used literally. The member listings are printed on alternating gray and white backgrounds to keep them visually separate.

Member availability and flags

Each member listing is a single line that defines the API for that member. These listings use Java syntax, so their meaning is immediately clear to any Java programmer. There is some auxiliary information associated with each member synopsis, however, that requires explanation.

Recall that each quick-reference entry begins with a title section that includes the release in which the class was first defined. When a member is introduced into a class after the initial release of the class, the version in which the member was introduced appears, in small print, to the left of the member synopsis. For example, if a class was first introduced in Java 1.1, but had a new method added in Version 1.2 of Java 2, the title contains the string "Java 1.1", and the listing for the new member is preceded by the number "1.2". Furthermore, if a member has been deprecated, that fact is indicated with a hash mark (#) to the left of the member synopsis.

The area to the right of the member synopsis is used to display a variety of flags that provide additional information about the member. Some of these flags indicate additional specification details that do not appear in the member API itself. Other flags contain implementation-specific information. This information can be quite useful in understanding the class and in debugging your code, but be aware that it may differ between implementations. The implementation-specific flags displayed in this book are based on Sun's implementation of Java for Microsoft Windows.

The following flags may be displayed to the right of a member synopsis:

native
An implementation-specific flag that indicates that a method is implemented in native code. Although native is a Java keyword and can appear in method signatures, it is part of the method implementation, not part of its specification. Therefore, this information is included with the member flags, rather than as part of the member listing. This flag is useful as a hint about the expected performance of a method.

synchronized
An implementation-specific flag that indicates that a method implementation is declared synchronized, meaning that it obtains a lock on the object or class before executing. Like the native keyword, the synchronized keyword is part of the method implementation, not part of the specification, so it appears as a flag, not in the method synopsis itself. This flag is a useful hint that the method is probably implemented in a thread-safe manner.

Whether or not a method is thread-safe is part of the method specification, and this information *should* appear (although it often does not) in the method documentation. There are a number of different ways to make a method thread-safe, however, and declaring the method with the synchronized keyword is only one possible implementation. In other words, a method that does not bear the synchronized flag can still be thread-safe.

Overrides:
Indicates that a method overrides a method in one of its superclasses. The flag is followed by the name of the superclass that the method overrides. This is a specification detail, not an implementation detail. As we'll see in the next section, overriding methods are usually grouped together in their own section of the class synopsis. The Overrides: flag is only used when an overriding method is not grouped in that way.

Implements:
Indicates that a method implements a method in an interface. The flag is followed by the name of the interface that is implemented. This is a specification detail, not an implementation detail. As we'll see in the next section, methods that implement an interface are usually grouped into a special section of the class synopsis. The Implements: flag is only used for methods that are not grouped in this way.

How To

empty

Indicates that the implementation of the method has an empty body. This can be a hint to the programmer that the method may need to be overridden in a subclass.

constant

An implementation flag that indicates that a method has a trivial implementation. Only methods with a void return type can be truly empty. Any method declared to return a value must have at least a return statement. The "constant" flag indicates that the method implementation is empty except for a return statement that returns a constant value. Such a method might have a body like return null; or return false;. Like the "empty" flag, this flag indicates that a method may need to be overridden.

default:

This flag is used with property accessor methods that read the value of a property (i.e., methods whose names begins with "get" and take no arguments). The flag is followed by the default value of the property. Strictly speaking, default property values are a specification detail. In practice, however, these defaults are not always documented, and care should be taken, because the default values may change between implementations.

Not all property accessors have a "default:" flag. A default value is determined by dynamically loading the class in question, instantiating it using a no-argument constructor, and then calling the method to find out what it returns. This technique can be used only on classes that can be dynamically loaded and instantiated and that have no-argument constructors, so default values are shown for those classes only. Furthermore, note that when a class is instantiated using a different constructor, the default values for its properties may be different.

bound

This flag is used with property accessor methods for bound properties of JavaBeans components. The presence of this flag means that calling the method generates a java.beans.PropertyChangeEvent. This is a specification detail, but it is sometimes not documented. Information about bound properties is obtained from the BeanInfo object for the class.

constrained

Indicates that a JavaBeans component property is constrained. In other words, the method may throw a java.beans.PropertyVetoException. This is a specification detail, not an implementation detail.

expert

Indicates that the BeanInfo object for this class specifies that this method is intended for use by experts only. This hint is intended for visual programming tools, but users of this book may find the hint useful as well.

hidden

Indicates that the BeanInfo object for this class specifies that this method is for internal use only. This is a hint that visual programming tools should hide the property or event from the programmer. This book does not hide these methods, of course, but this flag does indicate that you should probably avoid using the method.

preferred

Indicates that the BeanInfo object for this class specifies that this method is an accessor for a default or preferred property or event. This is a hint to visual programming tools to display the property or event in a prominent way, and it may also be a useful hint to readers of this book.

= For static final fields, this flag is followed by the constant value of the field. Only constants of primitive and String types and constants with the value null are displayed. Some constant values are specification details, while others are implementation details. The reason that symbolic constants are defined, however, is so you can write code that does not rely directly upon the constant value. Use this flag to help you understand the class, but do not rely upon the constant values in your own programs.

Functional grouping of members

Within a class synopsis, the members are not listed in strict alphabetical order. Instead, they are broken down into functional groups and listed alphabetically within each group. Constructors, methods, fields, and inner classes are all listed separately. Instance methods are kept separate from static (class) methods. Constants are separated from non-constant fields. Public members are listed separately from protected members. Grouping members by category breaks a class down into smaller, more comprehensible segments, making the class easier to understand. This grouping also makes it easier for you to find a desired member.

Functional groups are separated from each other in a class synopsis with Java comments, such as "// Public Constructors", "// Inner Classes", and "// Methods Implementing Servlet". The various functional categories are as follows (in the order in which they appear in a class synopsis):

Constructors

Displays the constructors for the class. Public constructors and protected constructors are displayed separately in subgroupings. If a class defines no constructor at all, the Java compiler adds a default no-argument constructor that is displayed here. If a class defines only private constructors, it cannot be instantiated, so a special, empty grouping entitled "No Constructor" indicates this fact. Constructors are listed first because the first thing you do with most classes is instantiate them by calling a constructor.

Constants

Displays all of the constants (i.e., fields that are declared static and final) defined by the class. Public and protected constants are displayed in separate subgroups. Constants are listed here, near the top of the class synopsis, because constant values are often used throughout the class as legal values for method parameters and return values.

Inner Classes

Groups all of the inner classes and interfaces defined by the class or interface. For each inner class, there is a single-line synopsis. Each inner class also has its own quick-reference entry that includes a full class synopsis for the inner class. Like constants, inner classes are listed near the top of the class synopsis because they are often used by a number of other members of the class.

Static Methods

Lists the static methods (class methods) of the class, broken down into subgroups for public static methods and protected static methods.

Event Listener Registration Methods

Lists the public instance methods that register and deregister event listener objects with the class. The names of these methods begin with the words "add" and "remove" and end in "Listener". These methods are always passed a java.util.EventListener object. The methods are typically defined in pairs, so the pairs are listed together. The methods are listed alphabetically by event name, rather than by method name.

Property Accessor Methods

Lists the public instance methods that set or query the value of a property or attribute of the class. The names of these methods begin with the words "set", "get", and "is", and their signatures follow the patterns set out in the JavaBeans specification. Although the naming conventions and method signature patterns are defined for JavaBeans, classes and interfaces throughout the Java platform define property accessor methods that follow these conventions and patterns. Looking at a class in terms of the properties it defines can be a powerful tool for understanding the class, so property methods are grouped together in this section.

Property accessor methods are listed alphabetically by property name, not by method name. This means that the "set", "get", and "is" methods for a property all appear together. This book defines a property accessor method in a somewhat more general way than the JavaBeans specification does. A method is considered to be a property accessor if it follows the JavaBeans conventions itself or if it has the same name as a method that follows those conventions. Consider the setSize() method of the Component class. There are two versions of this method, and, since they have the same name, they obviously share a purpose and deserve to be grouped together. However, only one version of the method strictly follows the JavaBeans signature patterns. The relaxed definition of what constitutes a property accessor method allows these two methods to be listed together, as they should be.

Public Instance Methods

Contains all of the public instance methods that are not grouped elsewhere.

Implementing Methods

Groups the methods that implement the same interface. There is one subgroup for each interface implemented by the class. Methods that are defined by the same interface are almost always related to each other, so this is a useful functional grouping of methods.

Note that if an interface method is also an event registration method or a property accessor method, it is listed both in this group and in the event or property group. This situation does not arise often, but when it does, all of the functional groupings are important and useful enough to warrant the duplicate listing. When an interface method is listed in the event or property group, it displays an "Implements:" flag that specifies the name of the interface of which it is part.

Overriding Methods

Groups the methods that override methods of a superclass broken down into subgroups by superclass. This is typically a useful grouping, because it helps to make it clear how a class modifies the default behavior of its superclasses. In practice, it is also often true that methods that override the same superclass are functionally related to each other.

Sometimes a method that overrides a superclass is also a property accessor method or (more rarely) an event registration method. When this happens, the method is grouped with the property or event methods and displays a flag that indicates which superclass it overrides. The method is not listed with other overriding methods, however. Note that this is different from interface methods, which, because they are more strongly functionally related, may have duplicate listings in both groups.

Protected Instance Methods

Contains all of the protected instance methods that are not grouped elsewhere.

Fields

Lists all the non-constant fields of the class, breaking them down into subgroups for public and protected static fields and public and protected instance fields. Many classes do not define any publicly accessible fields. For those that do, many object-oriented programmers prefer not to use those fields directly, but instead to use accessor methods when such methods are available.

Deprecated Members

Deprecated methods and deprecated fields are grouped at the very bottom of the class synopsis. Use of these members is strongly discouraged.

Class Hierarchy

For any class or interface that has a non-trivial class hierarchy, the class synopsis is followed by a **Hierarchy** section. This section lists all of the superclasses of the class, as well as any interfaces implemented by those superclasses. It may also list any interfaces extended by an interface. In the hierarchy listing, arrows indicate superclass to subclass relationships, while the interfaces implemented by a class follow the class name in parentheses. For example, the following hierarchy indicates that java.awt.AWTException extends Exception which extends Throwable (which implements Serializable) which extends Object:

Object→Throwable(Serializable)→Exception→AWTException

If a class has subclasses, the "Hierarchy" section is followed by a "Subclasses" section that lists those subclasses. If an interface has implementations, the "Hierarchy" section is followed by an "Implementations" section that lists those implementations. While the "Hierarchy" section shows ancestors of the class, the "Subclasses" or "Implementations" section shows descendants.

Cross References

The class hierarchy section of a quick-reference entry is followed by a number of optional "cross reference" sections that indicate other, related classes and methods that may be of interest. These sections are the following:

Passed To
> This section lists all of the methods and constructors that are passed an object of this type as an argument. This is useful when you have an object of a given type and want to figure out what you can do with it.

Returned By
> This section lists all of the methods (but not constructors) that return an object of this type. This is useful when you know that you want to work with an object of this type, but don't know how to obtain one.

Thrown By
> For checked exception classes, this section lists all of the methods and constructors that throw exceptions of this type. This material helps you figure out when a given exception or error may be thrown. Note, however, that this section is based on the exception types listed in the throws clauses of methods and constructors. Subclasses of RuntimeException and Error do not have to be listed in throws clauses, so it is not possible to generate a complete cross reference of methods that throw these types of unchecked exceptions.

Type Of
> This section lists all of the fields and constants that are of this type, which can help you figure out how to obtain an object of this type.

A Note About Class Names

Throughout the quick reference, you'll notice that classes are sometimes referred to by class name alone and at other times referred to by class name and package name. If package names were always used, the class synopses would become long and hard to read. On the other hand, if package names were never used, it would sometimes be difficult to know what class was being referred to. The rules for including or omitting the package name are complex. They can be summarized approximately as follows, however:

- If the class name alone is ambiguous, the package name is always used.

- If the class is part of the java.lang package or is a very commonly used class like java.io.Serializable or java.awt.Component, the package name is omitted.

- If the class being referred to is part of the current package (and has a quick-ref entry in the current chapter), the package name is omitted. The package name is also omitted if the class being referred to is part of a package that contains the current package.

CHAPTER 8

The java.applet Package

The java.applet package is a small but important package that defines the Applet class—the superclass of all applets. It also defines the AppletContext and AppletStub interfaces, which are implemented by web browsers and other applet viewers. Finally, for lack of a better place, this package contains the AudioClip interface, which represents a sound to be played. Figure 8-1 shows the class hierarchy of this package. See Chapter 7, *Applets*, for more details about applets.

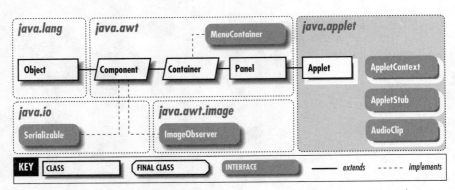

Figure 8-1: The java.applet package

Applet   Java 1.0

java.applet   *serializable AWT component PJ1.1*

This class implements an applet. To create your own applet, you should create a subclass of this class and override some or all of the following methods. Note that you never need to call these methods—they are called when appropriate by a web browser or other applet viewer.

init() should perform any initialization for the applet; it is called when the applet first starts. destroy() should free up any resources that the applet is holding; it is called when the applet is about to be permanently stopped. start() is called to make applet start doing whatever it is that it does. Often, it starts a thread to perform an animation or similar task. stop() should temporarily stop the applet from executing. It is called when the applet temporarily becomes hidden or nonvisible.

getAppletInfo() should return text suitable for display in an **About** dialog posted by the web browser or applet viewer. getParameterInfo() should return an arbitrary-length array of three-element arrays of strings, where each element describes one of the parameters that this applet understands. The three elements of each parameter description are strings that specify the parameter's name, type, and description, respectively.

In addition to these methods, an applet typically overrides several of the methods of java.awt.Component, notably the paint() method to draw the applet on the screen.

There are also several Applet methods that you do not override but may call from applet code: showStatus() displays text in the web browser or applet viewer's status line. getImage() and getAudioClip() read image (GIF and JPEG formats) and audio files (AU format) over the network and return corresponding Java objects. getParameter() looks up the value of a parameter specified with a <PARAM> tag within an <APPLET>/</APPLET> pair. getCodeBase() returns the base URL from which the applet's code was loaded, while getDocumentBase() returns the base URL from which the HTML document containing the applet was loaded. Finally, getAppletContext() returns an AppletContext object.

```
public class Applet extends java.awt.Panel {
// Public Constructors
    public Applet();
// Public Class Methods
1.2 public static final AudioClip newAudioClip(java.net.URL url);
// Property Accessor Methods (by property name)
    public boolean isActive();                                              default:false
    public AppletContext getAppletContext();
    public String getAppletInfo();                                  constant default:null
    public java.net.URL getCodeBase();
    public java.net.URL getDocumentBase();
1.1 public java.util.Locale getLocale();                              Overrides:Component
    public String[ ][ ] getParameterInfo();                         constant default:null
// Public Instance Methods
    public void destroy();                                                       empty
    public AudioClip getAudioClip(java.net.URL url);
    public AudioClip getAudioClip(java.net.URL url, String name);
    public java.awt.Image getImage(java.net.URL url);
    public java.awt.Image getImage(java.net.URL url, String name);
    public String getParameter(String name);
    public void init();                                                          empty
    public void play(java.net.URL url);
    public void play(java.net.URL url, String name);
    public final void setStub(AppletStub stub);
    public void showStatus(String msg);
    public void start();                                                         empty
    public void stop();                                                          empty
// Public Methods Overriding Component
    public void resize(java.awt.Dimension d);
    public void resize(int width, int height);
}
```

Hierarchy: Object→ Component(java.awt.image.ImageObserver, java.awt.MenuContainer, Serializable)→ Container→ java.awt.Panel→ Applet

Subclasses: javax.swing.JApplet

Passed To: java.beans.AppletInitializer.{activate(), initialize()}, org.omg.CORBA.ORB.{init(), set_parameters()}

Returned By: AppletContext.getApplet()

AppletContext
Java 1.0

java.applet
PJ1.1

This interface defines the methods that allow an applet to interact with the context in which it runs (usually a web browser or an applet viewer). The getAppletContext() method of Applet returns an object that implements the AppletContext interface. You can use an AppletContext to take advantage of a web browser's cache or display a message to the user in the web browser or applet viewer's message area. The getAudioClip() and getImage() methods may make use of a web browser's caching mechanism. showDocument() and showStatus() give an applet a small measure of control over the appearance of the browser or applet viewer. The getApplet() and getApplets() methods allow an applet to find out what other applets are running at the same time.

```
public abstract interface AppletContext {
// Public Instance Methods
    public abstract Applet getApplet(String name);
    public abstract java.util.Enumeration getApplets();
    public abstract AudioClip getAudioClip(java.net.URL url);
    public abstract java.awt.Image getImage(java.net.URL url);
    public abstract void showDocument(java.net.URL url);
    public abstract void showDocument(java.net.URL url, String target);
    public abstract void showStatus(String status);
}
```

Returned By: Applet.getAppletContext(), AppletStub.getAppletContext()

AppletStub
Java 1.0

java.applet
PJ1.1

This is an internal interface used when implementing an applet viewer.

```
public abstract interface AppletStub {
// Property Accessor Methods (by property name)
    public abstract boolean isActive();
    public abstract AppletContext getAppletContext();
    public abstract java.net.URL getCodeBase();
    public abstract java.net.URL getDocumentBase();
// Public Instance Methods
    public abstract void appletResize(int width, int height);
    public abstract String getParameter(String name);
}
```

Passed To: Applet.setStub()

AudioClip
Java 1.0

java.applet
PJ1.1

This interface describes the essential methods that an audio clip must have. The getAudioClip() methods of Applet and AppletContext both return an object that implements this interface. The current Java SDK implementation of this interface works only with sounds encoded in AU format. The AudioClip interface is in the java.applet package only because there is no better place for it.

```
public abstract interface AudioClip {
// Public Instance Methods
    public abstract void loop();
    public abstract void play();
    public abstract void stop();
}
```

Returned By: Applet.{getAudioClip(), newAudioClip()}, AppletContext.getAudioClip()

CHAPTER 9

The java.awt Package

The java.awt package is the main package of the AWT, or Abstract Windowing Toolkit. It contains classes for graphics, including the Java 2D graphics capabilities introduced in the Java 2 platform, and also defines the basic graphical user interface (GUI) framework for Java. java.awt also includes a number of heavyweight GUI objects, many of which have been superseded by the javax.swing package. java.awt also has a number of important subpackages.

The most important graphics classes in java.awt are Graphics and its Java 2D extension, Graphics2D. These classes represent a drawing surface, maintain a set of drawing attributes, and define methods for drawing and filling lines, shapes, and text. Classes that represent graphics attributes include Color, Font, Paint, Stroke, and Composite. The Image class and Shape interface represent things that you can draw using a Graphics object and the various graphics attributes. Figure 9-1 shows the graphics classes of this package.

The most important class for GUIs is Component, which represents a single graphical element in a GUI. Container is a kind of component that can contain other components. The LayoutManager interface and its various implementations are used to position components within their containers. Figure 9-2 shows the GUI classes of this package, and Figure 9-3 shows the event, exception, and security classes.

See Chapter 4, *Graphics with AWT and Java 2D*, for an introduction to Java graphics with AWT and Java 2D and Chapter 2, *Swing and AWT Architecture*, for an introduction to the GUI framework defined by the java.awt package.

ActiveEvent   Java 1.2

java.awt

This interface is implemented by events that know how to dispatch themselves. When the event dispatch system encounters an ActiveEvent on the event queue, it simply invokes the dispatch() method of the event, instead of attempting to dispatch the event on its own. This interface is implemented by java.awt.event.InvocationEvent, which is used by the invokeLater() and invokeAndWait() methods of EventQueue.

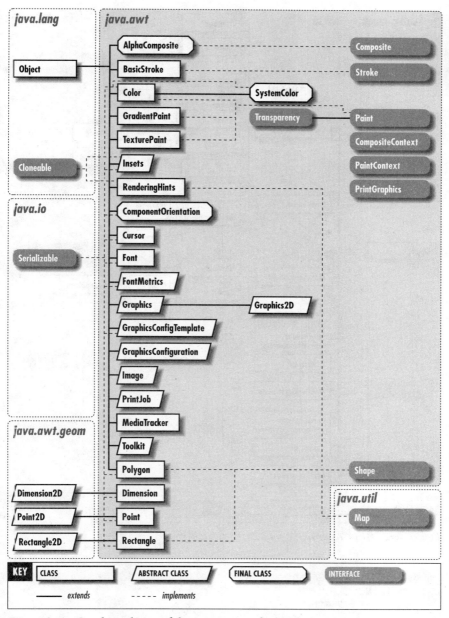

Figure 9-1: Graphics classes of the java.awt package

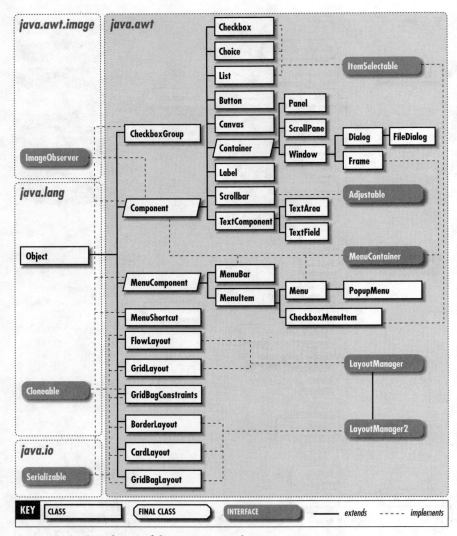

Figure 9-2: GUI classes of the java.awt package

```
public abstract interface ActiveEvent {
// Public Instance Methods
    public abstract void dispatch();
}
```

Implementations: java.awt.event.InvocationEvent

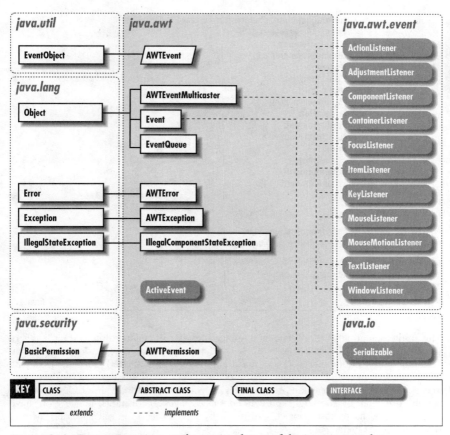

Figure 9-3: Event, exception, and security classes of the java.awt package

Adjustable

java.awt

PJ1.1

This interface defines the methods that should be implemented by an object that maintains a user-adjustable numeric value. The adjustable value has specified minimum and maximum values, and it may be incremented or decremented either a unit at a time or a block at a time. An Adjustable object generates an AdjustmentEvent when it is adjusted and maintains a list of AdjustmentListener objects interested in being notified when such an event occurs.

This interface abstracts the essential functionality of the Scrollbar and javax.swing.JScrollBar components.

```
public abstract interface Adjustable {
// Public Constants
    public static final int HORIZONTAL;                                               =0
    public static final int VERTICAL;                                                 =1
// Event Registration Methods (by event name)
    public abstract void addAdjustmentListener(java.awt.event.AdjustmentListener l);
```

```
    public abstract void removeAdjustmentListener(java.awt.event.AdjustmentListener l);
// Property Accessor Methods (by property name)
    public abstract int getBlockIncrement();
    public abstract void setBlockIncrement(int b);
    public abstract int getMaximum();
    public abstract void setMaximum(int max);
    public abstract int getMinimum();
    public abstract void setMinimum(int min);
    public abstract int getOrientation();
    public abstract int getUnitIncrement();
    public abstract void setUnitIncrement(int u);
    public abstract int getValue();
    public abstract void setValue(int v);
    public abstract int getVisibleAmount();
    public abstract void setVisibleAmount(int v);
}
```

Implementations: Scrollbar, javax.swing.JScrollBar

Passed To: java.awt.event.AdjustmentEvent.AdjustmentEvent(),
java.awt.peer.ScrollPanePeer.{setUnitIncrement(), setValue()}

Returned By: ScrollPane.{getHAdjustable(), getVAdjustable()},
java.awt.event.AdjustmentEvent.getAdjustable()

AlphaComposite   Java 1.2

java.awt

This implementation of the Composite interface blends colors according to their levels of
alpha transparency. AlphaComposite does not have a public constructor, but you can
obtain a shared immutable instance by calling the static getInstance() method, specifying
the desired compositing rule (one of the eight integer constants defined by the class),
and specifying an alpha value. Alternatively, if you use an alpha value of 1.0, you can
simply use one of the eight predefined AlphaComposite constants. Once you have
obtained an AlphaComposite object, you use it by passing it to the setComposite() method
of a Graphics2D object.

The most common way to use an AlphaComposite object is to specify the SRC_OVER compositing rule and an alpha value greater than 0 but less than 1. This causes the source
colors you draw to be given the specified level of alpha transparency, so that they are
blended with whatever colors already exist on the screen, making the destination colors
appear to show through the translucent source colors. This technique allows you to
achieve transparency effects using opaque colors when you are drawing onto a drawing surface, like a screen, that does not have an alpha channel.

The other compositing rules of AlphaComposite are best understood when both the
source (your drawing) and the destination (the drawing surface) have alpha channels.
For example, you can create translucent Color objects with the four-argument version of
the Color() constructor, and you can create an off-screen image with an alpha channel
by passing the constant TYPE_INT_ARGB to the java.awt.image.BufferedImage() constructor.
(Once your compositing operation has been performed in an off-screen image with an
alpha channel, you can view the results by copying the contents of the image to the
screen, of course.) When your source and destination have alpha channels built in, you
do not usually specify an alpha value for the AlphaComposite itself. If you do, however,
the transparency values of the source colors are multiplied by this alpha value.

AlphaComposite supports the following compositing rules:

SRC Replace the colors of the destination with the colors of the source, ignoring the destination colors and the transparency of the source.

SRC_OVER
Combine the source and destination colors combined based on the transparency of the source, so that the source appears to be drawn over the destination.

DST_OVER
Combine the source and destination colors based on the transparency of the destination, so that the source appears to be drawn underneath the destination.

SRC_IN
Draw the colors of the source using the transparency values of the destination, completely ignoring the colors of the destination.

SRC_OUT
Draw the colors of the source using the inverse transparency values of the destination.

DST_IN
Modify the colors of the destination using the alpha values of the source and ignoring the colors of the source.

DST_OUT
Modify the colors of the destination using the inverted alpha values of the source and ignoring the colors of the source.

CLEAR
Ignore the color and transparency of both the destination and the source. This clears the destination by making it a fully transparent black.

```
public final class AlphaComposite implements Composite {
// No Constructor
// Public Constants
    public static final AlphaComposite Clear;
    public static final int CLEAR;                                  =1
    public static final int DST_IN;                                 =6
    public static final int DST_OUT;                                =8
    public static final int DST_OVER;                               =4
    public static final AlphaComposite DstIn;
    public static final AlphaComposite DstOut;
    public static final AlphaComposite DstOver;
    public static final AlphaComposite Src;
    public static final int SRC;                                    =2
    public static final int SRC_IN;                                 =5
    public static final int SRC_OUT;                                =7
    public static final int SRC_OVER;                               =3
    public static final AlphaComposite SrcIn;
    public static final AlphaComposite SrcOut;
    public static final AlphaComposite SrcOver;
// Public Class Methods
    public static AlphaComposite getInstance(int rule);
    public static AlphaComposite getInstance(int rule, float alpha);
// Public Instance Methods
    public float getAlpha();
    public int getRule();
```

```
// Methods Implementing Composite
   public CompositeContext createContext(java.awt.image.ColorModel srcColorModel,
                                java.awt.image.ColorModel dstColorModel, RenderingHints hints);
// Public Methods Overriding Object
   public boolean equals(Object obj);
   public int hashCode();
}
```

Hierarchy: Object→ AlphaComposite(Composite)

Returned By: AlphaComposite.getInstance()

Type Of: AlphaComposite.{Clear, DstIn, DstOut, DstOver, Src, SrcIn, SrcOut, SrcOver}

AWTError   Java 1.0

java.awt   *serializable error PJ1.1*

Signals that an error has occurred in the java.awt package.

```
public class AWTError extends Error {
// Public Constructors
   public AWTError(String msg);
}
```

Hierarchy: Object→ Throwable(Serializable)→ Error→ AWTError

AWTEvent   Java 1.1

java.awt   *serializable event PJ1.1*

This abstract class serves as the root event type for all AWT events in Java 1.1 and supersedes the Event class that was used in Java 1.0.

Each AWTEvent has a source object, as all EventObject objects do. You can query the source of an event with the inherited getSource() method. The AWTEvent class adds an event type, or ID, for every AWT event. Use getID() to query the type of an event. Subclasses of AWTEvent define various constants for this type field.

The various _MASK constants are used by applets and custom components that call the enableEvents() method of Component to receive various event types without having to register EventListener objects.

```
public abstract class AWTEvent extends java.util.EventObject {
// Public Constructors
   public AWTEvent(Event event);
   public AWTEvent(Object source, int id);
// Public Constants
   public static final long ACTION_EVENT_MASK;                              =128
   public static final long ADJUSTMENT_EVENT_MASK;                          =256
   public static final long COMPONENT_EVENT_MASK;                             =1
   public static final long CONTAINER_EVENT_MASK;                             =2
   public static final long FOCUS_EVENT_MASK;                                 =4
1.2 public static final long INPUT_METHOD_EVENT_MASK;                       =2048
   public static final long ITEM_EVENT_MASK;                                =512
   public static final long KEY_EVENT_MASK;                                   =8
   public static final long MOUSE_EVENT_MASK;                                =16
   public static final long MOUSE_MOTION_EVENT_MASK;                         =32
   public static final int RESERVED_ID_MAX;                                =1999
   public static final long TEXT_EVENT_MASK;                               =1024
   public static final long WINDOW_EVENT_MASK;                               =64
```

```
// Public Instance Methods
  public int getID();
  public String paramString();
// Public Methods Overriding EventObject
  public String toString();
// Protected Methods Overriding Object
1.2 protected void finalize() throws Throwable;
// Protected Instance Methods
  protected void consume();
  protected boolean isConsumed();
// Protected Instance Fields
  protected boolean consumed;
  protected int id;
}
```

Hierarchy: Object→ java.util.EventObject(Serializable)→ AWTEvent

Subclasses: java.awt.event.ActionEvent, java.awt.event.AdjustmentEvent, java.awt.event.ComponentEvent, java.awt.event.InputMethodEvent, java.awt.event.InvocationEvent, java.awt.event.ItemEvent, java.awt.event.TextEvent, javax.swing.event.AncestorEvent, javax.swing.event.InternalFrameEvent

Passed To: Too many methods to list.

Returned By: Component.coalesceEvents(), EventQueue.{getNextEvent(), peekEvent()}

AWTEventMulticaster   Java 1.1

java.awt   *PJ1.1*

AWTEventMulticaster is a convenience class used when writing a custom AWT component. It provides an easy way to maintain a list of AWT EventListener objects and notify the listeners on that list when an event occurs.

AWTEventMulticaster implements each of the event listener interfaces defined in the java.awt.event package, which means that an AWTEventMulticaster object can serve as any desired type of event listener. (It also means that the class defines quite a few methods.) AWTEventMulticaster implements what amounts to a linked list of EventListener objects. When you invoke one of the EventListener methods of an AWTEventMulticaster, it invokes the same method on all of the EventListener objects in the linked list.

Rather than instantiate an AWTEventMulticaster object directly, you use the static add() and remove() methods of the class to add and remove EventListener objects from the linked list. Calling add() or remove() returns an AWTEventMulticaster with the appropriate EventListener object registered or deregistered. Using an AWTEventMulticaster is somewhat non-intuitive, so here is some example code that shows its use:

```
public class MyList extends Component {   // a class that sends ItemEvents
  // The head of a linked list of AWTEventMulticaster objects
  protected ItemListener listener = null;
  public void addItemListener(ItemListener l) {    // add a listener
    listener = AWTEventMulticaster.add(listener, l);
  }
  public void removeItemListener(ItemListener l) {  // remove a listener
    listener = AWTEventMulticaster.remove(listener, l);
  }
  protected void fireItemEvent(ItemEvent e) {    // notify all listeners
    if (listener != null) listener.itemStateChanged(e);
  }
  // The rest of the class goes here
}
```

public class **AWTEventMulticaster** implements java.awt.event.ActionListener, java.awt.event.AdjustmentListener,
   java.awt.event.ComponentListener, java.awt.event.ContainerListener, java.awt.event.FocusListener,
   java.awt.event.InputMethodListener, java.awt.event.ItemListener, java.awt.event.KeyListener,
   java.awt.event.MouseListener, java.awt.event.MouseMotionListener, java.awt.event.TextListener,
   java.awt.event.WindowListener {
// *Protected Constructors*
 protected **AWTEventMulticaster**(java.util.EventListener *a*, java.util.EventListener *b*);
// *Public Class Methods*
 public static java.awt.event.ActionListener **add**(java.awt.event.ActionListener *a*, java.awt.event.ActionListener *b*);
 public static java.awt.event.AdjustmentListener **add**(java.awt.event.AdjustmentListener *a*,
              java.awt.event.AdjustmentListener *b*);
 public static java.awt.event.ComponentListener **add**(java.awt.event.ComponentListener *a*,
              java.awt.event.ComponentListener *b*);
 public static java.awt.event.ContainerListener **add**(java.awt.event.ContainerListener *a*,
              java.awt.event.ContainerListener *b*);
 public static java.awt.event.FocusListener **add**(java.awt.event.FocusListener *a*, java.awt.event.FocusListener *b*);
1.2 public static java.awt.event.InputMethodListener **add**(java.awt.event.InputMethodListener *a*,
              java.awt.event.InputMethodListener *b*);
 public static java.awt.event.ItemListener **add**(java.awt.event.ItemListener *a*, java.awt.event.ItemListener *b*);
 public static java.awt.event.KeyListener **add**(java.awt.event.KeyListener *a*, java.awt.event.KeyListener *b*);
 public static java.awt.event.MouseListener **add**(java.awt.event.MouseListener *a*, java.awt.event.MouseListener *b*);
 public static java.awt.event.MouseMotionListener **add**(java.awt.event.MouseMotionListener *a*,
              java.awt.event.MouseMotionListener *b*);
 public static java.awt.event.TextListener **add**(java.awt.event.TextListener *a*, java.awt.event.TextListener *b*);
 public static java.awt.event.WindowListener **add**(java.awt.event.WindowListener *a*, java.awt.event.WindowListener *b*);
 public static java.awt.event.ActionListener **remove**(java.awt.event.ActionListener *l*,
              java.awt.event.ActionListener *oldl*);
 public static java.awt.event.AdjustmentListener **remove**(java.awt.event.AdjustmentListener *l*,
              java.awt.event.AdjustmentListener *oldl*);
 public static java.awt.event.ComponentListener **remove**(java.awt.event.ComponentListener *l*,
              java.awt.event.ComponentListener *oldl*);
 public static java.awt.event.ContainerListener **remove**(java.awt.event.ContainerListener *l*,
              java.awt.event.ContainerListener *oldl*);
 public static java.awt.event.FocusListener **remove**(java.awt.event.FocusListener *l*, java.awt.event.FocusListener *oldl*);
1.2 public static java.awt.event.InputMethodListener **remove**(java.awt.event.InputMethodListener *l*,
              java.awt.event.InputMethodListener *oldl*);
 public static java.awt.event.ItemListener **remove**(java.awt.event.ItemListener *l*, java.awt.event.ItemListener *oldl*);
 public static java.awt.event.KeyListener **remove**(java.awt.event.KeyListener *l*, java.awt.event.KeyListener *oldl*);
 public static java.awt.event.MouseListener **remove**(java.awt.event.MouseListener *l*,
              java.awt.event.MouseListener *oldl*);
 public static java.awt.event.MouseMotionListener **remove**(java.awt.event.MouseMotionListener *l*,
              java.awt.event.MouseMotionListener *oldl*);
 public static java.awt.event.TextListener **remove**(java.awt.event.TextListener *l*, java.awt.event.TextListener *oldl*);
 public static java.awt.event.WindowListener **remove**(java.awt.event.WindowListener *l*,
              java.awt.event.WindowListener *oldl*);
// *Protected Class Methods*
 protected static java.util.EventListener **addInternal**(java.util.EventListener *a*, java.util.EventListener *b*);
 protected static java.util.EventListener **removeInternal**(java.util.EventListener *l*, java.util.EventListener *oldl*);
 protected static void **save**(java.io.ObjectOutputStream *s*, String *k*, java.util.EventListener *l*)
  throws java.io.IOException;
// *Methods Implementing ActionListener*
 public void **actionPerformed**(java.awt.event.ActionEvent *e*);
// *Methods Implementing AdjustmentListener*
 public void **adjustmentValueChanged**(java.awt.event.AdjustmentEvent *e*);
// *Methods Implementing ComponentListener*
 public void **componentHidden**(java.awt.event.ComponentEvent *e*);
 public void **componentMoved**(java.awt.event.ComponentEvent *e*);

```
    public void componentResized(java.awt.event.ComponentEvent e);
    public void componentShown(java.awt.event.ComponentEvent e);
// Methods Implementing ContainerListener
    public void componentAdded(java.awt.event.ContainerEvent e);
    public void componentRemoved(java.awt.event.ContainerEvent e);
// Methods Implementing FocusListener
    public void focusGained(java.awt.event.FocusEvent e);
    public void focusLost(java.awt.event.FocusEvent e);
// Methods Implementing InputMethodListener
1.2 public void caretPositionChanged(java.awt.event.InputMethodEvent e);
1.2 public void inputMethodTextChanged(java.awt.event.InputMethodEvent e);
// Methods Implementing ItemListener
    public void itemStateChanged(java.awt.event.ItemEvent e);
// Methods Implementing KeyListener
    public void keyPressed(java.awt.event.KeyEvent e);
    public void keyReleased(java.awt.event.KeyEvent e);
    public void keyTyped(java.awt.event.KeyEvent e);
// Methods Implementing MouseListener
    public void mouseClicked(java.awt.event.MouseEvent e);
    public void mouseEntered(java.awt.event.MouseEvent e);
    public void mouseExited(java.awt.event.MouseEvent e);
    public void mousePressed(java.awt.event.MouseEvent e);
    public void mouseReleased(java.awt.event.MouseEvent e);
// Methods Implementing MouseMotionListener
    public void mouseDragged(java.awt.event.MouseEvent e);
    public void mouseMoved(java.awt.event.MouseEvent e);
// Methods Implementing TextListener
    public void textValueChanged(java.awt.event.TextEvent e);
// Methods Implementing WindowListener
    public void windowActivated(java.awt.event.WindowEvent e);
    public void windowClosed(java.awt.event.WindowEvent e);
    public void windowClosing(java.awt.event.WindowEvent e);
    public void windowDeactivated(java.awt.event.WindowEvent e);
    public void windowDeiconified(java.awt.event.WindowEvent e);
    public void windowIconified(java.awt.event.WindowEvent e);
    public void windowOpened(java.awt.event.WindowEvent e);
// Protected Instance Methods
    protected java.util.EventListener remove(java.util.EventListener oldl);
    protected void saveInternal(java.io.ObjectOutputStream s, String k) throws java.io.IOException;
// Protected Instance Fields
    protected final java.util.EventListener a;
    protected final java.util.EventListener b;
}
```

Hierarchy: Object → AWTEventMulticaster(java.awt.event.ActionListener(java.util.EventListener),
java.awt.event.AdjustmentListener(java.util.EventListener),
java.awt.event.ComponentListener(java.util.EventListener),
java.awt.event.ContainerListener(java.util.EventListener), java.awt.event.FocusListener(java.util.EventListener),
java.awt.event.InputMethodListener(java.util.EventListener), java.awt.event.ItemListener(java.util.EventListener),
java.awt.event.KeyListener(java.util.EventListener), java.awt.event.MouseListener(java.util.EventListener),
java.awt.event.MouseMotionListener(java.util.EventListener), java.awt.event.TextListener(java.util.EventListener),
java.awt.event.WindowListener(java.util.EventListener))

AWTException   Java 1.0

java.awt   *serializable checked PJ1.1*

Signals that an exception has occurred in the java.awt package.

```
public class AWTException extends Exception {
// Public Constructors
     public AWTException(String msg);
}
```

Hierarchy: Object→ Throwable(Serializable)→ Exception→ AWTException

Thrown By: Cursor.getSystemCustomCursor()

AWTPermission   Java 1.2

java.awt   *serializable permission*

This class encapsulates permissions for performing various AWT-related operations; applications do not typically use it. The name, or target, of a permission should be one of the following values: accessClipboard, accessEventQueue, listenToAllAWTEvents, or showWindowWithoutWarningBanner. Alternatively, a name of * implies all of these values. AWTPermission does not use actions, so the *actions* argument to the constructor should be null.

```
public final class AWTPermission extends java.security.BasicPermission {
// Public Constructors
     public AWTPermission(String name);
     public AWTPermission(String name, String actions);
}
```

Hierarchy: Object→ java.security.Permission(java.security.Guard, Serializable)→ java.security.BasicPermission(Serializable)→ AWTPermission

BasicStroke   Java 1.2

java.awt

This class defines properties that control how lines are drawn. By default, lines are one-pixel wide and solid. To change these attributes, pass a BasicStroke (or another implementation of Stroke) to the setStroke() method of a Graphics2D object. BasicStroke supports the following line attribute properties:

lineWidth

The thickness of the line.

endCap

The end cap style of the line. CAP_BUTT specifies that a line ends exactly at its end points, without caps. CAP_SQUARE causes a line to end with square caps that extend beyond the end points by a distance equal to one-half of the line width. CAP_ROUND specifies that a line ends with round caps with a radius of one-half of the line width.

lineJoin

The join style when two line segments meet at the vertex of a shape. JOIN_MITER specifies that the outside edges of the two line segments are extended as far as necessary until they intersect. JOIN_BEVEL causes the outside corners of the vertex to be joined with a straight line. JOIN_ROUND specifies that the vertex is rounded with a curve that has a radius of half the line width.

miterLimit

The maximum length of the miter used to connect two intersecting line segments. When two lines intersect at an acute angle and the line join style is JOIN_MITER, the length of the miter gets progressively longer as the angle between the lines gets

---

smaller. This property imposes a maximum length on the miter; beyond this length, the miter is squared off.

dashArray

The pattern of dashes and spaces that make up a dashed line. This attribute is an array, where the first element and all the additional odd elements specify the lengths of dashes. The second element and all the additional even elements specify the lengths of the spaces. When the dash pattern is complete, it starts over at the beginning of the array, of course.

dashPhase

The distance into the dash pattern that line drawing begins. Note that this value is not an index into the dash array, but a distance. For example, if you've specified a dash of length 5 followed by a space of length 3 and want to begin your line with the space rather than the dash, you set this property to 5.

See Stroke for a discussion of how line drawing is performed in Java 2D.

```
public class BasicStroke implements Stroke {
// Public Constructors
    public BasicStroke();
    public BasicStroke(float width);
    public BasicStroke(float width, int cap, int join);
    public BasicStroke(float width, int cap, int join, float miterlimit);
    public BasicStroke(float width, int cap, int join, float miterlimit, float[ ] dash, float dash_phase);
// Public Constants
    public static final int CAP_BUTT;                                          =0
    public static final int CAP_ROUND;                                         =1
    public static final int CAP_SQUARE;                                        =2
    public static final int JOIN_BEVEL;                                        =2
    public static final int JOIN_MITER;                                        =0
    public static final int JOIN_ROUND;                                        =1
// Property Accessor Methods (by property name)
    public float[ ] getDashArray();                                    default:null
    public float getDashPhase();                                        default:0.0
    public int getEndCap();                                               default:2
    public int getLineJoin();                                             default:0
    public float getLineWidth();                                        default:1.0
    public float getMiterLimit();                                      default:10.0
// Methods Implementing Stroke
    public Shape createStrokedShape(Shape s);
// Public Methods Overriding Object
    public boolean equals(Object obj);
    public int hashCode();
}
```

Hierarchy: Object→ BasicStroke(Stroke)

BorderLayout   Java 1.0

java.awt   *serializable layout manager PJ1.1*

A LayoutManager that arranges components that have been added to their Container (using the Container.add() method) with the names "North", "South", "East", "West", and "Center". These named components are arranged along the edges and in the center of the container. The *hgap* and *vgap* arguments to the BorderLayout constructor specify the desired horizontal and vertical spacing between adjacent components.

In Java 1.1, five constants were defined to represent these strings. In Java 1.2, an additional four constants have been added to represent the four sides of the container in a way that is independent of writing direction. For example, BEFORE_LINE_BEGINS is the same as WEST in locales where text is drawn from left to right, but is the same as EAST in locales where text is drawn from right to left.

Note that an application should never call the LayoutManager methods of this class directly; the Container for which the BorderLayout is registered does this.

In Java 1.1, five constants were defined to represent these strings. In Java 1.2, an additional four constants have been added to represent the four sides of the container in a way that is independent of writing direction. For example, BEFORE_LINE_BEGINS is the same as WEST in locales where text is drawn from left to right but is the same as EAST in locales where text is drawn right to left.

```
public class BorderLayout implements LayoutManager2, Serializable {
// Public Constructors
    public BorderLayout();
    public BorderLayout(int hgap, int vgap);
// Public Constants
1.2 public static final String AFTER_LAST_LINE;                              ="Last"
1.2 public static final String AFTER_LINE_ENDS;                              ="After"
1.2 public static final String BEFORE_FIRST_LINE;                            ="First"
1.2 public static final String BEFORE_LINE_BEGINS;                           ="Before"
1.1 public static final String CENTER;                                       ="Center"
1.1 public static final String EAST;                                         ="East"
1.1 public static final String NORTH;                                        ="North"
1.1 public static final String SOUTH;                                        ="South"
1.1 public static final String WEST;                                         ="West"
// Property Accessor Methods (by property name)
1.1 public int getHgap();                                                   default:0
1.1 public void setHgap(int hgap);
1.1 public int getVgap();                                                   default:0
1.1 public void setVgap(int vgap);
// Methods Implementing LayoutManager
    public void layoutContainer(Container target);
    public Dimension minimumLayoutSize(Container target);
    public Dimension preferredLayoutSize(Container target);
    public void removeLayoutComponent(Component comp);
// Methods Implementing LayoutManager2
1.1 public void addLayoutComponent(Component comp, Object constraints);
1.1 public float getLayoutAlignmentX(Container parent);
1.1 public float getLayoutAlignmentY(Container parent);
1.1 public void invalidateLayout(Container target);                            empty
1.1 public Dimension maximumLayoutSize(Container target);
// Public Methods Overriding Object
    public String toString();
// Deprecated Public Methods
#   public void addLayoutComponent(String name, Component comp);  Implements:LayoutManager
}
```

Hierarchy: Object→ BorderLayout(LayoutManager2(LayoutManager), Serializable)

Button

Java 1.0

java.awt

serializable AWT component PJ1.1

This class represents a GUI push button that displays a specified textual label. Use setActionCommand() to specify an identifying string that is included in the ActionEvent events generated by the button.

```
public class Button extends Component {
// Public Constructors
    public Button();
    public Button(String label);
// Event Registration Methods (by event name)
1.1 public void addActionListener(java.awt.event.ActionListener l);           synchronized
1.1 public void removeActionListener(java.awt.event.ActionListener l);        synchronized
// Property Accessor Methods (by property name)
1.1 public String getActionCommand();                                         default:""
1.1 public void setActionCommand(String command);
    public String getLabel();                                                 default:""
    public void setLabel(String label);
// Public Methods Overriding Component
    public void addNotify();
// Protected Methods Overriding Component
    protected String paramString();
1.1 protected void processEvent(AWTEvent e);
// Protected Instance Methods
1.1 protected void processActionEvent(java.awt.event.ActionEvent e);
}
```

Hierarchy: Object→ Component(java.awt.image.ImageObserver, MenuContainer, Serializable)→ Button

Passed To: Toolkit.createButton()

Canvas

Java 1.0

java.awt

serializable AWT component PJ1.1

A Component that does no default drawing or event handling on its own. You can subclass it to display any kind of drawing or image and handle any kind of user input event. Canvas inherits the event-handling methods of its superclass. In Java 1.1, you can also subclass Component directly to create a lightweight component, instead of having to subclass Canvas.

```
public class Canvas extends Component {
// Public Constructors
    public Canvas();
1.2 public Canvas(GraphicsConfiguration config);
// Public Methods Overriding Component
    public void addNotify();
    public void paint(Graphics g);
}
```

Hierarchy: Object→ Component(java.awt.image.ImageObserver, MenuContainer, Serializable)→ Canvas

Passed To: Toolkit.createCanvas()

CardLayout

Java 1.0

java.awt

serializable layout manager PJ1.1

A LayoutManager that makes each of the components it manages as large as the container and ensures that only one is visible at a time. The standard LayoutManager methods are called by the Container object and should not be called directly by applet or application code. first(), last(), next(), previous(), and show() make a particular Component in the Container visible. The names with which the components are added to the container are used only by the show() method.

```
public class CardLayout implements LayoutManager2, Serializable {
// Public Constructors
     public CardLayout();
     public CardLayout(int hgap, int vgap);
// Property Accessor Methods (by property name)
1.1 public int getHgap();                                                       default:0
1.1 public void setHgap(int hgap);
1.1 public int getVgap();                                                       default:0
1.1 public void setVgap(int vgap);
// Public Instance Methods
     public void first(Container parent);
     public void last(Container parent);
     public void next(Container parent);
     public void previous(Container parent);
     public void show(Container parent, String name);
// Methods Implementing LayoutManager
     public void layoutContainer(Container parent);
     public Dimension minimumLayoutSize(Container parent);
     public Dimension preferredLayoutSize(Container parent);
     public void removeLayoutComponent(Component comp);
// Methods Implementing LayoutManager2
1.1 public void addLayoutComponent(Component comp, Object constraints);
1.1 public float getLayoutAlignmentX(Container parent);
1.1 public float getLayoutAlignmentY(Container parent);
1.1 public void invalidateLayout(Container target);                             empty
1.1 public Dimension maximumLayoutSize(Container target);
// Public Methods Overriding Object
     public String toString();
// Deprecated Public Methods
#    public void addLayoutComponent(String name, Component comp);    Implements:LayoutManager
}
```

Hierarchy: Object→ CardLayout(LayoutManager2(LayoutManager), Serializable)

Checkbox   Java 1.0

java.awt   *serializable AWT component PJ1.1*

This class represents a GUI checkbox with a textual label. The Checkbox maintains a boolean state—whether it is checked or not. The checkbox may optionally be part of a CheckboxGroup that enforces radio button behavior.

```
public class Checkbox extends Component implements ItemSelectable {
// Public Constructors
     public Checkbox();
     public Checkbox(String label);
1.1 public Checkbox(String label, boolean state);
     public Checkbox(String label, CheckboxGroup group, boolean state);
1.1 public Checkbox(String label, boolean state, CheckboxGroup group);
// Event Registration Methods (by event name)
1.1 public void addItemListener(java.awt.event.ItemListener l);       Implements:ItemSelectable synchronized
1.1 public void removeItemListener(java.awt.event.ItemListener l);    Implements:ItemSelectable synchronized
// Property Accessor Methods (by property name)
     public CheckboxGroup getCheckboxGroup();                                   default:null
     public void setCheckboxGroup(CheckboxGroup g);
     public String getLabel();                                                  default:""
```

```
      public void setLabel(String label);
1.1 public Object[ ] getSelectedObjects();                          Implements:ItemSelectable default:null
      public boolean getState();                                                           default:false
      public void setState(boolean state);
// Methods Implementing ItemSelectable
1.1 public void addItemListener(java.awt.event.ItemListener l);                            synchronized
1.1 public Object[ ] getSelectedObjects();                                                  default:null
1.1 public void removeItemListener(java.awt.event.ItemListener l);                         synchronized
// Public Methods Overriding Component
      public void addNotify();
// Protected Methods Overriding Component
      protected String paramString();
1.1 protected void processEvent(AWTEvent e);
// Protected Instance Methods
1.1 protected void processItemEvent(java.awt.event.ItemEvent e);
}
```

Hierarchy: Object→ Component(java.awt.image.ImageObserver, MenuContainer, Serializable)→ Checkbox(ItemSelectable)

Passed To: CheckboxGroup.{setCurrent(), setSelectedCheckbox()}, Toolkit.createCheckbox()

Returned By: CheckboxGroup.{getCurrent(), getSelectedCheckbox()}

CheckboxGroup   Java 1.0
java.awt   serializable PJ1.1

A CheckboxGroup object enforces mutual exclusion (also known as radio button behavior) among any number of Checkbox buttons. A Checkbox component can specify a CheckboxGroup object when created or with its setCheckboxGroup() method. If a Checkbox within a CheckboxGroup object is selected, the CheckboxGroup ensures that the previously selected Checkbox becomes unselected.

```
public class CheckboxGroup implements Serializable {
// Public Constructors
      public CheckboxGroup();
// Property Accessor Methods (by property name)
1.1 public Checkbox getSelectedCheckbox();                                                  default:null
1.1 public void setSelectedCheckbox(Checkbox box);
// Public Methods Overriding Object
      public String toString();
// Deprecated Public Methods
#    public Checkbox getCurrent();                                                           default:null
#    public void setCurrent(Checkbox box);                                                 synchronized
}
```

Hierarchy: Object→ CheckboxGroup(Serializable)

Passed To: Checkbox.{Checkbox(), setCheckboxGroup()}, java.awt.peer.CheckboxPeer.setCheckboxGroup()

Returned By: Checkbox.getCheckboxGroup()

CheckboxMenuItem   Java 1.0
java.awt   serializable AWT component PJ1.1(opt)

This class represents a checkbox with a textual label in a GUI menu. It maintains a boolean state—whether it is checked or not. See also MenuItem.

```
public class CheckboxMenuItem extends MenuItem implements ItemSelectable {
// Public Constructors
1.1 public CheckboxMenuItem();
    public CheckboxMenuItem(String label);
1.1 public CheckboxMenuItem(String label, boolean state);
// Event Registration Methods (by event name)
1.1 public void addItemListener(java.awt.event.ItemListener l);        Implements:ItemSelectable synchronized
1.1 public void removeItemListener(java.awt.event.ItemListener l);     Implements:ItemSelectable synchronized
// Property Accessor Methods (by property name)
1.1 public Object[ ] getSelectedObjects();          Implements:ItemSelectable synchronized default:null
    public boolean getState();                                                    default:false
    public void setState(boolean b);                                             synchronized
// Methods Implementing ItemSelectable
1.1 public void addItemListener(java.awt.event.ItemListener l);                  synchronized
1.1 public Object[ ] getSelectedObjects();                             synchronized default:null
1.1 public void removeItemListener(java.awt.event.ItemListener l);               synchronized
// Public Methods Overriding MenuItem
    public void addNotify();
    public String paramString();
// Protected Methods Overriding MenuItem
1.1 protected void processEvent(AWTEvent e);
// Protected Instance Methods
1.1 protected void processItemEvent(java.awt.event.ItemEvent e);
}
```

Hierarchy: Object → MenuComponent(Serializable) → MenuItem → CheckboxMenuItem(ItemSelectable)

Passed To: Toolkit.createCheckboxMenuItem()

Choice   Java 1.0

java.awt   *serializable AWT component PJ1.1*

This class represents an option menu or dropdown list. The addItem() method adds an item with the specified label to a Choice menu. getSelectedIndex() returns the numerical position of the selected item in the menu, while getSelectedItem() returns the label of the selected item.

```
public class Choice extends Component implements ItemSelectable {
// Public Constructors
    public Choice();
// Event Registration Methods (by event name)
1.1 public void addItemListener(java.awt.event.ItemListener l);        Implements:ItemSelectable synchronized
1.1 public void removeItemListener(java.awt.event.ItemListener l);     Implements:ItemSelectable synchronized
// Property Accessor Methods (by property name)
1.1 public int getItemCount();                                                    default:0
    public int getSelectedIndex();                                               default:-1
    public String getSelectedItem();                                   synchronized default:null
1.1 public Object[ ] getSelectedObjects();          Implements:ItemSelectable synchronized default:null
// Public Instance Methods
1.1 public void add(String item);
    public void addItem(String item);
    public String getItem(int index);
1.1 public void insert(String item, int index);
1.1 public void remove(String item);
1.1 public void remove(int position);
1.1 public void removeAll();
    public void select(String str);                                             synchronized
    public void select(int pos);                                                synchronized
```

```
// Methods Implementing ItemSelectable
1.1 public void addItemListener(java.awt.event.ItemListener l);                                synchronized
1.1 public Object[ ] getSelectedObjects();                                     synchronized default:null
1.1 public void removeItemListener(java.awt.event.ItemListener l);                             synchronized
// Public Methods Overriding Component
    public void addNotify();
// Protected Methods Overriding Component
    protected String paramString();
1.1 protected void processEvent(AWTEvent e);
// Protected Instance Methods
1.1 protected void processItemEvent(java.awt.event.ItemEvent e);
// Deprecated Public Methods
 #  public int countItems();
}
```

Hierarchy: Object→ Component(java.awt.image.ImageObserver, MenuContainer, Serializable)→ Choice(ItemSelectable)

Passed To: Toolkit.createChoice()

Color   Java 1.0
java.awt   serializable PJ1.1

This class describes a color in terms of the individual components of that color. These components are either float values that range between 0 and 1 or 8-bit integers that range from 0 to 255. Prior to Java 1.2, only the RGB (red, green, blue) color space was supported. With the advent of Java 2D, the Color class has been extended to support alpha transparency and arbitrary java.awt.color.ColorSpace objects. In addition, the Java 1.2 Color class implements the Paint interface and is used to perform Java 2D drawing and filling operations that use solid colors.

Color objects can be obtained in a number of ways. The Color() constructors allow color components to be directly specified. The class also defines several color constants. The SystemColor subclass defines other useful Color constants that are related to standard colors used on the system desktop. The static methods HSBtoRGB() and RGBtoHSB() convert between the RGB color space and the HSB (hue, saturation, brightness) color space and can be used to create colors specified using the more intuitive HSB color components. brighter() and darker() return variants on the current color and are useful for creating shading effects.

An RGB color can be expressed as a 24-bit number, where the top 8 bits specifies the red component, the middle 8 bits specifies the green component, and the low 8 bits specifies the blue component. Colors are often represented using a string representation of this 24-bit number. It is particularly common to use a hexadecimal representation for a color, since it keeps the red, green, and blue components distinct. For example, the string "0xFF0000" represents a bright red color: the red component has a value of 255, and both the green and blue components are 0. The static decode() method converts color strings encoded in this way to Color objects. Each getColor() method looks up the specified key in the system properties list and then decodes the value and returns the resulting Color or the specified default color, if no color is found in the properties list.

getRGB() returns the red, green, and blue components of a color as a 24-bit number. getRed(), getBlue(), getGreen(), and getAlpha() return the individual components of a color as integers. getComponents() is a generalized method that returns the color and transparency components of a color in a float array, using an optionally specified ColorSpace. getColorComponents() is similar but returns only the color components, not the transparency component. getRGBComponents() returns the color and alpha components as float values using the RGB color space. getRGBColorComponents() does the same but does not return the alpha component. Each of these methods either fills in the elements of a float[] array you provide or allocates one of its own, if you pass null.

```
public class Color implements Paint, Serializable {
// Public Constructors
    public Color(int rgb);
1.2 public Color(int rgba, boolean hasalpha);
1.2 public Color(java.awt.color.ColorSpace cspace, float[ ] components, float alpha);
    public Color(float r, float g, float b);
    public Color(int r, int g, int b);
1.2 public Color(int r, int g, int b, int a);
1.2 public Color(float r, float g, float b, float a);
// Public Constants
    public static final Color black;
    public static final Color blue;
    public static final Color cyan;
    public static final Color darkGray;
    public static final Color gray;
    public static final Color green;
    public static final Color lightGray;
    public static final Color magenta;
    public static final Color orange;
    public static final Color pink;
    public static final Color red;
    public static final Color white;
    public static final Color yellow;
// Public Class Methods
1.1 public static Color decode(String nm) throws NumberFormatException;
    public static Color getColor(String nm);
    public static Color getColor(String nm, Color v);
    public static Color getColor(String nm, int v);
    public static Color getHSBColor(float h, float s, float b);
    public static int HSBtoRGB(float hue, float saturation, float brightness);
    public static float[ ] RGBtoHSB(int r, int g, int b, float[ ] hsbvals);
// Property Accessor Methods (by property name)
1.2 public int getAlpha();
    public int getBlue();
1.2 public java.awt.color.ColorSpace getColorSpace();
    public int getGreen();
    public int getRed();
    public int getRGB();
1.2 public int getTransparency();                                          Implements:Transparency
// Public Instance Methods
    public Color brighter();
    public Color darker();
1.2 public float[ ] getColorComponents(float[ ] compArray);
1.2 public float[ ] getColorComponents(java.awt.color.ColorSpace cspace, float[ ] compArray);
1.2 public float[ ] getComponents(float[ ] compArray);
1.2 public float[ ] getComponents(java.awt.color.ColorSpace cspace, float[ ] compArray);
1.2 public float[ ] getRGBColorComponents(float[ ] compArray);
1.2 public float[ ] getRGBComponents(float[ ] compArray);
// Methods Implementing Paint
1.2 public PaintContext createContext(java.awt.image.ColorModel cm, Rectangle r,          synchronized
                        java.awt.geom.Rectangle2D r2d,
                        java.awt.geom.AffineTransform xform, RenderingHints hints);
// Methods Implementing Transparency
1.2 public int getTransparency();
```

```
// Public Methods Overriding Object
    public boolean equals(Object obj);
    public int hashCode();
    public String toString();
}
```

Hierarchy: Object→ Color(Paint(Transparency), Serializable)

Subclasses: SystemColor, javax.swing.plaf.ColorUIResource

Passed To: Too many methods to list.

Returned By: Too many methods to list.

Type Of: Too many fields to list.

Component   Java 1.0

java.awt   *serializable AWT component PJ1.1(mod)*

Component is the superclass of all GUI components (except menu components) in the java.awt package. You cannot instantiate a Component directly; you must use a subclass.

Component defines many methods. Some of these are intended to be implemented by subclasses, including some that are for handling events. Other methods are used internally by the AWT. And many are useful utility methods for working with GUI components. getParent() returns the Container that contains a Component. setBackground(), setForeground(), and setFont() set the specified display attributes of a component. hide(), show(), enable(), and disable() perform the specified actions for a component. createImage() creates either an Image object from a specified ImageProducer or an off-screen image that can be drawn into and used for double-buffering during animation. Component also has quite a few deprecated methods, as a result of the Java 1.1 event model and the introduction of the JavaBeans method-naming conventions. The class defines numerous methods for handling many types of events, using the 1.0 and 1.1 event models, in both their high-level and low-level forms.

In Personal Java environments, the setCursor() method can be ignored. Also, the Personal Java API supports the isDoubleBuffered() method, even though it is not part of the Java 1.1 API from which Personal Java is derived.

```
public abstract class Component implements java.awt.image.ImageObserver, MenuContainer, Serializable {
// Protected Constructors
    protected Component();
// Public Constants
1.1 public static final float BOTTOM_ALIGNMENT;                                =1.0
1.1 public static final float CENTER_ALIGNMENT;                                =0.5
1.1 public static final float LEFT_ALIGNMENT;                                  =0.0
1.1 public static final float RIGHT_ALIGNMENT;                                 =1.0
1.1 public static final float TOP_ALIGNMENT;                                   =0.0
// Event Registration Methods (by event name)
1.1 public void addComponentListener(java.awt.event.ComponentListener l);              synchronized
1.1 public void removeComponentListener(java.awt.event.ComponentListener l);           synchronized
1.1 public void addFocusListener(java.awt.event.FocusListener l);                      synchronized
1.1 public void removeFocusListener(java.awt.event.FocusListener l);                   synchronized
1.2 public void addInputMethodListener(java.awt.event.InputMethodListener l);          synchronized
1.2 public void removeInputMethodListener(java.awt.event.InputMethodListener l);       synchronized
1.1 public void addKeyListener(java.awt.event.KeyListener l);                          synchronized
1.1 public void removeKeyListener(java.awt.event.KeyListener l);                       synchronized
1.1 public void addMouseListener(java.awt.event.MouseListener l);                      synchronized
1.1 public void removeMouseListener(java.awt.event.MouseListener l);                   synchronized
1.1 public void addMouseMotionListener(java.awt.event.MouseMotionListener l);          synchronized
```

1.1 public void **removeMouseMotionListener**(java.awt.event.MouseMotionListener *l*);   *synchronized*
1.2 public void **addPropertyChangeListener**(java.beans.PropertyChangeListener *listener*);   *synchronized*
1.2 public void **removePropertyChangeListener**(java.beans.PropertyChangeListener *listener*); *synchronized*
// Property Accessor Methods (by property name)
1.1 public float **getAlignmentX**( );
1.1 public float **getAlignmentY**( );
   public Color **getBackground**( );
   public void **setBackground**(Color *c*);
1.1 public Rectangle **getBounds**( );
1.2 public Rectangle **getBounds**(Rectangle *rv*);
1.1 public void **setBounds**(Rectangle *r*);
1.1 public void **setBounds**(int *x*, int *y*, int *width*, int *height*);
   public java.awt.image.ColorModel **getColorModel**( );
1.2 public ComponentOrientation **getComponentOrientation**( );
1.2 public void **setComponentOrientation**(ComponentOrientation *o*);
1.1 public Cursor **getCursor**( );
1.1 public void **setCursor**(Cursor *cursor*);   *synchronized*
1.2 public boolean **isDisplayable**( );
1.2 public boolean **isDoubleBuffered**( );   *constant*
1.2 public java.awt.dnd.DropTarget **getDropTarget**( );   *synchronized*
1.2 public void **setDropTarget**(java.awt.dnd.DropTarget *dt*);   *synchronized*
   public boolean **isEnabled**( );
1.1 public void **setEnabled**(boolean *b*);
1.1 public boolean **isFocusTraversable**( );
   public Font **getFont**( );   *Implements:MenuContainer*
   public void **setFont**(Font *f*);
   public Color **getForeground**( );
   public void **setForeground**(Color *c*);
   public Graphics **getGraphics**( );
1.2 public int **getHeight**( );
1.2 public java.awt.im.InputContext **getInputContext**( );
1.2 public java.awt.im.InputMethodRequests **getInputMethodRequests**( );   *constant*
1.2 public boolean **isLightweight**( );
1.1 public java.util.Locale **getLocale**( );
1.1 public void **setLocale**(java.util.Locale *l*);
1.1 public Point **getLocation**( );
1.2 public Point **getLocation**(Point *rv*);
1.1 public void **setLocation**(Point *p*);
1.1 public void **setLocation**(int *x*, int *y*);
1.1 public Point **getLocationOnScreen**( );
1.1 public Dimension **getMaximumSize**( );
1.1 public Dimension **getMinimumSize**( );
1.1 public String **getName**( );
1.1 public void **setName**(String *name*);
1.2 public boolean **isOpaque**( );
   public Container **getParent**( );
1.1 public Dimension **getPreferredSize**( );
   public boolean **isShowing**( );
1.1 public Dimension **getSize**( );
1.2 public Dimension **getSize**(Dimension *rv*);
1.1 public void **setSize**(Dimension *d*);
1.1 public void **setSize**(int *width*, int *height*);
   public Toolkit **getToolkit**( );
1.1 public final Object **getTreeLock**( );
   public boolean **isValid**( );
   public boolean **isVisible**( );
1.1 public void **setVisible**(boolean *b*);
1.2 public int **getWidth**( );

```
1.2 public int getX( );
1.2 public int getY( );
// Public Instance Methods
1.1 public void add(PopupMenu popup);                                           synchronized
    public void addNotify( );
1.2 public void addPropertyChangeListener(String propertyName,                  synchronized
                              java.beans.PropertyChangeListener listener);
    public int checkImage(Image image, java.awt.image.ImageObserver observer);
    public int checkImage(Image image, int width, int height, java.awt.image.ImageObserver observer);
1.1 public boolean contains(Point p);
1.1 public boolean contains(int x, int y);
    public Image createImage(java.awt.image.ImageProducer producer);
    public Image createImage(int width, int height);
1.1 public final void dispatchEvent(AWTEvent e);
1.1 public void doLayout( );
1.2 public void enableInputMethods(boolean enable);
1.1 public Component getComponentAt(Point p);
1.1 public Component getComponentAt(int x, int y);
    public FontMetrics getFontMetrics(Font font);
1.2 public boolean hasFocus( );
    public void invalidate( );
    public void list( );
1.1 public void list(java.io.PrintWriter out);
    public void list(java.io.PrintStream out);
1.1 public void list(java.io.PrintWriter out, int indent);
    public void list(java.io.PrintStream out, int indent);
    public void paint(Graphics g);                                              empty
    public void paintAll(Graphics g);
    public boolean prepareImage(Image image, java.awt.image.ImageObserver observer);
    public boolean prepareImage(Image image, int width, int height, java.awt.image.ImageObserver observer);
    public void print(Graphics g);
    public void printAll(Graphics g);
    public void removeNotify( );
1.2 public void removePropertyChangeListener(String propertyName,               synchronized
                              java.beans.PropertyChangeListener listener);
    public void repaint( );
    public void repaint(long tm);
    public void repaint(int x, int y, int width, int height);
    public void repaint(long tm, int x, int y, int width, int height);
    public void requestFocus( );
1.1 public void transferFocus( );
    public void update(Graphics g);
    public void validate( );
// Methods Implementing ImageObserver
    public boolean imageUpdate(Image img, int flags, int x, int y, int w, int h);
// Methods Implementing MenuContainer
    public Font getFont( );
1.1 public void remove(MenuComponent popup);                                    synchronized
// Public Methods Overriding Object
    public String toString( );
// Protected Instance Methods
1.2 protected AWTEvent coalesceEvents(AWTEvent existingEvent, AWTEvent newEvent);
1.1 protected final void disableEvents(long eventsToDisable);
1.1 protected final void enableEvents(long eventsToEnable);
1.2 protected void firePropertyChange(String propertyName, Object oldValue, Object newValue);
    protected String paramString( );
1.1 protected void processComponentEvent(java.awt.event.ComponentEvent e);
1.1 protected void processEvent(AWTEvent e);
```

```
1.1  protected void processFocusEvent(java.awt.event.FocusEvent e);
1.2  protected void processInputMethodEvent(java.awt.event.InputMethodEvent e);
1.1  protected void processKeyEvent(java.awt.event.KeyEvent e);
1.1  protected void processMouseEvent(java.awt.event.MouseEvent e);
1.1  protected void processMouseMotionEvent(java.awt.event.MouseEvent e);
     // Deprecated Public Methods
#    public boolean action(Event evt, Object what);                              constant
#    public Rectangle bounds();
#    public void deliverEvent(Event e);
#    public void disable();
#    public void enable();
#    public void enable(boolean b);
#    public java.awt.peer.ComponentPeer getPeer();
#    public boolean gotFocus(Event evt, Object what);                           constant
#    public boolean handleEvent(Event evt);
#    public void hide();
#    public boolean inside(int x, int y);
#    public boolean keyDown(Event evt, int key);                                constant
#    public boolean keyUp(Event evt, int key);                                  constant
#    public void layout();                                                         empty
#    public Component locate(int x, int y);
#    public Point location();
#    public boolean lostFocus(Event evt, Object what);                          constant
#    public Dimension minimumSize();
#    public boolean mouseDown(Event evt, int x, int y);                         constant
#    public boolean mouseDrag(Event evt, int x, int y);                         constant
#    public boolean mouseEnter(Event evt, int x, int y);                        constant
#    public boolean mouseExit(Event evt, int x, int y);                         constant
#    public boolean mouseMove(Event evt, int x, int y);                         constant
#    public boolean mouseUp(Event evt, int x, int y);                           constant
#    public void move(int x, int y);
#    public void nextFocus();
#    public boolean postEvent(Event e);                            Implements:MenuContainer
#    public Dimension preferredSize();
#    public void reshape(int x, int y, int width, int height);
#    public void resize(Dimension d);
#    public void resize(int width, int height);
#    public void show();
#    public void show(boolean b);
#    public Dimension size();
}
```

Hierarchy: Object→ Component(java.awt.image.ImageObserver, MenuContainer, Serializable)

Subclasses: Button, Canvas, Checkbox, Choice, Container, Label, java.awt.List, Scrollbar, TextComponent, javax.swing.Box.Filler

Passed To: Too many methods to list.

Returned By: Too many methods to list.

Type Of: Too many fields to list.

ComponentOrientation
Java 1.2

java.awt
serializable

This class encapsulates differences in the way characters in GUI components are arranged into lines and the way lines are grouped into blocks. In western languages like English, characters are arranged left to right and lines are arranged top to bottom, but this is not true throughout the world. In Hebrew, for example, characters are arranged from right to left, and in traditional Chinese, characters are arranged from top to bottom.

The isHorizontal() and isLeftToRight() methods specify the necessary orientation information. The class defines two constants for commonly used orientation types. Authors of AWT, Swing, and JavaBeans components may want to take orientation into account when developing their components (see the getComponentOrientation() method of Component). Applications that use these components should typically not have to worry about this class.

You can query the default orientation for a given java.util.Locale by calling the static getOrientation() method. Set the componentOrientation property of all components in a window by passing a ResourceBundle object to the applyResourceBundle() method of a Window. This looks up the "Orientation" resource in the bundle and, if it is not found, uses the default orientation for the locale of the bundle.

```
public final class ComponentOrientation implements Serializable {
// No Constructor
// Public Constants
    public static final ComponentOrientation LEFT_TO_RIGHT;
    public static final ComponentOrientation RIGHT_TO_LEFT;
    public static final ComponentOrientation UNKNOWN;
// Public Class Methods
    public static ComponentOrientation getOrientation(java.util.ResourceBundle bdl);
    public static ComponentOrientation getOrientation(java.util.Locale locale);
// Public Instance Methods
    public boolean isHorizontal();
    public boolean isLeftToRight();
}
```

Hierarchy: Object→ ComponentOrientation(Serializable)

Passed To: Component.setComponentOrientation()

Returned By: Component.getComponentOrientation(), ComponentOrientation.getOrientation()

Type Of: ComponentOrientation.{LEFT_TO_RIGHT, RIGHT_TO_LEFT, UNKNOWN}

Composite   Java 1.2
java.awt

This interface defines how two colors are combined to yield a composite color. When Java 2D performs a drawing operation, it uses a Composite object to combine the colors it wants to draw with the colors that already exist on the screen or in the off-screen image.

The default compositing operation is to draw the new color on top of the color already on the screen. If the new color is fully opaque, the existing color is ignored. If the new color is partially transparent, however, it is combined with the color already on the screen to produce a composite color. To specify a different compositing operation, pass a Composite object to the setComposite() method of a Graphics2D object.

AlphaComposite is a commonly used implementation of Composite; it combines colors in a number of possible ways based on their alpha-transparency levels. AlphaComposite is suitable for most uses; very few applications should have to define a custom implementation of Composite.

Note that the only method of Composite, createContext(), does not perform compositing itself. Instead, it returns a CompositeContext object suitable for compositing colors encoded using the specified color models and rendering hints. It is the CompositeContext object that performs the actual work of combining colors.

```
public abstract interface Composite {
// Public Instance Methods
    public abstract CompositeContext createContext(java.awt.image.ColorModel srcColorModel,
                                                   java.awt.image.ColorModel dstColorModel,
                                                   RenderingHints hints);
}
```

Implementations: AlphaComposite

Passed To: Graphics2D.setComposite()

Returned By: Graphics2D.getComposite()

CompositeContext   Java 1.2

java.awt

This interface defines the methods that do the actual work of compositing colors. The CompositeContext interface is used internally by Java 2D; applications never need to call CompositeContext methods. And only applications that implement a custom Composite class need to implement this interface.

A CompositeContext object holds the state for a particular compositing operation (in multi-threaded programs, there may be several compositing operations in progress at once). A Graphics2D object creates CompositeContext objects as needed by calling the createContext() method of its Composite object.

Once a CompositeContext object has been created, its compose() method is responsible for combining the colors of the first two Raster objects passed to it and storing the resulting colors in the specified WriteableRaster. (This WriteableRaster is usually the same object as one of the first two arguments.) The dispose() method should free any resources held by the CompositeContext. It is called when the Graphics2D no longer requires the Composite-Context.

```
public abstract interface CompositeContext {
// Public Instance Methods
    public abstract void compose(java.awt.image.Raster src, java.awt.image.Raster dstIn,
                                 java.awt.image.WritableRaster dstOut);
    public abstract void dispose();
}
```

Returned By: AlphaComposite.createContext(), Composite.createContext()

Container   Java 1.0

java.awt   *serializable AWT component PJ1.1*

This class implements a component that can contain other components. You cannot instantiate Container directly but must use one of its subclasses, such as Panel, Frame, or Dialog. Once a Container is created, you can set its LayoutManager with setLayout(), add components to it with add(), and remove them with remove(). getComponents() returns an array of the components contained in a Container. locate() determines within which contained component a specified point falls. list() produces helpful debugging output.

```
public class Container extends Component {
// Public Constructors
    public Container();
// Event Registration Methods (by event name)
1.1 public void addContainerListener(java.awt.event.ContainerListener l);        synchronized
1.1 public void removeContainerListener(java.awt.event.ContainerListener l);     synchronized
```

```
// Property Accessor Methods (by property name)
1.1 public float getAlignmentX();                                          Overrides:Component default:0.5
1.1 public float getAlignmentY();                                          Overrides:Component default:0.5
1.1 public int getComponentCount();                                                            default:0
    public Component[ ] getComponents();
1.2 public void setCursor(Cursor cursor);                                  Overrides:Component synchronized
1.2 public void setFont(Font f);                                               Overrides:Component
1.1 public Insets getInsets();
    public LayoutManager getLayout();                                                       default:null
    public void setLayout(LayoutManager mgr);
1.1 public Dimension getMaximumSize();                                        Overrides:Component
1.1 public Dimension getMinimumSize();                                        Overrides:Component
1.1 public Dimension getPreferredSize();                                      Overrides:Component
// Public Instance Methods
    public Component add(Component comp);
1.1 public void add(Component comp, Object constraints);
    public Component add(String name, Component comp);
    public Component add(Component comp, int index);
1.1 public void add(Component comp, Object constraints, int index);
1.2 public Component findComponentAt(Point p);
1.2 public Component findComponentAt(int x, int y);
    public Component getComponent(int n);
1.1 public boolean isAncestorOf(Component c);
    public void paintComponents(Graphics g);
    public void printComponents(Graphics g);
    public void remove(Component comp);
1.1 public void remove(int index);
    public void removeAll();
// Public Methods Overriding Component
    public void addNotify();
1.1 public void doLayout();
1.1 public Component getComponentAt(Point p);
1.1 public Component getComponentAt(int x, int y);
1.1 public void invalidate();
1.1 public void list(java.io.PrintWriter out, int indent);
    public void list(java.io.PrintStream out, int indent);
1.1 public void paint(Graphics g);
1.1 public void print(Graphics g);
    public void removeNotify();
1.1 public void update(Graphics g);
    public void validate();
// Protected Methods Overriding Component
    protected String paramString();
1.1 protected void processEvent(AWTEvent e);
// Protected Instance Methods
1.1 protected void addImpl(Component comp, Object constraints, int index);
1.1 protected void processContainerEvent(java.awt.event.ContainerEvent e);
1.1 protected void validateTree();
// Deprecated Public Methods
#   public int countComponents();
#   public void deliverEvent(Event e);                                       Overrides:Component
#   public Insets insets();
#   public void layout();                                                    Overrides:Component
#   public Component locate(int x, int y);                                   Overrides:Component
#   public Dimension minimumSize();                                          Overrides:Component
#   public Dimension preferredSize();                                        Overrides:Component
}
```

Hierarchy: Object→ Component(java.awt.image.ImageObserver, MenuContainer, Serializable)→ Container

Subclasses: Panel, ScrollPane, Window, javax.swing.Box, javax.swing.CellRendererPane, javax.swing.JComponent, javax.swing.tree.DefaultTreeCellEditor.EditorContainer

Passed To: Too many methods to list.

Returned By: Too many methods to list.

Type Of: javax.swing.JRootPane.contentPane, javax.swing.tree.DefaultTreeCellEditor.editingContainer

Cursor

Java 1.1

java.awt

serializable PJ1.1

This class represents a mouse cursor. It defines a number of constants, which represent the 14 predefined cursors provided by Java 1.0 and Java 1.1. You can pass one of these constants to the constructor to create a cursor of the specified type. Call getType() to determine the type of an existing Cursor object. Since there are only a fixed number of available cursors, the static method getPredefinedCursor() is more efficient than the Cursor() constructor—it maintains a cache of Cursor objects that can be reused. The static getDefaultCursor() method returns the default cursor for the underlying system.

In Java 1.2, the Cursor class has a new getSystemCustomCursor() method that returns a named cursor defined by a system administrator in a systemwide *cursors.properties* file. Since there is no way to query the list of system-specific custom cursors, however, this method is rarely used. Instead, you can create your own custom cursor by calling the createCustomCursor() method of the Toolkit object. You should first check whether custom cursors are supported by calling the getBestCursorSize() method of Toolkit. If this method indicates a width or height of 0, custom cursors are not supported (by either the Java implementation or the underlying windowing system).

```
public class Cursor implements Serializable {
// Public Constructors
     public Cursor(int type);
// Protected Constructors
1.2  protected Cursor(String name);
// Public Constants
     public static final int CROSSHAIR_CURSOR;                              =1
1.2  public static final int CUSTOM_CURSOR;                                 =-1
     public static final int DEFAULT_CURSOR;                                =0
     public static final int E_RESIZE_CURSOR;                               =11
     public static final int HAND_CURSOR;                                   =12
     public static final int MOVE_CURSOR;                                   =13
     public static final int N_RESIZE_CURSOR;                               =8
     public static final int NE_RESIZE_CURSOR;                              =7
     public static final int NW_RESIZE_CURSOR;                              =6
     public static final int S_RESIZE_CURSOR;                               =9
     public static final int SE_RESIZE_CURSOR;                              =5
     public static final int SW_RESIZE_CURSOR;                              =4
     public static final int TEXT_CURSOR;                                   =2
     public static final int W_RESIZE_CURSOR;                               =10
     public static final int WAIT_CURSOR;                                   =3
// Public Class Methods
     public static Cursor getDefaultCursor();
     public static Cursor getPredefinedCursor(int type);
1.2  public static Cursor getSystemCustomCursor(String name) throws AWTException;
// Public Instance Methods
1.2  public String getName();
     public int getType();
```

```
// Public Methods Overriding Object
1.2 public String toString();
// Protected Class Fields
    protected static Cursor[ ] predefined;
// Protected Instance Fields
1.2 protected String name;
}
```

Hierarchy: Object→ Cursor(Serializable)

Passed To: Too many methods to list.

Returned By: Too many methods to list.

Type Of: Cursor.predefined, java.awt.dnd.DragSource.{DefaultCopyDrop, DefaultCopyNoDrop, DefaultLinkDrop, DefaultLinkNoDrop, DefaultMoveDrop, DefaultMoveNoDrop}

Dialog
java.awt

Java 1.0

serializable AWT component PJ1.1(mod)

This class represents a dialog box window. A Dialog can be modal, so that it blocks user input to all other windows until dismissed. It is optional whether a dialog has a title and whether it is resizable. A Dialog object is a Container, so you can add Component objects to it in the normal way with the add() method. The default LayoutManager for Dialog is BorderLayout. You can specify a different LayoutManager object with setLayout(). Call the pack() method of Window to initiate layout management of the dialog and set its initial size appropriately. Call show() to pop a dialog up and setVisible(false) to pop it down. For modal dialogs, show() blocks until the dialog is dismissed. Event handling continues while show() is blocked, using a new event dispatcher thread. In Java 1.0, show() is inherited from Window. Call the Window.dispose() method when the Dialog is no longer needed so that its window system resources may be reused.

In Personal Java environments, support for modeless dialogs is optional, and the Dialog() constructors can throw an exception if you attempt to create a modeless dialog. Also, the setResizable() method is optional, and calls to it can be ignored.

```
public class Dialog extends Window {
// Public Constructors
1.1 public Dialog(Frame owner);
1.2 public Dialog(Dialog owner);
1.2 public Dialog(Dialog owner, String title);
1.1 public Dialog(Frame owner, String title);
    public Dialog(Frame owner, boolean modal);
    public Dialog(Frame owner, String title, boolean modal);
1.2 public Dialog(Dialog owner, String title, boolean modal);
// Property Accessor Methods (by property name)
    public boolean isModal();
1.1 public void setModal(boolean b);
    public boolean isResizable();
    public void setResizable(boolean resizable);
    public String getTitle();
    public void setTitle(String title);                                    synchronized
// Public Methods Overriding Window
    public void addNotify();
1.2 public void dispose();
1.2 public void hide();
1.1 public void show();
```

```
// Protected Methods Overriding Container
    protected String paramString();
}
```

Hierarchy: Object→ Component(java.awt.image.ImageObserver, MenuContainer, Serializable)→ Container→ Window→ Dialog

Subclasses: FileDialog, javax.swing.JDialog

Passed To: Dialog.Dialog(), Toolkit.createDialog(), javax.swing.JDialog.JDialog()

Dimension   Java 1.0

java.awt   *cloneable serializable PJ1.1*

This class contains two integer fields that describe a width and a height of something. The fields are public and can be manipulated directly.

In Java 1.0 and Java 1.1, Dimension is a subclass of Object. In Java 1.2, with the introduction of Java 2D, it has become a concrete subclass of java.awt.geom.Dimension2D. Contrast Dimension with Dimension2D,which represents the width and height with double values.

```
public class Dimension extends java.awt.geom.Dimension2D implements Serializable {
// Public Constructors
    public Dimension();
    public Dimension(Dimension d);
    public Dimension( nt width, int height);
// Public Instance Methods
1.1 public Dimension getSize();
1.1 public void setSize(Dimension d);
1.1 public void setSize(int width, int height);
// Public Methods Overriding Dimension2D
1.2 public double getHeight();                                           default:0.0
1.2 public double getWidth();                                            default:0.0
1.2 public void setSize(double width, double height);
// Public Methods Overriding Object
1.1 public boolean equals(Object obj);
    public String toString();
// Public Instance Fields
    public int height;
    public int width;
}
```

Hierarchy: Object→ java.awt.geom.Dimension2D(Cloneable)→ Dimension(Serializable)

Subclasses: javax.swing.plaf.DimensionUIResource

Passed To: Too many methods to list.

Returned By: Too many methods to list.

Type Of: javax.swing.JTable.preferredViewportSize

Event   Java 1.0

java.awt   *serializable PJ1.1*

This class contains public instance variables that describe some kind of GUI event. In Java 1.1, this class has been superseded by AWTEvent and the java.awt.event package.

The class contains a large number of constants. Some of the constants specify the event type and are values for the id variable. Other constants are values for keys, such as the function keys, that do not have ASCII (Latin-1) values and are set on the key field. Other constants are mask values that are ORed into the modifiers field to describe the state of the modifier keys on the keyboard. The target field is very important—it is the object for which the event occurred. The when field specifies when the event occurred. The x and y fields specify the mouse coordinates at which it occurred. Finally, the arg field is a value specific to the type of the event. Not all fields have valid values for all types of events.

```
public class Event implements Serializable {
// Public Constructors
    public Event(Object target, int id, Object arg);
    public Event(Object target, long when, int id, int x, int y, int key, int modifiers);
    public Event(Object target, long when, int id, int x, int y, int key, int modifiers, Object arg);
// Public Constants
    public static final int ACTION_EVENT;                                    =1001
    public static final int ALT_MASK;                                           =8
1.1 public static final int BACK_SPACE;                                         =8
1.1 public static final int CAPS_LOCK;                                       =1022
    public static final int CTRL_MASK;                                          =2
1.1 public static final int DELETE;                                           =127
    public static final int DOWN;                                            =1005
    public static final int END;                                             =1001
1.1 public static final int ENTER;                                             =10
1.1 public static final int ESCAPE;                                            =27
    public static final int F1;                                              =1008
    public static final int F10;                                             =1017
    public static final int F11;                                             =1018
    public static final int F12;                                             =1019
    public static final int F2;                                              =1009
    public static final int F3;                                              =1010
    public static final int F4;                                              =1011
    public static final int F5;                                              =1012
    public static final int F6;                                              =1013
    public static final int F7;                                              =1014
    public static final int F8;                                              =1015
    public static final int F9;                                              =1016
    public static final int GOT_FOCUS;                                       =1004
    public static final int HOME;                                            =1000
1.1 public static final int INSERT;                                          =1025
    public static final int KEY_ACTION;                                       =403
    public static final int KEY_ACTION_RELEASE;                               =404
    public static final int KEY_PRESS;                                        =401
    public static final int KEY_RELEASE;                                      =402
    public static final int LEFT;                                            =1006
    public static final int LIST_DESELECT;                                    =702
    public static final int LIST_SELECT;                                      =701
    public static final int LOAD_FILE;                                       =1002
    public static final int LOST_FOCUS;                                      =1005
    public static final int META_MASK;                                          =4
    public static final int MOUSE_DOWN;                                       =501
    public static final int MOUSE_DRAG;                                       =506
    public static final int MOUSE_ENTER;                                      =504
    public static final int MOUSE_EXIT;                                       =505
    public static final int MOUSE_MOVE;                                       =503
    public static final int MOUSE_UP;                                         =502
1.1 public static final int NUM_LOCK;                                        =1023
1.1 public static final int PAUSE;                                           =1024
    public static final int PGDN;                                            =1003
    public static final int PGUP;                                            =1002
1.1 public static final int PRINT_SCREEN;                                    =1020
    public static final int RIGHT;                                           =1007
```

public static final int **SAVE_FILE**;	=1003
public static final int **SCROLL_ABSOLUTE**;	=605
1.1 public static final int **SCROLL_BEGIN**;	=606
1.1 public static final int **SCROLL_END**;	=607
public static final int **SCROLL_LINE_DOWN**;	=602
public static final int **SCROLL_LINE_UP**;	=601
1.1 public static final int **SCROLL_LOCK**;	=1021
public static final int **SCROLL_PAGE_DOWN**;	=604
public static final int **SCROLL_PAGE_UP**;	=603
public static final int **SHIFT_MASK**;	=1
1.1 public static final int **TAB**;	=9
public static final int **UP**;	=1004
public static final int **WINDOW_DEICONIFY**;	=204
public static final int **WINDOW_DESTROY**;	=201
public static final int **WINDOW_EXPOSE**;	=202
public static final int **WINDOW_ICONIFY**;	=203
public static final int **WINDOW_MOVED**;	=205

```
// Public Instance Methods
    public boolean controlDown();
    public boolean metaDown();
    public boolean shiftDown();
    public void translate(int x, int y);
// Public Methods Overriding Object
    public String toString();
// Protected Instance Methods
    protected String paramString();
// Public Instance Fields
    public Object arg;
    public int clickCount;
    public Event evt;
    public int id;
    public int key;
    public int modifiers;
    public Object target;
    public long when;
    public int x;
    public int y;
}
```

Hierarchy: Object → Event(Serializable)

Passed To: Too many methods to list.

Type Of: Event.evt

EventQueue

	Java 1.1
java.awt	*PJ1.1*

This class implements an event queue for AWT events in Java 1.1. When an EventQueue is created, a new thread is automatically created and started to remove events from the front of the queue and dispatch them to the appropriate component. It is this thread, created by the EventQueue, that notifies event listeners and executes most of the code in a typical GUI-driven application.

An application can create and use its own private EventQueue, but all AWT events are placed on and dispatched from a single system EventQueue. Use the getSystemEventQueue() method of the Toolkit class to get the system EventQueue object.

getNextEvent() removes and returns the event at the front of the queue. It blocks if there are no events in the queue. peekEvent() returns the event at the front of the queue without removing it from the queue. Passed an optional AWTEvent id field, it returns the first event of the specified type. Finally, postEvent() places a new event on the end of the event queue.

In Java 1.2, EventQueue defines three useful static methods. isDispatchThread() returns true if the calling thread is the AWT event dispatch thread. To avoid thread-safety issues, all modifications to AWT and Swing components should be done from this dispatch thread. If another thread needs to operate on a component, it should wrap the desired operation in a Runnable object and pass that object to invokeLater() or invokeAndWait(). These methods bundle the Runnable object into an ActiveEvent that is placed on the queue. When the ActiveEvent reaches the head of the queue, the Runnable code is invoked by the event dispatch thread and can safely modify any AWT and Swing components. invokeLater() returns immediately, while invokeAndWait() blocks until the Runnable code has been run. It is an error to call invokeAndWait() from the event dispatch thread itself. See also ActiveEvent and javax.swing.SwingUtilities. Except for these useful static methods, most applications do not need to use the EventQueue class at all; they can simply rely on the system to dispatch events automatically.

```
public class EventQueue {
// Public Constructors
     public EventQueue();
// Public Class Methods
1.2 public static void invokeAndWait(Runnable runnable) throws InterruptedException,
          java.lang.reflect.InvocationTargetException;
1.2 public static void invokeLater(Runnable runnable);
1.2 public static boolean isDispatchThread();
// Public Instance Methods
     public AWTEvent getNextEvent() throws InterruptedException;              synchronized
     public AWTEvent peekEvent();                                            synchronized
     public AWTEvent peekEvent(int id);                                      synchronized
     public void postEvent(AWTEvent theEvent);
1.2 public void push(EventQueue newEventQueue);                              synchronized
// Protected Instance Methods
1.2 protected void dispatchEvent(AWTEvent event);
1.2 protected void pop() throws java.util.EmptyStackException;
}
```

Passed To: EventQueue.push()

Returned By: Toolkit.{getSystemEventQueue(), getSystemEventQueueImpl()}

FileDialog   Java 1.0
java.awt   *serializable AWT component PJ1.1(opt)*

This class represents a file selection dialog box. The constants LOAD and SAVE are values of an optional constructor argument that specifies whether the dialog should be an **Open File** dialog or a **Save As** dialog. You may specify a FilenameFilter object to control the files that are displayed in the dialog.

The inherited show() method pops the dialog up. For dialogs of this type, show() blocks, not returning until the user has selected a file and dismissed the dialog (which pops down automatically—you don't have to call hide()). Once show() has returned, use get-File() to get the name of the file the user selected.

```
public class FileDialog extends Dialog {
// Public Constructors
1.1 public FileDialog(Frame parent);
     public FileDialog(Frame parent, String title);
     public FileDialog(Frame parent, String title, int mode);
```

```
// Public Constants
   public static final int LOAD;                                                            =0
   public static final int SAVE;                                                            =1
// Property Accessor Methods (by property name)
   public String getDirectory();
   public void setDirectory(String dir);
   public String getFile();
   public void setFile(String file);
   public java.io.FilenameFilter getFilenameFilter();
   public void setFilenameFilter(java.io.FilenameFilter filter);                   synchronized
   public int getMode();
1.1 public void setMode(int mode);
// Public Methods Overriding Dialog
   public void addNotify();
// Protected Methods Overriding Dialog
   protected String paramString();
}
```

Hierarchy: Object→ Component(java.awt.image.ImageObserver, MenuContainer, Serializable)→
Container→ Window→ Dialog→ FileDialog

Passed To: Toolkit.createFileDialog()

FlowLayout   Java 1.0

java.awt   *serializable layout manager PJ1.1*

A LayoutManager that arranges components in a container likes words on a page: from
left to right and top to bottom. It fits as many components as it can in a row before
moving on to the next row. The constructor allows you to specify one of five constants
as an alignment value for the rows. LEFT, CENTER, and RIGHT specify left, center, and right
alignment, obviously. LEADING and TRAILING alignment are the same as LEFT and RIGHT
alignment in locales where writing is done left to right, but they have the opposite
meaning in locales where writing is done primarily right to left. You can also specify
the horizontal spacing between components and the vertical spacing between rows.

Applications should never call the LayoutManager methods of this class directly; the Container for which the FlowLayout is registered does this.

```
public class FlowLayout implements LayoutManager, Serializable {
// Public Constructors
   public FlowLayout();
   public FlowLayout(int align);
   public FlowLayout(int align, int hgap, int vgap);
// Public Constants
   public static final int CENTER;                                                         =1
1.2 public static final int LEADING;                                                        =3
   public static final int LEFT;                                                           =0
   public static final int RIGHT;                                                          =2
1.2 public static final int TRAILING;                                                       =4
// Property Accessor Methods (by property name)
1.1 public int getAlignment();                                                       default:1
1.1 public void setAlignment(int align);
1.1 public int getHgap();                                                            default:5
1.1 public void setHgap(int hgap);
1.1 public int getVgap();                                                            default:5
1.1 public void setVgap(int vgap);
// Methods Implementing LayoutManager
   public void addLayoutComponent(String name, Component comp);                        empty
```

```
    public void layoutContainer(Container target);
    public Dimension minimumLayoutSize(Container target);
    public Dimension preferredLayoutSize(Container target);
    public void removeLayoutComponent(Component comp);                        empty
// Public Methods Overriding Object
    public String toString();
}
```

Hierarchy: Object → FlowLayout(LayoutManager, Serializable)

Font

Java 1.0

java.awt   *serializable PJ1.1*

This class represents a font. The Font() constructor is passed a name, a style, and a point size. The style should be one of the constants PLAIN, BOLD, or ITALIC or the sum BOLD+ITALIC.

The allowed font names have changed with each release of Java. In Java 1.0, the supported font names are "TimesRoman", "Helvetica", "Courier", "Dialog", "DialogInput", and "Symbol". In Java 1.1, "serif", "sansserif", and "monospaced" should be used in preference to the first three names.

With the introduction of Java 2D, you may continue to use these logical names, but you are not limited to them. In Java 1.2, you may specify the name of any font family available on the system. These are names such as "Times New Roman," "Arial," "New Century Schoolbook," "Bookman," and so on. You can obtain a list of available font families by calling the getAvailableFontFamilyNames() method of GraphicsEnvironment. You may also pass the name of a specific font face to the Font() constructor. These are names such as "Copperplate DemiBold Oblique." When you specify the name of a specific font face, you typically specify a font style of PLAIN, since the style you want is implicit in the name.

With Java 1.2, you can also create a font by passing a Map object that contains attribute names and values to either the Font() constructor or the static getFont() method. The attribute names and values are defined by java.awt.font.TextAttribute. The TextAttribute constants FAMILY, WEIGHT, POSTURE, and SIZE identify the attributes of interest.

In Java 1.2, new fonts can be derived from old fonts in a variety of ways, using the deriveFont() methods. Most generally, the glyphs of a font may all be transformed with the specified AffineTransform.

If you need to know the height or width (or other metrics) of characters or strings drawn using a Font, call the getFontMetrics() method of a Graphics object to obtain a FontMetrics object. The methods of this object return font measurement information as integer values. In Java 1.2, you can obtain higher-precision floating-point font measurements with the getLineMetrics(), getMaxCharBounds(), and getStringBounds() methods of a Font. These methods require a FontRenderContext, which is obtained by calling the getFontRenderContext() method of Graphics2D.

The canDisplay() method tests whether a Font can display a given character (i.e., whether the font contains a glyph for that character). canDisplayUpTo() tests whether the Font can display all the characters in a string and returns the index of the first character it cannot display.

```
public class Font implements Serializable {
// Public Constructors
1.2 public Font(java.util.Map attributes);
    public Font(String name, int style, int size);
```

```
// Public Constants
    public static final int BOLD;                                                              =1
1.2 public static final int CENTER_BASELINE;                                                   =1
1.2 public static final int HANGING_BASELINE;                                                  =2
    public static final int ITALIC;                                                            =2
    public static final int PLAIN;                                                             =0
1.2 public static final int ROMAN_BASELINE;                                                    =0
// Public Class Methods
1.1 public static Font decode(String str);
1.2 public static Font getFont(java.util.Map attributes);
    public static Font getFont(String nm);
    public static Font getFont(String nm, Font font);
// Property Accessor Methods (by property name)
1.2 public java.util.Map getAttributes();
1.2 public java.text.AttributedCharacterIterator.Attribute[ ] getAvailableAttributes();
    public boolean isBold();
    public String getFamily();
1.2 public String getFamily(java.util.Locale l);
1.2 public String getFontName();
1.2 public String getFontName(java.util.Locale l);
    public boolean isItalic();
1.2 public float getItalicAngle();
1.2 public int getMissingGlyphCode();
    public String getName();
1.2 public int getNumGlyphs();
    public boolean isPlain();
1.2 public String getPSName();
    public int getSize();
1.2 public float getSize2D();
    public int getStyle();
1.2 public java.awt.geom.AffineTransform getTransform();
// Public Instance Methods
1.2 public boolean canDisplay(char c);
1.2 public int canDisplayUpTo(String str);
1.2 public int canDisplayUpTo(char[ ] text, int start, int limit);
1.2 public int canDisplayUpTo(java.text.CharacterIterator iter, int start, int limit);
1.2 public java.awt.font.GlyphVector createGlyphVector(java.awt.font.FontRenderContext frc,
                                                    java.text.CharacterIterator ci);
1.2 public java.awt.font.GlyphVector createGlyphVector(java.awt.font.FontRenderContext frc, char[ ] chars);
1.2 public java.awt.font.GlyphVector createGlyphVector(java.awt.font.FontRenderContext frc, int[ ] glyphCodes);
1.2 public java.awt.font.GlyphVector createGlyphVector(java.awt.font.FontRenderContext frc, String str);
1.2 public Font deriveFont(float size);
1.2 public Font deriveFont(int style);
1.2 public Font deriveFont(java.awt.geom.AffineTransform trans);
1.2 public Font deriveFont(java.util.Map attributes);
1.2 public Font deriveFont(int style, java.awt.geom.AffineTransform trans);
1.2 public Font deriveFont(int style, float size);
1.2 public byte getBaselineFor(char c);
1.2 public java.awt.font.LineMetrics getLineMetrics(String str, java.awt.font.FontRenderContext frc);
1.2 public java.awt.font.LineMetrics getLineMetrics(char[ ] chars, int beginIndex, int limit,
                                                    java.awt.font.FontRenderContext frc);
1.2 public java.awt.font.LineMetrics getLineMetrics(java.text.CharacterIterator ci, int beginIndex, int limit,
                                                    java.awt.font.FontRenderContext frc);
1.2 public java.awt.font.LineMetrics getLineMetrics(String str, int beginIndex, int limit,
                                                    java.awt.font.FontRenderContext frc);
1.2 public java.awt.geom.Rectangle2D getMaxCharBounds(java.awt.font.FontRenderContext frc);
1.2 public java.awt.geom.Rectangle2D getStringBounds(String str, java.awt.font.FontRenderContext frc);
1.2 public java.awt.geom.Rectangle2D getStringBounds(char[ ] chars, int beginIndex, int limit,
                                                    java.awt.font.FontRenderContext frc);
```

```
1.2  public java.awt.geom.Rectangle2D getStringBounds(java.text.CharacterIterator ci, int beginIndex, int limit,
                                                       java.awt.font.FontRenderContext frc);
1.2  public java.awt.geom.Rectangle2D getStringBounds(String str, int beginIndex, int limit,
                                                       java.awt.font.FontRenderContext frc);
1.2  public boolean hasUniformLineMetrics();                                                         constant
// Public Methods Overriding Object
     public boolean equals(Object obj);
     public int hashCode();
     public String toString();
// Protected Methods Overriding Object
1.2  protected void finalize() throws Throwable;
// Protected Instance Fields
     protected String name;
1.2  protected float pointSize;
     protected int size;
     protected int style;
// Deprecated Public Methods
1.1# public java.awt.peer.FontPeer getPeer();
}
```

Hierarchy: Object→ Font(Serializable)

Subclasses: javax.swing.plaf.FontUIResource

Passed To: Too many methods to list.

Returned By: Too many methods to list.

Type Of: FontMetrics.font, javax.swing.border.TitledBorder.titleFont, javax.swing.tree.DefaultTreeCellEditor.font

FontMetrics   Java 1.0

java.awt   *serializable PJ1.1*

This class represents font metrics for a specified Font. The methods allow you to determine the overall metrics for the font (ascent, descent, and so on) and compute the width of strings that are to be displayed in a particular font. The FontMetrics() constructor is protected; you can obtain a FontMetrics object for a font with the getFontMetrics() method of Component, Graphics, or Toolkit.

In Java 1.2, with the introduction of Java 2D, you can obtain more precise (floating-point) metrics using the getLineMetrics(), getMaxCharBounds(), and getStringBounds() methods of FontMetrics or a Font object itself. See also java.awt.font.LineMetrics.

```
public abstract class FontMetrics implements Serializable {
// Protected Constructors
     protected FontMetrics(Font font);
// Property Accessor Methods (by property name)
     public int getAscent();
     public int getDescent();                                                                        constant
     public Font getFont();
     public int getHeight();
     public int getLeading();                                                                        constant
     public int getMaxAdvance();                                                                     constant
     public int getMaxAscent();
     public int getMaxDescent();
     public int[ ] getWidths();
// Public Instance Methods
     public int bytesWidth(byte[ ] data, int off, int len);
     public int charsWidth(char[ ] data, int off, int len);
     public int charWidth(int ch);
```

```
    public int charWidth(char ch);
1.2 public java.awt.font.LineMetrics getLineMetrics(String str, Graphics context);
1.2 public java.awt.font.LineMetrics getLineMetrics(char[ ] chars, int beginIndex, int limit, Graphics context);
1.2 public java.awt.font.LineMetrics getLineMetrics(java.text.CharacterIterator ci, int beginIndex, int limit,
                                                                   Graphics context);
1.2 public java.awt.font.LineMetrics getLineMetrics(String str, int beginIndex, int limit, Graphics context);
1.2 public java.awt.geom.Rectangle2D getMaxCharBounds(Graphics context);
1.2 public java.awt.geom.Rectangle2D getStringBounds(String str, Graphics context);
1.2 public java.awt.geom.Rectangle2D getStringBounds(char[ ] chars, int beginIndex, int limit, Graphics context);
1.2 public java.awt.geom.Rectangle2D getStringBounds(java.text.CharacterIterator ci, int beginIndex, int limit,
                                                                   Graphics context);
1.2 public java.awt.geom.Rectangle2D getStringBounds(String str, int beginIndex, int limit, Graphics context);
1.2 public boolean hasUniformLineMetrics();
    public int stringWidth(String str);
// Public Methods Overriding Object
    public String toString();
// Protected Instance Fields
    protected Font font;
// Deprecated Public Methods
#   public int getMaxDecent();
}
```

Hierarchy: Object→ FontMetrics(Serializable)

Passed To: javax.swing.SwingUtilities.{computeStringWidth(), layoutCompoundLabel()}, javax.swing.text.Utilities.{getBreakLocation(), getTabbedTextOffset(), getTabbedTextWidth()}

Returned By: Too many methods to list.

Type Of: javax.swing.text.PlainView.metrics

Frame   Java 1.0

java.awt   *serializable AWT component PJ1.1(mod)*

This class represents an optionally resizable top-level application window with a title-bar and other platform-dependent window decorations. setTitle() specifies a title, set-MenuBar() specifies a menu bar, setCursor() specifies a cursor, and setIconImage() specifies an icon for the window. Call the pack() method of Window to initiate layout management of the window and set its initial size appropriately. Call the show() method of Window to make the window appear and be brought to the top of the window stack. Call setVisible(false) to make the window disappear. Call setState(Frame.ICONIFIED) to iconify the window, and call setState(Frame.NORMAL) to deiconify it. Use getState() to determine whether the window is iconified or not. Call the static getFrames() method to obtain an array of all Frame objects that have been created by the application or applet. Call the dispose() method when the Frame is no longer needed, so that it can release its window system resources for reuse.

The constants defined by this class specify various cursor types. As of Java 1.1, these constants and the cursor methods of Frame are deprecated in favor of the Cursor class and cursor methods of Component.

Personal Java environments can support only a single Frame object, and any calls to the Frame() constructor after the first can throw an exception.

```
public class Frame extends Window implements MenuContainer {
// Public Constructors
    public Frame();
    public Frame(String title);
```

```
// Public Constants
1.2 public static final int ICONIFIED;                                              =1
1.2 public static final int NORMAL;                                                 =0
// Public Class Methods
1.2 public static Frame[ ] getFrames();
// Property Accessor Methods (by property name)
    public Image getIconImage();                                            default:null
    public void setIconImage(Image image);                                 synchronized
    public MenuBar getMenuBar();                                            default:null
    public void setMenuBar(MenuBar mb);
    public boolean isResizable();                                           default:true
    public void setResizable(boolean resizable);
1.2 public int getState();                                        synchronized default:0
1.2 public void setState(int state);                                       synchronized
    public String getTitle();                                               default:""
    public void setTitle(String title);                                    synchronized
// Methods Implementing MenuContainer
    public void remove(MenuComponent m);
// Public Methods Overriding Window
    public void addNotify();
// Protected Methods Overriding Window
1.2 protected void finalize() throws Throwable;
// Public Methods Overriding Container
1.2 public void removeNotify();
// Protected Methods Overriding Container
    protected String paramString();
// Deprecated Public Methods
#   public int getCursorType();                                              default:0
#   public void setCursor(int cursorType);                                 synchronized
// Deprecated Public Fields
#   public static final int CROSSHAIR_CURSOR;                                     =1
#   public static final int DEFAULT_CURSOR;                                      =0
#   public static final int E_RESIZE_CURSOR;                                    =11
#   public static final int HAND_CURSOR;                                        =12
#   public static final int MOVE_CURSOR;                                        =13
#   public static final int N_RESIZE_CURSOR;                                     =8
#   public static final int NE_RESIZE_CURSOR;                                    =7
#   public static final int NW_RESIZE_CURSOR;                                    =6
#   public static final int S_RESIZE_CURSOR;                                     =9
#   public static final int SE_RESIZE_CURSOR;                                    =5
#   public static final int SW_RESIZE_CURSOR;                                    =4
#   public static final int TEXT_CURSOR;                                         =2
#   public static final int W_RESIZE_CURSOR;                                    =10
#   public static final int WAIT_CURSOR;                                         =3
}
```

Hierarchy: Object→ Component(java.awt.image.ImageObserver, MenuContainer, Serializable)→ Container→ Window→ Frame(MenuContainer)

Subclasses: javax.swing.JFrame

Passed To: Too many methods to list.

Returned By: Frame.getFrames(), javax.swing.JOptionPane.{getFrameForComponent(), getRootFrame()}

GradientPaint
java.awt
Java 1.2

This implementation of Paint fills shapes with a color gradient. To use a GradientPaint object for filling shapes, pass it to the setPaint() method of a Graphics2D object.

The color of the fill varies linearly between a color C1 and another color C2. The orientation of the color gradient is defined by a line between points P1 and P2. For example, if these points define a horizontal line, the color of the fill varies from left to right. If P1 is at the upper left of a rectangle and P2 is at the lower right, the fill color varies from upper left to lower right.

Color C1 is always used at point P1 and color C2 is used at P2. If the area to be filled includes points outside of the fill region defined by P1 and P2, these points can be filled in one of two ways. If the GradientPaint object is created with the *cyclic* constructor argument set to true, colors repeatedly cycle from C1 to C2 and back to C1 again. If *cyclic* is specified as false or if this argument is omitted, the gradient does not repeat. When an acyclic GradientPaint object is used, all points beyond P1 are given the color C1, and all points beyond C2 are given the color P2.

```
public class GradientPaint implements Paint {
// Public Constructors
    public GradientPaint(java.awt.geom.Point2D pt1, Color color1, java.awt.geom.Point2D pt2, Color color2);
    public GradientPaint(java.awt.geom.Point2D pt1, Color color1, java.awt.geom.Point2D pt2, Color color2,
                    boolean cyclic);
    public GradientPaint(float x1, float y1, Color color1, float x2, float y2, Color color2);
    public GradientPaint(float x1, float y1, Color color1, float x2, float y2, Color color2, boolean cyclic);
// Property Accessor Methods (by property name)
    public Color getColor1();
    public Color getColor2();
    public boolean isCyclic();
    public java.awt.geom.Point2D getPoint1();
    public java.awt.geom.Point2D getPoint2();
    public int getTransparency();                                          Implements:Transparency
// Methods Implementing Paint
    public PaintContext createContext(java.awt.image.ColorModel cm, Rectangle deviceBounds,
                    java.awt.geom.Rectangle2D userBounds, java.awt.geom.AffineTransform xform,
                    RenderingHints hints);
// Methods Implementing Transparency
    public int getTransparency();
}
```

Hierarchy: Object→ GradientPaint(Paint(Transparency))

Graphics
java.awt
Java 1.0
PJ1.1(mod)

This abstract class defines a device-independent interface to graphics. It specifies methods for drawing lines, filling areas, painting images, copying areas, and clipping graphics output. Specific subclasses of Graphics are implemented for different platforms and different graphics output devices. A Graphics object cannot be created directly through a constructor—it must either be obtained with the getGraphics() method of a Component or an Image or copied from an existing Graphics object with create(). When a Graphics object is no longer needed, you should call dispose() to free up the window system resources it uses.

In Personal Java environments, the setXORMode() method may be unsupported.

```
public abstract class Graphics {
// Protected Constructors
    protected Graphics();
// Property Accessor Methods (by property name)
1.1 public abstract Shape getClip();
1.1 public abstract void setClip(Shape clip);
1.1 public abstract void setClip(int x, int y, int width, int height);
1.1 public abstract Rectangle getClipBounds();
1.2 public Rectangle getClipBounds(Rectangle r);
    public abstract Color getColor();
    public abstract void setColor(Color c);
    public abstract Font getFont();
    public abstract void setFont(Font font);
    public FontMetrics getFontMetrics();
    public abstract FontMetrics getFontMetrics(Font f);
// Public Instance Methods
    public abstract void clearRect(int x, int y, int width, int height);
    public abstract void clipRect(int x, int y, int width, int height);
    public abstract void copyArea(int x, int y, int width, int height, int dx, int dy);
    public abstract Graphics create();
    public Graphics create(int x, int y, int width, int height);
    public abstract void dispose();
    public void draw3DRect(int x, int y, int width, int height, boolean raised);
    public abstract void drawArc(int x, int y, int width, int height, int startAngle, int arcAngle);
    public void drawBytes(byte[ ] data, int offset, int length, int x, int y);
    public void drawChars(char[ ] data, int offset, int length, int x, int y);
    public abstract boolean drawImage(Image img, int x, int y, java.awt.image.ImageObserver observer);
    public abstract boolean drawImage(Image img, int x, int y, Color bgcolor, java.awt.image.ImageObserver observer);
    public abstract boolean drawImage(Image img, int x, int y, int width, int height,
                                      java.awt.image.ImageObserver observer);
    public abstract boolean drawImage(Image img, int x, int y, int width, int height, Color bgcolor,
                                      java.awt.image.ImageObserver observer);
1.1 public abstract boolean drawImage(Image img, int dx1, int dy1, int dx2, int dy2, int sx1, int sy1, int sx2, int sy2,
                                      java.awt.image.ImageObserver observer);
1.1 public abstract boolean drawImage(Image img, int dx1, int dy1, int dx2, int dy2, int sx1, int sy1, int sx2, int sy2,
                                      Color bgcolor, java.awt.image.ImageObserver observer);
    public abstract void drawLine(int x1, int y1, int x2, int y2);
    public abstract void drawOval(int x, int y, int width, int height);
    public void drawPolygon(Polygon p);
    public abstract void drawPolygon(int[ ] xPoints, int[ ] yPoints, int nPoints);
1.1 public abstract void drawPolyline(int[ ] xPoints, int[ ] yPoints, int nPoints);
    public void drawRect(int x, int y, int width, int height);
    public abstract void drawRoundRect(int x, int y, int width, int height, int arcWidth, int arcHeight);
1.2 public abstract void drawString(java.text.AttributedCharacterIterator iterator, int x, int y);
    public abstract void drawString(String str, int x, int y);
    public void fill3DRect(int x, int y, int width, int height, boolean raised);
    public abstract void fillArc(int x, int y, int width, int height, int startAngle, int arcAngle);
    public abstract void fillOval(int x, int y, int width, int height);
    public void fillPolygon(Polygon p);
    public abstract void fillPolygon(int[ ] xPoints, int[ ] yPoints, int nPoints);
    public abstract void fillRect(int x, int y, int width, int height);
    public abstract void fillRoundRect(int x, int y, int width, int height, int arcWidth, int arcHeight);
1.2 public boolean hitClip(int x, int y, int width, int height);
    public abstract void setPaintMode();
    public abstract void setXORMode(Color c1);
    public abstract void translate(int x, int y);
// Public Methods Overriding Object
    public void finalize();
```

```
   public String toString();
// Deprecated Public Methods
#   public Rectangle getClipRect();
}
```

Subclasses: Graphics2D, javax.swing.DebugGraphics

Passed To: Too many methods to list.

Returned By: Component.getGraphics(), Graphics.create(), Image.getGraphics(), PrintJob.getGraphics(), java.awt.image.BufferedImage.getGraphics(), java.awt.peer.ComponentPeer.getGraphics(), javax.swing.DebugGraphics.create(), javax.swing.JComponent.{getComponentGraphics(), getGraphics()}

Graphics2D   Java 1.2
java.awt

This class is the Java 2D graphics context that encapsulates all drawing and filling operations. It generalizes and extends the Graphics class. A number of attributes control how the Graphics2D object performs drawing and filling operations. You can set these attributes with the following methods:

setBackground()
> Specifies the background color used by the clearRect() method of the Graphics object. Prior to Java 2D, the background color could not be set.

setClip()
> Sets the clipping region, outside of which no drawing is done. This method is inherited from the Graphics object. Use setClip() to establish an initial clipping region and then use clip() to narrow that region by intersecting it with other regions.

setComposite()
> Specifies a Composite object (typically an instance of AlphaComposite) that should be used to combine drawing colors with the colors that are already present on the drawing surface.

setFont()
> Sets the default Font object used to draw text. This is a Graphics method, inherited by Graphics2D.

setPaint()
> Specifies the Paint object that controls the color or pattern used for drawing. See Color, GradientPaint, and TexturePaint.

setRenderingHints()
> Sets hints about how drawing should be done. This method allows you to turn antialiasing and color dithering on and off, for example. You can also set hints with addRenderingHints() and setRenderingHint().

setStroke()
> Specifies the Stroke object (typically an instance of BasicStroke) used to trace the outline of shapes that are drawn. The Stroke object effectively defines the pen that is used for drawing operations.

setTransform()
> Sets the AffineTransform object used to convert from user coordinates to device coordinates. Note that you do not usually call setTransform() directly, but instead modify the current transform with transform() or the more specific rotate(), scale(), shear(), and translate() methods.

Once you have used these methods to configure a Graphics2D object as desired, you can proceed to draw with it. The following methods are commonly used:

draw()
> Draw the outline of a Shape, using the line style specified by the current Stroke object and the color or pattern specified by the current Paint object. The java.awt.geom package contains a number of commonly used implementations of the Shape interface.

fill() Fill the interior of a Shape, using the color or pattern specified by the current Paint object.

drawString()
> Draw the specified text using the specified Font object and Paint object. drawGlyph-Vector() is similar. See also the drawString() methods inherited from Graphics.

drawImage()
> Draw an Image with an optional filtering operation and/or an optional transformation. Also drawRenderableImage() and drawRenderedImage(). See also the drawImage() methods inherited from Graphics.

```
public abstract class Graphics2D extends Graphics {
// Protected Constructors
    protected Graphics2D();
// Property Accessor Methods (by property name)
    public abstract Color getBackground();
    public abstract void setBackground(Color color);
    public abstract Composite getComposite();
    public abstract void setComposite(Composite comp);
    public abstract GraphicsConfiguration getDeviceConfiguration();
    public abstract java.awt.font.FontRenderContext getFontRenderContext();
    public abstract Paint getPaint();
    public abstract void setPaint(Paint paint);
    public abstract RenderingHints getRenderingHints();
    public abstract void setRenderingHints(java.util.Map hints);
    public abstract Stroke getStroke();
    public abstract void setStroke(Stroke s);
    public abstract java.awt.geom.AffineTransform getTransform();
    public abstract void setTransform(java.awt.geom.AffineTransform Tx);
// Public Instance Methods
    public abstract void addRenderingHints(java.util.Map hints);
    public abstract void clip(Shape s);
    public abstract void draw(Shape s);
    public abstract void drawGlyphVector(java.awt.font.GlyphVector g, float x, float y);
    public abstract boolean drawImage(Image img, java.awt.geom.AffineTransform xform,
                                      java.awt.image.ImageObserver obs);
    public abstract void drawImage(java.awt.image.BufferedImage img, java.awt.image.BufferedImageOp op, int x,
                                   int y);
    public abstract void drawRenderableImage(java.awt.image.renderable.RenderableImage img,
                                             java.awt.geom.AffineTransform xform);
    public abstract void drawRenderedImage(java.awt.image.RenderedImage img,
                                           java.awt.geom.AffineTransform xform);
    public abstract void drawString(java.text.AttributedCharacterIterator iterator, float x, float y);
    public abstract void drawString(String s, float x, float y);
    public abstract void fill(Shape s);
    public abstract Object getRenderingHint(RenderingHints.Key hintKey);
    public abstract boolean hit(Rectangle rect, Shape s, boolean onStroke);
    public abstract void rotate(double theta);
```

```
    public abstract void rotate(double theta, double x, double y);
    public abstract void scale(double sx, double sy);
    public abstract void setRenderingHint(RenderingHints.Key hintKey, Object hintValue);
    public abstract void shear(double shx, double shy);
    public abstract void transform(java.awt.geom.AffineTransform Tx);
    public abstract void translate(double tx, double ty);
// Public Methods Overriding Graphics
    public void draw3DRect(int x, int y, int width, int height, boolean raised);
    public abstract void drawString(java.text.AttributedCharacterIterator iterator, int x, int y);
    public abstract void drawString(String str, int x, int y);
    public void fill3DRect(int x, int y, int width, int height, boolean raised);
    public abstract void translate(int x, int y);
}
```

Hierarchy: Object→ Graphics→ Graphics2D

Passed To: java.awt.font.GraphicAttribute.draw(), java.awt.font.ImageGraphicAttribute.draw(), java.awt.font.ShapeGraphicAttribute.draw(), java.awt.font.TextLayout.draw()

Returned By: GraphicsEnvironment.createGraphics(), java.awt.image.BufferedImage.createGraphics()

GraphicsConfigTemplate   Java 1.2

java.awt   *serializable*

This abstract class is designed to support a matching operation that selects the best configuration from an array of GraphicsConfiguration objects. The best configuration is defined as the one that most closely matches the desired criteria. GraphicsConfigTemplate does not define what those criteria might be, however: the criteria and the matching algorithm are left entirely to the concrete subclass that provides definitions of the abstract methods.

This class in not commonly used. There are not any implementations of GraphicsConfigTemplate built into Java 1.2. On many platforms, such as Windows, a screen has only one available GraphicsConfiguration, so there is never a need to try to find the best one.

```
public abstract class GraphicsConfigTemplate implements Serializable {
// Public Constructors
    public GraphicsConfigTemplate();
// Public Constants
    public static final int PREFERRED;                                    =2
    public static final int REQUIRED;                                     =1
    public static final int UNNECESSARY;                                  =3
// Public Instance Methods
    public abstract GraphicsConfiguration getBestConfiguration(GraphicsConfiguration[ ] gc);
    public abstract boolean isGraphicsConfigSupported(GraphicsConfiguration gc);
}
```

Hierarchy: Object→ GraphicsConfigTemplate(Serializable)

Passed To: GraphicsDevice.getBestConfiguration()

GraphicsConfiguration   Java 1.2

java.awt

This class describes a configuration of a graphics device. It stores information about the available resolution and colors of the device.

Resolution information is stored in the form of AffineTransform objects. getDefaultTransform() returns the default transform used to map user coordinates to device coordinates. For screen devices, this is usually an identity transform: by default, user coordinates are measured in screen pixels. For printers, the default transform is such that 72 units in user space maps to one inch on the printed page. getNormalizingTransform() returns an AffineTransform that, when concatenated to the default transform, yields a coordinate system in which 72 units of user space equal one inch on the screen or on a printed piece of paper. (For printers, this normalizing transform is obviously the identity transform, since the default transform is already 72 units to the inch.)

Color information about the device is returned by getColorModel(), in the form of a java.awt.image.ColorModel object. A ColorModel maps pixel values to their individual color components. The zero-argument form of getColorModel() returns the default color model for the configuration. If you pass one of the constants defined by the Transparency interface, the method returns a ColorModel object suitable for the configuration and the specified level of transparency.

createCompatibleImage() creates an off-screen BufferedImage object with the specified size and transparency that is compatible with the device color model. However, that most applications create off-screen images using a higher-level method, such as the createImage() method of Component.

See also GraphicsDevice and GraphicsEnvironment.

```
public abstract class GraphicsConfiguration {
// Protected Constructors
    protected GraphicsConfiguration();
// Property Accessor Methods (by property name)
    public abstract java.awt.image.ColorModel getColorModel();
    public abstract java.awt.image.ColorModel getColorModel(int transparency);
    public abstract java.awt.geom.AffineTransform getDefaultTransform();
    public abstract GraphicsDevice getDevice();
    public abstract java.awt.geom.AffineTransform getNormalizingTransform();
// Public Instance Methods
    public abstract java.awt.image.BufferedImage createCompatibleImage(int width, int height);
    public abstract java.awt.image.BufferedImage createCompatibleImage(int width, int height, int transparency);
}
```

Passed To: Canvas.Canvas(), GraphicsConfigTemplate.{getBestConfiguration(), isGraphicsConfigSupported()}

Returned By: Graphics2D.getDeviceConfiguration(), GraphicsConfigTemplate.getBestConfiguration(), GraphicsDevice.{getBestConfiguration(), getConfigurations(), getDefaultConfiguration()}

GraphicsDevice   Java 1.2

java.awt

The GraphicsDevice class represents a device capable of displaying graphics, such as a computer monitor, a printer, or an off-screen image.

A GraphicsDevice object stores the type of the device (getType()) and an identifying string (getIDString()). More importantly, it contains a list of possible configurations of the device. For example, a screen may be configured at different resolutions and color depths. This configuration information is stored by the GraphicsDevice as GraphicsConfiguration objects.

GraphicsDevice does not have a public constructor. Instances that represent screen devices can be obtained by calling the getDefaultScreenDevice() method of GraphicsEnvironment. More generally, the GraphicsDevice used by any Graphics2D object can be obtained by calling getDeviceConfiguration() on that object to obtain a GraphicsConfiguration, and then calling getDevice() on that object to get its GraphicsDevice.

```
public abstract class GraphicsDevice {
// Protected Constructors
    protected GraphicsDevice();
// Public Constants
    public static final int TYPE_IMAGE_BUFFER;                                        =2
    public static final int TYPE_PRINTER;                                             =1
    public static final int TYPE_RASTER_SCREEN;                                       =0
// Property Accessor Methods (by property name)
    public abstract Graph csConfiguration[ ] getConfigurations();
    public abstract Graph csConfiguration getDefaultConfiguration();
    public abstract String getIDstring();
    public abstract int getType();
// Public Instance Methods
    public GraphicsConfiguration getBestConfiguration(GraphicsConfigTemplate gct);
}
```

Returned By: GraphicsConfiguration.getDevice(), GraphicsEnvironment.{getDefaultScreenDevice(), getScreenDevices()}

GraphicsEnvironment   Java 1.2

java.awt

This class describes a Java 2D graphics environment. This class does not have a public constructor; use getLocalGraphicsEnvironment() to obtain the GraphicsEnvironment object that represents the environment available to the Java VM.

A graphics environment consists of a list of available screens and a list of available fonts. The screens are represented by GraphicsDevice objects. Use getDefaultScreenDevice() to obtain information about the default screen. Although the GraphicsDevice class can also describe printers and off-screen images, the methods of GraphicsEnvironment return only screen devices. Therefore, it is not possible to use the GraphicsEnvironment class to query the available printers.

getAllFonts() returns a list of all fonts available on the system. Use caution when calling this method, however, because on some systems it can take a long time to enumerate all installed fonts. Note that the fonts returned by this method all have a size of 1 unit; a font must be scaled to the desired size by calling deriveFont() on the Font. When possible, it is usually better to call getAvailableFontFamilyNames() to list available font families, then create only the individual Font objects desired.

See also GraphicsDevice and GraphicsConfiguration.

```
public abstract class GraphicsEnvironment {
// Protected Constructors
    protected GraphicsEnvironment();
// Public Class Methods
    public static GraphicsEnvironment getLocalGraphicsEnvironment();
// Property Accessor Methods (by property name)
    public abstract Font[ ] getAllFonts();
    public abstract String[ ] getAvailableFontFamilyNames();
    public abstract String[ ] getAvailableFontFamilyNames(java.util.Locale l);
    public abstract GraphicsDevice getDefaultScreenDevice();
    public abstract GraphicsDevice[ ] getScreenDevices();
// Public Instance Methods
    public abstract Graphics2D createGraphics(java.awt.image.BufferedImage img);
}
```

Returned By: GraphicsEnvironment.getLocalGraphicsEnvironment()

GridBagConstraints

java.awt

This class encapsulates the instance variables that tell a GridBagLayout how to position a given Component within its Container:

gridx, gridy
> The grid position of the component. The RELATIVE constant specifies a position to the right of or below the previous component.

gridwidth, gridheight
> The height and width of the component in grid cells. The constant REMAINDER specifies that the component is the last one and should get all remaining cells.

fill The dimensions of a component that should grow when the space available for it is larger than its default size. Legal values are the constants NONE, BOTH, HORIZONTAL, and VERTICAL.

ipadx, ipady
> Internal padding to add on each side of the component in each dimension. This padding increases the size of the component beyond its default minimum size.

insets
> An Insets object that specifies margins to appear on all sides of the component.

anchor
> How the component should be displayed within its grid cells when it is smaller than those cells. The CENTER constant and the compass-point constants are legal values.

weightx, weighty
> How extra space in the container should be distributed among its components in the X and Y dimensions. Larger weights specify that a component should receive a proportionally larger amount of extra space. A 0 weight indicates that the component should not receive any extra space. These weights specify the resizing behavior of the component and its container.

See also GridBagLayout.

```
public class GridBagConstraints implements Cloneable, Serializable {
// Public Constructors
    public GridBagConstraints();
1.2 public GridBagConstraints(int gridx, int gridy, int gridwidth, int gridheight, double weightx, double weighty,
                               int anchor, int fill, Insets insets, int ipadx, int ipady);
// Public Constants
    public static final int BOTH;                                                              =1
    public static final int CENTER;                                                           =10
    public static final int EAST;                                                             =13
    public static final int HORIZONTAL;                                                        =2
    public static final int NONE;                                                              =0
    public static final int NORTH;                                                            =11
    public static final int NORTHEAST;                                                        =12
    public static final int NORTHWEST;                                                        =18
    public static final int RELATIVE;                                                         =-1
    public static final int REMAINDER;                                                         =0
    public static final int SOUTH;                                                            =15
    public static final int SOUTHEAST;                                                        =14
    public static final int SOUTHWEST;                                                        =16
    public static final int VERTICAL;                                                          =3
```

```
      public static final int WEST;                                            =17
// Public Methods Overriding Object
      public Object clone();
// Public Instance Fields
      public int anchor;
      public int fill;
      public int gridheight;
      public int gridwidth;
      public int gridx;
      public int gridy;
      public Insets insets;
      public int ipadx;
      public int ipady;
      public double weightx;
      public double weighty;
}
```

Hierarchy: Object → GridBagConstraints(Cloneable, Serializable)

Passed To: GridBagLayout.{AdjustForGravity(), setConstraints()}

Returned By: GridBagLayout.{getConstraints(), lookupConstraints()}

Type Of: GridBagLayout.defaultConstraints

GridBagLayout   Java 1.0
java.awt   *serializable layout manager PJ1.1*

The most complicated and most powerful LayoutManager in the java.awt package. Grid-BagLayout divides a container into a grid of rows and columns (that need not have the same width and height) and places the components into this grid, adjusting the size of the grid cells as necessary to ensure that components do not overlap. Each component controls how it is positioned within this grid by specifying a number of variables (or constraints) in a GridBagConstraints object. Do not confuse this class with the much simpler GridLayout, which arranges components in a grid of equally sized cells.

Use setConstraints() to specify a GridBagConstraints object for each of the components in the container. Or, as of Java 1.1, specify the GridBagConstraints object when adding the component to the container with add(). The variables in this object specify the position of the component in the grid and the number of horizontal and vertical grid cells that the component occupies and also control other important aspects of component layout. See GridBagConstraints for more information on these constraint variables. setConstraints() makes a copy of the constraints object, so you may reuse a single object in your code.

Applications should never call the LayoutManager methods of this class directly; the Container for which the GridBagLayout is registered does this.

```
public class GridBagLayout implements LayoutManager2, Serializable {
// Public Constructors
      public GridBagLayout();
// Protected Constants
      protected static final int MAXGRIDSIZE;                                  =512
      protected static final int MINSIZE;                                      =1
      protected static final int PREFERREDSIZE;                                =2
// Property Accessor Methods (by property name)
      public int[ ][ ] getLayoutDimensions();
      public Point getLayoutOrigin();
      public double[ ][ ] getLayoutWeights();
```

```
// Public Instance Methods
   public GridBagConstraints getConstraints(Component comp);
   public Point location(int x, int y);
   public void setConstraints(Component comp, GridBagConstraints constraints);
// Methods Implementing LayoutManager
   public void addLayoutComponent(String name, Component comp);                empty
   public void layoutContainer(Container parent);
   public Dimension minimumLayoutSize(Container parent);
   public Dimension preferredLayoutSize(Container parent);
   public void removeLayoutComponent(Component comp);
// Methods Implementing LayoutManager2
11 public void addLayoutComponent(Component comp, Object constraints);
11 public float getLayoutAlignmentX(Container parent);
11 public float getLayoutAlignmentY(Container parent);
11 public void invalidateLayout(Container target);                             empty
1.1 public Dimension maximumLayoutSize(Container target);
// Public Methods Overriding Object
   public String toString();
// Protected Instance Methods
   protected void AdjustForGravity(GridBagConstraints constraints, Rectangle r);
   protected void ArrangeGrid(Container parent);
   protected GridBagLayoutInfo GetLayoutInfo(Container parent, int sizeflag);
   protected Dimension GetMinSize(Container parent, GridBagLayoutInfo info);
   protected GridBagConstraints lookupConstraints(Component comp);
// Public Instance Fields
   public double[ ] columnWeights;
   public int[ ] columnWidths;
   public int[ ] rowHeights;
   public double[ ] rowWeights;
// Protected Instance Fields
   protected java.util.Hashtable comptable;
   protected GridBagConstraints defaultConstraints;
   protected GridBagLayoutInfo layoutInfo;
}
```

Hierarchy: Object→ GridBagLayout(LayoutManager2(LayoutManager), Serializable)

GridLayout   Java 1.0

java.awt   *serializable layout manager PJ1.1*

A LayoutManager that divides a Container into a specified number of equally sized rows
and columns and arranges the components in those rows and columns, left to right and
top to bottom. If either the number of rows or the number of columns is set to 0, its
value is computed from the other dimension and the total number of components. Do
not confuse this class with the more flexible and complicated GridBagLayout.

Applications should never call the LayoutManager methods of this class directly; the Container for which the GridLayout is registered does this.

```
public class GridLayout implements LayoutManager, Serializable {
// Public Constructors
1.1 public GridLayout();
   public GridLayout(int rows, int cols);
   public GridLayout(int rows, int cols, int hgap, int vgap);
// Property Accessor Methods (by property name)
1.1 public int getColumns();                                              default:0
1.1 public void setColumns(int cols);
1.1 public int getHgap();                                                 default:0
```

```
1.1 public void setHgap(int hgap);
1.1 public int getRows();                                                    default:1
1.1 public void setRows(int rows);
1.1 public int getVgap();                                                    default:0
1.1 public void setVgap(int vgap);
// Methods Implementing LayoutManager
    public void addLayoutComponent(String name, Component comp);             empty
    public void layoutContainer(Container parent);
    public Dimension minimumLayoutSize(Container parent);
    public Dimension preferredLayoutSize(Container parent);
    public void removeLayoutComponent(Component comp);                       empty
// Public Methods Overriding Object
    public String toString();
}
```

Hierarchy: Object→ GridLayout(LayoutManager, Serializable)

IllegalComponentStateException   Java 1.1

java.awt   *serializable unchecked PJ1.1*

Signals that an AWT component is not in the appropriate state for some requested operation (e.g., it hasn't been added to a container yet or is currently hidden).

```
public class IllegalComponentStateException extends java.lang.IllegalStateException {
// Public Constructors
    public IllegalComponentStateException();
    public IllegalComponentStateException(String s);
}
```

Hierarchy: Object→ Throwable(Serializable)→ Exception→ RuntimeException→
java.lang.IllegalStateException→ IllegalComponentStateException

Thrown By: AccessibleContext.getLocale()

Image   Java 1.0

java.awt   *PJ1.1*

This abstract class represents a displayable image in a platform-independent way. An
Image object cannot be instantiated directly through a constructor; it must be obtained
through a method like the getImage() method of Applet or the createImage() method of
Component. getSource() method returns the ImageProducer object that produces the image
data. getGraphics() returns a Graphics object that can be used for drawing into off-screen
images (but not images that are downloaded or generated by an ImageProducer).

```
public abstract class Image {
// Public Constructors
    public Image();
// Public Constants
1.1 public static final int SCALE_AREA_AVERAGING;                              =16
1.1 public static final int SCALE_DEFAULT;                                      =1
1.1 public static final int SCALE_FAST;                                         =2
1.1 public static final int SCALE_REPLICATE;                                     =8
1.1 public static final int SCALE_SMOOTH;                                        =4
    public static final Object UndefinedProperty;
// Property Accessor Methods (by property name)
    public abstract Graphics getGraphics();
    public abstract java.awt.image.ImageProducer getSource();
```

```
// Public Instance Methods
    public abstract void flush( );
    public abstract int getHeight(java.awt.image.ImageObserver observer);
    public abstract Object getProperty(String name, java.awt.image.ImageObserver observer);
1.1 public Image getScaledInstance(int width, int height, int hints);
    public abstract int getWidth(java.awt.image.ImageObserver observer);
}
```

Subclasses: java.awt.image.BufferedImage

Passed To: Too many methods to list.

Returned By: Too many methods to list.

Type Of: javax.swing.JViewport.backingStoreImage

Insets   Java 1.0

java.awt   *cloneable serializable PJ1.1*

This class holds four values that represent the top, left, bottom, and right margins, in pixels, of a Container or other Component. An object of this type can be specified in a GridBagConstraints layout object and is returned by Container.insets(), which queries the margins of a container.

```
public class Insets implements Cloneable, Serializable {
// Public Constructors
    public Insets(int top, int left, int bottom, int right);
// Public Methods Overriding Object
    public Object clone( );
1.1 public boolean equals(Object obj);
    public String toString( );
// Public Instance Fields
    public int bottom;
    public int left;
    public int right;
    public int top;
}
```

Hierarchy: Object→ Insets(Cloneable, Serializable)

Subclasses: javax.swing.plaf.InsetsUIResource

Passed To: Too many methods to list.

Returned By: Too many methods to list.

Type Of: GridBagConstraints.insets

ItemSelectable   Java 1.1

java.awt   *PJ1.1*

This interface abstracts the functionality of an AWT component that presents one or more items to the user and allows the user to select none, one, or several of them. It is implemented by several components in the AWT and Swing.

getSelectedObjects() returns an array of selected objects or null, if none are selected. addItemListener() and removeItemListener() are standard methods for adding and removing ItemListener objects to be notified when an item is selected.

```
public .ne 10 abstract interface ItemSelectable {
// Event Registration Methods (by event name)
    public abstract void addItemListener(java.awt.event.ItemListener l);
```

```
    public abstract void removeItemListener(java.awt.event.ItemListener l);
// Public Instance Methods
    public abstract Object[ ] getSelectedObjects();
}
```

Implementations: Checkbox, CheckboxMenuItem, Choice, java.awt.List, javax.swing.AbstractButton, javax.swing.ButtonModel, javax.swing.JComboBox

Passed To: java.awt.event.ItemEvent.ItemEvent()

Returned By: java.awt.event.ItemEvent.getItemSelectable()

Label   Java 1.0

java.awt   *serializable AWT component PJ1.1*

This class is a Component that displays a single specified line of read-only text. The constant values specify the text alignment within the component and can be specified in a call to the constructor or used with setAlignment().

```
public class Label extends Component {
// Public Constructors
    public Label();
    public Label(String text);
    public Label(String text, int alignment);
// Public Constants
    public static final int CENTER;                                                      =1
    public static final int LEFT;                                                        =0
    public static final int RIGHT;                                                       =2
// Property Accessor Methods (by property name)
    public int getAlignment();                                                    default:0
    public void setAlignment(int alignment);                                  synchronized
    public String getText();                                                     default:""
    public void setText(String text);
// Public Methods Overriding Component
    public void addNotify();
// Protected Methods Overriding Component
    protected String paramString();
}
```

Hierarchy: Object→ Component(java.awt.image.ImageObserver, MenuContainer, Serializable)→ Label

Passed To: Toolkit.createLabel()

LayoutManager   Java 1.0

java.awt   *layout manager PJ1.1*

This interface defines the methods necessary for a class to be able to arrange Component objects within a Container object. Most programs use one of the existing classes that implement this interface: BorderLayout, CardLayout, FlowLayout, GridBagConstraints, GridBagLayout, or GridLayout.

To define a new class that lays out components, you must implement each of the methods defined by this interface. addLayoutComponent() is called when a component is added to the container. removeLayoutComponent() is called when a component is removed. layoutContainer() should perform the actual positioning of components by setting the size and position of each component in the specified container. minimumLayoutSize() should return the minimum container width and height that the LayoutManager needs in order to lay out its components. preferredLayoutSize() should return the optimal container width and height for the LayoutManager to lay out its components.

As of Java 1.1, layout managers should implement the LayoutManager2 interface, which is an extension of this one. A Java applet or application never directly calls any of these LayoutManager methods—the Container object for which the LayoutManager is registered does that.

```
public abstract interface LayoutManager {
// Public Instance Methods
    public abstract void addLayoutComponent(String name, Component comp);
    public abstract void layoutContainer(Container parent);
    public abstract Dimension minimumLayoutSize(Container parent);
    public abstract Dimension preferredLayoutSize(Container parent);
    public abstract void removeLayoutComponent(Component comp);
}
```

Implementations: FlowLayout, GridLayout, LayoutManager2, javax.swing.ScrollPaneLayout, javax.swing.ViewportLayout

Passed To: Container.setLayout(), Panel.Panel(), ScrollPane.setLayout(), javax.swing.Box.setLayout(), javax.swing.JApplet.setLayout(), javax.swing.JDialog.setLayout(), javax.swing.JFrame.setLayout(), javax.swing.JInternalFrame.setLayout(), javax.swing.JPanel.JPanel(), javax.swing.JScrollPane.setLayout(), javax.swing.JWindow.setLayout()

Returned By: Container.getLayout(), javax.swing.JRootPane.createRootLayout(), javax.swing.JViewport.createLayoutManager()

LayoutManager2   Java 1.1

java.awt   *layout manager PJ1.1*

This interface is an extension of the LayoutManager interface. It defines additional layout management methods for layout managers that perform constraint-based layout. Grid-BagLayout is an example of a constraint-based layout manager—each component added to the layout is associated with a GridBagConstraints object that specifies the constraints on how the component is to be laid out.

Java programs do not directly invoke the methods of this interface—they are used by the Container object for which the layout manager is registered.

```
public abstract interface LayoutManager2 extends LayoutManager {
// Public Instance Methods
    public abstract void addLayoutComponent(Component comp, Object constraints);
    public abstract float getLayoutAlignmentX(Container target);
    public abstract float getLayoutAlignmentY(Container target);
    public abstract void invalidateLayout(Container target);
    public abstract Dimension maximumLayoutSize(Container target);
}
```

Hierarchy: (LayoutManager2(LayoutManager))

Implementations: BorderLayout, CardLayout, GridBagLayout, javax.swing.BoxLayout, javax.swing.JRootPane.RootLayout, javax.swing.OverlayLayout

List   Java 1.0

java.awt   *serializable AWT component PJ1.1*

This class is a Component that graphically displays a list of strings. The list is scrollable if necessary. The constructor takes optional arguments that specify the number of visible rows in the list and whether selection of more than one item is allowed. The various instance methods allow strings to be added and removed from the List and allow the selected item or items to be queried.

```
public class List extends Component implements ItemSelectable {
```
```
// Public Constructors
     public List();
1.1  public List(int rows);
     public List(int rows, boolean multipleMode);
// Event Registration Methods (by event name)
1.1  public void addActionListener(java.awt.event.ActionListener l);                          synchronized
1.1  public void removeActionListener(java.awt.event.ActionListener l);                       synchronized
1.1  public void addItemListener(java.awt.event.ItemListener l);            Implements:ItemSelectable synchronized
1.1  public void removeItemListener(java.awt.event.ItemListener l);         Implements:ItemSelectable synchronized
// Property Accessor Methods (by property name)
1.1  public int getItemCount();                                                                default:0
1.1  public String[ ] getItems();                                                              synchronized
1.1  public Dimension getMinimumSize();                                               Overrides:Component
1.1  public Dimension getMinimumSize(int rows);
1.1  public boolean isMultipleMode();                                                        default:false
1.1  public void setMultipleMode(boolean b);
1.1  public Dimension getPreferredSize();                                             Overrides:Component
1.1  public Dimension getPreferredSize(int rows);
     public int getRows();                                                                     default:4
     public int getSelectedIndex();                                                 synchronized default:-1
     public int[ ] getSelectedIndexes();                                                       synchronized
     public String getSelectedItem();                                              synchronized default:null
     public String[ ] getSelectedItems();                                                      synchronized
1.1  public Object[ ] getSelectedObjects();                                          Implements:ItemSelectable
     public int getVisibleIndex();                                                             default:-1
// Public Instance Methods
1.1  public void add(String item);
1.1  public void add(String item, int index);
     public void deselect(int index);                                                          synchronized
     public String getItem(int index);
1.1  public boolean isIndexSelected(int index);
     public void makeVisible(int index);                                                       synchronized
1.1  public void remove(String item);                                                          synchronized
1.1  public void remove(int position);
1.1  public void removeAll();
     public void replaceItem(String newValue, int index);                                      synchronized
     public void select(int index);
// Methods Implementing ItemSelectable
1.1  public void addItemListener(java.awt.event.ItemListener l);                               synchronized
1.1  public Object[ ] getSelectedObjects();
1.1  public void removeItemListener(java.awt.event.ItemListener l);                            synchronized
// Public Methods Overriding Component
     public void addNotify();
     public void removeNotify();
// Protected Methods Overriding Component
     protected String paramString();
1.1  protected void processEvent(AWTEvent e);
// Protected Instance Methods
1.1  protected void processActionEvent(java.awt.event.ActionEvent e);
1.1  protected void processItemEvent(java.awt.event.ItemEvent e);
// Deprecated Public Methods
#    public void addItem(String item);
#    public void addItem(String item, int index);                                             synchronized
#    public boolean allowsMultipleSelections();
#    public void clear();                                                                      synchronized
```

```
#   public int countItems();
#   public void delItem(int position);
#   public void delItems(int start, int end);                              synchronized
#   public boolean isSelected(int index);
#   public Dimension minimumSize();                                   Overrides:Component
#   public Dimension minimumSize(int rows);
#   public Dimension preferredSize();                                 Overrides:Component
#   public Dimension preferredSize(int rows);
#   public void setMultipleSelections(boolean b);                          synchronized
}
```

Hierarchy: Object→ Component(java.awt.image.ImageObserver, MenuContainer, Serializable)→ java.awt.List(ItemSelectable)

Passed To: Toolkit.createList()

MediaTracker   Java 1.0

java.awt   *serializable PJ1.1*

This class provides a convenient way to asynchronously load and keep track of the status of any number of Image objects. You can use it to load one or more images and then wait until those images have been completely loaded and are ready to be used.

The addImage() method registers an image to be loaded and tracked, assigning it a specified identifier value. waitForID() loads all the images that have been assigned the specified identifier and returns when they have all finished loading or it receives an error. isErrorAny() and isErrorID() check whether any errors have occurred while loading images. statusAll() and statusID() return the status of all images and of all images with the specified identifier, respectively. The return value of each of these methods is one of the defined constants.

```
public class MediaTracker implements Serializable {
// Public Constructors
    public MediaTracker(Component comp);
// Public Constants
    public static final int ABORTED;                                              =2
    public static final int COMPLETE;                                             =8
    public static final int ERRORED;                                              =4
    public static final int LOADING;                                              =1
// Public Instance Methods
    public void addImage(Image image, int id);
    public void addImage(Image image, int id, int w, int h);               synchronized
    public boolean checkAll();
    public boolean checkAll(boolean load);
    public boolean checkID(int id);
    public boolean checkID(int id, boolean load);
    public Object[] getErrorsAny();                                        synchronized
    public Object[] getErrorsID(int id);                                   synchronized
    public boolean isErrorAny();                                           synchronized
    public boolean isErrorID(int id);                                      synchronized
1.1 public void removeImage(Image image);                                  synchronized
1.1 public void removeImage(Image image, int id);                          synchronized
1.1 public void removeImage(Image image, int id, int width, int height);   synchronized
    public int statusAll(boolean load);
    public int statusID(int id, boolean load);
    public void waitForAll() throws InterruptedException;
    public boolean waitForAll(long ms) throws InterruptedException;        synchronized
    public void waitForID(int id) throws InterruptedException;
```

public boolean **waitForID**(int *id*, long *ms*) throws InterruptedException;   *synchronized*
}

Hierarchy: Object→ MediaTracker(Serializable)

Type Of: javax.swing.ImageIcon.tracker

Menu   Java 1.0

java.awt   *serializable AWT component PJ1.1(opt)*

This class represents a pulldown menu pane that appears within a MenuBar. Each Menu
has a label that appears in the MenuBar and can optionally be a tear-off menu. The add()
and addSeparator() methods add individual items to a Menu.

```
public class Menu extends MenuItem implements MenuContainer {
// Public Constructors
1.1 public Menu();
    public Menu(String label);
    public Menu(String label, boolean tearOff);
// Property Accessor Methods (by property name)
1.1 public int getItemCount();                                                              default:0
    public boolean isTearOff();                                                          default:false
// Public Instance Methods
    public void add(String label);
    public MenuItem add(MenuItem mi);
    public void addSeparator();
    public MenuItem getItem(int index);
1.1 public void insert(String label, int index);
1.1 public void insert(MenuItem menuitem, int index);
1.1 public void insertSeparator(int index);
    public void remove(int index);
1.1 public void removeAll();
// Methods Implementing MenuContainer
    public void remove(MenuComponent item);
// Public Methods Overriding MenuItem
    public void addNotify();
1.1 public String paramString();
// Public Methods Overriding MenuComponent
    public void removeNotify();
// Deprecated Public Methods
#   public int countItems();
}
```

Hierarchy: Object→ MenuComponent(Serializable)→ MenuItem→ Menu(MenuContainer)

Subclasses: PopupMenu

Passed To: MenuBar.{add(), setHelpMenu()}, Toolkit.createMenu(),
java.awt.peer.MenuBarPeer.{addHelpMenu(), addMenu()}

Returned By: MenuBar.{add(), getHelpMenu(), getMenu()}

MenuBar   Java 1.0

java.awt   *serializable AWT component PJ1.1(opt)*

This class represents a menu bar. add() adds Menu objects to the menu bar, and setHelp-
Menu() adds a **Help** menu in a reserved location of the menu bar. A MenuBar object may
be displayed within a Frame by passing it to the setMenuBar() of the Frame.

```
public class MenuBar extends MenuComponent implements MenuContainer {
// Public Constructors
    public MenuBar();
// Property Accessor Methods (by property name)
    public Menu getHelpMenu();                                              default:null
    public void setHelpMenu(Menu m);
1.1 public int getMenuCount();                                              default:0
// Public Instance Methods
    public Menu add(Menu m);
    public void addNotify();
1.1 public void deleteShortcut(MenuShortcut s);
    public Menu getMenu(int i);
1.1 public MenuItem getShortcutMenuItem(MenuShortcut s);
    public void remove(int index);
1.1 public java.util.Enumeration shortcuts();                              synchronized
// Methods Implementing MenuContainer
    public void remove(MenuComponent m);
// Public Methods Overriding MenuComponent
    public void removeNotify();
// Deprecated Public Methods
#   public int countMenus();
}
```

Hierarchy: Object → MenuComponent(Serializable) → MenuBar(MenuContainer)

Passed To: Frame.setMenuBar(), Toolkit.createMenuBar(), java.awt.peer.FramePeer.setMenuBar()

Returned By: Frame.getMenuBar()

MenuComponent   Java 1.0

java.awt   serializable AWT component PJ1.1

This class is the superclass of all menu-related classes: You never need to instantiate a MenuComponent directly. setFont() specifies the font to be used for all text within the menu component.

```
public abstract class MenuComponent implements Serializable {
// Public Constructors
    public MenuComponent();
// Property Accessor Methods (by property name)
    public Font getFont();
    public void setFont(Font f);
1.1 public String getName();
1.1 public void setName(String name);
    public MenuContainer getParent();
// Public Instance Methods
1.1 public final void dispatchEvent(AWTEvent e);
    public void removeNotify();
// Public Methods Overriding Object
    public String toString();
// Protected Instance Methods
1.1 protected final Object getTreeLock();
    protected String paramString();
1.1 protected void processEvent(AWTEvent e);                               empty
// Deprecated Public Methods
#   public java.awt.peer.MenuComponentPeer getPeer();
#   public boolean postEvent(Event evt);
}
```

Hierarchy: Object→ MenuComponent(Serializable)

Subclasses: MenuBar, MenuItem

Passed To: Component.remove(), Frame.remove(), Menu.remove(), MenuBar.remove(), MenuContainer.remove()

MenuContainer

java.awt

Java 1.0

PJ1.1

This interface defines the methods necessary for MenuContainer types, such as Menu, Frame, and MenuBar objects. Unless you implement new menulike components, you never need to use it.

```
public abstract interface MenuContainer {
// Public Instance Methods
    public abstract Font getFont();
    public abstract void remove(MenuComponent comp);
// Deprecated Public Methods
#   public abstract boolean postEvent(Event evt);
}
```

Implementations: Component, Frame, Menu, MenuBar

Returned By: MenuComponent.getParent()

MenuItem

java.awt

Java 1.0

serializable AWT component PJ1.1

This class encapsulates a menu item with a specified textual label. A MenuItem can be added to a menu pane with the add() method of Menu. The disable() method makes an item nonselectable; you might use it to gray out a menu item when the command it represents is not valid in the current context. The enable() method makes an item selectable again. In Java 1.1, use setActionCommand() to specify an identifying string that is included in ActionEvent events generated by the menu item.

```
public class MenuItem extends MenuComponent {
// Public Constructors
1.1 public MenuItem();
    public MenuItem(String label);
1.1 public MenuItem(String label, MenuShortcut s);
// Event Registration Methods (by event name)
1.1 public void addActionListener(java.awt.event.ActionListener l);              synchronized
1.1 public void removeActionListener(java.awt.event.ActionListener l);           synchronized
// Property Accessor Methods (by property name)
1.1 public String getActionCommand();                                           default:""
1.1 public void setActionCommand(String command);
    public boolean isEnabled();                                                 default:true
1.1 public void setEnabled(boolean b);                                          synchronized
    public String getLabel();                                                   default:""
    public void setLabel(String label);                                         synchronized
1.1 public MenuShortcut getShortcut();                                          default:null
1.1 public void setShortcut(MenuShortcut s);
// Public Instance Methods
    public void addNotify();
1.1 public void deleteShortcut();
// Public Methods Overriding MenuComponent
    public String paramString();
// Protected Methods Overriding MenuComponent
1.1 protected void processEvent(AWTEvent e);
```

```
// Protected Instance Methods
1.1 protected final void disableEvents(long eventsToDisable);
1.1 protected final void enableEvents(long eventsToEnable);
1.1 protected void processActionEvent(java.awt.event.ActionEvent e);
// Deprecated Public Methods
#    public void disable();                                          synchronized
#    public void enable();                                           synchronized
#    public void enable(boolean b);
}
```

Hierarchy: Object→ MenuComponent(Serializable)→ MenuItem

Subclasses: CheckboxMenuItem, Menu

Passed To: Menu.{add(), insert()}, Toolkit.createMenuItem(), java.awt.peer.MenuPeer.addItem()

Returned By: Menu.{add(), getItem()}, MenuBar.getShortcutMenuItem()

MenuShortcut

Java 1.1

java.awt

serializable PJ1.1(opt)

This class represents a keystroke used to select a MenuItem without actually pulling down the menu. A MenuShortcut object can be specified for a MenuItem when the MenuItem is created or by calling the item's setShortcut() method. The keystroke sequence for the menu shortcut automatically appears in the label for the menu item, so you do not need to add this information yourself.

When you create a MenuShortcut, you specify the keycode of the shortcut—this is one of the VK_ constants defined by java.awt.event.KeyEvent and is not always the same as a corresponding character code. You may optionally specify a boolean value that, if true, indicates that the MenuShortcut requires the Shift key to be held down.

Note that menu shortcuts are triggered in a platform-dependent way. When you create a shortcut, you specify only the keycode and an optional Shift modifier. The shortcut is not triggered, however, unless an additional modifier key is held down. On Windows platforms, for example, the Ctrl key is used for menu shortcuts. You can query the platform-specific menu shortcut key with the getMenuShortcutKeyMask() method of Toolkit.

```
public class MenuShortcut implements Serializable {
// Public Constructors
     public MenuShortcut(int key);
     public MenuShortcut(int key, boolean useShiftModifier);
// Public Instance Methods
     public boolean equals(MenuShortcut s);
     public int getKey();
     public boolean usesShiftModifier();
// Public Methods Overriding Object
1.2  public boolean equals(Object obj);
1.2  public int hashCode();
     public String toString();
// Protected Instance Methods
     protected String paramString();
}
```

Hierarchy: Object→ MenuShortcut(Serializable)

Passed To: MenuBar.{deleteShortcut(), getShortcutMenuItem()}, MenuItem.{MenuItem(), setShortcut()}, MenuShortcut.equals()

Returned By: MenuItem.getShortcut()

Paint

Java 1.2

java.awt

This interface defines a color or pattern used by Java 2D in drawing and filling operations. Color is the simplest implementation: it performs drawing and filling using a solid color. GradientPaint and TexturePaint are two other commonly used implementations. Most applications can simply use these predefined Paint implementations and do not need to implement this interface themselves.

Because a single Paint object may be used by different threads with different Graphics2D objects, the Paint object does not perform painting operations itself. Instead, it defines a createContext() method that returns a PaintContext object that is capable of performing painting in a particular context. See PaintContext for details.

```
public abstract interface Paint extends Transparency {
// Public Instance Methods
    public abstract PaintContext createContext(java.awt.image.ColorModel cm, Rectangle deviceBounds,
                                        java.awt.geom.Rectangle2D userBounds,
                                        java.awt.geom.AffineTransform xform, RenderingHints hints);
}
```

Hierarchy: (Paint(Transparency))

Implementations: Color, GradientPaint, TexturePaint

Passed To: Graphics2D.setPaint()

Returned By: Graphics2D.getPaint()

PaintContext

Java 1.2

java.awt

This interface defines the methods that do the actual work of computing the colors to be used in Java 2D drawing and filling operations. PaintContext is used internally by Java 2D; applications never need to call any of its methods. Only applications that implement custom Paint objects need to implement this interface.

A Graphics2D object creates a PaintContext object by calling the createContext() method of its Paint object. The getRaster() method of the PaintContext is called to perform the actual painting; this method must return a java.awt.image.Raster object that contains the appropriate colors for the specified rectangle. The Graphics2D object calls dispose() when the PaintContext is no longer needed. The dispose() method should release any system resources held by the PaintContext.

```
public abstract interface PaintContext {
// Public Instance Methods
    public abstract void dispose();
    public abstract java.awt.image.ColorModel getColorModel();
    public abstract java.awt.image.Raster getRaster(int x, int y, int w, int h);
}
```

Returned By: Color.createContext(), GradientPaint.createContext(), Paint.createContext(), SystemColor.createContext(), TexturePaint.createContext()

Panel

Java 1.0

java.awt

serializable AWT component PJ1.1

This class is a Container that is itself contained within a container. Unlike Frame and Dialog, Panel is a container that does not create a separate window of its own. Panel is suitable for holding portions of a larger interface within a parent Frame or Dialog or within another Panel. (Because Applet is a subclass of Panel, applets are displayed in a Panel that is contained within a web browser or applet viewer.) The default LayoutManager for a Panel is FlowLayout.

```
public class Panel extends Container {
// Public Constructors
    public Panel();
1.1 public Panel(LayoutManager layout);
// Public Methods Overriding Container
    public void addNotify();
}
```

Hierarchy: Object→ Component(java.awt.image.ImageObserver, MenuContainer, Serializable)→ Container→ Panel

Subclasses: java.applet.Applet

Passed To: Toolkit.createPanel()

Point

java.awt

Java 1.0

cloneable serializable PJ1.1

This class holds the integer X and Y coordinates of a two-dimensional point. The move() and setLocation() methods set the coordinates, and the translate() method adds specified values to the coordinates. Also, the x and y fields are public and may be manipulated directly.

In Java 1.0 and Java 1.1, Point is a subclass of Object. In Java 1.2, with the introduction of Java 2D, Point has become a concrete subclass of java.awt.geom.Point2D. Contrast Point with Point2D.Float and Point2D.Double, which use float and double fields to represent the coordinates of the point.

```
public class Point extends java.awt.geom.Point2D implements Serializable {
// Public Constructors
1.1 public Point();
1.1 public Point(Point p);
    public Point(int x, int y);
// Public Instance Methods
1.1 public Point getLocation();
    public void move(int x, int y);
1.1 public void setLocation(Point p);
1.1 public void setLocation(int x, int y);
    public void translate(int x, int y);
// Public Methods Overriding Point2D
    public boolean equals(Object obj);
1.2 public double getX();                                                    default:0.0
1.2 public double getY();                                                    default:0.0
1.2 public void setLocation(double x, double y);
// Public Methods Overriding Object
    public String toString();
// Public Instance Fields
    public int x;
    public int y;
}
```

Hierarchy: Object→ java.awt.geom.Point2D(Cloneable)→ Point(Serializable)

Passed To: Too many methods to list.

Returned By: Too many methods to list.

Type Of: javax.swing.JViewport.lastPaintPosition

Polygon
Java 1.0

java.awt
serializable shape PJ1.1

This class defines a polygon as an array of points. The points of the polygon can be passed to the constructor or specified with addPoint(). getBoundingBox() returns the smallest Rectangle that contains the polygon, and inside() tests whether a specified point is within the Polygon. Note that the arrays of X and Y points and the number of points in the polygon (not necessarily the same as the array size) are defined as public variables. Polygon objects are used when drawing polygons with the drawPolygon() and fillPolygon() methods of Graphics. In Java 2, Polygon has become part of the Java 2D API. It implements the Shape interface and can be passed to the draw() and fill() method of a Graphics2D object.

```
public class Polygon implements Serializable, Shape {
// Public Constructors
    public Polygon();
    public Polygon(int[ ] xpoints, int[ ] ypoints, int npoints);
// Public Instance Methods
    public void addPoint(int x, int y);
1.1 public boolean contains(Point p);
1.1 public boolean contains(int x, int y);
1.1 public void translate(int deltaX, int deltaY);
// Methods Implementing Shape
1.2 public boolean contains(java.awt.geom.Rectangle2D r);
1.2 public boolean contains(java.awt.geom.Point2D p);
1.2 public boolean contains(double x, double y);
1.2 public boolean contains(double x, double y, double w, double h);
1.1 public Rectangle getBounds();
1.2 public java.awt.geom.Rectangle2D getBounds2D();                              default:Rectangle2D.Float
1.2 public java.awt.geom.PathIterator getPathIterator(java.awt.geom.AffineTransform at);
1.2 public java.awt.geom.PathIterator getPathIterator(java.awt.geom.AffineTransform at, double flatness);
1.2 public boolean intersects(java.awt.geom.Rectangle2D r);
1.2 public boolean intersects(double x, double y, double w, double h);
// Public Instance Fields
    public int npoints;
    public int[ ] xpoints;
    public int[ ] ypoints;
// Protected Instance Fields
    protected Rectangle bounds;
// Deprecated Public Methods
#   public Rectangle getBoundingBox();
#   public boolean inside(int x, int y);
}
```

Hierarchy: Object → Polygon(Serializable, Shape)

Passed To: Graphics.{drawPolygon(), fillPolygon()}

PopupMenu
Java 1.1

java.awt
serializable AWT component PJ1.1(mod)

PopupMenu is a simple subclass of Menu that represents a popup menu rather than a pulldown menu. You create a PopupMenu just as you would create a Menu object. The main difference is that a popup menu must be popped up in response to a user event by calling its show() method. Another difference is that, unlike a Menu, which can only appear within a MenuBar or another Menu, a PopupMenu can be associated with any component in a graphical user interface. A PopupMenu is associated with a component by calling the add() method of the component.

Popup menus are popped up by the user in different ways on different platforms. In order to hide this platform dependency, the MouseEvent class defines the isPopupTrigger() method. If this method returns true, the specified MouseEvent represents the platform-specific popup menu trigger event, and you should use the show() method to display your PopupMenu. Note that the X and Y coordinates passed to show() should be in the coordinate system of the specified Component.

Support for nested popup menus is optional in Personal Java environments, and the inherited add() method may throw an exception if you attempt to add a Menu child to a PopupMenu.

```
public class PopupMenu extends Menu {
// Public Constructors
    public PopupMenu();
    public PopupMenu(String label);
// Public Instance Methods
    public void show(Component origin, int x, int y);
// Public Methods Overriding Menu
    public void addNotify();
}
```

Hierarchy: Object→ MenuComponent(Serializable)→ MenuItem→ Menu(MenuContainer)→ PopupMenu

Passed To: Component.add(), Toolkit.createPopupMenu()

PrintGraphics   Java 1.1

java.awt   PJ1.1

The Graphics object returned by the getGraphics() method of PrintJob always implements this PrintGraphics interface. You can use this fact to distinguish a Graphics object that draws to the screen from one that generates hardcopy. This is a useful thing to do in a paint() method, when you want to generate hardcopy that differs somewhat from what is being displayed on-screen.

The getPrintJob() method defined by this interface can be used to return the PrintJob with which the PrintGraphics object is associated.

```
public abstract interface PrintGraphics {
// Public Instance Methods
    public abstract PrintJob getPrintJob();
}
```

PrintJob   Java 1.1

java.awt   PJ1.1

A PrintJob object represents a single printing session, or job. The job may consist of one or more individual pages.

PrintJob is abstract, so it cannot be instantiated directly. Instead, you must call the get-PrintJob() method of the Toolkit object. Calling this method posts an appropriate print dialog box to request information from the user, such as which printer should be used. An application has no control over this process, but may pass a Properties object in which the dialog stores the user's printing preferences. This Properties object can then be reused when initiating subsequent print jobs.

Once a PrintJob object has been obtained from the Toolkit object, you call the getGraphics() method of PrintJob to obtain a Graphics object. Any drawing done with this Graphics object is printed, instead of displayed on-screen. The object returned by getGraphics()

implements the PrintGraphics interface. Do not make any assumptions about the initial state of the Graphics object; in particular, note that you must specify a font before you can draw any text.

When you are done drawing all the desired output on a page, call the dispose() method of the Graphics object to force the current page to be printed. You can call getGraphics() and dispose() repeatedly to print any number of pages required by your application. However, if the lastPageFirst() method returns true, the user has requested that pages be printed in reverse order. It is up to your application to implement this feature.

The getPageDimension() method returns the size of the page in pixels. getPageResolution() returns the resolution of the page in pixels per inch. This resolution is closer to a screen resolution (70 to 100 pixels per inch) than a typical printer resolution (300 to 600 pixels per inch). This means that on-screen drawings can be drawn directly to the printer without scaling. It also means, however, that you cannot take full advantage of the extra resolution provided by printers.

When you are done with a PrintJob and have called dispose() on the Graphics object returned by getGraphics(), you should call end() to terminate the job.

As of Java 1.2, the PrintJob class has been superseded by a more complete printing API provided in the java.awt.print package.

```
public abstract class PrintJob {
// Public Constructors
    public PrintJob();
// Property Accessor Methods (by property name)
    public abstract Graphics getGraphics();
    public abstract Dimension getPageDimension();
    public abstract int getPageResolution();
// Public Instance Methods
    public abstract void end();
    public abstract boolean lastPageFirst();
// Public Methods Overriding Object
    public void finalize();
}
```

Returned By: PrintGraphics.getPrintJob(), Toolkit.getPrintJob()

Rectangle   Java 1.0

java.awt   *cloneable serializable shape PJ1.1*

This class defines a rectangle using four integer values: the X and Y coordinates of its upper-left corner and its width and height. The instance methods perform various tests and transformations on the rectangle. The x, y, width, and height methods are public and may thus be manipulated directly. Rectangle is used for a variety of purposes throughout java.awt and related packages.

In Java 1.0 and Java 1.1, Rectangle is a subclass of Object. In Java 2, with the introduction of Java 2D, Rectangle has become a concrete subclass of java.awt.geom.Rectangle2D. Contrast Rectangle with Rectangle2D.Float and Rectangle2D.Double, which use float and double fields to represent the coordinates of the rectangle.

```
public class Rectangle extends java.awt.geom.Rectangle2D implements Serializable, Shape {
// Public Constructors
    public Rectangle();
1.1 public Rectangle(Rectangle r);
    public Rectangle(Dimension d);
    public Rectangle(Point p);
    public Rectangle(int width, int height);
```

```
      public Rectangle(Point p, Dimension d);
      public Rectangle(int x, int y, int width, int height);
// Property Accessor Methods (by property name)
1.1 public Rectangle getBounds();                                    Implements:Shape
1.1 public void setBounds(Rectangle r);
1.1 public void setBounds(int x, int y, int width, int height);
1.2 public java.awt.geom.Rectangle2D getBounds2D();                  Implements:Shape default:Rectangle
      public boolean isEmpty();                                      Overrides:RectangularShape default:true
1.2 public double getHeight();                                       Overrides:RectangularShape default:0.0
1.1 public Point getLocation();
1.1 public void setLocation(Point p);
1.1 public void setLocation(int x, int y);
1.1 public Dimension getSize();
1.1 public void setSize(Dimension d);
1.1 public void setSize(int width, int height);
1.2 public double getWidth();                                        Overrides:RectangularShape default:0.0
1.2 public double getX();                                            Overrides:RectangularShape default:0.0
1.2 public double getY();                                            Overrides:RectangularShape default:0.0
// Public Instance Methods
      public void add(Rectangle r);
      public void add(Point pt);
      public void add(int newx, int newy);
1.2 public boolean contains(Rectangle r);
1.1 public boolean contains(Point p);
1.1 public boolean contains(int x, int y);
1.2 public boolean contains(int X, int Y, int W, int H);
      public void grow(int h, int v);
      public Rectangle intersection(Rectangle r);
      public boolean intersects(Rectangle r);
      public void translate(int x, int y);
      public Rectangle union(Rectangle r);
// Methods Implementing Shape
1.1 public Rectangle getBounds();
1.2 public java.awt.geom.Rectangle2D getBounds2D();                  default:Rectangle
// Public Methods Overriding Rectangle2D
1.2 public java.awt.geom.Rectangle2D createIntersection(java.awt.geom.Rectangle2D r);
1.2 public java.awt.geom.Rectangle2D createUnion(java.awt.geom.Rectangle2D r);
      public boolean equals(Object obj);
1.2 public int outcode(double x, double y);
1.2 public void setRect(double x, double y, double width, double height);
// Public Methods Overriding Object
      public String toString();
// Public Instance Fields
      public int height;
      public int width;
      public int x;
      public int y;
// Deprecated Public Methods
#     public boolean inside(int x, int y);
#     public void move(int x, int y);
#     public void reshape(int x, int y, int width, int height);
#     public void resize(int width, int height);
}
```

Hierarchy: Object→ java.awt.geom.RectangularShape(Cloneable, Shape) →
java.awt.geom.Rectangle2D → Rectangle(Serializable, Shape)

Subclasses: javax.swing.text.DefaultCaret

Passed To: Too many methods to list.

Returned By: Too many methods to list.

Type Of: Polygon.bounds

RenderingHints

java.awt

cloneable collection

This class contains a set of key-to-value mappings that provide hints to Java 2D about the speed-versus-quality trade-offs it should make. The constants that begin with KEY_ are the hints, while the constants that begin with VALUE_ are the values that may be specified for those hints. Use put() to add a hint to the RenderingHints object. Once you have specified all desired hints, pass the RenderingHints object to the setRenderingHints() or addRenderingHints() method of a Graphics2D object. If you want to set only a single rendering hint, you don't need to create a RenderingHints object at all; you can simply pass a key and value to the setRenderingHint() method of Graphics2D.

```
public class RenderingHints implements Cloneable, java.util.Map {
// Public Constructors
    public RenderingHints(java.util.Map init);
    public RenderingHints(RenderingHints.Key key, Object value);
// Public Constants
    public static final RenderingHints.Key KEY_ALPHA_INTERPOLATION;
    public static final RenderingHints.Key KEY_ANTIALIASING;
    public static final RenderingHints.Key KEY_COLOR_RENDERING;
    public static final RenderingHints.Key KEY_DITHERING;
    public static final RenderingHints.Key KEY_FRACTIONALMETRICS;
    public static final RenderingHints.Key KEY_INTERPOLATION;
    public static final RenderingHints.Key KEY_RENDERING;
    public static final RenderingHints.Key KEY_TEXT_ANTIALIASING;
    public static final Object VALUE_ALPHA_INTERPOLATION_DEFAULT;
    public static final Object VALUE_ALPHA_INTERPOLATION_QUALITY;
    public static final Object VALUE_ALPHA_INTERPOLATION_SPEED;
    public static final Object VALUE_ANTIALIAS_DEFAULT;
    public static final Object VALUE_ANTIALIAS_OFF;
    public static final Object VALUE_ANTIALIAS_ON;
    public static final Object VALUE_COLOR_RENDER_DEFAULT;
    public static final Object VALUE_COLOR_RENDER_QUALITY;
    public static final Object VALUE_COLOR_RENDER_SPEED;
    public static final Object VALUE_DITHER_DEFAULT;
    public static final Object VALUE_DITHER_DISABLE;
    public static final Object VALUE_DITHER_ENABLE;
    public static final Object VALUE_FRACTIONALMETRICS_DEFAULT;
    public static final Object VALUE_FRACTIONALMETRICS_OFF;
    public static final Object VALUE_FRACTIONALMETRICS_ON;
    public static final Object VALUE_INTERPOLATION_BICUBIC;
    public static final Object VALUE_INTERPOLATION_BILINEAR;
    public static final Object VALUE_INTERPOLATION_NEAREST_NEIGHBOR;
    public static final Object VALUE_RENDER_DEFAULT;
    public static final Object VALUE_RENDER_QUALITY;
    public static final Object VALUE_RENDER_SPEED;
    public static final Object VALUE_TEXT_ANTIALIAS_DEFAULT;
    public static final Object VALUE_TEXT_ANTIALIAS_OFF;
    public static final Object VALUE_TEXT_ANTIALIAS_ON;
// Inner Classes
    public abstract static class Key;
// Public Instance Methods
    public void add(RenderingHints hints);
```

```
// Methods Implementing Map
    public void clear();
    public boolean containsKey(Object key);
    public boolean containsValue(Object value);
    public java.util.Set entrySet();
    public boolean equals(Object o);
    public Object get(Object key);
    public int hashCode();
    public boolean isEmpty();
    public java.util.Set keySet();
    public Object put(Object key, Object value);
    public void putAll(java.util.Map m);
    public Object remove(Object key);
    public int size();
    public java.util.Collection values();
// Public Methods Overriding Object
    public Object clone();
    public String toString();
}
```

Hierarchy: Object → RenderingHints(Cloneable, java.util.Map)

Passed To: Too many methods to list.

Returned By: Graphics2D.getRenderingHints(), java.awt.image.AffineTransformOp.getRenderingHints(), java.awt.image.BandCombineOp.getRenderingHints(), java.awt.image.BufferedImageOp.getRenderingHints(), java.awt.image.ColorConvertOp.getRenderingHints(), java.awt.image.ConvolveOp.getRenderingHints(), java.awt.image.LookupOp.getRenderingHints(), java.awt.image.RasterOp.getRenderingHints(), java.awt.image.RescaleOp.getRenderingHints(), java.awt.image.renderable.RenderContext.getRenderingHints()

RenderingHints.Key   Java 1.2

java.awt

This class is the type of the KEY_ constants defined by RenderingHints.

```
public abstract static class RenderingHints.Key {
// Protected Constructors
    protected Key(int privatekey);
// Public Instance Methods
    public abstract boolean isCompatibleValue(Object val);
// Public Methods Overriding Object
    public final boolean equals(Object o);
    public final int hashCode();
// Protected Instance Methods
    protected final int intKey();
}
```

Passed To: Graphics2D.{getRenderingHint(), setRenderingHint()}, RenderingHints.RenderingHints()

Type Of: RenderingHints.{KEY_ALPHA_INTERPOLATION, KEY_ANTIALIASING, KEY_COLOR_RENDERING, KEY_DITHERING, KEY_FRACTIONALMETRICS, KEY_INTERPOLATION, KEY_RENDERING, KEY_TEXT_ANTIALIASING}

Scrollbar   Java 1.0

java.awt   *serializable AWT component PJ1.1(opt)*

This Component represents a graphical scrollbar. setValue() sets the displayed value of the scrollbar. setValues() sets the displayed value, the page size, and the minimum and maximum values. The constants HORIZONTAL and VERTICAL are legal values for the scrollbar orientation.

```
public class Scrollbar extends Component implements Adjustable {
// Public Constructors
     public Scrollbar();
     public Scrollbar(int orientation);
     public Scrollbar(int orientation, int value, int visible, int minimum, int maximum);
// Public Constants
     public static final int HORIZONTAL;                                                  =0
     public static final int VERTICAL;                                                    =1
// Event Registration Methods (by event name)
1.1 public void addAdjustmentListener(java.awt.event.AdjustmentListener l);    Implements:Adjustable synchronized
1.1 public void removeAdjustmentListener(                                      Implements:Adjustable synchronized
                                java.awt.event.AdjustmentListener l);
// Property Accessor Methods (by property name)
1.1 public int getBlockIncrement();                                      Implements:Adjustable default:10
1.1 public void setBlockIncrement(int v);                                         Implements:Adjustable
     public int getMaximum();                                            Implements:Adjustable default:100
1.1 public void setMaximum(int newMaximum);                                       Implements:Adjustable
     public int getMinimum();                                            Implements:Adjustable default:0
1.1 public void setMinimum(int newMinimum);                                       Implements:Adjustable
     public int getOrientation();                                        Implements:Adjustable default:1
1.1 public void setOrientation(int orientation);
1.1 public int getUnitIncrement();                                       Implements:Adjustable default:1
1.1 public void setUnitIncrement(int v);                                          Implements:Adjustable
     public int getValue();                                              Implements:Adjustable default:0
     public void setValue(int newValue);                                          Implements:Adjustable
1.1 public int getVisibleAmount();                                       Implements:Adjustable default:10
1.1 public void setVisibleAmount(int newAmount);                                  Implements:Adjustable
// Public Instance Methods
     public void setValues(int value, int visible, int minimum, int maximum);              synchronized
// Public Methods Overriding Component
     public void addNotify();
// Protected Methods Overriding Component
     protected String paramString();
1.1 protected void processEvent(AWTEvent e);
// Protected Instance Methods
1.1 protected void processAdjustmentEvent(java.awt.event.AdjustmentEvent e);
// Deprecated Public Methods
#   public int getLineIncrement();                                                       default:1
#   public int getPageIncrement();                                                      default:10
#   public int getVisible();                                                            default:10
#   public void setLineIncrement(int v);                                               synchronized
#   public void setPageIncrement(int v);                                               synchronized
}
```

Hierarchy: Object→ Component(java.awt.image.ImageObserver, MenuContainer, Serializable)→ Scrollbar(Adjustable)

Passed To: Toolkit.createScrollbar()

ScrollPane   Java 1.1

java.awt   *serializable AWT component PJ1.1(mod)*

This Container class creates horizontal and vertical scrollbars surrounding a viewport and allows a single child component to be displayed and scrolled within this viewport. Typically, the child of the ScrollPane is larger than the ScrollPane itself, so scrollbars allow the user to select the currently visible portion.

When you call the ScrollPane() constructor, you may optionally specify a scrollbar display policy, which should be one of the three constants defined by this class. If you do not specify a policy, ScrollPane uses the SCROLLBARS_AS_NEEDED policy. Personal Java environments may provide a scrolling mechanism other than scrollbars. In this case, the scrollbar display policy may be ignored.

A program can programmatically scroll the child within the viewport by calling setScroll-Position(). getHAdjustable() and getVAdjustable() return the horizontal and vertical Adjustable objects that control scrolling (typically these are not actually instances of Scrollbar). You can use these Adjustable objects to specify the unit and block increment values for the scrollbars. You can also directly set the Adjustable value as an alternative to calling setScrollPosition(), but you should not set other values of an Adjustable object.

Use setSize() to set the size of the ScrollPane container. You may want to take the size of the scrollbars into account when computing the overall container size—use getHScroll-barHeight() and getVScrollbarWidth() to obtain these values.

ScrollPane overrides the printComponents() method of Container, so that when a ScrollPane is printed, the entire child component, rather than only the currently visible portion, is printed.

```
public class ScrollPane extends Container {
// Public Constructors
    public ScrollPane();
    public ScrollPane(int scrollbarDisplayPolicy);
// Public Constants
    public static final int SCROLLBARS_ALWAYS;                              =1
    public static final int SCROLLBARS_AS_NEEDED;                          =0
    public static final int SCROLLBARS_NEVER;                              =2
// Property Accessor Methods (by property name)
    public Adjustable getHAdjustable();
    public int getHScrollbarHeight();                                default:0
    public final void setLayout(LayoutManager mgr);          Overrides:Container
    public int getScrollbarDisplayPolicy();                          default:0
    public Point getScrollPosition();
    public void setScrollPosition(Point p);
    public void setScrollPosition(int x, int y);
    public Adjustable getVAdjustable();
    public Dimension getViewportSize();
    public int getVScrollbarWidth();                                 default:0
// Public Methods Overriding Container
    public void addNotify();
    public void doLayout();
    public String paramString();
    public void printComponents(Graphics g);
// Protected Methods Overriding Container
    protected final void addImpl(Component comp, Object constraints, int index);
// Deprecated Public Methods
#   public void layout();                                     Overrides:Container
}
```

Hierarchy: Object→ Component(java.awt.image.ImageObserver, MenuContainer, Serializable)→ Container→ ScrollPane

Passed To: Toolkit.createScrollPane()

Shape   Java 1.1

java.awt   shape PJ1.1

This interface is one of the most important in all of Java 2D. It defines methods necessary for generalized operations on shapes, such as drawing, filling, and insideness testing. The package java.awt.geom contains a number of useful implementations of this interface, including GeneralPath, which can be used to describe arbitrary shapes composed of line and curve segments. java.awt.Polygon and java.awt.Rectangle are also important implementations of Shape. Most applications can rely on these predefined implementations and do not need to implement this interface themselves.

getBounds() and getBounds2D() return rectangular bounding boxes that completely enclose a Shape. contains() and intersects() test whether the shape contains or intersects a specified point or rectangle. The most important method of the Shape interface, however, is getPathIterator(). This method returns a java.awt.geom.PathIterator object that traces the outline of the shape using line and curve segments. The two-argument version of this method returns a PathIterator that is guaranteed to trace the outline using only straight line segments and no curves. The *flatness* argument is a measure of how closely the line segments must approximate the actual outline. Smaller values of *flatness* require increasingly accurate approximations.

The Shape interface was first defined in Java 1.1. In that version of the language it contained only the getBounds() method. The interface is so central to Java 2D and has grown so much since the Java 1.1 version, however, that it should generally be considered to be new in Java 1.2.

```
public abstract interface Shape {
// Public Instance Methods
1.2 public abstract boolean contains(java.awt.geom.Point2D p);
1.2 public abstract boolean contains(java.awt.geom.Rectangle2D r);
1.2 public abstract boolean contains(double x, double y);
1.2 public abstract boolean contains(double x, double y, double w, double h);
    public abstract Rectangle getBounds();
1.2 public abstract java.awt.geom.Rectangle2D getBounds2D();
1.2 public abstract java.awt.geom.PathIterator getPathIterator(java.awt.geom.AffineTransform at);
1.2 public abstract java.awt.geom.PathIterator getPathIterator(java.awt.geom.AffineTransform at, double flatness);
1.2 public abstract boolean intersects(java.awt.geom.Rectangle2D r);
1.2 public abstract boolean intersects(double x, double y, double w, double h);
}
```

Implementations: Polygon, Rectangle, java.awt.geom.Area, java.awt.geom.CubicCurve2D, java.awt.geom.GeneralPath, java.awt.geom.Line2D, java.awt.geom.QuadCurve2D, java.awt.geom.RectangularShape

Passed To: Too many methods to list.

Returned By: Too many methods to list.

Stroke   Java 1.2

java.awt

This interface defines how Java 2D draws the outline of a shape. It is responsible for graphical attributes such as line width and dash pattern. However, the Stroke is not responsible for the color or texture of the outline—those are the responsibility of the Paint interface. By default, lines are solid and are one pixel wide. To specify a different line style, pass a Stroke object to the setStroke() method of a Graphics2D object.

Mathematically, the outline of a shape is an infinitely thin line. Because it has no thickness, it cannot be drawn. The Stroke interface is responsible for defining how such infinitely thin outlines are drawn. The createStrokedShape() method is passed the Shape that is to be drawn. It returns a new Shape that places a finite width around the infinitely thin boundaries of the specified shape. The outline of the original shape can then be drawn by filling the interior of the returned shape.

BasicStroke implements Stroke and is the only implementation needed by most programs. Some programs may define their own implementations to achieve special effects not possible with BasicStroke, however.

```
public abstract interface Stroke {
// Public Instance Methods
    public abstract Shape createStrokedShape(Shape p);
}
```

Implementations: BasicStroke

Passed To: Graphics2D.setStroke()

Returned By: Graphics2D.getStroke()

SystemColor   Java 1.1

java.awt   serializable PJ1.1

Instances of the SystemColor class represent colors used in the system desktop. You can use these colors to produce applications and custom components that fit well in the desktop color scheme. On platforms that allow the desktop colors to be modified dynamically, the actual colors represented by these symbolic system colors may be dynamically updated.

The SystemColor class does not have a constructor, but it defines constant SystemColor objects that represent each of the symbolic colors used by the system desktop. If you need to compare a SystemColor object to a regular Color object, use the getRGB() method of both objects and compare the resulting values.

```
public final class SystemColor extends Color implements Serializable {
// No Constructor
// Public Constants
    public static final int ACTIVE_CAPTION;                          =1
    public static final int ACTIVE_CAPTION_BORDER;                   =3
    public static final int ACTIVE_CAPTION_TEXT;                     =2
    public static final SystemColor activeCaption;
    public static final SystemColor activeCaptionBorder;
    public static final SystemColor activeCaptionText;
    public static final SystemColor control;
    public static final int CONTROL;                                =17
    public static final int CONTROL_DK_SHADOW;                      =22
    public static final int CONTROL_HIGHLIGHT;                      =19
    public static final int CONTROL_LT_HIGHLIGHT;                   =20
    public static final int CONTROL_SHADOW;                         =21
    public static final int CONTROL_TEXT;                           =18
    public static final SystemColor controlDkShadow;
    public static final SystemColor controlHighlight;
    public static final SystemColor controlLtHighlight;
    public static final SystemColor controlShadow;
    public static final SystemColor controlText;
    public static final SystemColor desktop;
    public static final int DESKTOP;                                 =0
    public static final int INACTIVE_CAPTION;                        =4
    public static final int INACTIVE_CAPTION_BORDER;                 =6
    public static final int INACTIVE_CAPTION_TEXT;                   =5
    public static final SystemColor inactiveCaption;
    public static final SystemColor inactiveCaptionBorder;
    public static final SystemColor inactiveCaptionText;
    public static final SystemColor info;
    public static final int INFO;                                   =24
```

```
      public static final int INFO_TEXT;                                           =25
      public static final SystemColor infoText;
      public static final SystemColor menu;
      public static final int MENU;                                                =10
      public static final int MENU_TEXT;                                           =11
      public static final SystemColor menuText;
      public static final int NUM_COLORS;                                          =26
      public static final SystemColor scrollbar;
      public static final int SCROLLBAR;                                           =23
      public static final int TEXT;                                                =12
      public static final SystemColor text;
      public static final int TEXT_HIGHLIGHT;                                      =14
      public static final int TEXT_HIGHLIGHT_TEXT;                                 =15
      public static final int TEXT_INACTIVE_TEXT;                                  =16
      public static final int TEXT_TEXT;                                           =13
      public static final SystemColor textHighlight;
      public static final SystemColor textHighlightText;
      public static final SystemColor textInactiveText;
      public static final SystemColor textText;
      public static final int WINDOW;                                              =7
      public static final SystemColor window;
      public static final int WINDOW_BORDER;                                       =8
      public static final int WINDOW_TEXT;                                         =9
      public static final SystemColor windowBorder;
      public static final SystemColor windowText;
// Public Methods Overriding Color
1.2 public PaintContext createContext(java.awt.image.ColorModel cm, Rectangle r, java.awt.geom.Rectangle2D r2d,
                                      java.awt.geom.AffineTransform xform, RenderingHints hints);
      public int getRGB();
      public String toString();
}
```

Hierarchy: Object→ Color(Paint(Transparency), Serializable)→ SystemColor(Serializable)

Type Of: Too many fields to list.

TextArea   Java 1.0

java.awt   *serializable AWT component PJ1.1(mod)*

This class is a GUI component that displays and optionally edits multiline text. The
appendText(), insertText(), and replaceText() methods provide various techniques for specifying text to appear in the TextArea. Many important TextArea methods are defined by its
TextComponent superclass. See also TextComponent and TextField.

The four-argument version of the TextArea() constructor allows you to specify a scrollbar
display policy for the TextArea object. Personal Java environments can define a scrolling
mechanism other than scrollbars. In this case, the scrollbar display policy can be
ignored.

```
public class TextArea extends TextComponent {
// Public Constructors
      public TextArea();
      public TextArea(String text);
      public TextArea(int rows, int columns);
      public TextArea(String text, int rows, int columns);
1.1 public TextArea(String text, int rows, int columns, int scrollbars);
// Public Constants
1.1 public static final int SCROLLBARS_BOTH;                                     =0
1.1 public static final int SCROLLBARS_HORIZONTAL_ONLY;                          =2
```

```
1.1 public static final int SCROLLBARS_NONE;                                                =3
1.1 public static final int SCROLLBARS_VERTICAL_ONLY;                                       =1
// Property Accessor Methods (by property name)
    public int getColumns();                                                         default:0
1.1 public void setColumns(int columns);
1.1 public Dimension getMinimumSize();                                       Overrides:Component
1.1 public Dimension getMinimumSize(int rows, int columns);
1.1 public Dimension getPreferredSize();                                     Overrides:Component
1.1 public Dimension getPreferredSize(int rows, int columns);
    public int getRows();                                                            default:0
1.1 public void setRows(int rows);
1.1 public int getScrollbarVisibility();                                              default:0
// Public Instance Methods
1.1 public void append(String str);
1.1 public void insert(String str, int pos);
1.1 public void replaceRange(String str, int start, int end);
// Protected Methods Overriding TextComponent
    protected String paramString();
// Public Methods Overriding Component
    public void addNotify();
// Deprecated Public Methods
#   public void appendText(String str);                                            synchronized
#   public void insertText(String str, int pos);                                   synchronized
#   public Dimension minimumSize();                                     Overrides:Component
#   public Dimension minimumSize(int rows, int columns);
#   public Dimension preferredSize();                                   Overrides:Component
#   public Dimension preferredSize(int rows, int columns);
#   public void replaceText(String str, int start, int end);                       synchronized
}
```

Hierarchy: Object→ Component(java.awt.image.ImageObserver, MenuContainer, Serializable)→ TextComponent→ TextArea

Passed To: Toolkit.createTextArea()

TextComponent   Java 1.0

java.awt   serializable AWT component PJ1.1

This class is the superclass of the TextArea and TextField components. It cannot be instantiated itself but provides methods that are common to these two component types. setEditable() specifies whether the text in the component is editable. getText() returns the text in the component, and setText() specifies text to be displayed. getSelectedText() returns the currently selected text in the component, and getSelectionStart() and getSelectionEnd() return the extents of the selected region of text. select() and selectAll() select some and all of the text displayed in the text component, respectively.

See also TextField and TextArea.

```
public class TextComponent extends Component {
// No Constructor
// Event Registration Methods (by event name)
1.1 public void addTextListener(java.awt.event.TextListener l);                synchronized
1.1 public void removeTextListener(java.awt.event.TextListener l);             synchronized
// Property Accessor Methods (by property name)
1.1 public int getCaretPosition();                                            synchronized
1.1 public void setCaretPosition(int position);                               synchronized
    public boolean isEditable();
    public void setEditable(boolean b);                                       synchronized
```

```
        public String getSelectedText();                                          synchronized
        public int getSelectionEnd();                                             synchronized
1.1 public void setSelectionEnd(int selectionEnd);                                synchronized
        public int getSelectionStart();                                           synchronized
1.1 public void setSelectionStart(int selectionStart);                            synchronized
        public String getText();                                                  synchronized
        public void setText(String t);                                            synchronized
// Public Instance Methods
        public void select(int selectionStart, int selectionEnd);                 synchronized
        public void selectAll();                                                  synchronized
// Public Methods Overriding Component
        public void removeNotify();
// Protected Methods Overriding Component
        protected String paramString();
1.1 protected void processEvent(AWTEvent e);
// Protected Instance Methods
1.1 protected void processTextEvent(java.awt.event.TextEvent e);
// Protected Instance Fields
1.1 protected transient java.awt.event.TextListener textListener;
}
```

Hierarchy: Object→ Component(java.awt.image.ImageObserver, MenuContainer, Serializable)→ TextComponent

Subclasses: TextArea, TextField

TextField   Java 1.0

java.awt   *serializable AWT component PJ1.1*

This Component displays a single line of optionally editable text. Most of its interesting methods are defined by its TextComponent superclass. Use setEchoChar() to specify a character to be echoed when requesting sensitive input, such as a password.

See also TextComponent and TextArea.

```
public class TextField extends TextComponent {
// Public Constructors
        public TextField();
        public TextField(int columns);
        public TextField(String text);
        public TextField(String text, int columns);
// Event Registration Methods (by event name)
1.1 public void addActionListener(java.awt.event.ActionListener l);              synchronized
1.1 public void removeActionListener(java.awt.event.ActionListener l);           synchronized
// Property Accessor Methods (by property name)
        public int getColumns();                                                 default:0
1.1 public void setColumns(int columns);                                        synchronized
        public char getEchoChar();                                              default:\0
1.1 public void setEchoChar(char c);
1.1 public Dimension getMinimumSize();                                    Overrides:Component
1.1 public Dimension getMinimumSize(int columns);
1.1 public Dimension getPreferredSize();                                  Overrides:Component
1.1 public Dimension getPreferredSize(int columns);
1.2 public void setText(String t);                                     Overrides:TextComponent
// Public Instance Methods
        public boolean echoCharIsSet();
// Protected Methods Overriding TextComponent
        protected String paramString();
1.1 protected void processEvent(AWTEvent e);
```

```
// Public Methods Overriding Component
    public void addNotify( );
// Protected Instance Methods
1.1 protected void processActionEvent(java.awt.event.ActionEvent e);
// Deprecated Public Methods
#   public Dimension minimumSize( );                                    Overrides:Component
#   public Dimension minimumSize(int columns);
#   public Dimension preferredSize( );                                  Overrides:Component
#   public Dimension preferredSize(int columns);
#   public void setEchoCharacter(char c);                               synchronized
}
```

Hierarchy: Object→ Component(java.awt.image.ImageObserver, MenuContainer, Serializable)→
TextComponent→ TextField

Passed To: Toolkit.createTextField()

TexturePaint   Java 1.2

java.awt

This implementation of Paint is used to perform Java 2D drawing and filling operations
with a texture or pattern of colors defined in a BufferedImage object.

When you create a TexturePaint object, you must specify the BufferedImage that defines the
texture. You must also specify a rectangle that defines both the initial position of the
image and the tile size with which the image is replicated. Typically, you specify a rectangle with its upper-left corner at (0,0) and a width and height equal to the width and
height of the image

```
public class TexturePaint implements Paint {
// Public Constructors
    public TexturePaint(java.awt.image.BufferedImage txtr, java.awt.geom.Rectangle2D anchor);
// Public Instance Methods
    public java.awt.geom.Rectangle2D getAnchorRect( );
    public java.awt.image.BufferedImage getImage( );
// Methods Implementing Paint
    public PaintContext createContext(java.awt.image.ColorModel cm, Rectangle deviceBounds,
                        java.awt.geom.Rectangle2D userBounds, java.awt.geom.AffineTransform xform,
                        RenderingHints hints);
// Methods Implementing Transparency
    public int getTransparency( );
}
```

Hierarchy: Object→ TexturePaint(Paint(Transparency))

Toolkit   Java 1.0

java.awt   PJ1.1(mod)

This abstract class defines methods that, when implemented, create platform-dependent
peers for each of the Component types in java.awt. Java supports its platform-independent
GUI interface by implementing a subclass of Toolkit for each platform. Portable programs
should never use these methods to create peers directly—they should use the Component classes themselves. A Toolkit object cannot be instantiated directly. The getToolkit()
method of Component returns the Toolkit being used for a particular component.

The Toolkit class also defines methods that you can use directly. The static method getDe-
faultToolkit() returns the default Toolkit that is in use. getScreenSize() returns the screen size
in pixels, and getScreenResolution() returns the resolution in dots per inch. sync() flushes
all pending graphics output, which can be useful for animation. Other methods of

interest include beep(), getSystemClipboard(), createCustomCursor(), and addAWTEventListener(). getPrintJob() is part of the Java 1.1 printing API. In Personal Java environments, printing support is optional, and this method can throw an exception.

```
public abstract class Toolkit {
// Public Constructors
    public Toolkit();
// Public Class Methods
    public static Toolkit getDefaultToolkit();                                       synchronized
1.1 public static String getProperty(String key, String defaultValue);
// Protected Class Methods
1.1 protected static Container getNativeContainer(Component c);
// Event Registration Methods (by event name)
1.2 public void removeAWTEventListener(java.awt.event.AWTEventListener listener);
// Property Accessor Methods (by property name)
    public abstract java.awt.image.ColorModel getColorModel();
1.2 public int getMaximumCursorColors();                                             constant
1.1 public int getMenuShortcutKeyMask();                                             constant
    public abstract int getScreenResolution();
    public abstract Dimension getScreenSize();
1.1 public abstract java.awt.datatransfer.Clipboard getSystemClipboard();
1.1 public final EventQueue getSystemEventQueue();
// Public Instance Methods
1.2 public void addAWTEventListener(java.awt.event.AWTEventListener listener, long eventMask);
1.2 public void addPropertyChangeListener(String name, java.beans.PropertyChangeListener pcl);  synchronized
1.1 public abstract void beep();
    public abstract int checkImage(Image image, int width, int height, java.awt.image.ImageObserver observer);
1.2 public Cursor createCustomCursor(Image cursor, Point hotSpot, String name)
            throws IndexOutOfBoundsException;
1.2 public java.awt.dnd.DragGestureRecognizer createDragGestureRecognizer(          constant
                            Class abstractRecognizerClass,
                            java.awt.dnd.DragSource ds,
                            Component c, int srcActions,
                            java.awt.dnd.DragGestureListener dgl);
1.2 public abstract java.awt.dnd.peer.DragSourceContextPeer createDragSourceContextPeer(
                            java.awt.dnd.DragGestureEvent dge)
            throws java.awt.dnd.InvalidDnDOperationException;
1.2 public abstract Image createImage(java.net.URL url);
1.1 public Image createImage(byte[] imagedata);
1.2 public abstract Image createImage(String filename);
    public abstract Image createImage(java.awt.image.ImageProducer producer);
1.1 public abstract Image createImage(byte[] imagedata, int imageoffset, int imagelength);
1.2 public Dimension getBestCursorSize(int preferredWidth, int preferredHeight);
1.2 public final Object getDesktopProperty(String propertyName);                     synchronized
    public abstract Image getImage(java.net.URL url);
    public abstract Image getImage(String filename);
1.1 public abstract PrintJob getPrintJob(Frame frame, String jobtitle, java.util.Properties props);
    public abstract boolean prepareImage(Image image, int width, int height,
                            java.awt.image.ImageObserver observer);
1.2 public void removePropertyChangeListener(String name,                            synchronized
                            java.beans.PropertyChangeListener pcl);
    public abstract void sync();
// Protected Instance Methods
    protected abstract java.awt.peer.ButtonPeer createButton(Button target);
    protected abstract java.awt.peer.CanvasPeer createCanvas(Canvas target);
    protected abstract java.awt.peer.CheckboxPeer createCheckbox(Checkbox target);
    protected abstract java.awt.peer.CheckboxMenuItemPeer createCheckboxMenuItem(
                            CheckboxMenuItem target);
    protected abstract java.awt.peer.ChoicePeer createChoice(Choice target);
```

1.1 protected java.awt.peer.LightweightPeer **createComponent**(Component *target*);
   protected abstract java.awt.peer.DialogPeer **createDialog**(Dialog *target*);
   protected abstract java.awt.peer.FileDialogPeer **createFileDialog**(FileDialog *target*);
   protected abstract java.awt.peer.FramePeer **createFrame**(Frame *target*);
   protected abstract java.awt.peer.LabelPeer **createLabel**(Label *target*);
   protected abstract java.awt.peer.ListPeer **createList**(java.awt.List *target*);
   protected abstract java.awt.peer.MenuPeer **createMenu**(Menu *target*);
   protected abstract java.awt.peer.MenuBarPeer **createMenuBar**(MenuBar *target*);
   protected abstract java.awt.peer.MenuItemPeer **createMenuItem**(MenuItem *target*);
   protected abstract java.awt.peer.PanelPeer **createPanel**(Panel *target*);
1.1 protected abstract java.awt.peer.PopupMenuPeer **createPopupMenu**(PopupMenu *target*);
   protected abstract java.awt.peer.ScrollbarPeer **createScrollbar**(Scrollbar *target*);
1.1 protected abstract java.awt.peer.ScrollPanePeer **createScrollPane**(ScrollPane *target*);
   protected abstract java.awt.peer.TextAreaPeer **createTextArea**(TextArea *target*);
   protected abstract java.awt.peer.TextFieldPeer **createTextField**(TextField *target*);
   protected abstract java.awt.peer.WindowPeer **createWindow**(Window *target*);
1.1 protected abstract EventQueue **getSystemEventQueueImpl**( );
1.2 protected void **initializeDesktopProperties**( );   *empty*
1.2 protected Object **lazilyLoadDesktopProperty**(String *name*);   *constant*
1.1 protected void **loadSystemColors**(int[ ] *systemColors*);   *empty*
1.2 protected final void **setDesktopProperty**(String *name*, Object *newValue*);   *synchronized*
// Protected Instance Fields
1.2 protected final java.util.Map **desktopProperties**;
1.2 protected final java.beans.PropertyChangeSupport **desktopPropsSupport**;
// Deprecated Public Methods
public abstract String[ ] **getFontList**( );
public abstract FontMetrics **getFontMetrics**(Font *font*);
// Deprecated Protected Methods
1.1# protected abstract java.awt.peer.FontPeer **getFontPeer**(String *name*, int *style*);
}

Returned By: Component.getToolkit(), Toolkit.getDefaultToolkit(), Window.getToolkit(),
java.awt.peer.ComponentPeer.getToolkit()

Transparency   Java 1.2

java.awt

The integer constants defined by this interface identify the three types of transparency
supported by Java 2D. Although the Transparency interface is implemented only by a
couple of Java 2D classes, the constants it defines are more widely used. These constants are:

OPAQUE
   All colors are fully opaque, with no transparency. The alpha value of every pixel is
   1.0.

BITMASK
   Colors are either fully opaque or fully transparent, as specified by the bits in a bit
   mask. That is, each pixel has 1 bit associated with it that specifies whether the
   pixel is opaque (alpha is 1.0) or transparent (alpha is 0.0).

TRANSLUCENT
   Colors may be totally opaque, totally transparent, or translucent. This model of
   transparency uses an alpha channel that is wider than 1 bit and supports a number
   of alpha transparency levels between 1.0 and 0.0.

```
public abstract interface Transparency {
// Public Constants
    public static final int BITMASK;                                          =2
    public static final int OPAQUE;                                           =1
    public static final int TRANSLUCENT;                                      =3
// Public Instance Methods
    public abstract int getTransparency();
}
```

Implementations: Paint, java.awt.image.ColorModel

Window   Java 1.0

java.awt   *serializable AWT component PJ1.1(mod)*

This class represents a top-level window with no borders or menu bar. Window is a Container with BorderLayout as its default layout manager. Window is rarely used directly; its subclasses Frame and Dialog are more commonly useful.

show() (which overrides the show() method of Component) makes a Window visible and brings it to the front of other windows. toFront() brings a window to the front, and toBack() buries a window beneath others. pack() is an important method that initiates layout management for the window, setting the window size to match the preferred size of the components contained within the window. getToolkit() returns the Toolkit() in use for this window. Call dispose() when a Window is no longer needed, to free its window system resources.

Although the Window class is part of the Personal Java API, Personal Java implementations can prohibit the creation of Window objects. In this case, the Window() constructor throws an exception.

```
public class Window extends Container {
// Public Constructors
1.2 public Window(Window owner);
    public Window(Frame owner);
// Event Registration Methods (by event name)
1.1 public void addWindowListener(java.awt.event.WindowListener l);          synchronized
1.1 public void removeWindowListener(java.awt.event.WindowListener l);       synchronized
// Property Accessor Methods (by property name)
1.1 public Component getFocusOwner();
1.2 public java.awt.im.InputContext getInputContext();                  Overrides:Component
1.1 public java.util.Locale getLocale();                               Overrides:Component
1.2 public Window[ ] getOwnedWindows();
1.2 public Window getOwner();
1.1 public boolean isShowing();                                        Overrides:Component
    public Toolkit getToolkit();                                       Overrides:Component
    public final String getWarningString();
// Public Instance Methods
1.2 public void applyResourceBundle(java.util.ResourceBundle rb);
1.2 public void applyResourceBundle(String rbName);
    public void dispose();
    public void pack();
    public void toBack();
    public void toFront();
// Public Methods Overriding Container
    public void addNotify();
1.2 public void setCursor(Cursor cursor);                                    synchronized
// Protected Methods Overriding Container
1.1 protected void processEvent(AWTEvent e);
```

```
// Public Methods Overriding Component
1.2 public void hide( );
    public void show( );
// Protected Methods Overriding Object
1.2 protected void finalize( ) throws Throwable;
// Protected Instance Methods
1.1 protected void processWindowEvent(java.awt.event.WindowEvent e);
// Deprecated Public Methods
1.1# public boolean postEvent(Event e);                              Overrides:Component
}
```

Hierarchy: Object→ Component(java.awt.image.ImageObserver, MenuContainer, Serializable)→ Container→ Window

Subclasses: Dialog, Frame, javax.swing.JWindow

Passed To: Toolkit.createWindow(), Window.Window(), java.awt.event.WindowEvent.WindowEvent(), javax.swing.JWindow.JWindow()

Returned By: Window.{getOwnedWindows(), getOwner()}, java.awt.event.WindowEvent.getWindow(), javax.swing.SwingUtilities.windowForComponent()

CHAPTER 10

The java.awt.color Package

The java.awt.color package includes the abstract ColorSpace class, which defines methods necessary for converting colors between arbitrary color spaces. The package also contains implementations of the ColorSpace class based on data contained in ICC profile files. (The ICC is the international color standards body.) Most applications do not need to use this package; it is required only for applications that perform sophisticated image processing or require extremely accurate device-independent color display. Figure 10-1 shows the class hierarchy of this package, which is new in Java 1.2.

This package does not contain classes for representing colors. See the java.awt.Color class instead.

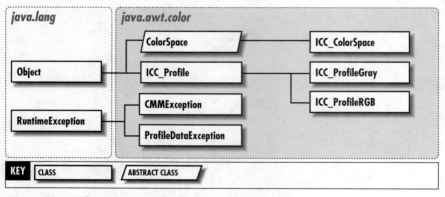

Figure 10–1: The java.awt.color package

CMMException
Java 1.2

java.awt.color *serializable unchecked*

Signals that an error has occurred in the internal color space management code.

```
public class CMMException extends RuntimeException {
// Public Constructors
    public CMMException(String s);
}
```

Hierarchy: Object→ Throwable(Serializable)→ Exception→ RuntimeException→ CMMException

ColorSpace
Java 1.2

java.awt.color

This abstract class encapsulates a color space: a system of representing colors using some number of floating-point color components. For examples, sRGB is a proposed standard color space that represents colors in terms of red, green, and blue components, while CIEXYZ is an international standard color space that represents colors in terms of three color components named X, Y, and Z. Typically, only applications that are doing image processing or are concerned with very precise color reproduction need to use this class.

ColorSpace does not have a public constructor. You can obtain an instance by calling the static getInstance() method and passing in one of the CS_ constants to specify the type of color space you want. Alternatively, implement and instantiate your own concrete subclass. Each ColorSpace object has methods to convert a color to and from the standard sRGB and CIEXYZ color spaces. This ensures that any color, regardless of its color space, can be converted to the red, green, and blue values used by computer display devices. It also ensures that a color represented in an arbitrary color space can be transformed to any other color space by first converting to an intermediate CIEXYZ representation.

```
public abstract class ColorSpace {
// Protected Constructors
    protected ColorSpace(int type, int numcomponents);
// Public Constants
    public static final int CS_CIEXYZ;                      =1001
    public static final int CS_GRAY;                        =1003
    public static final int CS_LINEAR_RGB;                  =1004
    public static final int CS_PYCC;                        =1002
    public static final int CS_sRGB;                        =1000
    public static final int TYPE_2CLR;                        =12
    public static final int TYPE_3CLR;                        =13
    public static final int TYPE_4CLR;                        =14
    public static final int TYPE_5CLR;                        =15
    public static final int TYPE_6CLR;                        =16
    public static final int TYPE_7CLR;                        =17
    public static final int TYPE_8CLR;                        =18
    public static final int TYPE_9CLR;                        =19
    public static final int TYPE_ACLR;                        =20
    public static final int TYPE_BCLR;                        =21
    public static final int TYPE_CCLR;                        =22
    public static final int TYPE_CMY;                         =11
    public static final int TYPE_CMYK;                         =9
    public static final int TYPE_DCLR;                        =23
    public static final int TYPE_ECLR;                        =24
    public static final int TYPE_FCLR;                        =25
    public static final int TYPE_GRAY;                         =6
```

```
    public static final int TYPE_HLS;                                      =8
    public static final int TYPE_HSV;                                      =7
    public static final int TYPE_Lab;                                      =1
    public static final int TYPE_Luv;                                      =2
    public static final int TYPE_RGB;                                      =5
    public static final int TYPE_XYZ;                                      =0
    public static final int TYPE_YCbCr;                                    =3
    public static final int TYPE_Yxy;                                      =4
// Public Class Methods
    public static ColorSpace getInstance(int colorspace);
// Public Instance Methods
    public abstract float[ ] fromCIEXYZ(float[ ] colorvalue);
    public abstract float[ ] fromRGB(float[ ] rgbvalue);
    public String getName(int idx);
    public int getNumComponents();
    public int getType();
    public boolean isCS_sRGB();
    public abstract float[ ] toCIEXYZ(float[ ] colorvalue);
    public abstract float[ ] toRGB(float[ ] colorvalue);
}
```

Subclasses: ICC_ColorSpace

Passed To: Color.{Color(), getColorComponents(), getComponents()},
java.awt.image.ColorConvertOp.ColorConvertOp(), java.awt.image.ColorModel.ColorModel(),
java.awt.image.ComponentColorModel.ComponentColorModel(),
java.awt.image.DirectColorModel.DirectColorModel(), java.awt.image.PackedColorModel.PackedColorModel()

Returned By: Color.getColorSpace(), ColorSpace.getInstance(), java.awt.image.ColorModel.getColorSpace()

ICC_ColorSpace   Java 1.2

java.awt.color

This concrete subclass of ColorSpace defines a color space based on an ICC_Profile object
that represents color space profile data in a format defined by the International Color
Consortium (ICC). See *http://www.color.org* for information about ICC standards.

```
public class ICC_ColorSpace extends ColorSpace {
// Public Constructors
    public ICC_ColorSpace(ICC_Profile profile);
// Public Instance Methods
    public ICC_Profile getProfile();
// Public Methods Overriding ColorSpace
    public float[ ] fromCIEXYZ(float[ ] colorvalue);
    public float[ ] fromRGB(float[ ] rgbvalue);
    public float[ ] toCIEXYZ(float[ ] colorvalue);
    public float[ ] toRGB(float[ ] colorvalue);
}
```

Hierarchy: Object→ ColorSpace→ ICC_ColorSpace

ICC_Profile

Java 1.2

java.awt.color

This class represents an International Color Consortium (ICC) color space profile. For details about the profile format, see the ICC Profile Format Specification, Version 3.4, at *http://www.color.org*. Only applications working with custom or specialized color spaces ever need to use this class.

ICC_Profile does not have a public constructor. Obtain an instance by calling the static getInstance() method. There are versions of this method that read profile data from a java.io.InputStream, a string, and an array of bytes. The fourth version of this method takes one of the CS_ constants defined by the ColorSpace class and reads a built-in profile for that color space. (In Sun's Java 1.2 implementation, the profile data for these built-in standard color spaces is in the directory *jre/lib/cmm*.)

```
public class ICC_Profile {
// No Constructor
// Public Constants
    public static final int CLASS_ABSTRACT;                          =5
    public static final int CLASS_COLORSPACECONVERSION;              =4
    public static final int CLASS_DEVICELINK;                        =3
    public static final int CLASS_DISPLAY;                           =1
    public static final int CLASS_INPUT;                             =0
    public static final int CLASS_NAMEDCOLOR;                        =6
    public static final int CLASS_OUTPUT;                            =2
    public static final int icAbsoluteColorimetric;                  =3
    public static final int icCurveCount;                            =8
    public static final int icCurveData;                             =12
    public static final int icHdrAttributes;                         =56
    public static final int icHdrCmmId;                              =4
    public static final int icHdrColorSpace;                         =16
    public static final int icHdrCreator;                            =80
    public static final int icHdrDate;                               =24
    public static final int icHdrDeviceClass;                        =12
    public static final int icHdrFlags;                              =44
    public static final int icHdrIlluminant;                         =68
    public static final int icHdrMagic;                              =36
    public static final int icHdrManufacturer;                       =48
    public static final int icHdrModel;                              =52
    public static final int icHdrPcs;                                =20
    public static final int icHdrPlatform;                           =40
    public static final int icHdrRenderingIntent;                    =64
    public static final int icHdrSize;                               =0
    public static final int icHdrVersion;                            =8
    public static final int icPerceptual;                            =0
    public static final int icRelativeColorimetric;                  =1
    public static final int icSaturation;                            =2
    public static final int icSigAbstractClass;               =1633842036
    public static final int icSigAToB0Tag;                    =1093812784
    public static final int icSigAToB1Tag;                    =1093812785
    public static final int icSigAToB2Tag;                    =1093812786
    public static final int icSigBlueColorantTag;             =1649957210
    public static final int icSigBlueTRCTag;                  =1649693251
    public static final int icSigBToA0Tag;                    =1110589744
    public static final int icSigBToA1Tag;                    =1110589745
    public static final int icSigBToA2Tag;                    =1110589746
    public static final int icSigCalibrationDateTimeTag;      =1667329140
    public static final int icSigCharTargetTag;               =1952543335
    public static final int icSigCmyData;                     =1129142560
```

```
public static final int icSigCmykData;                      =1129142603
public static final int icSigColorSpaceClass;               =1936744803
public static final int icSigCopyrightTag;                  =1668313716
public static final int icSigDeviceMfgDescTag;              =1684893284
public static final int icSigDeviceModelDescTag;            =1684890724
public static final int icSigDisplayClass;                  =1835955314
public static final int icSigGamutTag;                      =1734438260
public static final int icSigGrayData;                      =1196573017
public static final int icSigGrayTRCTag;                    =1800688195
public static final int icSigGreenColorantTag;              =1733843290
public static final int icSigGreenTRCTag;                   =1733579331
public static final int icSigHead;                          =1751474532
public static final int icSigHlsData;                       =1212961568
public static final int icSigHsvData;                       =1213421088
public static final int icSigInputClass;                    =1935896178
public static final int icSigLabData;                       =1281450528
public static final int icSigLinkClass;                     =1818848875
public static final int icSigLuminanceTag;                  =1819635049
public static final int icSigLuvData;                       =1282766368
public static final int icSigMeasurementTag;                =1835360627
public static final int icSigMediaBlackPointTag;            =1651208308
public static final int icSigMediaWhitePointTag;            =2004119668
public static final int icSigNamedColor2Tag;                =1852009522
public static final int icSigNamedColorClass;               =1852662636
public static final int icSigOutputClass;                   =1886549106
public static final int icSigPreview0Tag;                   =1886545200
public static final int icSigPreview1Tag;                   =1886545201
public static final int icSigPreview2Tag;                   =1886545202
public static final int icSigProfileDescriptionTag;         =1684370275
public static final int icSigProfileSequenceDescTag;        =1886610801
public static final int icSigPs2CRD0Tag;                    =1886610480
public static final int icSigPs2CRD1Tag;                    =1886610481
public static final int icSigPs2CRD2Tag;                    =1886610482
public static final int icSigPs2CRD3Tag;                    =1886610483
public static final int icSigPs2CSATag;                     =1886597747
public static final int icSigPs2RenderingIntentTag;         =1886597737
public static final int icSigRedColorantTag;                =1918392666
public static final int icSigRedTRCTag;                     =1918128707
public static final int icSigRgbData;                       =1380401696
public static final int icSigScreeningDescTag;              =1935897188
public static final int icSigScreeningTag;                  =1935897198
public static final int icSigSpace2CLR;                     =843271250
public static final int icSigSpace3CLR;                     =860048466
public static final int icSigSpace4CLR;                     =876825682
public static final int icSigSpace5CLR;                     =893602898
public static final int icSigSpace6CLR;                     =910380114
public static final int icSigSpace7CLR;                     =927157330
public static final int icSigSpace8CLR;                     =943934546
public static final int icSigSpace9CLR;                     =960711762
public static final int icSigSpaceACLR;                     =1094929490
public static final int icSigSpaceBCLR;                     =1111706706
public static final int icSigSpaceCCLR;                     =1128483922
public static final int icSigSpaceDCLR;                     =1145261138
public static final int icSigSpaceECLR;                     =1162038354
public static final int icSigSpaceFCLR;                     =1178815570
public static final int icSigTechnologyTag;                 =1952801640
public static final int icSigUcrBgTag;                      =1650877472
public static final int icSigViewingCondDescTag;            =1987405156
```

```
   public static final int icSigViewingConditionsTag;                          =1986618743
   public static final int icSigXYZData;                                        =1482250784
   public static final int icSigYCbCrData;                                      =1497588338
   public static final int icSigYxyData;                                        =1501067552
   public static final int icTagReserved;                                                =4
   public static final int icTagType;                                                    =0
   public static final int icXYZNumberX;                                                 =8
// Public Class Methods
   public static ICC_Profile getInstance(java.io.InputStream s) throws java.io.IOException;
   public static ICC_Profile getInstance(String fileName) throws java.io.IOException;
   public static ICC_Profile getInstance(byte[ ] data);
   public static ICC_Profile getInstance(int cspace);
// Property Accessor Methods (by property name)
   public int getColorSpaceType();
   public byte[ ] getData();
   public byte[ ] getData(int tagSignature);
   public int getMajorVersion();
   public int getMinorVersion();
   public int getNumComponents();
   public int getPCSType();
   public int getProfileClass();
// Public Instance Methods
   public void setData(int tagSignature, byte[ ] tagData);
   public void write(String fileName) throws java.io.IOException;
   public void write(java.io.OutputStream s) throws java.io.IOException;
// Protected Methods Overriding Object
   protected void finalize();
}
```

Subclasses: ICC_ProfileGray, ICC_ProfileRGB

Passed To: ICC_ColorSpace.ICC_ColorSpace(), java.awt.image.ColorConvertOp.ColorConvertOp()

Returned By: ICC_ColorSpace.getProfile(), ICC_Profile.getInstance(),
java.awt.image.ColorConvertOp.getICC_Profiles()

ICC_ProfileGray   Java 1.2

java.awt.color

A specialized subclass of ICC_Profile that is used to represent certain grayscale color
spaces that meet criteria that allow color space conversions to be optimized. Applications never need to use this class.

```
public class ICC_ProfileGray extends ICC_Profile {
// No Constructor
// Public Instance Methods
   public float getGamma();
   public short[ ] getTRC();
// Public Methods Overriding ICC_Profile
   public float[ ] getMediaWhitePoint();
}
```

Hierarchy: Object → ICC_Profile → ICC_ProfileGray

ICC_ProfileRGB   Java 1.2

java.awt.color

A specialized subclass of ICC_Profile that is used to represent certain RGB color spaces
that meet criteria that allow color space conversions to be optimized. Applications
never need to use this class.

```
public class ICC_ProfileRGB extends ICC_Profile {
// No Constructor
// Public Constants
    public static final int BLUECOMPONENT;                              =2
    public static final int GREENCOMPONENT;                             =1
    public static final int REDCOMPONENT;                               =0
// Public Instance Methods
    public float[ ][ ] getMatrix( );
// Public Methods Overriding ICC_Profile
    public float getGamma(int component);
    public float[ ] getMediaWhitePoint( );
    public short[ ] getTRC(int component);
}
```

Hierarchy: Object→ ICC_Profile→ ICC_ProfileRGB

ProfileDataException   Java 1.2

java.awt.color   *serializable unchecked*

Signals that an error occurred while reading ICC profile data.

```
public class ProfileDataException extends RuntimeException {
// Public Constructors
    public ProfileDataException(String s);
}
```

Hierarchy: Object→ Throwable(Serializable)→ Exception→ RuntimeException→ ProfileDataException

CHAPTER 11

The java.awt.datatransfer Package

The java.awt.datatransfer package contains classes and interfaces that define a framework for user-driven interapplication and intra-application data transfer. It also contains classes that support data transfer through cut-and-paste. The Java 2 platform java.awt.dnd package implements drag-and-drop using the framework defined by this package.

The Transferable interface is implemented by any class that allows data to be transferred. The DataFlavor class defines the type of data to be transferred. Clipboard and ClipboardOwner are used for implementing cut-and-paste. StringSelection is a utility class that enables easy data transfer of strings. Figure 11-1 shows the class hierarchy of this package. See Chapter 6, *Data Transfer*, for more details about data transfer.

Clipboard   Java 1.1
java.awt.datatransfer   PJ1.1

This class represents a clipboard on which data may be transferred using the cut-and-paste metaphor. When data is cut, it should be encapsulated in a Transferable object and registered with a Clipboard object by calling setContents(). A Clipboard can hold only a single piece of data at a time, so a ClipboardOwner object must be specified when data is placed on the clipboard. This object is notified that it no longer owns the clipboard when the data is replaced by other, more recent, data.

When a paste is requested by the user, an application requests the data on the clipboard by calling getContents(), which returns a Transferable object. The methods of this object can be used to negotiate a mutually compatible data format and then actually transfer the data.

A clipboard name is passed to the Clipboard() constructor and may be retrieved with getName(). This name is not actually used in Java 1.1, however.

Note that while an application can create its own private Clipboard objects for intra-application cut-and-paste, it is more common for an application to use the system clipboard to enable cut-and-paste between applications. You can obtain the system

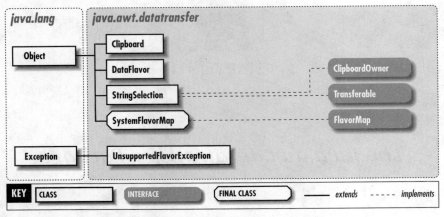

Figure 11-1: The java.awt.datatransfer package

clipboard by calling the getSystemClipboard() method of the current Toolkit object. Untrusted applet code is not allowed to access the system clipboard, so untrusted applets cannot participate in interapplication cut-and-paste.

```
public class Clipboard {
// Public Constructors
    public Clipboard(String name);
// Public Instance Methods
    public Transferable getContents(Object requestor);                    synchronized
    public String getName();
    public void setContents(Transferable contents, ClipboardOwner owner); synchronized
// Protected Instance Fields
    protected Transferable contents;
    protected ClipboardOwner owner;
}
```

Passed To: ClipboardOwner.lostOwnership(), StringSelection.lostOwnership()

Returned By: Toolkit.getSystemClipboard()

ClipboardOwner   Java 1.1
java.awt.datatransfer   PJ1.1

This interface defines the single method that an object that places data on a clipboard must implement. This method is used to notify the object when its data on the clipboard has been replaced by other, more recent, data. An object that places data on a clipboard must remain ready to satisfy requests for that data until lostOwnership() is called.

```
public abstract interface ClipboardOwner {
// Public Instance Methods
    public abstract void lostOwnership(Clipboard clipboard, Transferable contents);
}
```

Implementations: StringSelection

Passed To: Clipboard.setContents()

Type Of: Clipboard.owner

DataFlavor

java.awt.datatransfer

cloneable serializable PJ1.1

This class defines a data format for the purpose of data transfer through Transferable objects. A DataFlavor is characterized by three values. The first is a descriptive human-readable name, passed to a DataFlavor() constructor or set with setHumanPresentableName(). The second value is a MIME type that specifies the data format, while the third is the representation class of the data. This third value is the class of object that is returned by the getTransferData() method of Transferable when data is actually transferred.

In Java 1.1, you can specify either a MIME type or a representation class, but not both. If you specify a MIME type, the representation class is java.io.InputStream, and data is transferred through an input stream. If, on the other hand, you use a Class object to specify the representation class, the MIME type is automatically set to the special value:

> application/x-java-serialized-object class=*classname*

In this case, data is transferred through object serialization.

The plainTextFlavor and stringFlavor constants are predefined DataFlavor objects for transferring text. They illustrate these two distinctly different types of data transfer. plainTextFlavor is "text/plain" data transferred through an input stream, while stringFlavor is a String object transferred directly through serialization.

In Java 1.2, DataFlavor provides several new ways to specify data formats. First, the MIME type constant "application/x-java-serialized-object" is now available as the constant javaSerializedObjectMimeType. Two similar MIME type constants have also been defined. javaJVMLocalObjectMimeType represents a local reference to a Java object. Data flavors of this type can be used only for transfers within a single Java VM. javaRemoteObjectMimeType is a MIME type that represents a remote reference to a java.rmi.Remote object. In this case, a reference to the object, rather than the object data itself, is transferred. This reference can be used with RMI. Note that all three of these MIME type constants are incomplete as is. In order to use them, you must add class=*classname* to the MIME type string, specifying the class name of the object or remote object being transferred.

Another change in Java 1.2 is the addition of the predefined DataFlavor javaFileListFlavor. This DataFlavor represents a list of filenames and is transferred as a java.util.List object containing java.io.File objects. javaFileListFlavor has been added because files and groups of files are commonly used with the drag-and-drop interface of the java.awt.dnd package.

```
public class DataFlavor implements Cloneable, java.io.Externalizable {
// Public Constructors
1.2 public DataFlavor( );
1.2 public DataFlavor(String mimeType) throws ClassNotFoundException;
    public DataFlavor(Class representationClass, String humanPresentableName);
    public DataFlavor(String mimeType, String humanPresentableName);
1.2 public DataFlavor(String mimeType, String humanPresentableName, ClassLoader classLoader)
        throws ClassNotFoundException;
// Public Constants
1.2 public static final DataFlavor javaFileListFlavor;
1.2 public static final String javaJVMLocalObjectMimeType;          ="application/x-java-jvm-local-objectref"
1.2 public static final String javaRemoteObjectMimeType;                 ="application/x-java-remote-object"
1.2 public static final String javaSerializedObjectMimeType;           ="application/x-java-serialized-object"
    public static final DataFlavor plainTextFlavor;
    public static final DataFlavor stringFlavor;
// Protected Class Methods
1.2 protected static final Class tryToLoadClass(String className, ClassLoader fallback)
        throws ClassNotFoundException;
```

```
// Property Accessor Methods (by property name)
1.2 public boolean isFlavorJavaFileListType();                                        default:false
1.2 public boolean isFlavorRemoteObjectType();
1.2 public boolean isFlavorSerializedObjectType();
    public String getHumanPresentableName();                                          default:null
    public void setHumanPresentableName(String humanPresentableName);
    public String getMimeType();
1.2 public boolean isMimeTypeSerializedObject();                                       default:false
1.2 public String getPrimaryType();
    public Class getRepresentationClass();                                             default:null
1.2 public boolean isRepresentationClassInputStream();
1.2 public boolean isRepresentationClassRemote();
1.2 public boolean isRepresentationClassSerializable();
1.2 public String getSubType();
// Public Instance Methods
1.2 public boolean equals(String s);
    public boolean equals(DataFlavor dataFlavor);
1.2 public String getParameter(String paramName);
    public boolean isMimeTypeEqual(String mimeType);
    public final boolean isMimeTypeEqual(DataFlavor dataFlavor);
// Methods Implementing Externalizable
1.2 public void readExternal(java.io.ObjectInput is) throws java.io.IOException,       synchronized
        ClassNotFoundException;
1.2 public void writeExternal(java.io.ObjectOutput os) throws java.io.IOException;      synchronized
// Public Methods Overriding Object
1.2 public Object clone() throws CloneNotSupportedException;
1.2 public boolean equals(Object o);
1.2 public String toString();
// Deprecated Protected Methods
 #    protected String normalizeMimeType(String mimeType);
 #    protected String normalizeMimeTypeParameter(String parameterName, String parameterValue);
}
```

Hierarchy: Object→ DataFlavor(Cloneable, java.io.Externalizable(Serializable))

Passed To: DataFlavor.{equals(), isMimeTypeEqual()}, FlavorMap.getNativesForFlavors(), StringSelection.{getTransferData(), isDataFlavorSupported()}, SystemFlavorMap.{encodeDataFlavor(), getNativesForFlavors()}, Transferable.{getTransferData(), isDataFlavorSupported()}, UnsupportedFlavorException.UnsupportedFlavorException(), java.awt.dnd.DropTargetContext.isDataFlavorSupported(), java.awt.dnd.DropTargetContext.TransferableProxy.{getTransferData(), isDataFlavorSupported()}, java.awt.dnd.DropTargetDragEvent.isDataFlavorSupported(), java.awt.dnd.DropTargetDropEvent.isDataFlavorSupported()

Returned By: StringSelection.getTransferDataFlavors(), SystemFlavorMap.decodeDataFlavor(), Transferable.getTransferDataFlavors(), java.awt.dnd.DropTargetContext.getCurrentDataFlavors(), java.awt.dnd.DropTargetContext.TransferableProxy.getTransferDataFlavors(), java.awt.dnd.DropTargetDragEvent.getCurrentDataFlavors(), java.awt.dnd.DropTargetDropEvent.getCurrentDataFlavors(), java.awt.dnd.peer.DropTargetContextPeer.getTransferDataFlavors()

Type Of: DataFlavor.{javaFileListFlavor, plainTextFlavor, stringFlavor}

FlavorMap

Java 1.2

java.awt.datatransfer

This interface defines methods that map between Java DataFlavor objects and platform-dependent strings that represent the data transfer type to the native system. getFlavorsForNatives() returns a java.util.Map object that maps from native data format names to DataFlavor objects. getNativesForFlavors() returns a Map from DataFlavor objects to native data format names. For both these methods, you may specify either an array of the desired keys or null, to obtain a Map that contains all known key-to-value mappings.

```
public abstract interface FlavorMap {
// Public Instance Methods
    public abstract java.util.Map getFlavorsForNatives(String[ ] natives);
    public abstract java.util.Map getNativesForFlavors(DataFlavor[ ] flavors);
}
```

Implementations: SystemFlavorMap

Passed To: java.awt.dnd.DragSource.startDrag(), java.awt.dnd.DropTarget.{DropTarget(), setFlavorMap()}

Returned By: SystemFlavorMap.getDefaultFlavorMap(), java.awt.dnd.DragSource.getFlavorMap(), java.awt.dnd.DropTarget.getFlavorMap()

StringSelection

Java 1.1

java.awt.datatransfer

PJ1.1

This convenience class implements the Transferable and ClipboardOwner interfaces in order to make it easy to transfer String values through the AWT data transfer mechanism. StringSelection can transfer String values using either the DataFlavor.stringFlavor or DataFlavor.plainTextFlavor data flavors.

To create a StringSelection object, simply pass the String you want to transfer to the StringSelection() constructor. You can then make the StringSelection available for transfer by passing it to the setContents() method of the Clipboard. You need never call the methods of StringSelection yourself.

```
public class StringSelection implements ClipboardOwner, Transferable {
// Public Constructors
    public StringSelection(String data);
// Methods Implementing ClipboardOwner
    public void lostOwnership(Clipboard clipboard, Transferable contents);             empty
// Methods Implementing Transferable
    public Object getTransferData(DataFlavor flavor) throws UnsupportedFlavorException,   synchronized
        java.io.IOException;
    public DataFlavor[ ] getTransferDataFlavors();                                      synchronized
    public boolean isDataFlavorSupported(DataFlavor flavor);
}
```

Hierarchy: Object→ StringSelection(ClipboardOwner, Transferable)

SystemFlavorMap

Java 1.2

java.awt.datatransfer

This FlavorMap implementation reads the mappings from DataFlavor objects to native data format names for the system from an external file. In Sun's Java SDK implementation, for example, this class reads the *flavormap.properties* file.

SystemFlavorMap does not have a public constructor. You can obtain an instance by calling getDefaultFlavorMap(). SystemFlavorMap also defines several static methods that you can use without instantiating the class.

```
public final class SystemFlavorMap implements FlavorMap {
// No Constructor
// Public Class Methods
    public static DataFlavor decodeDataFlavor(String atom) throws ClassNotFoundException;
    public static String decodeJavaMIMEType(String atom);
    public static String encodeDataFlavor(DataFlavor df);
    public static String encodeJavaMIMEType(String mimeType);
    public static FlavorMap getDefaultFlavorMap();
    public static boolean isJavaMIMEType(String atom);
// Methods Implementing FlavorMap
    public java.util.Map getFlavorsForNatives(String[ ] natives);                       synchronized
    public java.util.Map getNativesForFlavors(DataFlavor[ ] flavors);                    synchronized
}
```

Hierarchy: Object→ SystemFlavorMap(FlavorMap)

Transferable   Java 1.1
java.awt.datatransfer   PJ1.1

This interface defines the methods that a class must define if it is to act as the source object in a data transfer operation.

getTransferDataFlavors() should return an array of DataFlavor objects that specify the data types or formats in which the object can provide its data. The DataFlavor objects should be ordered from best format (most richly descriptive) to worst format. isDataFlavorSupported() must return a boolean value that indicates whether it can transfer data using a specified DataFlavor. Finally, getTransferData() must return an object that represents the data formatted as required by the specified DataFlavor.

StringSelection is a predefined class that implements the Transferable interface for the transfer of string data.

```
public abstract interface Transferable {
// Public Instance Methods
    public abstract Object getTransferData(DataFlavor flavor) throws UnsupportedFlavorException, java.io.IOException;
    public abstract DataFlavor[ ] getTransferDataFlavors();
    public abstract boolean isDataFlavorSupported(DataFlavor flavor);
}
```

Implementations: StringSelection, java.awt.dnd.DropTargetContext.TransferableProxy

Passed To: Clipboard.setContents(), ClipboardOwner.lostOwnership(), StringSelection.lostOwnership(), java.awt.dnd.DragGestureEvent.startDrag(), java.awt.dnd.DragSource.{createDragSourceContext(), startDrag()}, java.awt.dnd.DragSourceContext.DragSourceContext(), java.awt.dnd.DropTargetContext.createTransferableProxy()

Returned By: Clipboard.getContents(), java.awt.dnd.DragSourceContext.getTransferable(), java.awt.dnd.DropTargetContext.{createTransferableProxy(), getTransferable()}, java.awt.dnd.DropTargetDropEvent.getTransferable(), java.awt.dnd.peer.DropTargetContextPeer.getTransferable()

Type Of: Clipboard.contents, java.awt.dnd.DropTargetContext.TransferableProxy.transferable

UnsupportedFlavorException   Java 1.1
java.awt.datatransfer   *serializable checked PJ1.1*

Signals that a Transferable object cannot provide data in the requested format.

```
public class UnsupportedFlavorException extends Exception {
// Public Constructors
    public UnsupportedFlavorException(DataFlavor flavor);
}
```

Hierarchy: Object→ Throwable(Serializable)→ Exception→ UnsupportedFlavorException

Thrown By: StringSelection.getTransferData(), Transferable.getTransferData(), java.awt.dnd.DropTargetContext.TransferableProxy.getTransferData()

CHAPTER 12

The java.awt.dnd Package

The java.awt.dnd package contains classes and interfaces that support data transfer through the drag-and-drop metaphor; the package is new in Java 1.2. This functionality is built upon the data transfer framework of the java.awt.datatransfer package.

A DragSource object is a proxy for an object that initiates a drag, while a DropTarget object is a proxy for an object that wishes to accept drops. All inter-object communication during the drag process is done through the various event classes defined by this package. Figure 12-1 shows the class hierarchy of this package. See Chapter 6, *Data Transfer*, for more details on drag-and-drop.

Autoscroll   Java 1.2

java.awt.dnd

This interface allows a scrollable component to scroll itself as part of the drag-and-drop process, so that a user can drop an object anywhere within the component's scrollable content. Consider, for example, the problem of cutting a paragraph of text from the top of a long document and dragging it down to the bottom of the same document. While the drag-and-drop operation is in progress, the user obviously cannot operate the scrollbar, since the mouse is already in use. So some other technique is necessary to enable scrolling during a drag-and-drop operation.

The Autoscroll interface enables this specialized form of scrolling. When an object is first dragged over a component that implements Autoscroll, the drag-and-drop system calls the component's getAutoscrollInsets() method. This defines an autoscroll region at the edges of the component. If, during the drag, the user places the mouse within this autoscroll region and holds it there (for a platform-dependent amount of time), the drag-and-drop system begins to call the autoscroll() method repeatedly (at a platform-dependent repetition rate) until the user once again moves the mouse. The autoscroll() method of the component is responsible for scrolling the content. The direction of the scroll is determined by the position of the mouse pointer, which is passed as an argument to autoscroll().

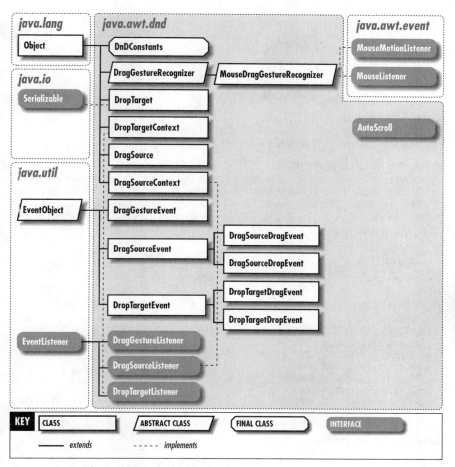

Figure 12–1: The java.awt.dnd package

```
pub ic abstract interface Autoscroll {
// Public Instance Methods
    public abstract void autoscroll(Point cursorLocn);
    public abstract Insets getAutoscrollInsets();
}
```

DnDConstants   Java 1.2

java.awt.dnd

Successful completion of a drag-and-drop operation can result in a number of different types of actions being performed. This interface defines constants that represent the possible actions:

ACTION_COPY

This is the most common action: the dragged object is to be copied in some way. ACTION_COPY is also used as a default action when there is only one possible action, even if that action is not really a copy.

ACTION_MOVE

The dragged object is to be copied by the destination. The source object deletes its copy after the object is successfully transferred.

ACTION_COPY_OR_MOVE

This constant is the combination of ACTION_COPY and ACTION_MOVE. Many drop targets can accept drops of either type; this constant is used to indicate that fact.

ACTION_LINK or ACTION_REFERENCE

These two constants are synonyms. They indicate that the destination object should create a link to the transferred object or share a reference to the transferred object with the source object. Note that this action has a particularly vague meaning; its use is not recommended except for intra-application drag-and-drop of specialized data types.

ACTION_NONE

This constant specifies that no actions are supported. It is used internally by the drag-and-drop API but is not commonly used by application-level code.

```
public final class DnDConstants {
// No Constructor
// Public Constants
    public static final int ACTION_COPY;                        =1
    public static final int ACTION_COPY_OR_MOVE;                =3
    public static final int ACTION_LINK;              =1073741824
    public static final int ACTION_MOVE;                        =2
    public static final int ACTION_NONE;                        =0
    public static final int ACTION_REFERENCE;         =1073741824
}
```

DragGestureEvent   Java 1.2

java.awt.dnd   *serializable event*

This event type is fired by a DragGestureRecognizer and sent to the dragGestureRecognized() method of a DragGestureListener. Unlike many event classes, which are merely holders of event information, DragGestureEvent also defines the startDrag() method, which can be used to initiate the drag-and-drop process.

When the dragGestureRecognized() method is invoked, it should start the drag-and-drop process by invoking this startDrag() method, passing in the initial drag cursor to display, the Transferable data to transfer, and the DragSourceListener that monitors the drag process. If there is to be an image dragged along with the drag cursor, the image and its offset from the cursor hotspot may also be passed to startDrag().

The other methods of DragGestureEvent() are accessor methods that return information about the event. Most applications do not need to call them.

```
public class DragGestureEvent extends java.util.EventObject {
// Public Constructors
    public DragGestureEvent(DragGestureRecognizer dgr, int act, Point ori, java.util.List evs);
// Property Accessor Methods (by property name)
    public Component getComponent();
```

```
    public int getDragAction();
    public Point getDragOrigin();
    public DragSource getDragSource();
    public DragGestureRecognizer getSourceAsDragGestureRecognizer();
    public java.awt.event.InputEvent getTriggerEvent();
// Public Instance Methods
    public java.util.Iterator iterator();
    public void startDrag(Cursor dragCursor, java.awt.datatransfer.Transferable transferable, DragSourceListener dsl)
        throws InvalidDnDOperationException;
    public void startDrag(Cursor dragCursor, Image dragImage, Point imageOffset,
                    java.awt.datatransfer.Transferable transferable, DragSourceListener dsl)
        throws InvalidDnDOperationException;
    public Object[ ] toArray();
    public Object[ ] toArray(Object[ ] array);
}
```

Hierarchy: Object → java.util.EventObject(Serializable) → DragGestureEvent

Passed To: Toolkit.createDragSourceContextPeer(), DragGestureListener.dragGestureRecognized(),
DragSource.{createDragSourceContext(), startDrag()}, DragSourceContext.DragSourceContext()

Returned By: DragSourceContext.getTrigger()

DragGestureListener

Java 1.2

java.awt.dnd

event listener

This interface defines the method that is invoked by a DragGestureRecognizer when the
user initiates a drag-and-drop action. When dragGestureRecognized() is called, the DragGestureListener should prepare a Transferable object to be transferred through the drag-and-
drop process and then initiate that process by calling the startDrag() method of the
DragGestureEvent object.

You do not typically pass a DragGestureListener to an addDragGestureListener() method.
Instead, you specify the DragGestureListener when you call the createDefaultDragGestureRec-
ognizer() method of a DragSource object. This method creates a DragGestureRecognizer and
automatically registers the DragGestureListener with it.

```
public abstract interface DragGestureListener extends java.util.EventListener {
// Public Instance Methods
    public abstract void dragGestureRecognized(DragGestureEvent dge);
}
```

Hierarchy: (DragGestureListener(java.util.EventListener))

Passed To: Toolkit.createDragGestureRecognizer(), DragGestureRecognizer.{addDragGestureListener(),
DragGestureRecognizer(), removeDragGestureListener()}, DragSource.{createDefaultDragGestureRecognizer(),
createDragGestureRecognizer()}, MouseDragGestureRecognizer.MouseDragGestureRecognizer()

Type Of: DragGestureRecognizer.dragGestureListener

DragGestureRecognizer

Java 1.2

java.awt.dnd

Drag-and-drop operations may be initiated in different ways on different native platforms. This abstract class is the superclass of the platform-dependent classes that are
used to recognize the platform-dependent gesture used to begin a drag. As an abstract
class, you cannot instantiate a DragGestureRecognizer directly. Instead, you typically create
a DragGestureRecognizer by calling the createDefaultDragGestureRecognizer() method of a Drag-
Source object. If you want to allow the user to initiate drags with nonstandard gestures,

you may implement your own DragGestureRecognizer subclass and instantiate it by calling the createDragGestureRecognizer() method of java.awt.Toolkit.

When you create a DragGestureRecognizer, you specify the Component it is to look for drag gestures over and the DragGestureListener it is to notify when it recognizes one. The creation process automatically links these three objects together, so you typically never need to do anything with a DragGestureRecognizer other than create it.

One additional piece of information you must supply when you create a DragGestureRecognizer is a bit mask of allowed drag actions. ACTION_COPY, ACTION_MOVE, and ACTION_LINK actions are usually initiated with different gestures (different modifier keys). A DragGestureRecognizer must know which actions are available so it can know which gestures to recognize and which to ignore.

```
public abstract class DragGestureRecognizer {
// Protected Constructors
    protected DragGestureRecognizer(DragSource ds);
    protected DragGestureRecognizer(DragSource ds, Component c);
    protected DragGestureRecognizer(DragSource ds, Component c, int sa);
    protected DragGestureRecognizer(DragSource ds, Component c, int sa, DragGestureListener dgl);
// Event Registration Methods (by event name)
    public void addDragGestureListener(DragGestureListener dgl)          synchronized
        throws java.util.TooManyListenersException;
    public void removeDragGestureListener(DragGestureListener dgl);      synchronized
// Property Accessor Methods (by property name)
    public Component getComponent();                                     synchronized
    public void setComponent(Component c);                              synchronized
    public DragSource getDragSource();
    public int getSourceActions();                                      synchronized
    public void setSourceActions(int actions);                          synchronized
    public java.awt.event.InputEvent getTriggerEvent();
// Public Instance Methods
    public void resetRecognizer();
// Protected Instance Methods
    protected void appendEvent(java.awt.event.InputEvent awtie);        synchronized
    protected void fireDragGestureRecognized(int dragAction, Point p);  synchronized
    protected abstract void registerListeners();
    protected abstract void unregisterListeners();
// Protected Instance Fields
    protected Component component;
    protected DragGestureListener dragGestureListener;
    protected DragSource dragSource;
    protected java.util.ArrayList events;
    protected int sourceActions;
}
```

Subclasses: MouseDragGestureRecognizer

Passed To: DragGestureEvent.DragGestureEvent()

Returned By: Toolkit.createDragGestureRecognizer(),
DragGestureEvent.getSourceAsDragGestureRecognizer(), DragSource.{createDefaultDragGestureRecognizer(),
createDragGestureRecognizer()}

DragSource   Java 1.2
java.awt.dnd

This class coordinates the initiation of drag-and-drop operations. Despite the central role it plays in the drag-and-drop system, it is not used much in typical drag-and-drop code.

You can create a DragSource object by calling the constructor, but because the DragSource object does not hold any state, you can continually reuse a single object. Call the static getDefaultDragSource() method to obtain a reference to a shared default DragSource object.

Once you have obtained a DragSource object, call createDefaultDragGestureRecognizer() to create and register a DragGestureRecognizer object that detects user gestures that should initiate drags. If you want to drag an image that represents the dragged data along with the drag cursor, you may also call the isDragImageSupported() method to find out whether that option is supported on the native platform.

After you have called these two methods, you typically never need to use the Drag-Source again. The startDrag() method of the DragSource is responsible for initiating a drag action, but it is easier to invoke it through the startDrag() utility method of the DragGes-tureEvent class instead.

```
public class DragSource {
// Public Constructors
    public DragSource();
// Public Constants
    public static final Cursor DefaultCopyDrop;
    public static final Cursor DefaultCopyNoDrop;
    public static final Cursor DefaultLinkDrop;
    public static final Cursor DefaultLinkNoDrop;
    public static final Cursor DefaultMoveDrop;
    public static final Cursor DefaultMoveNoDrop;
// Public Class Methods
    public static DragSource getDefaultDragSource();
    public static boolean isDragImageSupported();
// Public Instance Methods
    public DragGestureRecognizer createDefaultDragGestureRecognizer(Component c, int actions,
                                        DragGestureListener dgl);
    public DragGestureRecognizer createDragGestureRecognizer(Class recognizerAbstractClass, Component c,
                                        int actions, DragGestureListener dgl);
    public java.awt.datatransfer.FlavorMap getFlavorMap();                    default:SystemFlavorMap
    public void startDrag(DragGestureEvent trigger, Cursor dragCursor, java.awt.datatransfer.Transferable transferable,
                                        DragSourceListener dsl) throws InvalidDnDOperationException;
    public void startDrag(DragGestureEvent trigger, Cursor dragCursor, java.awt.datatransfer.Transferable transferable,
                                        DragSourceListener dsl, java.awt.datatransfer.FlavorMap flavorMap)
        throws InvalidDnDOperationException;
    public void startDrag(DragGestureEvent trigger, Cursor dragCursor, Image dragImage, Point dragOffset,
                                        java.awt.datatransfer.Transferable transferable, DragSourceListener dsl)
        throws InvalidDnDOperationException;
    public void startDrag(DragGestureEvent trigger, Cursor dragCursor, Image dragImage, Point imageOffset,
                                        java.awt.datatransfer.Transferable transferable, DragSourceListener dsl,
                                        java.awt.datatransfer.FlavorMap flavorMap) throws InvalidDnDOperationException;
// Protected Instance Methods
    protected DragSourceContext createDragSourceContext(java.awt.dnd.peer.DragSourceContextPeer dscp,
                                        DragGestureEvent dgl, Cursor dragCursor,
                                        Image dragImage, Point imageOffset,
                                        java.awt.datatransfer.Transferable t,
                                        DragSourceListener dsl);
}
```

Passed To: Toolkit.createDragGestureRecognizer(), DragGestureRecognizer.DragGestureRecognizer(), MouseDragGestureRecognizer.MouseDragGestureRecognizer()

Returned By: DragGestureEvent.getDragSource(), DragGestureRecognizer.getDragSource(), DragSource.getDefaultDragSource(), DragSourceContext.getDragSource()

Type Of: DragGestureRecognizer.dragSource

DragSourceContext   Java 1.2

java.awt.dnd

This class contains state information about a drag operation currently in progress. It is the DragSourceContext that is responsible for communicating with the native drag-and-drop system of the underlying platform and relaying drag-and-drop events to the DragSourceListener. Although this is an important class, it does its work in the background, and you typically do not need to use it. If you do want to use it, for example, to perform cursor animation with the setCursor() method, you may obtain the current DragSourceContext from any DragSourceEvent object.

```
public class DragSourceContext implements DragSourceListener {
// Public Constructors
    public DragSourceContext(java.awt.dnd.peer.DragSourceContextPeer dscp, DragGestureEvent trigger,
                Cursor dragCursor, Image dragImage, Point offset, java.awt.datatransfer.Transferable t,
                DragSourceListener dsl);
// Protected Constants
    protected static final int CHANGED;                                          =3
    protected static final int DEFAULT;                                          =0
    protected static final int ENTER;                                            =1
    protected static final int OVER;                                             =2
// Event Registration Methods (by event name)
    public void addDragSourceListener(DragSourceListener dsl)                     synchronized
        throws java.util.TooManyListenersException;
    public void removeDragSourceListener(DragSourceListener dsl);                 synchronized
// Property Accessor Methods (by property name)
    public Component getComponent();
    public Cursor getCursor();
    public void setCursor(Cursor c);
    public DragSource getDragSource();
    public int getSourceActions();
    public java.awt.datatransfer.Transferable getTransferable();
    public DragGestureEvent getTrigger();
// Public Instance Methods
    public void transferablesFlavorsChanged();
// Methods Implementing DragSourceListener
    public void dragDropEnd(DragSourceDropEvent dsde);                            synchronized
    public void dragEnter(DragSourceDragEvent dsde);                             synchronized
    public void dragExit(DragSourceEvent dse);                                   synchronized
    public void dragOver(DragSourceDragEvent dsde);                             synchronized
    public void dropActionChanged(DragSourceDragEvent dsde);                     synchronized
// Protected Instance Methods
    protected void updateCurrentCursor(int dropOp, int targetAct, int status);
}
```

Hierarchy: Object→ DragSourceContext(DragSourceListener(java.util.EventListener))

Passed To: DragSourceDragEvent.DragSourceDragEvent(), DragSourceDropEvent.DragSourceDropEvent(), DragSourceEvent.DragSourceEvent(), java.awt.dnd.peer.DragSourceContextPeer.startDrag()

Returned By: DragSource.createDragSourceContext(), DragSourceEvent.getDragSourceContext()

DragSourceDragEvent
java.awt.dnd

Java 1.2

serializable event

This event type is fired by a DragSourceContext and passed to the dragEnter(), dragOver(), dragExit(), and dragActionChanged() methods of a DragSourceListener. These methods may use the notification as an opportunity to perform drag-over animation effects, by changing the cursor, for example.

isLocalDropTarget() specifies whether the drop target currently under the cursor is in the same Java VM as the drag source. getUserAction() returns the current drag action selected by the user. This is usually a function of the modifier keys the user is holding down; these modifiers are available from getGestureModifiers(). getTargetActions() returns a bit mask of the actions that the drop target can support, and getDropAction() is the intersection of the user action with the set of target actions.

```java
public class DragSourceDragEvent extends DragSourceEvent {
// Public Constructors
    public DragSourceDragEvent(DragSourceContext dsc, int dropAction, int actions, int modifiers);
// Property Accessor Methods (by property name)
    public int getDropAction();
    public int getGestureModifiers();
    public int getTargetActions();
    public int getUserAction();
}
```

Hierarchy: Object→ java.util.EventObject(Serializable)→ DragSourceEvent→ DragSourceDragEvent

Passed To: DragSourceContext.{dragEnter(), dragOver(), dropActionChanged()},
DragSourceListener.{dragEnter(), dragOver(), dropActionChanged()}

DragSourceDropEvent
java.awt.dnd

Java 1.2

serializable event

This event type is fired by the DragSourceContext and is passed to the dragDropEnd() method of a DragSourceListener to signify that the drag-and-drop operation is complete. getDropSuccess() returns true if the drop occurs and the data is successfully transferred. It returns false if the drag is cancelled, if the drop is performed over an invalid drop target, or if the data transfer is not successful. getDropAction() returns the action (see DnD-Constants) that is actually performed. The user's selected action may change during the drag, so this value may not be the same as the initially selected action.

```java
public class DragSourceDropEvent extends DragSourceEvent {
// Public Constructors
    public DragSourceDropEvent(DragSourceContext dsc);
    public DragSourceDropEvent(DragSourceContext dsc, int action, boolean success);
// Public Instance Methods
    public int getDropAction();
    public boolean getDropSuccess();
}
```

Hierarchy: Object→ java.util.EventObject(Serializable)→ DragSourceEvent→ DragSourceDropEvent

Passed To: DragSourceContext.dragDropEnd(), DragSourceListener.dragDropEnd()

DragSourceEvent
java.awt.dnd

Java 1.2

serializable event

This class is the superclass of event types fired by a DragSourceContext to notify a DragSourceListener about events in the drag-and-drop process. Although applications typically do not need to do so, they can call getDragSourceContext() or getSource() to obtain a reference to the current DragSourceContext. This object can be used, for example, to perform drag over animation effects by changing the current drag cursor. If you are writing a DragSourceListener that handles drags on more than one component, you can determine which component initiated the drag by calling getSource() to obtain a DragSourceContext and then calling its getComponent() method.

See also DragSourceDragEvent and DragSourceDropEvent.

```
public class DragSourceEvent extends java.util.EventObject {
// Public Constructors
    public DragSourceEvent(DragSourceContext dsc);
// Public Instance Methods
    public DragSourceContext getDragSourceContext();
}
```

Hierarchy: Object→ java.util.EventObject(Serializable)→ DragSourceEvent

Subclasses: DragSourceDragEvent, DragSourceDropEvent

Passed To: DragSourceContext.dragExit(), DragSourceListener.dragExit()

DragSourceListener   Java 1.2
java.awt.dnd   *event listener*

This interface is implemented by objects that allow data to be transferred through drag-and-drop and want to be notified about the progress of the drag-and-drop process. The methods of this interface are invoked by a DragSourceContext at various interesting points during the drag-and-drop. The methods are passed a DragSourceDragEvent or a DragSource-DropEvent, both of which are subclasses of DragSourceEvent. The methods are:

dragDropEnd()

Invoked when the drag-and-drop operation is complete and has ended in success or failure. This is the only method that is passed a DragSourceDropEvent, instead of a DragSourceDragEvent. If the drag is of type ACTION_MOVE and the getDropSuccess() method of DragSourceDropEvent returns true, the DragSourceListener knows that the data has been safely transferred to the drop target and should delete the source copy of that data.

dragEnter()

Called when the drag cursor has entered an active drop target that has indicated an interest in and capability to receive a drop. This method should initiate any custom drag over effects.

dragExit()

Invoked when the drag cursor has left a receptive drop target. This method should terminate any custom drag over effects.

dragOver()

Called continuously while the mouse remains within a receptive drop target. Because this method is called very frequently, it should not perform any lengthy operations.

dropActionChanged()

Invoked if the user changes his desired drop action, typically by changing the keyboard modifiers she is holding down. If you are displaying a custom drag cursor, this method may need to modify the currently displayed cursor.

```
public abstract interface DragSourceListener extends java.util.EventListener {
// Public Instance Methods
    public abstract void dragDropEnd(DragSourceDropEvent dsde);
    public abstract void dragEnter(DragSourceDragEvent dsde);
    public abstract void dragExit(DragSourceEvent dse);
    public abstract void dragOver(DragSourceDragEvent dsde);
    public abstract void dropActionChanged(DragSourceDragEvent dsde);
}
```

Hierarchy: (DragSourceListener(java.util.EventListener))

Implementations: DragSourceContext

Passed To: DragGestureEvent.startDrag(), DragSource.{createDragSourceContext(), startDrag()}, DragSourceContext.{addDragSourceListener(), DragSourceContext(), removeDragSourceListener()}

DropTarget
Java 1.2

java.awt.dnd *serializable*

This class holds the state necessary for a Component to accept drops. Create a DropTarget by specifying the Component with which it is to be associated and the DropTargetListener that responds to interesting events during a drag-and-drop operation. You may optionally specify a bit mask of drop actions that this DropTarget can support and a boolean value that indicates whether the DropTarget is currently active. If you do not specify these optional values, your DropTarget supports ACTION_COPY_OR_MOVE and is active.

Once you have created a DropTarget, you often never have to do anything else with it. The DropTarget() constructor automatically connects the DropTarget with the Component it serves and the DropTargetListener it notifies, so you do not have to perform any of the registration yourself. In fact, the only time you typically need to use the DropTarget object you create is if you need to activate or deactivate it with setActive().

```
public class DropTarget implements DropTargetListener, Serializable {
// Public Constructors
    public DropTarget();
    public DropTarget(Component c, DropTargetListener dtl);
    public DropTarget(Component c, int ops, DropTargetListener dtl);
    public DropTarget(Component c, int ops, DropTargetListener dtl, boolean act);
    public DropTarget(Component c, int ops, DropTargetListener dtl, boolean act, java.awt.datatransfer.FlavorMap fm);
// Inner Classes
    protected static class DropTargetAutoScroller implements java.awt.event.ActionListener;
// Event Registration Methods (by event name)
    public void addDropTargetListener(DropTargetListener dtl)                              synchronized
        throws java.util.TooManyListenersException;
    public void removeDropTargetListener(DropTargetListener dtl);                          synchronized
// Property Accessor Methods (by property name)
    public boolean isActive();                                              synchronized default:true
    public void setActive(boolean isActive);                                              synchronized
    public Component getComponent();                                        synchronized default:null
    public void setComponent(Component c);                                                synchronized
    public int getDefaultActions();                                           synchronized default:3
    public void setDefaultActions(int ops);                                               synchronized
    public DropTargetContext getDropTargetContext();
    public java.awt.datatransfer.FlavorMap getFlavorMap();                        default:SystemFlavorMap
    public void setFlavorMap(java.awt.datatransfer.FlavorMap fm);
// Public Instance Methods
    public void addNotify(java.awt.peer.ComponentPeer peer);
    public void removeNotify(java.awt.peer.ComponentPeer peer);
```

java.awt.dnd

```
// Methods Implementing DropTargetListener
   public void dragEnter(DropTargetDragEvent dtde);                                    synchronized
   public void dragExit(DropTargetEvent dte);                                          synchronized
   public void dragOver(DropTargetDragEvent dtde);                                     synchronized
   public void drop(DropTargetDropEvent dtde);                                         synchronized
   public void dropActionChanged(DropTargetDragEvent dtde);
// Protected Instance Methods
   protected void clearAutoscroll();
   protected DropTarget.DropTargetAutoScroller createDropTargetAutoScroller(Component c, Point p);
   protected DropTargetContext createDropTargetContext();
   protected void initializeAutoscrolling(Point p);
   protected void updateAutoscroll(Point dragCursorLocn);
}
```

Hierarchy: Object→ DropTarget(DropTargetListener(java.util.EventListener), Serializable)

Passed To: Component.setDropTarget(), java.awt.dnd.peer.DropTargetPeer.{addDropTarget(), removeDropTarget()}

Returned By: Component.getDropTarget(), DropTargetContext.getDropTarget(), java.awt.dnd.peer.DropTargetContextPeer.getDropTarget()

DropTarget.DropTargetAutoScroller   Java 1.2

java.awt.dnd

This protected inner class implements autoscrolling behavior for a drop target. If the drop target is associated with a component that implements Autoscroll, this class invokes the autoscroll() method of that component as appropriate. Applications never need to use this class directly. Applications that want to override the default autoscrolling behavior can subclass this class and override the createDropTargetAutoScroller() method of DropTarget to return an instance of the subclass.

```
protected static class DropTarget.DropTargetAutoScroller implements java.awt.event.ActionListener {
// Protected Constructors
   protected DropTargetAutoScroller(Component c, Point p);
// Methods Implementing ActionListener
   public void actionPerformed(java.awt.event.ActionEvent e);                          synchronized
// Protected Instance Methods
   protected void stop();
   protected void updateLocation(Point newLocn);                                       synchronized
}
```

Returned By: DropTarget.createDropTargetAutoScroller()

DropTargetContext   Java 1.2

java.awt.dnd

This class contains state information about a drag operation currently in progress above a DropTarget. The DropTargetContext is responsible for communicating with the native drag-and-drop system of the underlying platform and relaying drag-and-drop events from that native system to the DropTargetListener.

Although this is an important class, it does its work internally, and application-level code does not typically need to use it. DropTargetContext does define some important methods, such as acceptDrag() and acceptDrop(), but these are typically invoked through the utility methods of DropTargetDragEvent and DropTargetDropEvent. If you ever do need to use a DropTargetContext directly, it is available from any DropTargetEvent.

```
public class DropTargetContext {
// No Constructor
// Inner Classes
    protected class TransferableProxy implements java.awt.datatransfer.Transferable;
// Public Instance Methods
    public void addNotify(java.awt.dnd.peer.DropTargetContextPeer dtcp);                synchronized
    public void dropComplete(boolean success) throws InvalidDnDOperationException;
    public Component getComponent();
    public DropTarget getDropTarget();
    public void removeNotify();                                                         synchronized
// Protected Instance Methods
    protected void acceptDrag(int dragOperation);
    protected void acceptDrop(int dropOperation);
    protected java.awt.datatransfer.Transferable createTransferableProxy(java.awt.datatransfer.Transferable t,
                                     boolean local);
    protected java.awt.datatransfer.DataFlavor[ ] getCurrentDataFlavors();
    protected java.util.List getCurrentDataFlavorsAsList();
    protected int getTargetActions();
    protected java.awt.datatransfer.Transferable getTransferable() throws             synchronized
        InvalidDnDOperationException;
    protected boolean isDataFlavorSupported(java.awt.datatransfer.DataFlavor df);
    protected void rejectDrag();
    protected void rejectDrop();
    protected void setTargetActions(int actions);
}
```

Passed To: DropTargetDragEvent.DropTargetDragEvent(), DropTargetDropEvent.DropTargetDropEvent(),
DropTargetEvent.DropTargetEvent()

Returned By: DropTarget.{createDropTargetContext(), getDropTargetContext()},
DropTargetEvent.getDropTargetContext()

Type Of: DropTargetEvent.context

DropTargetContext.TransferableProxy   Java 1.2

java.awt.dnd

This protected inner class is used by the protected createTransferableProxy() method of
DropTargetContext. Applications never need to use this class. This class is not defined by
the JFC drag-and-drop specification and its inclusion in the public API of java.awt.dnd
was probably unintentional.

```
protected class DropTargetContext.TransferableProxy implements java.awt.datatransfer.Transferable {
// No Constructor
// Methods Implementing Transferable
    public Object getTransferData(java.awt.datatransfer.DataFlavor df)                 synchronized
        throws java.awt.datatransfer.UnsupportedFlavorException, java.io.IOException;
    public java.awt.datatransfer.DataFlavor[ ] getTransferDataFlavors();               synchronized
    public boolean isDataFlavorSupported(java.awt.datatransfer.DataFlavor flavor);     synchronized
// Protected Instance Fields
    protected boolean isLocal;
    protected java.awt.datatransfer.Transferable transferable;
}
```

DropTargetDragEvent   Java 1.2

java.awt.dnd   *serializable event*

This event is fired by a DropTargetContext and passed to the dragEnter(), dragOver(), and
dropActionChanged() methods of a DropTargetListener. Each of these methods should use

getDropAction(), getCurrentDataFlavors(), and related methods to check whether the drop target knows how to handle the drag action and is able to interpret the data formats offered. If so, the method should call acceptDrag(). If not, it should call rejectDrag(). See DropTargetListener for further details.

```
public class DropTargetDragEvent extends DropTargetEvent {
// Public Constructors
    public DropTargetDragEvent(DropTargetContext dtc, Point cursorLocn, int dropAction, int srcActions);
// Property Accessor Methods (by property name)
    public java.awt.datatransfer.DataFlavor[ ] getCurrentDataFlavors();
    public java.util.List getCurrentDataFlavorsAsList();
    public int getDropAction();
    public Point getLocation();
    public int getSourceActions();
// Public Instance Methods
    public void acceptDrag(int dragOperation);
    public boolean isDataFlavorSupported(java.awt.datatransfer.DataFlavor df);
    public void rejectDrag();
}
```

Hierarchy: Object→ java.util.EventObject(Serializable)→ DropTargetEvent→ DropTargetDragEvent

Passed To: DropTarget.{dragEnter(), dragOver(), dropActionChanged()}, DropTargetListener.{dragEnter(), dragOver(), dropActionChanged()}

DropTargetDropEvent   Java 1.2
java.awt.dnd   *serializable event*

This event is fired by a DropTargetContext and delivered to the drop() method of a DropTargetListener. This method should call getDropAction() to ensure that it is able to perform the requested action. It should also call getCurrentDataFlavors() or isDataFlavorSupported() to ensure that it can interpret the data that is transferred. If it cannot perform the action or interpret the data, it should call rejectDrag() and return.

If the DropTargetListener can perform the action and interpret the data, it should accept the drop. It does this in a four-step process. First, it calls acceptDrop() to signal that it accepts the drop. Second, it calls getTransferable() to obtain a java.awt.datatransfer.Transferable object. Third, it calls the getTransferData() method of Transferable to actually transfer the data.

Finally, if the data transfer fails for any reason, the DropTargetListener should pass false to the dropComplete() method of the DropTargetDropEvent, indicating that the drop action is complete but that it was not successful. If the data transfer is successful and the data has been safely and completely transferred, the drop() method should pass true to the dropComplete() method. This notifies the system that the data has been successfully transferred. The notification is passed on to the DragSourceListener, which can then complete its part of the action. For example, if the action is ACTION_MOVE, the DragSourceListener deletes its copy of the data once it receives notification that the DropTargetListener has successfully copied it.

```
public class DropTargetDropEvent extends DropTargetEvent {
// Public Constructors
    public DropTargetDropEvent(DropTargetContext dtc, Point cursorLocn, int dropAction, int srcActions);
    public DropTargetDropEvent(DropTargetContext dtc, Point cursorLocn, int dropAction, int srcActions,
                               boolean isLocal);
// Property Accessor Methods (by property name)
    public java.awt.datatransfer.DataFlavor[ ] getCurrentDataFlavors();
    public java.util.List getCurrentDataFlavorsAsList();
    public int getDropAction();
```

```
    public boolean isLocalTransfer();
    public Point getLocation();
    public int getSourceActions();
    public java.awt.datatransfer.Transferable getTransferable();
// Public Instance Methods
    public void acceptDrop(int dropAction);
    public void dropComplete(boolean success);
    public boolean isDataFlavorSupported(java.awt.datatransfer.DataFlavor df);
    public void rejectDrop();
}
```

Hierarchy: Object→ java.util.EventObject(Serializable)→ DropTargetEvent→ DropTargetDropEvent

Passed To: DropTarget.drop(), DropTargetListener.drop()

DropTargetEvent   Java 1.2

java.awt.dnd   *serializable event*

This class is the superclass of both DropTargetDragEvent and DropTargetDropEvent. getDropTargetContext() returns the DropTargetContext object that generated the event, and getSource() returns the corresponding DropTarget object. Applications rarely need to use these methods, however.

```
public class DropTargetEvent extends java.util.EventObject {
// Public Constructors
    public DropTargetEvent(DropTargetContext dtc);
// Public Instance Methods
    public DropTargetContext getDropTargetContext();
// Protected Instance Fields
    protected DropTargetContext context;
}
```

Hierarchy: Object→ java.util.EventObject(Serializable)→ DropTargetEvent

Subclasses: DropTargetDragEvent, DropTargetDropEvent

Passed To: DropTarget.dragExit(), DropTargetListener.dragExit()

DropTargetListener   Java 1.2

java.awt.dnd   *event listener*

This interface is implemented by objects that want to be able to receive dropped data. Its methods are invoked by a DropTargetContext at various interesting points in the drag-and-drop process. The methods of this interface are passed a DropTargetEvent or one of its subclasses, a DropTargetDragEvent or a DropTargetDropEvent. The methods are:

dragEnter()
> Invoked when a drag enters the Component associated with the DropTargetListener. This method should call getDropAction() to determine whether it can perform the requested action and either getCurrentDataFlavors() or isDataFlavorSupported() to determine whether it can interpret the data that is being offered. If so, it should call the acceptDrag() method of the event object. If not, it should call the rejectDrag() method.

> If this method accepts the drag, it may also perform or initiate custom graphical drag under effects on the associated Component. These effects provide feedback to the user that the drop target Component is interested in receiving the drop.

dragExit()

> Called when a previously accepted drag leaves the DropTarget. If the dragEnter() method performed any custom drag under effects, this method should undo them.

dragOver()

> Invoked continuously while the mouse pointer remains over the DragTarget. In most cases, this method need not do anything. If the DropTarget is a complex one that is capable of accepting drags in some regions but not in other regions, this method should behave like dragEnter() and call the acceptDrag() or rejectDrag() methods of the event object to inform the system whether a drag is possible at the current location. In this case, this method is also responsible for any custom drag under graphical effects.

drop()

> Called when data is dropped over the DropTarget. This method should determine whether the DropTarget can accept the drop and call the acceptDrop() or rejectDrop() method of the DropTargetDropEvent event object. If it accepts the drop, it must then transfer the data, perform the requested action, and call dropComplete(). See DropTargetDropEvent for details on this process. This method need not undo your drag under effects; the dragExit() method is invoked for this purpose.

dropActionChanged()

> Invoked when the user changes the requested action in mid-drag. This typically occurs if the user changes the modifier keys currently held down. This method should behave like dragEnter() to evaluate whether the drop target can perform the requested action on the offered data and then call acceptDrag() or rejectDrag() and begin or end custom drag under effects, as appropriate.

```
public abstract interface DropTargetListener extends java.util.EventListener {
// Public Instance Methods
    public abstract void dragEnter(DropTargetDragEvent dtde);
    public abstract void dragExit(DropTargetEvent dte);
    public abstract void dragOver(DropTargetDragEvent dtde);
    public abstract void drop(DropTargetDropEvent dtde);
    public abstract void dropActionChanged(DropTargetDragEvent dtde);
}
```

Hierarchy: (DropTargetListener(java.util.EventListener))

Implementations: DropTarget

Passed To: DropTarget.{addDropTargetListener(), DropTarget(), removeDropTargetListener()}

InvalidDnDOperationException   Java 1.2

java.awt.dnd   *serializable unchecked*

Signals that a misconfiguration or error of some sort prevents a drag-and-drop operation from completing normally. This exception is thrown by methods throughout the java.awt.dnd package.

```
public class InvalidDnDOperationException extends java.lang.IllegalStateException {
// Public Constructors
    public InvalidDnDOperationException();
    public InvalidDnDOperationException(String msg);
}
```

Hierarchy: Object→ Throwable(Serializable)→ Exception→ RuntimeException→
java.lang.IllegalStateException→ InvalidDnDOperationException

Thrown By: Toolkit.createDragSourceContextPeer(), DragGestureEvent.startDrag(), DragSource.startDrag(), DropTargetContext.{dropComplete(), getTransferable()}, java.awt.dnd.peer.DragSourceContextPeer.{setCursor(), startDrag()}, java.awt.dnd.peer.DropTargetContextPeer.getTransferable()

MouseDragGestureRecognizer   Java 1.2
java.awt.dnd

This class is a DragGestureRecognizer that is designed to recognize mouse gestures (as opposed, for example, to keyboard gestures). Like DragGestureRecognizer, this is an abstract class and cannot be instantiated. The createDefaultDragGestureRecognizer() method of DragSource returns a platform-specific concrete subclass of this class. Most applications do not need to use this class. Applications that want to support custom drag-and-drop gestures may find it convenient to subclass this class.

```
public abstract class MouseDragGestureRecognizer extends DragGestureRecognizer
        implements java.awt.event.MouseListener, java.awt.event.MouseMotionListener {
// Protected Constructors
    protected MouseDragGestureRecognizer(DragSource ds);
    protected MouseDragGestureRecognizer(DragSource ds, Component c);
    protected MouseDragGestureRecognizer(DragSource ds, Component c, int act);
    protected MouseDragGestureRecognizer(DragSource ds, Component c, int act, DragGestureListener dgl);
// Methods Implementing MouseListener
    public void mouseClicked(java.awt.event.MouseEvent e);                              empty
    public void mouseEntered(java.awt.event.MouseEvent e);                             empty
    public void mouseExited(java.awt.event.MouseEvent e);                              empty
    public void mousePressed(java.awt.event.MouseEvent e);                             empty
    public void mouseReleased(java.awt.event.MouseEvent e);                            empty
// Methods Implementing MouseMotionListener
    public void mouseDragged(java.awt.event.MouseEvent e);                             empty
    public void mouseMoved(java.awt.event.MouseEvent e);                              empty
// Protected Methods Overriding DragGestureRecognizer
    protected void registerListeners();
    protected void unregisterListeners();
}
```

Hierarchy: Object→ DragGestureRecognizer→
MouseDragGestureRecognizer(java.awt.event.MouseListener(java.util.EventListener),
java.awt.event.MouseMotionListener(java.util.EventListener))

CHAPTER 13

The java.awt.dnd.peer Package

The interfaces of the java.awt.dnd.peer package precisely specify the native drag-and-drop capabilities that are required to implement the java.awt.dnd package. Application-level code never needs to use this package. Figure 13-1 shows the class hierarchy of this package.

Figure 13–1: The java.awt.dnd.peer package

DragSourceContextPeer   Java 1.2

java.awt.dnd.peer

This interface defines methods that the java.awt.dnd.DragSourceContext class uses to communicate with the underlying native drag-and-drop subsystem. Application-level code never uses this interface.

```
public abstract interface DragSourceContextPeer {
// Public Instance Methods
    public abstract Cursor getCursor();
    public abstract void setCursor(Cursor c) throws InvalidDnDOperationException;
    public abstract void startDrag(DragSourceContext dsc, Cursor c, Image dragImage, Point imageOffset)
        throws InvalidDnDOperationException;
    public abstract void transferablesFlavorsChanged();
}
```

Passed To: DragSource.createDragSourceContext(), DragSourceContext.DragSourceContext()

Returned By: Toolkit.createDragSourceContextPeer()

DropTargetContextPeer   Java 1.2

java.awt.dnd.peer

This interface defines methods that the java.awt.dnd.DropTargetContext class uses to communicate with the underlying native drag-and-drop subsystem. Application-level code
never uses this interface.

```
public abstract interface DropTargetContextPeer {
// Property Accessor Methods (by property name)
    public abstract DropTarget getDropTarget();
    public abstract int getTargetActions();
    public abstract void setTargetActions(int actions);
    public abstract java.awt.datatransfer.Transferable getTransferable() throws InvalidDnDOperationException;
    public abstract boolean isTransferableJVMLocal();
    public abstract java.awt.datatransfer.DataFlavor[ ] getTransferDataFlavors();
// Public Instance Methods
    public abstract void acceptDrag(int dragAction);
    public abstract void acceptDrop(int dropAction);
    public abstract void dropComplete(boolean success);
    public abstract void rejectDrag();
    public abstract void rejectDrop();
}
```

Passed To: DropTargetContext.addNotify()

DropTargetPeer   Java 1.2

java.awt.dnd.peer

This interface defines methods that the java.awt.dnd.DropTarget class uses to communicate
with the underlying native drag-and-drop subsystem. Application-level code never uses
this interface.

```
public abstract interface DropTargetPeer {
// Public Instance Methods
    public abstract void addDropTarget(DropTarget dt);
    public abstract void removeDropTarget(DropTarget dt);
}
```

CHAPTER 14

The java.awt.event Package

The java.awt.event package defines classes and interfaces used for event handling in the AWT and Swing. The members of this package fall into three categories:

Events
> The classes with names ending in "Event" represent specific types of events, generated by the AWT or by one of the AWT or Swing components.

Listeners
> The interfaces in this package are all event listeners; their names end with "Listener". These interfaces define the methods that must be implemented by any object that wants to be notified when a particular event occurs. Note that there is a Listener interface for each Event class.

Adapters
> Each of the classes with a name ending in "Adapter" provides a no-op implementation for an event listener interface that defines more than one method. When you are interested in only a single method of an event listener interface, it is easier to subclass an Adapter class than to implement all of the methods of the corresponding Listener interface.

Figure 14-1 shows the class hierarchy of this package.

The Swing user-interface components use some of these event classes and interfaces and also define others in the javax.swing.event package. The java.beans package also defines a few commonly used event classes and listener interfaces. Note that this package is part of the Java 1.1 event model. In Java 1.0, events were represented by the java.awt.Event class. See Chapter 2, *Swing and AWT Architecture*, for an introduction to events and event handling.

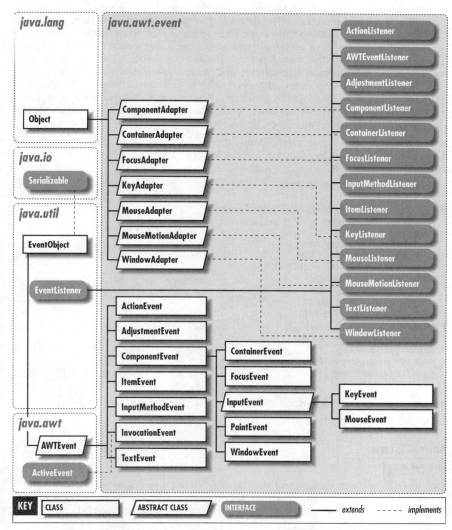

Figure 14–1: The java.awt.event package

ActionEvent

java.awt.event   *serializable event PJ1.1*

An object of this class represents a high-level action event generated by an AWT component. Instead of representing a direct user event, such as a mouse or keyboard event, ActionEvent represents some sort of action performed by the user on an AWT component.

The getID() method returns the type of action that has occurred. For AWT-generated action events, this type is always ActionEvent.ACTION_PERFORMED; custom components can generate action events of other types.

The getActionCommand() method returns a String that serves as a kind of name for the action that the event represents. The Button and MenuItem components have a setActionCommand() method that allows the programmer to specify an action command string to be included with any action events generated by those components. It is this value that is returned by the getActionCommand() method. When more than one Button or other component notifies the same ActionListener, you can use getActionCommand() to help determine the appropriate response to the event. This is generally a better technique than using the source object returned by getSource(). If no action command string is explicitly set, getActionCommand() returns the label of the Button or MenuItem. Internationalized programs should not rely on these labels being constant.

getModifiers() returns a value that indicates the keyboard modifiers that were in effect when the action event was triggered. Use the various _MASK constants, along with the & operator, to decode this value.

```
public class ActionEvent extends AWTEvent {
// Public Constructors
    public ActionEvent(Object source, int id, String command);
    public ActionEvent(Object source, int id, String command, int modifiers);
// Public Constants
    public static final int ACTION_FIRST;                              =1001
    public static final int ACTION_LAST;                               =1001
    public static final int ACTION_PERFORMED;                          =1001
    public static final int ALT_MASK;                                     =8
    public static final int CTRL_MASK;                                    =2
    public static final int META_MASK;                                    =4
    public static final int SHIFT_MASK;                                   =1
// Public Instance Methods
    public String getActionCommand();
    public int getModifiers();
// Public Methods Overriding AWTEvent
    public String paramString();
}
```

Hierarchy: Object→ java.util.EventObject(Serializable)→ AWTEvent→ ActionEvent

Passed To: Too many methods to list.

ActionListener   Java 1.1

java.awt.event   *event listener PJ1.1*

This interface defines the method that an object must implement to listen for action events on AWT components. When an ActionEvent occurs, an AWT component notifies its registered ActionListener objects by invoking their actionPerformed() methods.

```
public abstract interface ActionListener extends java.util.EventListener {
// Public Instance Methods
    public abstract void actionPerformed(ActionEvent e);
}
```

Hierarchy: (ActionListener(java.util.EventListener))

Implementations: AWTEventMulticaster, java.awt.dnd.DropTarget.DropTargetAutoScroller, javax.swing.Action, javax.swing.DefaultCellEditor.EditorDelegate, javax.swing.JComboBox, javax.swing.ToolTipManager.insideTimerAction, javax.swing.ToolTipManager.outsideTimerAction, javax.swing.ToolTipManager.stillInsideTimerAction, javax.swing.text.html.FormView, javax.swing.tree.DefaultTreeCellEditor

Passed To: Too many methods to list.

Returned By: AWTEventMulticaster.{add(), remove()}, javax.swing.AbstractButton.createActionListener(), javax.swing.JComponent.getActionForKeyStroke()

Type Of: javax.swing.AbstractButton.actionListener

AdjustmentEvent
Java 1.1

java.awt.event
serializable event PJ1.1

An event of this type indicates that an adjustment has been made to an Adjustable object—usually, this means that the user has interacted with a Scrollbar component.

The getValue() method returns the new value of the Adjustable object. This is usually the most important piece of information stored in the event. getAdjustable() returns the Adjustable object that was the source of the event. It is a convenient alternative to the inherited getSource() method.

The getID() method returns the type of an AdjustmentEvent. The standard AWT components only generate adjustment events of the type AdjustmentEvent.ADJUST-MENT_VALUE_CHANGED. There are several types of adjustments that can be made to an Adjustable object, however, and the getAdjustmentType() method returns one of five constants to indicate which type has occurred. UNIT_INCREMENT indicates that the Adjustable value has been incremented by one unit, as in a scroll-line-down operation. UNIT_DECREMENT indicates the opposite: scroll-line-up. BLOCK_INCREMENT and BLOCK_DEC-REMENT indicate that the Adjustable object has been incremented or decremented by multiple units, as in a scroll-page-down or scroll-page-up operation. Finally, the TRACK constant indicates that the Adjustable value has been set to an absolute value unrelated to its previous value, as when the user drags a scrollbar to a new position.

```
public class AdjustmentEvent extends AWTEvent {
// Public Constructors
    public AdjustmentEvent(Adjustable source, int id, int type, int value);
// Public Constants
    public static final int ADJUSTMENT_FIRST;                      =601
    public static final int ADJUSTMENT_LAST;                       =601
    public static final int ADJUSTMENT_VALUE_CHANGED;              =601
    public static final int BLOCK_DECREMENT;                       =3
    public static final int BLOCK_INCREMENT;                       =4
    public static final int TRACK;                                 =5
    public static final int UNIT_DECREMENT;                        =2
    public static final int UNIT_INCREMENT;                        =1
// Public Instance Methods
    public Adjustable getAdjustable();
    public int getAdjustmentType();
    public int getValue();
// Public Methods Overriding AWTEvent
    public String paramString();
}
```

Hierarchy: Object→ java.util.EventObject(Serializable)→ AWTEvent→ AdjustmentEvent

Passed To: AWTEventMulticaster.adjustmentValueChanged(), Scrollbar.processAdjustmentEvent(), AdjustmentListener.adjustmentValueChanged()

AdjustmentListener
Java 1.1

java.awt.event
event listener PJ1.1

This interface defines the method that an object must implement to listen for adjustment events on AWT components. When an AdjustmentEvent occurs, an AWT component notifies its registered AdjustmentListener objects by invoking their adjustmentValueChanged() methods.

```
public abstract interface AdjustmentListener extends java.util.EventListener {
// Public Instance Methods
    public abstract void adjustmentValueChanged(AdjustmentEvent e);
}
```

Hierarchy: (AdjustmentListener(java.util.EventListener))

Implementations: AWTEventMulticaster

Passed To: Adjustable.{addAdjustmentListener(), removeAdjustmentListener()}, AWTEventMulticaster.{add(), remove()}, Scrollbar.{addAdjustmentListener(), removeAdjustmentListener()}, javax.swing.JScrollBar.{addAdjustmentListener(), removeAdjustmentListener()}

Returned By: AWTEventMulticaster.{add(), remove()}

AWTEventListener   Java 1.2

java.awt.event   *event listener*

This interface is implemented by objects, such as GUI macro recorders, that want to be notified of all AWT events that occur on Component and MenuComponent objects throughout the system. Register an AWTEventListener with the addAWTEventListener() method of Toolkit.

```
public abstract interface AWTEventListener extends java.util.EventListener {
// Public Instance Methods
    public abstract void eventDispatched(AWTEvent event);
}
```

Hierarchy: (AWTEventListener(java.util.EventListener))

Passed To: Toolkit.{addAWTEventListener(), removeAWTEventListener()}

ComponentAdapter   Java 1.1

java.awt.event   *event adapter PJ1.1*

This class is a trivial implementation of ComponentListener; it provides empty bodies for each of the methods of that interface. When you are not interested in all of these methods, it is often easier to subclass ComponentAdapter than it is to implement ComponentListener from scratch.

```
public abstract class ComponentAdapter implements ComponentListener {
// Public Constructors
    public ComponentAdapter();
// Methods Implementing ComponentListener
    public void componentHidden(ComponentEvent e);                          empty
    public void componentMoved(ComponentEvent e);                           empty
    public void componentResized(ComponentEvent e);                         empty
    public void componentShown(ComponentEvent e);                           empty
}
```

Hierarchy: Object→ ComponentAdapter(ComponentListener(java.util.EventListener))

Subclasses: javax.swing.JViewport.ViewListener

ComponentEvent   Java 1.1

java.awt.event   *serializable event PJ1.1*

An event of this type serves as notification that the source Component has been moved, resized, shown, or hidden. Note that this event is a notification only: the AWT handles these Component operations internally, and the recipient of the event need take no action itself.

getComponent() returns the component that was moved, resized, shown, or hidden. It is simply a convenient alternative to getSource(). getID() returns one of four COMPONENT_ constants to indicate what operation was performed on the Component.

```
public class ComponentEvent extends AWTEvent {
// Public Constructors
    public ComponentEvent(Component source, int id);
// Public Constants
    public static final int COMPONENT_FIRST;                =100
    public static final int COMPONENT_HIDDEN;               =103
    public static final int COMPONENT_LAST;                 =103
    public static final int COMPONENT_MOVED;                =100
    public static final int COMPONENT_RESIZED;              =101
    public static final int COMPONENT_SHOWN;                =102
// Public Instance Methods
    public Component getComponent();
// Public Methods Overriding AWTEvent
    public String paramString();
}
```

Hierarchy: Object→ java.util.EventObject(Serializable)→ AWTEvent→ ComponentEvent

Subclasses: ContainerEvent, FocusEvent, InputEvent, PaintEvent, WindowEvent

Passed To: AWTEventMulticaster.{componentHidden(), componentMoved(), componentResized(), componentShown()}, Component.processComponentEvent(), ComponentAdapter.{componentHidden(), componentMoved(), componentResized(), componentShown()}, ComponentListener.{componentHidden(), componentMoved(), componentResized(), componentShown()}, javax.swing.JViewport.ViewListener.componentResized()

ComponentListener   Java 1.1
java.awt.event   *event listener PJ1.1*

This interface defines the methods that an object must implement to listen for component events on AWT components. When a ComponentEvent occurs, an AWT component notifies its registered ComponentListener objects by invoking one of their methods. An easy way to implement this interface is by subclassing the ComponentAdapter class.

```
public abstract interface ComponentListener extends java.util.EventListener {
// Public Instance Methods
    public abstract void componentHidden(ComponentEvent e);
    public abstract void componentMoved(ComponentEvent e);
    public abstract void componentResized(ComponentEvent e);
    public abstract void componentShown(ComponentEvent e);
}
```

Hierarchy: (ComponentListener(java.util.EventListener))

Implementations: AWTEventMulticaster, ComponentAdapter

Passed To: AWTEventMulticaster.{add(), remove()}, Component.{addComponentListener(), removeComponentListener()}

Returned By: AWTEventMulticaster.{add(), remove()}

ContainerAdapter   Java 1.1
java.awt.event   *event adapter PJ1.1*

This class is a trivial implementation of ContainerListener; it provides empty bodies for each of the methods of that interface. When you are not interested in all of these methods, it is often easier to subclass ContainerAdapter than it is to implement ContainerListener from scratch.

java.awt. event

```
public abstract class ContainerAdapter implements ContainerListener {
// Public Constructors
    public ContainerAdapter();
// Methods Implementing ContainerListener
    public void componentAdded(ContainerEvent e);                          empty
    public void componentRemoved(ContainerEvent e);                        empty
}
```

Hierarchy: Object→ ContainerAdapter(ContainerListener(java.util.EventListener))

ContainerEvent   Java 1.1

java.awt.event   *serializable event PJ1.1*

An event of this type serves as notification that the source Container has had a child added to it or removed from it. Note that this event is a notification only; the AWT adds or removes the child internally, and the recipient of this event need take no action itself.

getChild() returns the child Component that was added or removed, and getContainer() returns the Container to which it was added or from which it was removed. getContainer() is simply a convenient alternative to getSource(). getID() returns the constant COMPONENT_ADDED or COMPONENT_REMOVED to indicate whether the specified child was added or removed.

```
public class ContainerEvent extends ComponentEvent {
// Public Constructors
    public ContainerEvent(Component source, int id, Component child);
// Public Constants
    public static final int COMPONENT_ADDED;                               =300
    public static final int COMPONENT_REMOVED;                             =301
    public static final int CONTAINER_FIRST;                               =300
    public static final int CONTAINER_LAST;                                =301
// Public Instance Methods
    public Component getChild();
    public Container getContainer();
// Public Methods Overriding ComponentEvent
    public String paramString();
}
```

Hierarchy: Object→ java.util.EventObject(Serializable)→ AWTEvent→ ComponentEvent→ ContainerEvent

Passed To: AWTEventMulticaster.{componentAdded(), componentRemoved()},
Container.processContainerEvent(), ContainerAdapter.{componentAdded(), componentRemoved()},
ContainerListener.{componentAdded(), componentRemoved()},
javax.swing.JComponent.AccessibleJComponent.AccessibleContainerHandler.{componentAdded(),
componentRemoved()}

ContainerListener   Java 1.1

java.awt.event   *event listener PJ1.1*

This interface defines the methods that an object must implement to listen for container events on AWT components. When a ContainerEvent occurs, an AWT component notifies its registered ContainerListener objects by invoking one of their methods. An easy way to implement this interface is by subclassing the ContainerAdapter class.

```
public abstract interface ContainerListener extends java.util.EventListener {
// Public Instance Methods
    public abstract void componentAdded(ContainerEvent e);
```

```
    public abstract void componentRemoved(ContainerEvent e);
}
```

Hierarchy: (ContainerListener(java.util.EventListener))

Implementations: AWTEventMulticaster, ContainerAdapter,
javax.swing.JComponent.AccessibleJComponent.AccessibleContainerHandler

Passed To: AWTEventMulticaster.{add(), remove()}, Container.{addContainerListener(),
removeContainerListener()}

Returned By: AWTEventMulticaster.{add(), remove()}

Type Of: javax.swing.JComponent.AccessibleJComponent.accessibleContainerHandler

FocusAdapter

Java 1.1

java.awt.event

event adapter PJ1.1

This class is a trivial implementation of FocusListener; it provides empty bodies for each
of the methods of that interface. When you are not interested in all of these methods, it
is often easier to subclass FocusAdapter than it is to implement FocusListener from scratch.

```
public abstract class FocusAdapter implements FocusListener {
// Public Constructors
    public FocusAdapter();
// Methods Implementing FocusListener
    public void focusGained(FocusEvent e);                                    empty
    public void focusLost(FocusEvent e);                                      empty
}
```

Hierarchy: Object→ FocusAdapter(FocusListener(java.util.EventListener))

FocusEvent

Java 1.1

java.awt.event

serializable event PJ1.1

An event of this type indicates that a Component has gained or lost focus on a temporary
or permanent basis. Use the inherited getComponent() method to determine which component has gained or lost focus. Use getID() to determine the type of focus event; it
returns FOCUS_GAINED or FOCUS_LOST.

When focus is lost, you can call isTemporary() to determine whether it is a temporary loss
of focus. Temporary focus loss occurs when the window that contains the component
loses focus, for example, or when focus is temporarily diverted to a popup menu or a
scrollbar. Similarly, you can also use isTemporary() to determine whether focus is being
granted to a component on a temporary basis.

```
public class FocusEvent extends ComponentEvent {
// Public Constructors
    public FocusEvent(Component source, int id);
    public FocusEvent(Component source, int id, boolean temporary);
// Public Constants
    public static final int FOCUS_FIRST;                                     =1004
    public static final int FOCUS_GAINED;                                    =1004
    public static final int FOCUS_LAST;                                      =1005
    public static final int FOCUS_LOST;                                      =1005
// Public Instance Methods
    public boolean isTemporary();
// Public Methods Overriding ComponentEvent
    public String paramString();
}
```

Hierarchy: Object→ java.util.EventObject(Serializable)→ AWTEvent→ ComponentEvent→ FocusEvent

Passed To: AWTEventMulticaster.{focusGained(), focusLost()}, Component.processFocusEvent(), FocusAdapter.{focusGained(), focusLost()}, FocusListener.{focusGained(), focusLost()}, javax.swing.JComponent.processFocusEvent(), javax.swing.text.DefaultCaret.{focusGained(), focusLost()}

FocusListener
java.awt.event

Java 1.1

event listener PJ1.1

This interface defines the methods that an object must implement to listen for focus events on AWT components. When a FocusEvent occurs, an AWT component notifies its registered FocusListener objects by invoking one of their methods. An easy way to implement this interface is by subclassing the FocusAdapter class.

```
public abstract interface FocusListener extends java.util.EventListener {
// Public Instance Methods
    public abstract void focusGained(FocusEvent e);
    public abstract void focusLost(FocusEvent e);
}
```

Hierarchy: (FocusListener(java.util.EventListener))

Implementations: AWTEventMulticaster, FocusAdapter, javax.swing.text.DefaultCaret

Passed To: Too many methods to list.

Returned By: AWTEventMulticaster.{add(), remove()}

InputEvent
java.awt.event

Java 1.1

serializable event PJ1.1

This abstract class serves as the superclass for the raw user input event types MouseEvent and KeyEvent. Use the inherited getComponent() method to determine in which component the event occurred. Use getWhen() to obtain a timestamp for the event. Use getModifiers() to determine which keyboard modifier keys or mouse buttons were down when the event occurred. You can decode the getModifiers() return value using the various _MASK constants defined by this class. The class also defines four convenience methods for determining the state of keyboard modifiers.

As of Java 1.1, input events are delivered to the appropriate listener objects before they are delivered to the AWT components themselves. If a listener calls the consume() method of the event, the event is not passed on to the component. For example, if a listener registered on a Button consumes a mouse click, it prevents the button itself from responding to that event. You can use isConsumed() to test whether some other listener object has already consumed the event.

```
public abstract class InputEvent extends ComponentEvent {
// No Constructor
// Public Constants
1.2 public static final int ALT_GRAPH_MASK;                              =32
    public static final int ALT_MASK;                                     =8
    public static final int BUTTON1_MASK;                                =16
    public static final int BUTTON2_MASK;                                 =8
    public static final int BUTTON3_MASK;                                 =4
    public static final int CTRL_MASK;                                    =2
    public static final int META_MASK;                                    =4
    public static final int SHIFT_MASK;                                   =1
// Property Accessor Methods (by property name)
    public boolean isAltDown();
1.2 public boolean isAltGraphDown();
```

```
    public boolean isConsumed();                                    Overrides:AWTEvent
    public boolean isControlDown();
    public boolean isMetaDown();
    public int getModifiers();
    public boolean isShiftDown();
    public long getWhen();
// Public Methods Overriding AWTEvent
    public void consume();
}
```

Hierarchy: Object→ java.util.EventObject(Serializable)→ AWTEvent→ ComponentEvent→ InputEvent

Subclasses: KeyEvent, MouseEvent

Passed To: java.awt.dnd.DragGestureRecognizer.appendEvent()

Returned By: java.awt.dnd.DragGestureEvent.getTriggerEvent(),
java.awt.dnd.DragGestureRecognizer.getTriggerEvent()

InputMethodEvent   Java 1.2

java.awt.event   *serializable event*

Events of this type are sent from an input method to the text input component or text composition window that is using the services of the input method. An InputMethodEvent is generated each time the user makes an edit to the text that is being composed. Input method details are usually hidden by text input components. Application-level code should never have to use this class.

The getText() method returns a java.text.AttributedCharacterIterator that contains the current input method text. getCommittedCharacterCount() specifies how many characters of that text have been fully composed and committed, so that they are ready to be integrated into the text input component. The input method does not send these committed characters again. Any characters returned by the iterator beyond the specified number of committed characters are characters that are still undergoing composition and are not ready to be integrated into the text input component. These characters may be repeated in future InputMethodEvent objects, as the user continues to edit them.

```
public class InputMethodEvent extends AWTEvent {
// Public Constructors
    public InputMethodEvent(Component source, int id, java.awt.font.TextHitInfo caret,
                        java.awt.font.TextHitInfo visiblePosition);
    public InputMethodEvent(Component source, int id, java.text.AttributedCharacterIterator text,
                        int committedCharacterCount, java.awt.font.TextHitInfo caret,
                        java.awt.font.TextHitInfo visiblePosition);
// Public Constants
    public static final int CARET_POSITION_CHANGED;                          =1101
    public static final int INPUT_METHOD_FIRST;                              =1100
    public static final int INPUT_METHOD_LAST;                               =1101
    public static final int INPUT_METHOD_TEXT_CHANGED;                       =1100
// Property Accessor Methods (by property name)
    public java.awt.font.TextHitInfo getCaret();
    public int getCommittedCharacterCount();
    public boolean isConsumed();                                    Overrides:AWTEvent
    public java.text.AttributedCharacterIterator getText();
    public java.awt.font.TextHitInfo getVisiblePosition();
// Public Methods Overriding AWTEvent
    public void consume();
    public String paramString();
}
```

Hierarchy: Object→ java.util.EventObject(Serializable)→ AWTEvent→ InputMethodEvent

Passed To: AWTEventMulticaster.{caretPositionChanged(), inputMethodTextChanged()}, Component.processInputMethodEvent(), InputMethodListener.{caretPositionChanged(), inputMethodTextChanged()}, javax.swing.text.JTextComponent.processInputMethodEvent()

InputMethodListener

java.awt.event

Java 1.2

event listener

This interface defines the methods that a text input component must define in order to receive notifications from an input method. caretPositionChanged() is invoked when the user has moved the editing cursor. inputMethodTextChanged() is invoked when the user has edited text being composed by the input method.

Input method details are usually hidden by text input components. Application-level code should never have to use or implement this interface.

```
public abstract interface InputMethodListener extends java.util.EventListener {
// Public Instance Methods
    public abstract void caretPositionChanged(InputMethodEvent event);
    public abstract void inputMethodTextChanged(InputMethodEvent event);
}
```

Hierarchy: (InputMethodListener(java.util.EventListener))

Implementations: AWTEventMulticaster

Passed To: AWTEventMulticaster.{add(), remove()}, Component.{addInputMethodListener(), removeInputMethodListener()}, javax.swing.text.JTextComponent.addInputMethodListener()

Returned By: AWTEventMulticaster.{add(), remove()}

InvocationEvent

java.awt.event

Java 1.2

serializable event

An event of this type is not generated by an asynchronous external event, such as user input. Instead, an InvocationEvent is placed on the event queue by the invokeLater() and invokeAndWait() methods of EventQueue. InvocationEvent implements java.awt.ActiveEvent, which means that it is an event that knows how to dispatch itself, with its own dispatch() method. When an InvocationEvent reaches the front of the event queue, its dispatch() method is called, and this invokes the run() method of the Runnable object specified when the InvocationEvent was created. This technique provides a simple method for running arbitrary code from the event dispatch thread.

Applications need not be concerned with these details; they can simply use the invoke-Later() and invokeAndWait() methods of EventQueue.

```
public class InvocationEvent extends AWTEvent implements ActiveEvent {
// Public Constructors
    public InvocationEvent(Object source, Runnable runnable);
    public InvocationEvent(Object source, Runnable runnable, Object notifier, boolean catchExceptions);
// Protected Constructors
    protected InvocationEvent(Object source, int id, Runnable runnable, Object notifier, boolean catchExceptions);
// Public Constants
    public static final int INVOCATION_DEFAULT;                                    =1200
    public static final int INVOCATION_FIRST;                                      =1200
    public static final int INVOCATION_LAST;                                       =1200
// Public Instance Methods
    public Exception getException();
```

```
// Methods Implementing ActiveEvent
    public void dispatch();
// Public Methods Overriding AWTEvent
    public String paramString();
// Protected Instance Fields
    protected boolean catchExceptions;
    protected Object notifier;
    protected Runnable runnable;
}
```

Hierarchy: Object→ java.util.EventObject(Serializable)→ AWTEvent→ InvocationEvent(ActiveEvent)

ItemEvent   Java 1.1

java.awt.event   *serializable event PJ1.1*

An event of this type indicates that an item within an ItemSelectable component has had its selection state changed. getItemSelectable() is a convenient alternative to getSource() that returns the ItemSelectable object that originated the event. getItem() returns an object that represents the item that was selected or deselected.

getID() returns the type of the ItemEvent. The standard AWT components always generate item events of type ITEM_STATE_CHANGED. The getStateChange() method returns the new selection state of the item: it returns one of the constants SELECTED or DESELECTED. (This value can be misleading for Checkbox components that are part of a CheckboxGroup. If the user attempts to deselect a selected component, a DESELECTED event is delivered, but the CheckboxGroup immediately reselects the component to enforce its requirement that at least one Checkbox be selected at all times.)

```
public class ItemEvent extends AWTEvent {
// Public Constructors
    public ItemEvent(ItemSelectable source, int id, Object item, int stateChange);
// Public Constants
    public static final int DESELECTED;                                      =2
    public static final int ITEM_FIRST;                                    =701
    public static final int ITEM_LAST;                                     =701
    public static final int ITEM_STATE_CHANGED;                            =701
    public static final int SELECTED;                                        =1
// Public Instance Methods
    public Object getItem();
    public ItemSelectable getItemSelectable();
    public int getStateChange();
// Public Methods Overriding AWTEvent
    public String paramString();
}
```

Hierarchy: Object→ java.util.EventObject(Serializable)→ AWTEvent→ ItemEvent

Passed To: AWTEventMulticaster.itemStateChanged(), Checkbox.processItemEvent(),
CheckboxMenuItem.processItemEvent(), Choice.processItemEvent(), java.awt.List.processItemEvent(),
ItemListener.itemStateChanged(), javax.swing.AbstractButton.fireItemStateChanged(),
javax.swing.DefaultButtonModel.fireItemStateChanged(),
javax.swing.DefaultCellEditor.EditorDelegate.itemStateChanged(),
javax.swing.JComboBox.fireItemStateChanged(),
javax.swing.JToggleButton.AccessibleJToggleButton.itemStateChanged()

*java.awt.
event*

ItemListener

Java 1.1

java.awt.event

event listener PJ1.1

This interface defines the method that an object must implement to listen for item events on AWT components. When an ItemEvent occurs, an AWT component notifies its registered ItemListener objects by invoking their itemStateChanged() methods.

```
public abstract interface ItemListener extends java.util.EventListener {
// Public Instance Methods
    public abstract void itemStateChanged(ItemEvent e);
}
```

Hierarchy: (ItemListener(java.util.EventListener))

Implementations: AWTEventMulticaster, javax.swing.DefaultCellEditor.EditorDelegate, javax.swing.JToggleButton.AccessibleJToggleButton

Passed To: Too many methods to list.

Returned By: AWTEventMulticaster.{add(), remove()}, javax.swing.AbstractButton.createItemListener()

Type Of: javax.swing.AbstractButton.itemListener

KeyAdapter

Java 1.1

java.awt.event

event adapter PJ1.1

This class is a trivial implementation of KeyListener; it provides empty bodies for each of the methods of that interface. When you are not interested in all of these methods, it is often easier to subclass KeyAdapter than it is to implement KeyListener from scratch.

```
public abstract class KeyAdapter implements KeyListener {
// Public Constructors
    public KeyAdapter();
// Methods Implementing KeyListener
    public void keyPressed(KeyEvent e);                                          empty
    public void keyReleased(KeyEvent e);                                         empty
    public void keyTyped(KeyEvent e);                                            empty
}
```

Hierarchy: Object → KeyAdapter(KeyListener(java.util.EventListener))

KeyEvent

Java 1.1

java.awt.event

serializable event PJ1.1

An event of this type indicates that the user has pressed or released a key on the keyboard. Call getID() to determine the particular type of key event that has occurred. The constant KEY_PRESSED indicates that a key has been pressed, while the constant KEY_RELEASED indicates that a key has been released. Not all keystrokes actually correspond to or generate Unicode characters. Modifier keys and function keys, for example, do not correspond to characters. Furthermore, for internationalized input, multiple keystrokes are sometimes required to generate a single character of input. Therefore, getID() returns a third constant, KEY_TYPED, to indicate a KeyEvent that actually contains a character value.

For KEY_PRESSED and KEY_RELEASED key events, use getKeyCode() to obtain the virtual keycode of the key that was pressed or released. KeyEvent defines a number of VK_ constants that represent these virtual keys. Note that not all keys on all keyboards have corresponding constants in the KeyEvent class, and not all keyboards can generate all of the virtual keycodes defined by this class. As of Java 1.1, the VK_ constants for letter keys, number keys, and some other keys have the same values as the ASCII encodings of the letters and numbers. You should not rely on this to always be the case, however.

If the key that was pressed or released corresponds directly to a Unicode character, you can obtain that character by calling getKeyChar(). If there is not a corresponding Unicode character, this method returns the constant CHAR_UNDEFINED. The isActionKey() method returns true if the key that was pressed or released does not have a corresponding character.

For KEY_TYPED key events, use getKeyChar() to return the Unicode character that was typed. If you call getKeyCode() for this type of key event, it returns VK_UNDEFINED.

See InputEvent for information on inherited methods you can use to obtain the keyboard modifiers that were down during the event and other important methods. Use getComponent(), inherited from ComponentEvent, to determine over what component the event occurred. The static method getKeyText() returns a (possibly localized) textual name for a given keycode. The static method getKeyModifiersText() returns a (possibly localized) textual description for a set of modifiers.

KeyEvent has methods that allow you to change the keycode, key character, or modifiers of an event. These methods, along with the consume() method, allow a KeyListener to perform filtering of key events before they are passed to the underlying AWT component.

```java
public class KeyEvent extends InputEvent {
// Public Constructors
    public KeyEvent(Component source, int id, long when, int modifiers, int keyCode);
    public KeyEvent(Component source, int id, long when, int modifiers, int keyCode, char keyChar);
// Public Constants
    public static final char CHAR_UNDEFINED;                         ='\uFFFF'
    public static final int KEY_FIRST;                               =400
    public static final int KEY_LAST;                                =402
    public static final int KEY_PRESSED;                             =401
    public static final int KEY_RELEASED;                            =402
    public static final int KEY_TYPED;                               =400
    public static final int VK_0;                                    =48
    public static final int VK_1;                                    =49
    public static final int VK_2;                                    =50
    public static final int VK_3;                                    =51
    public static final int VK_4;                                    =52
    public static final int VK_5;                                    =53
    public static final int VK_6;                                    =54
    public static final int VK_7;                                    =55
    public static final int VK_8;                                    =56
    public static final int VK_9;                                    =57
    public static final int VK_A;                                    =65
    public static final int VK_ACCEPT;                               =30
    public static final int VK_ADD;                                  =107
1.2 public static final int VK_AGAIN;                                =65481
1.2 public static final int VK_ALL_CANDIDATES;                       =256
1.2 public static final int VK_ALPHANUMERIC;                         =240
    public static final int VK_ALT;                                  =18
1.2 public static final int VK_ALT_GRAPH;                            =65406
1.2 public static final int VK_AMPERSAND;                            =150
1.2 public static final int VK_ASTERISK;                             =151
1.2 public static final int VK_AT;                                   =512
    public static final int VK_B;                                    =66
    public static final int VK_BACK_QUOTE;                           =192
    public static final int VK_BACK_SLASH;                           =92
    public static final int VK_BACK_SPACE;                           =8
1.2 public static final int VK_BRACELEFT;                            =161
1.2 public static final int VK_BRACERIGHT;                           =162
    public static final int VK_C;                                    =67
    public static final int VK_CANCEL;                               =3
```

public static final int **VK_CAPS_LOCK**;	=20
1.2 public static final int **VK_CIRCUMFLEX**;	=514
public static final int **VK_CLEAR**;	=12
public static final int **VK_CLOSE_BRACKET**;	=93
1.2 public static final int **VK_CODE_INPUT**;	=258
1.2 public static final int **VK_COLON**;	=513
public static final int **VK_COMMA**;	=44
1.2 public static final int **VK_COMPOSE**;	=65312
public static final int **VK_CONTROL**;	=17
public static final int **VK_CONVERT**;	=28
1.2 public static final int **VK_COPY**;	=65485
1.2 public static final int **VK_CUT**;	=65489
public static final int **VK_D**;	=68
1.2 public static final int **VK_DEAD_ABOVEDOT**;	=134
1.2 public static final int **VK_DEAD_ABOVERING**;	=136
1.2 public static final int **VK_DEAD_ACUTE**;	=129
1.2 public static final int **VK_DEAD_BREVE**;	=133
1.2 public static final int **VK_DEAD_CARON**;	=138
1.2 public static final int **VK_DEAD_CEDILLA**;	=139
1.2 public static final int **VK_DEAD_CIRCUMFLEX**;	=130
1.2 public static final int **VK_DEAD_DIAERESIS**;	=135
1.2 public static final int **VK_DEAD_DOUBLEACUTE**;	=137
1.2 public static final int **VK_DEAD_GRAVE**;	=128
1.2 public static final int **VK_DEAD_IOTA**;	=141
1.2 public static final int **VK_DEAD_MACRON**;	=132
1.2 public static final int **VK_DEAD_OGONEK**;	=140
1.2 public static final int **VK_DEAD_SEMIVOICED_SOUND**;	=143
1.2 public static final int **VK_DEAD_TILDE**;	=131
1.2 public static final int **VK_DEAD_VOICED_SOUND**;	=142
public static final int **VK_DECIMAL**;	=110
public static final int **VK_DELETE**;	=127
public static final int **VK_DIVIDE**;	=111
1.2 public static final int **VK_DOLLAR**;	=515
public static final int **VK_DOWN**;	=40
public static final int **VK_E**;	=69
public static final int **VK_END**;	=35
public static final int **VK_ENTER**;	=10
public static final int **VK_EQUALS**;	=61
public static final int **VK_ESCAPE**;	=27
1.2 public static final int **VK_EURO_SIGN**;	=516
1.2 public static final int **VK_EXCLAMATION_MARK**;	=517
public static final int **VK_F**;	=70
public static final int **VK_F1**;	=112
public static final int **VK_F10**;	=121
public static final int **VK_F11**;	=122
public static final int **VK_F12**;	=123
1.2 public static final int **VK_F13**;	=61440
1.2 public static final int **VK_F14**;	=61441
1.2 public static final int **VK_F15**;	=61442
1.2 public static final int **VK_F16**;	=61443
1.2 public static final int **VK_F17**;	=61444
1.2 public static final int **VK_F18**;	=61445
1.2 public static final int **VK_F19**;	=61446
public static final int **VK_F2**;	=113
1.2 public static final int **VK_F20**;	=61447
1.2 public static final int **VK_F21**;	=61448
1.2 public static final int **VK_F22**;	=61449
1.2 public static final int **VK_F23**;	=61450

1 2 public static final int **VK_F24**;		=61451
public static final int **VK_F3**;		=114
public static final int **VK_F4**;		=115
public static final int **VK_F5**;		=116
public static final int **VK_F6**;		=117
public static final int **VK_F7**;		=118
public static final int **VK_F8**;		=119
public static final int **VK_F9**;		=120
public static final int **VK_FINAL**;		=24
1.2 public static final int **VK_FIND**;		=65488
1.2 public static final int **VK_FULL_WIDTH**;		=243
public static final int **VK_G**;		=71
1.2 public static final int **VK_GREATER**;		=160
public static final int **VK_H**;		=72
1.2 public static final int **VK_HALF_WIDTH**;		=244
public static final int **VK_HELP**;		=156
1.2 public static final int **VK_HIRAGANA**;		=242
public static final int **VK_HOME**;		=36
public static final int **VK_I**;		=73
public static final int **VK_INSERT**;		=155
1.2 public static final int **VK_INVERTED_EXCLAMATION_MARK**;		=518
public static final int **VK_J**;		=74
1.2 public static final int **VK_JAPANESE_HIRAGANA**;		=260
1.2 public static final int **VK_JAPANESE_KATAKANA**;		=259
1.2 public static final int **VK_JAPANESE_ROMAN**;		=261
public static final int **VK_K**;		=75
public static final int **VK_KANA**;		=21
public static final int **VK_KANJI**;		=25
1.2 public static final int **VK_KATAKANA**;		=241
1.2 public static final int **VK_KP_DOWN**;		=225
1.2 public static final int **VK_KP_LEFT**;		=226
1.2 public static final int **VK_KP_RIGHT**;		=227
1.2 public static final int **VK_KP_UP**;		=224
public static final int **VK_L**;		=76
public static final int **VK_LEFT**;		=37
1.2 public static final int **VK_LEFT_PARENTHESIS**;		=519
1.2 public static final int **VK_LESS**;		=153
public static final int **VK_M**;		=77
public static final int **VK_META**;		=157
1.2 public static final int **VK_MINUS**;		=45
public static final int **VK_MODECHANGE**;		=31
public static final int **VK_MULTIPLY**;		=106
public static final int **VK_N**;		=78
public static final int **VK_NONCONVERT**;		=29
public static final int **VK_NUM_LOCK**;		=144
1.2 public static final int **VK_NUMBER_SIGN**;		=520
public static final int **VK_NUMPAD0**;		=96
public static final int **VK_NUMPAD1**;		=97
public static final int **VK_NUMPAD2**;		=98
public static final int **VK_NUMPAD3**;		=99
public static final int **VK_NUMPAD4**;		=100
public static final int **VK_NUMPAD5**;		=101
public static final int **VK_NUMPAD6**;		=102
public static final int **VK_NUMPAD7**;		=103
public static final int **VK_NUMPAD8**;		=104
public static final int **VK_NUMPAD9**;		=105
public static final int **VK_O**;		=79
public static final int **VK_OPEN_BRACKET**;		=91

java.awt. event

```
    public static final int VK_P;                                =80
    public static final int VK_PAGE_DOWN;                        =34
    public static final int VK_PAGE_UP;                          =33
1.2 public static final int VK_PASTE;                          =65487
    public static final int VK_PAUSE;                            =19
    public static final int VK_PERIOD;                           =46
1.2 public static final int VK_PLUS;                            =521
1.2 public static final int VK_PREVIOUS_CANDIDATE;              =257
    public static final int VK_PRINTSCREEN;                     =154
1.2 public static final int VK_PROPS;                         =65482
    public static final int VK_Q;                                =81
    public static final int VK_QUOTE;                           =222
1.2 public static final int VK_QUOTEDBL;                        =152
    public static final int VK_R;                                =82
    public static final int VK_RIGHT;                            =39
1.2 public static final int VK_RIGHT_PARENTHESIS;               =522
1.2 public static final int VK_ROMAN_CHARACTERS;                =245
    public static final int VK_S;                                =83
    public static final int VK_SCROLL_LOCK;                     =145
    public static final int VK_SEMICOLON;                        =59
    public static final int VK_SEPARATER;                       =108
    public static final int VK_SHIFT;                            =16
    public static final int VK_SLASH;                            =47
    public static final int VK_SPACE;                            =32
1.2 public static final int VK_STOP;                          =65480
    public static final int VK_SUBTRACT;                        =109
    public static final int VK_T;                                =84
    public static final int VK_TAB;                               =9
    public static final int VK_U;                                =85
    public static final int VK_UNDEFINED;                         =0
1.2 public static final int VK_UNDERSCORE;                      =523
1.2 public static final int VK_UNDO;                          =65483
    public static final int VK_UP;                               =38
    public static final int VK_V;                                =86
    public static final int VK_W;                                =87
    public static final int VK_X;                                =88
    public static final int VK_Y;                                =89
    public static final int VK_Z;                                =90
// Public Class Methods
    public static String getKeyModifiersText(int modifiers);
    public static String getKeyText(int keyCode);
// Property Accessor Methods (by property name)
    public boolean isActionKey();
    public char getKeyChar();
    public void setKeyChar(char keyChar);
    public int getKeyCode();
    public void setKeyCode(int keyCode);
// Public Instance Methods
    public void setModifiers(int modifiers);
// Public Methods Overriding ComponentEvent
    public String paramString();
}
```

Hierarchy: Object→ java.util.EventObject(Serializable) → AWTEvent→ ComponentEvent→ InputEvent→ KeyEvent

Subclasses: javax.swing.event.MenuKeyEvent

Passed To: Too many methods to list.

KeyListener
Java 1.1

java.awt.event
event listener PJ1.1

This interface defines the methods that an object must implement to listen for key events on AWT components. When a KeyEvent occurs, an AWT component notifies its registered KeyListener objects by invoking one of their methods. An easy way to implement this interface is by subclassing the KeyAdapter class.

```
public abstract interface KeyListener extends java.util.EventListener {
// Public Instance Methods
    public abstract void keyPressed(KeyEvent e);
    public abstract void keyReleased(KeyEvent e);
    public abstract void keyTyped(KeyEvent e);
}
```

Hierarchy: (KeyListener(java.util.EventListener))

Implementations: AWTEventMulticaster, KeyAdapter

Passed To: AWTEventMulticaster.{add(), remove()}, Component.{addKeyListener(), removeKeyListener()}

Returned By: AWTEventMulticaster.{add(), remove()}

MouseAdapter
Java 1.1

java.awt.event
event adapter PJ1.1

This class is a trivial implementation of MouseListener; it provides empty bodies for each of the methods of that interface. When you are not interested in all of these methods, it is often easier to subclass MouseAdapter than it is to implement MouseListener from scratch.

```
public abstract class MouseAdapter implements MouseListener {
// Public Constructors
    public MouseAdapter();
// Methods Implementing MouseListener
    public void mouseClicked(MouseEvent e);                         empty
    public void mouseEntered(MouseEvent e);                         empty
    public void mouseExited(MouseEvent e);                          empty
    public void mousePressed(MouseEvent e);                         empty
    public void mouseReleased(MouseEvent e);                        empty
}
```

Hierarchy: Object → MouseAdapter(MouseListener(java.util.EventListener))

Subclasses: javax.swing.ToolTipManager, javax.swing.text.html.FormView.MouseEventListener, javax.swing.text.html.HTMLEditorKit.LinkController

MouseEvent
Java 1.1

java.awt.event
serializable event PJ1.1

An event of this type indicates that the user has moved the mouse or pressed one of the mouse buttons. Call getID() to determine the specific type of mouse event that has occurred. This method returns one of the following seven constants, which corresponds to a method in either the MouseListener or MouseMotionListener interface:

MOUSE_PRESSED
    The user has pressed a mouse button.

*java.awt.
event*

MOUSE_RELEASED

The user has released a mouse button.

MOUSE_CLICKED

The user has pressed and released a mouse button without any intervening mouse drag.

MOUSE_DRAGGED

The user has moved the mouse while holding a button down.

MOUSE_MOVED

The user has moved the mouse without holding any buttons down.

MOUSE_ENTERED

The mouse pointer has entered the component.

MOUSE_EXITED

The mouse pointer has left the component.

Use getX() and getY() or getPoint() to obtain the coordinates of the mouse event. Use translatePoint() to modify these coordinates by a specified amount.

Use getModifiers() and other methods and constants inherited from InputEvent to determine the mouse button or keyboard modifiers that were down when the event occurred. See InputEvent for details. Note that mouse button modifiers are not reported for MOUSE_RELEASED events, since, technically, the mouse button in question is no longer pressed.

Use getComponent(), inherited from ComponentEvent, to determine over which component the event occurred. For mouse events of type MOUSE_CLICKED, MOUSE_PRESSED, or MOUSE_RELEASED, call getClickCount() to determine how many consecutive clicks have occurred. If you are using popup menus, use isPopupTrigger() to test whether the current event represents the standard platform-dependent popup menu trigger event.

```
public class MouseEvent extends InputEvent {
// Public Constructors
    public MouseEvent(Component source, int id, long when, int modifiers, int x, int y, int clickCount,
                      boolean popupTrigger);
// Public Constants
    public static final int MOUSE_CLICKED;                                           =500
    public static final int MOUSE_DRAGGED;                                           =506
    public static final int MOUSE_ENTERED;                                           =504
    public static final int MOUSE_EXITED;                                            =505
    public static final int MOUSE_FIRST;                                             =500
    public static final int MOUSE_LAST;                                              =506
    public static final int MOUSE_MOVED;                                             =503
    public static final int MOUSE_PRESSED;                                           =501
    public static final int MOUSE_RELEASED;                                          =502
// Property Accessor Methods (by property name)
    public int getClickCount();
    public Point getPoint();
    public boolean isPopupTrigger();
    public int getX();
    public int getY();
// Public Instance Methods
    public void translatePoint(int x, int y);                                  synchronized
// Public Methods Overriding ComponentEvent
    public String paramString();
}
```

Hierarchy: Object→ java.util.EventObject(Serializable)→ AWTEvent→ ComponentEvent→ InputEvent→ MouseEvent

Subclasses: javax.swing.event.MenuDragMouseEvent

Passed To: Too many methods to list.

Returned By: javax.swing.SwingUtilities.convertMouseEvent()

MouseListener   Java 1.1
java.awt.event   *event listener PJ1.1*

This interface defines the methods that an object must implement to listen for mouse events on AWT components. When a MouseEvent occurs, an AWT component notifies its registered MouseListener objects (or MouseMotionListener objects, if the event involves mouse motion) by invoking one of their methods. An easy way to implement this interface is by subclassing the MouseAdapter class.

```
public abstract interface MouseListener extends java.util.EventListener {
// Public Instance Methods
    public abstract void mouseClicked(MouseEvent e);
    public abstract void mouseEntered(MouseEvent e);
    public abstract void mouseExited(MouseEvent e);
    public abstract void mousePressed(MouseEvent e);
    public abstract void mouseReleased(MouseEvent e);
}
```

Hierarchy: (MouseListener(java.util.EventListener))

Implementations: AWTEventMulticaster, java.awt.dnd.MouseDragGestureRecognizer, MouseAdapter, javax.swing.event.MouseInputListener, javax.swing.text.DefaultCaret

Passed To: AWTEventMulticaster.{add(), remove()}, Component.{addMouseListener(), removeMouseListener()}

Returned By: AWTEventMulticaster.{add(), remove()}

MouseMotionAdapter   Java 1.1
java.awt.event   *event adapter PJ1.1*

This class is a trivial implementation of MouseMotionListener; it provides empty bodies for each of the methods of that interface. When you are not interested in all of these methods, it is often easier to subclass MouseMotionAdapter than it is to implement MouseMotionListener from scratch.

```
public abstract class MouseMotionAdapter implements MouseMotionListener {
// Public Constructors
    public MouseMotionAdapter();
// Methods Implementing MouseMotionListener
    public void mouseDragged(MouseEvent e);                                empty
    public void mouseMoved(MouseEvent e);                                  empty
}
```

Hierarchy: Object→ MouseMotionAdapter(MouseMotionListener(java.util.EventListener))

MouseMotionListener   Java 1.1
java.awt.event   *event listener PJ1.1*

This interface defines the methods that an object must implement to listen for mouse motion events on AWT components. When a MouseEvent involving a mouse drag or mouse motion with no buttons down occurs, an AWT component notifies its registered

java.awt. event

MouseMotionListener objects by invoking one of their methods. An easy way to implement this is by subclassing the MouseMotionAdapter class.

```
public abstract interface MouseMotionListener extends java.util.EventListener {
// Public Instance Methods
    public abstract void mouseDragged(MouseEvent e);
    public abstract void mouseMoved(MouseEvent e);
}
```

Hierarchy: (MouseMotionListener(java.util.EventListener))

Implementations: AWTEventMulticaster, java.awt.dnd.MouseDragGestureRecognizer, MouseMotionAdapter, javax.swing.ToolTipManager, javax.swing.event.MouseInputListener, javax.swing.text.DefaultCaret

Passed To: AWTEventMulticaster.{add(), remove()}, Component.{addMouseMotionListener(), removeMouseMotionListener()}

Returned By: AWTEventMulticaster.{add(), remove()}

PaintEvent   Java 1.1

java.awt.event   *serializable event PJ1.1*

An event of this type indicates that a component should have its update() method invoked. (The update() method typically, by default, invokes the paint() method.)

PaintEvent differs from the other event types in java.awt.event in that it does not have a corresponding EventListener interface. PaintEvent is essentially for internal use by the AWT redisplay framework, so your programs should not try to handle it the way they handle other events. Instead, applets and custom components should simply override their paint() and/or update() methods to redraw themselves appropriately. AWT automatically invokes update() (which typically invokes paint()) when a PaintEvent arrives.

Although you do not typically use PaintEvent, redraw events are implemented through this class for simplicity, so that they are on equal footing with other event types and so that advanced programs can manipulate them through the EventQueue.

```
public class PaintEvent extends ComponentEvent {
// Public Constructors
    public PaintEvent(Component source, int id, Rectangle updateRect);
// Public Constants
    public static final int PAINT;                                    =800
    public static final int PAINT_FIRST;                              =800
    public static final int PAINT_LAST;                               =801
    public static final int UPDATE;                                   =801
// Public Instance Methods
    public Rectangle getUpdateRect();
    public void setUpdateRect(Rectangle updateRect);
// Public Methods Overriding ComponentEvent
    public String paramString();
}
```

Hierarchy: Object→ java.util.EventObject(Serializable)→ AWTEvent→ ComponentEvent→ PaintEvent

TextEvent   Java 1.1

java.awt.event   *serializable event PJ1.1*

An event of this type indicates that the user has edited the text value that appears in a TextField, TextArea, or other TextComponent. This event is triggered by any change to the displayed text. Note that this is not the same as the ActionEvent sent by the TextField object when the user edits the text and strikes the **Return** key.

Use the inherited getSource() to determine the object that was the source of this event. You have to cast that object to its TextComponent type. Call getID() to determine the type of a TextEvent. The standard AWT components always generate text events of type TEXT_VALUE_CHANGED.

```
public class TextEvent extends AWTEvent {
// Public Constructors
    public TextEvent(Object source, int id);
// Public Constants
    public static final int TEXT_FIRST;                              =900
    public static final int TEXT_LAST;                               =900
    public static final int TEXT_VALUE_CHANGED;                      =900
// Public Methods Overriding AWTEvent
    public String paramString();
}
```

Hierarchy: Object→ java.util.EventObject(Serializable)→ AWTEvent→ TextEvent

Passed To: AWTEventMulticaster.textValueChanged(), TextComponent.processTextEvent(), TextListener.textValueChanged()

TextListener   Java 1.1

java.awt.event   *event listener PJ1.1*

This interface defines the method that an object must implement to listen for text events on AWT components. When a TextEvent occurs, an AWT component notifies its registered TextListener objects by invoking their textValueChanged() methods.

```
public abstract interface TextListener extends java.util.EventListener {
// Public Instance Methods
    public abstract void textValueChanged(TextEvent e);
}
```

Hierarchy: (TextListener(java.util.EventListener))

Implementations: AWTEventMulticaster

Passed To: AWTEventMulticaster.{add(), remove()}, TextComponent.{addTextListener(), removeTextListener()}

Returned By: AWTEventMulticaster.{add(), remove()}

Type Of: TextComponent.textListener

WindowAdapter   Java 1.1

java.awt.event   *event adapter PJ1.1*

This class is a trivial implementation of WindowListener; it provides empty bodies for each of the methods of that interface. When you are not interested in all of these methods, it is often easier to subclass WindowAdapter than it is to implement WindowListener from scratch.

```
public abstract class WindowAdapter implements WindowListener {
// Public Constructors
    public WindowAdapter();
// Methods Implementing WindowListener
    public void windowActivated(WindowEvent e);                      empty
    public void windowClosed(WindowEvent e);                         empty
    public void windowClosing(WindowEvent e);                        empty
    public void windowDeactivated(WindowEvent e);                    empty
    public void windowDeiconified(WindowEvent e);                    empty
    public void windowIconified(WindowEvent e);                      empty
```

java.awt. event

```
    public void windowOpened(WindowEvent e);                                    empty
}
```

Hierarchy: Object→ WindowAdapter(WindowListener(java.util.EventListener))

Subclasses: javax.swing.JMenu.WinListener

WindowEvent
java.awt.event

An event of this type indicates that an important action has occurred for a Window object. Call getWindow() to determine the Window object that is the source of this event. Call getID() to determine the specific type of event that has occurred. Each of the following seven constants corresponds to one of the methods of the WindowListener interface:

WINDOW_OPENED

Indicates that the window has been created and opened; it is delivered only the first time that a window is opened.

WINDOW_CLOSING

Indicates that the user has requested that the window be closed through the system menu, through a close button on the window's border, or by invoking a platform-defined keystroke, such as **Alt-F4** in Windows. The application should respond to this event by calling hide() or dispose() on the Window object.

WINDOW_CLOSED

Delivered after a window is closed by a call to hide() or dispose().

WINDOW_ICONIFIED

Delivered when the user iconifies the window.

WINDOW_DEICONIFIED

Delivered when the user deiconifies the window.

WINDOW_ACTIVATED

Delivered when the window is activated—that is, when it is given the keyboard focus and becomes the active window.

WINDOW_DEACTIVATED

Delivered when the window ceases to be the active window, typically when the user activates some other window.

```
public class WindowEvent extends ComponentEvent {
// Public Constructors
    public WindowEvent(Window source, int id);
// Public Constants
    public static final int WINDOW_ACTIVATED;                                   =205
    public static final int WINDOW_CLOSED;                                      =202
    public static final int WINDOW_CLOSING;                                     =201
    public static final int WINDOW_DEACTIVATED;                                 =206
    public static final int WINDOW_DEICONIFIED;                                 =204
    public static final int WINDOW_FIRST;                                       =200
    public static final int WINDOW_ICONIFIED;                                   =203
    public static final int WINDOW_LAST;                                        =206
    public static final int WINDOW_OPENED;                                      =200
// Public Instance Methods
    public Window getWindow();
```

```
// Public Methods Overriding ComponentEvent
    public String paramString( );
}
```

Hierarchy: Object→ java.util.EventObject(Serializable)→ AWTEvent→ ComponentEvent→ WindowEvent

Passed To: Too many methods to list.

WindowListener

Java 1.1

java.awt.event

event listener PJ1.1

This interface defines the methods that an object must implement to listen for window events on AWT components. When a WindowEvent occurs, an AWT component notifies its registered WindowListener objects by invoking one of their methods. An easy way to implement this interface is by subclassing the WindowAdapter class.

```
public abstract interface WindowListener extends java.util.EventListener {
// Public Instance Methods
    public abstract void windowActivated(WindowEvent e);
    public abstract void windowClosed(WindowEvent e);
    public abstract void windowClosing(WindowEvent e);
    public abstract void windowDeactivated(WindowEvent e);
    public abstract void windowDeiconified(WindowEvent e);
    public abstract void windowIconified(WindowEvent e);
    public abstract void windowOpened(WindowEvent e);
}
```

Hierarchy: (WindowListener(java.util.EventListener))

Implementations: AWTEventMulticaster, WindowAdapter

Passed To: AWTEventMulticaster.{add(), remove()}, Window.{addWindowListener(), removeWindowListener()}

Returned By: AWTEventMulticaster.{add(), remove()}

*java.awt.
event*

CHAPTER 15

The java.awt.font Package

The java.awt.font package contains classes and interfaces related to fonts; it is new in Java 1.2. Note, however, that the Font class itself is part of the java.awt package. This package contains low-level classes for obtaining information about the measurements of font glyphs and lines of text. It also contains classes for the low-level layout of text. LineMetrics and TextLayout are the two most important classes in this package. Figure 15-1 shows the class hierarchy of this package.

Most programs can rely on the higher-level text display features of java.awt and javax.swing and do not have to use this package.

FontRenderContext   Java 1.2

java.awt.font

This class stores the information necessary to precisely measure the size of text. It is used by a number of Font methods and also by TextLayout and LineBreakMeasurer. Although FontRenderContext has a public constructor, it is more common to obtain a FontRenderContext by calling the getFontRenderContext() method of a Graphics2D object.

```
public class FontRenderContext {
// Public Constructors
    public FontRenderContext(java.awt.geom.AffineTransform tx, boolean isAntiAliased,
                             boolean usesFractionalMetrics);
// Protected Constructors
    protected FontRenderContext();
// Property Accessor Methods (by property name)
    public boolean isAntiAliased();
    public java.awt.geom.AffineTransform getTransform();
// Public Instance Methods
    public boolean usesFractionalMetrics();
}
```

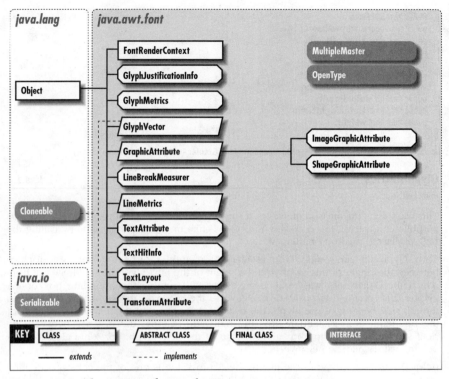

Figure 15-1: The java.awt.font package

Passed To: Too many methods to list.

Returned By: Graphics2D.getFontRenderContext(), GlyphVector.getFontRenderContext()

GlyphJustificationInfo

Java 1.2

java.awt.font

This class contains information about how much whitespace may be added to or removed from the left and right sides of a glyph without unduly compromising the appearance of the text output. This information is used by algorithms that perform fill justification to force a line of text to an exact size. Only applications that perform high-end typography need to use this class.

```
public final class GlyphJustificationInfo {
// Public Constructors
    public GlyphJustificationInfo(float weight, boolean growAbsorb, int growPriority, float growLeftLimit,
                          float growRightLimit, boolean shrinkAbsorb, int shrinkPriority, float shrinkLeftLimit,
                          float shrinkRightLimit);
// Public Constants
    public static final int PRIORITY_INTERCHAR;                                      =2
    public static final int PRIORITY_KASHIDA;                                        =0
    public static final int PRIORITY_NONE;                                           =3
    public static final int PRIORITY_WHITESPACE;                                     =1
```

```
// Public Instance Fields
    public final boolean growAbsorb;
    public final float growLeftLimit;
    public final int growPriority;
    public final float growRightLimit;
    public final boolean shrinkAbsorb;
    public final float shrinkLeftLimit;
    public final int shrinkPriority;
    public final float shrinkRightLimit;
    public final float weight;
}
```

Returned By: GlyphVector.getGlyphJustificationInfo(), GraphicAttribute.getJustificationInfo()

GlyphMetrics   Java 1.2

java.awt.font

This class contains measurements for a single glyph of a font. Although GlyphMetrics has a public constructor, the only way to obtain actual metrics for a glyph is by calling the getGlyphMetrics() method of a GlyphVector.

Each glyph has an origin. The getAdvance() method returns the standard distance between the origin of this glyph and the origin of the next glyph in the GlyphVector from which the GlyphMetrics was obtained. getBounds2D() returns the bounding box of the glyph. This rectangle is positioned relative to the origin of the glyph. getLSB() returns the left-side bearing of the glyph: the distance between the origin and the left side of the bounding box. getRSB() returns the right-side bearing: the distance between the right side of the bounding box and the start of the next glyph. For some glyphs, these bearing values may be negative.

getType() returns the type of the glyph; the return value is one of the constants defined by the class. Most glyphs are of STANDARD type. Glyphs with no visible representation are of type WHITESPACE. Glyphs that represent more than one character have type LIGATURE. Accents and other diacritical marks that modify other glyphs have type COMBINING. Finally, when one character is represented by two or more glyphs, the extra glyph or glyphs have the type COMPONENT.

```
public final class GlyphMetrics {
// Public Constructors
    public GlyphMetrics(float advance, java.awt.geom.Rectangle2D bounds, byte glyphType);
// Public Constants
    public static final byte COMBINING;                                    =2
    public static final byte COMPONENT;                                    =3
    public static final byte LIGATURE;                                     =1
    public static final byte STANDARD;                                     =0
    public static final byte WHITESPACE;                                   =4
// Property Accessor Methods (by property name)
    public float getAdvance();
    public java.awt.geom.Rectangle2D getBounds2D();
    public boolean isCombining();
    public boolean isComponent();
    public boolean isLigature();
    public float getLSB();
    public float getRSB();
    public boolean isStandard();
```

```
    public int getType();
    public boolean isWhitespace();
}
```

Returned By: GlyphVector.getGlyphMetrics()

GlyphVector   Java 1.2

java.awt.font   *cloneable*

This class represents an array of glyphs taken from a single font that are to be drawn on a single line. You obtain a GlyphVector by calling the createGlyphVector() method of a Font object, and you draw a GlyphVector with the drawGlyphVector() method of a Graphics2D object.

When a string is drawn using the drawString() method of Graphics or Graphics2D, the characters of the string first must be converted to font glyphs, and then those glyphs must be drawn. Thus, if a string is to be drawn repeatedly, it can be more efficient to separate these two steps, converting the string to a GlyphVector once and then drawing that GlyphVector multiple times.

```
public abstract class GlyphVector implements Cloneable {
// Public Constructors
    public GlyphVector();
// Property Accessor Methods (by property name)
    public abstract Font getFont();
    public abstract FontRenderContext getFontRenderContext();
    public abstract java.awt.geom.Rectangle2D getLogicalBounds();
    public abstract int getNumGlyphs();
    public abstract Shape getOutline();
    public abstract Shape getOutline(float x, float y);
    public abstract java.awt.geom.Rectangle2D getVisualBounds();
// Public Instance Methods
    public abstract boolean equals(GlyphVector set);
    public abstract int getGlyphCode(int glyphIndex);
    public abstract int[ ] getGlyphCodes(int beginGlyphIndex, int numEntries, int[ ] codeReturn);
    public abstract GlyphJustificationInfo getGlyphJustificationInfo(int glyphIndex);
    public abstract Shape getGlyphLogicalBounds(int glyphIndex);
    public abstract GlyphMetrics getGlyphMetrics(int glyphIndex);
    public abstract Shape getGlyphOutline(int glyphIndex);
    public abstract java.awt.geom.Point2D getGlyphPosition(int glyphIndex);
    public abstract float[ ] getGlyphPositions(int beginGlyphIndex, int numEntries, float[ ] positionReturn);
    public abstract java.awt.geom.AffineTransform getGlyphTransform(int glyphIndex);
    public abstract Shape getGlyphVisualBounds(int glyphIndex);
    public abstract void performDefaultLayout();
    public abstract void setGlyphPosition(int glyphIndex, java.awt.geom.Point2D newPos);
    public abstract void setGlyphTransform(int glyphIndex, java.awt.geom.AffineTransform newTX);
}
```

Hierarchy: Object→ GlyphVector(Cloneable)

Passed To: Graphics2D.drawGlyphVector(), GlyphVector.equals()

Returned By: Font.createGlyphVector()

GraphicAttribute   Java 1.2

java.awt.font

This abstract class represents a graphic to be embedded in a line of text in lieu of a regular font glyph. A GraphicAttribute is used as the value of an TextAttribute.CHAR_REPLACEMENT attribute in a java.text.AttributedString or java.text.AttributedCharacterIterator. Most applications use one of the two subclasses ImageGraphicAttribute and ShapeGraphicAttribute. Few applications need to create custom subclasses of their own.

The draw() method is responsible for actually drawing the desired graphic. The other methods return various measurements for the graphic. The constants are possible alignment values returned by getAligment().

```
public abstract class GraphicAttribute {
// Protected Constructors
    protected GraphicAttribute(int alignment);
// Public Constants
    public static final int BOTTOM_ALIGNMENT;                              =-2
    public static final int CENTER_BASELINE;                               =1
    public static final int HANGING_BASELINE;                              =2
    public static final int ROMAN_BASELINE;                                =0
    public static final int TOP_ALIGNMENT;                                 =-1
// Property Accessor Methods (by property name)
    public abstract float getAdvance();
    public final int getAlignment();
    public abstract float getAscent();
    public java.awt.geom.Rectangle2D getBounds();
    public abstract float getDescent();
    public GlyphJustificationInfo getJustificationInfo();
// Public Instance Methods
    public abstract void draw(Graphics2D graphics, float x, float y);
}
```

Subclasses: ImageGraphicAttribute, ShapeGraphicAttribute

ImageGraphicAttribute

Java 1.2

java.awt.font

This concrete subclass of GraphicAttribute allows an image to be drawn within a string of text. Create an ImageGraphicAttribute by specifying an image to draw, an alignment (one of the constants defined by GraphicAttribute), and, optionally, an origin for the image. The origin coordinates are relative to the image itself. Use the ImageGraphicAttribute by specifying it as the value of a TextAttribute.CHAR_REPLACEMENT attribute in a java.text.AttributedString or java.text.AttributedCharacterIterator.

See also ShapeGraphicAttribute.

```
public final class ImageGraphicAttribute extends GraphicAttribute {
// Public Constructors
    public ImageGraphicAttribute(Image image, int alignment);
    public ImageGraphicAttribute(Image image, int alignment, float originX, float originY);
// Public Instance Methods
    public boolean equals(ImageGraphicAttribute rhs);
// Public Methods Overriding GraphicAttribute
    public void draw(Graphics2D graphics, float x, float y);
    public float getAdvance();
    public float getAscent();
    public java.awt.geom.Rectangle2D getBounds();
    public float getDescent();
// Public Methods Overriding Object
    public boolean equals(Object rhs);
    public int hashCode();
}
```

Hierarchy: Object→ GraphicAttribute→ ImageGraphicAttribute

Passed To: ImageGraphicAttribute.equals()

LineBreakMeasurer
Java 1.2

java.awt.font

This class breaks a paragraph of text into individual lines of a specified width, where each line is represented by a TextLayout object. When you create a LineBreakMeasurer, you must specify the paragraph to be broken with a java.text.AttributedCharacterIterator, which is usually is obtained from a java.text.AttributedString. You may optionally specify a java.text.BreakIterator to indicate where line breaks are allowed. The default is to use the line breaking rules of the current locale. You must also pass a FontRenderContext to the LineBreakMeasurer() constructor. The FontRenderContext is usually obtained with the get-FontRenderContext() method of Graphics2D.

Once you have created a LineBreakMeasurer for your paragraph, you use it by repeatedly calling nextLayout() to create TextLayout objects that represent lines. nextLayout() returns null when it reaches the end of the paragraph. The desired width of each line is passed as an argument to nextLayout(). This allows the first line of a paragraph to be made shorter than the following lines, for example.

```
public final class LineBreakMeasurer {
// Public Constructors
    public LineBreakMeasurer(java.text.AttributedCharacterIterator text, FontRenderContext frc);
    public LineBreakMeasurer(java.text.AttributedCharacterIterator text, java.text.BreakIterator breakIter,
                             FontRenderContext frc);
// Public Instance Methods
    public void deleteChar(java.text.AttributedCharacterIterator newParagraph, int deletePos);
    public int getPosition();
    public void insertChar(java.text.AttributedCharacterIterator newParagraph, int insertPos);
    public TextLayout nextLayout(float maxAdvance);
    public TextLayout nextLayout(float wrappingWidth, int offsetLimit, boolean requireNextWord);
    public int nextOffset(float maxAdvance);
    public int nextOffset(float wrappingWidth, int offsetLimit, boolean requireNextWord);
    public void setPosition(int newPosition);
}
```

LineMetrics
Java 1.2

java.awt.font

This class provides access to various measurements for the characters in a font. The name LineMetrics is somewhat confusing; it refers to the general line metrics of a font, not the metrics of some particular line of text rendered with the font. LineMetrics provides more accurate metrics than java.awt.FontMetrics and also includes some metrics that are simply not available through that class.

Obtain a LineMetrics object by calling one of the getLineMetrics() methods of Font or Font-Metrics. These methods require that you supply some form of text to measure. The returned LineMetrics object does not contain the width of that text, but the font measurements it does return may depend on the content of the text. For example, the metrics for English text may differ from metrics for Japanese text. (Note, however, that the initial implementation from Sun simply ignores the text you specify.) If the supplied text contains characters from more than one language, the returned metrics may apply only to a prefix of the text. The getNumChars() method returns the length of this prefix.

Once you have obtained a LineMetrics object, you can call its various accessor methods to obtain information about the font. getAscent() returns the distance between the baseline and the top of the tallest character. getDescent() returns the distance between the baseline and the bottom of the lowest descender. getLeading() returns the recommended interline spacing for the font (so named for the strips of lead that used to be placed between rows of movable type). getHeight() returns the distance between the baseline of one line and the baseline of the next. It is equal to the sum of the ascent, descent, and leading. getUnderlineOffset() returns the recommended position of an underline, relative to the baseline for the font, and getUnderlineThickness() returns the recommended thickness of an underline. Two similar methods return the position and thickness of lines used to strike through characters in the font.

```
public abstract class LineMetrics {
// Public Constructors
    public LineMetrics();
// Property Accessor Methods (by property name)
    public abstract float getAscent();
    public abstract int getBaselineIndex();
    public abstract float[ ] getBaselineOffsets();
    public abstract float getDescent();
    public abstract float getHeight();
    public abstract float getLeading();
    public abstract int getNumChars();
    public abstract float getStrikethroughOffset();
    public abstract float getStrikethroughThickness();
    public abstract float getUnderlineOffset();
    public abstract float getUnderlineThickness();
}
```

Returned By: Font.getLineMetrics(), FontMetrics.getLineMetrics()

MultipleMaster   Java 1.2

java.awt.font

This interface describes capabilities of Type 1 Multiple Master fonts. If a Font object represents a Multiple Master font, it implements the MultipleMaster interface. Most fonts have only one parameter that you can vary: the point size. A Multiple Master font is a generalization that allows you to vary any number of design axes of the font. These design axes may be things such as font weight, average glyph width, italic angle, and so forth. The methods of the MultipleMaster interface allow you to query the names, defaults, and valid ranges of these design axes and derive new versions of the font by specifying values for each axis.

```
public abstract interface MultipleMaster {
// Property Accessor Methods (by property name)
    public abstract float[ ] getDesignAxisDefaults();
    public abstract String[ ] getDesignAxisNames();
    public abstract float[ ] getDesignAxisRanges();
    public abstract int getNumDesignAxes();
// Public Instance Methods
    public abstract Font deriveMMFont(float[ ] axes);
    public abstract Font deriveMMFont(float[ ] glyphWidths, float avgStemWidth, float typicalCapHeight,
                        float typicalXHeight, float italicAngle);
}
```

OpenType   Java 1.2

java.awt.font

This interface is implemented by Font objects that represent OpenType and TrueType fonts. It allows access to tables of raw font data. You should use this interface only if you are intimately familiar with the font data format for OpenType and TrueType fonts.

```
public abstract interface OpenType {
// Public Constants
   public static final int TAG_ACNT;                                      =1633906292
   public static final int TAG_AVAR;                                      =1635148146
   public static final int TAG_BASE;                                      =1111577413
   public static final int TAG_BDAT;                                      =1650745716
   public static final int TAG_BLOC;                                      =1651273571
   public static final int TAG_BSLN;                                      =1651731566
   public static final int TAG_CFF;                                       =1128678944
   public static final int TAG_CMAP;                                      =1668112752
   public static final int TAG_CVAR;                                      =1668702578
   public static final int TAG_CVT;                                       =1668707360
   public static final int TAG_DSIG;                                      =1146308935
   public static final int TAG_EBDT;                                      =1161970772
   public static final int TAG_EBLC;                                      =1161972803
   public static final int TAG_EBSC;                                      =1161974595
   public static final int TAG_FDSC;                                      =1717859171
   public static final int TAG_FEAT;                                      =1717920116
   public static final int TAG_FMTX;                                      =1718449272
   public static final int TAG_FPGM;                                      =1718642541
   public static final int TAG_FVAR;                                      =1719034226
   public static final int TAG_GASP;                                      =1734439792
   public static final int TAG_GDEF;                                      =1195656518
   public static final int TAG_GLYF;                                      =1735162214
   public static final int TAG_GPOS;                                      =1196445523
   public static final int TAG_GSUB;                                      =1196643650
   public static final int TAG_GVAR;                                      =1735811442
   public static final int TAG_HDMX;                                      =1751412088
   public static final int TAG_HEAD;                                      =1751474532
   public static final int TAG_HHEA;                                      =1751672161
   public static final int TAG_HMTX;                                      =1752003704
   public static final int TAG_JSTF;                                      =1246975046
   public static final int TAG_JUST;                                      =1786082164
   public static final int TAG_KERN;                                      =1801810542
   public static final int TAG_LCAR;                                      =1818452338
   public static final int TAG_LOCA;                                      =1819239265
   public static final int TAG_LTSH;                                      =1280594760
   public static final int TAG_MAXP;                                      =1835104368
   public static final int TAG_MMFX;                                      =1296909912
   public static final int TAG_MMSD;                                      =1296913220
   public static final int TAG_MORT;                                      =1836020340
   public static final int TAG_NAME;                                      =1851878757
   public static final int TAG_OPBD;                                      =1836020340
   public static final int TAG_OS2;                                       =1330851634
   public static final int TAG_PCLT;                                      =1346587732
   public static final int TAG_POST;                                      =1886352244
   public static final int TAG_PREP;                                      =1886545264
   public static final int TAG_PROP;                                      =1886547824
   public static final int TAG_TRAK;                                      =1953653099
   public static final int TAG_TYP1;                                      =1954115633
   public static final int TAG_VDMX;                                      =1447316824
   public static final int TAG_VHEA;                                      =1986553185
   public static final int TAG_VMTX;                                      =1986884728
// Public Instance Methods
   public abstract byte[ ] getFontTable(String strSfntTag);
   public abstract byte[ ] getFontTable(int sfntTag);
   public abstract byte[ ] getFontTable(String strSfntTag, int offset, int count);
   public abstract byte[ ] getFontTable(int sfntTag, int offset, int count);
```

```
    public abstract int getFontTableSize(String strSfntTag);
    public abstract int getFontTableSize(int sfntTag);
    public abstract int getVersion();
}
```

ShapeGraphicAttribute   Java 1.2

java.awt.font

This concrete subclass of GraphicAttribute allows an arbitrary shape to be drawn within a string of text. Create a ShapeGraphicAttribute by specifying a shape to draw and an alignment (one of the constants defined by GraphicAttribute) that specifies how the shape is aligned with the rest of the text. Pass true for the third argument, *stroke*, if the shape should simply be drawn, or pass false if the shape should be filled. Use the ShapeGraphicAttribute by specifying it as the value of a TextAttribute.CHAR_REPLACEMENT attribute in a java.text.AttributedString or java.text.AttributedCharacterIterator

See also ImageGraphicAttribute.

```
public final class ShapeGraphicAttribute extends GraphicAttribute {
// Public Constructors
    public ShapeGraphicAttribute(Shape shape, int alignment, boolean stroke);
// Public Constants
    public static final boolean FILL;                                      =false
    public static final boolean STROKE;                                    =true
// Public Instance Methods
    public boolean equals(ShapeGraphicAttribute rhs);
// Public Methods Overriding GraphicAttribute
    public void draw(Graphics2D graphics, float x, float y);
    public float getAdvance();
    public float getAscent();
    public java.awt.geom.Rectangle2D getBounds();
    public float getDescent();
// Public Methods Overriding Object
    public boolean equals(Object rhs);
    public int hashCode();
}
```

Hierarchy: Object→ GraphicAttribute→ ShapeGraphicAttribute

Passed To: ShapeGraphicAttribute.equals()

TextAttribute   Java 1.2

java.awt.font   *serializable*

This class defines constants that serve as attribute names and attribute values for use with java.text.AttributedString and java.text.AttributedCharacterIterator objects. The constants of type TextAttribute serve as attribute names. The other constants define commonly used values for those attributes. Note that the value of the CHAR_REPLACEMENT attribute should be a GraphicAttribute object, and the value of the TRANSFORM attribute should be a TransformAttribute object.

```
public final class TextAttribute extends java.text.AttributedCharacterIterator.Attribute {
// Protected Constructors
    protected TextAttribute(String name);
// Public Constants
    public static final TextAttribute BACKGROUND;
    public static final TextAttribute BIDI_EMBEDDING;
    public static final TextAttribute CHAR_REPLACEMENT;
```

```
   public static final TextAttribute FAMILY;
   public static final TextAttribute FONT;
   public static final TextAttribute FOREGROUND;
   public static final TextAttribute INPUT_METHOD_HIGHLIGHT;
   public static final TextAttribute JUSTIFICATION;
   public static final Float JUSTIFICATION_FULL;
   public static final Float JUSTIFICATION_NONE;
   public static final TextAttribute POSTURE;
   public static final Float POSTURE_OBLIQUE;
   public static final Float POSTURE_REGULAR;
   public static final TextAttribute RUN_DIRECTION;
   public static final Boolean RUN_DIRECTION_LTR;
   public static final Boolean RUN_DIRECTION_RTL;
   public static final TextAttribute SIZE;
   public static final TextAttribute STRIKETHROUGH;
   public static final Boolean STRIKETHROUGH_ON;
   public static final TextAttribute SUPERSCRIPT;
   public static final Integer SUPERSCRIPT_SUB;
   public static final Integer SUPERSCRIPT_SUPER;
   public static final TextAttribute SWAP_COLORS;
   public static final Boolean SWAP_COLORS_ON;
   public static final TextAttribute TRANSFORM;
   public static final TextAttribute UNDERLINE;
   public static final Integer UNDERLINE_ON;
   public static final TextAttribute WEIGHT;
   public static final Float WEIGHT_BOLD;
   public static final Float WEIGHT_DEMIBOLD;
   public static final Float WEIGHT_DEMILIGHT;
   public static final Float WEIGHT_EXTRA_LIGHT;
   public static final Float WEIGHT_EXTRABOLD;
   public static final Float WEIGHT_HEAVY;
   public static final Float WEIGHT_LIGHT;
   public static final Float WEIGHT_MEDIUM;
   public static final Float WEIGHT_REGULAR;
   public static final Float WEIGHT_SEMIBOLD;
   public static final Float WEIGHT_ULTRABOLD;
   public static final TextAttribute WIDTH;
   public static final Float WIDTH_CONDENSED;
   public static final Float WIDTH_EXTENDED;
   public static final Float WIDTH_REGULAR;
   public static final Float WIDTH_SEMI_CONDENSED;
   public static final Float WIDTH_SEMI_EXTENDED;
// Protected Methods Overriding AttributedCharacterIterator.Attribute
   protected Object readResolve() throws java.io.InvalidObjectException;
}
```

Hierarchy: Object→ java.text.AttributedCharacterIterator.Attribute(Serializable) → TextAttribute

Type Of: Too many fields to list.

TextHitInfo   Java 1.2

java.awt.font

This class encapsulates the position of a character within a string of text and the bias, or side, of the character. The hitTestChar() method of TextLayout takes the position of a mouse click and returns a TextHitInfo that specifies where the click occurred.

getCharIndex() returns the position of the character that was hit. getInsertionIndex() returns the position at which characters should be inserted or deleted. This may or may not be the same as the value returned by getCharIndex(). isLeadingEdge() specifies whether the hit was on the leading edge of the character.

If you want to place the insertion cursor at the position of the mouse click, it is not sufficient to know which character was clicked on; you must also know whether the leading edge or the trailing edge of the character was clicked on. This is particularly important when working with bidirectional text, such as Arabic or Hebrew. If the TextHitInfo specifies that the trailing edge was selected, the insertion cursor should be placed before the character. Otherwise, it should be placed after the character.

In bidirectional text, positioning the cursor correctly in response to user requests to move it left or right can be quite tricky. TextHitInfo is also returned by the getNextLeftHit() and getNextRightHit() methods of TextLayout, to help solve this problem.

```
public final class TextHitInfo {
// No Constructor
// Public Class Methods
    public static TextHitInfo afterOffset(int offset);
    public static TextHitInfo beforeOffset(int offset);
    public static TextHitInfo leading(int charIndex);
    public static TextHitInfo trailing(int charIndex);
// Property Accessor Methods (by property name)
    public int getCharIndex();
    public int getInsertionIndex();
    public boolean isLeadingEdge();
    public TextHitInfo getOtherHit();
// Public Instance Methods
    public boolean equals(TextHitInfo hitInfo);
    public TextHitInfo getOffsetHit(int delta);
// Public Methods Overriding Object
    public boolean equals(Object obj);
    public int hashCode();
    public String toString();
}
```

Passed To: Too many methods to list.

Returned By: Too many methods to list.

TextLayout   Java 1.2
java.awt.font   *cloneable*

This class represents and displays a line of styled, possibly bidirectional, text and provides algorithms for the visual manipulation of that text. This is a powerful and complex class. Many applications prefer to use high-level Swing components, such as JTextField and JTextPane, to handle text display and editing. Some applications may want to use the lower-level GlyphVector class for maximum text drawing speed.

Using the TextLayout() constructor, you can create a TextLayout from a java.text.AttributedCharacterIterator, from a string and a font, or from a string and a java.util.Map of attributes. All versions of the constructor also require a FontRenderContext, obtained with the getFontRenderContext() method of Graphics2D.

Once you have created a TextLayout, you can draw it by calling its draw() method. TextLayout also provides various other methods to support applications that allow the user to edit the text. If the user clicks on the text, you can determine what character was clicked on with hitTestChar(), which returns a TextHitInfo. Once you have an insertion position specified with a TextHitInfo, you can obtain a Shape appropriate for use as an insertion cursor by calling getCaretShape(). The returned shape is relative to the origin of the TextLayout, and it takes into account whether the text is italic. getCaretShapes() is passed a character index within the TextLayout; it returns an array of one or two Shape objects that represent insertion cursors for that character position. Usually this array contains only one cursor, but in bidirectional text, it may contain both a primary insertion cursor and a secondary insertion cursor.

If the user selects text by clicking and dragging with the mouse, you can call getVisual-HighlightShape() to determine how to highlight the selected text. This method returns a Shape object suitable for drawing the highlighted regions. Alternatively, you can use get-LogicalHighlightShape() to highlight a specified contiguous group of characters in the Text-Layout. Note, however, that in bidirectional text, this logical highlight might map to two visually disjoint regions.

```
public final class TextLayout implements Cloneable {
// Public Constructors
    public TextLayout(java.text.AttributedCharacterIterator text, FontRenderContext frc);
    public TextLayout(String string, Font font, FontRenderContext frc);
    public TextLayout(String string, java.util.Map attributes, FontRenderContext frc);
// Public Constants
    public static final TextLayout.CaretPolicy DEFAULT_CARET_POLICY;
// Inner Classes
    public static class CaretPolicy;
// Property Accessor Methods (by property name)
    public float getAdvance();
    public float getAscent();
    public byte getBaseline();
    public float[ ] getBaselineOffsets();
    public java.awt.geom.Rectangle2D getBounds();
    public int getCharacterCount();
    public float getDescent();
    public float getLeading();
    public boolean isLeftToRight();
    public boolean isVertical();
    public float getVisibleAdvance();
// Public Instance Methods
    public void draw(Graphics2D g2, float x, float y);
    public boolean equals(TextLayout rhs);
    public Shape getBlackBoxBounds(int firstEndpoint, int secondEndpoint);
    public float[ ] getCaretInfo(TextHitInfo hit);
    public float[ ] getCaretInfo(TextHitInfo hit, java.awt.geom.Rectangle2D bounds);
    public Shape getCaretShape(TextHitInfo hit);
    public Shape getCaretShape(TextHitInfo hit, java.awt.geom.Rectangle2D bounds);
    public Shape[ ] getCaretShapes(int offset);
    public Shape[ ] getCaretShapes(int offset, java.awt.geom.Rectangle2D bounds);
    public Shape[ ] getCaretShapes(int offset, java.awt.geom.Rectangle2D bounds, TextLayout.CaretPolicy policy);
    public byte getCharacterLevel(int index);
    public TextLayout getJustifiedLayout(float justificationWidth);
    public Shape getLogicalHighlightShape(int firstEndpoint, int secondEndpoint);
    public Shape getLogicalHighlightShape(int firstEndpoint, int secondEndpoint,
                                java.awt.geom.Rectangle2D bounds);
    public int[ ] getLogicalRangesForVisualSelection(TextHitInfo firstEndpoint, TextHitInfo secondEndpoint);
    public TextHitInfo getNextLeftHit(int offset);
    public TextHitInfo getNextLeftHit(TextHitInfo hit);
    public TextHitInfo getNextLeftHit(int offset, TextLayout.CaretPolicy policy);
    public TextHitInfo getNextRightHit(int offset);
    public TextHitInfo getNextRightHit(TextHitInfo hit);
    public TextHitInfo getNextRightHit(int offset, TextLayout.CaretPolicy policy);
    public Shape getOutline(java.awt.geom.AffineTransform tx);
    public Shape getVisualHighlightShape(TextHitInfo firstEndpoint, TextHitInfo secondEndpoint);
    public Shape getVisualHighlightShape(TextHitInfo firstEndpoint, TextHitInfo secondEndpoint,
                                java.awt.geom.Rectangle2D bounds);
```

```
    public TextHitInfo getVisualOtherHit(TextHitInfo hit);
    public TextHitInfo hitTestChar(float x, float y);
    public TextHitInfo hitTestChar(float x, float y, java.awt.geom.Rectangle2D bounds);
// Public Methods Overriding Object
    public boolean equals(Object obj);
    public int hashCode();
    public String toString();
// Protected Methods Overriding Object
    protected Object clone();
// Protected Instance Methods
    protected void handleJustify(float justificationWidth);                          empty
}
```

Hierarchy: Object → TextLayout(Cloneable)

Passed To: TextLayout.equals(), TextLayout.CaretPolicy.getStrongCaret()

Returned By: LineBreakMeasurer.nextLayout(), TextLayout.getJustifiedLayout()

TextLayout.CaretPolicy   Java 1.2

java.awt.font

This class defines a policy for deciding which insertion position is the dominant one in
bidirectional text. Most applications never need to use this class.

If you want to specify a policy other than the default, you should subclass this class
and override getStrongCaret() to choose between two TextHitInfo objects, returning the one
that represents the dominant insertion position. Then pass an instance of your subclass
to the getCaretShapes(), getNextLeftHit(), and getNextRightHit() methods of TextLayout.

```
public static class TextLayout.CaretPolicy {
// Public Constructors
    public CaretPolicy();
// Public Instance Methods
    public TextHitInfo getStrongCaret(TextHitInfo hit1, TextHitInfo hit2, TextLayout layout);
}
```

Passed To: TextLayout.{getCaretShapes(), getNextLeftHit(), getNextRightHit()}

Type Of: TextLayout.DEFAULT_CARET_POLICY

TextLine.TextLineMetrics   Java 1.2

java.awt.font

This public inner class is defined within a private class. It was inadvertently included in
the public API of java.awt.font but should be considered private.

```
public static final class TextLine.TextLineMetrics {
// Public Constructors
    public TextLineMetrics(float ascent, float descent, float leading, float advance);
// Public Instance Fields
    public final float advance;
    public final float ascent;
    public final float descent;
    public final float leading;
}
```

TransformAttribute

java.awt.font

serializable

This class is a simple immutable wrapper around a java.awt.geom.AffineTransform. This wrapper makes it safe to use a transform as the value of a TextAttribute.TRANSFORM attribute.

```
public final class TransformAttribute implements Serializable {
// Public Constructors
    public TransformAttribute(java.awt.geom.AffineTransform transform);
// Public Instance Methods
    public java.awt.geom.AffineTransform getTransform();
}
```

Hierarchy: Object→ TransformAttribute(Serializable)

CHAPTER 16

The java.awt.geom Package

The java.awt.geom package contains Java 2D classes and interfaces related to shapes and geometry; the package is new in Java 1.2. Most of the classes in this package are java.awt.Shape implementations that can be drawn and filled by a java.awt.Graphics2D object. Note that some implementations store data using single-precision floating-point coordinates, while others use double-precision coordinates. Other important classes include AffineTransform, Area, GeneralPath, and PathIterator. Figure 16-1 shows the class hierarchy of this package.

AffineTransform   Java 1.2

java.awt.geom   *cloneable serializable*

An AffineTransform represents an arbitrary linear transformation of a point, vector, shape, or coordinate system by any combination of translation, rotation, scaling, flipping, and skewing. This is one of the most fundamental classes in Java 2D: the Java 2D rendering process uses an AffineTransform to convert from user coordinate space to the coordinate space of the physical device. In addition to this implicit use of AffineTransform, the class is often used explicitly in Java 2D programming.

The transformations specified by AffineTransform objects are quite general. But they are all linear: straight lines remain straight, and parallel lines remain parallel under any AffineTransform. Although it is possible to imagine more general, nonlinear, transformations, Java 2D works only with affine transformations. AffineTransform is not an implementation of some more general Transform interface.

Mathematically, an affine transformation is represented by a 2-by-3 matrix of six numbers. The AffineTransform class has constructors and methods that allow you to work with this matrix directly, but unless you remember your linear algebra, you typically use the higher-level methods of this class.

You can use a constructor to create an AffineTransform, but it is usually easier to use one of the static methods to create an AffineTransform suitable for rotation about the origin, rotation about an arbitrary point, scaling, shearing, or translation. Or, if you have an existing AffineTransform object that you want to reuse, you can use one of the setTo()

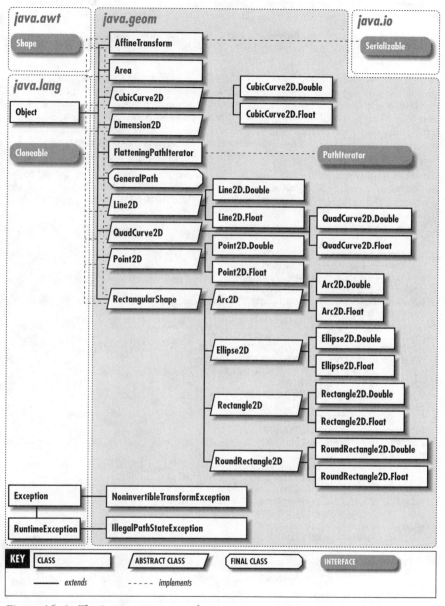

Figure 16-1: The java.awt.geom package

methods to specify a rotation, scale, shear, or translation to replace the existing transform. Note that a flip transform is simply scaling by -1.0 in the X or Y dimension.

Often, however, you have an AffineTransform that you want to transform further. The rotate(), scale(), shear(), and translate() methods do this. Or, more generally, you can use concatenate() or preConcatenate() to transform one AffineTransform by another.

Once an AffineTransform object is set to the desired transformation, the transform() method can be used to transform points, or arrays of points, in the desired way. deltaTransform() transforms a point or array of points, leaving out any translation component of the transform. This is useful for transforming dimensions and position-independent vectors, rather than transforming absolute coordinates. inverseTransform() performs the inverse of the transformation specified by an AffineTransform. Finally, createTransformedShape() returns a java.awt.Shape that represents a transformed version of the specified Shape.

isIdentity() returns true if an AffineTransform is an identity transform—that is, if it performs no transform at all. getType() returns a value that provides basic information about the transform. The value returned is TYPE_IDENTITY, TYPE_GENERAL_TRANSFORM, or a bitmask of the remaining type constants.

```
public class AffineTransform implements Cloneable, Serializable {
// Public Constructors
    public AffineTransform();
    public AffineTransform(double[ ] flatmatrix);
    public AffineTransform(float[ ] flatmatrix);
    public AffineTransform(AffineTransform Tx);
    public AffineTransform(double m00, double m10, double m01, double m11, double m02, double m12);
    public AffineTransform(float m00, float m10, float m01, float m11, float m02, float m12);
// Public Constants
    public static final int TYPE_FLIP;                                          =64
    public static final int TYPE_GENERAL_ROTATION;                              =16
    public static final int TYPE_GENERAL_SCALE;                                 =4
    public static final int TYPE_GENERAL_TRANSFORM;                             =32
    public static final int TYPE_IDENTITY;                                      =0
    public static final int TYPE_MASK_ROTATION;                                 =24
    public static final int TYPE_MASK_SCALE;                                    =6
    public static final int TYPE_QUADRANT_ROTATION;                             =8
    public static final int TYPE_TRANSLATION;                                   =1
    public static final int TYPE_UNIFORM_SCALE;                                 =2
// Public Class Methods
    public static AffineTransform getRotateInstance(double theta);
    public static AffineTransform getRotateInstance(double theta, double x, double y);
    public static AffineTransform getScaleInstance(double sx, double sy);
    public static AffineTransform getShearInstance(double shx, double shy);
    public static AffineTransform getTranslateInstance(double tx, double ty);
// Property Accessor Methods (by property name)
    public double getDeterminant();                                       default:1.0
    public boolean isIdentity();                                          default:true
    public double getScaleX();                                            default:1.0
    public double getScaleY();                                            default:1.0
    public double getShearX();                                            default:0.0
    public double getShearY();                                            default:0.0
    public double getTranslateX();                                        default:0.0
    public double getTranslateY();                                        default:0.0
    public int getType();                                                 default:0
// Public Instance Methods
    public void concatenate(AffineTransform Tx);
    public AffineTransform createInverse() throws NoninvertibleTransformException;
    public Shape createTransformedShape(Shape pSrc);
```

```
    public Point2D deltaTransform(Point2D ptSrc, Point2D ptDst);
    public void deltaTransform(double[ ] srcPts, int srcOff, double[ ] dstPts, int dstOff, int numPts);
    public void getMatrix(double[ ] flatmatrix);
    public Point2D inverseTransform(Point2D ptSrc, Point2D ptDst) throws NoninvertibleTransformException;
    public void inverseTransform(double[ ] srcPts, int srcOff, double[ ] dstPts, int dstOff, int numPts)
        throws NoninvertibleTransformException;
    public void preConcatenate(AffineTransform Tx);
    public void rotate(double theta);
    public void rotate(double theta, double x, double y);
    public void scale(double sx, double sy);
    public void setToIdentity();
    public void setToRotation(double theta);
    public void setToRotation(double theta, double x, double y);
    public void setToScale(double sx, double sy);
    public void setToShear(double shx, double shy);
    public void setToTranslation(double tx, double ty);
    public void setTransform(AffineTransform Tx);
    public void setTransform(double m00, double m10, double m01, double m11, double m02, double m12);
    public void shear(double shx, double shy);
    public Point2D transform(Point2D ptSrc, Point2D ptDst);
    public void transform(float[ ] srcPts, int srcOff, float[ ] dstPts, int dstOff, int numPts);
    public void transform(Point2D[ ] ptSrc, int srcOff, Point2D[ ] ptDst, int dstOff, int numPts);
    public void transform(float[ ] srcPts, int srcOff, double[ ] dstPts, int dstOff, int numPts);
    public void transform(double[ ] srcPts, int srcOff, double[ ] dstPts, int dstOff, int numPts);
    public void transform(double[ ] srcPts, int srcOff, float[ ] dstPts, int dstOff, int numPts);
    public void translate(double tx, double ty);
// Public Methods Overriding Object
    public Object clone();
    public boolean equals(Object obj);
    public int hashCode();
    public String toString();
}
```

Hierarchy: Object→ AffineTransform(Cloneable, Serializable)

Passed To: Too many methods to list.

Returned By: Font.getTransform(), Graphics2D.getTransform(),
GraphicsConfiguration.{getDefaultTransform(), getNormalizingTransform()},
java.awt.font.FontRenderContext.getTransform(), java.awt.font.GlyphVector.getGlyphTransform(),
java.awt.font.TransformAttribute.getTransform(), AffineTransform.{createInverse(), getRotateInstance(),
getScaleInstance(), getShearInstance(), getTranslateInstance()},
java.awt.image.AffineTransformOp.getTransform(), java.awt.image.renderable.RenderContext.getTransform()

Arc2D   Java 1.2

java.awt.geom   *cloneable shape*

This abstract class is a java.awt.Shape that represents an arc. The arc is defined as a portion of an ellipse, where the ellipse is defined by a rectangle. The start and end points of the arc on that ellipse are defined by a start angle and an extent angle, measured in degrees counterclockwise from the positive X axis. Unless the ellipse is actually a perfect circle, the specified angles are not true angles: a line drawn from the center of the ellipse to the upper-right corner of the bounding rectangle is always considered to form a 45-degree angle with the X axis, regardless of the true angle it forms.

In addition to the coordinates of the rectangle and the angles that specify the start and end points of the arc, the shape of an Arc2D is also specified by its arcType property. If the type of the arc is specified as CHORD, the two end points are joined by a straight line. If the type is specified as PIE, each of the two end points is joined to the center of the ellipse, forming a wedge, or slice of pie. If the type is specified as OPEN, the end points are not joined and the resulting shape is an open curve that does not enclose a region.

Arc2D is an abstract class and cannot be instantiated. Arc2D.Float and Arc2D.Double are concrete subclasses that use float and double fields to store arc coordinates and angles.

```
public abstract class Arc2D extends RectangularShape {
// Protected Constructors
    protected Arc2D(int type);
// Public Constants
    public static final int CHORD;                                          =1
    public static final int OPEN;                                           =0
    public static final int PIE;                                            =2
// Inner Classes
    public static class Double extends Arc2D;
    public static class Float extends Arc2D;
// Property Accessor Methods (by property name)
    public abstract double getAngleExtent();
    public abstract void setAngleExtent(double angExt);
    public abstract double getAngleStart();
    public void setAngleStart(Point2D p);
    public abstract void setAngleStart(double angSt);
    public int getArcType();
    public void setArcType(int type);
    public Rectangle2D getBounds2D();                        Overrides:RectangularShape
    public Point2D getEndPoint();
    public Point2D getStartPoint();
// Public Instance Methods
    public boolean containsAngle(double angle);
    public void setAngles(Point2D p1, Point2D p2);
    public void setAngles(double x1, double y1, double x2, double y2);
    public void setArc(Arc2D a);
    public void setArc(Rectangle2D rect, double angSt, double angExt, int closure);
    public void setArc(Point2D loc, Dimension2D size, double angSt, double angExt, int closure);
    public abstract void setArc(double x, double y, double w, double h, double angSt, double angExt, int closure);
    public void setArcByCenter(double x, double y, double radius, double angSt, double angExt, int closure);
    public void setArcByTangent(Point2D p1, Point2D p2, Point2D p3, double radius);
// Public Methods Overriding RectangularShape
    public boolean contains(Rectangle2D r);
    public boolean contains(double x, double y);
    public boolean contains(double x, double y, double w, double h);
    public PathIterator getPathIterator(AffineTransform at);
    public boolean intersects(double x, double y, double w, double h);
    public void setFrame(double x, double y, double w, double h);
// Protected Instance Methods
    protected abstract Rectangle2D makeBounds(double x, double y, double w, double h);
}
```

Hierarchy: Object → RectangularShape(Cloneable, Shape) → Arc2D

Subclasses: Arc2D.Double, Arc2D.Float

Passed To: Arc2D.setArc()

Arc2D.Double   Java 1.2

java.awt.geom   *cloneable shape*

This class is a concrete implementation of Arc2D that uses double fields to store the coordinates and angles of the arc. For efficiency, these x, y, width, height, start, and extent fields are declared public and may be used directly by Java programs. See Arc2D for more information.

```
public static class Arc2D.Double extends Arc2D {
// Public Constructors
    public Double();
    public Double(int type);
    public Double(Rectangle2D ellipseBounds, double start, double extent, int type);
    public Double(double x, double y, double w, double h, double start, double extent, int type);
// Public Methods Overriding Arc2D
    public double getAngleExtent();                                                    default:0.0
    public double getAngleStart();                                                     default:0.0
    public void setAngleExtent(double angExt);
    public void setAngleStart(double angSt);
    public void setArc(double x, double y, double w, double h, double angSt, double angExt, int closure);
// Protected Methods Overriding Arc2D
    protected Rectangle2D makeBounds(double x, double y, double w, double h);
// Public Methods Overriding RectangularShape
    public double getHeight();                                                         default:0.0
    public double getWidth();                                                          default:0.0
    public double getX();                                                              default:0.0
    public double getY();                                                              default:0.0
    public boolean isEmpty();                                                          default:true
// Public Instance Fields
    public double extent;
    public double height;
    public double start;
    public double width;
    public double x;
    public double y;
}
```

Arc2D.Float

Java 1.2

java.awt.geom

cloneable shape

This class is a concrete implementation of Arc2D that uses float fields to store the coordinates and angles of the arc. For efficiency, these x, y, width, height, start, and extent fields are declared public and may be used directly by Java programs. See Arc2D for more information.

```
public static class Arc2D.Float extends Arc2D {
// Public Constructors
    public Float();
    public Float(int type);
    public Float(Rectangle2D ellipseBounds, float start, float extent, int type);
    public Float(float x, float y, float w, float h, float start, float extent, int type);
// Public Methods Overriding Arc2D
    public double getAngleExtent();                                                    default:0.0
    public double getAngleStart();                                                     default:0.0
    public void setAngleExtent(double angExt);
    public void setAngleStart(double angSt);
    public void setArc(double x, double y, double w, double h, double angSt, double angExt, int closure);
// Protected Methods Overriding Arc2D
    protected Rectangle2D makeBounds(double x, double y, double w, double h);
// Public Methods Overriding RectangularShape
    public double getHeight();                                                         default:0.0
    public double getWidth();                                                          default:0.0
    public double getX();                                                              default:0.0
    public double getY();                                                              default:0.0
```

```
    public boolean isEmpty();                                                    default:true
// Public Instance Fields
    public float extent;
    public float height;
    public float start;
    public float width;
    public float x;
    public float y;
}
```

Area   Java 1.2

java.awt.geom   *cloneable shape*

Area is an implementation of java.awt.Shape that represents an arbitrary enclosed area. The Area() constructor is passed an arbitrary Shape that defines the initial area. If this Shape object represents an open curve that does not enclose an area, the curve is automatically closed with a straight line between the end points. Once an Area object has been created, it can be combined with another Area object with the add(), subtract(), intersect(), and exclusiveOr() methods. For example, you can construct an Area object that represents a hexagon minus the intersection of two circles.

```
public class Area implements Cloneable, Shape {
// Public Constructors
    public Area();
    public Area(Shape s);
// Property Accessor Methods (by property name)
    public Rectangle getBounds();                                        Implements:Shape
    public Rectangle2D getBounds2D();          Implements:Shape default:Rectangle2D.Double
    public boolean isEmpty();                                                default:true
    public boolean isPolygonal();                                            default:true
    public boolean isRectangular();                                          default:true
    public boolean isSingular();                                             default:true
// Public Instance Methods
    public void add(Area rhs);
    public Area createTransformedArea(AffineTransform t);
    public boolean equals(Area other);
    public void exclusiveOr(Area rhs);
    public void intersect(Area rhs);
    public void reset();
    public void subtract(Area rhs);
    public void transform(AffineTransform t);
// Methods Implementing Shape
    public boolean contains(Point2D p);
    public boolean contains(Rectangle2D p);
    public boolean contains(double x, double y);
    public boolean contains(double x, double y, double w, double h);
    public Rectangle getBounds();
    public Rectangle2D getBounds2D();                              default:Rectangle2D.Double
    public PathIterator getPathIterator(AffineTransform at);
    public PathIterator getPathIterator(AffineTransform at, double flatness);
    public boolean intersects(Rectangle2D p);
    public boolean intersects(double x, double y, double w, double h);
// Public Methods Overriding Object
    public Object clone();
}
```

Hierarchy: Object→ Area(Cloneable, Shape)

Passed To: Area.{add(), equals(), exclusiveOr(), intersect(), subtract()}

Returned By: Area.createTransformedArea()

CubicCurve2D

java.awt.geom

Java 1.2

cloneable shape

This abstract class is a java.awt.Shape that represents a smooth cubic Bezier curve (or spline) between end points p1 (x1, y1) and p2 (x2, y2). The precise shape of the curve is defined by two control points, cp1 (ctrlx1, ctrly1) and cp2 (ctrlx2, ctrly2). Note that the curve does not pass through cp1 and cp2 but that it does remain inside the quadrilateral defined by p1, cp1, cp2, and p2.

CubicCurve2D does not itself enclose an area, so the contains() methods test whether a point or rectangle is within the area defined by the curve and the straight line between its end points.

CubicCurve2D is an abstract class and cannot be instantiated. CubicCurve2D.Float and CubicCurve2D.Double are concrete subclasses that use float and double fields to store the end points and control points. See also QuadCurve2D, which is a quadratic Bezier curve that uses only a single control point.

```
public abstract class CubicCurve2D implements Cloneable, Shape {
// Protected Constructors
     protected CubicCurve2D();
// Inner Classes
     public static class Double extends CubicCurve2D;
     public static class Float extends CubicCurve2D;
// Public Class Methods
     public static double getFlatness(double[ ] coords, int offset);
     public static double getFlatness(double x1, double y1, double ctrlx1, double ctrly1, double ctrlx2, double ctrly2,
                                double x2, double y2);
     public static double getFlatnessSq(double[ ] coords, int offset);
     public static double getFlatnessSq(double x1, double y1, double ctrlx1, double ctrly1, double ctrlx2,
                                double ctrly2, double x2, double y2);
     public static int solveCubic(double[ ] eqn);
     public static void subdivide(CubicCurve2D src, CubicCurve2D left, CubicCurve2D right);
     public static void subdivide(double[ ] src, int srcoff, double[ ] left, int leftoff, double[ ] right, int rightoff);
// Property Accessor Methods (by property name)
     public Rectangle getBounds();                                              Implements:Shape
     public abstract Rectangle2D getBounds2D();                                 Implements:Shape
     public abstract Point2D getCtrlP1();
     public abstract Point2D getCtrlP2();
     public abstract double getCtrlX1();
     public abstract double getCtrlX2();
     public abstract double getCtrlY1();
     public abstract double getCtrlY2();
     public double getFlatness();
     public double getFlatnessSq();
     public abstract Point2D getP1();
     public abstract Point2D getP2();
     public abstract double getX1();
     public abstract double getX2();
     public abstract double getY1();
     public abstract double getY2();
// Public Instance Methods
     public void setCurve(CubicCurve2D c);
     public void setCurve(double[ ] coords, int offset);
     public void setCurve(Point2D[ ] pts, int offset);
```

```
    public void setCurve(Point2D p1, Point2D cp1, Point2D cp2, Point2D p2);
    public abstract void setCurve(double x1, double y1, double ctrlx1, double ctrly1, double ctrlx2, double ctrly2,
                double x2, double y2);
    public void subdivide(CubicCurve2D left, CubicCurve2D right);
// Methods Implementing Shape
    public boolean contains(Point2D p);
    public boolean contains(Rectangle2D r);
    public boolean contains(double x, double y);
    public boolean contains(double x, double y, double w, double h);
    public Rectangle getBounds();
    public abstract Rectangle2D getBounds2D();
    public PathIterator getPathIterator(AffineTransform at);
    public PathIterator getPathIterator(AffineTransform at, double flatness);
    public boolean intersects(Rectangle2D r);
    public boolean intersects(double x, double y, double w, double h);
// Public Methods Overriding Object
    public Object clone();
}
```

Hierarchy: Object→ CubicCurve2D(Cloneable, Shape)

Subclasses: CubicCurve2D.Double, CubicCurve2D.Float

Passed To: CubicCurve2D.{setCurve(), subdivide()}

CubicCurve2D.Double

java.awt.geom

Java 1.2

cloneable shape

This class is a concrete implementation of CubicCurve2D that uses double fields to store the end points and control points of the curve. The X and Y coordinates of these four points are stored in public fields and may be used directly by Java programs. See Cubic-Curve2D for more information.

```
public static class CubicCurve2D.Double extends CubicCurve2D {
// Public Constructors
    public Double();
    public Double(double x1, double y1, double ctrlx1, double ctrly1, double ctrlx2, double ctrly2, double x2,
                double y2);
// Public Methods Overriding CubicCurve2D
    public Rectangle2D getBounds2D();                                                default:Rectangle2D.Double
    public Point2D getCtrlP1();                                                          default:Point2D.Double
    public Point2D getCtrlP2();                                                          default:Point2D.Double
    public double getCtrlX1();                                                                   default:0.0
    public double getCtrlX2();                                                                   default:0.0
    public double getCtrlY1();                                                                   default:0.0
    public double getCtrlY2();                                                                   default:0.0
    public Point2D getP1();                                                              default:Point2D.Double
    public Point2D getP2();                                                              default:Point2D.Double
    public double getX1();                                                                       default:0.0
    public double getX2();                                                                       default:0.0
    public double getY1();                                                                       default:0.0
    public double getY2();                                                                       default:0.0
    public void setCurve(double x1, double y1, double ctrlx1, double ctrly1, double ctrlx2, double ctrly2, double x2,
                double y2);
// Public Instance Fields
    public double ctrlx1;
    public double ctrlx2;
    public double ctrly1;
    public double ctrly2;
```

```
    public double x1;
    public double x2;
    public double y1;
    public double y2;
}
```

CubicCurve2D.Float

java.awt.geom   *cloneable shape*

This class is a concrete implementation of CubicCurve2D that uses float fields to store the end points and control points of the curve. The X and Y coordinates of these four points are stored in public fields and may be used directly by Java programs. See Cubic-Curve2D for more information.

```
public static class CubicCurve2D.Float extends CubicCurve2D {
// Public Constructors
    public Float();
    public Float(float x1, float y1, float ctrlx1, float ctrly1, float ctrlx2, float ctrly2, float x2, float y2);
// Public Instance Methods
    public void setCurve(float x1, float y1, float ctrlx1, float ctrly1, float ctrlx2, float ctrly2, float x2, float y2);
// Public Methods Overriding CubicCurve2D
    public Rectangle2D getBounds2D();                              default:Rectangle2D.Float
    public Point2D getCtrlP1();                                       default:Point2D.Float
    public Point2D getCtrlP2();                                       default:Point2D.Float
    public double getCtrlX1();                                              default:0.0
    public double getCtrlX2();                                              default:0.0
    public double getCtrlY1();                                              default:0.0
    public double getCtrlY2();                                              default:0.0
    public Point2D getP1();                                          default:Point2D.Float
    public Point2D getP2();                                          default:Point2D.Float
    public double getX1();                                                 default:0.0
    public double getX2();                                                 default:0.0
    public double getY1();                                                 default:0.0
    public double getY2();                                                 default:0.0
    public void setCurve(double x1, double y1, double ctrlx1, double ctrly1, double ctrlx2, double ctrly2, double x2,
                     double y2);
// Public Instance Fields
    public float ctrlx1;
    public float ctrlx2;
    public float ctrly1;
    public float ctrly2;
    public float x1;
    public float x2;
    public float y1;
    public float y2;
}
```

Dimension2D

java.awt.geom   *cloneable*

This class represents a two-dimensional size in terms of its width and height. The accessor methods defined by this class query and set the width and height using values of type double. Note, however, that this class is abstract and does not actually store a size itself. java.awt.Dimension is a concrete subclass that stores a width and height as integers.

```
public abstract class Dimension2D implements Cloneable {
// Protected Constructors
    protected Dimension2D( );
// Property Accessor Methods (by property name)
    public abstract double getHeight( );
    public abstract double getWidth( );
// Public Instance Methods
    public void setSize(Dimension2D d);
    public abstract void setSize(double width, double height);
// Public Methods Overriding Object
    public Object clone( );
}
```

Hierarchy: Object→ Dimension2D(Cloneable)

Subclasses: Dimension

Passed To: Arc2D.setArc(), Dimension2D.setSize(), RectangularShape.setFrame()

Ellipse2D
Java 1.2

java.awt.geom
cloneable shape

This abstract class is a java.awt.Shape that represents an ellipse (or a circle). Ellipse2D is a subclass of RectangularShape, and for this reason, the ellipse is defined by its bounding rectangle. The width and height of the bounding rectangle specify the length of the two axes of the ellipse. (If the width and height are equal, the ellipse is a circle.) The X and Y coordinates of the ellipse specify the upper-left corner of the bounding rectangle; note that this point actually falls outside of the ellipse. The setFrameFromCenter() method, inherited from RectangularShape, allows you to define the ellipse by specifying the center and one corner. Note that Ellipse2D can only represent ellipses whose axes are parallel to the X and Y axes of the coordinate system. In order to work with rotated ellipses, use the createTransformedShape() method of AffineTransform or some other transformation method.

Ellipse2D is an abstract class and cannot be instantiated. The concrete subclasses Ellipse2D.Double and Ellipse2D.Float represent ellipses using double and float fields to contain the rectangular coordinates.

```
public abstract class Ellipse2D extends RectangularShape {
// Protected Constructors
    protected Ellipse2D( );
// Inner Classes
    public static class Double extends Ellipse2D;
    public static class Float extends Ellipse2D;
// Public Methods Overriding RectangularShape
    public boolean contains(double x, double y);
    public boolean contains(double x, double y, double w, double h);
    public PathIterator getPathIterator(AffineTransform at);
    public boolean intersects(double x, double y, double w, double h);
}
```

Hierarchy: Object→ RectangularShape(Cloneable, Shape)→ Ellipse2D

Subclasses: Ellipse2D.Double, Ellipse2D.Float

Ellipse2D.Double
Java 1.2

java.awt.geom
cloneable shape

This class is a concrete implementation of Ellipse2D that uses double fields to store the coordinates of the bounding rectangle of the ellipse. These x, y, width, height fields are declared public and may be used directly by Java programs. See Ellipse2D for more information.

```
public static class Ellipse2D.Double extends Ellipse2D {
// Public Constructors
    public Double();
    public Double(double x, double y, double w, double h);
// Public Methods Overriding RectangularShape
    public Rectangle2D getBounds2D();                                    default:Rectangle2D.Double
    public double getHeight();                                                       default:0.0
    public double getWidth();                                                        default:0.0
    public double getX();                                                            default:0.0
    public double getY();                                                            default:0.0
    public boolean isEmpty();                                                        default:true
    public void setFrame(double x, double y, double w, double h);
// Public Instance Fields
    public double height;
    public double width;
    public double x;
    public double y;
}
```

Ellipse2D.Float

Java 1.2

java.awt.geom

cloneable shape

This class is a concrete implementation of Ellipse2D that uses float fields to store the coordinates of the bounding rectangle of the ellipse. Note that these x, y, width, height fields are declared public and may be used directly by Java programs. See Ellipse2D for more information.

```
public static class Ellipse2D.Float extends Ellipse2D {
// Public Constructors
    public Float();
    public Float(float x, float y, float w, float h);
// Public Instance Methods
    public void setFrame(float x, float y, float w, float h);
// Public Methods Overriding RectangularShape
    public Rectangle2D getBounds2D();                                      default:Rectangle2D.Float
    public double getHeight();                                                       default:0.0
    public double getWidth();                                                        default:0.0
    public double getX();                                                            default:0.0
    public double getY();                                                            default:0.0
    public boolean isEmpty();                                                        default:true
    public void setFrame(double x, double y, double w, double h);
// Public Instance Fields
    public float height;
    public float width;
    public float x;
    public float y;
}
```

FlatteningPathIterator

Java 1.2

java.awt.geom

This class is a PathIterator that flattens the curves returned by another PathIterator, approximating them with straight-line segments that are easier to work with. The currentSegment() methods of FlatteningPathIterator are guaranteed never to return SEG_QUADTO or SEG_CUBICTO curve segments.

The flatness of a cubic or quadratic curve is the distance from the curve to its control points. Smaller distances imply flatter curves (i.e., curves that are closer to a straight line). The *flatness* argument to the FlatteningPathIterator() constructor specifies how flat a curve must be before it is approximated with a flat line. Smaller values of flatness result in increasingly accurate approximations of the curves.

When a FlatteningPathIterator encounters a curve that is not flat enough to approximate with a straight line, it subdivides the curve into two curves, each of which is flatter than the original curve. This process of subdivision continues recursively until the subdivided curves are flat enough to be approximated with line segments, up to the number of times specified by the *limit* argument. If *limit* is not specified, a default of 10 is used, which means that no curve is broken down into more than 1,024 separate line segments.

You should rarely need to use a FlatteningPathIterator explicitly in Java 2D programming. The two-argument version of the getPathIterator() method of Shape takes a *flatness* argument and returns a flattened path that does not contain any curves. Implementations of this method typically use FlatteningPathIterator internally.

```
public class FlatteningPathIterator implements PathIterator {
// Public Constructors
    public FlatteningPathIterator(PathIterator src, double flatness);
    public FlatteningPathIterator(PathIterator src, double flatness, int limit);
// Public Instance Methods
    public double getFlatness();
    public int getRecursionLimit();
// Methods Implementing PathIterator
    public int currentSegment(double[ ] coords);
    public int currentSegment(float[ ] coords);
    public int getWindingRule();
    public boolean isDone();
    public void next();
}
```

Hierarchy: Object→ FlatteningPathIterator(PathIterator)

GeneralPath
java.awt.geom

Java 1.2

cloneable shape

This class represents an arbitrary path or shape that consists of any number of line segments and quadratic and cubic Bezier curves. After creating a GeneralPath object, you must define a current point by calling moveTo(). Once an initial current point is established, you can create the path by calling lineTo(), quadTo(), and curveTo(). These methods draw line segments, quadratic curves, and cubic curves from the current point to a new point (which becomes the new current point).

The shape defined by a GeneralPath need not be closed, although you may close it by calling the closePath() method, which appends a line segment between the current point and the initial point. Similarly, the path need not be continuous: you can call moveTo() at any time to change the current point without adding a connecting line or curve to the path. The append() method allows you to add a Shape or PathIterator to a GeneralPath, optionally connecting it to the current point with a straight line.

The GeneralPath() constructor allows you to specify an estimate of the number of path segments that will be added. Specifying an accurate estimate can increase efficiency. It also allows you to specify the winding rule to use for the path. A winding rule is used to determine what points are contained within a GeneralPath. The choice of winding rules matters only for those paths that intersect themselves. The two choices are WIND_EVEN_ODD and WIND_NON_ZERO.

Note the close correspondence between the path elements (lines, quadratic curves, and cubic curves) that may be appended to a GeneralPath and those that are enumerated by a PathIterator object.

```
public final class GeneralPath implements Cloneable, Shape {
// Public Constructors
    public GeneralPath();
    public GeneralPath(int rule);
    public GeneralPath(Shape s);
    public GeneralPath(int rule, int initialCapacity);
// Public Constants
    public static final int WIND_EVEN_ODD;                                              =0
    public static final int WIND_NON_ZERO;                                              =1
// Property Accessor Methods (by property name)
    public Rectangle getBounds();                                               Implements:Shape
    public Rectangle2D getBounds2D();               Implements:Shape synchronized default:Rectangle2D.Float
    public Point2D getCurrentPoint();                                  synchronized default:null
    public int getWindingRule();                                       synchronized default:1
    public void setWindingRule(int rule);
// Public Instance Methods
    public void append(Shape s, boolean connect);
    public void append(PathIterator pi, boolean connect);
    public void closePath();                                                       synchronized
    public Shape createTransformedShape(AffineTransform at);                         synchronized
    public void curveTo(float x1, float y1, float x2, float y2, float x3, float y3);  synchronized
    public void lineTo(float x, float y);                                          synchronized
    public void moveTo(float x, float y);                                          synchronized
    public void quadTo(float x1, float y1, float x2, float y2);                     synchronized
    public void reset();                                                           synchronized
    public void transform(AffineTransform at);
// Methods Implementing Shape
    public boolean contains(Rectangle2D r);
    public boolean contains(Point2D p);
    public boolean contains(double x, double y);
    public boolean contains(double x, double y, double w, double h);
    public Rectangle getBounds();
    public Rectangle2D getBounds2D();                                  synchronized default:Rectangle2D.Float
    public PathIterator getPathIterator(AffineTransform at);
    public PathIterator getPathIterator(AffineTransform at, double flatness);
    public boolean intersects(Rectangle2D r);
    public boolean intersects(double x, double y, double w, double h);
// Public Methods Overriding Object
    public Object clone();
}
```

Hierarchy: Object→ GeneralPath(Cloneable, Shape)

IllegalPathStateException   Java 1.2

java.awt.geom   *serializable unchecked*

Signals that a path is not in an appropriate state for some requested operation. This exception is thrown if you attempt to append a path segment to a GeneralPath before performing an initial moveTo().

```
public class IllegalPathStateException extends RuntimeException {
// Public Constructors
    public IllegalPathStateException();
    public IllegalPathStateException(String s);
}
```

Hierarchy: Object→ Throwable(Serializable)→ Exception→ RuntimeException→
IllegalPathStateException

Line2D

java.awt.geom

cloneable shape

This abstract class is a java.awt.Shape that represents a line segment between two end points. Line2D defines various methods for computing the distance between a point and a line or line segment and for computing the position of a point relative to a line. Note, however, that the setLine() method for specifying the end points of the line segment is abstract. The concrete subclasses Line2D.Double and Line2D.Float use double and float fields to store the coordinates of the end points. They define the setLine() method and constructors that accept the line segment end points as arguments. Since a line does not contain an area, the contains() methods of Line2D and of its subclasses always return false.

```
public abstract class Line2D implements Cloneable, Shape {
// Protected Constructors
    protected Line2D();
// Inner Classes
    public static class Double extends Line2D;
    public static class Float extends Line2D;
// Public Class Methods
    public static boolean linesIntersect(double X1, double Y1, double X2, double Y2, double X3, double Y3,
                                          double X4, double Y4);
    public static double ptLineDist(double X1, double Y1, double X2, double Y2, double PX, double PY);
    public static double ptLineDistSq(double X1, double Y1, double X2, double Y2, double PX, double PY);
    public static double ptSegDist(double X1, double Y1, double X2, double Y2, double PX, double PY);
    public static double ptSegDistSq(double X1, double Y1, double X2, double Y2, double PX, double PY);
    public static int relativeCCW(double X1, double Y1, double X2, double Y2, double PX, double PY);
// Property Accessor Methods (by property name)
    public Rectangle getBounds();                                                      Implements:Shape
    public abstract Rectangle2D getBounds2D();                                          Implements:Shape
    public abstract Point2D getP1();
    public abstract Point2D getP2();
    public abstract double getX1();
    public abstract double getX2();
    public abstract double getY1();
    public abstract double getY2();
// Public Instance Methods
    public boolean intersectsLine(Line2D l);
    public boolean intersectsLine(double X1, double Y1, double X2, double Y2);
    public double ptLineDist(Point2D pt);
    public double ptLineDist(double PX, double PY);
    public double ptLineDistSq(Point2D pt);
    public double ptLineDistSq(double PX, double PY);
    public double ptSegDist(Point2D pt);
    public double ptSegDist(double PX, double PY);
    public double ptSegDistSq(Point2D pt);
    public double ptSegDistSq(double PX, double PY);
    public int relativeCCW(Point2D p);
    public int relativeCCW(double PX, double PY);
    public void setLine(Line2D l);
    public void setLine(Point2D p1, Point2D p2);
    public abstract void setLine(double X1, double Y1, double X2, double Y2);
// Methods Implementing Shape
    public boolean contains(Point2D p);                                                      constant
    public boolean contains(Rectangle2D r);                                                  constant
```

```
    public boolean contains(double x, double y);                                                constant
    public boolean contains(double x, double y, double w, double h);                             constant
    public Rectangle getBounds();
    public abstract Rectangle2D getBounds2D();
    public PathIterator getPathIterator(AffineTransform at);
    public PathIterator getPathIterator(AffineTransform at, double flatness);
    public boolean intersects(Rectangle2D r);
    public boolean intersects(double x, double y, double w, double h);
// Public Methods Overriding Object
    public Object clone();
}
```

Hierarchy: Object→ Line2D(Cloneable, Shape)

Subclasses: Line2D.Double, Line2D.Float

Passed To: Line2D.{intersectsLine(), setLine()}, Rectangle2D.intersectsLine()

Line2D.Double   Java 1.2

java.awt.geom   *cloneable shape*

This class is a concrete implementation of Line2D that uses double fields to store the end points of the line segment. These end points are stored in public fields and may be directly set and queried by programs. See Line2D for more information.

```
public static class Line2D.Double extends Line2D {
// Public Constructors
    public Double();
    public Double(Point2D p1, Point2D p2);
    public Double(double X1, double Y1, double X2, double Y2);
// Public Methods Overriding Line2D
    public Rectangle2D getBounds2D();                                    default:Rectangle2D.Double
    public Point2D getP1();                                                  default:Point2D.Double
    public Point2D getP2();                                                  default:Point2D.Double
    public double getX1();                                                           default:0.0
    public double getX2();                                                           default:0.0
    public double getY1();                                                           default:0.0
    public double getY2();                                                           default:0.0
    public void setLine(double X1, double Y1, double X2, double Y2);
// Public Instance Fields
    public double x1;
    public double x2;
    public double y1;
    public double y2;
}
```

Line2D.Float   Java 1.2

java.awt.geom   *cloneable shape*

This class is a concrete implementation of Line2D that uses float fields to store the end points of the line segment. These end points are stored in public fields and may be directly set and queried by programs. See Line2D for more information.

```
public static class Line2D.Float extends Line2D {
// Public Constructors
    public Float();
    public Float(Point2D p1, Point2D p2);
    public Float(float X1, float Y1, float X2, float Y2);
```

```
// Public Instance Methods
    public void setLine(float X1, float Y1, float X2, float Y2);
// Public Methods Overriding Line2D
    public Rectangle2D getBounds2D();                                    default:Rectangle2D.Float
    public Point2D getP1();                                                  default:Point2D.Float
    public Point2D getP2();                                                  default:Point2D.Float
    public double getX1();                                                         default:0.0
    public double getX2();                                                         default:0.0
    public double getY1();                                                         default:0.0
    public double getY2();                                                         default:0.0
    public void setLine(double X1, double Y1, double X2, double Y2);
// Public Instance Fields
    public float x1;
    public float x2;
    public float y1;
    public float y2;
}
```

NoninvertibleTransformException

Java 1.2

java.awt.geom

serializable checked

Thrown when the inverse of a noninvertible AffineTransform is required. An example of a noninvertible transformation is scaling the X dimension by a factor of 0. This maps all points onto a vertical line, leaving no information about transforming those points back to their original locations. This transform is noninvertible because division by zero is not possible.

```
public class NoninvertibleTransformException extends Exception {
// Public Constructors
    public NoninvertibleTransformException(String s);
}
```

Hierarchy: Object→ Throwable(Serializable)→ Exception→ NoninvertibleTransformException

Thrown By: AffineTransform.{createInverse(), inverseTransform()}

PathIterator

Java 1.2

java.awt.geom

This interface is the basic Java 2D mechanism for defining arbitrary shapes. The most important requirement of the java.awt.Shape interface is that every shape be able to return a PathIterator that traverses the outline of the shape. The information returned by a PathIterator is sufficient to allow the Java 2D rendering engine to stroke (draw) or fill arbitrarily complex shapes.

A PathIterator breaks a shape or path down into individual path segments. The currentSegment() method returns the current segment. The next() method moves the iterator on to the next segment, and isDone() returns true if there are no more segments left to iterate. getWindingRule() returns the winding rule for the shape—this value is used to determine which points are inside complex self-intersecting shapes. The two possible values are WIND_EVEN_ODD and WIND_NON_ZERO.

currentSegment() is the most important method of PathIterator. Its return value, one of the five integer constants whose names begin with SEG, specifies the type of the current segment. currentSegment() returns the coordinates of the current segment in the float or double array passed as an argument. This array must have at least six elements. The segment types and their meanings are as follows:

SEG_MOVETO

Defines a path starting point rather than an actual segment. The current point of the path is set to the X,Y point specified in the first two elements of the array. This is the first segment type of all paths. Paths may be disjoint, and may have more than one SEG_MOVETO segment.

SEG_LINETO

Defines a line between the current point and the X,Y end point stored in the first two elements of the array. The end point of the line segment becomes the new current point.

SEG_QUADTO

Defines a quadratic Bezier curve between the current point and an end point stored in the third and fourth elements of the array, using a control point stored in the first and second elements of the array. The end point of the curve becomes the current point.

SEG_CUBICTO

Defines a cubic Bezier curve between the current point and an end point stored in the fifth and sixth elements of the array, using two control points stored in the first through fourth elements of the array. The end point of the curve becomes the current point.

SEG_CLOSE

Specifies that the path should be closed by drawing a straight line from the current point back to the point specified by the most recent SEG_MOVETO segment. No values are stored in the array for this segment type.

```
public abstract interface PathIterator {
// Public Constants
    public static final int SEG_CLOSE;                              =4
    public static final int SEG_CUBICTO;                            =3
    public static final int SEG_LINETO;                             =1
    public static final int SEG_MOVETO;                             =0
    public static final int SEG_QUADTO;                             =2
    public static final int WIND_EVEN_ODD;                          =0
    public static final int WIND_NON_ZERO;                          =1
// Public Instance Methods
    public abstract int currentSegment(float[ ] coords);
    public abstract int currentSegment(double[ ] coords);
    public abstract int getWindingRule();
    public abstract boolean isDone();
    public abstract void next();
}
```

Implementations: FlatteningPathIterator

Passed To: FlatteningPathIterator.FlatteningPathIterator(), GeneralPath.append()

Returned By: Too many methods to list.

Point2D   **Java 1.2**

java.awt.geom   *cloneable*

java.awt. geom

This abstract class represents a point in two-dimensional space. It has methods for getting and setting the X and Y coordinates of the point as double values and for computing the distance between points.

Point2D is abstract; it does not store actual coordinates and cannot be instantiated. You must use one of its concrete subclasses instead. Point2D.Double stores the coordinates of a point using double fields, while Point2D.Float stores the coordinates using float fields. Finally, java.awt.Point stores the coordinates using int fields.

```
public abstract class Point2D implements Cloneable {
// Protected Constructors
    protected Point2D();
// Inner Classes
    public static class Double extends Point2D;
    public static class Float extends Point2D;
// Public Class Methods
    public static double distance(double X1, double Y1, double X2, double Y2);
    public static double distanceSq(double X1, double Y1, double X2, double Y2);
// Property Accessor Methods (by property name)
    public abstract double getX();
    public abstract double getY();
// Public Instance Methods
    public double distance(Point2D pt);
    public double distance(double PX, double PY);
    public double distanceSq(Point2D pt);
    public double distanceSq(double PX, double PY);
    public void setLocation(Point2D p);
    public abstract void setLocation(double x, double y);
// Public Methods Overriding Object
    public Object clone();
    public boolean equals(Object obj);
    public int hashCode();
}
```

Hierarchy: Object → Point2D(Cloneable)

Subclasses: Point, Point2D.Double, Point2D.Float

Passed To: Too many methods to list.

Returned By: Too many methods to list.

Point2D.Double   Java 1.2

java.awt.geom   *cloneable*

This class is a concrete implementation of Point2D that stores the X and Y coordinates of a point using double fields. These fields are public and can be queried and set directly, without using accessor methods.

```
public static class Point2D.Double extends Point2D {
// Public Constructors
    public Double();
    public Double(double x, double y);
// Public Methods Overriding Point2D
    public double getX();                                  default:0.0
    public double getY();                                  default:0.0
    public void setLocation(double x, double y);
// Public Methods Overriding Object
    public String toString();
// Public Instance Fields
    public double x;
    public double y;
}
```

Point2D.Float

Java 1.2

java.awt.geom
cloneable

This class is a concrete implementation of Point2D that stores the X and Y coordinates of a point using float fields. These fields are public and can be queried and set directly, without using accessor methods.

```
public static class Point2D.Float extends Point2D {
// Public Constructors
    public Float();
    public Float(float x, float y);
// Public Instance Methods
    public void setLocation(float x, float y);
// Public Methods Overriding Point2D
    public double getX();                                              default:0.0
    public double getY();                                              default:0.0
    public void setLocation(double x, double y);
// Public Methods Overriding Object
    public String toString();
// Public Instance Fields
    public float x;
    public float y;
}
```

QuadCurve2D

Java 1.2

java.awt.geom
cloneable shape

This abstract class is a java.awt.Shape that represents a smooth quadratic Bezier curve (or spline) between end points p1 (x1, y1) and p2 (x2, y2). The precise shape of the curve is defined by a control point, cp (ctrlx, ctrly). Note that the curve does not pass through cp but that it does remain inside the triangle defined by p1, cp, and p2.

QuadCurve2D does not itself enclose an area, so the contains() methods test whether a point or rectangle is within the area defined by the curve and the straight line between its end points.

QuadCurve2D is an abstract class and cannot be instantiated. QuadCurve2D.Float and Quad-Curve2D.Double are concrete subclasses that use float and double fields to store the end points and control point. See also CubicCurve2D, which is a cubic Bezier curve that uses two control points.

```
public abstract class QuadCurve2D implements Cloneable, Shape {
// Protected Constructors
    protected QuadCurve2D();
// Inner Classes
    public static class Double extends QuadCurve2D;
    public static class Float extends QuadCurve2D;
// Public Class Methods
    public static double getFlatness(double[] coords, int offset);
    public static double getFlatness(double x1, double y1, double ctrlx, double ctrly, double x2, double y2);
    public static double getFlatnessSq(double[] coords, int offset);
    public static double getFlatnessSq(double x1, double y1, double ctrlx, double ctrly, double x2, double y2);
    public static int solveQuadratic(double[] eqn);
    public static void subdivide(QuadCurve2D src, QuadCurve2D left, QuadCurve2D right);
    public static void subdivide(double[] src, int srcoff, double[] left, int leftoff, double[] right, int rightoff);
// Property Accessor Methods (by property name)
    public Rectangle getBounds();                                      Implements:Shape
    public abstract Rectangle2D getBounds2D();                         Implements:Shape
    public abstract Point2D getCtrlPt();
```

java.awt. geom

```
    public abstract double getCtrlX();
    public abstract double getCtrlY();
    public double getFlatness();
    public double getFlatnessSq();
    public abstract Point2D getP1();
    public abstract Point2D getP2();
    public abstract double getX1();
    public abstract double getX2();
    public abstract double getY1();
    public abstract double getY2();
// Public Instance Methods
    public void setCurve(QuadCurve2D c);
    public void setCurve(double[ ] coords, int offset);
    public void setCurve(Point2D[ ] pts, int offset);
    public void setCurve(Point2D p1, Point2D cp, Point2D p2);
    public abstract void setCurve(double x1, double y1, double ctrlx, double ctrly, double x2, double y2);
    public void subdivide(QuadCurve2D left, QuadCurve2D right);
// Methods Implementing Shape
    public boolean contains(Point2D p);
    public boolean contains(Rectangle2D r);
    public boolean contains(double x, double y);
    public boolean contains(double x, double y, double w, double h);
    public Rectangle getBounds();
    public abstract Rectangle2D getBounds2D();
    public PathIterator getPathIterator(AffineTransform at);
    public PathIterator getPathIterator(AffineTransform at, double flatness);
    public boolean intersects(Rectangle2D r);
    public boolean intersects(double x, double y, double w, double h);
// Public Methods Overriding Object
    public Object clone();
}
```

Hierarchy: Object→ QuadCurve2D(Cloneable, Shape)

Subclasses: QuadCurve2D.Double, QuadCurve2D.Float

Passed To: QuadCurve2D.{setCurve(), subdivide()}

QuadCurve2D.Double   Java 1.2

java.awt.geom   *cloneable shape*

This class is a concrete implementation of QuadCurve2D that uses double fields to store
the end points and control point of the curve. The X and Y coordinates of these three
points are stored in public fields and may be used directly by Java programs. See Quad-
Curve2D for more information.

```
public static class QuadCurve2D.Double extends QuadCurve2D {
// Public Constructors
    public Double();
    public Double(double x1, double y1, double ctrlx, double ctrly, double x2, double y2);
// Public Methods Overriding QuadCurve2D
    public Rectangle2D getBounds2D();                       default:Rectangle2D.Double
    public Point2D getCtrlPt();                                default:Point2D.Double
    public double getCtrlX();                                          default:0.0
    public double getCtrlY();                                          default:0.0
    public Point2D getP1();                                    default:Point2D.Double
    public Point2D getP2();                                    default:Point2D.Double
    public double getX1();                                             default:0.0
    public double getX2();                                             default:0.0
```

```
    public double getY1();                                                         default:0.0
    public double getY2();                                                         default:0.0
    public void setCurve(double x1, double y1, double ctrlx, double ctrly, double x2, double y2);
// Public Instance Fields
    public double ctrlx;
    public double ctrly;
    public double x1;
    public double x2;
    public double y1;
    public double y2;
}
```

QuadCurve2D.Float   Java 1.2

java.awt.geom   *cloneable shape*

This class is a concrete implementation of QuadCurve2D that uses float fields to store the
end points and control point of the curve. The X and Y coordinates of these three
points are stored in public fields and may be used directly by Java programs. See Quad-
Curve2D for more information.

```
public static class QuadCurve2D.Float extends QuadCurve2D {
// Public Constructors
    public Float();
    public Float(float x1, float y1, float ctrlx, float ctrly, float x2, float y2);
// Public Instance Methods
    public void setCurve(float x1, float y1, float ctrlx, float ctrly, float x2, float y2);
// Public Methods Overriding QuadCurve2D
    public Rectangle2D getBounds2D();                               default:Rectangle2D.Float
    public Point2D getCtrlPt();                                        default:Point2D.Float
    public double getCtrlX();                                                   default:0.0
    public double getCtrlY();                                                   default:0.0
    public Point2D getP1();                                            default:Point2D.Float
    public Point2D getP2();                                            default:Point2D.Float
    public double getX1();                                                      default:0.0
    public double getX2();                                                      default:0.0
    public double getY1();                                                      default:0.0
    public double getY2();                                                      default:0.0
    public void setCurve(double x1, double y1, double ctrlx, double ctrly, double x2, double y2);
// Public Instance Fields
    public float ctrlx;
    public float ctrly;
    public float x1;
    public float x2;
    public float y1;
    public float y2;
}
```

Rectangle2D   Java 1.2

java.awt.geom   *cloneable shape*

This abstract java.awt.Shape represents a rectangle specified by the location of its upper-
left corner, its width, and its height. Various methods compute intersections and unions
of rectangles, test whether a rectangle contains a point or contains another rectangle,
and test whether a rectangle intersects a line or another rectangle. The outcode() method
determines the spatial relationship between a point and a rectangle. The return value is
the sum of the OUT_ constants that specify which edges of the rectangle a point is outside of. A value of 0 means that the point is inside the rectangle, of course. Other

interesting methods include setFrameFromDiagonal() and setFrameFromCenter(), inherited from RectangularShape.

Rectangle2D is an abstract class that does not define any fields to store the size and position of the rectangle and cannot be instantiated. Choose a concrete subclass based on the type of data fields you desire: Rectangle2D.Double uses double fields, Rectangle2D.Float uses float fields, and java.awt.Rectangle uses int fields.

```
public abstract class Rectangle2D extends RectangularShape {
// Protected Constructors
    protected Rectangle2D();
// Public Constants
    public static final int OUT_BOTTOM;                                    =8
    public static final int OUT_LEFT;                                      =1
    public static final int OUT_RIGHT;                                     =4
    public static final int OUT_TOP;                                       =2
// Inner Classes
    public static class Double extends Rectangle2D;
    public static class Float extends Rectangle2D;
// Public Class Methods
    public static void intersect(Rectangle2D src1, Rectangle2D src2, Rectangle2D dest);
    public static void union(Rectangle2D src1, Rectangle2D src2, Rectangle2D dest);
// Public Instance Methods
    public void add(Point2D pt);
    public void add(Rectangle2D r);
    public void add(double newx, double newy);
    public abstract Rectangle2D createIntersection(Rectangle2D r);
    public abstract Rectangle2D createUnion(Rectangle2D r);
    public boolean intersectsLine(Line2D l);
    public boolean intersectsLine(double x1, double y1, double x2, double y2);
    public int outcode(Point2D p);
    public abstract int outcode(double x, double y);
    public void setRect(Rectangle2D r);
    public abstract void setRect(double x, double y, double w, double h);
// Public Methods Overriding RectangularShape
    public boolean contains(double x, double y);
    public boolean contains(double x, double y, double w, double h);
    public Rectangle2D getBounds2D();
    public PathIterator getPathIterator(AffineTransform at);
    public PathIterator getPathIterator(AffineTransform at, double flatness);
    public boolean intersects(double x, double y, double w, double h);
    public void setFrame(double x, double y, double w, double h);
// Public Methods Overriding Object
    public boolean equals(Object obj);
    public int hashCode();
}
```

Hierarchy: Object→ RectangularShape(Cloneable, Shape)→ Rectangle2D

Subclasses: Rectangle, Rectangle2D.Double, Rectangle2D.Float

Passed To: Too many methods to list.

Returned By: Too many methods to list.

Rectangle2D.Double   Java 1.2

java.awt.geom   *cloneable shape*

This concrete subclass of Rectangle2D stores the position and size of the rectangle in fields of type double. These fields are declared public and can be set and queried directly without relying on accessor methods.

```
public static class Rectangle2D.Double extends Rectangle2D {
// Public Constructors
    public Double();
    public Double(double x, double y, double w, double h);
// Public Methods Overriding Rectangle2D
    public Rectangle2D createIntersection(Rectangle2D r);
    public Rectangle2D createUnion(Rectangle2D r);
    public Rectangle2D getBounds2D();                                    default:Rectangle2D.Double
    public int outcode(double x, double y);
    public void setRect(Rectangle2D r);
    public void setRect(double x, double y, double w, double h);
// Public Methods Overriding RectangularShape
    public double getHeight();                                           default:0.0
    public double getWidth();                                            default:0.0
    public double getX();                                                default:0.0
    public double getY();                                               default:0.0
    public boolean isEmpty();                                            default:true
// Public Methods Overriding Object
    public String toString();
// Public Instance Fields
    public double height;
    public double width;
    public double x;
    public double y;
}
```

Rectangle2D.Float

java.awt.geom   *cloneable shape*

This concrete subclass of Rectangle2D stores the position and size of the rectangle in fields of type float. These fields are declared public and can be set and queried directly without relying on accessor methods.

```
public static class Rectangle2D.Float extends Rectangle2D {
// Public Constructors
    public Float();
    public Float(float x, float y, float w, float h);
// Public Instance Methods
    public void setRect(float x, float y, float w, float h);
// Public Methods Overriding Rectangle2D
    public Rectangle2D createIntersection(Rectangle2D r);
    public Rectangle2D createUnion(Rectangle2D r);
    public Rectangle2D getBounds2D();                                    default:Rectangle2D.Float
    public int outcode(double x, double y);
    public void setRect(Rectangle2D r);
    public void setRect(double x, double y, double w, double h);
// Public Methods Overriding RectangularShape
    public double getHeight();                                           default:0.0
    public double getWidth();                                            default:0.0
    public double getX();                                                default:0.0
    public double getY();                                                default:0.0
    public boolean isEmpty();                                            default:true
// Public Methods Overriding Object
    public String toString();
// Public Instance Fields
    public float height;
    public float width;
```

java.awt. geom

```
    public float x;
    public float y;
}
```

RectangularShape   Java 1.2

java.awt.geom   *cloneable shape*

This abstract class is the base class for several java.awt.Shape implementations that have
a rectangular outline or bounding box. Its methods allow you to set and query the size
and position of the bounding rectangle in several interesting ways.

```
public abstract class RectangularShape implements Cloneable, Shape {
// Protected Constructors
    protected RectangularShape();
// Property Accessor Methods (by property name)
    public Rectangle getBounds();                                      Implements:Shape
    public abstract Rectangle2D getBounds2D();                         Implements:Shape
    public double getCenterX();
    public double getCenterY();
    public abstract boolean isEmpty();
    public Rectangle2D getFrame();
    public void setFrame(Rectangle2D r);
    public void setFrame(Point2D loc, Dimension2D size);
    public abstract void setFrame(double x, double y, double w, double h);
    public abstract double getHeight();
    public double getMaxX();
    public double getMaxY();
    public double getMinX();
    public double getMinY();
    public abstract double getWidth();
    public abstract double getX();
    public abstract double getY();
// Public Instance Methods
    public void setFrameFromCenter(Point2D center, Point2D corner);
    public void setFrameFromCenter(double centerX, double centerY, double cornerX, double cornerY);
    public void setFrameFromDiagonal(Point2D p1, Point2D p2);
    public void setFrameFromDiagonal(double x1, double y1, double x2, double y2);
// Methods Implementing Shape
    public boolean contains(Point2D p);
    public boolean contains(Rectangle2D r);
    public abstract boolean contains(double x, double y);
    public abstract boolean contains(double x, double y, double w, double h);
    public Rectangle getBounds();
    public abstract Rectangle2D getBounds2D();
    public abstract PathIterator getPathIterator(AffineTransform at);
    public PathIterator getPathIterator(AffineTransform at, double flatness);
    public boolean intersects(Rectangle2D r);
    public abstract boolean intersects(double x, double y, double w, double h);
// Public Methods Overriding Object
    public Object clone();
}
```

Hierarchy: Object→ RectangularShape(Cloneable, Shape)

Subclasses: Arc2D, Ellipse2D, Rectangle2D, RoundRectangle2D

RoundRectangle2D

java.awt.geom

cloneable shape

This abstract java.awt.Shape represents a rectangle with rounded corners, specified by the position of the upper-left corner (before rounding), the width and height of the rectangle, and the width and height of the arc used to round the corners. RoundRectangle2D is abstract and may not be instantiated. Use the concrete subclasses RoundRectangle2D.Double and RoundRectangle2D.Float, depending on the precision you desire for the rectangle coordinates and dimensions.

```
public abstract class RoundRectangle2D extends RectangularShape {
// Protected Constructors
    protected RoundRectangle2D();
// Inner Classes
    public static class Double extends RoundRectangle2D;
    public static class Float extends RoundRectangle2D;
// Property Accessor Methods (by property name)
    public abstract double getArcHeight();
    public abstract double getArcWidth();
// Public Instance Methods
    public void setRoundRect(RoundRectangle2D rr);
    public abstract void setRoundRect(double x, double y, double w, double h, double arcWidth, double arcHeight);
// Public Methods Overriding RectangularShape
    public boolean contains(double x, double y);
    public boolean contains(double x, double y, double w, double h);
    public PathIterator getPathIterator(AffineTransform at);
    public boolean intersects(double x, double y, double w, double h);
    public void setFrame(double x, double y, double w, double h);
}
```

Hierarchy: Object→ RectangularShape(Cloneable, Shape)→ RoundRectangle2D

Subclasses: RoundRectangle2D.Double, RoundRectangle2D.Float

Passed To: RoundRectangle2D.setRoundRect(), RoundRectangle2D.Double.setRoundRect(), RoundRectangle2D.Float.setRoundRect()

RoundRectangle2D.Double

java.awt.geom

cloneable shape

This concrete subclass of RoundRectangle2D stores the position and size of the rectangle and the size of the rounded corners in fields of type double. These fields are declared public and can be set and queried directly without relying on accessor methods.

```
public static class RoundRectangle2D.Double extends RoundRectangle2D {
// Public Constructors
    public Double();
    public Double(double x, double y, double w, double h, double arcw, double arch);
// Public Methods Overriding RoundRectangle2D
    public double getArcHeight();                                         default:0.0
    public double getArcWidth();                                          default:0.0
    public void setRoundRect(RoundRectangle2D rr);
    public void setRoundRect(double x, double y, double w, double h, double arcw, double arch);
// Public Methods Overriding RectangularShape
    public Rectangle2D getBounds2D();                      default:Rectangle2D.Double
    public double getHeight();                                            default:0.0
    public double getWidth();                                             default:0.0
    public double getX();                                                 default:0.0
    public double getY();                                                 default:0.0
```

java.awt. geom

```
    public boolean isEmpty();                                                    default:true
// Public Instance Fields
    public double archeight;
    public double arcwidth;
    public double height;
    public double width;
    public double x;
    public double y;
}
```

RoundRectangle2D.Float

Java 1.2

java.awt.geom

cloneable shape

This concrete subclass of RoundRectangle2D stores the position and size of the rectangle
and the size of the rounded corners in fields of type float. These fields are declared
public and can be set and queried directly without relying on accessor methods.

```
public static class RoundRectangle2D.Float extends RoundRectangle2D {
// Public Constructors
    public Float();
    public Float(float x, float y, float w, float h, float arcw, float arch);
// Public Instance Methods
    public void setRoundRect(float x, float y, float w, float h, float arcw, float arch);
// Public Methods Overriding RoundRectangle2D
    public double getArcHeight();                                                default:0.0
    public double getArcWidth();                                                 default:0.0
    public void setRoundRect(RoundRectangle2D rr);
    public void setRoundRect(double x, double y, double w, double h, double arcw, double arch);
// Public Methods Overriding RectangularShape
    public Rectangle2D getBounds2D();                             default:Rectangle2D.Float
    public double getHeight();                                                   default:0.0
    public double getWidth();                                                    default:0.0
    public double getX();                                                        default:0.0
    public double getY();                                                        default:0.0
    public boolean isEmpty();                                                    default:true
// Public Instance Fields
    public float archeight;
    public float arcwidth;
    public float height;
    public float width;
    public float x;
    public float y;
}
```

CHAPTER 17

The java.awt.im Package

The java.awt.im package contains classes and interfaces used by input methods and by the text-editing user interface components that interact with input methods. Most applications rely on GUI components that have input method support built in and do not need to use this package directly. In other words, input method details are usually hidden by text input components, and application-level code should never have to use these classes and interfaces. Figure 17-1 shows the class hierarchy of this package, which is new in Java 1.2.

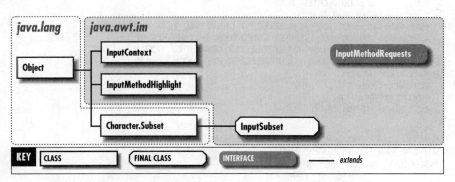

Figure 17–1: The java.awt.im package

InputContext   Java 1.2

java.awt.im

This class serves as an intermediary between input methods and the text input components that use them. An InputContext stores the state related to one pending text composition operation. By default, there is one InputContext per Window. Components can obtain this shared input context with the Component.getInputContext() method. Components that need a private InputContext can create their own with InputContext.getInstance().

```
public class InputContext {
// Protected Constructors
    protected InputContext();
// Public Class Methods
    public static InputContext getInstance();
// Property Accessor Methods (by property name)
    public Object getInputMethodControlObject();                              constant
// Public Instance Methods
    public void dispatchEvent(AWTEvent event);                    synchronized empty
    public void dispose();                                                      empty
    public void endComposition();                                 synchronized empty
    public void removeNotify(Component client);                                 empty
    public boolean selectInputMethod(java.util.Locale locale);              constant
    public void setCharacterSubsets(Character.Subset[ ] subsets);               empty
}
```

Returned By: Component.getInputContext(), Window.getInputContext(), InputContext.getInstance()

InputMethodHighlight   Java 1.2

java.awt.im

This class defines the highlighted or unhighlighted state of text being processed by an input method. For input methods, highlighting can be used to distinguish converted from unconverted text, as well as to distinguish selected from unselected text. Input-MethodHighlight objects are used as attribute values returned by java.text.AttributedCharacterIt-erator objects. Note the various InputMethodHighlight constants predefined by this class.

```
public class InputMethodHighlight {
// Public Constructors
    public InputMethodHighlight(boolean selected, int state);
    public InputMethodHighlight(boolean selected, int state, int variation);
// Public Constants
    public static final int CONVERTED_TEXT;                                        =1
    public static final int RAW_TEXT;                                              =0
    public static final InputMethodHighlight SELECTED_CONVERTED_TEXT_HIGHLIGHT;
    public static final InputMethodHighlight SELECTED_RAW_TEXT_HIGHLIGHT;
    public static final InputMethodHighlight UNSELECTED_CONVERTED_TEXT_HIGHLIGHT;
    public static final InputMethodHighlight UNSELECTED_RAW_TEXT_HIGHLIGHT;
// Public Instance Methods
    public int getState();
    public int getVariation();
    public boolean isSelected();
}
```

Type Of: InputMethodHighlight.{SELECTED_CONVERTED_TEXT_HIGHLIGHT,
SELECTED_RAW_TEXT_HIGHLIGHT, UNSELECTED_CONVERTED_TEXT_HIGHLIGHT,
UNSELECTED_RAW_TEXT_HIGHLIGHT}

InputMethodRequests   Java 1.2

java.awt.im

This interface defines the methods that a component must implement in order to accept text input from input methods. A component need not implement these methods directly, but it must return an object that implements this interface from a getInputMethod-Requests() method.

```
public abstract interface InputMethodRequests {
// Public Instance Methods
    public abstract java.text.AttributedCharacterIterator cancelLatestCommittedText(
                                           java.text.AttributedCharacterIterator.Attribute[ ] attributes);
    public abstract java.text.AttributedCharacterIterator getCommittedText(int beginIndex, int endIndex,
                                           java.text.AttributedCharacterIterator.Attribute[ ] attributes);
    public abstract int getCommittedTextLength();
    public abstract int getInsertPositionOffset();
    public abstract java.awt.font.TextHitInfo getLocationOffset(int x, int y);
    public abstract java.text.AttributedCharacterIterator getSelectedText(
                                           java.text.AttributedCharacterIterator.Attribute[ ] attributes);
    public abstract Rectangle getTextLocation(java.awt.font.TextHitInfo offset);
}
```

Returned By: Component.getInputMethodRequests(),
javax.swing.text.JTextComponent.getInputMethodRequests()

InputSubset

java.awt.im

This class defines Character$Subset constants that are useful to input methods.

```
public final class InputSubset extends Character.Subset {
// No Constructor
// Public Constants
    public static final InputSubset HALFWIDTH_KATAKANA;
    public static final InputSubset HANJA;
    public static final InputSubset KANJI;
    public static final InputSubset LATIN;
    public static final InputSubset LATIN_DIGITS;
    public static final InputSubset SIMPLIFIED_HANZI;
    public static final InputSubset TRADITIONAL_HANZI;
}
```

Hierarchy: Object→ Character.Subset→ InputSubset

Type Of: InputSubset.{HALFWIDTH_KATAKANA, HANJA, KANJI, LATIN, LATIN_DIGITS, SIMPLIFIED_HANZI, TRADITIONAL_HANZI}

CHAPTER 18

The java.awt.image Package

The java.awt.image package contains classes and interfaces for manipulating images. Note that the java.awt.Image class itself is not part of this package. In Java 1.0 and Java 1.1, the image processing model was optimized for streaming image data loaded over a network and processed on the fly. It involved the ImageProducer, ImageConsumer, and ImageObserver interfaces and the ImageFilter class. This image-processing model is complex and difficult to use. Much of it has been superseded in Java 1.2.

In Java 2D, the image-processing model has been extended (and simplified) to accommodate image data that is stored and manipulated in memory. The key pieces of this new image-processing model are the BufferedImage class, which represents an image in memory, and the BufferedImageOp interface, which represents an image-processing operation. Every BufferedImage contains a Raster object that hold the pixels of the image and a ColorModel object that can interpret those pixel values as Color objects. A Raster object, in turn, contains a DataBuffer that holds the raw image data and a SampleModel object that knows how to extract pixel values from that raw data.

Figure 18-1 shows the class hierarchy of this package. See Chapter 4, *Graphics with AWT and Java 2D*, for a discussion of images and image processing.

AffineTransformOp   Java 1.2

java.awt.image

This class is a BufferedImageOp and a RasterOp that performs an arbitrary java.awt.geom.AffineTransform on a BufferedImage or Raster. To create an AffineTransformOp, you must specify the desired AffineTransform and the interpolation mode to use when interpolation is necessary to determine the pixel or color values of the destination. TYPE_NEAREST_NEIGHBOR is the quicker form of interpolation, but TYPE_BILINEAR produces better results. You may also specify the type of interpolation to use by specifying a java.awt.RenderingHints object that contains an interpolation hint.

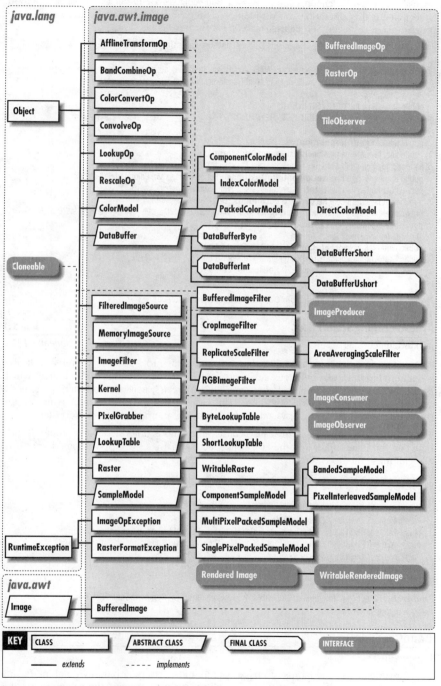

Figure 18-1: The java.awt.image package

To use an AffineTransformOp, simply pass a BufferedImage or Raster to the filter() method. Note that for this operation the destination image or raster cannot be the same as the source image or raster. See BufferedImageOp for further details.

```
public class AffineTransformOp implements BufferedImageOp, RasterOp {
// Public Constructors
    public AffineTransformOp(java.awt.geom.AffineTransform xform, RenderingHints hints);
    public AffineTransformOp(java.awt.geom.AffineTransform xform, int interpolationType);
// Public Constants
    public static final int TYPE_BILINEAR;                                          =2
    public static final int TYPE_NEAREST_NEIGHBOR;                                  =1
// Public Instance Methods
    public final int getInterpolationType();
    public final java.awt.geom.AffineTransform getTransform();
// Methods Implementing BufferedImageOp
    public BufferedImage createCompatibleDestImage(BufferedImage src, ColorModel destCM);
    public final BufferedImage filter(BufferedImage src, BufferedImage dst);
    public final java.awt.geom.Rectangle2D getBounds2D(BufferedImage src);
    public final java.awt.geom.Point2D getPoint2D(java.awt.geom.Point2D srcPt, java.awt.geom.Point2D dstPt);
    public final RenderingHints getRenderingHints();
// Methods Implementing RasterOp
    public WritableRaster createCompatibleDestRaster(Raster src);
    public final WritableRaster filter(Raster src, WritableRaster dst);
    public final java.awt.geom.Rectangle2D getBounds2D(Raster src);
}
```

Hierarchy: Object→ AffineTransformOp(BufferedImageOp, RasterOp)

AreaAveragingScaleFilter

Java 1.1

java.awt.image

cloneable PJ1.1

This class implements an ImageFilter that scales an image to a specified pixel size. It uses a scaling algorithm that averages adjacent pixel values when shrinking an image, which produces relatively smooth scaled images. Its superclass, ReplicateScaleFilter, implements a faster, less smooth scaling algorithm. The easiest way to use this filter is to call the getScaledInstance() method of java.awt.Image, specifying an appropriate hint constant.

The methods of this class are ImageConsumer methods intended for communication between the image filter and the FilteredImageSource that uses it. Applications do not usually call these methods directly.

```
public class AreaAveragingScaleFilter extends ReplicateScaleFilter {
// Public Constructors
    public AreaAveragingScaleFilter(int width, int height);
// Public Methods Overriding ReplicateScaleFilter
    public void setPixels(int x, int y, int w, int h, ColorModel model, int[ ] pixels, int off, int scansize);
    public void setPixels(int x, int y, int w, int h, ColorModel model, byte[ ] pixels, int off, int scansize);
// Public Methods Overriding ImageFilter
    public void setHints(int hints);
}
```

Hierarchy: Object→ ImageFilter(Cloneable, ImageConsumer)→ ReplicateScaleFilter→ AreaAveragingScaleFilter

BandCombineOp

Java 1.2

java.awt.image

This RasterOp allows the bands of image data in a Raster to be arbitrarily combined using a matrix. For example, you can use a BandCombineOp to convert three bands of color image data to a single band of grayscale image data. The number of columns of the matrix should be equal to the number of bands in the source raster or the number of bands plus one, if you are adding constant values as part of the combination. The number of rows in the matrix should be equal to the number of bands in the destination Raster.

As an example, consider the following matrix with four columns and three rows, used to convert a Raster with three bands to another three-banded raster:

$$\begin{bmatrix} m11 & m21 & m31 & c1 \\ m12 & m22 & m32 & c2 \\ m13 & m23 & m33 & c3 \end{bmatrix}$$

This matrix is used to convert the source bands s1, s2, and s3 into destination bands d1, d2, and d3, using the following formulas:

$$d1 = s1*m11 + s2*m21 + s3*m31 + c1;$$
$$d2 = s1*m12 + s2*m22 + s3*m32 + c2;$$
$$d3 = s1*m13 + s2*m23 + s3*m33 + c3;$$

If the constants c1, c2, and c3 are all 0, they can be omitted from the vector.

After creating a BandCombineOp for a specified vector, you perform the operation by passing a source and optional destination Raster to the filter() method. Because this operation processes each pixel independently, you can specify the same Raster object as both source and destination. BandCombineOp does *not* implement BufferedImageOp and cannot be used to process BufferedImage objects. See RasterOp for further details.

```
public class BandCombineOp implements RasterOp {
// Public Constructors
    public BandCombineOp(float[ ][ ] matrix, RenderingHints hints);
// Public Instance Methods
    public final float[ ][ ] getMatrix();
// Methods Implementing RasterOp
    public WritableRaster createCompatibleDestRaster(Raster src);
    public WritableRaster filter(Raster src, WritableRaster dst);
    public final java.awt.geom.Rectangle2D getBounds2D(Raster src);
    public final java.awt.geom.Point2D getPoint2D(java.awt.geom.Point2D srcPt, java.awt.geom.Point2D dstPt);
    public final RenderingHints getRenderingHints();
}
```

Hierarchy: Object → BandCombineOp(RasterOp)

BandedSampleModel

java.awt.image

This SampleModel represents image data stored so that each color component is in a separate data element of a DataBuffer and each band of color components is in a separate bank of the DataBuffer. For example, it can be used to represent RGB colors stored in three separate banks of short values. Most applications never need to use this class. See SampleModel for further information.

```
public final class BandedSampleModel extends ComponentSampleModel {
// Public Constructors
    public BandedSampleModel(int dataType, int w, int h, int numBands);
    public BandedSampleModel(int dataType, int w, int h, int scanlineStride, int[ ] bankIndices, int[ ] bandOffsets);
// Public Methods Overriding ComponentSampleModel
    public SampleModel createCompatibleSampleModel(int w, int h);
    public DataBuffer createDataBuffer();
    public SampleModel createSubsetSampleModel(int[ ] bands);
```

```
    public Object getDataElements(int x, int y, Object obj, DataBuffer data);
    public int[ ] getPixel(int x, int y, int[ ] iArray, DataBuffer data);
    public int[ ] getPixels(int x, int y, int w, int h, int[ ] iArray, DataBuffer data);
    public int getSample(int x, int y, int b, DataBuffer data);
    public int[ ] getSamples(int x, int y, int w, int h, int b, int[ ] iArray, DataBuffer data);
    public void setDataElements(int x, int y, Object obj, DataBuffer data);
    public void setPixel(int x, int y, int[ ] iArray, DataBuffer data);
    public void setPixels(int x, int y, int w, int h, int[ ] iArray, DataBuffer data);
    public void setSample(int x, int y, int b, int s, DataBuffer data);
    public void setSamples(int x, int y, int w, int h, int b, int[ ] iArray, DataBuffer data);
}
```

Hierarchy: Object→ SampleModel→ ComponentSampleModel→ BandedSampleModel

BufferedImage   Java 1.2

java.awt.image

This is the central class in the simplified, immediate-mode imaging API introduced in Java 1.2 as part of Java 2D. A BufferedImage represents an image as a rectangular array of pixels in a Raster object and a ColorModel object that is capable of interpreting the pixel values of the Raster. BufferedImage extends java.awt.Image and can therefore be used anywhere that an Image can. However, a BufferedImage always holds its image data in memory, so there is no need for the complicated ImageObserver interface to handle asynchronous notifications as image data loads over a network.

If you know the data format of the image you need, you can create a BufferedImage by calling the BufferedImage() constructor. For example, to create an off-screen image with an alpha channel for use in complex color compositing operations, you can call BufferedImage() with the desired image size and an image type of TYPE_INT_ARGB. If you want to create an off-screen image and you do not need an alpha channel, it is easier to simply call the createImage() method of a java.awt.Component. Although this method is declared to return an Image, in Java 1.2 it is guaranteed to return a BufferedImage. The advantage to using this method is that it creates a BufferedImage with a type that is the same as (or can be efficiently converted to) the type used on your screen. If you do not have a Component handy, you can achieve the same effect by calling the createCompatibleImage() method of the java.awt.GraphicsConfiguration object that represents your screen configuration.

Once you have created a BufferedImage, you can call createGraphics() to obtain a Graphics2D object that you can use to draw into the image. You can draw a BufferedImage onto the screen or into any other image, using any of the drawImage() methods of Graphics or Graphics2D. You can perform image processing on a BufferedImage by passing it to the filter() method of any BufferedImageOp object. Finally, you can query and set individual pixels (or blocks of pixels) in a BufferedImage with getRGB() and setRGB(). These methods use the default ARGB color model: each pixel contains 8 bits of alpha, red, green, and blue data.

BufferedImage implements WritableRenderedImage, which in turn implements RenderedImage. These interfaces are used primarily by the forthcoming Java Advanced Imaging (JAI) API (javax.jai.*). Their methods allow an image to be divided up into multiple rectangular tiles. The BufferedImage class defines each image as a single tile, so most of these methods have trivial implementations. Most applications can simply ignore the RenderedImage and WritableRenderedImage methods of this class.

```
public class BufferedImage extends Image implements WritableRenderedImage {
// Public Constructors
    public BufferedImage(int width, int height, int imageType);
```

```
        public BufferedImage(ColorModel cm, WritableRaster raster, boolean isRasterPremultiplied,
                        java.util.Hashtable properties);
        public BufferedImage(int width, int height, int imageType, IndexColorModel cm);
// Public Constants
        public static final int TYPE_3BYTE_BGR;                                              =5
        public static final int TYPE_4BYTE_ABGR;                                             =6
        public static final int TYPE_4BYTE_ABGR_PRE;                                         =7
        public static final int TYPE_BYTE_BINARY;                                            =12
        public static final int TYPE_BYTE_GRAY;                                              =10
        public static final int TYPE_BYTE_INDEXED;                                           =13
        public static final int TYPE_CUSTOM;                                                 =0
        public static final int TYPE_INT_ARGB;                                               =2
        public static final int TYPE_INT_ARGB_PRE;                                           =3
        public static final int TYPE_INT_BGR;                                                =4
        public static final int TYPE_INT_RGB;                                                =1
        public static final int TYPE_USHORT_555_RGB;                                         =9
        public static final int TYPE_USHORT_565_RGB;                                         =8
        public static final int TYPE_USHORT_GRAY;                                            =11
// Property Accessor Methods (by property name)
        public boolean isAlphaPremultiplied();
        public WritableRaster getAlphaRaster();
        public ColorModel getColorModel();                                  Implements:RenderedImage
        public Raster getData();                                            Implements:RenderedImage
        public Raster getData(Rectangle rect);                              Implements:RenderedImage
        public void setData(Raster r);                              Implements:WritableRenderedImage
        public Graphics getGraphics();                                                Overrides:Image
        public int getHeight();                                             Implements:RenderedImage
        public int getHeight(ImageObserver observer);                                 Overrides:Image
        public int getMinTileX();                                  Implements:RenderedImage constant
        public int getMinTileY();                                  Implements:RenderedImage constant
        public int getMinX();                                               Implements:RenderedImage
        public int getMinY();                                               Implements:RenderedImage
        public int getNumXTiles();                                 Implements:RenderedImage constant
        public int getNumYTiles();                                 Implements:RenderedImage constant
        public String[ ] getPropertyNames();                       Implements:RenderedImage constant
        public WritableRaster getRaster();
        public SampleModel getSampleModel();                                Implements:RenderedImage
        public ImageProducer getSource();                                             Overrides:Image
        public java.util.Vector getSources();                      Implements:RenderedImage constant
        public int getTileGridXOffset();                                    Implements:RenderedImage
        public int getTileGridYOffset();                                    Implements:RenderedImage
        public int getTileHeight();                                         Implements:RenderedImage
        public int getTileWidth();                                          Implements:RenderedImage
        public int getType();
        public int getWidth();                                              Implements:RenderedImage
        public int getWidth(ImageObserver observer);                                  Overrides:Image
        public Point[ ] getWritableTileIndices();                  Implements:WritableRenderedImage
// Public Instance Methods
        public void coerceData(boolean isAlphaPremultiplied);
        public Graphics2D createGraphics();
        public int getRGB(int x, int y);
        public int[ ] getRGB(int startX, int startY, int w, int h, int[ ] rgbArray, int offset, int scansize);
        public BufferedImage getSubimage(int x, int y, int w, int h);
        public void setRGB(int x, int y, int rgb);                                        synchronized
        public void setRGB(int startX, int startY, int w, int h, int[ ] rgbArray, int offset, int scansize);
// Other Methods Implementing RenderedImage
        public WritableRaster copyData(WritableRaster outRaster);
        public Object getProperty(String name);
```

```
    public Raster getTile(int tileX, int tileY);
// Methods Implementing WritableRenderedImage
    public void addTileObserver(TileObserver to);                                            empty
    public WritableRaster getWritableTile(int tileX, int tileY);
    public Point[ ] getWritableTileIndices();
    public boolean hasTileWriters();                                                      constant
    public boolean isTileWritable(int tileX, int tileY);
    public void releaseWritableTile(int tileX, int tileY);                                    empty
    public void removeTileObserver(TileObserver to);                                          empty
    public void setData(Raster r);
// Public Methods Overriding Image
    public void flush();                                                                      empty
    public Object getProperty(String name, ImageObserver observer);
// Public Methods Overriding Object
    public String toString();
}
```

Hierarchy: Object→ Image → BufferedImage(WritableRenderedImage(RenderedImage))

Passed To: Too many methods to list.

Returned By: Too many methods to list.

BufferedImageFilter   Java 1.2

java.awt.image   *cloneable*

This class allows a Java 1.2 BufferedImageOp image-processing operation to be used as an
ImageFilter in the Java 1.0 and Java 1.1 image processing model. Create a BufferedImage-
Filter by passing a BufferedImageOp to the constructor. Then use the resulting BufferedImageFilter with a FilteredImageSource exactly as you would use RGBImageFilter, CropImageFilter,
or any other Java 1.0 or Java 1.1 image filter.

```
public class BufferedImageFilter extends ImageFilter implements Cloneable {
// Public Constructors
    public BufferedImageFilter(BufferedImageOp op);
// Public Instance Methods
    public BufferedImageOp getBufferedImageOp();
// Public Methods Overriding ImageFilter
    public void imageComplete(int status);
    public void setColorModel(ColorModel model);
    public void setDimensions(int width, int height);
    public void setPixels(int x, int y, int w, int h, ColorModel model, int[ ] pixels, int off, int scansize);
    public void setPixels(int x, int y, int w, int h, ColorModel model, byte[ ] pixels, int off, int scansize);
}
```

Hierarchy: Object→ ImageFilter(Cloneable, ImageConsumer)→ BufferedImageFilter(Cloneable)

BufferedImageOp   Java 1.2

java.awt.image

This interface describes an image-processing operation that can be performed on any
BufferedImage. Java 2D includes a number of versatile implementations of this interface
that most applications can rely for all their image-processing needs.

To use a BufferedImageOp, call its filter() method. This method processes a specified
source image and stores the results in a specified destination image. If no destination
image is specified, the method creates and returns an appropriate one. You can pass a
source image to getBounds2D() to get the bounding box of the destination image that
would be produced if that source image were to be passed to filter(). Given a point in a

(hypothetical) source image, getPoint2D() returns the corresponding point in the destination image. If a destination Point2D object is provided, it is used to return the destination point; otherwise a Point2D object is allocated for this purpose. getRenderingHints() returns the rendering hints associated with this implementation of BufferedImageOp, or null if it has no rendering hints. Finally, createCompatibleDestImage() is an internal method that implementations must define but that applications never need to call.

```
public abstract interface BufferedImageOp {
// Public Instance Methods
    public abstract BufferedImage createCompatibleDestImage(BufferedImage src, ColorModel destCM);
    public abstract BufferedImage filter(BufferedImage src, BufferedImage dest);
    public abstract java.awt.geom.Rectangle2D getBounds2D(BufferedImage src);
    public abstract java.awt.geom.Point2D getPoint2D(java.awt.geom.Point2D srcPt, java.awt.geom.Point2D dstPt);
    public abstract RenderingHints getRenderingHints();
}
```

Implementations: AffineTransformOp, ColorConvertOp, ConvolveOp, LookupOp, RescaleOp

Passed To: Graphics2D.drawImage(), BufferedImageFilter.BufferedImageFilter()

Returned By: BufferedImageFilter.getBufferedImageOp()

ByteLookupTable

java.awt.image

This concrete subclass of LookupTable contains one or more byte arrays that serve as lookup tables for a LookupOp image-processing operation. Applications never need to use a ByteLookupTable directly; they need to create one only to pass to the LookupOp() constructor. Create a ByteLookupTable by passing the byte array or arrays to the ByteLookupTable() constructor, along with an offset that is subtracted from each source color component before the lookup is performed. See also LookupTable.

```
public class ByteLookupTable extends LookupTable {
// Public Constructors
    public ByteLookupTable(int offset, byte[ ][ ] data);
    public ByteLookupTable(int offset, byte[ ] data);
// Public Instance Methods
    public final byte[ ][ ] getTable();
    public byte[ ] lookupPixel(byte[ ] src, byte[ ] dst);
// Public Methods Overriding LookupTable
    public int[ ] lookupPixel(int[ ] src, int[ ] dst);
}
```

Hierarchy: Object → LookupTable → ByteLookupTable

ColorConvertOp

java.awt.image

This class is a BufferedImageOp and a RasterOp that converts the colors of a BufferedImage or a Raster from one color space to another color space. If the filter() method is called with two distinct source and destination BufferedImage objects specified, it converts the colors from the java.awt.color.ColorSpace of the source image to the ColorSpace of the destination image. If no destination image is passed to filter(), the destination ColorSpace must have been specified when the ColorConvertOp() constructor was called. Finally, if this ColorConvertOp is to be used to filter Raster object, both the source and destination color spaces must be specified, either in the form of ColorSpace objects or as an array of two java.awt.color.ICC_PROFILE objects.

In addition to optionally specifying the source and destination color spaces when you invoke the ColorConvertOp() constructor, you may also specify a RenderingHints object. If the hints object is non-null, the ColorConvertOp may use the color rendering and dithering hints it contains.

To use a ColorConvertOp, simply pass a source and optional destination image or raster to the filter() method. Because the ColorConvertOp works on each pixel of the image or raster independently, you may specify the same object for both source and destination. In this case, the image or raster is modified in place. See BufferedImageOp for further details.

```
public class ColorConvertOp implements BufferedImageOp, RasterOp {
// Public Constructors
    public ColorConvertOp(RenderingHints hints);
    public ColorConvertOp(java.awt.color.ICC_Profile[ ] profiles, RenderingHints hints);
    public ColorConvertOp(java.awt.color.ColorSpace cspace, RenderingHints hints);
    public ColorConvertOp(java.awt.color.ColorSpace srcCspace, java.awt.color.ColorSpace dstCspace,
                    RenderingHints hints);
// Public Instance Methods
    public final java.awt.color.ICC_Profile[ ] getICC_Profiles();
// Methods Implementing BufferedImageOp
    public BufferedImage createCompatibleDestImage(BufferedImage src, ColorModel destCM);
    public final BufferedImage filter(BufferedImage src, BufferedImage dest);
    public final java.awt.geom.Rectangle2D getBounds2D(BufferedImage src);
    public final java.awt.geom.Point2D getPoint2D(java.awt.geom.Point2D srcPt, java.awt.geom.Point2D dstPt);
    public final RenderingHints getRenderingHints();
// Methods Implementing RasterOp
    public WritableRaster createCompatibleDestRaster(Raster src);
    public final WritableRaster filter(Raster src, WritableRaster dest);
    public final java.awt.geom.Rectangle2D getBounds2D(Raster src);
}
```

Hierarchy: Object→ ColorConvertOp(BufferedImageOp, RasterOp)

ColorModel   Java 1.0

java.awt.image   PJ1.1

This abstract class defines a scheme for representing colors as pixels. The primary job of a ColorModel object is to extract individual color components from pixel values. Most applications do not need to work with ColorModel objects directly; those that do usually need only to instantiate an appropriate ColorModel subclass for use by some other method or constructor.

In Java 1.0 and 1.1, this is a fairly simple class: pixel values are supplied as int values, and the getRed(), getGreen(), getBlue(), and getAlpha() methods return the red, green, blue, and alpha components of the pixel. The getRGB() method converts a pixel to the pixel format used by the default ARGB color model. This color model is returned by the static getRGBDefault() method; it packs 8-bit color and alpha components into a 32-bit int in 0xAARRGGBB format.

With the introduction of Java 2D in Java 1.2, this class has become more complicated. Now the ColorModel is not tied to the default RGB java.awt.color.ColorSpace and provides methods for extracting color components from any color space. The getComponents() method and its variants return an array of color components for a given pixel value. If the ColorModel is defined in terms of the CMYK color space, for example, these components are not red, green, and blue, but cyan, magenta, yellow, and black. Note, however, that because every ColorSpace can convert colors to the default RGB color space, the getRed(), getGreen(), getBlue(), and getRGB() methods still work, regardless of color space.

Another generalization to the ColorModel class in Java 1.2 is that pixel values are no longer assumed to fit in int values. Each method that extracts color components from pixels comes in two forms. In the first, the pixel value is specified as an int. In the second form, it is specified as a Object. This object is an array of primitive values. The type of these values is known as the transfer type of the color model and is specified by one of the constants DataBuffer.TYPE_BYTE, Databuffer.TYPE_USHORT, or DataBuffer.TYPE_INT. In simple cases, the elements of the transfer type arrays contain color components, and the ColorModel object provides a trivial mapping between pixel values and color component values.

Other ColorModel additions in Java 1.2 include the implementation of the Transparency interface and its getTransparency() method. This method returns a Transparency constant that specifies the level of transparency supported by the ColorModel. For ColorModel objects that support transparency, the isAlphaPremultiplied() method specifies whether the color components have been premultiplied by the alpha component. (Premultiplication makes alpha compositing operations more efficient.) Also, the getNormalizedComponents() and getUnnormalizedComponents() convert back and forth between normalized and unnormalized color component values. A normalized component is a float value between 0.0 and 1.0 that has not been premultiplied by an alpha value. An unnormalized component is an integral value with a range that depends on the number of bits used by the color model, possibly premultiplied by the alpha value.

There are a number of ColorModel subclasses, suitable for distinctly different types of color models. See also ComponentColorModel, DirectColorModel, IndexColorModel, and PackedColorModel.

```
public abstract class ColorModel implements Transparency {
// Public Constructors
     public ColorModel(int bits);
// Protected Constructors
1.2 protected ColorModel(int pixel_bits, int[] bits, java.awt.color.ColorSpace cspace, boolean hasAlpha,
                    boolean isAlphaPremultiplied, int transparency, int transferType);
// Public Class Methods
     public static ColorModel getRGBdefault();
// Property Accessor Methods (by property name)
1.2 public final boolean isAlphaPremultiplied();
1.2 public final java.awt.color.ColorSpace getColorSpace();
1.2 public int[] getComponentSize();
1.2 public int getComponentSize(int componentIdx);
1.2 public int getNumColorComponents();
1.2 public int getNumComponents();
     public int getPixelSize();
1.2 public int getTransparency();                                              Implements:Transparency
// Public Instance Methods
1.2 public ColorModel coerceData(WritableRaster raster, boolean isAlphaPremultiplied);
1.2 public SampleModel createCompatibleSampleModel(int w, int h);
1.2 public WritableRaster createCompatibleWritableRaster(int w, int h);
1.2 public int getAlpha(Object inData);
     public abstract int getAlpha(int pixel);
1.2 public WritableRaster getAlphaRaster(WritableRaster raster);                         constant
1.2 public int getBlue(Object inData);
     public abstract int getBlue(int pixel);
1.2 public int[] getComponents(int pixel, int[] components, int offset);
1.2 public int[] getComponents(Object pixel, int[] components, int offset);
1.2 public int getDataElement(int[] components, int offset);
1.2 public Object getDataElements(int rgb, Object pixel);
1.2 public Object getDataElements(int[] components, int offset, Object obj);
1.2 public int getGreen(Object inData);
     public abstract int getGreen(int pixel);
1.2 public float[] getNormalizedComponents(int[] components, int offset, float[] normComponents,
                    int normOffset);
```

```
    public abstract int getRed(int pixel);
1.2 public int getRed(Object inData);
    public int getRGB(int pixel);
1.2 public int getRGB(Object inData);
1.2 public int[ ] getUnnormalizedComponents(float[ ] normComponents, int normOffset, int[ ] components,
                                            int offset);
1.2 public final boolean hasAlpha();
1.2 public boolean isCompatibleRaster(Raster raster);
1.2 public boolean isCompatibleSampleModel(SampleModel sm);
// Methods Implementing Transparency
1.2 public int getTransparency();
// Public Methods Overriding Object
1.2 public boolean equals(Object obj);
    public void finalize();                                                      empty
1.2 public String toString();
// Protected Instance Fields
    protected int pixel_bits;
1.2 protected int transferType;
}
```

Hierarchy: Object → ColorModel(Transparency)

Subclasses: ComponentColorModel, IndexColorModel, PackedColorModel

Passed To: Too many methods to list.

Returned By: Component.getColorModel(), GraphicsConfiguration.getColorModel(), PaintContext.getColorModel(), Toolkit.getColorModel(), BufferedImage.getColorModel(), ColorModel.{coerceData(), getRGBdefault()}, ComponentColorModel.coerceData(), DirectColorModel.coerceData(), PixelGrabber.getColorModel(), RenderedImage.getColorModel(), java.awt.peer.ComponentPeer.getColorModel()

Type Of: RGBImageFilter.{newmodel, origmodel}

ComponentColorModel   Java 1.2

java.awt.image

This ColorModel is used with image data in which the color and transparency components of pixels are stored separately, instead of being combined together into a single int value. This class works only with pixel values specified as an array of primitive values of the specified transfer type. The number of elements in these pixel arrays must match the number of color and transparency components in the specified color space. This class performs the trivial mapping between the array elements of the pixel value and the color components of the color it represents. The methods of this class that are passed int pixel values can throw IllegalArgumentException. Only applications that are doing custom image processing need to use this, or any, ColorModel.

```
public class ComponentColorModel extends ColorModel {
// Public Constructors
    public ComponentColorModel(java.awt.color.ColorSpace colorSpace, int[ ] bits, boolean hasAlpha,
                                boolean isAlphaPremultiplied, int transparency, int transferType);
// Public Methods Overriding ColorModel
    public ColorModel coerceData(WritableRaster raster, boolean isAlphaPremultiplied);
    public SampleModel createCompatibleSampleModel(int w, int h);
    public WritableRaster createCompatibleWritableRaster(int w, int h);
    public boolean equals(Object obj);
    public int getAlpha(Object inData);
    public int getAlpha(int pixel);
    public WritableRaster getAlphaRaster(WritableRaster raster);
```

```
    public int getBlue(Object inData);
    public int getBlue(int pixel);
    public int[ ] getComponents(Object pixel, int[ ] components, int offset);
    public int[ ] getComponents(int pixel, int[ ] components, int offset);
    public int getDataElement(int[ ] components, int offset);
    public Object getDataElements(int rgb, Object pixel);
    public Object getDataElements(int[ ] components, int offset, Object obj);
    public int getGreen(Object inData);
    public int getGreen(int pixel);
    public int getRed(int pixel);
    public int getRed(Object inData);
    public int getRGB(int pixel);
    public int getRGB(Object inData);
    public boolean isCompatibleRaster(Raster raster);
    public boolean isCompatibleSampleModel(SampleModel sm);
}
```

Hierarchy: Object→ ColorModel(Transparency)→ ComponentColorModel

ComponentSampleModel   Java 1.2

java.awt.image

This SampleModel represents image data stored so that each component of each pixel is stored in a separate element of the DataBuffer. The arguments to the ComponentSample-Model allow great flexibility in this model. For example, it can represent RGB values interleaved into a single bank of bytes or ARGB values stored in four separate banks of bytes. Additionally, it can handle offsets at the end of scanlines and an offset at the beginning of each bank.

Java 2D defines two subclasses of ComponentSampleModel that are more efficient for particular types of image data. When each band of pixel components is stored in a separate bank of the DataBuffer, it is easier and more efficient to use the BandedSampleModel subclass. When the components of a pixel are stored in adjacent data elements of a single bank of the DataBuffer, it is easier and more efficient to use PixelInterleavedSample-Model.

Most applications never need to use this class or its subclasses. See SampleModel for further information.

```
public class ComponentSampleModel extends SampleModel {
// Public Constructors
    public ComponentSampleModel(int dataType, int w, int h, int pixelStride, int scanlineStride, int[ ] bandOffsets);
    public ComponentSampleModel(int dataType, int w, int h, int pixelStride, int scanlineStride, int[ ] bankIndices,
                                int[ ] bandOffsets);
// Property Accessor Methods (by property name)
    public final int[ ] getBandOffsets();
    public final int[ ] getBankIndices();
    public final int getNumDataElements();                                          Overrides:SampleModel
    public final int getPixelStride();
    public final int[ ] getSampleSize();                                            Overrides:SampleModel
    public final int getSampleSize(int band);                                       Overrides:SampleModel
    public final int getScanlineStride();
// Public Instance Methods
    public int getOffset(int x, int y);
    public int getOffset(int x, int y, int b);
// Public Methods Overriding SampleModel
    public SampleModel createCompatibleSampleModel(int w, int h);
    public DataBuffer createDataBuffer();
```

```
    public SampleModel createSubsetSampleModel(int[ ] bands);
    public Object getDataElements(int x, int y, Object obj, DataBuffer data);
    public int[ ] getPixel(int x, int y, int[ ] iArray, DataBuffer data);
    public int[ ] getPixels(int x, int y, int w, int h, int[ ] iArray, DataBuffer data);
    public int getSample(int x, int y, int b, DataBuffer data);
    public int[ ] getSamples(int x, int y, int w, int h, int b, int[ ] iArray, DataBuffer data);
    public void setDataElements(int x, int y, Object obj, DataBuffer data);
    public void setPixel(int x, int y, int[ ] iArray, DataBuffer data);
    public void setPixels(int x, int y, int w, int h, int[ ] iArray, DataBuffer data);
    public void setSample(int x, int y, int b, int s, DataBuffer data);
    public void setSamples(int x, int y, int w, int h, int b, int[ ] iArray, DataBuffer data);
// Protected Instance Fields
    protected int[ ] bandOffsets;
    protected int[ ] bankIndices;
    protected int numBands;
    protected int numBanks;
    protected int pixelStride;
    protected int scanlineStride;
}
```

Hierarchy: Object→ SampleModel→ ComponentSampleModel

Subclasses: BandedSampleModel, PixelInterleavedSampleModel

ConvolveOp   Java 1.2

java.awt.image

This class is a BufferedImageOp and a RasterOp that performs an arbitrary convolution on an image. Convolution is a versatile image-processing operation that can be used, for example, to blur or sharpen an image or perform edge detection on an image. The convolution to be performed is specified by a matrix of floating-point numbers, in the form of a Kernel object. Because convolution looks at the neighbors of each pixel in an image, special care must be taken when operating on the pixels at the edges of the image. By default, a ConvolveOp uses imaginary color components of all zeros when it reaches the edges of an image. You can pass EDGE_NO_OP to the constructor to specify that the edges of the image should simply be left unprocessed. Finally, you can pass a RenderingHints object to the ConvolveOp() constructor. If this argument is not null, the ConvolveOp may use its color and dithering hints.

To use a ConvolveOp, simply pass a source and optional destination image or raster to its filter() method. Note that you cannot specify the same object as both source and destination. See BufferedImageOp for further details.

```
public class ConvolveOp implements BufferedImageOp, RasterOp {
// Public Constructors
    public ConvolveOp(Kernel kernel);
    public ConvolveOp(Kernel kernel, int edgeCondition, RenderingHints hints);
// Public Constants
    public static final int EDGE_NO_OP;                                            =1
    public static final int EDGE_ZERO_FILL;                                        =0
// Public Instance Methods
    public int getEdgeCondition();
    public final Kernel getKernel();
// Methods Implementing BufferedImageOp
    public BufferedImage createCompatibleDestImage(BufferedImage src, ColorModel destCM);
    public final BufferedImage filter(BufferedImage src, BufferedImage dst);
    public final java.awt.geom.Rectangle2D getBounds2D(BufferedImage src);
    public final java.awt.geom.Point2D getPoint2D(java.awt.geom.Point2D srcPt, java.awt.geom.Point2D dstPt);
```

```
    public final RenderingHints getRenderingHints();
// Methods Implementing RasterOp
    public WritableRaster createCompatibleDestRaster(Raster src);
    public final WritableRaster filter(Raster src, WritableRaster dst);
    public final java.awt.geom.Rectangle2D getBounds2D(Raster src);
}
```

Hierarchy: Object→ ConvolveOp(BufferedImageOp, RasterOp)

CropImageFilter
Java 1.0

java.awt.image
cloneable PJ1.1

This class implements an ImageFilter that crops an image to a specified rectangle. The methods defined by this class are used for communication between the filter and its FilteredImageSource and should never be called directly.

```
public class CropImageFilter extends ImageFilter {
// Public Constructors
    public CropImageFilter(int x, int y, int w, int h);
// Public Methods Overriding ImageFilter
    public void setDimensions(int w, int h);
    public void setPixels(int x, int y, int w, int h, ColorModel model, int[ ] pixels, int off, int scansize);
    public void setPixels(int x, int y, int w, int h, ColorModel model, byte[ ] pixels, int off, int scansize);
    public void setProperties(java.util.Hashtable props);
}
```

Hierarchy: Object→ ImageFilter(Cloneable, ImageConsumer)→ CropImageFilter

DataBuffer
Java 1.2

java.awt.image

This abstract class stores image data at the lowest level. A DataBuffer stores one or more arrays, or banks, of data of a specified size and a given type. The Raster class uses a DataBuffer to store image data and a SampleModel to interpret the storage format of that data. Most applications never need to use DataBuffer objects directly.

Specific concrete subclasses of DataBuffer are implemented for specific types of data. See also DataBufferByte, DataBufferShort, DataBufferUShort, and DataBufferInt.

```
public abstract class DataBuffer {
// Protected Constructors
    protected DataBuffer(int dataType, int size);
    protected DataBuffer(int dataType, int size, int numBanks);
    protected DataBuffer(int dataType, int size, int numBanks, int[ ] offsets);
    protected DataBuffer(int dataType, int size, int numBanks, int offset);
// Public Constants
    public static final int TYPE_BYTE;                                             =0
    public static final int TYPE_DOUBLE;                                           =5
    public static final int TYPE_FLOAT;                                            =4
    public static final int TYPE_INT;                                              =3
    public static final int TYPE_SHORT;                                            =2
    public static final int TYPE_UNDEFINED;                                        =32
    public static final int TYPE_USHORT;                                           =1
// Public Class Methods
    public static int getDataTypeSize(int type);
// Property Accessor Methods (by property name)
    public int getDataType();
    public int getNumBanks();
```

```
      public int getOffset();
      public int[ ] getOffsets();
      public int getSize();
// Public Instance Methods
      public int getElem(int i);
      public abstract int getElem(int bank, int i);
      public double getElemDouble(int i);
      public double getElemDouble(int bank, int i);
      public float getElemFloat(int i);
      public float getElemFloat(int bank, int i);
      public void setElem(int i, int val);
      public abstract void setElem(int bank, int i, int val);
      public void setElemDouble(int i, double val);
      public void setElemDouble(int bank, int i, double val);
      public void setElemFloat(int i, float val);
      public void setElemFloat(int bank, int i, float val);
// Protected Instance Fields
      protected int banks;
      protected int dataType;
      protected int offset;
      protected int[ ] offsets;
      protected int size;
}
```

Subclasses: DataBufferByte, DataBufferInt, DataBufferShort, DataBufferUShort

Passed To: Too many methods to list.

Returned By: BandedSampleModel.createDataBuffer(), ComponentSampleModel.createDataBuffer(), MultiPixelPackedSampleModel.createDataBuffer(), Raster.getDataBuffer(), SampleModel.createDataBuffer(), SinglePixelPackedSampleModel.createDataBuffer()

Type Of: Raster.dataBuffer

DataBufferByte   Java 1.2

java.awt.image

This class stores image data in one or more byte arrays. The arrays, or banks, of data can be passed directly to the DataBufferByte() constructor, or they can be created by the constructor. You may specify an offset into each array at which the data begins. getElem() and setElem() allow you to get and set the values of a particular element of a particular bank. Most applications never use this class directly.

```
public final class DataBufferByte extends DataBuffer {
// Public Constructors
      public DataBufferByte(int size);
      public DataBufferByte(byte[ ][ ] dataArray, int size);
      public DataBufferByte(byte[ ] dataArray, int size);
      public DataBufferByte(int size, int numBanks);
      public DataBufferByte(byte[ ][ ] dataArray, int size, int[ ] offsets);
      public DataBufferByte(byte[ ] dataArray, int size, int offset);
// Public Instance Methods
      public byte[ ][ ] getBankData();
      public byte[ ] getData();
      public byte[ ] getData(int bank);
// Public Methods Overriding DataBuffer
      public int getElem(int i);
      public int getElem(int bank, int i);
      public void setElem(int i, int val);
```

```
    public void setElem(int bank, int i, int val);
}
```

Hierarchy: Object→ DataBuffer→ DataBufferByte

DataBufferInt

java.awt.image

This class stores image data in one or more int arrays. The arrays, or banks, of data can be passed directly to the DataBufferInt() constructor, or they can be created by the constructor. You may specify an offset into each array at which the data begins. getElem() and setElem() allow you to get and set the values of a particular element of a particular bank. Most applications never use this class directly.

```
public final class DataBufferInt extends DataBuffer {
// Public Constructors
    public DataBufferInt(int size);
    public DataBufferInt(int[ ][ ] dataArray, int size);
    public DataBufferInt(int[ ] dataArray, int size);
    public DataBufferInt(int size, int numBanks);
    public DataBufferInt(int[ ][ ] dataArray, int size, int[ ] offsets);
    public DataBufferInt(int[ ] dataArray, int size, int offset);
// Public Instance Methods
    public int[ ][ ] getBankData( );
    public int[ ] getData( );
    public int[ ] getData(int bank);
// Public Methods Overriding DataBuffer
    public int getElem(int i);
    public int getElem(int bank, int i);
    public void setElem(int i, int val);
    public void setElem(int bank, int i, int val);
}
```

Hierarchy: Object→ DataBuffer→ DataBufferInt

DataBufferShort

java.awt.image

This class stores image data in one or more short arrays. The arrays, or banks, of data can be passed directly to the DataBufferShort() constructor, or they can be created by the constructor. You may specify an offset into each array at which the data begins. getElem() and setElem() allow you to get and set the values of a particular element of a particular bank. Most applications never use this class directly.

```
public final class DataBufferShort extends DataBuffer {
// Public Constructors
    public DataBufferShort(int size);
    public DataBufferShort(short[ ][ ] dataArray, int size);
    public DataBufferShort(short[ ] dataArray, int size);
    public DataBufferShort(int size, int numBanks);
    public DataBufferShort(short[ ][ ] dataArray, int size, int[ ] offsets);
    public DataBufferShort(short[ ] dataArray, int size, int offset);
// Public Instance Methods
    public short[ ][ ] getBankData( );
    public short[ ] getData( );
    public short[ ] getData(int bank);
// Public Methods Overriding DataBuffer
    public int getElem(int i);
```

```
    public int getElem(int bank, int i);
    public void setElem(int i, int val);
    public void setElem(int bank, int i, int val);
}
```

Hierarchy: Object→ DataBuffer→ DataBufferShort

DataBufferUShort
Java 1.2

java.awt.image

This class stores unsigned image data in one or more short arrays. The arrays, or banks, of data can be passed directly to the DataBufferUShort() constructor, or they can be created by the constructor. You may specify an offset into each array at which the data begins. getElem() and setElem() allow you to get and set the values of a particular element of a particular bank. Most applications never use this class directly.

```
public final class DataBufferUShort extends DataBuffer {
// Public Constructors
    public DataBufferUShort(int size);
    public DataBufferUShort(short[ ][ ] dataArray, int size);
    public DataBufferUShort(short[ ] dataArray, int size);
    public DataBufferUShort(int size, int numBanks);
    public DataBufferUShort(short[ ][ ] dataArray, int size, int[ ] offsets);
    public DataBufferUShort(short[ ] dataArray, int size, int offset);
// Public Instance Methods
    public short[ ][ ] getBankData();
    public short[ ] getData();
    public short[ ] getData(int bank);
// Public Methods Overriding DataBuffer
    public int getElem(int i);
    public int getElem(int bank, int i);
    public void setElem(int i, int val);
    public void setElem(int bank, int i, int val);
}
```

Hierarchy: Object→ DataBuffer→ DataBufferUShort

DirectColorModel
Java 1.0

java.awt.image
PJ1.1

This ColorModel works only with RGB color spaces. It extracts red, green, blue, and, optionally, alpha values directly from the bits of the pixel, using bitmasks to specify which bits correspond to which color components. The default RGB color model is a DirectColorModel. Only applications that are doing custom image processing need to use this, or any, ColorModel.

Prior to Java 1.2, this class extended ColorModel directly. In Java 1.2, it extends PackedColorModel, which itself extends ColorModel. The Java 1.2 methods of this class that accept pixel values as an array of a primitive transfer type expect that array argument to have a length of 1.

```
public class DirectColorModel extends PackedColorModel {
// Public Constructors
    public DirectColorModel(int bits, int rmask, int gmask, int bmask);
    public DirectColorModel(int bits, int rmask, int gmask, int bmask, int amask);
1.2 public DirectColorModel(java.awt.color.ColorSpace space, int bits, int rmask, int gmask, int bmask, int amask,
                            boolean isAlphaPremultiplied, int transferType);
```

```
// Property Accessor Methods (by property name)
   public final int getAlphaMask();
   public final int getBlueMask();
   public final int getGreenMask();
   public final int getRedMask();
// Public Methods Overriding ColorModel
1.2 public final ColorModel coerceData(WritableRaster raster, boolean isAlphaPremultiplied);
1.2 public final WritableRaster createCompatibleWritableRaster(int w, int h);
1.2 public int getAlpha(Object inData);
   public final int getAlpha(int pixel);
1.2 public final int getBlue(Object inData);
   public final int getBlue(int pixel);
1.2 public final int[ ] getComponents(Object pixel, int[ ] components, int offset);
1.2 public final int[ ] getComponents(int pixel, int[ ] components, int offset);
1.2 public int getDataElement(int[ ] components, int offset);
1.2 public Object getDataElements(int rgb, Object pixel);
1.2 public Object getDataElements(int[ ] components, int offset, Object obj);
1.2 public int getGreen(Object inData);
   public final int getGreen(int pixel);
1.2 public int getRed(Object inData);
   public final int getRed(int pixel);
   public final int getRGB(int pixel);
1.2 public int getRGB(Object inData);
1.2 public boolean isCompatibleRaster(Raster raster);
1.2 public String toString();
}
```

Hierarchy: Object → ColorModel(Transparency) → PackedColorModel → DirectColorModel

FilteredImageSource   Java 1.0

java.awt.image   PJ1.1

This class is an ImageProducer that produces image data filtered from some other Image-Producer. A FilteredImageSource is created with a specified ImageProducer and a specified ImageFilter. For example, an applet might use the following code to download and crop an image:

```
Image full_image = getImage(getDocumentBase(), "images/1.gif");
ImageFilter cropper = new CropImageFilter(10, 10, 100, 100);
ImageProducer prod = new FilteredImageSource(full_image.getSource(), cropper);
Image cropped_image = createImage(prod);
```

The methods of this class are the standard ImageProducer methods that you can invoke to add and remove ImageConsumer objects.

```
public class FilteredImageSource implements ImageProducer {
// Public Constructors
   public FilteredImageSource(ImageProducer orig, ImageFilter imgf);
// Methods Implementing ImageProducer
   public void addConsumer(ImageConsumer ic);                          synchronized
   public boolean isConsumer(ImageConsumer ic);                        synchronized
   public void removeConsumer(ImageConsumer ic);                       synchronized
   public void requestTopDownLeftRightResend(ImageConsumer ic);
   public void startProduction(ImageConsumer ic);
}
```

Hierarchy: Object → FilteredImageSource(ImageProducer)

ImageConsumer

Java 1.0

java.awt.image

PJ1.1

This interface defines the methods necessary for a class that consumes image data to communicate with a class that produces image data. The methods defined by this interface should never be called by a program directly; instead, they are invoked by an ImageProducer to pass the image data and other information about the image to the ImageConsumer. The constants defined by this interface are values passed to the setHints() and imageComplete() methods. Unless you want to do low-level manipulation of image data, you never need to use or implement an ImageConsumer.

```
public abstract interface ImageConsumer {
// Public Constants
    public static final int COMPLETESCANLINES;                                              =4
    public static final int IMAGEABORTED;                                                   =4
    public static final int IMAGEERROR;                                                     =1
    public static final int RANDOMPIXELORDER;                                               =1
    public static final int SINGLEFRAME;                                                    =16
    public static final int SINGLEFRAMEDONE;                                                =2
    public static final int SINGLEPASS;                                                     =8
    public static final int STATICIMAGEDONE;                                                =3
    public static final int TOPDOWNLEFTRIGHT;                                               =2
// Public Instance Methods
    public abstract void imageComplete(int status);
    public abstract void setColorModel(ColorModel model);
    public abstract void setDimensions(int width, int height);
    public abstract void setHints(int hintflags);
    public abstract void setPixels(int x, int y, int w, int h, ColorModel model, int[ ] pixels, int off, int scansize);
    public abstract void setPixels(int x, int y, int w, int h, ColorModel model, byte[ ] pixels, int off, int scansize);
    public abstract void setProperties(java.util.Hashtable props);
}
```

Implementations: ImageFilter, PixelGrabber

Passed To: Too many methods to list.

Type Of: ImageFilter.consumer

ImageFilter

Java 1.0

java.awt.image

cloneable PJ1.1

This class is used in conjunction with a FilteredImageSource. It accepts image data through the ImageConsumer interface and passes it on to an ImageConsumer specified by the controlling FilteredImageSource. ImageFilter is the superclass of all image filters; it performs no filtering itself. You must subclass it to perform the desired filtering. See also CropImageFilter and RGBImageFilter. The ImageFilter methods are the ImageConsumer methods invoked by an ImageProducer. You should not call them directly. See FilteredImageSource for an example of using an ImageFilter.

```
public class ImageFilter implements Cloneable, ImageConsumer {
// Public Constructors
    public ImageFilter();
// Public Instance Methods
    public ImageFilter getFilterInstance(ImageConsumer ic);
    public void resendTopDownLeftRight(ImageProducer ip);
// Methods Implementing ImageConsumer
    public void imageComplete(int status);
    public void setColorModel(ColorModel model);
    public void setDimensions(int width, int height);
```

```
    public void setHints(int hints);
    public void setPixels(int x, int y, int w, int h, ColorModel model, int[ ] pixels, int off, int scansize);
    public void setPixels(int x, int y, int w, int h, ColorModel model, byte[ ] pixels, int off, int scansize);
    public void setProperties(java.util.Hashtable props);
// Public Methods Overriding Object
    public Object clone( );
// Protected Instance Fields
    protected ImageConsumer consumer;
}
```

Hierarchy: Object→ ImageFilter(Cloneable, ImageConsumer)

Subclasses: BufferedImageFilter, CropImageFilter, ReplicateScaleFilter, RGBImageFilter

Passed To: FilteredImageSource.FilteredImageSource()

Returned By: ImageFilter.getFilterInstance()

ImageObserver   Java 1.0

java.awt.image   *PJ1.1*

This interface defines a method and associated constants used by classes that want to receive information asynchronously about the status of an image. Many methods that query information about an image take an ImageObserver as an argument. If the specified information is not available when requested, it is passed to the ImageObserver when it becomes available. Component implements this interface, and components are the most commonly used image observers.

```
public abstract interface ImageObserver {
// Public Constants
    public static final int ABORT;                                  =128
    public static final int ALLBITS;                                 =32
    public static final int ERROR;                                   =64
    public static final int FRAMEBITS;                               =16
    public static final int HEIGHT;                                   =2
    public static final int PROPERTIES;                               =4
    public static final int SOMEBITS;                                 =8
    public static final int WIDTH;                                    =1
// Public Instance Methods
    public abstract boolean imageUpdate(Image img, int infoflags, int x, int y, int width, int height);
}
```

Implementations: Component

Passed To: Too many methods to list.

Returned By: javax.swing.ImageIcon.getImageObserver()

ImageProducer   Java 1.0

java.awt.image   *PJ1.1*

This interface defines the methods that any class that produces image data must define to enable communication with ImageConsumer classes. An ImageConsumer registers itself as interested in a producer's image by calling the addConsumer() method. Most applications never need to use or implement this interface.

```
public abstract interface ImageProducer {
// Public Instance Methods
    public abstract void addConsumer(ImageConsumer ic);
    public abstract boolean isConsumer(ImageConsumer ic);
```

```
    public abstract void removeConsumer(ImageConsumer ic);
    public abstract void requestTopDownLeftRightResend(ImageConsumer ic);
    public abstract void startProduction(ImageConsumer ic);
}
```

Implementations: FilteredImageSource, MemoryImageSource,
java.awt.image.renderable.RenderableImageProducer

Passed To: Component.createImage(), Toolkit.createImage(), FilteredImageSource.FilteredImageSource(),
ImageFilter.resendTopDownLeftRight(), PixelGrabber.PixelGrabber(),
java.awt.peer.ComponentPeer.createImage()

Returned By: Image.getSource(), BufferedImage.getSource()

ImagingOpException   Java 1.2

java.awt.image   *serializable unchecked*

Thrown by the filter() methods of BufferedImageOp and RasterOp if, for any reason, they
are unable to filter the specified image.

```
public class ImagingOpException extends RuntimeException {
// Public Constructors
    public ImagingOpException(String s);
}
```

Hierarchy: Object→ Throwable(Serializable)→ Exception→ RuntimeException→ ImagingOpException

IndexColorModel   Java 1.0

java.awt.image   *PJ1.1*

This ColorModel is used with RGB color spaces and determines the red, green, blue, and,
optionally, alpha components of a pixel by using the pixel value as an index into colormap arrays. If no array of alpha values is specified, all pixels are fully opaque, except
for one optionally specified reserved value that is fully transparent. This color model is
useful when working with image data that is defined in terms of a colormap. Only
applications that are doing custom image processing need to use this, or any, Color-
Model.

```
public class IndexColorModel extends ColorModel {
// Public Constructors
    public IndexColorModel(int bits, int size, byte[ ] cmap, int start, boolean hasalpha);
    public IndexColorModel(int bits, int size, byte[ ] r, byte[ ] g, byte[ ] b);
    public IndexColorModel(int bits, int size, byte[ ] cmap, int start, boolean hasalpha, int trans);
    public IndexColorModel(int bits, int size, byte[ ] r, byte[ ] g, byte[ ] b, byte[ ] a);
    public IndexColorModel(int bits, int size, byte[ ] r, byte[ ] g, byte[ ] b, int trans);
1.2 public IndexColorModel(int bits, int size, int[ ] cmap, int start, boolean hasalpha, int trans, int transferType);
// Public Instance Methods
1.2 public BufferedImage convertToIntDiscrete(Raster raster, boolean forceARGB);
    public final void getAlphas(byte[ ] a);
    public final void getBlues(byte[ ] b);
    public final void getGreens(byte[ ] g);
    public final int getMapSize();
    public final void getReds(byte[ ] r);
1.2 public final void getRGBs(int[ ] rgb);
    public final int getTransparentPixel();
// Public Methods Overriding ColorModel
1.2 public SampleModel createCompatibleSampleModel(int w, int h);
1.2 public WritableRaster createCompatibleWritableRaster(int w, int h);
1.2 public void finalize();
```

```
    public final int getAlpha(int pixel);
    public final int getBlue(int pixel);
1.2 public int[ ] getComponents(Object pixel, int[ ] components, int offset);
1.2 public int[ ] getComponents(int pixel, int[ ] components, int offset);
1.2 public int[ ] getComponentSize( );
1.2 public int getDataElement(int[ ] components, int offset);
1.2 public Object getDataElements(int rgb, Object pixel);
1.2 public Object getDataElements(int[ ] components, int offset, Object pixel);
    public final int getGreen(int pixel);
    public final int getRed(int pixel);
    public final int getRGB(int pixel);
1.2 public int getTransparency( );
1.2 public boolean isCompatibleRaster(Raster raster);
1.2 public boolean isCompatibleSampleModel(SampleModel sm);
1.2 public String toString( );
}
```

Hierarchy: Object→ ColorModel(Transparency)→ IndexColorModel

Passed To: BufferedImage.BufferedImage(), RGBImageFilter.filterIndexColorModel()

Returned By: RGBImageFilter.filterIndexColorModel()

Kernel   Java 1.2

java.awt.image   *cloneable*

This class represents a matrix of float values, for use with the ConvolveOp image-processing operation. Convolution is performed by combining a pixel value with the values of the pixels that surround it. The convolution kernel specifies the relative contribution of each pixel to the end result. For example, to blur an image, you can use a kernel like this:

$$\begin{bmatrix} 0.111 & 0.111 & 0.111 \\ 0.111 & 0.111 & 0.111 \\ 0.111 & 0.111 & 0.111 \end{bmatrix}$$

This matrix specifies that the destination pixel is composed of one-ninth (0.111) of the source pixel plus one-ninth of each of the eight pixels that surround it.

To create a Kernel, pass the width and height of the kernel to the constructor, along with the array of float values that comprise the kernel. The array should be organized by rows. Note that a Kernel need not have a square array. Kernels typically have an odd number of rows and columns and are placed symmetrically about the source pixel being processed. However, if the number of rows or columns is even, the origin of the Kernel is such that the extra row or column is to the bottom or the right of the pixel being processed.

```
public class Kernel implements Cloneable {
// Public Constructors
    public Kernel(int width, int height, float[ ] data);
// Property Accessor Methods (by property name)
    public final int getHeight( );
    public final int getWidth( );
    public final int getXOrigin( );
    public final int getYOrigin( );
// Public Instance Methods
    public final float[ ] getKernelData(float[ ] data);
```

```
// Public Methods Overriding Object
    public Object clone();
}
```

Hierarchy: Object→ Kernel(Cloneable)

Passed To: ConvolveOp.ConvolveOp()

Returned By: ConvolveOp.getKernel()

LookupOp   Java 1.2

java.awt.image

This class is a BufferedImageOp and RasterOp that processes an image by one or more lookup tables to convert the value of each component of each pixel to a new value. LookupOp is useful for operations such as brightening or darkening an image, reducing the number of colors in an image, or thresholding an image. When you create a LookupOp object, you specify the lookup table or tables with a LookupTable object, typically a ByteLookupTable or ShortLookupTable. If the LookupTable contains one table, that table is used for all color bands of the image (but not alpha bands). Otherwise, the LookupTable should contain one table for each color band or one table for each of the color and transparency bands. If you specify a RenderingHints object when you create a LookupOp, the operation may use the color rendering and dithering hints it contains.

To use a LookupOp, simply pass a source and optional destination image or raster to the filter() method. Because LookupOp processes pixels independently of each other, you can use the same objects as both source and destination. Because of the nature of lookup tables, however, you cannot use LookupOp with images that use an IndexColorModel. If the lookup tables used by a LookupOp describe a simple linear function, you can also use a RescaleOp to achieve the same effect. See BufferedImageOp for further details.

```
public class LookupOp implements BufferedImageOp, RasterOp {
// Public Constructors
    public LookupOp(LookupTable lookup, RenderingHints hints);
// Public Instance Methods
    public final LookupTable getTable();
// Methods Implementing BufferedImageOp
    public BufferedImage createCompatibleDestImage(BufferedImage src, ColorModel destCM);
    public final BufferedImage filter(BufferedImage src, BufferedImage dst);
    public final java.awt.geom.Rectangle2D getBounds2D(BufferedImage src);
    public final java.awt.geom.Point2D getPoint2D(java.awt.geom.Point2D srcPt, java.awt.geom.Point2D dstPt);
    public final RenderingHints getRenderingHints();
// Methods Implementing RasterOp
    public WritableRaster createCompatibleDestRaster(Raster src);
    public final WritableRaster filter(Raster src, WritableRaster dst);
    public final java.awt.geom.Rectangle2D getBounds2D(Raster src);
}
```

Hierarchy: Object→ LookupOp(BufferedImageOp, RasterOp)

LookupTable   Java 1.2

java.awt.image

This abstract class defines one or more lookup tables used by the LookupOp image-processing operation. lookupPixel() performs the table-lookup operation. This method is passed an array of color component source values. It transforms this array into a new array of destination values by replacing each source value with the value found in the appropriate lookup table at the index that corresponds to the source value. Note, however, that an offset may be specified for the lookup tables. If so, the offset is subtracted from the source values before the lookup is performed. See the concrete subclasses ByteLookupTable and ShortLookupTable.

```
public abstract class LookupTable {
// Protected Constructors
    protected LookupTable(int offset, int numComponents);
// Public Instance Methods
    public int getNumComponents();
    public int getOffset();
    public abstract int[ ] lookupPixel(int[ ] src, int[ ] dest);
}
```

Subclasses: ByteLookupTable, ShortLookupTable

Passed To: LookupOp.LookupOp()

Returned By: LookupOp.getTable()

MemoryImageSource

Java 1.0

java.awt.image

PJ1.1

This class is an ImageProducer that produces an image from data stored in memory. The various constructors specify image data, color model, array offset, scanline length, and properties in slightly different ways. The instance methods implement the standard ImageProducer interface that allows an ImageConsumer object to register interest in the image.

```
public class MemoryImageSource implements ImageProducer {
// Public Constructors
    public MemoryImageSource(int w, int h, int[ ] pix, int off, int scan);
    public MemoryImageSource(int w, int h, ColorModel cm, int[ ] pix, int off, int scan);
    public MemoryImageSource(int w, int h, ColorModel cm, byte[ ] pix, int off, int scan);
    public MemoryImageSource(int w, int h, int[ ] pix, int off, int scan, java.util.Hashtable props);
    public MemoryImageSource(int w, int h, ColorModel cm, byte[ ] pix, int off, int scan, java.util.Hashtable props);
    public MemoryImageSource(int w, int h, ColorModel cm, int[ ] pix, int off, int scan, java.util.Hashtable props);
// Public Instance Methods
1.1 public void newPixels();
1.1 public void newPixels(byte[ ] newpix, ColorModel newmodel, int offset, int scansize);      synchronized
1.1 public void newPixels(int[ ] newpix, ColorModel newmodel, int offset, int scansize);        synchronized
1.1 public void newPixels(int x, int y, int w, int h);                                          synchronized
1.1 public void newPixels(int x, int y, int w, int h, boolean framenotify);                     synchronized
1.1 public void setAnimated(boolean animated);                                                  synchronized
1.1 public void setFullBufferUpdates(boolean fullbuffers);                                      synchronized
// Methods Implementing ImageProducer
    public void addConsumer(ImageConsumer ic);                                                  synchronized
    public boolean isConsumer(ImageConsumer ic);                                                synchronized
    public void removeConsumer(ImageConsumer ic);                                               synchronized
    public void requestTopDownLeftRightResend(ImageConsumer ic);                                     empty
    public void startProduction(ImageConsumer ic);
}
```

Hierarchy: Object→ MemoryImageSource(ImageProducer)

MultiPixelPackedSampleModel

Java 1.2

java.awt.image

This SampleModel knows how to interpret single-banded image data in a DataBuffer that is organized so that more than one pixel is packed into a single element of the data buffer. For example, a MultiPixelPackedSampleModel can be used to represent a monochrome image in which eight pixels are packed in a byte or 8-bit indexed color data in which four pixels are packed into an int. Most applications never need to use this class. See also SampleModel for further information.

```
public class MultiPixelPackedSampleModel extends SampleModel {
// Public Constructors
    public MultiPixelPackedSampleModel(int dataType, int w, int h, int numberOfBits);
    public MultiPixelPackedSampleModel(int dataType, int w, int h, int numberOfBits, int scanlineStride,
                                       int dataBitOffset);
// Public Instance Methods
    public int getBitOffset(int x);
    public int getDataBitOffset();
    public int getOffset(int x, int y);
    public int getPixelBitStride();
    public int getScanlineStride();
// Public Methods Overriding SampleModel
    public SampleModel createCompatibleSampleModel(int w, int h);
    public DataBuffer createDataBuffer();
    public int getNumDataElements();                                                             constant
    public SampleModel createSubsetSampleModel(int[ ] bands);
    public Object getDataElements(int x, int y, Object obj, DataBuffer data);
    public int[ ] getPixel(int x, int y, int[ ] iArray, DataBuffer data);
    public int getSample(int x, int y, int b, DataBuffer data);
    public int[ ] getSampleSize();
    public int getSampleSize(int band);
    public int getTransferType();
    public void setDataElements(int x, int y, Object obj, DataBuffer data);
    public void setPixel(int x, int y, int[ ] iArray, DataBuffer data);
    public void setSample(int x, int y, int b, int s, DataBuffer data);
}
```

Hierarchy: Object → SampleModel → MultiPixelPackedSampleModel

PackedColorModel   Java 1.2

java.awt.image

This abstract ColorModel is used with image data in which color component and transparency values are packed into contiguous bits of a byte, short, or int. It uses bitmasks and bit-shifting operations to extract the color and transparency components from the pixel value. DirectColorModel is a concrete subclass that works with RGB color spaces. Only applications that are doing custom image processing need to use this, or any, ColorModel.

```
public abstract class PackedColorModel extends ColorModel {
// Public Constructors
    public PackedColorModel(java.awt.color.ColorSpace space, int bits, int[ ] colorMaskArray, int alphaMask,
                            boolean isAlphaPremultiplied, int trans, int transferType);
    public PackedColorModel(java.awt.color.ColorSpace space, int bits, int rmask, int gmask, int bmask, int amask,
                            boolean isAlphaPremultiplied, int trans, int transferType);
// Public Instance Methods
    public final int getMask(int index);
    public final int[ ] getMasks();
// Public Methods Overriding ColorModel
    public SampleModel createCompatibleSampleModel(int w, int h);
    public boolean equals(Object obj);
    public WritableRaster getAlphaRaster(WritableRaster raster);
    public boolean isCompatibleSampleModel(SampleModel sm);
}
```

java.awt.
image

Hierarchy: Object→ ColorModel(Transparency)→ PackedColorModel

Subclasses: DirectColorModel

PixelGrabber

Java 1.0

java.awt.image

PJ1.1

This class is an ImageConsumer that extracts a specified rectangular array of pixels (in the default RGB color model) from a specified Image or ImageProducer and stores them in a specified array (using the specified offset into the array and specified scanline size). Use this class when you want to inspect or manipulate the data of an image or some rectangular portion of an image.

The method grabPixels() makes the PixelGrabber start grabbing pixels. status() returns the status of the pixel-grabbing process. The return value uses the same flag value constants that the ImageObserver class does. The remaining methods are the standard ImageConsumer methods and should not be called directly.

```
public class PixelGrabber implements ImageConsumer {
// Public Constructors
1.1  public PixelGrabber(Image img, int x, int y, int w, int h, boolean forceRGB);
     public PixelGrabber(ImageProducer ip, int x, int y, int w, int h, int[ ] pix, int off, int scansize);
     public PixelGrabber(Image img, int x, int y, int w, int h, int[ ] pix, int off, int scansize);
// Property Accessor Methods (by property name)
1.1  public ColorModel getColorModel();                                              synchronized
     public void setColorModel(ColorModel model);                      Implements:ImageConsumer empty
1.1  public int getHeight();                                                         synchronized
1.1  public Object getPixels();                                                      synchronized
1.1  public int getStatus();                                                         synchronized
1.1  public int getWidth();                                                          synchronized
// Public Instance Methods
1.1  public void abortGrabbing();                                                    synchronized
     public boolean grabPixels() throws InterruptedException;
     public boolean grabPixels(long ms) throws InterruptedException;                 synchronized
1.1  public void startGrabbing();                                                    synchronized
     public int status();                                                            synchronized
// Methods Implementing ImageConsumer
     public void imageComplete(int status);                                          synchronized
     public void setColorModel(ColorModel model);                                    empty
     public void setDimensions(int width, int height);
     public void setHints(int hints);                                                empty
     public void setPixels(int srcX, int srcY, int srcW, int srcH, ColorModel model, int[ ] pixels, int srcOff, int srcScan);
     public void setPixels(int srcX, int srcY, int srcW, int srcH, ColorModel model, byte[ ] pixels, int srcOff, int srcScan);
     public void setProperties(java.util.Hashtable props);                           empty
}
```

Hierarchy: Object→ PixelGrabber(ImageConsumer)

PixelInterleavedSampleModel

Java 1.2

java.awt.image

This SampleModel represents image data stored so that each component of each pixel is stored in a separate element of the DataBuffer and all pixel components are stored in the same bank of the DataBuffer. For example, it can be used to represent RGB pixels in which the red, green, and blue components are interleaved into a single bank of byte values. Most applications never need to use this class or its subclasses. See SampleModel for further information.

```
public class PixelInterleavedSampleModel extends ComponentSampleModel {
// Public Constructors
    public PixelInterleavedSampleModel(int dataType, int w, int h, int pixelStride, int scanlineStride,
                                       int[ ] bandOffsets);
// Public Methods Overriding ComponentSampleModel
    public SampleModel createCompatibleSampleModel(int w, int h);
    public SampleModel createSubsetSampleModel(int[ ] bands);
}
```

Hierarchy: Object→ SampleModel→ ComponentSampleModel→ PixelInterleavedSampleModel

Raster   Java 1.2
java.awt.image

This class represents a rectangular array of pixels. A Raster is composed of a DataBuffer that contains raw pixel data and a matching SampleModel that knows how to extract pixel data from that DataBuffer. A Raster object is used within a BufferedImage object, which also contains a ColorModel object to interpret the pixel values of the Raster as colors. Most applications can simply used BufferedImage objects and never have to work with Raster objects directly.

Raster does not have any public constructors. You can call the static method createRaster() or createWritableRaster() to create a Raster using arbitrary DataBuffer and SampleModel objects. However, you usually obtain more efficient results if you use createBandedRaster(), createInterleavedRaster(), or createPackedRaster() to create a Raster using one of the data formats supported by the built-in DataBuffer and SampleModel subclasses.

Raster contains a number of methods to read individual pixels and blocks of pixels. Note, however, that there are no methods to set pixel values. If you want to modify pixels in a Raster, you must use the WritableRaster subclass. A Raster can have a parent Raster that contains the actual data. The createChild() method uses this feature to return a Raster object that represents a rectangular subset of the current raster. (It can also return a child Raster that contains only a subset of the bands of the parent raster: for example, a Raster that contains only the alpha band of transparency values of its parent.) Finally, while BufferedImage objects have only a width and height, Raster objects have a size and location. Thus, you can specify an origin when you create a Raster.

```
public class Raster {
// Protected Constructors
    protected Raster(SampleModel sampleModel, Point origin);
    protected Raster(SampleModel sampleModel, DataBuffer dataBuffer, Point origin);
    protected Raster(SampleModel sampleModel, DataBuffer dataBuffer, Rectangle aRegion,
                     Point sampleModelTranslate, Raster parent);
// Public Class Methods
    public static WritableRaster createBandedRaster(int dataType, int w, int h, int bands, Point location);
    public static WritableRaster createBandedRaster(int dataType, int w, int h, int scanlineStride, int[ ] bankIndices,
                                       int[ ] bandOffsets, Point location);
    public static WritableRaster createBandedRaster(DataBuffer dataBuffer, int w, int h, int scanlineStride,
                                       int[ ] bankIndices, int[ ] bandOffsets, Point location);
    public static WritableRaster createInterleavedRaster(int dataType, int w, int h, int bands, Point location);
    public static WritableRaster createInterleavedRaster(int dataType, int w, int h, int scanlineStride, int pixelStride,
                                       int[ ] bandOffsets, Point location);
    public static WritableRaster createInterleavedRaster(DataBuffer dataBuffer, int w, int h, int scanlineStride,
                                       int pixelStride, int[ ] bandOffsets, Point location);
    public static WritableRaster createPackedRaster(DataBuffer dataBuffer, int w, int h, int bitsPerPixel,
                                       Point location);
    public static WritableRaster createPackedRaster(int dataType, int w, int h, int[ ] bandMasks, Point location);
```

```
    public static WritableRaster createPackedRaster(DataBuffer dataBuffer, int w, int h, int scanlineStride,
                                        int[ ] bandMasks, Point location);
    public static WritableRaster createPackedRaster(int dataType, int w, int h, int bands, int bitsPerBand,
                                        Point location);
    public static Raster createRaster(SampleModel sm, DataBuffer db, Point location);
    public static WritableRaster createWritableRaster(SampleModel sm, Point location);
    public static WritableRaster createWritableRaster(SampleModel sm, DataBuffer db, Point location);
// Property Accessor Methods (by property name)
    public Rectangle getBounds();
    public DataBuffer getDataBuffer();
    public final int getHeight();
    public final int getMinX();
    public final int getMinY();
    public final int getNumBands();
    public final int getNumDataElements();
    public Raster getParent();
    public SampleModel getSampleModel();
    public final int getSampleModelTranslateX();
    public final int getSampleModelTranslateY();
    public final int getTransferType();
    public final int getWidth();
// Public Instance Methods
    public Raster createChild(int parentX, int parentY, int width, int height, int childMinX, int childMinY,
                                        int[ ] bandList);
    public WritableRaster createCompatibleWritableRaster();
    public WritableRaster createCompatibleWritableRaster(Rectangle rect);
    public WritableRaster createCompatibleWritableRaster(int w, int h);
    public WritableRaster createCompatibleWritableRaster(int x, int y, int w, int h);
    public Raster createTranslatedChild(int childMinX, int childMinY);
    public Object getDataElements(int x, int y, Object outData);
    public Object getDataElements(int x, int y, int w, int h, Object outData);
    public int[ ] getPixel(int x, int y, int[ ] iArray);
    public float[ ] getPixel(int x, int y, float[ ] fArray);
    public double[ ] getPixel(int x, int y, double[ ] dArray);
    public int[ ] getPixels(int x, int y, int w, int h, int[ ] iArray);
    public float[ ] getPixels(int x, int y, int w, int h, float[ ] fArray);
    public double[ ] getPixels(int x, int y, int w, int h, double[ ] dArray);
    public int getSample(int x, int y, int b);
    public double getSampleDouble(int x, int y, int b);
    public float getSampleFloat(int x, int y, int b);
    public int[ ] getSamples(int x, int y, int w, int h, int b, int[ ] iArray);
    public float[ ] getSamples(int x, int y, int w, int h, int b, float[ ] fArray);
    public double[ ] getSamples(int x, int y, int w, int h, int b, double[ ] dArray);
// Protected Instance Fields
    protected DataBuffer dataBuffer;
    protected int height;
    protected int minX;
    protected int minY;
    protected int numBands;
    protected int numDataElements;
    protected Raster parent;
    protected SampleModel sampleModel;
    protected int sampleModelTranslateX;
    protected int sampleModelTranslateY;
    protected int width;
}
```

Subclasses: WritableRaster

Passed To: Too many methods to list.

Returned By: PaintContext.getRaster(), BufferedImage.{getData(), getTile()}, Raster.{createChild(), createRaster(), createTranslatedChild(), getParent()}, RenderedImage.{getData(), getTile()}

Type Of: Raster.parent

RasterFormatException
Java 1.2

java.awt.image
serializable unchecked

Signals that a Raster is improperly configured.

```
public class RasterFormatException extends RuntimeException {
// Public Constructors
    public RasterFormatException(String s);
}
```

Hierarchy: Object→ Throwable(Serializable)→ Exception→ RuntimeException→ RasterFormatException

RasterOp
Java 1.2

java.awt.image

This interface defines an image-processing operation that can be performed on a Raster. It is very similar to the BufferedImageOp, except that the operation is performed directly on the uninterpreted pixels of Raster data, rather than on the color values of a Buffered-Image. Many of the implementations of BufferedImageOp are also implementations of RasterOp. See BufferedImageOp for details.

```
public abstract interface RasterOp {
// Public Instance Methods
    public abstract WritableRaster createCompatibleDestRaster(Raster src);
    public abstract WritableRaster filter(Raster src, WritableRaster dest);
    public abstract java.awt.geom.Rectangle2D getBounds2D(Raster src);
    public abstract java.awt.geom.Point2D getPoint2D(java.awt.geom.Point2D srcPt, java.awt.geom.Point2D dstPt);
    public abstract RenderingHints getRenderingHints();
}
```

Implementations: AffineTransformOp, BandCombineOp, ColorConvertOp, ConvolveOp, LookupOp, RescaleOp

RenderedImage
Java 1.2

java.awt.image

This interface describes the methods of rendered images. RenderedImage exists primarily for use by the forthcoming Java Advanced Imaging API (javax.jai.*), but it is also implemented (through WritableRenderedImage) by BufferedImage, meaning that BufferedImage images will be able to interoperate with JAI-rendered images.

The getSources() method and the tile-related methods of RenderedImage are used in the JAI, and are not of interest in Java 2D. BufferedImage objects contain only a single tile, so the BufferedImage class defines implementations of these methods. Methods that are of interest include getData(), getSampleModel(), and getColorModel(). These methods return a copy of the Raster that contains pixels, the SampleModel that specifies the internal organization of the Raster, and the ColorModel that specifies how to interpret the pixels as colors, respectively. getWidth(), getHeight(), and copyData() are also useful in Java 2D programs.

```
public abstract interface RenderedImage {
// Property Accessor Methods (by property name)
    public abstract ColorModel getColorModel();
    public abstract Raster getData();
    public abstract Raster getData(Rectangle rect);
    public abstract int getHeight();
    public abstract int getMinTileX();
    public abstract int getMinTileY();
    public abstract int getMinX();
    public abstract int getMinY();
    public abstract int getNumXTiles();
    public abstract int getNumYTiles();
    public abstract String[ ] getPropertyNames();
    public abstract SampleModel getSampleModel();
    public abstract java.util.Vector getSources();
    public abstract int getTileGridXOffset();
    public abstract int getTileGridYOffset();
    public abstract int getTileHeight();
    public abstract int getTileWidth();
    public abstract int getWidth();
// Public Instance Methods
    public abstract WritableRaster copyData(WritableRaster raster);
    public abstract Object getProperty(String name);
    public abstract Raster getTile(int tileX, int tileY);
}
```

Implementations: WritableRenderedImage

Passed To: Graphics2D.drawRenderedImage()

Returned By: java.awt.image.renderable.ContextualRenderedImageFactory.create(),
java.awt.image.renderable.ParameterBlock.getRenderedSource(),
java.awt.image.renderable.RenderableImage.{createDefaultRendering(), createRendering(),
createScaledRendering()}, java.awt.image.renderable.RenderableImageOp.{createDefaultRendering(),
createRendering(), createScaledRendering()}, java.awt.image.renderable.RenderedImageFactory.create()

ReplicateScaleFilter   Java 1.1

java.awt.image   cloneable PJ1.1

This class implements an ImageFilter that scales an image to a specified pixel size. It uses
a simple scaling algorithm in which rows and columns of image pixels are duplicated
or omitted as necessary to achieve the desired size. See AreaAveragingScaleFilter for a scaling filter that results in smoother images. The methods of this class are ImageConsumer
methods used for communication between the image filter and the FilteredImageSource
that uses it. Applications usually do not call these methods directly. The easiest way to
use this filter is to call the getScaledInstance() method of Image, specifying an appropriate
hint constant.

```
public class ReplicateScaleFilter extends ImageFilter {
// Public Constructors
    public ReplicateScaleFilter(int width, int height);
// Public Methods Overriding ImageFilter
    public void setDimensions(int w, int h);
    public void setPixels(int x, int y, int w, int h, ColorModel model, int[ ] pixels, int off, int scansize);
    public void setPixels(int x, int y, int w, int h, ColorModel model, byte[ ] pixels, int off, int scansize);
    public void setProperties(java.util.Hashtable props);
// Protected Instance Fields
    protected int destHeight;
```

```
    protected int destWidth;
    protected Object outpixbuf;
    protected int[ ] srccols;
    protected int srcHeight;
    protected int[ ] srcrows;
    protected int srcWidth;
}
```

Hierarchy: Object→ ImageFilter(Cloneable, ImageConsumer)→ ReplicateScaleFilter

Subclasses: AreaAveragingScaleFilter

RescaleOp   Java 1.2

java.awt.image

This class is a BufferedImageOp and a RasterOp that performs a linear scaling on the components of each pixel in an image by multiplying them by a scale factor and adding a constant. When you create a RescaleOp, you specify either a single scale factor and a single offset or an array of scale factors and an array of constants. If only one scale factor and constant are specified, then all color bands of the image are rescaled identically. Otherwise, there should be one scale factor and constant for each color band or for each color band plus the alpha transparency band. In this case, each color band, and possibly the alpha band, is rescaled independently.

To use a RescaleOp, simply pass a source and optional destination image or raster to the filter() method. Because RescaleOp processes pixels independently of each other, you can use the same objects as both source and destination. Because of the nature of the rescaling, however, you cannot use LookupOp with images that use an IndexColorModel. RescaleOp performs a linear rescaling. If you want to perform a nonlinear rescaling, you can do so with a LookupOp and a LookupTable that describes the desired scaling. See BufferedImageOp for further details.

```
public class RescaleOp implements BufferedImageOp, RasterOp {
// Public Constructors
    public RescaleOp(float scaleFactor, float offset, RenderingHints hints);
    public RescaleOp(float[ ] scaleFactors, float[ ] offsets, RenderingHints hints);
// Public Instance Methods
    public final int getNumFactors();
    public final float[ ] getOffsets(float[ ] offsets);
    public final float[ ] getScaleFactors(float[ ] scaleFactors);
// Methods Implementing BufferedImageOp
    public BufferedImage createCompatibleDestImage(BufferedImage src, ColorModel destCM);
    public final BufferedImage filter(BufferedImage src, BufferedImage dst);
    public final java.awt.geom.Rectangle2D getBounds2D(BufferedImage src);
    public final java.awt.geom.Point2D getPoint2D(java.awt.geom.Point2D srcPt, java.awt.geom.Point2D dstPt);
    public final RenderingHints getRenderingHints();
// Methods Implementing RasterOp
    public WritableRaster createCompatibleDestRaster(Raster src);
    public final WritableRaster filter(Raster src, WritableRaster dst);
    public final java.awt.geom.Rectangle2D getBounds2D(Raster src);
}
```

Hierarchy: Object→ RescaleOp(BufferedImageOp, RasterOp)

RGBImageFilter   Java 1.0

java.awt.image   *cloneable PJ1.1*

This abstract class is an ImageFilter that provides an easy way to implement filters that modify the colors of an image. To create a color filter that modifies the colors of an

---

image, you should subclass RGBImageFilter and provide a definition of filterRGB() that converts the input pixel value (in the default RGB color model) to an output value. If the conversion does not depend on the location of the pixel, set the canFilterIndexColorModel variable to true so that the RGBImageFilter can save time by filtering the colormap of an image that uses an IndexColorModel, instead of filtering each pixel of the image.

```
public abstract class RGBImageFilter extends ImageFilter {
// Public Constructors
    public RGBImageFilter();
// Public Instance Methods
    public IndexColorModel filterIndexColorModel(IndexColorModel icm);
    public abstract int filterRGB(int x, int y, int rgb);
    public void filterRGBPixels(int x, int y, int w, int h, int[ ] pixels, int off, int scansize);
    public void substituteColorModel(ColorModel oldcm, ColorModel newcm);
// Public Methods Overriding ImageFilter
    public void setColorModel(ColorModel model);
    public void setPixels(int x, int y, int w, int h, ColorModel model, int[ ] pixels, int off, int scansize);
    public void setPixels(int x, int y, int w, int h, ColorModel model, byte[ ] pixels, int off, int scansize);
// Protected Instance Fields
    protected boolean canFilterIndexColorModel;
    protected ColorModel newmodel;
    protected ColorModel origmodel;
}
```

Hierarchy: Object→ ImageFilter(Cloneable, ImageConsumer)→ RGBImageFilter

Subclasses: javax.swing.GrayFilter

SampleModel

Java 1.2

java.awt.image

This abstract class defines methods for extracting the pixels of an image from an arbitrary DataBuffer, regardless of how those pixels are stored in the DataBuffer. Image data is stored in a Raster object, which consists of a DataBuffer to hold the raw data and a SampleModel to interpret the storage format. Only appliations that read or write image data directly from files or other sources ever need to use this class. See also the concrete subclasses ComponentSampleModel, SinglePixelPackedSampleModel, and MultiPixelPackedSampleModel.

```
public abstract class SampleModel {
// Public Constructors
    public SampleModel(int dataType, int w, int h, int numBands);
// Property Accessor Methods (by property name)
    public final int getDataType();
    public final int getHeight();
    public final int getNumBands();
    public abstract int getNumDataElements();
    public abstract int[ ] getSampleSize();
    public abstract int getSampleSize(int band);
    public int getTransferType();
    public final int getWidth();
// Public Instance Methods
    public abstract SampleModel createCompatibleSampleModel(int w, int h);
    public abstract DataBuffer createDataBuffer();
    public abstract SampleModel createSubsetSampleModel(int[ ] bands);
    public abstract Object getDataElements(int x, int y, Object obj, DataBuffer data);
    public Object getDataElements(int x, int y, int w, int h, Object obj, DataBuffer data);
    public int[ ] getPixel(int x, int y, int[ ] iArray, DataBuffer data);
    public float[ ] getPixel(int x, int y, float[ ] fArray, DataBuffer data);
```

```
     public double[ ] getPixel(int x, int y, double[ ] dArray, DataBuffer data);
     public int[ ] getPixels(int x, int y, int w, int h, int[ ] iArray, DataBuffer data);
     public float[ ] getPixels(int x, int y, int w, int h, float[ ] fArray, DataBuffer data);
     public double[ ] getPixels(int x, int y, int w, int h, double[ ] dArray, DataBuffer data);
     public abstract int getSample(int x, int y, int b, DataBuffer data);
     public double getSampleDouble(int x, int y, int b, DataBuffer data);
     public float getSampleFloat(int x, int y, int b, DataBuffer data);
     public int[ ] getSamples(int x, int y, int w, int h, int b, int[ ] iArray, DataBuffer data);
     public float[ ] getSamples(int x, int y, int w, int h, int b, float[ ] fArray, DataBuffer data);
     public double[ ] getSamples(int x, int y, int w, int h, int b, double[ ] dArray, DataBuffer data);
     public abstract void setDataElements(int x, int y, Object obj, DataBuffer data);
     public void setDataElements(int x, int y, int w, int h, Object obj, DataBuffer data);
     public void setPixel(int x, int y, int[ ] iArray, DataBuffer data);
     public void setPixel(int x, int y, float[ ] fArray, DataBuffer data);
     public void setPixel(int x, int y, double[ ] dArray, DataBuffer data);
     public void setPixels(int x, int y, int w, int h, int[ ] iArray, DataBuffer data);
     public void setPixels(int x, int y, int w, int h, float[ ] fArray, DataBuffer data);
     public void setPixels(int x, int y, int w, int h, double[ ] dArray, DataBuffer data);
     public abstract void setSample(int x, int y, int b, int s, DataBuffer data);
     public void setSample(int x, int y, int b, float s, DataBuffer data);
     public void setSample(int x, int y, int b, double s, DataBuffer data);
     public void setSamples(int x, int y, int w, int h, int b, int[ ] iArray, DataBuffer data);
     public void setSamples(int x, int y, int w, int h, int b, float[ ] fArray, DataBuffer data);
     public void setSamples(int x, int y, int w, int h, int b, double[ ] dArray, DataBuffer data);
// Protected Instance Fields
     protected int dataType;
     protected int height;
     protected int numBands;
     protected int width;
}
```

Subclasses: ComponentSampleModel, MultiPixelPackedSampleModel, SinglePixelPackedSampleModel

Passed To: ColorModel.isCompatibleSampleModel(), ComponentColorModel.isCompatibleSampleModel(), IndexColorModel.isCompatibleSampleModel(), PackedColorModel.isCompatibleSampleModel(), Raster.{createRaster(), createWritableRaster(), Raster()}, WritableRaster.WritableRaster()

Returned By: Too many methods to list.

Type Of: Raster.sampleModel

ShortLookupTable

Java 1.2

java.awt.image

This concrete subclass of LookupTable contains one or more short arrays that serve as lookup tables for a LookupOp image-processing operation. Applications never need to use a ShortLookupTable directly; they need to create one only to pass to the LookupOp() constructor. Create a ShortLookupTable by passing the short array or arrays to the Short-LookupTable() constructor, along with an offset that is subtracted from each source color component before the lookup is performed. See also ByteLookupTable().

```
public class ShortLookupTable extends LookupTable {
// Public Constructors
     public ShortLookupTable(int offset, short[ ][ ] data);
     public ShortLookupTable(int offset, short[ ] data);
// Public Instance Methods
     public final short[ ][ ] getTable();
     public short[ ] lookupPixel(short[ ] src, short[ ] dst);
```

```
// Public Methods Overriding LookupTable
    public int[ ] lookupPixel(int[ ] src, int[ ] dst);
}
```

Hierarchy: Object→ LookupTable→ ShortLookupTable

SinglePixelPackedSampleModel   Java 1.2

java.awt.image

This SampleModel knows how to interpret image data in a DataBuffer that is organized so
that each pixel is stored in a single data element and each data element contains
exactly one pixel. For example, it can be used to represent RGB and ARGB data
packed into a int element or 8-bit grayscale data stored in byte elements. The *bitMasks*
array passed to the constructor specifies the bitmask used to extract each color component from the data element. For example, to extract the red color component of an
RGB color from an int, you specify a bitmask of 0x00FF0000. Most applications never
need to use this class. See SampleModel for further information.

```
public class SinglePixelPackedSampleModel extends SampleModel {
// Public Constructors
    public SinglePixelPackedSampleModel(int dataType, int w, int h, int[ ] bitMasks);
    public SinglePixelPackedSampleModel(int dataType, int w, int h, int scanlineStride, int[ ] bitMasks);
// Public Instance Methods
    public int[ ] getBitMasks();
    public int[ ] getBitOffsets();
    public int getOffset(int x, int y);
    public int getScanlineStride();
// Public Methods Overriding SampleModel
    public SampleModel createCompatibleSampleModel(int w, int h);
    public int getNumDataElements();                                            constant
    public DataBuffer createDataBuffer();
    public SampleModel createSubsetSampleModel(int[ ] bands);
    public Object getDataElements(int x, int y, Object obj, DataBuffer data);
    public int[ ] getPixel(int x, int y, int[ ] iArray, DataBuffer data);
    public int[ ] getPixels(int x, int y, int w, int h, int[ ] iArray, DataBuffer data);
    public int getSample(int x, int y, int b, DataBuffer data);
    public int[ ] getSamples(int x, int y, int w, int h, int b, int[ ] iArray, DataBuffer data);
    public int[ ] getSampleSize();
    public int getSampleSize(int band);
    public void setDataElements(int x, int y, Object obj, DataBuffer data);
    public void setPixel(int x, int y, int[ ] iArray, DataBuffer data);
    public void setPixels(int x, int y, int w, int h, int[ ] iArray, DataBuffer data);
    public void setSample(int x, int y, int b, int s, DataBuffer data);
    public void setSamples(int x, int y, int w, int h, int b, int[ ] iArray, DataBuffer data);
}
```

Hierarchy: Object→ SampleModel→ SinglePixelPackedSampleModel

TileObserver   Java 1.2

java.awt.image

This interface is implemented by objects that wish to be notified when a WritableRenderedImage is about to be written to. It is used as part of the Java Advanced Imaging API
(javax.jai.*) and is not of interest to Java 2D programs. In particular, note that while
BufferedImage objects allow TileObserver objects to be registered, they never send out notifications to them. Only programs using the JAI will ever implement this interface. It is
used in the java.awt.image package simply for future compatibility with the JAI.

```
public abstract interface TileObserver {
// Public Instance Methods
    public abstract void tileUpdate(WritableRenderedImage source, int tileX, int tileY, boolean willBeWritable);
}
```

Passed To: BufferedImage.{addTileObserver(), removeTileObserver()},
WritableRenderedImage.{addTileObserver(), removeTileObserver()}

WritableRaster   Java 1.2

java.awt.image

This class extends Raster to add methods for setting pixel values in the Raster. It does
not have any public constructors. You create WritableRaster objects with the static methods defined by the Raster class. WritableRaster is used by BufferedImage, and, in practice,
most rasters used in a program are WritableRaster objects. Most applications can use the
features of BufferedImage and never need to use WritableRaster or Raster directly. See Raster
for more information.

```
public class WritableRaster extends Raster {
// Protected Constructors
    protected WritableRaster(SampleModel sampleModel, Point origin);
    protected WritableRaster(SampleModel sampleModel, DataBuffer dataBuffer, Point origin);
    protected WritableRaster(SampleModel sampleModel, DataBuffer dataBuffer, Rectangle aRegion,
                            Point sampleModelTranslate, WritableRaster parent);
// Public Instance Methods
    public WritableRaster createWritableChild(int parentX, int parentY, int w, int h, int childMinX, int childMinY,
                            int[ ] bandList);
    public WritableRaster createWritableTranslatedChild(int childMinX, int childMinY);
    public WritableRaster getWritableParent();
    public void setDataElements(int x, int y, Raster inRaster);
    public void setDataElements(int x, int y, Object inData);
    public void setDataElements(int x, int y, int w, int h, Object inData);
    public void setPixel(int x, int y, float[ ] fArray);
    public void setPixel(int x, int y, int[ ] iArray);
    public void setPixel(int x, int y, double[ ] dArray);
    public void setPixels(int x, int y, int w, int h, double[ ] dArray);
    public void setPixels(int x, int y, int w, int h, float[ ] fArray);
    public void setPixels(int x, int y, int w, int h, int[ ] iArray);
    public void setRect(Raster srcRaster);
    public void setRect(int dx, int dy, Raster srcRaster);
    public void setSample(int x, int y, int b, double s);
    public void setSample(int x, int y, int.b, float s);
    public void setSample(int x, int y, int b, int s);
    public void setSamples(int x, int y, int w, int h, int b, double[ ] dArray);
    public void setSamples(int x, int y, int w, int h, int b, float[ ] fArray);
    public void setSamples(int x, int y, int w, int h, int b, int[ ] iArray);
}
```

Hierarchy: Object→ Raster→ WritableRaster

Passed To: Too many methods to list.

Returned By: Too many methods to list.

WritableRenderedImage   Java 1.2

java.awt.image

This interface defines methods that allow image data to be written into a RenderedImage
in a way that allows for notification of updates. Most of the methods of this interface

exist for use with the forthcoming Java Advanced Imaging (JAI) API (javax.jai.*) and are not of interest to programs using Java 2D. Nevertheless, BufferedImage implements this interface, so that Java 2D BufferedImage objects can interoperate with future JAI Rendered-Image objects. BufferedImage objects contain only a single tile and provide trivial implementations of all the tile-related methods. setData() is the only method of interest to Java 2D programs.

```
public abstract interface WritableRenderedImage extends RenderedImage {
// Public Instance Methods
    public abstract void addTileObserver(TileObserver to);
    public abstract WritableRaster getWritableTile(int tileX, int tileY);
    public abstract Point[ ] getWritableTileIndices();
    public abstract boolean hasTileWriters();
    public abstract boolean isTileWritable(int tileX, int tileY);
    public abstract void releaseWritableTile(int tileX, int tileY);
    public abstract void removeTileObserver(TileObserver to);
    public abstract void setData(Raster r);
}
```

Hierarchy: (WritableRenderedImage(RenderedImage))

Implementations: BufferedImage

Passed To: TileObserver.tileUpdate()

CHAPTER 19

The java.awt.image.renderable Package

The java.awt.image.renderable package contains classes and interfaces used by the Java Advanced Imaging (JAI) standard extension (javax.jai.*). In general, these classes and interfaces are not of interest to Java 2D programs, but the package is part of the core Java platform so that the JAI can be tightly coupled to the core image-processing features. Only image-processing applications that use the JAI ever need to use the classes and interfaces in this package. Figure 19-1 shows the class hierarchy of this package, which is new in Java 1.2.

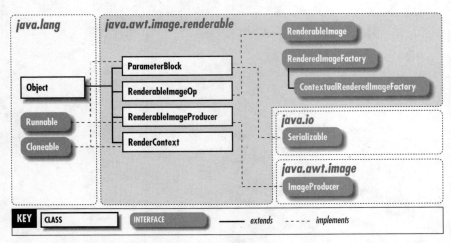

Figure 19–1: The java.awt.image.renderable package

ContextualRenderedImageFactory

java.awt.image.renderable

This interface is implemented by classes that, given a RenderContext and a ParameterBlock of arguments, can produce a java.awt.image.RenderedImage. Implementations of this interface are used to perform rendering-independent image filtering by RenderableImageOp.

```
public abstract interface ContextualRenderedImageFactory extends RenderedImageFactory {
// Public Instance Methods
    public abstract RenderedImage create(RenderContext renderContext, ParameterBlock paramBlock);
    public abstract java.awt.geom.Rectangle2D getBounds2D(ParameterBlock paramBlock);
    public abstract Object getProperty(ParameterBlock paramBlock, String name);
    public abstract String[ ] getPropertyNames();
    public abstract boolean isDynamic();
    public abstract RenderContext mapRenderContext(int i, RenderContext renderContext,
                                        ParameterBlock paramBlock, RenderableImage image);
}
```

Hierarchy: (ContextualRenderedImageFactory(RenderedImageFactory))

Passed To: RenderableImageOp.RenderableImageOp()

ParameterBlock

java.awt.image.renderable

cloneable serializable

This utility class maintains a list of parameter objects and a list of source objects for use by a RenderableImageOp. Various methods allow sources and parameters to added, set, and queried.

```
public class ParameterBlock implements Cloneable, Serializable {
// Public Constructors
    public ParameterBlock();
    public ParameterBlock(java.util.Vector sources);
    public ParameterBlock(java.util.Vector sources, java.util.Vector parameters);
// Property Accessor Methods (by property name)
    public int getNumParameters();                                                  default:0
    public int getNumSources();                                                     default:0
    public Class[ ] getParamClasses();
    public java.util.Vector getParameters();
    public void setParameters(java.util.Vector parameters);
    public java.util.Vector getSources();
    public void setSources(java.util.Vector sources);
// Public Instance Methods
    public ParameterBlock add(int i);
    public ParameterBlock add(float f);
    public ParameterBlock add(long l);
    public ParameterBlock add(short s);
    public ParameterBlock add(Object obj);
    public ParameterBlock add(double d);
    public ParameterBlock add(byte b);
    public ParameterBlock add(char c);
    public ParameterBlock addSource(Object source);
    public byte getByteParameter(int index);
    public char getCharParameter(int index);
    public double getDoubleParameter(int index);
    public float getFloatParameter(int index);
    public int getIntParameter(int index);
    public long getLongParameter(int index);
    public Object getObjectParameter(int index);
    public RenderableImage getRenderableSource(int index);
```

```
    public RenderedImage getRenderedSource(int index);
    public short getShortParameter(int index);
    public Object getSource(int index);
    public void removeParameters();
    public void removeSources();
    public ParameterBlock set(long l, int index);
    public ParameterBlock set(int i, int index);
    public ParameterBlock set(short s, int index);
    public ParameterBlock set(Object obj, int index);
    public ParameterBlock set(char c, int index);
    public ParameterBlock set(byte b, int index);
    public ParameterBlock set(float f, int index);
    public ParameterBlock set(double d, int index);
    public ParameterBlock setSource(Object source, int index);
    public Object shallowClone();
// Public Methods Overriding Object
    public Object clone();
// Protected Instance Fields
    protected java.util.Vector parameters;
    protected java.util.Vector sources;
}
```

Hierarchy: Object→ ParameterBlock(Cloneable, Serializable)

Passed To: ContextualRenderedImageFactory.{create(), getBounds2D(), getProperty(), mapRenderContext()}, RenderableImageOp.{RenderableImageOp(), setParameterBlock()}, RenderedImageFactory.create()

Returned By: Too many methods to list.

RenderableImage   Java 1.2

java.awt.image.renderable

This interface represents a rendering-independent (and resolution-independent) image. A RenderableImage may be passed to the drawRenderableImage() method of Graphics2D. However, a working, concrete implementation RenderableImage requires the forthcoming Java Advanced Imaging API. Java 2D programs that are not using the JAI will never use this interface.

```
public abstract interface RenderableImage {
// Public Constants
    public static final String HINTS_OBSERVED;                     ="HINTS_OBSERVED"
// Property Accessor Methods (by property name)
    public abstract boolean isDynamic();
    public abstract float getHeight();
    public abstract float getMinX();
    public abstract float getMinY();
    public abstract String[ ] getPropertyNames();
    public abstract java.util.Vector getSources();
    public abstract float getWidth();
// Public Instance Methods
    public abstract RenderedImage createDefaultRendering();
    public abstract RenderedImage createRendering(RenderContext renderContext);
    public abstract RenderedImage createScaledRendering(int w, int h, RenderingHints hints);
    public abstract Object getProperty(String name);
}
```

Implementations: RenderableImageOp

Passed To: Graphics2D.drawRenderableImage(), ContextualRenderedImageFactory.mapRenderContext(), RenderableImageProducer.RenderableImageProducer()

Returned By: ParameterBlock.getRenderableSource()

RenderableImageOp

Java 1.2

java.awt.image.renderable

This class defines an image-processing operation on a RenderableImage and is itself a RenderableImage, allowing processing operations to be pipelined, or streamed. Although this is a concrete class, the image-processing operation itself is defined in an external ContextualRenderedImageFactor object.

```
public class RenderableImageOp implements RenderableImage {
// Public Constructors
    public RenderableImageOp(ContextualRenderedImageFactory CRIF, ParameterBlock paramBlock);
// Public Instance Methods
    public ParameterBlock getParameterBlock();
    public ParameterBlock setParameterBlock(ParameterBlock paramBlock);
// Methods Implementing RenderableImage
    public RenderedImage createDefaultRendering();
    public RenderedImage createRendering(RenderContext renderContext);
    public RenderedImage createScaledRendering(int w, int h, RenderingHints hints);
    public float getHeight();
    public float getMinX();
    public float getMinY();
    public Object getProperty(String name);
    public String[ ] getPropertyNames();
    public java.util.Vector getSources();
    public float getWidth();
    public boolean isDynamic();
}
```

Hierarchy: Object→ RenderableImageOp(RenderableImage)

RenderableImageProducer

Java 1.2

java.awt.image.renderable

runnable

This class is an adapter that allows RenderableImage objects of the Java Advanced Imaging API to be used with the Java 1.0 ImageProducer/ImageConsumer image-processing model. The JAI is a forthcoming standard extension. This class exists in a core AWT package solely for future interoperability.

```
public class RenderableImageProducer implements ImageProducer, Runnable {
// Public Constructors
    public RenderableImageProducer(RenderableImage rdblImage, RenderContext rc);
// Public Instance Methods
    public void setRenderContext(RenderContext rc);                              synchronized
// Methods Implementing ImageProducer
    public void addConsumer(ImageConsumer ic);                                   synchronized
    public boolean isConsumer(ImageConsumer ic);                                 synchronized
    public void removeConsumer(ImageConsumer ic);                                synchronized
    public void requestTopDownLeftRightResend(ImageConsumer ic);                      empty
    public void startProduction(ImageConsumer ic);                               synchronized
```

```
// Methods Implementing Runnable
   public void run();
}
```

Hierarchy: Object→ RenderableImageProducer(ImageProducer, Runnable)

RenderContext

java.awt.image.renderable

This class contains the information necessary to produce a device-specific java.awt.-image.RenderedImage from a RenderableImage. That information is a transformation from user coordinates to device coordinates, an optional java.awt.Shape describing the area of interest in the RenderableImage, and an optional set of java.awt.RenderingHints.

```
public class RenderContext implements Cloneable {
// Public Constructors
   public RenderContext(java.awt.geom.AffineTransform usr2dev);
   public RenderContext(java.awt.geom.AffineTransform usr2dev, Shape aoi);
   public RenderContext(java.awt.geom.AffineTransform usr2dev, RenderingHints hints);
   public RenderContext(java.awt.geom.AffineTransform usr2dev, Shape aoi, RenderingHints hints);
// Public Instance Methods
   public void concetenateTransform(java.awt.geom.AffineTransform modTransform);
   public Shape getAreaOfInterest();
   public RenderingHints getRenderingHints();
   public java.awt.geom.AffineTransform getTransform();
   public void preConcetenateTransform(java.awt.geom.AffineTransform modTransform);
   public void setAreaOfInterest(Shape newAoi);
   public void setRenderingHints(RenderingHints hints);
   public void setTransform(java.awt.geom.AffineTransform newTransform);
// Public Methods Overriding Object
   public Object clone();
}
```

Hierarchy: Object→ RenderContext(Cloneable)

Passed To: ContextualRenderedImageFactory.{create(), mapRenderContext()}, RenderableImage.createRendering(), RenderableImageOp.createRendering(), RenderableImageProducer.{RenderableImageProducer(), setRenderContext()}

Returned By: ContextualRenderedImageFactory.mapRenderContext()

RenderedImageFactory

java.awt.image.renderable

This interface is implemented by classes that, given a ParameterBlock of arguments and a set of RenderingHints, can create RenderedImage objects, typically through the process of rendering a RenderableImage object. The subinterface ContextualRenderedImageFactory is used more often than RenderedImageFactory.

```
public abstract interface RenderedImageFactory {
// Public Instance Methods
   public abstract RenderedImage create(ParameterBlock paramBlock, RenderingHints hints);
}
```

Implementations: ContextualRenderedImageFactory

CHAPTER 20

The java.awt.peer Package

The interfaces in the java.awt.peer package define the native GUI capabilities that are required by the heavyweight AWT components of the java.awt package. Application-level code never needs to use this package. Because the package is rarely used and because the interfaces of this package closely mirror the component classes of java.awt, no descriptions are provided for the individual interfaces listed here. Figure 20-1 shows the class hierarchy of this package.

ButtonPeer

Java 1.0

java.awt.peer

PJ1.1

```
public abstract interface ButtonPeer extends ComponentPeer {
// Public Instance Methods
    public abstract void setLabel(String label);
}
```

CanvasPeer

Java 1.0

java.awt.peer

PJ1.1

```
public abstract interface CanvasPeer extends ComponentPeer {
}
```

CheckboxMenuItemPeer

Java 1.0

java.awt.peer

PJ1.1

```
public abstract interface CheckboxMenuItemPeer extends MenuItemPeer {
// Public Instance Methods
    public abstract void setState(boolean t);
}
```

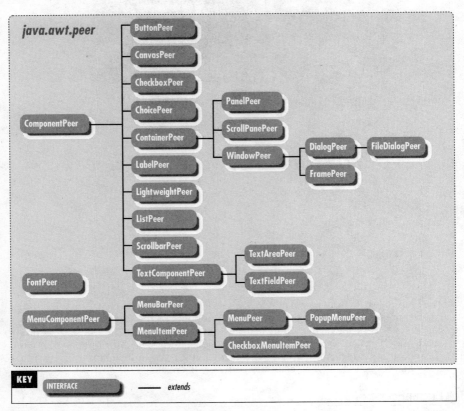

Figure 20–1: The java.awt.peer package

CheckboxPeer

Java 1.0

java.awt.peer

PJ1.1

```
public abstract interface CheckboxPeer extends ComponentPeer {
// Public Instance Methods
    public abstract void setCheckboxGroup(CheckboxGroup g);
    public abstract void setLabel(String label);
    public abstract void setState(boolean state);
}
```

ChoicePeer

Java 1.0

java.awt.peer

PJ1.1

```
public abstract interface ChoicePeer extends ComponentPeer {
// Public Instance Methods
1.1 public abstract void add(String item, int index);
    public abstract void addItem(String item, int index);
1.1 public abstract void remove(int index);
```

```
    public abstract void select(int index);
}
```

ComponentPeer

java.awt.peer

```
public abstract interface ComponentPeer {
// Property Accessor Methods (by property name)
    public abstract java.awt.image.ColorModel getColorModel();
1.1 public abstract boolean isFocusTraversable();
    public abstract Graphics getGraphics();
1.1 public abstract Point getLocationOnScreen();
1.1 public abstract Dimension getMinimumSize();
1.1 public abstract Dimension getPreferredSize();
    public abstract Toolkit getToolkit();
// Public Instance Methods
    public abstract int checkImage(Image img, int w, int h, java.awt.image.ImageObserver o);
    public abstract Image createImage(java.awt.image.ImageProducer producer);
    public abstract Image createImage(int width, int height);
    public abstract void disable();
    public abstract void dispose();
    public abstract void enable();
    public abstract FontMetrics getFontMetrics(Font font);
1.1 public abstract void handleEvent(AWTEvent e);
    public abstract void hide();
    public abstract Dimension minimumSize();
    public abstract void paint(Graphics g);
    public abstract Dimension preferredSize();
    public abstract boolean prepareImage(Image img, int w, int h, java.awt.image.ImageObserver o);
    public abstract void print(Graphics g);
    public abstract void repaint(long tm, int x, int y, int width, int height);
    public abstract void requestFocus();
    public abstract void reshape(int x, int y, int width, int height);
    public abstract void setBackground(Color c);
1.1 public abstract void setBounds(int x, int y, int width, int height);
1.1 public abstract void setCursor(Cursor cursor);
1.1 public abstract void setEnabled(boolean b);
    public abstract void setFont(Font f);
    public abstract void setForeground(Color c);
1.1 public abstract void setVisible(boolean b);
    public abstract void show();
}
```

ContainerPeer

java.awt.peer

```
public abstract interface ContainerPeer extends ComponentPeer {
// Public Instance Methods
1.1 public abstract void beginValidate();
1.1 public abstract void endValidate();
1.1 public abstract Insets getInsets();
```

```
    public abstract Insets insets();
}
```

DialogPeer

java.awt.peer

```
public abstract interface DialogPeer extends WindowPeer {
// Public Instance Methods
    public abstract void setResizable(boolean resizeable);
    public abstract void setTitle(String title);
}
```

FileDialogPeer

java.awt.peer

```
public abstract interface FileDialogPeer extends DialogPeer {
// Public Instance Methods
    public abstract void setDirectory(String dir);
    public abstract void setFile(String file);
    public abstract void setFilenameFilter(java.io.FilenameFilter filter);
}
```

FontPeer

java.awt.peer

```
public abstract interface FontPeer {
}
```

FramePeer

java.awt.peer

```
public abstract interface FramePeer extends WindowPeer {
// Property Accessor Methods (by property name)
1.2 public abstract int getState();
1.2 public abstract void setState(int state);
// Public Instance Methods
    public abstract void setIconImage(Image im);
    public abstract void setMenuBar(MenuBar mb);
    public abstract void setResizable(boolean resizeable);
    public abstract void setTitle(String title);
}
```

LabelPeer

java.awt.peer

```
public abstract interface LabelPeer extends ComponentPeer {
// Public Instance Methods
    public abstract void setAlignment(int alignment);
    public abstract void setText(String label);
}
```

LightweightPeer

java.awt.peer

```
public abstract interface LightweightPeer extends ComponentPeer {
}
```

ListPeer

java.awt.peer

```
public abstract interface ListPeer extends ComponentPeer {
// Public Instance Methods
1.1  public abstract void add(String item, int index);
     public abstract void addItem(String item, int index);
     public abstract void clear();
     public abstract void delItems(int start, int end);
     public abstract void deselect(int index);
1.1  public abstract Dimension getMinimumSize(int rows);
1.1  public abstract Dimension getPreferredSize(int rows);
     public abstract int[ ] getSelectedIndexes();
     public abstract void makeVisible(int index);
     public abstract Dimension minimumSize(int v);
     public abstract Dimension preferredSize(int v);
1.1  public abstract void removeAll();
     public abstract void select(int index);
1.1  public abstract void setMultipleMode(boolean b);
     public abstract void setMultipleSelections(boolean v);
}
```

MenuBarPeer

java.awt.peer

```
public abstract interface MenuBarPeer extends MenuComponentPeer {
// Public Instance Methods
     public abstract void addHelpMenu(Menu m);
     public abstract void addMenu(Menu m);
     public abstract void delMenu(int index);
}
```

MenuComponentPeer

java.awt.peer

```
public abstract interface MenuComponentPeer {
// Public Instance Methods
     public abstract void dispose();
}
```

*java.awt.
peer*

MenuItemPeer

Java 1.0

java.awt.peer

PJ1.1

```
public abstract interface MenuItemPeer extends MenuComponentPeer {
// Public Instance Methods
    public abstract void disable();
    public abstract void enable();
1.1 public abstract void setEnabled(boolean b);
    public abstract void setLabel(String label);
}
```

MenuPeer

Java 1.0

java.awt.peer

PJ1.1

```
public abstract interface MenuPeer extends MenuItemPeer {
// Public Instance Methods
    public abstract void addItem(MenuItem item);
    public abstract void addSeparator();
    public abstract void delItem(int index);
}
```

PanelPeer

Java 1.0

java.awt.peer

PJ1.1

```
public abstract interface PanelPeer extends ContainerPeer {
}
```

PopupMenuPeer

Java 1.1

java.awt.peer

PJ1.1

```
public abstract interface PopupMenuPeer extends MenuPeer {
// Public Instance Methods
    public abstract void show(Event e);
}
```

ScrollbarPeer

Java 1.0

java.awt.peer

PJ1.1

```
public abstract interface ScrollbarPeer extends ComponentPeer {
// Public Instance Methods
    public abstract void setLineIncrement(int l);
    public abstract void setPageIncrement(int l);
    public abstract void setValues(int value, int visible, int minimum, int maximum);
}
```

ScrollPanePeer

Java 1.1

java.awt.peer

PJ1.1

```
public abstract interface ScrollPanePeer extends ContainerPeer {
// Public Instance Methods
    public abstract void childResized(int w, int h);
    public abstract int getHScrollbarHeight();
    public abstract int getVScrollbarWidth();
    public abstract void setScrollPosition(int x, int y);
    public abstract void setUnitIncrement(Adjustable adj, int u);
    public abstract void setValue(Adjustable adj, int v);
}
```

TextAreaPeer

Java 1.0

java.awt.peer

PJ1.1

```
public abstract interface TextAreaPeer extends TextComponentPeer {
// Public Instance Methods
1.1  public abstract Dimension getMinimumSize(int rows, int columns);
1.1  public abstract Dimension getPreferredSize(int rows, int columns);
1.1  public abstract void insert(String text, int pos);
     public abstract void insertText(String txt, int pos);
     public abstract Dimension minimumSize(int rows, int cols);
     public abstract Dimension preferredSize(int rows, int cols);
1.1  public abstract void replaceRange(String text, int start, int end);
     public abstract void replaceText(String txt, int start, int end);
}
```

TextComponentPeer

Java 1.0

java.awt.peer

PJ1.1

```
public abstract interface TextComponentPeer extends ComponentPeer {
// Property Accessor Methods (by property name)
1.1  public abstract int getCaretPosition();
1.1  public abstract void setCaretPosition(int pos);
     public abstract int getSelectionEnd();
     public abstract int getSelectionStart();
     public abstract String getText();
     public abstract void setText(String l);
// Public Instance Methods
     public abstract void select(int selStart, int selEnd);
     public abstract void setEditable(boolean editable);
}
```

TextFieldPeer

Java 1.0

java.awt.peer

PJ1.1

```
public abstract interface TextFieldPeer extends TextComponentPeer {
// Public Instance Methods
1.1  public abstract Dimension getMinimumSize(int columns);
1.1  public abstract Dimension getPreferredSize(int columns);
     public abstract Dimension minimumSize(int cols);
     public abstract Dimension preferredSize(int cols);
```

```
1.1 public abstract void setEchoChar(char echoChar);
    public abstract void setEchoCharacter(char c);
}
```

WindowPeer   Java 1.0

java.awt.peer   PJ1.1

```
public abstract interface WindowPeer extends ContainerPeer {
// Public Constants
1.2 public static final int CONSUME_EVENT;                              =1
1.2 public static final int FOCUS_NEXT;                                 =2
1.2 public static final int FOCUS_PREVIOUS;                             =3
1.2 public static final int IGNORE_EVENT;                               =0
// Public Instance Methods
1.2 public abstract int handleFocusTraversalEvent(java.awt.event.KeyEvent e);
    public abstract void toBack();
    public abstract void toFront();
}
```

CHAPTER 21

The java.awt.print Package

The java.awt.print package contains classes and interfaces that support printing. It has been introduced in Java 1.2 and supersedes the PrintJob class of the java.awt package. The most important class in this package is PrinterJob; it coordinates the printing process. The Printable and Pageable interfaces represent printable objects or documents that can be printed with a PrinterJob. Figure 21-1 shows the class hierarchy of this package. See Chapter 5, *Printing*, for more details on printing.

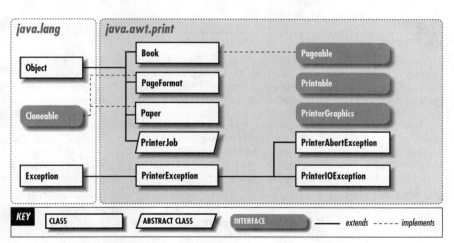

Figure 21-1: The java.awt.print package

Book

java.awt.print

This class implements a multi-page Pageable document out of individual single-page Printable objects. Each page of the Book can have its own PageFormat specified. You might use this class, for example, in a database-reporting application when you want to print a report that consists of single-page tables and graphs in mixed portrait and landscape modes.

The append() and setPage() methods allow you to specify the Printable pages that make up the book, along with their PageFormat objects. The remaining methods implement the Pageable interface and are used by a PrinterJob to print the Book.

As with all Pageable objects, the Printable objects added to a Book must print only a single page. (See Pageable for details.) Note that the three-argument version of append() takes a *numPages* argument. This argument does not specify the number of pages in the Printable; instead, it specifies the number of identical copies of the single-page Printable to be printed.

```
public class Book implements Pageable {
// Public Constructors
    public Book();
// Public Instance Methods
    public void append(Printable painter, PageFormat page);
    public void append(Printable painter, PageFormat page, int numPages);
    public void setPage(int pageIndex, Printable painter, PageFormat page) throws IndexOutOfBoundsException;
// Methods Implementing Pageable
    public int getNumberOfPages();                                                              default:0
    public PageFormat getPageFormat(int pageIndex) throws IndexOutOfBoundsException;
    public Printable getPrintable(int pageIndex) throws IndexOutOfBoundsException;
}
```

Hierarchy: Object→ Book(Pageable)

Pageable

java.awt.print

This interface is implemented by multipage documents that know how to print themselves in more sophisticated ways than the Printable interface allows. There are two primary differences between Pageable and Printable. The first is that a Pageable object knows how many pages are in the document and can print them in an arbitrary order. This allows a printer dialog to give the user the choice to print only a range of pages within the document. It also allows the user to request that the pages be printed in reverse order, which is useful on some printers that stack document pages in reverse order. The second difference between Pageable and Printable is that each page of a Pageable may have a different PageFormat associated with it. This is useful when a document contains pages in portrait orientation and some pages in landscape orientation, for example.

The heart of the Pageable interface is the method getPrintable(), which returns a Printable object able to print the specified page of the document. The Printable objects returned by this method are used differently and must be implemented differently than Printable objects that are designed to be printed alone. While standalone Printable objects may print multiple pages, the Printable objects returned by a Pageable represent only a single page. In other words, the getPrintable() method of Pageable is called once for every page in the document, and the Printable it returns is used to print only that one page.

The Pageable interface lends itself to two distinct implementation strategies. In the first, the getPrintable() method returns a different Printable object for each page of the document. This Printable object knows exactly what page to print and can ignore the *pageIndex* argument passed to its print() method. The second strategy is to implement a single Printable object and have the getPrintable() method always return this one object, regardless of page number. In this case, the print() method uses the *pageIndex* argument to decide what page to print. Note that a Printable implemented in this way must be more flexible than a standalone Printable object, since its pages may be printed in any order and are not guaranteed to be accessed sequentially.

Finally, as with standalone Printable objects, Printable objects returned by Pageable objects must be prepared to have their print() methods called multiple times for the same page number. This is a requirement for banded raster printing in low-memory environments. See Printable for details.

```
public abstract interface Pageable {
// Public Constants
    public static final int UNKNOWN_NUMBER_OF_PAGES;                                  =-1
// Public Instance Methods
    public abstract int getNumberOfPages();
    public abstract PageFormat getPageFormat(int pageIndex) throws IndexOutOfBoundsException;
    public abstract Printable getPrintable(int pageIndex) throws IndexOutOfBoundsException;
}
```

Implementations: Book

Passed To: PrinterJob.setPageable()

PageFormat

java.awt.print

cloneable

This class is a combination of a Paper object that specifies page size and imageable area with a field that specifies the orientation of the page. The orientation values are the following:

PORTRAIT

This is the normal orientation of a piece of paper. The origin is at the top left, with the X axis running from left to right and the Y axis running from top to bottom.

LANDSCAPE

This is the orientation that results from rotating a piece of paper 90 degrees clockwise. The origin is at the bottom left of the sheet of paper, with the X axis running from bottom to top and the Y axis running from left to right.

REVERSE_LANDSCAPE

This is the orientation that results from rotating a piece of paper 90 degrees counterclockwise. The origin is at the top right of the sheet of paper, with the X axis running from top to bottom and the Y axis running from right to left.

Printable and Pageable objects are not responsible for performing the rotations necessary to print in these orientations. The appropriate transform has already been done in the Graphics object passed to the print() method of Printable.

```
public class PageFormat implements Cloneable {
// Public Constructors
    public PageFormat();
// Public Constants
    public static final int LANDSCAPE;                                                =0
    public static final int PORTRAIT;                                                 =1
    public static final int REVERSE_LANDSCAPE;                                        =2
// Property Accessor Methods (by property name)
```

public double **getHeight**( );	*default:792.0*
public double **getImageableHeight**( );	*default:648.0*
public double **getImageableWidth**( );	*default:468.0*
public double **getImageableX**( );	*default:72.0*
public double **getImageableY**( );	*default:72.0*
public double[ ] **getMatrix**( );	
public int **getOrientation**( );	*default:1*
public void **setOrientation**(int *orientation*) throws IllegalArgumentException;	
public Paper **getPaper**( );	
public void **setPaper**(Paper *paper*);	
public double **getWidth**( );	*default:612.0*
// *Public Methods Overriding Object*	
public Object **clone**( );	

}

Hierarchy: Object→ PageFormat(Cloneable)

Passed To: Book.{append( ), setPage( )}, Printable.print( ), PrinterJob.{defaultPage( ), pageDialog( ), setPrintable( ), validatePage( )}

Returned By: Book getPageFormat( ), Pageable.getPageFormat( ), PrinterJob.{defaultPage( ), pageDialog( ), validatePage( )}

Paper   Java 1.2

java.awt.print   *cloneable*

This class describes the width, height, and imageable area of a piece of paper. The imageable area is the region of a page that should be printed on—the area inside the margins. Most printers cannot print all the way to the edges of the page and require margins of at least a quarter inch on all sides. All coordinates and sizes used by this class are measured in printer's points, where one point is defined as exactly 1/72nd of an inch.

public class **Paper** implements Cloneable {	
// *Public Constructors*	
public **Paper**( );	
// *Property Accessor Methods (by property name)*	
public double **getHeight**( );	*default:792.0*
public double **getImageableHeight**( );	*default:648.0*
public double **getImageableWidth**( );	*default:468.0*
public double **getImageableX**( );	*default:72.0*
public double **getImageableY**( );	*default:72.0*
public double **getWidth**( );	*default:612.0*
// *Public Instance Methods*	
public void **setImageableArea**(double *x*, double *y*, double *width*, double *height*);	
public void **setSize**(double *width*, double *height*);	
// *Public Methods Overriding Object*	
public Object **clone**( );	

}

Hierarchy: Object→ Paper(Cloneable)

Passed To: PageFormat.setPaper( )

Returned By: PageFormat.getPaper( )

Printable   Java 1.2

java.awt.print

This interface is implemented by objects that know how to print themselves. It should be implemented by objects that always print a single page, or by multipage documents that know how to print their pages in sequential order only. Multipage documents that are able to print their pages in arbitrary order should implement the somewhat more complex Pageable interface.

When a PrinterJob prints a Printable object, it calls the print() method one or more times to print the pages. This method should print the page specified by *pageIndex*, using the specified Graphics object and the page size and orientation specified in the PageFormat object.

The PrinterJob guarantees that it prints the pages of a Printable in strictly sequential order. The pageIndex argument begins at 0 and increases. After printing a page, the print() method should return the PAGE_EXISTS constant. Since the PrinterJob has no way of knowing how many pages there are in a Printable object, it keeps increasing the page number until the print() method returns the NO_SUCH_PAGE constant. When this value is returned, the PrinterJob knows that it has reached the end of the print job.

There is a very important twist in this communication protocol between PrinterJob and Printable. While the PrinterJob guarantees that it does not try to print pages out of order, it is allowed to print the same page multiple times. This means, for example, that the print() method may be called with a *pageIndex* argument of 0 three times in a row. Printable objects must be implemented with this possibility in mind. The reason that this is necessary is that, in some cases, printing is done into a very large (high-resolution) off-screen image, and this image data is then transferred to the printer. On systems with limited memory, this printing technique must be done in multiple passes, printing only a fraction, or band, of the page at each pass.

The Printable interface is also used by Pageable objects that know how to print their pages out of order. When a Printable object is returned by a Pageable object, the PrinterJob uses it differently than it does a standalone Printable object. See Pageable for details.

```
public abstract interface Printable {
// Public Constants
     public static final int NO_SUCH_PAGE;                                    =1
     public static final int PAGE_EXISTS;                                     =0
// Public Instance Methods
     public abstract int print(Graphics graphics, PageFormat pageFormat, int pageIndex) throws PrinterException;
}
```

Passed To: Book.{append(), setPage()}, PrinterJob.setPrintable()

Returned By: Book.getPrintable(), Pageable.getPrintable()

PrinterAbortException   Java 1.2

java.awt.print   *serializable checked*

Signals that a print job has been aborted, typically because of a user request to terminate it.

```
public class PrinterAbortException extends PrinterException {
// Public Constructors
     public PrinterAbortException();
```

```
    public PrinterAbortException(String msg);
}
```

Hierarchy: Object→ Throwable(Serializable)→ Exception→ PrinterException→ PrinterAbortException

PrinterException   Java 1.2

java.awt.print   *serializable checked*

This class serves as the superclass for all exceptions that may arise in the process of
printing. See the subclasses PrinterAbortException and PrinterIOException. PrinterException and
its subclasses are checked exceptions, they must be declared in the throws clauses of
methods that may throw them.

```
public class PrinterException extends Exception {
// Public Constructors
    public PrinterException();
    public PrinterException(String msg);
}
```

Hierarchy: Object→ Throwable(Serializable)→ Exception→ PrinterException

Subclasses: PrinterAbortException, PrinterIOException

Thrown By: Printable.print(), PrinterJob.print()

PrinterGraphics   Java 1.2

java.awt.print

This interface is implemented by any Graphics object that is passed to the print() method
of a Printable object. This means that a Printable can always cast its Graphics object to a
PrinterGraphics object and use the getPrinterJob() method to obtain the PrinterJob that is in
use.

```
public abstract interface PrinterGraphics {
// Public Instance Methods
    public abstract PrinterJob getPrinterJob();
}
```

PrinterIOException   Java 1.2

java.awt.print   *serializable checked*

Indicates that an I/O error occurred during the printing process. This usually means
that the PrinterJob had trouble communicating with the printer or print server.

```
public class PrinterIOException extends PrinterException {
// Public Constructors
    public PrinterIOException(java.io.IOException exception);
// Public Instance Methods
    public java.io.IOException getIOException();
}
```

Hierarchy: Object→ Throwable(Serializable)→ Exception→ PrinterException→ PrinterIOException

PrinterJob   Java 1.2

java.awt.print

This class controls printing of Printable and Pageable objects. Applications typically use
this class as follows:

- Create a PrinterJob by calling the static method getPrinterJob(). This requires appropriate security permissions, so untrusted applets cannot do this.

- Configure the PrinterJob, if desired, by calling setJobName() and setCopies().

- Interactive applications that want to give the user a choice about page orientation and margins should call pageDialog(), passing in a default PageFormat object. This method returns a new PageFormat object that contains the user's choices. While pageDialog() is suitable for simple single-page Printable objects, it typically is not necessary for more complex multipage documents, since these often have implicit or explicit margin sizes and page orientation already specified.

- Call setPrintable() or setPageable() to specify the object to be printed. You can use the PageFormat object returned by pageDialog(), defaultPage(), or validatePage() when creating the Printable or Pageable object used in this step. Or you can pass such a PageFormat object to the two-argument version of setPrintable().

- If your application is an interactive one, call printDialog() to give the user a chance to specify what range of pages to print or to cancel the print job. printDialog() configures the PrinterJob and returns true if the user wants to proceed with the print job. If printDialog() returns false, you should not continue with the print job. Noninteractive jobs that run unattended should skip this step.

- Finally, call print() to begin printing. If you are using more than one thread, you can abort the print job by calling cancel().

PrinterJob is the preferred class for printing in Java 1.2. Do not confuse it with java.awt.PrintJob, which was introduced in Java 1.1.

```
public abstract class PrinterJob {
// Public Constructors
    public PrinterJob();
// Public Class Methods
    public static PrinterJob getPrinterJob();
// Property Accessor Methods (by property name)
    public abstract boolean isCancelled();
    public abstract int getCopies();
    public abstract void setCopies(int copies);
    public abstract String getJobName();
    public abstract void setJobName(String jobName);
    public abstract String getUserName();
// Public Instance Methods
    public abstract void cancel();
    public PageFormat defaultPage();
    public abstract PageFormat defaultPage(PageFormat page);
    public abstract PageFormat pageDialog(PageFormat page);
    public abstract void print() throws PrinterException;
    public abstract boolean printDialog();
    public abstract void setPageable(Pageable document) throws NullPointerException;
    public abstract void setPrintable(Printable painter);
    public abstract void setPrintable(Printable painter, PageFormat format);
    public abstract PageFormat validatePage(PageFormat page);
}
```

Returned By: PrinterGraphics.getPrinterJob(), PrinterJob.getPrinterJob()

CHAPTER 22

The javax.accessibility Package

The javax.accessibility package contains classes and interfaces that define the contract between an accessible application and an assistive technology, such as a screen reader for the vision impaired. All accessible GUI components implement the Accessible interface and must be able to return an AccessibleContext object. AccessibleContext is the main entry point for an assistive technology to obtain information about the component. The methods of AccessibleContext return instances of many of the other classes and interfaces in this package. Figure 22-1 shows the class hierarchy of this package, which is new in Java 1.2.

Typically, only GUI component developers and developers of assistive technologies need to use this package. Chapter 3, *Swing Programming Topics*, contains an overview of accessibility.

Accessible

Java 1.2

javax.accessibility

accessible

This interface is the primary point of interaction between assistive technologies and accessible objects. All accessible objects implement the getAccessibleContext() method of this interface, providing a way for an assistive technology to obtain an AccessibleContext object that describes the accessible object. Component developers should implement this interface for their components, but application developers should never have to use it.

```
public abstract interface Accessible {
// Public Instance Methods
    public abstract AccessibleContext getAccessibleContext();
}
```

Implementations: Too many classes to list.

Passed To: AccessibleContext.setAccessibleParent(),
javax.swing.JTree.AccessibleJTree.AccessibleJTreeNode.AccessibleJTreeNode()

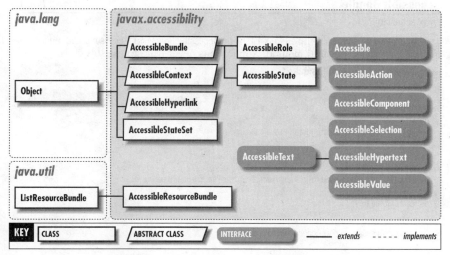

Figure 22–1: The javax.accessibility package

Returned By: Too many methods to list.

Type Of: AccessibleContext.accessibleParent

AccessibleAction   Java 1.2

javax.accessibility

This interface allows an assistive technology to obtain human-readable descriptions of the actions that an accessible object can perform and request that the object perform any one of them. Any accessible object that can perform one or more actions should return an AccessibleAction object from the getAccessibleAction() method of its AccessibleContext object. Applications never need to use or implement this interface.

```
public abstract interface AccessibleAction {
// Public Instance Methods
    public abstract boolean doAccessibleAction(int i);
    public abstract int getAccessibleActionCount();
    public abstract String getAccessibleActionDescription(int i);
}
```

Implementations: AccessibleHyperlink, javax.swing.AbstractButton.AccessibleAbstractButton, javax.swing.JComboBox.AccessibleJComboBox, javax.swing.JTree.AccessibleJTree.AccessibleJTreeNode

Returned By: AccessibleContext.getAccessibleAction(),
javax.swing.AbstractButton.AccessibleAbstractButton.getAccessibleAction(),
javax.swing.JComboBox.AccessibleJComboBox.getAccessibleAction(),
javax.swing.JList.AccessibleJList.AccessibleJListChild.getAccessibleAction(),
javax.swing.JTable.AccessibleJTable.AccessibleJTableCell.getAccessibleAction(),
javax.swing.JTree.AccessibleJTree.AccessibleJTreeNode.getAccessibleAction(),
javax.swing.table.JTableHeader.AccessibleJTableHeader.AccessibleJTableHeaderEntry.getAccessibleAction()

AccessibleBundle

Java 1.2

javax.accessibility

This class is the abstract superclass of both AccessibleRole and AccessibleState. It defines the localized toDisplayString() method. Applications never need to use this class.

```
public abstract class AccessibleBundle {
// Public Constructors
   public AccessibleBundle();
// Public Instance Methods
   public String toDisplayString();
   public String toDisplayString(java.util.Locale locale);
// Public Methods Overriding Object
   public String toString();
// Protected Instance Methods
   protected String toDisplayString(String resourceBundleName, java.util.Locale locale);
// Protected Instance Fields
   protected String key;
}
```

Subclasses: AccessibleRole, AccessibleState

AccessibleComponent

Java 1.2

javax.accessibility

This interface allows an assistive technology to query and set basic graphical attributes for an accessible object. Any accessible object that displays itself on the screen should return an object of this type from the getAccessibleComponent() method of its AccessibleContext. Applications never need to use or implement this interface.

```
public abstract interface AccessibleComponent {
// Event Registration Methods (by event name)
   public abstract void addFocusListener(java.awt.event.FocusListener l);
   public abstract void removeFocusListener(java.awt.event.FocusListener l);
// Property Accessor Methods (by property name)
   public abstract java.awt.Color getBackground();
   public abstract void setBackground(java.awt.Color c);
   public abstract java.awt.Rectangle getBounds();
   public abstract void setBounds(java.awt.Rectangle r);
   public abstract java.awt.Cursor getCursor();
   public abstract void setCursor(java.awt.Cursor cursor);
   public abstract boolean isEnabled();
   public abstract void setEnabled(boolean b);
   public abstract boolean isFocusTraversable();
   public abstract java.awt.Font getFont();
   public abstract void setFont(java.awt.Font f);
   public abstract java.awt.Color getForeground();
   public abstract void setForeground(java.awt.Color c);
   public abstract java.awt.Point getLocation();
   public abstract void setLocation(java.awt.Point p);
   public abstract java.awt.Point getLocationOnScreen();
   public abstract boolean isShowing();
   public abstract java.awt.Dimension getSize();
   public abstract void setSize(java.awt.Dimension d);
   public abstract boolean isVisible();
   public abstract void setVisible(boolean b);
// Public Instance Methods
   public abstract boolean contains(java.awt.Point p);
   public abstract Accessible getAccessibleAt(java.awt.Point p);
```

```
    public abstract java.awt.FontMetrics getFontMetrics(java.awt.Font f);
    public abstract void requestFocus();
}
```

Implementations: javax.swing.Box.AccessibleBox, javax.swing.Box.Filler.AccessibleBoxFiller, javax.swing.CellRendererPane.AccessibleCellRendererPane, javax.swing.JApplet.AccessibleJApplet, javax.swing.JComponent.AccessibleJComponent, javax.swing.JDialog.AccessibleJDialog, javax.swing.JFrame.AccessibleJFrame, javax.swing.JList.AccessibleJList.AccessibleJListChild, javax.swing.JPopupMenu.WindowPopup.AccessibleWindowPopup, javax.swing.JTable.AccessibleJTable.AccessibleJTableCell, javax.swing.JTree.AccessibleJTree.AccessibleJTreeNode, javax.swing.JWindow.AccessibleJWindow, javax.swing.table.JTableHeader.AccessibleJTableHeader.AccessibleJTableHeaderEntry

Returned By: AccessibleContext.getAccessibleComponent(),
javax.swing.Box.AccessibleBox.getAccessibleComponent(),
javax.swing.Box.Filler.AccessibleBoxFiller.getAccessibleComponent(),
javax.swing.CellRendererPane.AccessibleCellRendererPane.getAccessibleComponent(),
javax.swing.JApplet.AccessibleJApplet.getAccessibleComponent(),
javax.swing.JComponent.AccessibleJComponent.getAccessibleComponent(),
javax.swing.JDialog.AccessibleJDialog.getAccessibleComponent(),
javax.swing.JFrame.AccessibleJFrame.getAccessibleComponent(),
javax.swing.JList.AccessibleJList.AccessibleJListChild.getAccessibleComponent(),
javax.swing.JPopupMenu.WindowPopup.AccessibleWindowPopup.getAccessibleComponent(),
javax.swing.JTable.AccessibleJTable.AccessibleJTableCell.getAccessibleComponent(),
javax.swing.JTree.AccessibleJTree.AccessibleJTreeNode.getAccessibleComponent(),
javax.swing.JWindow.AccessibleJWindow.getAccessibleComponent(),
javax.swing.table.JTableHeader.AccessibleJTableHeader.AccessibleJTableHeaderEntry.getAccessibleComponent()

AccessibleContext

	Java 1.2
javax.accessibility	*accessible context*

This abstract class defines methods that provide basic information about an accessible object. Every Accessible object must be able to return an AccessibleContext to describe itself. The methods of AccessibleContext are largely self-explanatory. They allow an assistive technology to query the name, description, role, parent, children, and so on of the accessible object. In addition to this generic accessibility information, a number of AccessibleContext methods return more specialized objects that contain more specialized types of accessibility information. For example, if an accessible object is a GUI component, getAccessibleComponent() returns an AccessibleComponent object that contains further details about the accessible object. Applications never have to use this class.

```
public abstract class AccessibleContext {
// Public Constructors
    public AccessibleContext();
// Public Constants
    public static final String ACCESSIBLE_ACTIVE_DESCENDANT_PROPERTY;   ="AccessibleActiveDescendant"
    public static final String ACCESSIBLE_CARET_PROPERTY;                           ="AccessibleCaret"
    public static final String ACCESSIBLE_CHILD_PROPERTY;                           ="AccessibleChild"
    public static final String ACCESSIBLE_DESCRIPTION_PROPERTY;             ="AccessibleDescription"
    public static final String ACCESSIBLE_NAME_PROPERTY;                            ="AccessibleName"
    public static final String ACCESSIBLE_SELECTION_PROPERTY;                    ="AccessibleSelection"
    public static final String ACCESSIBLE_STATE_PROPERTY;                            ="AccessibleState"
    public static final String ACCESSIBLE_TEXT_PROPERTY;                              ="AccessibleText"
    public static final String ACCESSIBLE_VALUE_PROPERTY;                            ="AccessibleValue"
    public static final String ACCESSIBLE_VISIBLE_DATA_PROPERTY;           ="AccessibleVisibleData"
```

```
// Event Registration Methods (by event name)
    public void addPropertyChangeListener(java.beans.PropertyChangeListener listener);
    public void removePropertyChangeListener(java.beans.PropertyChangeListener listener);
// Property Accessor Methods (by property name)
    public AccessibleAction getAccessibleAction();                                          constant
    public abstract int getAccessibleChildrenCount();
    public AccessibleComponent getAccessibleComponent();                                    constant
    public String getAccessibleDescription();
    public void setAccessibleDescription(String s);
    public abstract int getAccessibleIndexInParent();
    public String getAccessibleName();
    public void setAccessibleName(String s);
    public Accessible getAccessibleParent();
    public void setAccessibleParent(Accessible a);
    public abstract AccessibleRole getAccessibleRole();
    public AccessibleSelection getAccessibleSelection();                                    constant
    public abstract AccessibleStateSet getAccessibleStateSet();
    public AccessibleText getAccessibleText();                                              constant
    public AccessibleValue getAccessibleValue();                                            constant
    public abstract java.util.Locale getLocale() throws java.awt.IllegalComponentStateException;
// Public Instance Methods
    public void firePropertyChange(String propertyName, Object oldValue, Object newValue);
    public abstract Accessible getAccessibleChild(int i);
// Protected Instance Fields
    protected String accessibleDescription;
    protected String accessibleName;
    protected Accessible accessibleParent;
}
```

Subclasses: javax.swing.Box.AccessibleBox, javax.swing.Box.Filler.AccessibleBoxFiller, javax.swing.CellRendererPane.AccessibleCellRendererPane, javax.swing.JApplet.AccessibleJApplet, javax.swing.JComponent.AccessibleJComponent, javax.swing.JDialog.AccessibleJDialog, javax.swing.JFrame.AccessibleJFrame, javax.swing.JList.AccessibleJList.AccessibleJListChild, javax.swing.JPopupMenu.WindowPopup.AccessibleWindowPopup, javax.swing.JTable.AccessibleJTable.AccessibleJTableCell, javax.swing.JTree.AccessibleJTree.AccessibleJTreeNode, javax.swing.JWindow.AccessibleJWindow, javax.swing.table.JTableHeader.AccessibleJTableHeader.AccessibleJTableHeaderEntry

Returned By: Too many methods to list.

Type Of: javax.swing.Box.accessibleContext, javax.swing.Box.Filler.accessibleContext, javax.swing.CellRendererPane.accessibleContext, javax.swing.JApplet.accessibleContext, javax.swing.JColorChooser.accessibleContext, javax.swing.JComponent.accessibleContext, javax.swing.JDialog.accessibleContext, javax.swing.JFileChooser.accessibleContext, javax.swing.JFrame.accessibleContext, javax.swing.JWindow.accessibleContext

AccessibleHyperlink   Java 1.2

javax.accessibility

This abstract class is an AccessibleAction that describes a hyperlink or set of hyperlinks, such as those found in an HTML image map. In addition to the AccessibleAction methods, this class defines getAccessibleActionObject(), which should return an object describing the link, typically a java.net.URL object. getAccessibleActionAnchor() should return the object that displays the link. For HTML hypertext, this is the string or image that appears between the HTML <A> and </A> tags. Applications never need to use this class.

```
public abstract class AccessibleHyperlink implements AccessibleAction {
// Public Constructors
    public AccessibleHyperlink();
// Property Accessor Methods (by property name)
    public abstract int getAccessibleActionCount();                          Implements:AccessibleAction
    public abstract int getEndIndex();
    public abstract int getStartIndex();
    public abstract boolean isValid();
// Public Instance Methods
    public abstract Object getAccessibleActionAnchor(int i);
    public abstract Object getAccessibleActionObject(int i);
// Methods Implementing AccessibleAction
    public abstract boolean doAccessibleAction(int i);
    public abstract int getAccessibleActionCount();
    public abstract String getAccessibleActionDescription(int i);
}
```

Hierarchy: Object → AccessibleHyperlink(AccessibleAction)

Subclasses: javax.swing.JEditorPane.JEditorPaneAccessibleHypertextSupport.HTMLLink

Returned By: AccessibleHypertext.getLink(),
javax.swing.JEditorPane.JEditorPaneAccessibleHypertextSupport.getLink()

AccessibleHypertext   Java 1.2
javax.accessibility

This interface extends AccessibleText. It allows an assistive technology to query the text
of an accessible object and the hyperlinks contained in that text. Accessible com-
ponents that display hyperlinked text should return an object of this type from the get-
AccessibleText() method of their AccessibleContext. The getLink() method of the
AccessibleHypertext object should return AccessibleHyperlink objects describing the links.
Applications never need to use or implement this interface.

```
public abstract interface AccessibleHypertext extends AccessibleText {
// Public Instance Methods
    public abstract AccessibleHyperlink getLink(int linkIndex);
    public abstract int getLinkCount();
    public abstract int getLinkIndex(int charIndex);
}
```

Hierarchy: (AccessibleHypertext(AccessibleText))

Implementations: javax.swing.JEditorPane.JEditorPaneAccessibleHypertextSupport

AccessibleResourceBundle   Java 1.2
javax.accessibility

This class is a java.util.ResourceBundle that contains all the localized strings for the
javax.accessibility package. It is used internally by the package and is not intended for use
by applications, components, or assistive technologies.

```
public class AccessibleResourceBundle extends java.util.ListResourceBundle {
// Public Constructors
    public AccessibleResourceBundle();
// Public Methods Overriding ListResourceBundle
    public Object[ ][ ] getContents();
}
```

Hierarchy: Object→ java.util.ResourceBundle→ java.util.ListResourceBundle→
AccessibleResourceBundle

AccessibleRole   Java 1.2

javax.accessibility

This class exists only to provide a type-safe enumeration of constants that may be legally returned by the getAccessibleRole() method of an AccessibleContext object. An AccessibleRole object describes the role or basic function of an accessible object. The predefined AccessibleRole objects describe the roles played by various Swing components. This set of predefined roles should be sufficient for most purposes, although a specialized component that performs a specialized role could create a new role constant for itself by subclassing AccessibleRole. AccessibleRole inherits toDisplayString() from it superclass. This method returns a localized human-readable string describing the role. Applications never need to use this class.

```
public class AccessibleRole extends AccessibleBundle {
// Protected Constructors
    protected AccessibleRole(String key);
// Public Constants
    public static final AccessibleRole ALERT;
    public static final AccessibleRole AWT_COMPONENT;
    public static final AccessibleRole CHECK_BOX;
    public static final AccessibleRole COLOR_CHOOSER;
    public static final AccessibleRole COLUMN_HEADER;
    public static final AccessibleRole COMBO_BOX;
    public static final AccessibleRole DESKTOP_ICON;
    public static final AccessibleRole DESKTOP_PANE;
    public static final AccessibleRole DIALOG;
    public static final AccessibleRole DIRECTORY_PANE;
    public static final AccessibleRole FILE_CHOOSER;
    public static final AccessibleRole FILLER;
    public static final AccessibleRole FRAME;
    public static final AccessibleRole GLASS_PANE;
    public static final AccessibleRole INTERNAL_FRAME;
    public static final AccessibleRole LABEL;
    public static final AccessibleRole LAYERED_PANE;
    public static final AccessibleRole LIST;
    public static final AccessibleRole MENU;
    public static final AccessibleRole MENU_BAR;
    public static final AccessibleRole MENU_ITEM;
    public static final AccessibleRole OPTION_PANE;
    public static final AccessibleRole PAGE_TAB;
    public static final AccessibleRole PAGE_TAB_LIST;
    public static final AccessibleRole PANEL;
    public static final AccessibleRole PASSWORD_TEXT;
    public static final AccessibleRole POPUP_MENU;
    public static final AccessibleRole PROGRESS_BAR;
    public static final AccessibleRole PUSH_BUTTON;
    public static final AccessibleRole RADIO_BUTTON;
    public static final AccessibleRole ROOT_PANE;
    public static final AccessibleRole ROW_HEADER;
    public static final AccessibleRole SCROLL_BAR;
    public static final AccessibleRole SCROLL_PANE;
    public static final AccessibleRole SEPARATOR;
    public static final AccessibleRole SLIDER;
    public static final AccessibleRole SPLIT_PANE;
    public static final AccessibleRole SWING_COMPONENT;
```

```
    public static final AccessibleRole TABLE;
    public static final AccessibleRole TEXT;
    public static final AccessibleRole TOGGLE_BUTTON;
    public static final AccessibleRole TOOL_BAR;
    public static final AccessibleRole TOOL_TIP;
    public static final AccessibleRole TREE;
    public static final AccessibleRole UNKNOWN;
    public static final AccessibleRole VIEWPORT;
    public static final AccessibleRole WINDOW;
}
```

Hierarchy: Object→ AccessibleBundle→ AccessibleRole

Returned By: Too many methods to list.

Type Of: Too many fields to list.

AccessibleSelection

Java 1.2

javax.accessibility

This interface allows an assistive technology to query and set the selection state of an accessible object that allows selection of items that are themselves accessible objects. An accessible object with selectable children should return an AccessibleSelection object from the getAccessibleSelection() method of its AccessibleContext. It should also be sure to implement Accessible objects to represent each of the selectable children. As an example, note that JTextComponent allows text to be selected, but this is not a selectable child, so it does not support the AccessibleSelection interface. On the other hand, JList allows selection of discrete child list items. It supports the AccessibleSelection interface and defines the JList.AccessibleJList.AccessibleJListChild to provide accessibility support for the individual items in the list. Applications never need to use or implement this interface.

```
public abstract interface AccessibleSelection {
// Public Instance Methods
    public abstract void addAccessibleSelection(int i);
    public abstract void clearAccessibleSelection();
    public abstract Accessible getAccessibleSelection(int i);
    public abstract int getAccessibleSelectionCount();
    public abstract boolean isAccessibleChildSelected(int i);
    public abstract void removeAccessibleSelection(int i);
    public abstract void selectAllAccessibleSelection();
}
```

Implementations: javax.swing.JList.AccessibleJList, javax.swing.JMenu.AccessibleJMenu, javax.swing.JMenuBar.AccessibleJMenuBar, javax.swing.JTabbedPane.AccessibleJTabbedPane, javax.swing.JTable.AccessibleJTable, javax.swing.JTree.AccessibleJTree, javax.swing.JTree.AccessibleJTree.AccessibleJTreeNode

Returned By: AccessibleContext.getAccessibleSelection(),
javax.swing.JList.AccessibleJList.getAccessibleSelection(),
javax.swing.JList.AccessibleJList.AccessibleJListChild.getAccessibleSelection(),
javax.swing.JMenu.AccessibleJMenu.getAccessibleSelection(),
javax.swing.JMenuBar.AccessibleJMenuBar.getAccessibleSelection(),
javax.swing.JTabbedPane.AccessibleJTabbedPane.getAccessibleSelection(),
javax.swing.JTable.AccessibleJTable.getAccessibleSelection(),
javax.swing.JTable.AccessibleJTable.AccessibleJTableCell.getAccessibleSelection(),
javax.swing.JTree.AccessibleJTree.getAccessibleSelection(),
javax.swing.JTree.AccessibleJTree.AccessibleJTreeNode.getAccessibleSelection(),
javax.swing.table.JTableHeader.AccessibleJTableHeader.AccessibleJTableHeaderEntry.getAccessibleSelection()

javax.
accessibility

AccessibleState

Java 1.2

javax.accessibility

This class exists to provide a type-safe enumeration of constants that describe the various states that accessible components may exist in. AccessibleState objects are aggregated into AccessibleStateSet objects, which are returned by the getAccessibleStateSet() method of an AccessibleContext. Every accessible object that is capable of existing in more than one state should return an appropriate set of AccessibleState constants from its AccessibleContext object. AccessibleState inherits toDisplayString() from it superclass. This method returns a localized human-readable string describing the role. Applications never need to use this class.

```
public class AccessibleState extends AccessibleBundle {
// Protected Constructors
    protected AccessibleState(String key);
// Public Constants
    public static final AccessibleState ACTIVE;
    public static final AccessibleState ARMED;
    public static final AccessibleState BUSY;
    public static final AccessibleState CHECKED;
    public static final AccessibleState COLLAPSED;
    public static final AccessibleState EDITABLE;
    public static final AccessibleState ENABLED;
    public static final AccessibleState EXPANDABLE;
    public static final AccessibleState EXPANDED;
    public static final AccessibleState FOCUSABLE;
    public static final AccessibleState FOCUSED;
    public static final AccessibleState HORIZONTAL;
    public static final AccessibleState ICONIFIED;
    public static final AccessibleState MODAL;
    public static final AccessibleState MULTI_LINE;
    public static final AccessibleState MULTISELECTABLE;
    public static final AccessibleState OPAQUE;
    public static final AccessibleState PRESSED;
    public static final AccessibleState RESIZABLE;
    public static final AccessibleState SELECTABLE;
    public static final AccessibleState SELECTED;
    public static final AccessibleState SHOWING;
    public static final AccessibleState SINGLE_LINE;
    public static final AccessibleState TRANSIENT;
    public static final AccessibleState VERTICAL;
    public static final AccessibleState VISIBLE;
}
```

Hierarchy: Object→ AccessibleBundle→ AccessibleState

Passed To: AccessibleStateSet.{AccessibleStateSet(), add(), addAll(), contains(), remove()}

Returned By: AccessibleStateSet.toArray()

Type Of: Too many fields to list.

AccessibleStateSet

Java 1.2

javax.accessibility

This class maintains a list of AccessibleState objects. Every accessible object that can exist in more than one state should return an appropriate AccessibleStateSet describing its current state from the getAccessibleStateSet() method of its AccessibleContext. Applications never need to use this class.

```
public class AccessibleStateSet {
// Public Constructors
    public AccessibleStateSet();
    public AccessibleStateSet(AccessibleState[ ] states);
// Public Instance Methods
    public boolean add(AccessibleState state);
    public void addAll(AccessibleState[ ] states);
    public void clear();
    public boolean contains(AccessibleState state);
    public boolean remove(AccessibleState state);
    public AccessibleState[ ] toArray();
// Public Methods Overriding Object
    public String toString();
// Protected Instance Fields
    protected java.util.Vector states;
}
```

Returned By: Too many methods to list.

AccessibleText

Java 1.2

javax.accessibility

This interface allows an assistive technology to query the textual contents, textual selection, and text-insertion positions of an accessible object that contains nonstatic text. An accessible object that contains nonstatic text should return an AccessibleText object from the getAccessibleText() method of its AccessibleContext. Note that components such as JButton and JLabel do not support this interface. They display only static text, and their contents are adequately described by the getAccessibleName() and getAccessibleDescription() methods of the AccessibleContext. Applications never need to use or implement this interface.

```
public abstract interface AccessibleText {
// Public Constants
    public static final int CHARACTER;                                        =1
    public static final int SENTENCE;                                         =3
    public static final int WORD;                                             =2
// Property Accessor Methods (by property name)
    public abstract int getCaretPosition();
    public abstract int getCharCount();
    public abstract String getSelectedText();
    public abstract int getSelectionEnd();
    public abstract int getSelectionStart();
// Public Instance Methods
    public abstract String getAfterIndex(int part, int index);
    public abstract String getAtIndex(int part, int index);
    public abstract String getBeforeIndex(int part, int index);
    public abstract javax.swing.text.AttributeSet getCharacterAttribute(int i);
    public abstract java.awt.Rectangle getCharacterBounds(int i);
    public abstract int getIndexAtPoint(java.awt.Point p);
}
```

Implementations: AccessibleHypertext, javax.swing.text.JTextComponent.AccessibleJTextComponent

Returned By: AccessibleContext.getAccessibleText(),
javax.swing.JEditorPane.AccessibleJEditorPaneHTML.getAccessibleText(),
javax.swing.JList.AccessibleJList.AccessibleJListChild.getAccessibleText(),
javax.swing.JTable.AccessibleJTable.AccessibleJTableCell.getAccessibleText(),

javax. accessibility

javax.swing.JTree.AccessibleJTree.AccessibleJTreeNode.getAccessibleText(),
javax.swing.table.JTableHeader.AccessibleJTableHeader.AccessibleJTableHeaderEntry.getAccessibleText(),
javax.swing.text.JTextComponent.AccessibleJTextComponent.getAccessibleText()

AccessibleValue

Java 1.2

javax.accessibility

This interface allows an assistive technology to set and query the numerical value displayed or maintained by an accessible object, such as a JScrollBar. It also allows an assistive technology to query the legal range of values supported by the accessible object. An accessible object that maintains a numerical value should return an AccessibleValue object from the getAccessibleValue() method of its AccessibleContext. Applications never need to use or implement this interface.

```
public abstract interface AccessibleValue {
// Public Instance Methods
    public abstract Number getCurrentAccessibleValue();
    public abstract Number getMaximumAccessibleValue();
    public abstract Number getMinimumAccessibleValue();
    public abstract boolean setCurrentAccessibleValue(Number n);
}
```

Implementations: javax.swing.AbstractButton.AccessibleAbstractButton,
javax.swing.JInternalFrame.AccessibleJInternalFrame,
javax.swing.JInternalFrame.JDesktopIcon.AccessibleJDesktopIcon,
javax.swing.JProgressBar.AccessibleJProgressBar, javax.swing.JScrollBar.AccessibleJScrollBar,
javax.swing.JSlider.AccessibleJSlider, javax.swing.JSplitPane.AccessibleJSplitPane

Returned By: AccessibleContext.getAccessibleValue(),
javax.swing.AbstractButton.AccessibleAbstractButton.getAccessibleValue(),
javax.swing.JInternalFrame.AccessibleJInternalFrame.getAccessibleValue(),
javax.swing.JInternalFrame.JDesktopIcon.AccessibleJDesktopIcon.getAccessibleValue(),
javax.swing.JList.AccessibleJList.AccessibleJListChild.getAccessibleValue(),
javax.swing.JProgressBar.AccessibleJProgressBar.getAccessibleValue(),
javax.swing.JScrollBar.AccessibleJScrollBar.getAccessibleValue(),
javax.swing.JSlider.AccessibleJSlider.getAccessibleValue(),
javax.swing.JSplitPane.AccessibleJSplitPane.getAccessibleValue(),
javax.swing.JTable.AccessibleJTable.AccessibleJTableCell.getAccessibleValue(),
javax.swing.JTree.AccessibleJTree.AccessibleJTreeNode.getAccessibleValue(),
javax.swing.table.JTableHeader.AccessibleJTableHeader.AccessibleJTableHeaderEntry.getAccessibleValue()

CHAPTER 23

The javax.swing Package

This large package contains the most important classes and interfaces of Swing. Swing is a core part of Java 1.2 and is also available as a standard extension to Java 1.1. The GUI component classes are at the heart of Swing. These classes have names that begin with the letter *J*. Figure 23-1 shows the hierarchy of Swing components in javax.swing. Note that this diagram does not show the fact that all the Swing components implement javax.accessibility.Accessible; see the individual class synopses for this information.

Most Swing components rely on a model object to hold their state information. Various interfaces define the methods that these state objects must implement, and various abstract and concrete classes implement these interfaces. These model interfaces and classes are recognizable by the word "Model" in their names. Figure 23-2 shows the model objects and layout managers in javax.swing.

Classes with the word "Manager" in their names typically manage some important part of the Swing user-interface or application environment. Other important classes and interfaces defined by this package include: Action, Icon, KeyStroke, Timer, and SwingUtilities. Figure 23-3 shows the rest of the classes and interfaces in javax.swing.

All Swing components are *accessible*, which means that they implement the javax.accessiblity.Accessible interface and define getAccessibleContext() methods. This method returns a javax.accessibility.AccessibleContext object that provides support to accessibility tools, such as screen readers for the vision impaired. Each accessible component has its own specific subclass of AccessibleContext, which is typically defined as a protected inner class of the component. These AccessibleContext inner classes have been omitted from this chapter and from Figure 23-1 because they contain little useful information and they detract from other, more important classes. Practically everything you need to know about an AccessibleContext subclass can be found in the single-line inner class synopsis that appears in the containing class, the *accessible* flag of the containing class, and in Chapter 22, *The javax.accessibility Package*.

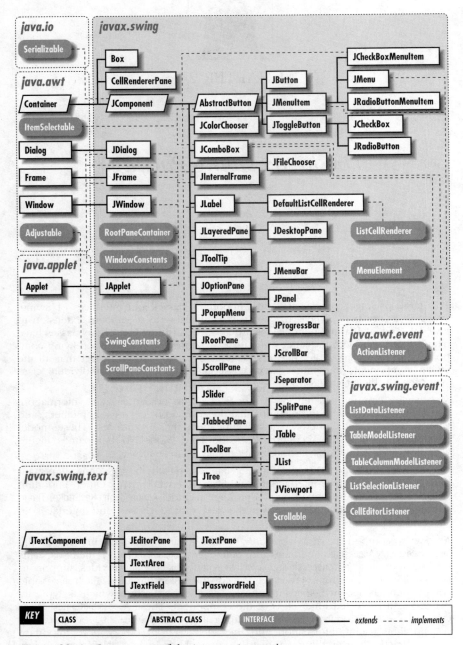

Figure 23-1: Components of the javax.swing package

See Chapter 2, *Swing and AWT Architecture*, for an overview of GUI programming in Java, and see Chapter 3, *Swing Programming Topics*, for detailed explanations of many important Swing components and capabilities.

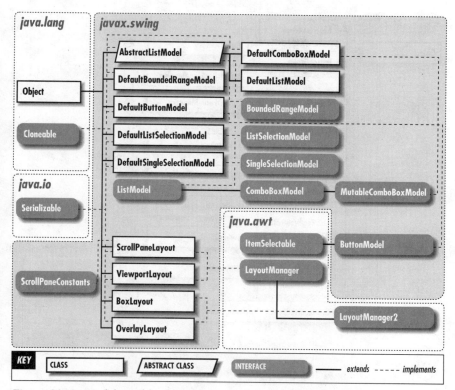

Figure 23–2: Models and layout managers of the java.swing package

AbstractAction

Java 1.2

javax.swing

cloneable serializable

This class implements all the methods of the Action interface except for the crucial actionPerformed() method that provides the substance of the action. Subclassing AbstractAction is one of the easiest ways to define Action objects for your application. Note the one- and two-argument constructors. These constructors automatically define name and icon attributes for the action and are simpler than using putValue().

```
public abstract class AbstractAction implements Action, Cloneable, Serializable {
// Public Constructors
    public AbstractAction();
    public AbstractAction(String name);
    public AbstractAction(String name, Icon icon);
// Event Registration Methods (by event name)
    public void addPropertyChangeListener(                     Implements:Action synchronized
                        java.beans.PropertyChangeListener listener);
    public void removePropertyChangeListener(                  Implements:Action synchronized
                        java.beans.PropertyChangeListener listener);
```

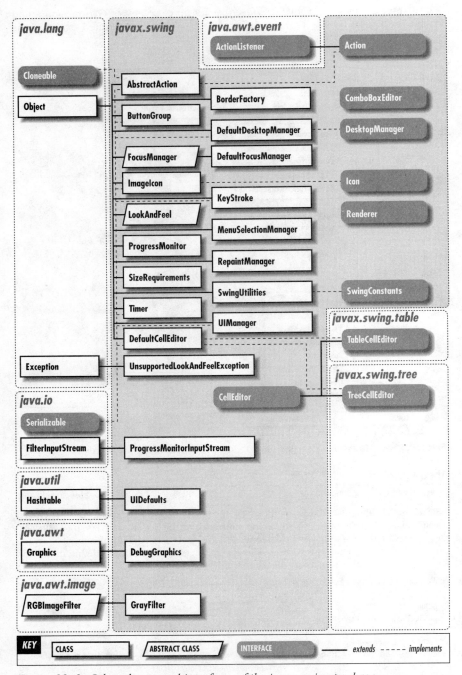

Figure 23-3: Other classes and interfaces of the javax.swing package

```
// Methods Implementing Action
   public void addPropertyChangeListener(java.beans.PropertyChangeListener listener);          synchronized
   public Object getValue(String key);
   public boolean isEnabled();
   public void putValue(String key, Object newValue);                                          synchronized
   public void removePropertyChangeListener(java.beans.PropertyChangeListener listener);        synchronized
   public void setEnabled(boolean newValue);                                                    synchronized
// Methods Implementing ActionListener
   public abstract void actionPerformed(java.awt.event.ActionEvent e);
// Protected Methods Overriding Object
   protected Object clone() throws CloneNotSupportedException;
// Protected Instance Methods
   protected void firePropertyChange(String propertyName, Object oldValue, Object newValue);
// Protected Instance Fields
   protected javax.swing.event.SwingPropertyChangeSupport changeSupport;
   protected boolean enabled;
}
```

Hierarchy: Object→ AbstractAction(Action(java.awt.event.ActionListener(java.util.EventListener)),
Cloneable, Serializable)

Subclasses: javax.swing.text.TextAction

AbstractButton
javax.swing

Java 1.2

serializable swing component

This class serves as the superclass for Swing components with buttonlike behavior. Because it is a general-purpose class, it defines a large number of properties. Like Swing labels, Swing buttons can display text and/or an icon, and several properties specify the relative positioning of the text and icon. (See JLabel for details on these positioning properties.) Swing buttons can display different icons when in different states. In addition to the default icon, AbstractButton has properties that specify icons to be displayed when the button is pressed, selected, disabled, disabled and selected, rolled over, and rolled over and selected. If the rolloverIcon property is specified and if the rolloverEnabled property is true, the rolloverIcon is displayed when the mouse is over the button.

By default, an AbstractButton displays a single line of text in a single font. However, as of Swing 1.1.1 and Java 1.2.2, if the text property begins with "<html>", the button text is formatted as HTML and may contain multiple fonts and multiple lines.

A Swing button may be enabled and disabled with setEnabled(). Disabled buttons are typically displayed with grayed-out graphics, although some other disabled icon can also be specified. A mnemonic can be specified with setMnemonic(). This causes the mnemonic character to be underlined in the button's text and allows the button to be operated via the keyboard.

Swing buttons generate three types of events. A java.awt.event.ActionEvent is generated when any button is pushed. A java.awt.event.ItemEvent is generated when a toggle-type button is selected or deselected. And a javax.swing.event.ChangeEvent is generated when the button's internal state changes—for example, when the mouse pointer enters the button or when the user arms the button by pressing the mouse button.

```
public abstract class AbstractButton extends JComponent implements java.awt.ItemSelectable, SwingConstants {
// Public Constructors
   public AbstractButton();
// Public Constants
   public static final String BORDER_PAINTED_CHANGED_PROPERTY;                    ="borderPainted"
```

public static final String **CONTENT_AREA_FILLED_CHANGED_PROPERTY**;	="contentAreaFilled"
public static final String **DISABLED_ICON_CHANGED_PROPERTY**;	="disabledIcon"
public static final String **DISABLED_SELECTED_ICON_CHANGED_PROPERTY**;	="disabledSelectedIcon"
public static final String **FOCUS_PAINTED_CHANGED_PROPERTY**;	="focusPainted"
public static final String **HORIZONTAL_ALIGNMENT_CHANGED_PROPERTY**;	="horizontalAlignment"
public static final String **HORIZONTAL_TEXT_POSITION_CHANGED_PROPERTY**;	="horizontalTextPosition"
public static final String **ICON_CHANGED_PROPERTY**;	="icon"
public static final String **MARGIN_CHANGED_PROPERTY**;	="margin"
public static final String **MNEMONIC_CHANGED_PROPERTY**;	="mnemonic"
public static final String **MODEL_CHANGED_PROPERTY**;	="model"
public static final String **PRESSED_ICON_CHANGED_PROPERTY**;	="pressedIcon"
public static final String **ROLLOVER_ENABLED_CHANGED_PROPERTY**;	="rolloverEnabled"
public static final String **ROLLOVER_ICON_CHANGED_PROPERTY**;	="rolloverIcon"
public static final String **ROLLOVER_SELECTED_ICON_CHANGED_PROPERTY**;	="rolloverSelectedIcon"
public static final String **SELECTED_ICON_CHANGED_PROPERTY**;	="selectedIcon"
public static final String **TEXT_CHANGED_PROPERTY**;	="text"
public static final String **VERTICAL_ALIGNMENT_CHANGED_PROPERTY**;	="verticalAlignment"
public static final String **VERTICAL_TEXT_POSITION_CHANGED_PROPERTY**;	="verticalTextPosition"

// Inner Classes
    protected abstract class **AccessibleAbstractButton** extends JComponent.AccessibleJComponent
        implements AccessibleAction, AccessibleValue;
    protected class **ButtonChangeListener** implements javax.swing.event.ChangeListener, Serializable;

// Event Registration Methods (by event name)
    public void **addActionListener**(java.awt.event.ActionListener *l*);
    public void **removeActionListener**(java.awt.event.ActionListener *l*);
    public void **addChangeListener**(javax.swing.event.ChangeListener *l*);
    public void **removeChangeListener**(javax.swing.event.ChangeListener *l*);
    public void **addItemListener**(java.awt.event.ItemListener *l*);   *Implements:ItemSelectable*
    public void **removeItemListener**(java.awt.event.ItemListener *l*);   *Implements:ItemSelectable*

// Property Accessor Methods (by property name)
    public String **getActionCommand**();
    public void **setActionCommand**(String *actionCommand*);
    public boolean **isBorderPainted**();
    public void **setBorderPainted**(boolean *b*);   *bound*
    public boolean **isContentAreaFilled**();
    public void **setContentAreaFilled**(boolean *b*);   *bound*
    public Icon **getDisabledIcon**();
    public void **setDisabledIcon**(Icon *disabledIcon*);   *bound*
    public Icon **getDisabledSelectedIcon**();
    public void **setDisabledSelectedIcon**(Icon *disabledSelectedIcon*);
    public boolean **isFocusPainted**();
    public void **setFocusPainted**(boolean *b*);   *bound*
    public int **getHorizontalAlignment**();
    public void **setHorizontalAlignment**(int *alignment*);   *bound*
    public int **getHorizontalTextPosition**();
    public void **setHorizontalTextPosition**(int *textPosition*);   *bound*
    public Icon **getIcon**();
    public void **setIcon**(Icon *defaultIcon*);   *bound*
    public java.awt.Insets **getMargin**();
    public void **setMargin**(java.awt.Insets *m*);   *bound*
    public int **getMnemonic**();
    public void **setMnemonic**(int *mnemonic*);   *bound*
    public void **setMnemonic**(char *mnemonic*);
    public ButtonModel **getModel**();
    public void **setModel**(ButtonModel *newModel*);   *bound*
    public Icon **getPressedIcon**();
    public void **setPressedIcon**(Icon *pressedIcon*);   *bound*
    public boolean **isRolloverEnabled**();

public void **setRolloverEnabled**(boolean *b*);	*bound*
public Icon **getRolloverIcon**();	
public void **setRolloverIcon**(Icon *rolloverIcon*);	*bound*
public Icon **getRolloverSelectedIcon**();	
public void **setRolloverSelectedIcon**(Icon *rolloverSelectedIcon*);	*bound*
public boolean **isSelected**();	
public void **setSelected**(boolean *b*);	
public Icon **getSelectedIcon**();	
public void **setSelectedIcon**(Icon *selectedIcon*);	*bound*
public Object[ ] **getSelectedObjects**();	*Implements:ItemSelectable synchronized*
public String **getText**();	
public void **setText**(String *text*);	*bound preferred*
public javax.swing.plaf.ButtonUI **getUI**();	
public void **setUI**(javax.swing.plaf.ButtonUI *ui*);	
public int **getVerticalAlignment**();	
public void **setVerticalAlignment**(int *alignment*);	*bound*
public int **getVerticalTextPosition**();	
public void **setVerticalTextPosition**(int *textPosition*);	*bound*

// *Public Instance Methods*
    public void **doClick**();
    public void **doClick**(int *pressTime*);
// *Methods Implementing ItemSelectable*
    public void **addItemListener**(java.awt.event.ItemListener *l*);

public Object[ ] **getSelectedObjects**();	*synchronized*

    public void **removeItemListener**(java.awt.event.ItemListener *l*);
// *Public Methods Overriding JComponent*
    public void **setEnabled**(boolean *b*);

public void **updateUI**();	*empty*

// *Protected Methods Overriding JComponent*
    protected void **paintBorder**(java.awt.Graphics *g*);
    protected String **paramString**();
// *Protected Instance Methods*
    protected int **checkHorizontalKey**(int *key*, String *exception*);
    protected int **checkVerticalKey**(int *key*, String *exception*);
    protected java.awt.event.ActionListener **createActionListener**();
    protected javax.swing.event.ChangeListener **createChangeListener**();
    protected java.awt.event.ItemListener **createItemListener**();
    protected void **fireActionPerformed**(java.awt.event.ActionEvent *event*);
    protected void **fireItemStateChanged**(java.awt.event.ItemEvent *event*);
    protected void **fireStateChanged**();
    protected void **init**(String *text*, Icon *icon*);
// *Protected Instance Fields*
    protected java.awt.event.ActionListener **actionListener**;
    protected transient javax.swing.event.ChangeEvent **changeEvent**;
    protected javax.swing.event.ChangeListener **changeListener**;
    protected java.awt.event.ItemListener **itemListener**;
    protected ButtonModel **model**;
// *Deprecated Public Methods*
\# public String **getLabel**();

\# public void **setLabel**(String *label*);	*bound*

}

javax.swing

Hierarchy: Object→ Component(java.awt.image.ImageObserver, java.awt.MenuContainer, Serializable) → Container→ JComponent(Serializable) → AbstractButton(java.awt.ItemSelectable, SwingConstants)

Subclasses: JButton, JMenuItem, JToggleButton

Passed To: ButtonGroup.{add(), remove()}

AbstractButton.ButtonChangeListener

javax.swing

Java 1.2

serializable

This protected inner class is a simple Serializable implementation of javax.swing.event.ChangeListener that AbstractButton uses internally to receive change notifications from its ButtonModel. Application-level code never needs to use this class.

```
protected class AbstractButton.ButtonChangeListener implements javax.swing.event.ChangeListener,
    Serializable {
// No Constructor
// Methods Implementing ChangeListener
    public void stateChanged(javax.swing.event.ChangeEvent e);
}
```

AbstractListModel

javax.swing

Java 1.2

serializable model

This abstract class provides a partial implementation of the ListModel interface. Subclassing AbstractListModel is usually easier than implementing ListModel from scratch. Note, however, that the DefaultListModel class is a usually an adequate ListModel implementation, so you shouldn't need to subclass AbstractListModel very often. Furthermore, the JList component provides convenience methods that often make it unnecessary to work with any kind of ListModel at all.

```
public abstract class AbstractListModel implements ListModel, Serializable {
// Public Constructors
    public AbstractListModel();
// Event Registration Methods (by event name)
    public void addListDataListener(javax.swing.event.ListDataListener l);          Implements:ListModel
    public void removeListDataListener(javax.swing.event.ListDataListener l);       Implements:ListModel
// Methods Implementing ListModel
    public void addListDataListener(javax.swing.event.ListDataListener l);
    public abstract Object getElementAt(int index);
    public abstract int getSize();
    public void removeListDataListener(javax.swing.event.ListDataListener l);
// Protected Instance Methods
    protected void fireContentsChanged(Object source, int index0, int index1);
    protected void fireIntervalAdded(Object source, int index0, int index1);
    protected void fireIntervalRemoved(Object source, int index0, int index1);
// Protected Instance Fields
    protected javax.swing.event.EventListenerList listenerList;
}
```

Hierarchy: Object → AbstractListModel(ListModel, Serializable)

Subclasses: DefaultComboBoxModel, DefaultListModel

Action

javax.swing

Java 1.2

event listener

An action is a single piece of application functionality, such as saving a file or printing a document. The actions performed by an application may be made available to the user in several different ways: in a pulldown or popup menu, in a toolbar, and from a keyboard binding, for example.

The Action interface extends java.awt.event.ActionListener and adds the ability to enable or disable the action. If an editor contains an empty document, its print action probably should not be enabled, for example. setEnabled() specifies whether the action is enabled. When an action is enabled or disabled, this change is broadcast by a java.beans.PropertyChangeEvent.

The Action interface also defines methods that associate attributes with an action. The putValue() method maps an arbitrary attribute name to an arbitrary attribute value. The getValue() method queries an attribute value. The constants defined by the Action interface specify predefined names for commonly used attributes. NAME and SMALL_ICON are the most commonly used. Finally, the actionPerformed() method, inherited from ActionListener, is responsible for performing the action.

JMenu, JPopupMenu, and JToolBar define methods that allow Action objects to be added to them. These methods query the action for its name and an icon that represents the action and use this information to present the action to the user. If the action is enabled, the component allows the user to invoke it. The JTextComponent and Keymap classes from the javax.swing.text package additionally provide techniques for mapping keystrokes to Action objects.

AbstractAction provides a useful starting point for defining your own Action classes.

```
public abstract interface Action extends java.awt.event.ActionListener {
// Public Constants
    public static final String DEFAULT;                                       ="Default"
    public static final String LONG_DESCRIPTION;                       ="LongDescription"
    public static final String NAME;                                            ="Name"
    public static final String SHORT_DESCRIPTION;                    ="ShortDescription"
    public static final String SMALL_ICON;                                  ="SmallIcon"
// Event Registration Methods (by event name)
    public abstract void addPropertyChangeListener(java.beans.PropertyChangeListener listener);
    public abstract void removePropertyChangeListener(java.beans.PropertyChangeListener listener);
// Public Instance Methods
    public abstract Object getValue(String key);
    public abstract boolean isEnabled();
    public abstract void putValue(String key, Object value);
    public abstract void setEnabled(boolean b);
}
```

Hierarchy: (Action(java.awt.event.ActionListener(java.util.EventListener)))

Implementations: AbstractAction

Passed To: JMenu.{add(), insert()}, JPopupMenu.{add(), insert()}, JToolBar.add(), javax.swing.text.JTextComponent.loadKeymap(), javax.swing.text.Keymap.{addActionForKeyStroke(), getKeyStrokesForAction(), setDefaultAction()}, javax.swing.text.TextAction.augmentList()

Returned By: JTextField.getActions(), javax.swing.text.DefaultEditorKit.getActions(), javax.swing.text.EditorKit.getActions(), javax.swing.text.JTextComponent.getActions(), javax.swing.text.Keymap.{getAction(), getBoundActions(), getDefaultAction()}, javax.swing.text.StyledEditorKit.getActions(), javax.swing.text.TextAction.augmentList(), javax.swing.text.html.HTMLEditorKit.getActions()

BorderFactory   Java 1.2

javax.swing

The static methods of this class return various types of Border objects. These methods may return previously created shared objects, making their use more memory-efficient than creating unshared Border objects with the new operator. See the various classes of the javax.swing.border package for more information on the types of borders supported by Swing.

```
public class BorderFactory {
// No Constructor
// Public Class Methods
    public static javax.swing.border.Border createBevelBorder(int type);
    public static javax.swing.border.Border createBevelBorder(int type, java.awt.Color highlight,
                                                              java.awt.Color shadow);
    public static javax.swing.border.Border createBevelBorder(int type, java.awt.Color highlightOuter,
                                                              java.awt.Color highlightInner,
                                                              java.awt.Color shadowOuter,
                                                              java.awt.Color shadowInner);
    public static javax.swing.border.CompoundBorder createCompoundBorder();
    public static javax.swing.border.CompoundBorder createCompoundBorder(
                                                              javax.swing.border.Border outsideBorder,
                                                              javax.swing.border.Border insideBorder);
    public static javax.swing.border.Border createEmptyBorder();
    public static javax.swing.border.Border createEmptyBorder(int top, int left, int bottom, int right);
    public static javax.swing.border.Border createEtchedBorder();
    public static javax.swing.border.Border createEtchedBorder(java.awt.Color highlight, java.awt.Color shadow);
    public static javax.swing.border.Border createLineBorder(java.awt.Color color);
    public static javax.swing.border.Border createLineBorder(java.awt.Color color, int thickness);
    public static javax.swing.border.Border createLoweredBevelBorder();
    public static javax.swing.border.MatteBorder createMatteBorder(int top, int left, int bottom, int right,
                                                              Icon tileIcon);
    public static javax.swing.border.MatteBorder createMatteBorder(int top, int left, int bottom, int right,
                                                              java.awt.Color color);
    public static javax.swing.border.Border createRaisedBevelBorder();
    public static javax.swing.border.TitledBorder createTitledBorder(javax.swing.border.Border border);
    public static javax.swing.border.TitledBorder createTitledBorder(String title);
    public static javax.swing.border.TitledBorder createTitledBorder(javax.swing.border.Border border, String title);
    public static javax.swing.border.TitledBorder createTitledBorder(javax.swing.border.Border border, String title,
                                                              int titleJustification, int titlePosition);
    public static javax.swing.border.TitledBorder createTitledBorder(javax.swing.border.Border border, String title,
                                                              int titleJustification, int titlePosition,
                                                              java.awt.Font titleFont);
    public static javax.swing.border.TitledBorder createTitledBorder(javax.swing.border.Border border, String title,
                                                              int titleJustification, int titlePosition,
                                                              java.awt.Font titleFont, java.awt.Color titleColor);
}
```

BoundedRangeModel   Java 1.2

javax.swing   *model*

This interface defines the data model used by the JScrollBar, JSlider, and JProgressBar components. The model is defined by four integer properties that obey the following relationship:

    minimum <= value <= value+extent <= maximum

The value property specifies the value currently displayed by the component. It must be between the values specified by the minimum and maximum properties. The extent property specifies the amount of data displayed. For JScrollBar components, this property specifies the size of the scrollbar thumb, or knob. Note the convenience method setRangeProperties() that sets all properties of the model at once.

When any value changes, interested listeners are notified with a javax.swing.event.ChangeEvent. One additional property defined by this interface is valueIsAdjusting. If this property is true, it means that a series of rapid property changes (such as those caused when the user drags the scrollbar) is in progress. This property is false for the last change in the series, so listeners can therefore choose to ignore transient changes that have this property set to true.

DefaultBoundedRangeModel is an implementation of this interface appropriate for most uses.

```
public abstract interface BoundedRangeModel {
// Event Registration Methods (by event name)
    public abstract void addChangeListener(javax.swing.event.ChangeListener x);
    public abstract void removeChangeListener(javax.swing.event.ChangeListener x);
// Property Accessor Methods (by property name)
    public abstract int getExtent();
    public abstract void setExtent(int newExtent);
    public abstract int getMaximum();
    public abstract void setMaximum(int newMaximum);
    public abstract int getMinimum();
    public abstract void setMinimum(int newMinimum);
    public abstract int getValue();
    public abstract void setValue(int newValue);
    public abstract boolean getValueIsAdjusting();
    public abstract void setValueIsAdjusting(boolean b);
// Public Instance Methods
    public abstract void setRangeProperties(int value, int extent, int min, int max, boolean adjusting);
}
```

Implementations: DefaultBoundedRangeModel

Passed To: JProgressBar.{JProgressBar(), setModel()}, JScrollBar.setModel(), JSlider.{JSlider(), setModel()}

Returned By: JProgressBar.getModel(), JScrollBar.getModel(), JSlider.getModel(), JTextField.getHorizontalVisibility()

Type Of: JProgressBar.model, JScrollBar.model, JSlider.sliderModel

Box   Java 1.2

javax.swing   *serializable accessible swing component*

This class is a container that uses the BoxLayout layout manager to arrange its children in a row or a column. Pass one of the constants BoxLayout.X_AXIS or BoxLayout.Y_AXIS to the constructor to create a horizontal or vertical box or use the static methods createHorizontalBox() and createVerticalBox(). A horizontal box attempts to lay out its children from left to right, one next to the other, at their preferred widths and tries to make each child as tall as the tallest child. A vertical box does the opposite: it lays out its children from top to bottom, trying both to maintain the preferred height of each child and to make all children as wide as the widest child.

The arrangement of children in a Box is often improved with the use of struts and glue: invisible components that exist only to improve the appearance of a layout. A horizontal strut has 0 height and has a specified value as its minimum, preferred, and maximum width. A vertical strut has 0 width and a fixed height. Struts are useful for inserting fixed amounts of space between components in a Box. Use createHorizontalStrut() and createVerticalStrut() to create struts.

Glue is a component with a preferred width or height of 0 but with an infinite maximum width or height. Glue is used to specify where extra space in a layout should go. For example, if you have three fixed-sized JButton components in a row that is wider than the sum of the button widths, placing glue between them forces them to be evenly spaced. Use createHorizontalGlue() and createVerticalGlue() to create glue components.

```
public class Box extends Container implements Accessible {
// Public Constructors
    public Box(int axis);
// Inner Classes
    protected class AccessibleBox extends AccessibleContext implements AccessibleComponent, Serializable;
    public static class Filler extends Component implements Accessible;
// Public Class Methods
    public static Component createGlue();
    public static Box createHorizontalBox();
    public static Component createHorizontalGlue();
    public static Component createHorizontalStrut(int width);
    public static Component createRigidArea(java.awt.Dimension d);
    public static Box createVerticalBox();
    public static Component createVerticalGlue();
    public static Component createVerticalStrut(int height);
// Property Accessor Methods (by property name)
    public AccessibleContext getAccessibleContext();                       Implements:Accessible
    public void setLayout(java.awt.LayoutManager l);                        Overrides:Container
// Methods Implementing Accessible
    public AccessibleContext getAccessibleContext();
// Protected Instance Fields
    protected AccessibleContext accessibleContext;
}
```

Hierarchy: Object→ Component(java.awt.image.ImageObserver, java.awt.MenuContainer, Serializable)→ Container→ Box(Accessible)

Returned By: Box.{createHorizontalBox(), createVerticalBox()}

Box.Filler

javax.swing

Java 1.2

serializable accessible swing component

This class implements the invisible component used to create struts and glue for use with the Box container. It allows you to create an invisible component with any specified minimum, preferred, and maximum sizes.

```
public static class Box.Filler extends Component implements Accessible {
// Public Constructors
    public Filler(java.awt.Dimension min, java.awt.Dimension pref, java.awt.Dimension max);
// Inner Classes
    protected class AccessibleBoxFiller extends AccessibleContext implements AccessibleComponent, Serializable;
// Property Accessor Methods (by property name)
    public AccessibleContext getAccessibleContext();                       Implements:Accessible
    public java.awt.Dimension getMaximumSize();                            Overrides:Component
    public java.awt.Dimension getMinimumSize();                            Overrides:Component
    public java.awt.Dimension getPreferredSize();                          Overrides:Component
// Public Instance Methods
    public void changeShape(java.awt.Dimension min, java.awt.Dimension pref, java.awt.Dimension max);
// Methods Implementing Accessible
    public AccessibleContext getAccessibleContext();
// Protected Instance Fields
    protected AccessibleContext accessibleContext;
}
```

BoxLayout

javax.swing

Java 1.2

serializable layout manager

This class is a layout manager that arranges its children into a row or a column. It is the layout manager used by the Box container. See Box for details.

```
public class BoxLayout implements java.awt.LayoutManager2, Serializable {
// Public Constructors
    public BoxLayout(Container target, int axis);
// Public Constants
    public static final int X_AXIS;                                                    =0
    public static final int Y_AXIS;                                                    =1
// Methods Implementing LayoutManager
    public void addLayoutComponent(String name, Component comp);                   empty
    public void layoutContainer(Container target);
    public java.awt.Dimension minimumLayoutSize(Container target);
    public java.awt.Dimension preferredLayoutSize(Container target);
    public void removeLayoutComponent(Component comp);                            empty
// Methods Implementing LayoutManager2
    public void addLayoutComponent(Component comp, Object constraints);           empty
    public float getLayoutAlignmentX(Container target);
    public float getLayoutAlignmentY(Container target);
    public void invalidateLayout(Container target);
    public java.awt.Dimension maximumLayoutSize(Container target);
}
```

Hierarchy: Object→ BoxLayout(java.awt.LayoutManager2(java.awt.LayoutManager), Serializable)

ButtonGroup   Java 1.2

javax.swing   *serializable*

This class enforces mutual exclusion (radio behavior) for a group of toggle buttons. Once buttons are added to a ButtonGroup with the add() method, mutual exclusion is automatic, and no further action is necessary.

```
public class ButtonGroup implements Serializable {
// Public Constructors
    public ButtonGroup();
// Property Accessor Methods (by property name)
    public java.util.Enumeration getElements();
    public ButtonModel getSelection();                                         default:null
// Public Instance Methods
    public void add(AbstractButton b);
    public boolean isSelected(ButtonModel m);
    public void remove(AbstractButton b);
    public void setSelected(ButtonModel m, boolean b);
// Protected Instance Fields
    protected java.util.Vector buttons;
}
```

Hierarchy: Object→ ButtonGroup(Serializable)

Passed To: ButtonModel.setGroup(), DefaultButtonModel.setGroup()

Type Of: DefaultButtonModel.group

ButtonModel   Java 1.2

javax.swing   *model*

This interface defines the model for Swing buttons. This model consists of five boolean properties that specify the current selection state of the button and three other properties that specify an optional mnemonic, ButtonGroup, and action command (a string passed with a java.awt.event.ActionEvent) for the button.

```
public abstract interface ButtonModel extends java.awt.ItemSelectable {
// Event Registration Methods (by event name)
    public abstract void addActionListener(java.awt.event.ActionListener l);
    public abstract void removeActionListener(java.awt.event.ActionListener l);
    public abstract void addChangeListener(javax.swing.event.ChangeListener l);
    public abstract void removeChangeListener(javax.swing.event.ChangeListener l);
    public abstract void addItemListener(java.awt.event.ItemListener l);
    public abstract void removeItemListener(java.awt.event.ItemListener l);
// Property Accessor Methods (by property name)
    public abstract String getActionCommand();
    public abstract void setActionCommand(String s);
    public abstract boolean isArmed();
    public abstract void setArmed(boolean b);
    public abstract boolean isEnabled();
    public abstract void setEnabled(boolean b);
    public abstract int getMnemonic();
    public abstract void setMnemonic(int key);
    public abstract boolean isPressed();
    public abstract void setPressed(boolean b);
    public abstract boolean isRollover();
    public abstract void setRollover(boolean b);
    public abstract boolean isSelected();
    public abstract void setSelected(boolean b);
// Public Instance Methods
    public abstract void setGroup(ButtonGroup group);
}
```

Hierarchy: (ButtonModel(java.awt.ItemSelectable))

Implementations: DefaultButtonModel

Passed To: AbstractButton.setModel(), ButtonGroup.{isSelected(), setSelected()}, JMenu.setModel()

Returned By: AbstractButton.getModel(), ButtonGroup.getSelection()

Type Of: AbstractButton.model

CellEditor   Java 1.2

javax.swing

This interface defines general methods that must be implemented by any cell editor object. isCellEditable() should return true if the cell is editable and if the specified event is an appropriate event to trigger an edit. (For example, some programs might require a double-click to edit a cell.) shouldSelectCell() should return true if the given event should cause the cell to become selected or false otherwise. However, this is only a minor secondary purpose of the method. Despite its name, the primary purpose of shouldSelect-Cell() is to cause the cell editor to begin editing the cell. The editor can use the specified event to set the initial state (e.g., cursor position) of the editor.

getCellEditorValue() returns the value being edited. cancelCellEditing() cancels an edit. stopCellEditing() instructs the editor to stop editing and accept a partially edited value. An editor may return false if it cannot accept the current value (because the partial value is not valid, for example). If the editor stops or cancels editing itself, it sends a javax.swing.event.ChangeEvent to any registered javax.swing.event.CellEditorListener objects.

javax.swing.table.TableCellEditor and javax.swing.tree.TreeCellEditor are table- and tree-specific cell editor interfaces; DefaultCellEditor is an implementation of both those interfaces.

```
public abstract interface CellEditor {
// Event Registration Methods (by event name)
    public abstract void addCellEditorListener(javax.swing.event.CellEditorListener l);
    public abstract void removeCellEditorListener(javax.swing.event.CellEditorListener l);
// Public Instance Methods
    public abstract void cancelCellEditing();
    public abstract Object getCellEditorValue();
    public abstract boolean isCellEditable(java.util.EventObject anEvent);
    public abstract boolean shouldSelectCell(java.util.EventObject anEvent);
    public abstract boolean stopCellEditing();
}
```

Implementations: javax.swing.table.TableCellEditor, javax.swing.tree.TreeCellEditor

CellRendererPane   Java 1.2

javax.swing   *serializable accessible swing component*

This class is used by Swing components that rely on cell renderer interfaces, such as
ListCellRenderer, javax.swing.table.TableCellRenderer, and javax.swing.tree.TreeCellRenderer. The
methods of this class are used to paint a single cell renderer component at various
specified locations within a container.

```
public class CellRendererPane extends Container implements Accessible {
// Public Constructors
    public CellRendererPane();
// Inner Classes
    protected class AccessibleCellRendererPane extends AccessibleContext implements AccessibleComponent,
        Serializable;
// Property Accessor Methods (by property name)
    public AccessibleContext getAccessibleContext();      Implements:Accessible default:AccessibleCellRendererPane
// Public Instance Methods
    public void paintComponent(java.awt.Graphics g, Component c, Container p, java.awt.Rectangle r);
    public void paintComponent(java.awt.Graphics g, Component c, Container p, int x, int y, int w, int h);
    public void paintComponent(java.awt.Graphics g, Component c, Container p, int x, int y, int w, int h,
                            boolean shouldValidate);
// Methods Implementing Accessible
    public AccessibleContext getAccessibleContext();                    default:AccessibleCellRendererPane
// Public Methods Overriding Container
    public void invalidate();                                                            empty
    public void paint(java.awt.Graphics g);                                              empty
    public void update(java.awt.Graphics g);                                             empty
// Protected Methods Overriding Container
    protected void addImpl(Component x, Object constraints, int index);
// Protected Instance Fields
    protected AccessibleContext accessibleContext;
}
```

Hierarchy: Object→ Component(java.awt.image.ImageObserver, java.awt.MenuContainer, Serializable)→
Container→ CellRendererPane(Accessible)

ComboBoxEditor   Java 1.2

javax.swing

This interface defines the methods that must be implemented by an object that wishes
to serve as the editor object for a JComboBox component. It is typically implemented as
part of a pluggable look-and-feel and is not normally used by application programmers.

```
public abstract interface ComboBoxEditor {
// Event Registration Methods (by event name)
    public abstract void addActionListener(java.awt.event.ActionListener l);
    public abstract void removeActionListener(java.awt.event.ActionListener l);
// Public Instance Methods
    public abstract Component getEditorComponent();
    public abstract Object getItem();
    public abstract void selectAll();
    public abstract void setItem(Object anObject);
}
```

Passed To: JComboBox.{configureEditor(), setEditor()}

Returned By: JComboBox.getEditor()

Type Of: JComboBox.editor

ComboBoxModel   Java 1.2

javax.swing   *model*

This interface defines the basic model used by the JComboBox component. The JComboBox allows the user to select a value from a list or type a value directly. Therefore, ComboBoxModel extends ListModel to add support for a selected item, in addition to the list of items that ListModel already supports. See also MutableComboBoxModel and Default-ComboBoxModel.

```
public abstract interface ComboBoxModel extends ListModel {
// Public Instance Methods
    public abstract Object getSelectedItem();
    public abstract void setSelectedItem(Object anItem);
}
```

Hierarchy: (ComboBoxModel(ListModel))

Implementations: MutableComboBoxModel

Passed To: JComboBox.{JComboBox(), setModel()}, JComboBox.KeySelectionManager.selectionForKey()

Returned By: JComboBox.getModel()

Type Of: JComboBox.dataModel

DebugGraphics   Java 1.2

javax.swing

This subclass of java.awt.Graphics reimplements most of the methods of its superclass to facilitate debugging of drawing operations. Instances of this class are rarely used directly; programs can enable graphics debugging by calling setDebugGraphicsOptions() on any Swing component.

```
public class DebugGraphics extends java.awt.Graphics {
// Public Constructors
    public DebugGraphics();
    public DebugGraphics(java.awt.Graphics graphics);
    public DebugGraphics(java.awt.Graphics graphics, JComponent component);
// Public Constants
    public static final int BUFFERED_OPTION;                              =4
    public static final int FLASH_OPTION;                                 =2
    public static final int LOG_OPTION;                                   =1
    public static final int NONE_OPTION;                                  =-1
```

```
// Public Class Methods
    public static java.awt.Color flashColor();
    public static int flashCount();
    public static int flashTime();
    public static java.io.PrintStream logStream();
    public static void setFlashColor(java.awt.Color flashColor);
    public static void setFlashCount(int flashCount);
    public static void setFlashTime(int flashTime);
    public static void setLogStream(java.io.PrintStream stream);
// Property Accessor Methods (by property name)
    public java.awt.Shape getClip();                                          Overrides:Graphics
    public void setClip(java.awt.Shape clip);                                 Overrides:Graphics
    public void setClip(int x, int y, int width, int height);                 Overrides:Graphics
    public java.awt.Rectangle getClipBounds();                                Overrides:Graphics
    public java.awt.Color getColor();                                         Overrides:Graphics
    public void setColor(java.awt.Color aColor);                              Overrides:Graphics
    public int getDebugOptions();                                                    default:0
    public void setDebugOptions(int options);
    public boolean isDrawingBuffer();                                            default:false
    public java.awt.Font getFont();                                           Overrides:Graphics
    public void setFont(java.awt.Font aFont);                                 Overrides:Graphics
    public java.awt.FontMetrics getFontMetrics();                            Overrides:Graphics
    public java.awt.FontMetrics getFontMetrics(java.awt.Font f);             Overrides:Graphics
// Public Methods Overriding Graphics
    public void clearRect(int x, int y, int width, int height);
    public void clipRect(int x, int y, int width, int height);
    public void copyArea(int x, int y, int width, int height, int destX, int destY);
    public java.awt.Graphics create();
    public java.awt.Graphics create(int x, int y, int width, int height);
    public void dispose();
    public void draw3DRect(int x, int y, int width, int height, boolean raised);
    public void drawArc(int x, int y, int width, int height, int startAngle, int arcAngle);
    public void drawBytes(byte[] data, int offset, int length, int x, int y);
    public void drawChars(char[] data, int offset, int length, int x, int y);
    public boolean drawImage(java.awt.Image img, int x, int y, java.awt.image.ImageObserver observer);
    public boolean drawImage(java.awt.Image img, int x, int y, java.awt.Color bgcolor,
                             java.awt.image.ImageObserver observer);
    public boolean drawImage(java.awt.Image img, int x, int y, int width, int height,
                             java.awt.image.ImageObserver observer);
    public boolean drawImage(java.awt.Image img, int x, int y, int width, int height, java.awt.Color bgcolor,
                             java.awt.image.ImageObserver observer);
    public boolean drawImage(java.awt.Image img, int dx1, int dy1, int dx2, int dy2, int sx1, int sy1, int sx2, int sy2,
                             java.awt.image.ImageObserver observer);
    public boolean drawImage(java.awt.Image img, int dx1, int dy1, int dx2, int dy2, int sx1, int sy1, int sx2, int sy2,
                             java.awt.Color bgcolor, java.awt.image.ImageObserver observer);
    public void drawLine(int x1, int y1, int x2, int y2);
    public void drawOval(int x, int y, int width, int height);
    public void drawPolygon(int[] xPoints, int[] yPoints, int nPoints);
    public void drawPolyline(int[] xPoints, int[] yPoints, int nPoints);
    public void drawRect(int x, int y, int width, int height);
    public void drawRoundRect(int x, int y, int width, int height, int arcWidth, int arcHeight);
    public void drawString(java.text.AttributedCharacterIterator iterator, int x, int y);
    public void drawString(String aString, int x, int y);
    public void fill3DRect(int x, int y, int width, int height, boolean raised);
    public void fillArc(int x, int y, int width, int height, int startAngle, int arcAngle);
    public void fillOval(int x, int y, int width, int height);
    public void fillPolygon(int[] xPoints, int[] yPoints, int nPoints);
    public void fillRect(int x, int y, int width, int height);
```

```
        public void fillRoundRect(int x, int y, int width, int height, int arcWidth, int arcHeight);
        public void setPaintMode();
        public void setXORMode(java.awt.Color aColor);
        public void translate(int x, int y);
}
```

Hierarchy: Object→ java.awt.Graphics→ DebugGraphics

DefaultBoundedRangeModel   Java 1.2

javax.swing   *serializable model*

This class is an implementation of the BoundedRangeModel appropriate for most uses. See
BoundedRangeModel for details.

```
public class DefaultBoundedRangeModel implements BoundedRangeModel, Serializable {
// Public Constructors
        public DefaultBoundedRangeModel();
        public DefaultBoundedRangeModel(int value, int extent, int min, int max);
// Event Registration Methods (by event name)
        public void addChangeListener(javax.swing.event.ChangeListener l);         Implements:BoundedRangeModel
        public void removeChangeListener(javax.swing.event.ChangeListener l);      Implements:BoundedRangeModel
// Methods Implementing BoundedRangeModel
        public void addChangeListener(javax.swing.event.ChangeListener l);
        public int getExtent();                                                             default:0
        public int getMaximum();                                                         default:100
        public int getMinimum();                                                            default:0
        public int getValue();                                                              default:0
        public boolean getValueIsAdjusting();                                            default:false
        public void removeChangeListener(javax.swing.event.ChangeListener l);
        public void setExtent(int n);
        public void setMaximum(int n);
        public void setMinimum(int n);
        public void setRangeProperties(int newValue, int newExtent, int newMin, int newMax, boolean adjusting);
        public void setValue(int n);
        public void setValueIsAdjusting(boolean b);
// Public Methods Overriding Object
        public String toString();
// Protected Instance Methods
        protected void fireStateChanged();
// Protected Instance Fields
        protected transient javax.swing.event.ChangeEvent changeEvent;
        protected javax.swing.event.EventListenerList listenerList;
}
```

Hierarchy: Object→ DefaultBoundedRangeModel(BoundedRangeModel, Serializable)

DefaultButtonModel   Java 1.2

javax.swing   *serializable model*

This class is a straightforward implementation of the ButtonModel interface that is suitable
for most uses. It is the default model for JButton and JMenuItem.

```
public class DefaultButtonModel implements ButtonModel, Serializable {
// Public Constructors
        public DefaultButtonModel();
// Public Constants
        public static final int ARMED;                                                         =1
        public static final int ENABLED;                                                       =8
```

```
      public static final int PRESSED;                                                =4
      public static final int ROLLOVER;                                               =16
      public static final int SELECTED;                                               =2
// Event Registration Methods (by event name)
      public void addActionListener(java.awt.event.ActionListener l);      Implements:ButtonModel
      public void removeActionListener(java.awt.event.ActionListener l);   Implements:ButtonModel
      public void addChangeListener(javax.swing.event.ChangeListener l);   Implements:ButtonModel
      public void removeChangeListener(javax.swing.event.ChangeListener l); Implements:ButtonModel
      public void addItemListener(java.awt.event.ItemListener l);          Implements:ButtonModel
      public void removeItemListener(java.awt.event.ItemListener l);       Implements:ButtonModel
// Methods Implementing ButtonModel
      public void addActionListener(java.awt.event.ActionListener l);
      public void addChangeListener(javax.swing.event.ChangeListener l);
      public void addItemListener(java.awt.event.ItemListener l);
      public String getActionCommand();                                         default:null
      public int getMnemonic();                                                   default:0
      public boolean isArmed();                                               default:false
      public boolean isEnabled();                                              default:true
      public boolean isPressed();                                             default:false
      public boolean isRollover();                                            default:false
      public boolean isSelected();                                            default:false
      public void removeActionListener(java.awt.event.ActionListener l);
      public void removeChangeListener(javax.swing.event.ChangeListener l);
      public void removeItemListener(java.awt.event.ItemListener l);
      public void setActionCommand(String actionCommand);
      public void setArmed(boolean b);
      public void setEnabled(boolean b);
      public void setGroup(ButtonGroup group);
      public void setMnemonic(int key);
      public void setPressed(boolean b);
      public void setRollover(boolean b);
      public void setSelected(boolean b);
// Methods Implementing ItemSelectable
      public Object[ ] getSelectedObjects();                            constant default:null
// Protected Instance Methods
      protected void fireActionPerformed(java.awt.event.ActionEvent e);
      protected void fireItemStateChanged(java.awt.event.ItemEvent e);
      protected void fireStateChanged();
// Protected Instance Fields
      protected String actionCommand;
      protected transient javax.swing.event.ChangeEvent changeEvent;
      protected ButtonGroup group;
      protected javax.swing.event.EventListenerList listenerList;
      protected int mnemonic;
      protected int stateMask;
}
```

Hierarchy: Object→ DefaultButtonModel(ButtonModel(java.awt.ItemSelectable), Serializable)

Subclasses: JToggleButton.ToggleButtonModel

DefaultCellEditor   Java 1.2

javax.swing   *serializable*

This class implements both the javax.swing.table.TableCellEditor and the javax.swing.tree.Tree-CellEditor interfaces. It is the default editor class used by JTable. Instances of this class can be created to use a specified JTextField, JCheckBox, or JComboBox as the editor component.

```
public class DefaultCellEditor implements Serializable, javax.swing.table.TableCellEditor,
      javax.swing.tree.TreeCellEditor {
```

```
// Public Constructors
    public DefaultCellEditor(JComboBox comboBox);
    public DefaultCellEditor(JTextField textField);
    public DefaultCellEditor(JCheckBox checkBox);
// Inner Classes
    protected class EditorDelegate implements java.awt.event.ActionListener, java.awt.event.ItemListener,
        Serializable;
// Event Registration Methods (by event name)
    public void addCellEditorListener(javax.swing.event.CellEditorListener l);           Implements:CellEditor
    public void removeCellEditorListener(javax.swing.event.CellEditorListener l);        Implements:CellEditor
// Public Instance Methods
    public int getClickCountToStart();
    public Component getComponent();
    public void setClickCountToStart(int count);
// Methods Implementing CellEditor
    public void addCellEditorListener(javax.swing.event.CellEditorListener l);
    public void cancelCellEditing();
    public Object getCellEditorValue();
    public boolean isCellEditable(java.util.EventObject anEvent);
    public void removeCellEditorListener(javax.swing.event.CellEditorListener l);
    public boolean shouldSelectCell(java.util.EventObject anEvent);
    public boolean stopCellEditing();
// Methods Implementing TableCellEditor
    public Component getTableCellEditorComponent(JTable table, Object value, boolean isSelected, int row,
                                                  int column);
// Methods Implementing TreeCellEditor
    public Component getTreeCellEditorComponent(JTree tree, Object value, boolean isSelected,
                                                  boolean expanded, boolean leaf, int row);
// Protected Instance Methods
    protected void fireEditingCanceled();
    protected void fireEditingStopped();
// Protected Instance Fields
    protected transient javax.swing.event.ChangeEvent changeEvent;
    protected int clickCountToStart;
    protected DefaultCellEditor.EditorDelegate delegate;
    protected JComponent editorComponent;
    protected javax.swing.event.EventListenerList listenerList;
}
```

Hierarchy: Object → DefaultCellEditor(Serializable, javax.swing.table.TableCellEditor(CellEditor), javax.swing.tree.TreeCellEditor(CellEditor))

DefaultCellEditor.EditorDelegate   Java 1.2

javax.swing   *serializable*

This DefaultCellEditor class can use a JTextField, JComboBox, or JCheckBox as the cell editor component. This protected inner class is used internally by DefaultCellEditor to encapsulate the differences between these three editor components. Application-level code never needs to use this class.

```
protected class DefaultCellEditor.EditorDelegate implements java.awt.event.ActionListener,
        java.awt.event.ItemListener, Serializable {
// Protected Constructors
    protected EditorDelegate();
// Property Accessor Methods (by property name)
    public Object getCellEditorValue();                                              constant
```

```
// Public Instance Methods
    public void cancelCellEditing();                                                    empty
    public boolean isCellEditable(java.util.EventObject anEvent);                        constant
    public void setValue(Object x);                                                      empty
    public boolean startCellEditing(java.util.EventObject anEvent);                      constant
    public boolean stopCellEditing();                                                    constant
// Methods Implementing ActionListener
    public void actionPerformed(java.awt.event.ActionEvent e);
// Methods Implementing ItemListener
    public void itemStateChanged(java.awt.event.ItemEvent e);
// Protected Instance Fields
    protected Object value;
}
```

Type Of: DefaultCellEditor.delegate

DefaultComboBoxModel   Java 1.2

javax.swing   *serializable model*

This MutableComboBoxModel implementation is the default model object used by the
JComboBox component. In addition to the methods of the MutableComboBoxModel, ComboBoxModel, and ListModel interfaces, DefaultComboBoxModel also implements methods to
remove all elements from the list and to find a specified element in the list.

```
public class DefaultComboBoxModel extends AbstractListModel implements MutableComboBoxModel,
        Serializable {
// Public Constructors
    public DefaultComboBoxModel();
    public DefaultComboBoxModel(Object[] items);
    public DefaultComboBoxModel(java.util.Vector v);
// Public Instance Methods
    public int getIndexOf(Object anObject);
    public void removeAllElements();
// Methods Implementing ComboBoxModel
    public Object getSelectedItem();                                                    default:null
    public void setSelectedItem(Object anObject);
// Methods Implementing ListModel
    public Object getElementAt(int index);
    public int getSize();                                                               default:0
// Methods Implementing MutableComboBoxModel
    public void addElement(Object anObject);
    public void insertElementAt(Object anObject, int index);
    public void removeElement(Object anObject);
    public void removeElementAt(int index);
}
```

Hierarchy: Object→ AbstractListModel(ListModel, Serializable)→
DefaultComboBoxModel(MutableComboBoxModel(ComboBoxModel(ListModel)), Serializable)

DefaultDesktopManager   Java 1.2

javax.swing   *serializable*

This class is a simple default implementation of the DesktopManager interface. It can be
used as a starting point for pluggable look-and-feel DesktopManager implementations. It
is also used to manage JInternalFrame components that are not within a JDesktopPane.
Appliations typically do not need to use this class.

```
public class DefaultDesktopManager implements DesktopManager, Serializable {
// Public Constructors
     public DefaultDesktopManager( );
// Methods Implementing DesktopManager
     public void activateFrame(JInternalFrame f);
     public void beginDraggingFrame(JComponent f);
     public void beginResizingFrame(JComponent f, int direction);
     public void closeFrame(JInternalFrame f);
     public void deactivateFrame(JInternalFrame f);
     public void deiconifyFrame(JInternalFrame f);
     public void dragFrame(JComponent f, int newX, int newY);
     public void endDraggingFrame(JComponent f);
     public void endResizingFrame(JComponent f);
     public void iconifyFrame(JInternalFrame f);
     public void maximizeFrame(JInternalFrame f);
     public void minimizeFrame(JInternalFrame f);
     public void openFrame(JInternalFrame f);
     public void resizeFrame(JComponent f, int newX, int newY, int newWidth, int newHeight);
     public void setBoundsForFrame(JComponent f, int newX, int newY, int newWidth, int newHeight);
// Protected Instance Methods
     protected java.awt.Rectangle getBoundsForIconOf(JInternalFrame f);
     protected java.awt.Rectangle getPreviousBounds(JInternalFrame f);
     protected void removeIconFor(JInternalFrame f);
     protected void setPreviousBounds(JInternalFrame f, java.awt.Rectangle r);
     protected void setWasIcon(JInternalFrame f, Boolean value);
     protected boolean wasIcon(JInternalFrame f);
}
```

Hierarchy: Object→ DefaultDesktopManager(DesktopManager, Serializable)

DefaultFocusManager   Java 1.2

javax.swing

This class is the default FocusManager used by Swing components. It uses the **Tab** and **Shift-Tab** keys to move focus forward and backward.

```
public class DefaultFocusManager extends FocusManager {
// Public Constructors
     public DefaultFocusManager( );
// Public Instance Methods
     public boolean compareTabOrder(Component a, Component b);
     public Component getComponentAfter(Container aContainer, Component aComponent);
     public Component getComponentBefore(Container aContainer, Component aComponent);
     public Component getFirstComponent(Container aContainer);
     public Component getLastComponent(Container aContainer);
// Public Methods Overriding FocusManager
     public void focusNextComponent(Component aComponent);
     public void focusPreviousComponent(Component aComponent);
     public void processKeyEvent(Component focusedComponent, java.awt.event.KeyEvent anEvent);
}
```

Hierarchy: Object→ FocusManager→ DefaultFocusManager

DefaultListCellRenderer   Java 1.2

javax.swing   *serializable accessible swing component*

This class is the default ListCellRenderer used by the JList component to render the items of the list. This class extends JLabel and uses JLabel features to render list items. Since JList uses this class by default, you should not have to instantiate or use it directly.

```
public class DefaultListCellRenderer extends JLabel implements ListCellRenderer, Serializable {
// Public Constructors
    public DefaultListCellRenderer();
// Inner Classes
    public static class UIResource extends DefaultListCellRenderer implements javax.swing.plaf.UIResource;
// Methods Implementing ListCellRenderer
    public Component getListCellRendererComponent(JList list, Object value, int index, boolean isSelected,
                                                  boolean cellHasFocus);
// Protected Class Fields
    protected static javax.swing.border.Border noFocusBorder;
}
```

Hierarchy: Object→ Component(java.awt.image.ImageObserver, java.awt.MenuContainer, Serializable)→
Container→ JComponent(Serializable)→ JLabel(Accessible, SwingConstants)→
DefaultListCellRenderer(ListCellRenderer, Serializable)

Subclasses: DefaultListCellRenderer.UIResource

DefaultListCellRenderer.UIResource   Java 1.2

javax.swing   *serializable accessible swing component*

This class is a trivial wrapper around DefaultListCellRenderer. It implements the empty
javax.swing.plaf.UIResource marker interface in order to distinguish cell renderers supplied
by a look-and-feel from cell renderers supplied by the user. Like all classes that implement UIResource, this class is used by implementors of custom look-and-feels. Applications do not need to use this class.

```
public static class DefaultListCellRenderer.UIResource extends DefaultListCellRenderer
       implements javax.swing.plaf.UIResource {
// Public Constructors
    public UIResource();
}
```

DefaultListModel   Java 1.2

javax.swing   *serializable model*

This class is a ListModel implementation that is based on AbstractListModel, with the addition of java.util.Vector methods for modifying the values contained in the list. This class is
suitable for most uses of the JList component, but you may on occasion want to implement a custom ListModel, probably by subclassing AbstractListModel.

```
public class DefaultListModel extends AbstractListModel {
// Public Constructors
    public DefaultListModel();
// Property Accessor Methods (by property name)
    public boolean isEmpty();                                          default:true
    public int getSize();                      Overrides:AbstractListModel default:0
    public void setSize(int newSize);
// Public Instance Methods
    public void add(int index, Object element);
    public void addElement(Object obj);
    public int capacity();
    public void clear();
    public boolean contains(Object elem);
    public void copyInto(Object[ ] anArray);
    public Object elementAt(int index);
    public java.util.Enumeration elements();
```

```
    public void ensureCapacity(int minCapacity);
    public Object firstElement();
    public Object get(int index);
    public int indexOf(Object elem);
    public int indexOf(Object elem, int index);
    public void insertElementAt(Object obj, int index);
    public Object lastElement();
    public int lastIndexOf(Object elem);
    public int lastIndexOf(Object elem, int index);
    public Object remove(int index);
    public void removeAllElements();
    public boolean removeElement(Object obj);
    public void removeElementAt(int index);
    public void removeRange(int fromIndex, int toIndex);
    public Object set(int index, Object element);
    public void setElementAt(Object obj, int index);
    public int size();
    public Object[ ] toArray();
    public void trimToSize();
// Public Methods Overriding AbstractListModel
    public Object getElementAt(int index);
// Public Methods Overriding Object
    public String toString();
}
```

Hierarchy: Object→ AbstractListModel(ListModel, Serializable)→ DefaultListModel

DefaultListSelectionModel   Java 1.2

javax.swing   *cloneable serializable model*

This class is the default implementation of the ListSelectionModel interface. It is used by JList and JTable components. Typical applications do not need to explicitly use this class or the ListSelectionModel interface.

```
public class DefaultListSelectionModel implements Cloneable, ListSelectionModel, Serializable {
// Public Constructors
    public DefaultListSelectionModel();
// Event Registration Methods (by event name)
    public void addListSelectionListener(javax.swing.event.ListSelectionListener l);    Implements:ListSelectionModel
    public void removeListSelectionListener(                                            Implements:ListSelectionModel
                            javax.swing.event.ListSelectionListener l);
// Public Instance Methods
    public boolean isLeadAnchorNotificationEnabled();                                                   default:true
    public void setLeadAnchorNotificationEnabled(boolean flag);
// Methods Implementing ListSelectionModel
    public void addListSelectionListener(javax.swing.event.ListSelectionListener l);
    public void addSelectionInterval(int index0, int index1);
    public void clearSelection();
    public int getAnchorSelectionIndex();                                                                 default:-1
    public int getLeadSelectionIndex();                                                                   default:-1
    public int getMaxSelectionIndex();                                                                    default:-1
    public int getMinSelectionIndex();                                                                    default:-1
    public int getSelectionMode();                                                                         default:2
    public boolean getValueIsAdjusting();                                                              default:false
    public void insertIndexInterval(int index, int length, boolean before);
    public boolean isSelectedIndex(int index);
    public boolean isSelectionEmpty();                                                                  default:true
    public void removeIndexInterval(int index0, int index1);
```

```
    public void removeListSelectionListener(javax.swing.event.ListSelectionListener l);
    public void removeSelectionInterval(int index0, int index1);
    public void setAnchorSelectionIndex(int anchorIndex);
    public void setLeadSelectionIndex(int leadIndex);
    public void setSelectionInterval(int index0, int index1);
    public void setSelectionMode(int selectionMode);
    public void setValueIsAdjusting(boolean isAdjusting);
// Public Methods Overriding Object
    public Object clone() throws CloneNotSupportedException;
    public String toString();
// Protected Instance Methods
    protected void fireValueChanged(boolean isAdjusting);
    protected void fireValueChanged(int firstIndex, int lastIndex);
    protected void fireValueChanged(int firstIndex, int lastIndex, boolean isAdjusting);
// Protected Instance Fields
    protected boolean leadAnchorNotificationEnabled;
    protected javax.swing.event.EventListenerList listenerList;
}
```

Hierarchy: Object→ DefaultListSelectionModel(Cloneable, ListSelectionModel, Serializable)

Type Of: javax.swing.tree.DefaultTreeSelectionModel.listSelectionModel

DefaultSingleSelectionModel   Java 1.2

javax.swing   *serializable model*

This class is the default implementation of the SingleSelectionModel interface. It is used by
JMenuBar, JPopupMenu, and JTabbedPane.

```
public class DefaultSingleSelectionModel implements Serializable, SingleSelectionModel {
// Public Constructors
    public DefaultSingleSelectionModel();
// Event Registration Methods (by event name)
    public void addChangeListener(javax.swing.event.ChangeListener l);        Implements:SingleSelectionModel
    public void removeChangeListener(javax.swing.event.ChangeListener l);     Implements:SingleSelectionModel
// Methods Implementing SingleSelectionModel
    public void addChangeListener(javax.swing.event.ChangeListener l);
    public void clearSelection();
    public int getSelectedIndex();                                            default:-1
    public boolean isSelected();                                              default:false
    public void removeChangeListener(javax.swing.event.ChangeListener l);
    public void setSelectedIndex(int index);
// Protected Instance Methods
    protected void fireStateChanged();
// Protected Instance Fields
    protected transient javax.swing.event.ChangeEvent changeEvent;
    protected javax.swing.event.EventListenerList listenerList;
}
```

Hierarchy: Object→ DefaultSingleSelectionModel(Serializable, SingleSelectionModel)

DesktopManager   Java 1.2

javax.swing

This interface defines the methods that must be defined by a pluggable look-and-feel to
manage JInternalFrame windows within a JDesktopPane container. Application programmers do not need to use this class.

```
public abstract interface DesktopManager {
// Public Instance Methods
    public abstract void activateFrame(JInternalFrame f);
    public abstract void beginDraggingFrame(JComponent f);
    public abstract void beginResizingFrame(JComponent f, int direction);
    public abstract void closeFrame(JInternalFrame f);
    public abstract void deactivateFrame(JInternalFrame f);
    public abstract void deiconifyFrame(JInternalFrame f);
    public abstract void dragFrame(JComponent f, int newX, int newY);
    public abstract void endDraggingFrame(JComponent f);
    public abstract void endResizingFrame(JComponent f);
    public abstract void iconifyFrame(JInternalFrame f);
    public abstract void maximizeFrame(JInternalFrame f);
    public abstract void minimizeFrame(JInternalFrame f);
    public abstract void openFrame(JInternalFrame f);
    public abstract void resizeFrame(JComponent f, int newX, int newY, int newWidth, int newHeight);
    public abstract void setBoundsForFrame(JComponent f, int newX, int newY, int newWidth, int newHeight);
}
```

Implementations: DefaultDesktopManager

Passed To: JDesktopPane.setDesktopManager()

Returned By: JDesktopPane.getDesktopManager()

FocusManager   Java 1.2

javax.swing

This abstract class defines three instance methods that must be implemented by an object that wants to manage keyboard focus for an application. It also defines static methods that manipulate the installed focus manager. Applications that mix AWT components with Swing components should call disableSwingFocusManager() to disable Swing's focus management and rely on the AWT focus manager. Call setCurrentManager() to replace the current focus manager with a custom manager of your own.

```
public abstract class FocusManager {
// Public Constructors
    public FocusManager();
// Public Constants
    public static final String FOCUS_MANAGER_CLASS_PROPERTY;        ="FocusManagerClassName"
// Public Class Methods
    public static void disableSwingFocusManager();
    public static FocusManager getCurrentManager();
    public static boolean isFocusManagerEnabled();
    public static void setCurrentManager(FocusManager aFocusManager);
// Public Instance Methods
    public abstract void focusNextComponent(Component aComponent);
    public abstract void focusPreviousComponent(Component aComponent);
    public abstract void processKeyEvent(Component focusedComponent, java.awt.event.KeyEvent anEvent);
}
```

Subclasses: DefaultFocusManager

Passed To: FocusManager.setCurrentManager()

Returned By: FocusManager.getCurrentManager()

GrayFilter

javax.swing

cloneable

This class is a java.awt.image.ImageFilter that converts a color image to a grayscale image, suitable for use as an icon that represents a disabled action or an unavailable option. In addition to the usual ImageFilter methods, GrayFilter provides the static createDisabledImage() method, which is all that most applications ever need to use. The AbstractButton and JLabel classes use GrayFilter to automatically create a grayscale version of an image, if no disabled image is explicitly provided.

```
public class GrayFilter extends java.awt.image.RGBImageFilter {
// Public Constructors
    public GrayFilter(boolean b, int p);
// Public Class Methods
    public static java.awt.Image createDisabledImage(java.awt.Image i);
// Public Methods Overriding RGBImageFilter
    public int filterRGB(int x, int y, int rgb);
}
```

Hierarchy: Object→ java.awt.image.ImageFilter(Cloneable, java.awt.image.ImageConsumer)→ java.awt.image.RGBImageFilter→ GrayFilter

Icon

javax.swing

This interface defines the Swing notion of an icon: an object that knows how to draw a graphic of a fixed width and height at a fixed location. Icons are most commonly implemented with images; see ImageIcon.

```
public abstract interface Icon {
// Public Instance Methods
    public abstract int getIconHeight();
    public abstract int getIconWidth();
    public abstract void paintIcon(Component c, java.awt.Graphics g, int x, int y);
}
```

Implementations: ImageIcon, javax.swing.plaf.IconUIResource

Passed To: Too many methods to list.

Returned By: Too many methods to list.

Type Of: JInternalFrame.frameIcon, JOptionPane.icon, javax.swing.border.MatteBorder.tileIcon, javax.swing.tree.DefaultTreeCellEditor.editingIcon, javax.swing.tree.DefaultTreeCellRenderer.{closedIcon, leafIcon, openIcon}

ImageIcon

javax.swing

serializable

This class is an implementation of the Icon interface that uses an Image to draw the icon. The various constructors allow the image to be specified as an Image object, as a URL, as a file name, or as an array of binary data. Every ImageIcon can have a short textual description that may be used for accessibility (e.g., to describe the icon to a blind user).

```
public class ImageIcon implements Icon, Serializable {
// Public Constructors
    public ImageIcon();
    public ImageIcon(java.awt.Image image);
    public ImageIcon(String filename);
    public ImageIcon(java.net.URL location);
```

```
    public ImageIcon(byte[ ] imageData);
    public ImageIcon(String filename, String description);
    public ImageIcon(java.net.URL location, String description);
    public ImageIcon(byte[ ] imageData, String description);
    public ImageIcon(java.awt.Image image, String description);
// Protected Constants
    protected static final Component component;
    protected static final java.awt.MediaTracker tracker;
// Property Accessor Methods (by property name)
    public String getDescription();                                          default:null
    public void setDescription(String description);
    public int getIconHeight();                               Implements:Icon default:-1
    public int getIconWidth();                                Implements:Icon default:-1
    public java.awt.Image getImage();                                        default:null
    public void setImage(java.awt.Image image);
    public int getImageLoadStatus();                                          default:0
    public java.awt.image.ImageObserver getImageObserver();                  default:null
    public void setImageObserver(java.awt.image.ImageObserver observer);
// Methods Implementing Icon
    public int getIconHeight();                                              default:-1
    public int getIconWidth();                                               default:-1
    public void paintIcon(Component c, java.awt.Graphics g, int x, int y);  synchronized
// Protected Instance Methods
    protected void loadImage(java.awt.Image image);
}
```

Hierarchy: Object→ ImageIcon(Icon, Serializable)

JApplet   Java 1.2

javax.swing   *serializable accessible swing component bean container*

This class is the Swing version of its superclass, java.applet.Applet. It creates a JRootPane as its sole child, and, like JFrame, JDialog, and similar classes, it implements RootPaneContainer. Calling add() or setLayout() on a JApplet raises an exception. Instead, call getContentPane() to obtain a reference to an internal container on which you can call add() and setLayout(). The default layout manager for this content pane is a BorderLayout. Because JApplet is a RootPaneContainer, it can display a Swing menubar. Use setJMenuBar() and getJMenuBar().

```
public class JApplet extends java.applet.Applet implements Accessible, RootPaneContainer {
// Public Constructors
    public JApplet();
// Inner Classes
    protected class AccessibleJApplet extends AccessibleContext implements AccessibleComponent, Serializable;
// Property Accessor Methods (by property name)
    public AccessibleContext getAccessibleContext();     Implements:Accessible default:AccessibleJApplet
    public Container getContentPane();               Implements:RootPaneContainer default:JPanel
    public void setContentPane(Container contentPane);   Implements:RootPaneContainer hidden
    public Component getGlassPane();                 Implements:RootPaneContainer default:JPanel
    public void setGlassPane(Component glassPane);       Implements:RootPaneContainer hidden
    public JMenuBar getJMenuBar();                                           default:null
    public void setJMenuBar(JMenuBar menuBar);                               hidden
    public JLayeredPane getLayeredPane();                Implements:RootPaneContainer
    public void setLayeredPane(JLayeredPane layeredPane); Implements:RootPaneContainer hidden
    public void setLayout(java.awt.LayoutManager manager);   Overrides:Container
    public JRootPane getRootPane();                      Implements:RootPaneContainer
// Methods Implementing Accessible
    public AccessibleContext getAccessibleContext();                 default:AccessibleJApplet
```

```
// Methods Implementing RootPaneContainer
    public Container getContentPane();                                          default:JPanel
    public Component getGlassPane();                                            default:JPanel
    public JLayeredPane getLayeredPane();
    public JRootPane getRootPane();
    public void setContentPane(Container contentPane);                          hidden
    public void setGlassPane(Component glassPane);                              hidden
    public void setLayeredPane(JLayeredPane layeredPane);                       hidden
// Public Methods Overriding Container
    public void remove(Component comp);
    public void update(java.awt.Graphics g);
// Protected Methods Overriding Container
    protected void addImpl(Component comp, Object constraints, int index);
    protected String paramString();
// Protected Methods Overriding Component
    protected void processKeyEvent(java.awt.event.KeyEvent e);
// Protected Instance Methods
    protected JRootPane createRootPane();
    protected boolean isRootPaneCheckingEnabled();
    protected void setRootPane(JRootPane root);                                 hidden
    protected void setRootPaneCheckingEnabled(boolean enabled);
// Protected Instance Fields
    protected AccessibleContext accessibleContext;
    protected JRootPane rootPane;
    protected boolean rootPaneCheckingEnabled;
}
```

Hierarchy: Object→ Component(java.awt.image.ImageObserver, java.awt.MenuContainer, Serializable)→ Container→ java.awt.Panel→ java.applet.Applet→ JApplet(Accessible, RootPaneContainer)

JButton   Java 1.2

javax.swing   *serializable accessible(action,value) swing component*

This class implements a push button. The constructors allow a textual label and/or an icon to be specified for the button. isDefaultButton() checks to see if the button is the default button registered with the setDefaultButton() method of JRootPane. A JButton generates a java.awt.event.ActionEvent when clicked. Most of the interesting properties and methods of JButton are implemented by AbstractButton. The default JButton model is DefaultButtonModel.

```
public class JButton extends AbstractButton implements Accessible {
// Public Constructors
    public JButton();
    public JButton(Icon icon);
    public JButton(String text);
    public JButton(String text, Icon icon);
// Inner Classes
    protected class AccessibleJButton extends AbstractButton.AccessibleAbstractButton;
// Property Accessor Methods (by property name)
    public AccessibleContext getAccessibleContext();       Implements:Accessible default:AccessibleJButton expert
    public boolean isDefaultButton();                                           default:false
    public boolean isDefaultCapable();                                          default:true
    public void setDefaultCapable(boolean defaultCapable);                      bound
    public String getUIClassID();               Overrides:JComponent default:"ButtonUI" expert
// Methods Implementing Accessible
    public AccessibleContext getAccessibleContext();              default:AccessibleJButton expert
```

```
// Public Methods Overriding AbstractButton
    public void updateUI();
// Protected Methods Overriding AbstractButton
    protected String paramString();
}
```

Hierarchy: Object→ Component(java.awt.image.ImageObserver, java.awt.MenuContainer, Serializable)→ Container→ JComponent(Serializable)→ AbstractButton(java.awt.ItemSelectable, SwingConstants)→ JButton(Accessible)

Passed To: JRootPane.setDefaultButton(), JToolBar.createActionChangeListener()

Returned By: JRootPane.getDefaultButton(), JToolBar.add()

Type Of: JRootPane.defaultButton

JCheckBox   Java 1.2

javax.swing   *serializable accessible(action,value) swing component*

This class implements a check button: a toggle button with default graphics that indicate that the button does not have mutually exclusive behavior. Because JCheckBox supplies its own default and selected icons, you typically do not use the constructors that take Icon arguments. The initial selection state of a JCheckBox can be specified in the call to the constructor. The state can also be set with setSelected() and queried with isSelected(). Use JRadioButton and ButtonGroup instead of JCheckBox if you want to display a set of mutually exclusive choices. The default JCheckBox model is JToggleButton.ToggleButton-Model. Note that java.awt.Checkbox is spelled with a lowercase b, while JCheckBox has an uppercase B.

```
public class JCheckBox extends JToggleButton implements Accessible {
// Public Constructors
    public JCheckBox();
    public JCheckBox(Icon icon);
    public JCheckBox(String text);
    public JCheckBox(String text, Icon icon);
    public JCheckBox(Icon icon, boolean selected);
    public JCheckBox(String text, boolean selected);
    public JCheckBox(String text, Icon icon, boolean selected);
// Inner Classes
    protected class AccessibleJCheckBox extends JToggleButton.AccessibleJToggleButton;
// Property Accessor Methods (by property name)
    public AccessibleContext getAccessibleContext();     Implements:Accessible default:AccessibleJCheckBox expert
    public String getUIClassID();                         Overrides:JToggleButton default:"CheckBoxUI" expert
// Methods Implementing Accessible
    public AccessibleContext getAccessibleContext();                      default:AccessibleJCheckBox expert
// Public Methods Overriding JToggleButton
    public void updateUI();
// Protected Methods Overriding JToggleButton
    protected String paramString();
}
```

Hierarchy: Object→ Component(java.awt.image.ImageObserver, java.awt.MenuContainer, Serializable)→ Container→ JComponent(Serializable)→ AbstractButton(java.awt.ItemSelectable, SwingConstants)→ JToggleButton(Accessible)→ JCheckBox(Accessible)

Passed To: DefaultCellEditor.DefaultCellEditor()

JCheckBoxMenuItem

javax.swing

serializable accessible(action,value) swing component

This class implements a check button that appears within a pulldown or popup menu. Its use is similar to that of JCheckBox. Use isSelected() to query the selection state of the menu item and setSelected() to select or deselect the item. For menu items with mutually-exclusive selection behavior, use JRadioButtonMenuItem instead. The default JCheckBoxMenuItem model is JToggleButton.ToggleButtonModel.

```
public class JCheckBoxMenuItem extends JMenuItem implements Accessible, SwingConstants {
// Public Constructors
    public JCheckBoxMenuItem();
    public JCheckBoxMenuItem(String text);
    public JCheckBoxMenuItem(Icon icon);
    public JCheckBoxMenuItem(String text, Icon icon);
    public JCheckBoxMenuItem(String text, boolean b);
    public JCheckBoxMenuItem(String text, Icon icon, boolean b);
// Inner Classes
    protected class AccessibleJCheckBoxMenuItem extends JMenuItem.AccessibleJMenuItem;
// Property Accessor Methods (by property name)
    public AccessibleContext                    Implements:Accessible default:AccessibleJCheckBoxMenuItem
        getAccessibleContext();
    public Object[ ] getSelectedObjects();          Overrides:AbstractButton synchronized default:null
    public boolean getState();                                             default:false
    public void setState(boolean b);                                  synchronized hidden
    public String getUIClassID();                                     Overrides:JMenuItem
// Methods Implementing Accessible
    public AccessibleContext getAccessibleContext();    default:AccessibleJCheckBoxMenuItem
// Protected Methods Overriding JMenuItem
    protected String paramString();
// Public Methods Overriding JComponent
    public void requestFocus();                                                empty
}
```

Hierarchy: Object→ Component(java.awt.image.ImageObserver, java.awt.MenuContainer, Serializable)→ Container→ JComponent(Serializable)→ AbstractButton(java.awt.ItemSelectable, SwingConstants)→ JMenuItem(Accessible, MenuElement)→ JCheckBoxMenuItem(Accessible, SwingConstants)

JColorChooser

javax.swing

serializable accessible swing component

This component allows the user to select a color. The easiest way to use it is to call the static showDialog() method, specifying a parent Component for the dialog, a title, and an initial default color. The method creates a JColorChooser in a modal JDialog and blocks until the user dismisses the dialog. If the user dismisses the dialog with the OK button, the method returns the selected color. If the user dismisses the dialog with the Cancel button, or in any other way, showDialog() returns null.

If you need more control over the color selection dialog, you can call createDialog(). This static method creates a JDialog that contains the JColorChooser component you specify. It allows you to specify java.awt.event.ActionListener objects to respond to the OK and Cancel buttons. It does not automatically display the dialog for you, nor does it wait for the user to make a selection.

You can also create and manipulate a JColorChooser on your own, placing it in any dialog or other container. You can register a java.beans.PropertyChangeListener object (with the inherited addPropertyChangeListener() method) to receive notification when the color property changes.

JColorChooser is highly customizable. You can specify how colors are selected by specifying a custom subclass of javax.swing.colorchooser.AbstractColorChooserPanel to addChocserPanel() or setChooserPanels(). And you can customize the way that colors are previewed by specifying an appropriate component to setPreviewPanel(). The default JColorChooser model is a javax.swing.colorchooser.DefaultColorSelectionModel.

```
public class JColorChooser extends JComponent implements Accessible {
// Public Constructors
    public JColorChooser();
    public JColorChooser(java.awt.Color initialColor);
    public JColorChooser(javax.swing.colorchooser.ColorSelectionModel model);
// Public Constants
    public static final String CHOOSER_PANELS_PROPERTY;                              ="chooserPanels"
    public static final String PREVIEW_PANEL_PROPERTY;                               ="previewPanel"
    public static final String SELECTION_MODEL_PROPERTY;                             ="selectionModel"
// Inner Classes
    protected class AccessibleJColorChooser extends JComponent.AccessibleJComponent;
// Public Class Methods
    public static JDialog createDialog(Component c, String title, boolean modal, JColorChooser chooserPane,
                                java.awt.event.ActionListener okListener,
                                java.awt.event.ActionListener cancelListener);
    public static java.awt.Color showDialog(Component component, String title, java.awt.Color initialColor);
// Property Accessor Methods (by property name)
    public AccessibleContext getAccessibleContext();            Implements:Accessible default:AccessibleJColorChooser
    public javax.swing.colorchooser.AbstractColorChooserPanel[ ] getChooserPanels();
    public void setChooserPanels(javax.swing.colorchooser.AbstractColorChooserPanel[ ] panels);       bound hidden
    public java.awt.Color getColor();
    public void setColor(int c);
    public void setColor(java.awt.Color color);
    public void setColor(int r, int g, int b);
    public JComponent getPreviewPanel();                                                        default:null
    public void setPreviewPanel(JComponent preview);                                          bound hidden
    public javax.swing.colorchooser.ColorSelectionModel getSelectionModel();     default:DefaultColorSelectionModel
    public void setSelectionModel(javax.swing.colorchooser.ColorSelectionModel newModel);      bound hidden
    public javax.swing.plaf.ColorChooserUI getUI();
    public void setUI(javax.swing.plaf.ColorChooserUI ui);                                    bound hidden
    public String getUIClassID();                               Overrides:JComponent default:"ColorChooserUI"
// Public Instance Methods
    public void addChooserPanel(javax.swing.colorchooser.AbstractColorChooserPanel panel);
    public javax.swing.colorchooser.AbstractColorChooserPanel removeChooserPanel(
                                javax.swing.colorchooser.AbstractColorChooserPanel panel);
// Methods Implementing Accessible
    public AccessibleContext getAccessibleContext();                             default:AccessibleJColorChooser
// Public Methods Overriding JComponent
    public void updateUI();
// Protected Methods Overriding JComponent
    protected String paramString();
// Protected Instance Fields
    protected AccessibleContext accessibleContext;
}
```

Hierarchy: Object→ Component(java.awt.image.ImageObserver, java.awt.MenuContainer, Serializable) →
Container→ JComponent(Serializable) → JColorChooser(Accessible)

Passed To: JColorChooser.createDialog(),
javax.swing.colorchooser.AbstractColorChooserPanel.{installChooserPanel(), uninstallChooserPanel()}

JComboBox

Java 1.2

javax.swing

serializable accessible(action) swing component

This class implements a combo box: a combination of a popup list of selectable items and an item editor that displays the selected value and, optionally, allows the user to enter an item that does not appear on the list. The editor is usually a text field, but a JComboBox can be configured to use another component as its ComboBoxEditor.

Typically, you create a JComboBox by passing a Vector or array of objects to a constructor. Alternatively, you can create an empty JComboBox and add items to it with addItem(). You can set and query the selection with setSelectedItem(), setSelectedIndex(), getSelectedItem(), and getSelectedIndex(). The JComboBox generates a java.awt.event.ActionEvent when the selection changes. The default JComboBox model is a private implementation of the ComboBox-Model interface. If you want to implement keyboard shortcuts for a JComboBox, implement the JComboBox.KeySelectionManager interface and pass an instance to the setKey-SelectionManager() method.

```
public class JComboBox extends JComponent implements Accessible, java.awt.event.ActionListener,
        java.awt.ItemSelectable, javax.swing.event.ListDataListener {
// Public Constructors
    public JComboBox();
    public JComboBox(java.util.Vector items);
    public JComboBox(ComboBoxModel aModel);
    public JComboBox(Object[ ] items);
// Inner Classes
    protected class AccessibleJComboBox extends JComponent.AccessibleJComponent implements
        AccessibleAction;
    public abstract static interface KeySelectionManager;
// Event Registration Methods (by event name)
    public void addActionListener(java.awt.event.ActionListener l);
    public void removeActionListener(java.awt.event.ActionListener l);
    public void addItemListener(java.awt.event.ItemListener aListener);              Implements:ItemSelectable
    public void removeItemListener(java.awt.event.ItemListener aListener);           Implements:ItemSelectable
// Property Accessor Methods (by property name)
    public AccessibleContext getAccessibleContext();        Implements:Accessible default:AccessibleJComboBox
    public String getActionCommand();                                   default:"comboBoxChanged"
    public void setActionCommand(String aCommand);
    public boolean isEditable();                                                    default:false
    public void setEditable(boolean aFlag);                                         preferred
    public ComboBoxEditor getEditor();
    public void setEditor(ComboBoxEditor anEditor);                                 expert
    public boolean isFocusTraversable();                        Overrides:JComponent default:false
    public int getItemCount();                                                      default:0
    public JComboBox.KeySelectionManager getKeySelectionManager();                  default:null
    public void setKeySelectionManager(JComboBox.KeySelectionManager aManager);     expert
    public boolean isLightWeightPopupEnabled();                                     default:true
    public void setLightWeightPopupEnabled(boolean aFlag);                          expert
    public int getMaximumRowCount();                                                default:8
    public void setMaximumRowCount(int count);                                      preferred
    public ComboBoxModel getModel();                            default:DefaultComboBoxModel
    public void setModel(ComboBoxModel aModel);                                     bound
    public boolean isPopupVisible();                                                default:false
    public void setPopupVisible(boolean v);
    public ListCellRenderer getRenderer();
    public void setRenderer(ListCellRenderer aRenderer);                            expert
    public int getSelectedIndex();                                                  default:-1
    public void setSelectedIndex(int anIndex);                                      preferred
    public Object getSelectedItem();                                                default:null
    public void setSelectedItem(Object anObject);                                   preferred
```

```
    public Object[ ] getSelectedObjects();                              Implements:ItemSelectable
    public javax.swing.plaf.ComboBoxUI getUI();
    public void setUI(javax.swing.plaf.ComboBoxUI ui);                                    expert
    public String getUIClassID();                       Overrides:JComponent default:"ComboBoxUI"
// Public Instance Methods
    public void addItem(Object anObject);
    public void configureEditor(ComboBoxEditor anEditor, Object anItem);
    public Object getItemAt(int index);
    public void hidePopup();
    public void insertItemAt(Object anObject, int index);
    public void removeAllItems();
    public void removeItem(Object anObject);
    public void removeItemAt(int anIndex);
    public boolean selectWithKeyChar(char keyChar);
    public void showPopup();
// Methods Implementing Accessible
    public AccessibleContext getAccessibleContext();            default:AccessibleJComboBox
// Methods Implementing ActionListener
    public void actionPerformed(java.awt.event.ActionEvent e);
// Methods Implementing ItemSelectable
    public void addItemListener(java.awt.event.ItemListener aListener);
    public Object[ ] getSelectedObjects();
    public void removeItemListener(java.awt.event.ItemListener aListener);
// Methods Implementing ListDataListener
    public void contentsChanged(javax.swing.event.ListDataEvent e);
    public void intervalAdded(javax.swing.event.ListDataEvent e);
    public void intervalRemoved(javax.swing.event.ListDataEvent e);
// Public Methods Overriding JComponent
    public void processKeyEvent(java.awt.event.KeyEvent e);
    public void setEnabled(boolean b);                                              preferred
    public void updateUI();
// Protected Methods Overriding JComponent
    protected String paramString();
// Protected Instance Methods
    protected JComboBox.KeySelectionManager createDefaultKeySelectionManager();
    protected void fireActionEvent();
    protected void fireItemStateChanged(java.awt.event.ItemEvent e);
    protected void installAncestorListener();
    protected void selectedItemChanged();
// Protected Instance Fields
    protected String actionCommand;
    protected ComboBoxModel dataModel;
    protected ComboBoxEditor editor;
    protected boolean isEditable;
    protected JComboBox.KeySelectionManager keySelectionManager;
    protected boolean lightWeightPopupEnabled;
    protected int maximumRowCount;
    protected ListCellRenderer renderer;
    protected Object selectedItemReminder;
}
```

Hierarchy: Object→ Component(java.awt.image.ImageObserver, java.awt.MenuContainer, Serializable)→
Container→ JComponent(Serializable)→ JComboBox(Accessible,
java.awt.event.ActionListener(java.util.EventListener), java.awt.ItemSelectable,
javax.swing.event.ListDataListener(java.util.EventListener))

Passed To: DefaultCellEditor.DefaultCellEditor(), javax.swing.plaf.ComboBoxUI.{isFocusTraversable(),
isPopupVisible(), setPopupVisible()}

JComponent.KeySelectionManager

javax.swing

This interface defines the method that must be implemented to bind characters to items in a JComboBox. Given a character, selectionForKey() should return the index of the item that should be selected or -1 if the character does not correspond to an item in the list.

```
public abstract static interface JComboBox.KeySelectionManager {
// Public Instance Methods
    public abstract int selectionForKey(char aKey, ComboBoxModel aModel);
}
```

Passed To: JComboBox.setKeySelectionManager()

Returned By: JComboBox.{createDefaultKeySelectionManager(), getKeySelectionManager()}

Type Of: JComboBox.keySelectionManager

JComponent

javax.swing

serializable swing component

JComponent is the root of the Swing component hierarchy. It inherits the properties and methods of java.awt.Component and java.awt.Container, including such commonly used properties as foreground, background, font, cursor, enabled, and visible.

In addition to these inherited properties, JComponent defines a number of new properties that are commonly used. The border property specifies a Border object that displays a border (or a blank space) around the component. doubleBuffered specifies whether the JComponent should automatically use double-buffering to reduce flickering during redraws. opaque specifies whether the component draws its background or lets its parent' background show through. toolTipText specifies the text to appear in a tooltip when the mouse pointer lingers over the component.

In addition to the standard get/set property accessor methods, JComponent also defines getClientProperty() and putClientProperty(). In effect, every JComponent maintains a hashtable that maps arbitrary property names to values. You can use this to associate arbitrary data with any Swing component. It is also occasionally used to specify properties that are specific to certain look-and-feels.

```
public abstract class JComponent extends Container implements Serializable {
// Public Constructors
    public JComponent();
// Public Constants
    public static final String TOOL_TIP_TEXT_KEY;                              ="ToolTipText"
    public static final int UNDEFINED_CONDITION;                               =-1
    public static final int WHEN_ANCESTOR_OF_FOCUSED_COMPONENT;                =1
    public static final int WHEN_FOCUSED;                                      =0
    public static final int WHEN_IN_FOCUSED_WINDOW;                            =2
// Inner Classes
    public abstract class AccessibleJComponent extends AccessibleContext implements AccessibleComponent,
        Serializable;
// Public Class Methods
    public static boolean isLightweightComponent(Component c);
// Event Registration Methods (by event name)
    public void addAncestorListener(javax.swing.event.AncestorListener listener);
    public void removeAncestorListener(javax.swing.event.AncestorListener listener);
    public void addPropertyChangeListener(                    Overrides:Component synchronized
                        java.beans.PropertyChangeListener listener);
    public void removePropertyChangeListener(                 Overrides:Component synchronized
                        java.beans.PropertyChangeListener listener);
```

public void **addVetoableChangeListener**(java.beans.VetoableChangeListener *listener*);	*synchronized*
public void **removeVetoableChangeListener**(java.beans.VetoableChangeListener *listener*);	*synchronized*

// *Property Accessor Methods (by property name)*

public AccessibleContext **getAccessibleContext**();	
public float **getAlignmentX**();	*Overrides:Container*
public void **setAlignmentX**(float *alignmentX*);	
public float **getAlignmentY**();	*Overrides:Container*
public void **setAlignmentY**(float *alignmentY*);	
public boolean **getAutoscrolls**();	
public void **setAutoscrolls**(boolean *autoscrolls*);	*expert*
public void **setBackground**(java.awt.Color *bg*);	*Overrides:Component bound preferred*
public javax.swing.border.Border **getBorder**();	
public void **setBorder**(javax.swing.border.Border *border*);	*bound preferred*
public int **getDebugGraphicsOptions**();	
public void **setDebugGraphicsOptions**(int *debugOptions*);	*preferred*
public boolean **isDoubleBuffered**();	*Overrides:Component*
public void **setDoubleBuffered**(boolean *aFlag*);	
public void **setEnabled**(boolean *enabled*);	*Overrides:Component bound preferred*
public boolean **isFocusCycleRoot**();	*constant*
public boolean **isFocusTraversable**();	*Overrides:Component*
public void **setForeground**(java.awt.Color *fg*);	*Overrides:Component bound preferred*
public java.awt.Graphics **getGraphics**(); .	*Overrides:Component*
public int **getHeight**();	*Overrides:Component*
public java.awt.Insets **getInsets**();	*Overrides:Container*
public java.awt.Insets **getInsets**(java.awt.Insets *insets*);	*expert*
public boolean **isManagingFocus**();	*constant*
public java.awt.Dimension **getMaximumSize**();	*Overrides:Container*
public void **setMaximumSize**(java.awt.Dimension *maximumSize*);	*bound*
public java.awt.Dimension **getMinimumSize**();	*Overrides:Container*
public void **setMinimumSize**(java.awt.Dimension *minimumSize*);	*bound*
public Component **getNextFocusableComponent**();	
public void **setNextFocusableComponent**(Component *aComponent*);	*expert*
public boolean **isOpaque**();	*Overrides:Component*
public void **setOpaque**(boolean *isOpaque*);	
public boolean **isOptimizedDrawingEnabled**();	*constant*
public boolean **isPaintingTile**();	
public java.awt.Dimension **getPreferredSize**();	*Overrides:Container*
public void **setPreferredSize**(java.awt.Dimension *preferredSize*);	*bound preferred*
public KeyStroke[ ] **getRegisteredKeyStrokes**();	
public boolean **isRequestFocusEnabled**();	
public void **setRequestFocusEnabled**(boolean *aFlag*);	*expert*
public JRootPane **getRootPane**();	
public String **getToolTipText**();	
public String **getToolTipText**(java.awt.event.MouseEvent *event*);	
public void **setToolTipText**(String *text*);	*preferred*
public Container **getTopLevelAncestor**();	
public String **getUIClassID**();	*expert*
public boolean **isValidateRoot**();	*constant*
public void **setVisible**(boolean *aFlag*);	*Overrides:Component*
public java.awt.Rectangle **getVisibleRect**();	
public int **getWidth**();	*Overrides:Component*
public int **getX**();	*Overrides:Component*
public int **getY**();	*Overrides:Component*

// *Public Instance Methods*

public void **computeVisibleRect**(java.awt.Rectangle *visibleRect*);	
public JToolTip **createToolTip**();	
public void **firePropertyChange**(String *propertyName*, long *oldValue*, long *newValue*);	
public void **firePropertyChange**(String *propertyName*, int *oldValue*, int *newValue*);	

public void **firePropertyChange**(String *propertyName*, boolean *oldValue*, boolean *newValue*);
public void **firePropertyChange**(String *propertyName*, short *oldValue*, short *newValue*);
public void **firePropertyChange**(String *propertyName*, char *oldValue*, char *newValue*);
public void **firePropertyChange**(String *propertyName*, byte *oldValue*, byte *newValue*);
public void **firePropertyChange**(String *propertyName*, float *oldValue*, float *newValue*);
public void **firePropertyChange**(String *propertyName*, double *oldValue*, double *newValue*);
public java.awt.event.ActionListener **getActionForKeyStroke**(KeyStroke *aKeyStroke*);
public final Object **getClientProperty**(Object *key*);
public int **getConditionForKeyStroke**(KeyStroke *aKeyStroke*);
public java.awt.Point **getToolTipLocation**(java.awt.event.MouseEvent *event*);   *constant*
public void **grabFocus**();
public void **paintImmediately**(java.awt.Rectangle *r*);
public void **paintImmediately**(int *x*, int *y*, int *w*, int *h*);
public final void **putClientProperty**(Object *key*, Object *value*);
public void **registerKeyboardAction**(java.awt.event.ActionListener *anAction*, KeyStroke *aKeyStroke*,
                    int *aCondition*);
public void **registerKeyboardAction**(java.awt.event.ActionListener *anAction*, String *aCommand*,
                    KeyStroke *aKeyStroke*, int *aCondition*);
public void **repaint**(java.awt.Rectangle *r*);
public boolean **requestDefaultFocus**();
public void **resetKeyboardActions**();
public void **revalidate**();
public void **scrollRectToVisible**(java.awt.Rectangle *aRect*);
public void **setFont**(java.awt.Font *font*);   *bound preferred*
public void **unregisterKeyboardAction**(KeyStroke *aKeyStroke*);
public void **updateUI**();   *empty*
// *Public Methods Overriding Container*
public void **addNotify**();
public void **paint**(java.awt.Graphics *g*);
public void **removeNotify**();
public void **update**(java.awt.Graphics *g*);
// *Protected Methods Overriding Container*
protected String **paramString**();
// *Public Methods Overriding Component*
public void **addPropertyChangeListener**(String *propertyName*,   *synchronized*
                    java.beans.PropertyChangeListener *listener*);
public boolean **contains**(int *x*, int *y*);
public java.awt.Rectangle **getBounds**(java.awt.Rectangle *rv*);
public java.awt.Point **getLocation**(java.awt.Point *rv*);
public java.awt.Dimension **getSize**(java.awt.Dimension *rv*);
public boolean **hasFocus**();
public void **removePropertyChangeListener**(String *propertyName*,   *synchronized*
                    java.beans.PropertyChangeListener *listener*);
public void **repaint**(long *tm*, int *x*, int *y*, int *width*, int *height*);
public void **requestFocus**();
public void **reshape**(int *x*, int *y*, int *w*, int *h*);
// *Protected Methods Overriding Component*
protected void **firePropertyChange**(String *propertyName*, Object *oldValue*, Object *newValue*);
protected void **processFocusEvent**(java.awt.event.FocusEvent *e*);
protected void **processKeyEvent**(java.awt.event.KeyEvent *e*);
protected void **processMouseMotionEvent**(java.awt.event.MouseEvent *e*);
// *Protected Instance Methods*
protected void **fireVetoableChange**(String *propertyName*, Object *oldValue*, Object *newValue*)
    throws java.beans.PropertyVetoException;
protected java.awt.Graphics **getComponentGraphics**(java.awt.Graphics *g*);
protected void **paintBorder**(java.awt.Graphics *g*);
protected void **paintChildren**(java.awt.Graphics *g*);
protected void **paintComponent**(java.awt.Graphics *g*);

```
            protected void processComponentKeyEvent(java.awt.event.KeyEvent e);                    empty
            protected void setUI(javax.swing.plaf.ComponentUI newUI);                              bound
// Protected Instance Fields
            protected AccessibleContext accessibleContext;
            protected javax.swing.event.EventListenerList listenerList;
            protected transient javax.swing.plaf.ComponentUI ui;
}
```

Hierarchy: Object→ Component(java.awt.image.ImageObserver, java.awt.MenuContainer, Serializable)→
Container→ JComponent(Serializable)

Subclasses: Too many classes to list.

Passed To: Too many methods to list.

Returned By: JColorChooser.getPreviewPanel(), JFileChooser.getAccessory(), JToolTip.getComponent(),
javax.swing.colorchooser.ColorChooserComponentFactory.getPreviewPanel(),
javax.swing.event.AncestorEvent.getComponent()

Type Of: DefaultCellEditor.editorComponent

JComponent.AccessibleJComponent   Java 1.2

javax.swing   *serializable accessible context*

This class provides default accessibility support for Swing components. It is typically
subclassed by component developers; application programmers never need to use it.

```
public abstract class JComponent.AccessibleJComponent extends AccessibleContext
        implements AccessibleComponent, Serializable {
// Protected Constructors
        protected AccessibleJComponent();
// Inner Classes
        protected class AccessibleContainerHandler implements java.awt.event.ContainerListener;
// Event Registration Methods (by event name)
        public void addFocusListener(java.awt.event.FocusListener l);         Implements:AccessibleComponent
        public void removeFocusListener(java.awt.event.FocusListener l);      Implements:AccessibleComponent
        public void addPropertyChangeListener(                                 Overrides:AccessibleContext
                            java.beans.PropertyChangeListener listener);
        public void removePropertyChangeListener(                             Overrides:AccessibleContext
                            java.beans.PropertyChangeListener listener);
// Methods Implementing AccessibleComponent
        public void addFocusListener(java.awt.event.FocusListener l);
        public boolean contains(java.awt.Point p);
        public Accessible getAccessibleAt(java.awt.Point p);
        public java.awt.Color getBackground();
        public java.awt.Rectangle getBounds();
        public java.awt.Cursor getCursor();
        public java.awt.Font getFont();
        public java.awt.FontMetrics getFontMetrics(java.awt.Font f);
        public java.awt.Color getForeground();
        public java.awt.Point getLocation();
        public java.awt.Point getLocationOnScreen();
        public java.awt.Dimension getSize();
        public boolean isEnabled();
        public boolean isFocusTraversable();
        public boolean isShowing();
        public boolean isVisible();
        public void removeFocusListener(java.awt.event.FocusListener l);
        public void requestFocus();
        public void setBackground(java.awt.Color c);
```

```
    public void setBounds(java.awt.Rectangle r);
    public void setCursor(java.awt.Cursor cursor);
    public void setEnabled(boolean b);
    public void setFont(java.awt.Font f);
    public void setForeground(java.awt.Color c);
    public void setLocation(java.awt.Point p);
    public void setSize(java.awt.Dimension d);
    public void setVisible(boolean b);
// Public Methods Overriding AccessibleContext
    public Accessible getAccessibleChild(int i);
    public int getAccessibleChildrenCount();
    public AccessibleComponent getAccessibleComponent();
    public String getAccessibleDescription();
    public int getAccessibleIndexInParent();
    public String getAccessibleName();
    public Accessible getAccessibleParent();
    public AccessibleRole getAccessibleRole();
    public AccessibleStateSet getAccessibleStateSet();
    public java.util.Locale getLocale();
// Protected Instance Methods
    protected String getBorderTitle(javax.swing.border.Border b);
// Protected Instance Fields
    protected java.awt.event.ContainerListener accessibleContainerHandler;
}
```

Subclasses: Too many classes to list.

JDesktopPane

Java 1.2

javax.swing   *serializable accessible swing component*

This class is a container for JInternalFrame windows. It provides window management
functionality appropriate for the currently installed look-and-feel.

```
public class JDesktopPane extends JLayeredPane implements Accessible {
// Public Constructors
    public JDesktopPane();
// Inner Classes
    protected class AccessibleJDesktopPane extends JComponent.AccessibleJComponent;
// Property Accessor Methods (by property name)
    public AccessibleContext getAccessibleContext();          Implements:Accessible default:AccessibleJDesktopPane
    public JInternalFrame[ ] getAllFrames();
    public DesktopManager getDesktopManager();                                default:DefaultDesktopManager
    public void setDesktopManager(DesktopManager d);
    public boolean isOpaque();                                Overrides:JComponent constant default:true
    public javax.swing.plaf.DesktopPaneUI getUI();
    public void setUI(javax.swing.plaf.DesktopPaneUI ui);
    public String getUIClassID();                             Overrides:JComponent default:"DesktopPaneUI"
// Public Instance Methods
    public JInternalFrame[ ] getAllFramesInLayer(int layer);
// Methods Implementing Accessible
    public AccessibleContext getAccessibleContext();                          default:AccessibleJDesktopPane
// Protected Methods Overriding JLayeredPane
    protected String paramString();
// Public Methods Overriding JComponent
    public void updateUI();
}
```

Hierarchy: Object→ Component(java.awt.image.ImageObserver, java.awt.MenuContainer, Serializable)→
Container→ JComponent(Serializable)→ JLayeredPane(Accessible)→ JDesktopPane(Accessible)

Returned By: JInternalFrame.getDesktopPane(), JInternalFrame.JDesktopIcon.getDesktopPane(), JOptionPane.getDesktopPaneForComponent()

JDialog
Java 1.2

javax.swing
serializable accessible swing component bean container

This class is used to display Swing dialog boxes. Every JDialog component has an automatically created JRootPane as its single child. Components must not be added directly to the JDialog component. Instead, they should be added to the container returned by getContentPane() method. The default layout manager of this content pane is java.awt.BorderLayout. Unlike its java.awt.Dialog superclass, JDialog can display a menubar. Specify one with setJMenuBar(). setDefaultCloseOperation() specifies how the JDialog should behave when the user attempts to close it. The argument should be one of the constants defined by the WindowConstants interface. The default is HIDE_ON_CLOSE. JDialog uses a native window. Use JInternalFrame for lightweight dialogs.

```
public class JDialog extends java.awt.Dialog implements Accessible, RootPaneContainer, WindowConstants {
// Public Constructors
     public JDialog();
     public JDialog(java.awt.Dialog owner);
     public JDialog(java.awt.Frame owner);
     public JDialog(java.awt.Dialog owner, String title);
     public JDialog(java.awt.Frame owner, boolean modal);
     public JDialog(java.awt.Frame owner, String title);
     public JDialog(java.awt.Dialog owner, boolean modal);
     public JDialog(java.awt.Frame owner, String title, boolean modal);
     public JDialog(java.awt.Dialog owner, String title, boolean modal);
// Inner Classes
     protected class AccessibleJDialog extends AccessibleContext implements AccessibleComponent, Serializable;
// Property Accessor Methods (by property name)
     public AccessibleContext getAccessibleContext();              Implements:Accessible default:AccessibleJDialog
     public Container getContentPane();                          Implements:RootPaneContainer default:JPanel
     public void setContentPane(Container contentPane);               Implements:RootPaneContainer hidden
     public int getDefaultCloseOperation();                                           default:1
     public void setDefaultCloseOperation(int operation);                               preferred
     public Component getGlassPane();                           Implements:RootPaneContainer default:JPanel
     public void setGlassPane(Component glassPane);                  Implements:RootPaneContainer hidden
     public JMenuBar getJMenuBar();                                                default:null
     public void setJMenuBar(JMenuBar menu);                                              hidden
     public JLayeredPane getLayeredPane();                            Implements:RootPaneContainer
     public void setLayeredPane(JLayeredPane layeredPane);            Implements:RootPaneContainer hidden
     public void setLayout(java.awt.LayoutManager manager);                     Overrides:Container
     public JRootPane getRootPane();                                 Implements:RootPaneContainer
// Public Instance Methods
     public void setLocationRelativeTo(Component c);
// Methods Implementing Accessible
     public AccessibleContext getAccessibleContext();                        default:AccessibleJDialog
// Methods Implementing RootPaneContainer
     public Container getContentPane();                                           default:JPanel
     public Component getGlassPane();                                             default:JPanel
     public JLayeredPane getLayeredPane();
     public JRootPane getRootPane();
     public void setContentPane(Container contentPane);                                  hidden
     public void setGlassPane(Component glassPane);                                      hidden
     public void setLayeredPane(JLayeredPane layeredPane);                               hidden
// Protected Methods Overriding Dialog
     protected String paramString();
```

```
// Protected Methods Overriding Window
    protected void processWindowEvent(java.awt.event.WindowEvent e);
// Public Methods Overriding Container
    public void remove(Component comp);
    public void update(java.awt.Graphics g);
// Protected Methods Overriding Container
    protected void addImpl(Component comp, Object constraints, int index);
// Protected Methods Overriding Component
    protected void processKeyEvent(java.awt.event.KeyEvent e);
// Protected Instance Methods
    protected JRootPane createRootPane();
    protected void dialogInit();
    protected boolean isRootPaneCheckingEnabled();
    protected void setRootPane(JRootPane root);                                      hidden
    protected void setRootPaneCheckingEnabled(boolean enabled);                      hidden
// Protected Instance Fields
    protected AccessibleContext accessibleContext;
    protected JRootPane rootPane;
    protected boolean rootPaneCheckingEnabled;
}
```

Hierarchy: Object→ Component(java.awt.image.ImageObserver, java.awt.MenuContainer, Serializable)→ Container→ java.awt.Window→ java.awt.Dialog→ JDialog(Accessible, RootPaneContainer, WindowConstants)

Returned By: JColorChooser.createDialog(), JOptionPane.createDialog()

JEditorPane

Java 1.2

javax.swing

serializable accessible(text,hypertext) swing component

This class is a subclass of javax.swing.text.JTextComponent that can be easily configured to display and edit different formatted-text content types using a javax.swing.text.EditorKit object. To configure a JEditorPane, call setEditorKit() to specify an appropriate editor kit for the desired content type. Alternatively, use the static registerEditorKitForContentType() to register a mapping between content types and their corresponding editor kits and then call setContentType(). With such a mapping in place, you may also use setPage() to specify a URL to be displayed. The JEditorPane determines the content type of the URL, installs an appropriate EditorKit, and loads the contents of the URL into the JEditorPane. Swing comes with two predefined EditorKit subclasses: javax.swing.text.html.HTMLEditorKit and javax.swing.text.rtf.RTFEditorKit.

```
public class JEditorPane extends javax.swing.text.JTextComponent {
// Public Constructors
    public JEditorPane();
    public JEditorPane(String url) throws java.io.IOException;
    public JEditorPane(java.net.URL initialPage) throws java.io.IOException;
    public JEditorPane(String type, String text);
// Inner Classes
    protected class AccessibleJEditorPane extends javax.swing.text.JTextComponent.AccessibleJTextComponent;
    protected class AccessibleJEditorPaneHTML extends JEditorPane.AccessibleJEditorPane;
    protected class JEditorPaneAccessibleHypertextSupport extends JEditorPane.AccessibleJEditorPane
        implements AccessibleHypertext;
// Public Class Methods
    public static javax.swing.text.EditorKit createEditorKitForContentType(String type);
    public static void registerEditorKitForContentType(String type, String classname);
    public static void registerEditorKitForContentType(String type, String classname, ClassLoader loader);
```

```
// Event Registration Methods (by event name)
    public void addHyperlinkListener(javax.swing.event.HyperlinkListener listener);          synchronized
    public void removeHyperlinkListener(javax.swing.event.HyperlinkListener listener);        synchronized
// Property Accessor Methods (by property name)
    public AccessibleContext getAccessibleContext();          Overrides:JTextComponent default:AccessibleJEditorPane
    public final String getContentType();                                                    default:"text/plain"
    public final void setContentType(String type);
    public final javax.swing.text.EditorKit getEditorKit();
    public void setEditorKit(javax.swing.text.EditorKit kit);                                 bound expert
    public boolean isManagingFocus();                        Overrides:JComponent constant default:true
    public java.net.URL getPage();                                                            default:null
    public void setPage(java.net.URL page) throws java.io.IOException;                        bound expert
    public void setPage(String url) throws java.io.IOException;
    public java.awt.Dimension getPreferredSize();                                             Overrides:JComponent
    public boolean getScrollableTracksViewportHeight();      Overrides:JTextComponent default:false
    public boolean getScrollableTracksViewportWidth();       Overrides:JTextComponent default:false
    public String getText();                                 Overrides:JTextComponent default:""
    public void setText(String t);                                                           Overrides:JTextComponent
    public String getUIClassID();                            Overrides:JComponent default:"EditorPaneUI"
// Public Instance Methods
    public void fireHyperlinkUpdate(javax.swing.event.HyperlinkEvent e);
    public javax.swing.text.EditorKit getEditorKitForContentType(String type);
    public void read(java.io.InputStream in, Object desc) throws java.io.IOException;
    public void setEditorKitForContentType(String type, javax.swing.text.EditorKit k);
// Public Methods Overriding JTextComponent
    public void replaceSelection(String content);
// Protected Methods Overriding JTextComponent
    protected String paramString();
    protected void processComponentKeyEvent(java.awt.event.KeyEvent e);
// Protected Instance Methods
    protected javax.swing.text.EditorKit createDefaultEditorKit();
    protected java.io.InputStream getStream(java.net.URL page) throws java.io.IOException;
    protected void scrollToReference(String reference);
}
```

Hierarchy: Object→ Component(java.awt.image.ImageObserver, java.awt.MenuContainer, Serializable)→ Container→ JComponent(Serializable)→ javax.swing.text.JTextComponent(Accessible, Scrollable)→ JEditorPane

Subclasses: JTextPane

Passed To: javax.swing.text.EditorKit.{deinstall(), install()}, javax.swing.text.StyledEditorKit.{deinstall(), install()}, javax.swing.text.StyledEditorKit.StyledTextAction.{getStyledDocument(), getStyledEditorKit(), setCharacterAttributes(), setParagraphAttributes()}, javax.swing.text.html.HTMLEditorKit.{deinstall(), install()}, javax.swing.text.html.HTMLEditorKit.HTMLTextAction.{getHTMLDocument(), getHTMLEditorKit()}, javax.swing.text.html.HTMLEditorKit.InsertHTMLTextAction.{insertAtBoundry(), insertHTML()}, javax.swing.text.html.HTMLEditorKit.LinkController.activateLink()

Returned By: javax.swing.text.StyledEditorKit.StyledTextAction.getEditor()

JFileChooser   Java 1.2

javax.swing   *serializable accessible swing component*

This component allows the user to select a file. After creating a JFileChooser component, and setting any desired properties, the easiest way to use it is to call showOpenDialog() or showSaveDialog(). These methods display the JFileChooser in a modal dialog box, using the component you specify as its parent. They also customize the Okay button to read **Open** or **Save** (or locale-appropriate equivalents). You can also call showDialog() and explicitly specify the text to appear in the Okay button. The methods return

APPROVE_OPTION if the user selects a file and clicks the **Save** or **Open** button. They return CANCEL_OPTION if the user clicks the **Cancel** button or otherwise dismisses the dialog. They return ERROR_OPTION if some sort of error or exception occurs during file selection. When the return value is APPROVE_OPTION, you can call getSelectedFile() to obtain a File object that represents the file the user selected.

Other commonly used JFileChooser properties are currentDirectory, which specifies the initial or most recently selected directory displayed by the JFileChooser, and fileSelection-Mode, which specifies whether the JFileChooser should allow the user to choose a file, a directory, or either. The legal values for the fileSelectionMode property are FILES_ONLY, DIRECTORIES_ONLY, and FILES_AND_DIRECTORIES.

You can selectively filter files, so that only certain choices are displayed to the user, by passing a javax.swing.filechooser.FileFilter object to setFileFilter(). This allows you, for example, to tell the JFileChooser to display only files that have an extension of *.htm* or *.html*. The default FileFilter is one that display all files. You can obtain an instance of it by calling getAcceptAllFileFilter(). You can provide a set of file filters for the user to choose from by setting the choosableFileFilters property to an array of FileFilter objects.

In addition to file filters, JFileChooser provides another powerful way to customize the file selection dialog. The accessory property allows you to specify a JComponent file selection accessory to be displayed within the JFileChooser. Such accessories are typically used as file previewers. For example, you might write an accessory to display a thumbnail version of a selected image file. The accessory object must register a PropertyChange-Listener on the JFileChooser, so that it can receive notification of changes in the selectedFile property.

```
public class JFileChooser extends JComponent implements Accessible {
// Public Constructors
    public JFileChooser();
    public JFileChooser(javax.swing.filechooser.FileSystemView fsv);
    public JFileChooser(java.io.File currentDirectory);
    public JFileChooser(String currentDirectoryPath);
    public JFileChooser(java.io.File currentDirectory, javax.swing.filechooser.FileSystemView fsv);
    public JFileChooser(String currentDirectoryPath, javax.swing.filechooser.FileSystemView fsv);
// Public Constants
    public static final String ACCESSORY_CHANGED_PROPERTY;              ="AccessoryChangedProperty"
    public static final String                                         ="ApproveButtonMnemonicChangedProperty"
        APPROVE_BUTTON_MNEMONIC_CHANGED_PROPERTY;
    public static final String                                         ="ApproveButtonTextChangedProperty"
        APPROVE_BUTTON_TEXT_CHANGED_PROPERTY;
    public static final String                                         ="ApproveButtonToolTipTextChangedProperty"
        APPROVE_BUTTON_TOOL_TIP_TEXT_CHANGED_PROPERTY;
    public static final int APPROVE_OPTION;                                                      =0
    public static final String APPROVE_SELECTION;                               ="ApproveSelection"
    public static final int CANCEL_OPTION;                                                       =1
    public static final String CANCEL_SELECTION;                                 ="CancelSelection"
    public static final String                                          ="ChoosableFileFilterChangedProperty"
        CHOOSABLE_FILE_FILTER_CHANGED_PROPERTY;
    public static final int CUSTOM_DIALOG;                                                       =2
    public static final String DIALOG_TITLE_CHANGED_PROPERTY;            ="DialogTitleChangedProperty"
    public static final String DIALOG_TYPE_CHANGED_PROPERTY;             ="DialogTypeChangedProperty"
    public static final int DIRECTORIES_ONLY;                                                    =1
    public static final String DIRECTORY_CHANGED_PROPERTY;                        ="directoryChanged"
    public static final int ERROR_OPTION;                                                       =-1
    public static final String FILE_FILTER_CHANGED_PROPERTY;                     ="fileFilterChanged"
    public static final String FILE_HIDING_CHANGED_PROPERTY;                     ="FileHidingChanged"
    public static final String FILE_SELECTION_MODE_CHANGED_PROPERTY;         ="fileSelectionChanged"
    public static final String FILE_SYSTEM_VIEW_CHANGED_PROPERTY;          ="FileSystemViewChanged"
```

javax.swing

public static final String **FILE_VIEW_CHANGED_PROPERTY**;	=*"fileViewChanged"*
public static final int **FILES_AND_DIRECTORIES**;	=2
public static final int **FILES_ONLY**;	=0
public static final String **MULTI_SELECTION_ENABLED_CHANGED_PROPERTY**;	=*"fileFilterChanged"*
public static final int **OPEN_DIALOG**;	=0
public static final int **SAVE_DIALOG**;	=1
public static final String **SELECTED_FILE_CHANGED_PROPERTY**;	=*"SelectedFileChangedProperty"*
public static final String **SELECTED_FILES_CHANGED_PROPERTY**;	=*"SelectedFilesChangedProperty"*

// Inner Classes
protected class **AccessibleJFileChooser** extends JComponent.AccessibleJComponent;

// Event Registration Methods (by event name)
public void **addActionListener**(java.awt.event.ActionListener *l*);
public void **removeActionListener**(java.awt.event.ActionListener *l*);

// Property Accessor Methods (by property name)

public javax.swing.filechooser.FileFilter **getAcceptAllFileFilter**();	
public AccessibleContext **getAccessibleContext**();	*Implements:Accessible default:AccessibleJFileChooser*
public JComponent **getAccessory**();	*default:null*
public void **setAccessory**(JComponent *newAccessory*);	*bound preferred*
public int **getApproveButtonMnemonic**();	*default:0*
public void **setApproveButtonMnemonic**(int *mnemonic*);	*bound preferred*
public void **setApproveButtonMnemonic**(char *mnemonic*);	
public String **getApproveButtonText**();	*default:null*
public void **setApproveButtonText**(String *approveButtonText*);	*bound preferred*
public String **getApproveButtonToolTipText**();	*default:null*
public void **setApproveButtonToolTipText**(String *toolTipText*);	*bound preferred*
public javax.swing.filechooser.FileFilter[ ] **getChoosableFileFilters**();	
public java.io.File **getCurrentDirectory**();	
public void **setCurrentDirectory**(java.io.File *dir*);	*bound preferred*
public String **getDialogTitle**();	*default:null*
public void **setDialogTitle**(String *dialogTitle*);	*bound preferred*
public int **getDialogType**();	*default:0*
public void **setDialogType**(int *dialogType*);	*bound preferred*
public boolean **isDirectorySelectionEnabled**();	*default:false*
public javax.swing.filechooser.FileFilter **getFileFilter**();	
public void **setFileFilter**(javax.swing.filechooser.FileFilter *filter*);	*bound preferred*
public boolean **isFileHidingEnabled**();	*default:true*
public void **setFileHidingEnabled**(boolean *b*);	*bound preferred*
public boolean **isFileSelectionEnabled**();	*default:true*
public int **getFileSelectionMode**();	*default:0*
public void **setFileSelectionMode**(int *mode*);	*bound preferred*
public javax.swing.filechooser.FileSystemView **getFileSystemView**();	
public void **setFileSystemView**(javax.swing.filechooser.FileSystemView *fsv*);	*bound expert*
public javax.swing.filechooser.FileView **getFileView**();	*default:null*
public void **setFileView**(javax.swing.filechooser.FileView *fileView*);	*bound preferred*
public boolean **isMultiSelectionEnabled**();	*default:false*
public void **setMultiSelectionEnabled**(boolean *b*);	*bound*
public java.io.File **getSelectedFile**();	*default:null*
public void **setSelectedFile**(java.io.File *file*);	*bound preferred*
public java.io.File[ ] **getSelectedFiles**();	
public void **setSelectedFiles**(java.io.File[ ] *selectedFiles*);	*bound*
public javax.swing.plaf.FileChooserUI **getUI**();	
public String **getUIClassID**();	*Overrides:JComponent default:"FileChooserUI" expert*

// Public Instance Methods

public boolean **accept**(java.io.File *f*);	
public void **addChoosableFileFilter**(javax.swing.filechooser.FileFilter *filter*);	*bound preferred*
public void **approveSelection**();	
public void **cancelSelection**();	
public void **changeToParentDirectory**();	

```
    public void ensureFileIsVisible(java.io.File f);
    public String getDescription(java.io.File f);
    public Icon getIcon(java.io.File f);
    public String getName(java.io.File f);
    public String getTypeDescription(java.io.File f);
    public boolean isTraversable(java.io.File f);
    public boolean removeChoosableFileFilter(javax.swing.filechooser.FileFilter f);
    public void rescanCurrentDirectory();
    public void resetChoosableFileFilters();
    public int showDialog(Component parent, String approveButtonText);
    public int showOpenDialog(Component parent);
    public int showSaveDialog(Component parent);
// Methods Implementing Accessible
    public AccessibleContext getAccessibleContext();                          default:AccessibleJFileChooser
// Public Methods Overriding JComponent
    public void updateUI();
// Protected Methods Overriding JComponent
    protected String paramString();
// Protected Instance Methods
    protected void fireActionPerformed(String command);
    protected void setup(javax.swing.filechooser.FileSystemView view);
// Protected Instance Fields
    protected AccessibleContext accessibleContext;
}
```

Hierarchy: Object→ Component(java.awt.image.ImageObserver, java.awt.MenuContainer, Serializable)→ Container→ JComponent(Serializable)→ JFileChooser(Accessible)

Passed To: javax.swing.plaf.FileChooserUI.{ensureFileIsVisible(), getAcceptAllFileFilter(), getApproveButtonText(), getDialogTitle(), getFileView(), rescanCurrentDirectory()}

JFrame   Java 1.2

javax.swing   *serializable accessible swing component bean container*

This class is used to display the main window (or windows) of a Swing application. Every JFrame has a single automatically created JRootPane child. You should not add children directly to the JFrame, but instead call getContentPane() and add children to the container returned by that method. Similarly, if you set a layout manager, you should do so on the container returned by getContentPane(). The default layout manager for this container is an instance of java.awt.BorderLayout.

The JFrame has two other features of interest. First, setJMenuBar() automatically places a specified menubar at the top of the window, leaving the content pane free for other application content. Second, setDefaultCloseOperation() specifies how the window should respond when the user attempts to close it (e.g., by typing **Alt-F4** in Windows). The argument to this method should be one of the constants defined by javax.swing.Window-Constants. The default is HIDE_ON_CLOSE. In addition to these features, JFrame also inherits useful methods from java.awt.Frame, including setCursor(), setIconImage(), setResizable(), and setTitle().

JFrame uses a heavyweight native window. To create a lightweight window that appears entirely within the confines of a containing window, you can use JInternalFrame.

```
public class JFrame extends java.awt.Frame implements Accessible, RootPaneContainer, WindowConstants {
// Public Constructors
    public JFrame();
    public JFrame(String title);
```

```
// Inner Classes
    protected class AccessibleJFrame extends AccessibleContext implements AccessibleComponent, Serializable;
// Property Accessor Methods (by property name)
    public AccessibleContext getAccessibleContext();                  Implements:Accessible default:AccessibleJFrame
    public Container getContentPane();                                Implements:RootPaneContainer default:JPanel
    public void setContentPane(Container contentPane);                Implements:RootPaneContainer hidden
    public int getDefaultCloseOperation();                                                           default:1
    public void setDefaultCloseOperation(int operation);                                             preferred
    public Component getGlassPane();                                  Implements:RootPaneContainer default:JPanel
    public void setGlassPane(Component glassPane);                    Implements:RootPaneContainer hidden
    public JMenuBar getJMenuBar();                                                                default:null
    public void setJMenuBar(JMenuBar menubar);                                                       hidden
    public JLayeredPane getLayeredPane();                                         Implements:RootPaneContainer
    public void setLayeredPane(JLayeredPane layeredPane);             Implements:RootPaneContainer hidden
    public void setLayout(java.awt.LayoutManager manager);                              Overrides:Container
    public JRootPane getRootPane();                                               Implements:RootPaneContainer
// Methods Implementing Accessible
    public AccessibleContext getAccessibleContext();                             default:AccessibleJFrame
// Methods Implementing RootPaneContainer
    public Container getContentPane();                                                    default:JPanel
    public Component getGlassPane();                                                      default:JPanel
    public JLayeredPane getLayeredPane();
    public JRootPane getRootPane();
    public void setContentPane(Container contentPane);                                               hidden
    public void setGlassPane(Component glassPane);                                                   hidden
    public void setLayeredPane(JLayeredPane layeredPane);                                            hidden
// Protected Methods Overriding Frame
    protected String paramString();
// Protected Methods Overriding Window
    protected void processWindowEvent(java.awt.event.WindowEvent e);
// Public Methods Overriding Container
    public void remove(Component comp);
    public void update(java.awt.Graphics g);
// Protected Methods Overriding Container
    protected void addImpl(Component comp, Object constraints, int index);
// Protected Methods Overriding Component
    protected void processKeyEvent(java.awt.event.KeyEvent e);
// Protected Instance Methods
    protected JRootPane createRootPane();
    protected void frameInit();
    protected boolean isRootPaneCheckingEnabled();
    protected void setRootPane(JRootPane root);                                                      hidden
    protected void setRootPaneCheckingEnabled(boolean enabled);                                      hidden
// Protected Instance Fields
    protected AccessibleContext accessibleContext;
    protected JRootPane rootPane;
    protected boolean rootPaneCheckingEnabled;
}
```

Hierarchy: Object→ Component(java.awt.image.ImageObserver, java.awt.MenuContainer, Serializable)→ Container→ java.awt.Window→ java.awt.Frame(java.awt.MenuContainer)→ JFrame(Accessible, RootPaneContainer, WindowConstants)

JInternalFrame   Java 1.2

javax.swing   *serializable accessible(value) swing component bean container*

This class is a lightweight Swing component that simulates a heavyweight native window, complete with titlebar and other window decorations appropriate to the installed

---

look-and-feel. Because it is a lightweight component, with no native window of its own, a JInternalFrame is constrained to stay within the bounds of its container. This container is typically a JDesktopPane. Within a JDesktopPane, a JInternalFrame can be moved, resized, iconified, and maximized, much like a JFrame can be.

JInternalFrame is like JFrame in many ways. A JInternalFrame has a JRootPane as its only child. Components should not be added directly to a JInternalFrame, but rather to the container returned by getContentPane(). setJMenuBar() specifies a menubar for the lightweight window, and setDefaultCloseOperation() specifies how it should respond when the user closes it. See JFrame for more on these two methods.

setTitle() sets the title displayed in the internal frame's titlebar. setFrameIcon() specifies a small image to be displayed in the titlebar and possibly also in the iconified representation of the JInternalFrame. setIconifiable() specifies whether the user is allowed to iconify the window, setIcon() actually iconifies or deiconifies the window, and isIcon() queries whether the window is currently iconified. setDesktopIcon() specifies the internal JInternalFrame.JDesktopIcon object used to represent the iconified version of the JInternalFrame. This last method should not be used by application-level code.

Similarly, setMaximizable() specifies whether the user can maximize the window, and setMaximum() maximizes the window. setResizable() specifies whether the window can be resized. setSelected() selects or deselects the window, and toFront() and toBack() move the window to the top and bottom of the stacking order relative to other JInternalFrame windows. Finally, as with all components, setVisible() makes the window visible or invisible.

```java
public class JInternalFrame extends JComponent implements Accessible, RootPaneContainer, WindowConstants {
// Public Constructors
    public JInternalFrame();
    public JInternalFrame(String title);
    public JInternalFrame(String title, boolean resizable);
    public JInternalFrame(String title, boolean resizable, boolean closable);
    public JInternalFrame(String title, boolean resizable, boolean closable, boolean maximizable);
    public JInternalFrame(String title, boolean resizable, boolean closable, boolean maximizable, boolean iconifiable);
// Public Constants
    public static final String CONTENT_PANE_PROPERTY;                      ="contentPane"
    public static final String FRAME_ICON_PROPERTY;                        ="frameIcon"
    public static final String GLASS_PANE_PROPERTY;                        ="glassPane"
    public static final String IS_CLOSED_PROPERTY;                         ="closed"
    public static final String IS_ICON_PROPERTY;                           ="icon"
    public static final String IS_MAXIMUM_PROPERTY;                        ="maximum"
    public static final String IS_SELECTED_PROPERTY;                       ="selected"
    public static final String LAYERED_PANE_PROPERTY;                      ="layeredPane"
    public static final String MENU_BAR_PROPERTY;                          ="menuBar"
    public static final String ROOT_PANE_PROPERTY;                         ="rootPane"
    public static final String TITLE_PROPERTY;                             ="title"
// Inner Classes
    protected class AccessibleJInternalFrame extends JComponent.AccessibleJComponent implements
        AccessibleValue;
    public static class JDesktopIcon extends JComponent implements Accessible;
// Event Registration Methods (by event name)
    public void addInternalFrameListener(javax.swing.event.InternalFrameListener l);
    public void removeInternalFrameListener(javax.swing.event.InternalFrameListener l);
// Property Accessor Methods (by property name)
    public AccessibleContext getAccessibleContext();      Implements:Accessible default:AccessibleJInternalFrame
    public boolean isClosable();                                                    default:false
    public void setClosable(boolean b);                                         bound preferred
    public boolean isClosed();                                                      default:false
    public void setClosed(boolean b) throws java.beans.PropertyVetoException;    bound constrained
    public Container getContentPane();                    Implements:RootPaneContainer default:JPanel
```

javax.swing

public void **setContentPane**(Container c);	*Implements:RootPaneContainer bound hidden*
public int **getDefaultCloseOperation**();	*default:1*
public void **setDefaultCloseOperation**(int *operation*);	
public JInternalFrame.JDesktopIcon **getDesktopIcon**();	
public void **setDesktopIcon**(JInternalFrame.JDesktopIcon *d*);	*bound*
public JDesktopPane **getDesktopPane**();	*default:null*
public Icon **getFrameIcon**();	
public void **setFrameIcon**(Icon *icon*);	*bound*
public Component **getGlassPane**();	*Implements:RootPaneContainer default:JPanel*
public void **setGlassPane**(Component *glass*);	*Implements:RootPaneContainer hidden*
public boolean **isIcon**();	*default:false*
public void **setIcon**(boolean *b*) throws java.beans.PropertyVetoException;	*bound constrained*
public boolean **isIconifiable**();	*default:false*
public void **setIconifiable**(boolean *b*);	
public JMenuBar **getJMenuBar**();	*default:null*
public void **setJMenuBar**(JMenuBar *m*);	*preferred*
public int **getLayer**();	*default:0*
public void **setLayer**(Integer *layer*);	*expert*
public JLayeredPane **getLayeredPane**();	*Implements:RootPaneContainer*
public void **setLayeredPane**(JLayeredPane *layered*);	*Implements:RootPaneContainer bound hidden*
public void **setLayout**(java.awt.LayoutManager *manager*);	*Overrides:Container*
public boolean **isMaximizable**();	*default:false*
public void **setMaximizable**(boolean *b*);	*bound preferred*
public boolean **isMaximum**();	*default:false*
public void **setMaximum**(boolean *b*) throws java.beans.PropertyVetoException;	*constrained*
public boolean **isResizable**();	*default:false*
public void **setResizable**(boolean *b*);	*bound preferred*
public JRootPane **getRootPane**();	*Implements:RootPaneContainer*
public boolean **isSelected**();	*default:false*
public void **setSelected**(boolean *selected*) throws java.beans.PropertyVetoException;	*bound constrained*
public String **getTitle**();	*default:""*
public void **setTitle**(String *title*);	
public javax.swing.plaf.InternalFrameUI **getUI**();	
public void **setUI**(javax.swing.plaf.InternalFrameUI *ui*);	*expert*
public String **getUIClassID**();	*Overrides:JComponent default:"InternalFrameUI"*
public final String **getWarningString**();	*constant default:null*

// *Public Instance Methods*

public void **dispose**();	
public void **moveToBack**();	
public void **moveToFront**();	
public void **pack**();	
public void **toBack**();	
public void **toFront**();	

// *Methods Implementing Accessible*

public AccessibleContext **getAccessibleContext**();	*default:AccessibleJInternalFrame*

// *Methods Implementing RootPaneContainer*

public Container **getContentPane**();	*default:JPanel*
public Component **getGlassPane**();	*default:JPanel*
public JLayeredPane **getLayeredPane**();	
public JRootPane **getRootPane**();	
public void **setContentPane**(Container *c*);	*bound hidden*
public void **setGlassPane**(Component *glass*);	*hidden*
public void **setLayeredPane**(JLayeredPane *layered*);	*bound hidden*

// *Public Methods Overriding JComponent*

public void **reshape**(int *x*, int *y*, int *width*, int *height*);	
public void **setVisible**(boolean *b*);	
public void **updateUI**();	

```
// Protected Methods Overriding JComponent
    protected void paintComponent(java.awt.Graphics g);
    protected String paramString();
// Public Methods Overriding Container
    public void remove(Component comp);
// Protected Methods Overriding Container
    protected void addImpl(Component comp, Object constraints, int index);
// Public Methods Overriding Component
    public void show();
// Protected Instance Methods
    protected JRootPane createRootPane();
    protected void fireInternalFrameEvent(int id);
    protected boolean isRootPaneCheckingEnabled();
    protected void setRootPane(JRootPane root);                                       hidden
    protected void setRootPaneCheckingEnabled(boolean enabled);
// Protected Instance Fields
    protected boolean closable;
    protected JInternalFrame.JDesktopIcon desktopIcon;
    protected Icon frameIcon;
    protected boolean iconable;
    protected boolean isClosed;
    protected boolean isIcon;
    protected boolean isMaximum;
    protected boolean isSelected;
    protected boolean maximizable;
    protected boolean resizable;
    protected JRootPane rootPane;
    protected boolean rootPaneCheckingEnabled;
    protected String title;
// Deprecated Public Methods
#   public JMenuBar getMenuBar();                                                 default:null
#   public void setMenuBar(JMenuBar m);
}
```

Hierarchy: Object→ Component(java.awt.image.ImageObserver, java.awt.MenuContainer, Serializable) → Container→ JComponent(Serializable)→ JInternalFrame(Accessible, RootPaneContainer, WindowConstants)

Passed To: Too many methods to list.

Returned By: JDesktopPane.{getAllFrames(), getAllFramesInLayer()}, JInternalFrame.JDesktopIcon.getInternalFrame(), JOptionPane.createInternalFrame()

JInternalFrame.JDesktopIcon   Java 1.2

javax.swing   *serializable accessible swing component*

This inner class represents an iconified version of a JInternalFrame to be displayed by a JDesktopPane. The appearance of the JDesktopIcon is left entirely to the current look-and-feel, and JDesktopIcon does not define any properties you can set to change its appearance. JDesktopIcon may be removed in future versions of Swing; it should not be used by application-level code.

```
public static class JInternalFrame.JDesktopIcon extends JComponent implements Accessible {
// Public Constructors
    public JDesktopIcon(JInternalFrame f);
// Inner Classes
    protected class AccessibleJDesktopIcon extends JComponent.AccessibleJComponent implements
        AccessibleValue;
```

javax.swing

```
// Property Accessor Methods (by property name)
    public AccessibleContext getAccessibleContext();                              Implements:Accessible
    public JDesktopPane getDesktopPane();
    public JInternalFrame getInternalFrame();
    public void setInternalFrame(JInternalFrame f);
    public javax.swing.plaf.DesktopIconUI getUI();
    public void setUI(javax.swing.plaf.DesktopIconUI ui);
    public String getUIClassID();                                                 Overrides:JComponent
// Methods Implementing Accessible
    public AccessibleContext getAccessibleContext();
// Public Methods Overriding JComponent
    public void updateUI();
}
```

Passed To: JInternalFrame.setDesktopIcon()

Returned By: JInternalFrame.getDesktopIcon()

Type Of: JInternalFrame.desktopIcon

JLabel   Java 1.2

javax.swing   *serializable accessible swing component*

This class displays a short string of text and/or an Icon. JLabel is a display-only component with no behavior, so the displayed text and/or icon does not respond to any input events. JLabel does not maintain any state and therefore does not use a model. By default, a JLabel displays a single line of text in a single font. However, as of Swing 1.1.1 and Java 1.2.2, if the text property begins with "<html>", the label is formatted as HTML text and may contain multiple fonts and multiple lines.

The icon, text, and font properties need no explanation. disabledIcon specifies an alternate icon to display when the JLabel is disabled. By default, a grayscale version of the regular icon is used. horizontalAlignment and verticalAlignment specify the justification of the label, and horizontalTextPosition and verticalTextPosition specify the position of the text relative to the icon. Each of these properties should be set to one of the LEFT, CENTER, RIGHT, TOP, or BOTTOM constants defined by the SwingConstants interface. The iconTextGap property specifies the number of pixels between the text and the icon.

Although JLabel does not have any behavior of its own, it can display a mnemonic character. If the displayedMnemonic property is set, the specified character is underlined in the label. If the labelFor property refers to another component, the JLabel requests keyboard focus for that component when the mnemonic is used. This is useful for labeling JTextField components, for example.

```
public class JLabel extends JComponent implements Accessible, SwingConstants {
// Public Constructors
    public JLabel();
    public JLabel(Icon image);
    public JLabel(String text);
    public JLabel(Icon image, int horizontalAlignment);
    public JLabel(String text, int horizontalAlignment);
    public JLabel(String text, Icon icon, int horizontalAlignment);
// Inner Classes
    protected class AccessibleJLabel extends JComponent.AccessibleJComponent;
// Property Accessor Methods (by property name)
    public AccessibleContext getAccessibleContext();       Implements:Accessible default:AccessibleJLabel expert
    public Icon getDisabledIcon();                                                            default:null
    public void setDisabledIcon(Icon disabledIcon);                                                bound
```

public int **getDisplayedMnemonic**( );	*default:0*
public void **setDisplayedMnemonic**(int *key*);	*bound*
public void **setDisplayedMnemonic**(char *aChar*);	
public int **getHorizontalAlignment**( );	*default:10*
public void **setHorizontalAlignment**(int *alignment*);	*bound*
public int **getHorizontalTextPosition**( );	*default:11*
public void **setHorizontalTextPosition**(int *textPosition*);	*bound expert*
public Icon **getIcon**( );	*default:null*
public void **setIcon**(Icon *icon*);	*bound preferred*
public int **getIconTextGap**( );	*default:4*
public void **setIconTextGap**(int *iconTextGap*);	*bound*
public Component **getLabelFor**( );	*default:null*
public void **setLabelFor**(Component *c*);	*bound*
public String **getText**( );	*default:""*
public void **setText**(String *text*);	*bound preferred*
public javax.swing.plaf.LabelUI **getUI**( );	
public void **setUI**(javax.swing.plaf.LabelUI *ui*);	*expert*
public String **getUIClassID**( );	*Overrides:JComponent default:"LabelUI"*
public int **getVerticalAlignment**( );	*default:0*
public void **setVerticalAlignment**(int *alignment*);	*bound*
public int **getVerticalTextPosition**( );	*default:0*
public void **setVerticalTextPosition**(int *textPosition*);	*bound expert*

// *Methods Implementing Accessible*

public AccessibleContext **getAccessibleContext**( );	*default:AccessibleJLabel expert*

// *Public Methods Overriding JComponent*
  public void **updateUI**( );
// *Protected Methods Overriding JComponent*
  protected String **paramString**( );
// *Protected Instance Methods*
  protected int **checkHorizontalKey**(int *key*, String *message*);
  protected int **checkVerticalKey**(int *key*, String *message*);
// *Protected Instance Fields*
  protected Component **labelFor**;
}

Hierarchy: Object→ Component(java.awt.image.ImageObserver, java.awt.MenuContainer, Serializable)→ Container→ JComponent(Serializable)→ JLabel(Accessible, SwingConstants)

Subclasses: DefaultListCellRenderer, javax.swing.table.DefaultTableCellRenderer, javax.swing.tree.DefaultTreeCellRenderer

JLayeredPane   Java 1.2

javax.swing   *serializable accessible swing component*

This class is a Swing container that layers its children according to a specified stacking order. When you add a child to a JLayeredPane, you specify an Integer as the constraints argument to the add() methods. This Integer object specifies the layer number for the child, where higher numbers are nearer the top of the stack. JLayeredPane defines a number of _LAYER constants as predefined layers. The layer of a child can also be set with setLayer(). If multiple children are in the same layer, their relative stacking order is determined by their insertion order. This position within a layer can be modified with setPosition(), moveToFront(), and moveToBack(). JLayeredPane is typically used without a layout manager; children have their size and position explicitly set.

All JFrame, JDialog, JApplet, and JInternalFrame objects contain a JRootPane which, in turn, contains a JLayeredPane. This internal JLayeredPane is used to correctly layer lightweight menus, dialogs, floating palettes, internal frames, and so forth.

```
public class JLayeredPane extends JComponent implements Accessible {
// Public Constructors
    public JLayeredPane();
// Public Constants
    public static final Integer DEFAULT_LAYER;
    public static final Integer DRAG_LAYER;
    public static final Integer FRAME_CONTENT_LAYER;
    public static final String LAYER_PROPERTY;                              ="layeredContainerLayer"
    public static final Integer MODAL_LAYER;
    public static final Integer PALETTE_LAYER;
    public static final Integer POPUP_LAYER;
// Inner Classes
    protected class AccessibleJLayeredPane extends JComponent.AccessibleJComponent;
// Public Class Methods
    public static int getLayer(JComponent c);
    public static JLayeredPane getLayeredPaneAbove(Component c);
    public static void putLayer(JComponent c, int layer);
// Property Accessor Methods (by property name)
    public AccessibleContext getAccessibleContext();           Implements:Accessible default:AccessibleJLayeredPane
    public boolean isOptimizedDrawingEnabled();                        Overrides:JComponent default:true
// Public Instance Methods
    public int getComponentCountInLayer(int layer);
    public Component[ ] getComponentsInLayer(int layer);
    public int getIndexOf(Component c);
    public int getLayer(Component c);
    public int getPosition(Component c);
    public int highestLayer();
    public int lowestLayer();
    public void moveToBack(Component c);
    public void moveToFront(Component c);
    public void setLayer(Component c, int layer);
    public void setLayer(Component c, int layer, int position);
    public void setPosition(Component c, int position);
// Methods Implementing Accessible
    public AccessibleContext getAccessibleContext();                  default:AccessibleJLayeredPane
// Public Methods Overriding JComponent
    public void paint(java.awt.Graphics g);
// Protected Methods Overriding JComponent
    protected String paramString();
// Public Methods Overriding Container
    public void remove(int index);
// Protected Methods Overriding Container
    protected void addImpl(Component comp, Object constraints, int index);
// Protected Instance Methods
    protected java.util.Hashtable getComponentToLayer();
    protected Integer getObjectForLayer(int layer);
    protected int insertIndexForLayer(int layer, int position);
}
```

Hierarchy: Object→ Component(java.awt.image.ImageObserver, java.awt.MenuContainer, Serializable)→ Container→ JComponent(Serializable)→ JLayeredPane(Accessible)

Subclasses: JDesktopPane

Passed To: JApplet.setLayeredPane(), JDialog.setLayeredPane(), JFrame.setLayeredPane(), JInternalFrame.setLayeredPane(), JRootPane.setLayeredPane(), JWindow.setLayeredPane(), RootPaneContainer.setLayeredPane()

Returned By: JApplet.getLayeredPane(), JDialog.getLayeredPane(), JFrame.getLayeredPane(), JInternalFrame.getLayeredPane(), JLayeredPane.getLayeredPaneAbove(), JRootPane.{createLayeredPane(), getLayeredPane()}, JWindow.getLayeredPane(), RootPaneContainer.getLayeredPane()

Type Of: JRootPane.layeredPane

JList   Java 1.2

javax.swing   *serializable accessible(selection) swing component*

This class displays a list of items (typically strings) and allows the user to select one or more of them. The objects to be displayed are stored in a ListModel object. Two JList constructors allow list items to be specified as a static array or Vector of objects, however. For a dynamic list of elements, you may want to use your own instance of Default-ListModel, which maintains a Vector-like list of objects. By default, JList displays lists of strings. To display other types of list items, define an appropriate ListCellRenderer class and pass an instance of it to setCellRenderer().

The selection state of the JList is maintained by a ListSelectionModel object. By default, JList uses a DefaultListSelectionModel object. Application programmers rarely need to work with the ListSelectionModel directly because JList provides a number of methods to query and set the selection state. setSelectionMode() specifies the types of selections allowed by the JList. Its argument should be one of the three constants defined by ListSelectionModel. SINGLE_SELECTION allows only a single item to be selected, while SINGLE_INTERVAL_SELEC-TION allows multiple items in a single contiguous block to be selected and MULTI-PLE_INTERVAL_SELECTION allows any number of items, contiguous or not, to be selected.

JList generates a javax.swing.event.ListSelectionEvent when the selection state changes and sends it to the valueChanged() methods of any registered javax.swing.event.ListSelectionListener objects.

```
public class JList extends JComponent implements Accessible, Scrollable {
// Public Constructors
    public JList();
    public JList(Object[ ] listData);
    public JList(ListModel dataModel);
    public JList(java.util.Vector listData);
// Inner Classes
    protected class AccessibleJList extends JComponent.AccessibleJComponent implements AccessibleSelection,
        javax.swing.event.ListDataListener, javax.swing.event.ListSelectionListener, java.beans.PropertyChangeListener;
// Event Registration Methods (by event name)
    public void addListSelectionListener(javax.swing.event.ListSelectionListener listener);
    public void removeListSelectionListener(javax.swing.event.ListSelectionListener listener);
// Property Accessor Methods (by property name)
    public AccessibleContext getAccessibleContext();              Implements:Accessible default:AccessibleJList
    public int getAnchorSelectionIndex();                                                    default:-1
    public ListCellRenderer getCellRenderer();              default:DefaultListCellRenderer.UIResource
    public void setCellRenderer(ListCellRenderer cellRenderer);                                  bound
    public int getFirstVisibleIndex();                                                       default:-1
    public int getFixedCellHeight();                                                         default:-1
    public void setFixedCellHeight(int height);                                                 bound
    public int getFixedCellWidth();                                                          default:-1
    public void setFixedCellWidth(int width);                                                   bound
    public int getLastVisibleIndex();                                                        default:-1
    public int getLeadSelectionIndex();                                                      default:-1
    public int getMaxSelectionIndex();                                                       default:-1
    public int getMinSelectionIndex();                                                       default:-1
    public ListModel getModel();
    public void setModel(ListModel model);                                                      bound
```

```
    public java.awt.Dimension getPreferredScrollableViewportSize();                    Implements:Scrollable
    public Object getPrototypeCellValue();                                                     default:null
    public void setPrototypeCellValue(Object prototypeCellValue);                                     bound
    public boolean getScrollableTracksViewportHeight();                   Implements:Scrollable default:false
    public boolean getScrollableTracksViewportWidth();                   Implements:Scrollable default:false
    public int getSelectedIndex();                                                             default:-1
    public void setSelectedIndex(int index);
    public int[ ] getSelectedIndices();
    public void setSelectedIndices(int[ ] indices);
    public Object getSelectedValue();                                                          default:null
    public Object[ ] getSelectedValues();
    public java.awt.Color getSelectionBackground();                                default:ColorUIResource
    public void setSelectionBackground(java.awt.Color selectionBackground);                           bound
    public boolean isSelectionEmpty();                                                        default:true
    public java.awt.Color getSelectionForeground();                                default:ColorUIRescurce
    public void setSelectionForeground(java.awt.Color selectionForeground);                           bound
    public int getSelectionMode();                                                             default:2
    public void setSelectionMode(int selectionMode);
    public ListSelectionModel getSelectionModel();                        default:DefaultListSelectionModel
    public void setSelectionModel(ListSelectionModel selectionModel);                                 bound
    public javax.swing.plaf.ListUI getUI();
    public void setUI(javax.swing.plaf.ListUI ui);
    public String getUIClassID();                                       Overrides:JComponent default:"ListUI"
    public boolean getValueIsAdjusting();                                                     default:false
    public void setValueIsAdjusting(boolean b);
    public int getVisibleRowCount();                                                           default:8
    public void setVisibleRowCount(int visibleRowCount);                                              bound
// Public Instance Methods
    public void addSelectionInterval(int anchor, int lead);
    public void clearSelection();
    public void ensureIndexIsVisible(int index);
    public java.awt.Rectangle getCellBounds(int index1, int index2);
    public java.awt.Point indexToLocation(int index);
    public boolean isSelectedIndex(int index);
    public int locationToIndex(java.awt.Point location);
    public void removeSelectionInterval(int index0, int index1);
    public void setListData(Object[ ] listData);
    public void setListData(java.util.Vector listData);
    public void setSelectedValue(Object anObject, boolean shouldScroll);
    public void setSelectionInterval(int anchor, int lead);
// Methods Implementing Accessible
    public AccessibleContext getAccessibleContext();                                default:AccessibleJList
// Methods Implementing Scrollable
    public java.awt.Dimension getPreferredScrollableViewportSize();
    public int getScrollableBlockIncrement(java.awt.Rectangle visibleRect, int orientation, int direction);
    public boolean getScrollableTracksViewportHeight();                                       default:false
    public boolean getScrollableTracksViewportWidth();                                        default:false
    public int getScrollableUnitIncrement(java.awt.Rectangle visibleRect, int orientation, int direction);
// Public Methods Overriding JComponent
    public void updateUI();
// Protected Methods Overriding JComponent
    protected String paramString();
// Protected Instance Methods
    protected ListSelectionModel createSelectionModel();
    protected void fireSelectionValueChanged(int firstIndex, int lastIndex, boolean isAdjusting);
}
```

Hierarchy: Object→ Component(java.awt.image.ImageObserver, java.awt.MenuContainer, Serializable)→ Container→ JComponent(Serializable)→ JList(Accessible, Scrollable)

Passed To: DefaultListCellRenderer.getListCellRendererComponent(),
JList.AccessibleJList.AccessibleJListChild.AccessibleJListChild(),
ListCellRenderer.getListCellRendererComponent(), javax.swing.plaf.ListUI.{getCellBounds(), indexToLocation(),
locationToIndex()}

JMenu   Java 1.2

javax.swing   *serializable accessible(action,selection,value) swing component*

This class implements a pulldown menu in a menubar or a pull-right menu nested
within another menu. As a subclass of JMenuItem, JMenu is effectively a menu button
with an associated JPopupMenu that appears when the button is activated. Menu items
can be added to a JMenu with the add(), insert(), addSeparator(), and insertSeparator() methods. Note that you can add String and Action objects in addition to regular JMenuItem
objects. In these cases, an appropriate JMenuItem is automatically created for the String or
Action. JMenu generates a javax.swing.event.MenuEvent when it is selected and when its
menu is popped up or down. The default JMenu model is DefaultButtonModel.

```
public class JMenu extends JMenuItem implements Accessible, MenuElement {
// Public Constructors
     public JMenu();
     public JMenu(String s);
     public JMenu(String s, boolean b);
// Inner Classes
     protected class AccessibleJMenu extends JMenuItem.AccessibleJMenuItem implements AccessibleSelection;
     protected class WinListener extends java.awt.event.WindowAdapter implements Serializable;
// Event Registration Methods (by event name)
     public void addMenuListener(javax.swing.event.MenuListener l);
     public void removeMenuListener(javax.swing.event.MenuListener l);
// Property Accessor Methods (by property name)
     public void setAccelerator(KeyStroke keyStroke);                    Overrides:JMenuItem hidden
     public AccessibleContext getAccessibleContext();     Implements:Accessible default:AccessibleJMenu
     public Component getComponent();                   Implements:MenuElement default:JMenu
     public int getDelay();                                              default:200
     public void setDelay(int d);                                             expert
     public int getItemCount();                                          default:0
     public int getMenuComponentCount();                                 default:0
     public Component[ ] getMenuComponents();
     public void setModel(ButtonModel newModel);          Overrides:AbstractButton bound expert hidden
     public JPopupMenu getPopupMenu();
     public boolean isPopupMenuVisible();                              default:false
     public void setPopupMenuVisible(boolean b);                         expert hidden
     public boolean isSelected();                    Overrides:AbstractButton default:false
     public void setSelected(boolean b);              Overrides:AbstractButton expert hidden
     public MenuElement[ ] getSubElements();                   Implements:MenuElement
     public boolean isTearOff();
     public boolean isTopLevelMenu();                                  default:false
     public String getUIClassID();                    Overrides:JMenuItem default:"MenuUI"
// Public Instance Methods
     public JMenuItem add(String s);
     public JMenuItem add(JMenuItem menuItem);
     public JMenuItem add(Action a);
     public void addSeparator();
     public JMenuItem getItem(int pos);
     public Component getMenuComponent(int n);
     public void insert(String s, int pos);
     public JMenuItem insert(JMenuItem mi, int pos);
     public JMenuItem insert(Action a, int pos);
     public void insertSeparator(int index);
```

```
      public boolean isMenuComponent(Component c);
      public void remove(JMenuItem item);
      public void setMenuLocation(int x, int y);
```
// Methods Implementing Accessible
```
      public AccessibleContext getAccessibleContext( );                    default:AccessibleJMenu
```
// Methods Implementing MenuElement
```
      public Component getComponent( );                                    default:JMenu
      public MenuElement[ ] getSubElements( );
      public void menuSelectionChanged(boolean isIncluded);
```
// Public Methods Overriding JMenuItem
```
      public void updateUI( );
```
// Protected Methods Overriding JMenuItem
```
      protected String paramString( );
```
// Public Methods Overriding AbstractButton
```
      public void doClick(int pressTime);
```
// Protected Methods Overriding JComponent
```
      protected void processKeyEvent(java.awt.event.KeyEvent e);
```
// Public Methods Overriding Container
```
      public Component add(Component c);
      public void remove(Component c);
      public void remove(int pos);
      public void removeAll( );
```
// Protected Instance Methods
```
      protected java.beans.PropertyChangeListener createActionChangeListener(JMenuItem b);
      protected JMenu.WinListener createWinListener(JPopupMenu p);
      protected void fireMenuCanceled( );
      protected void fireMenuDeselected( );
      protected void fireMenuSelected( );
```
// Protected Instance Fields
```
      protected JMenu.WinListener popupListener;
}
```

Hierarchy: Object→ Component(java.awt.image.ImageObserver, java.awt.MenuContainer, Serializable)→ Container→ JComponent(Serializable)→ AbstractButton(java.awt.ItemSelectable, SwingConstants)→ JMenuItem(Accessible, MenuElement)→ JMenu(Accessible, MenuElement)

Passed To: JMenuBar.{add(), setHelpMenu()}

Returned By: JMenuBar.{add(), getHelpMenu(), getMenu()}

JMenu.WinListener   Java 1.2

javax.swing   *serializable*

This protected inner class is a java.awt.event.WindowListener that is used internally by JMenu to determine when the popup window containing the menu items closes. Application-level code never needs to use this class.

```
protected class JMenu.WinListener extends java.awt.event.WindowAdapter implements Serializable {
```
// Public Constructors
```
      public WinListener(JPopupMenu p);
```
// Public Methods Overriding WindowAdapter
```
      public void windowClosing(java.awt.event.WindowEvent e);
}
```

Returned By: JMenu.createWinListener()

Type Of: JMenu.popupListener

JMenuBar

javax.swing

serializable accessible(selection) swing component

This class implements a menu bar. JMenu objects are placed in a JMenuBar with the add() method and can be removed with the remove() methods. A **Help** menu should be sing.ed out for special treatment (typically by placing it at the right-hand edge of the menu bar) with setHelpMenu(). JMenuBar uses a SingleSelectionModel object to keep track of which of its JMenuItem children (if any) is currently selected. By default, JMenuBar uses a DefaultSingleSelectionModel model object.

In AWT, the MenuBar class is not a Component. In Swing, JMenuBar is a JComponent and can be laid out in an application like any other component. Note, however, that JFrame, JDialog, JApplet, and JInternalFrame all have setJMenuBar() methods that automatically position a JMenuBar at the top of the window. This is the easiest and most common way to lay out a menu bar.

```
public class JMenuBar extends JComponent implements Accessible, MenuElement {
// Public Constructors
     public JMenuBar();
// Inner Classes
     protected class AccessibleJMenuBar extends JComponent.AccessibleJComponent implements
          AccessibleSelection;
// Property Accessor Methods (by property name)
     public AccessibleContext getAccessibleContext();        Implements:Accessible default:AccessibleJMenuBar
     public boolean isBorderPainted();                                                   default:true
     public void setBorderPainted(boolean b);                                                  bound
     public Component getComponent();                         Implements:MenuElement default:JMenuBar
     public JMenu getHelpMenu();
     public void setHelpMenu(JMenu menu);
     public boolean isManagingFocus();                      Overrides:JComponent constant default:true
     public java.awt.Insets getMargin();
     public void setMargin(java.awt.Insets m);                                                 bound
     public int getMenuCount();                                                            default:0
     public boolean isSelected();                                                      default:false
     public void setSelected(Component sel);
     public SingleSelectionModel getSelectionModel();            default:DefaultSingleSelectionModel
     public void setSelectionModel(SingleSelectionModel model);                                bound
     public MenuElement[ ] getSubElements();                              Implements:MenuElement
     public javax.swing.plaf.MenuBarUI getUI();
     public void setUI(javax.swing.plaf.MenuBarUI ui);
     public String getUIClassID();                          Overrides:JComponent default:"MenuBarUI"
// Public Instance Methods
     public JMenu add(JMenu c);
     public Component getComponentAtIndex(int i);
     public int getComponentIndex(Component c);
     public JMenu getMenu(int index);
// Methods Implementing Accessible
     public AccessibleContext getAccessibleContext();                  default:AccessibleJMenuBar
// Methods Implementing MenuElement
     public Component getComponent();                                         default:JMenuBar
     public MenuElement[ ] getSubElements();
     public void menuSelectionChanged(boolean isIncluded);                                 empty
     public void processKeyEvent(java.awt.event.KeyEvent e, MenuElement[ ] path,           empty
                     MenuSelectionManager manager);
     public void processMouseEvent(java.awt.event.MouseEvent event, MenuElement[ ] path,   empty
                     MenuSelectionManager manager);
// Public Methods Overriding JComponent
     public void addNotify();
```

```
    public void removeNotify( );
    public void updateUI( );
// Protected Methods Overriding JComponent
    protected void paintBorder(java.awt.Graphics g);
    protected String paramString( );
}
```

Hierarchy: Object→ Component(java.awt.image.ImageObserver, java.awt.MenuContainer, Serializable)→ Container→ JComponent(Serializable)→ JMenuBar(Accessible, MenuElement)

Passed To: JApplet.setJMenuBar(), JDialog.setJMenuBar(), JFrame.setJMenuBar(), JInternalFrame.{setJMenuBar(), setMenuBar()}, JRootPane.{setJMenuBar(), setMenuBar()}

Returned By: JApplet.getJMenuBar(), JDialog.getJMenuBar(), JFrame.getJMenuBar(), JInternalFrame.{getJMenuBar(), getMenuBar()}, JRootPane.{getJMenuBar(), getMenuBar()}

Type Of: JRootPane.menuBar

JMenuItem   Java 1.2

javax.swing   *serializable accessible(action,value) swing component*

This class implements an item in a pulldown or popup menu. As a subclass of Abstract-Button, it shares most of the properties of JButton. One new feature is that it allows an accelerator to be specified. An accelerator is a keyboard binding for the menu item. Like all Swing buttons, JMenuItem also supports a mnemonic. Accelerators differ from mnemonics in two important ways, however. First, accelerators can be used at any time, while menu item mnemonics can be used only when the menu that contains them is displayed. Second, accelerators are specified with a KeyStroke object, rather than a simple character. This allows complex bindings that include function keys and arbitrary modifier keys.

In addition to its AbstractButton functionality, JMenuItem also implements the MenuElement interface. The default JMenuItem model is DefaultButtonModel, and the UI delegate class is MenuItemUI.

```
public class JMenuItem extends AbstractButton implements Accessible, MenuElement {
// Public Constructors
    public JMenuItem( );
    public JMenuItem(Icon icon);
    public JMenuItem(String text);
    public JMenuItem(String text, Icon icon);
    public JMenuItem(String text, int mnemonic);
// Inner Classes
    protected class AccessibleJMenuItem extends AbstractButton.AccessibleAbstractButton implements
        javax.swing.event.ChangeListener;
// Event Registration Methods (by event name)
    public void addMenuDragMouseListener(javax.swing.event.MenuDragMouseListener l);
    public void removeMenuDragMouseListener(javax.swing.event.MenuDragMouseListener l);
    public void addMenuKeyListener(javax.swing.event.MenuKeyListener l);
    public void removeMenuKeyListener(javax.swing.event.MenuKeyListener l);
// Property Accessor Methods (by property name)
    public KeyStroke getAccelerator( );                                                 default:null
    public void setAccelerator(KeyStroke keyStroke);                               bound preferred
    public AccessibleContext getAccessibleContext( );        Implements:Accessible default:AccessibleJMenuItem
    public boolean isArmed( );                                                         default:false
    public void setArmed(boolean b);                                                         hidden
    public Component getComponent( );                        Implements:MenuElement default:JMenuItem
    public MenuElement[ ] getSubElements( );                               Implements:MenuElement
    public String getUIClassID( );                          Overrides:JComponent default:"MenuItemUI"
```

```
// Public Instance Methods
    public void processMenuDragMouseEvent(javax.swing.event.MenuDragMouseEvent e);
    public void processMenuKeyEvent(javax.swing.event.MenuKeyEvent e);
    public void setUI(javax.swing.plaf.MenuItemUI ui);                          bound expert hidden
// Methods Implementing Accessible
    public AccessibleContext getAccessibleContext();                  default:AccessibleJMenuItem
// Methods Implementing MenuElement
    public Component getComponent();                                         default:JMenuItem
    public MenuElement[ ] getSubElements();
    public void menuSelectionChanged(boolean isIncluded);
    public void processKeyEvent(java.awt.event.KeyEvent e, MenuElement[ ] path, MenuSelectionManager manager);
    public void processMouseEvent(java.awt.event.MouseEvent e, MenuElement[ ] path,
                                  MenuSelectionManager manager);
// Public Methods Overriding AbstractButton
    public void setEnabled(boolean b);                                        bound preferred
    public void updateUI();
// Protected Methods Overriding AbstractButton
    protected void init(String text, Icon icon);
    protected String paramString();
// Protected Instance Methods
    protected void fireMenuDragMouseDragged(javax.swing.event.MenuDragMouseEvent event);
    protected void fireMenuDragMouseEntered(javax.swing.event.MenuDragMouseEvent event);
    protected void fireMenuDragMouseExited(javax.swing.event.MenuDragMouseEvent event);
    protected void fireMenuDragMouseReleased(javax.swing.event.MenuDragMouseEvent event);
    protected void fireMenuKeyPressed(javax.swing.event.MenuKeyEvent event);
    protected void fireMenuKeyReleased(javax.swing.event.MenuKeyEvent event);
    protected void fireMenuKeyTyped(javax.swing.event.MenuKeyEvent event);
}
```

Hierarchy: Object→ Component(java.awt.image.ImageObserver, java.awt.MenuContainer, Serializable)→ Container→ JComponent(Serializable)→ AbstractButton(java.awt.ItemSelectable, SwingConstants)→ JMenuItem(Accessible, MenuElement)

Subclasses: JCheckBoxMenuItem, JMenu, JRadioButtonMenuItem

Passed To: JMenu.{add(), createActionChangeListener(), insert(), remove()}, JPopupMenu.{add(), createActionChangeListener()}

Returned By: JMenu.{add(), getItem(), insert()}, JPopupMenu.add()

JOptionPane   Java 1.2

javax.swing   *serializable accessible swing component bean container*

This component is used to display various types of simple dialog boxes to the user (yes, its name is misleading). It is almost always used through one of the show*XXX*Dialog() static methods. The fact that there are more than 20 of these methods demonstrates the highly-configurable nature of this class. The showInternal*XXX*Dialog() methods display dialogs in lightweight JInternalFrame windows. The other static methods display methods in heavyweight JDialog windows.

You can create and display a simple message dialog with showMessageDialog() and showInternalMessageDialog(). These methods display a dialog box that contains the specified message, an optional icon, and an **Okay** button that dismisses the dialog. The dialog is modal, meaning it blocks, returning only when the user has dismissed the dialog. The *parentComponent* argument specifies the component that serves as the parent of the dialog (the dialog typically pops up over this component), while *title* specifies a string to appear in the titlebar of the dialog. The *message* argument is more complex. It is declared as an Object. You typically pass a String value, which is automatically displayed in a JLabel. However, you can also specify an Icon, which is also displayed in a JLabel, or any JComponent, which is displayed as is. Furthermore, instead of specifying a single message object, you can specify an array of objects that contains any combination of strings, icons, and components. The *messageType* argument must be one of the constants WARNING_MESSAGE, QUESTION_MESSAGE, INFO_MESSAGE, ERROR_MESSAGE, or PLAIN_MESSAGE. These constants specify the basic type of message you are displaying. The current look-and-feel may customize the appearance of the dialog based on this value. Typically, the customization is limited to the display of one of a standard set of icons. If you'd like to override the default icon for the dialog, you can also explicitly specify an *icon* argument.

The showConfirmDialog() and showInternalConfirmDialog() methods are much like showMessageDialog() and showInternalMessageDialog(), except that they ask the user to make a choice and provide several push buttons that represent the options available to the user. (It is the options represented by these buttons from which the name JOptionPane derives.) For example, showConfirmDialog() can be used to display a dialog that asks "Do you really want to quit?" and allows the user to respond by pushing either a **Yes** button or a **No** button. The *parentComponent*, *title*, *message*, *messageType*, and *icon* arguments to these methods are the same as for the message dialogs. The confirm dialogs add an *optionType* argument and a return value. *optionType* specifies which buttons should appear in the dialog. It should be one of the constants DEFAULT_OPTION, YES_NO_OPTION, YES_NO_CANCEL_OPTION, or OK_CANCEL_OPTION. DEFAULT_OPTION provides a single **Okay** button; the others provide buttons as indicated by their names. Like the message dialogs, the confirm dialogs are modal, and the static methods that display them block until the user has dismissed the dialog. Since confirm dialogs present choices to the user, they have return values that indicate the choice the user selected. This return value is one of the constants OK_OPTION, CANCEL_OPTION, YES_OPTION, NO_OPTION, or CLOSED_OPTION. This last value indicates that the user closed the dialog window without selecting any of the available buttons; typically, it should be treated as a CANCEL_OPTION response.

showOptionDialog() and showInternalOptionDialog() are generalizations of the confirm dialog. They take an *options* argument, which specifies what buttons to display in the dialog box, and an *initialValue* argument, which specifies which of these buttons should be the default button. The *options* argument is an array of objects. Typically, you specify string values that the JOptionPane displays in JButton components. You can provide arbitrary components in the *options* array, but if you do so, you must arrange for each component to update the state of the JOptionPane by calling its setValue() method when selected.

The final category of dialogs are the input dialogs, created with showInputDialog() and showInternalInputDialog(). Most versions of these methods take the same arguments as the message dialogs. However, in addition to displaying a message, they also contain a JTextField in which the user can enter whatever input value is requested. These dialogs are modal, and the methods that display them block until the user has dismissed the dialog. If the user dismisses the dialog with the **Okay** button, the methods return the user's input as a String. If the user dismisses the dialog with the **Cancel** button, these methods return null. One version of both showInputDialog() and showInternalInputDialog() are different. These methods take additional *selectionValues* and *initialSelectionValue* arguments. Instead of asking the user to enter a string, they ask the user to choose among the values contained in the *selectionValues* array (presenting *initialSelectionValue* as the default value). The display of these values is left to the current look-and-feel, although they are typically displayed using a JComboBox or JList component. The *selectionValues* array typically contains strings, but it may also contain Icon objects or other objects that can be meaningfully displayed by JList and JComboBox components. When you pass an array of *selectionValues* to showInputDialog() or showInternalInputDialog(), the return value is the value the user has chosen or null, if the user selected the **Cancel** button.

Instead of using one of the static methods to display a JOptionPane dialog, you can also create a JOptionPane component, set properties as desired, and then create a dialog to contain it by calling the createDialog() or createInternalFrame() instance method.

```
public class JOptionPane extends JComponent implements Accessible {
// Public Constructors
    public JOptionPane( );
    public JOptionPane(Object message);
    public JOptionPane(Object message, int messageType);
    public JOptionPane(Object message, int messageType, int optionType);
    public JOptionPane(Object message, int messageType, int optionType, Icon icon);
    public JOptionPane(Object message, int messageType, int optionType, Icon icon, Object[ ] options);
    public JOptionPane(Object message, int messageType, int optionType, Icon icon, Object[ ] options,
                       Object initialValue);
// Public Constants
    public static final int CANCEL_OPTION;                                                      =2
    public static final int CLOSED_OPTION;                                                     =-1
    public static final int DEFAULT_OPTION;                                                    =-1
    public static final int ERROR_MESSAGE;                                                      =0
    public static final String ICON_PROPERTY;                                              ="icon"
    public static final int INFORMATION_MESSAGE;                                                =1
    public static final String INITIAL_SELECTION_VALUE_PROPERTY;              ="initialSelectionValue"
    public static final String INITIAL_VALUE_PROPERTY;                             ="initialValue"
    public static final String INPUT_VALUE_PROPERTY;                                 ="inputValue"
    public static final String MESSAGE_PROPERTY;                                        ="message"
    public static final String MESSAGE_TYPE_PROPERTY;                               ="messageType"
    public static final int NO_OPTION;                                                          =1
    public static final int OK_CANCEL_OPTION;                                                   =2
    public static final int OK_OPTION;                                                          =0
    public static final String OPTION_TYPE_PROPERTY;                                 ="optionType"
    public static final String OPTIONS_PROPERTY;                                        ="options"
    public static final int PLAIN_MESSAGE;                                                     =-1
    public static final int QUESTION_MESSAGE;                                                   =3
    public static final String SELECTION_VALUES_PROPERTY;                        ="selectionValues"
    public static final Object UNINITIALIZED_VALUE;
    public static final String VALUE_PROPERTY;                                            ="value"
    public static final String WANTS_INPUT_PROPERTY;                                 ="wantsInput"
    public static final int WARNING_MESSAGE;                                                    =2
    public static final int YES_NO_CANCEL_OPTION;                                               =1
    public static final int YES_NO_OPTION;                                                      =0
    public static final int YES_OPTION;                                                         =0
// Inner Classes
    protected class AccessibleJOptionPane extends JComponent.AccessibleJComponent;
// Public Class Methods
    public static JDesktopPane getDesktopPaneForComponent(Component parentComponent);
    public static java.awt.Frame getFrameForComponent(Component parentComponent);
    public static java.awt.Frame getRootFrame( );
    public static void setRootFrame(java.awt.Frame newRootFrame);
    public static int showConfirmDialog(Component parentComponent, Object message);
    public static int showConfirmDialog(Component parentComponent, Object message, String title, int optionType);
    public static int showConfirmDialog(Component parentComponent, Object message, String title, int optionType,
                       int messageType);
    public static int showConfirmDialog(Component parentComponent, Object message, String title, int optionType,
                       int messageType, Icon icon);
    public static String showInputDialog(Object message);
    public static String showInputDialog(Component parentComponent, Object message);
    public static String showInputDialog(Component parentComponent, Object message, String title,
                       int messageType);
    public static Object showInputDialog(Component parentComponent, Object message, String title,
                       int messageType, Icon icon, Object[ ] selectionValues,
                       Object initialSelectionValue);
    public static int showInternalConfirmDialog(Component parentComponent, Object message);
```

public static int **showInternalConfirmDialog**(Component *parentComponent*, Object *message*, String *title*,
int *optionType*);
public static int **showInternalConfirmDialog**(Component *parentComponent*, Object *message*, String *title*,
int *optionType*, int *messageType*);
public static int **showInternalConfirmDialog**(Component *parentComponent*, Object *message*, String *title*,
int *optionType*, int *messageType*, Icon *icon*);
public static String **showInternalInputDialog**(Component *parentComponent*, Object *message*);
public static String **showInternalInputDialog**(Component *parentComponent*, Object *message*, String *title*,
int *messageType*);
public static Object **showInternalInputDialog**(Component *parentComponent*, Object *message*, String *title*,
int *messageType*, Icon *icon*, Object[ ] *selectionValues*,
Object *initialSelectionValue*);
public static void **showInternalMessageDialog**(Component *parentComponent*, Object *message*);
public static void **showInternalMessageDialog**(Component *parentComponent*, Object *message*, String *title*,
int *messageType*);
public static void **showInternalMessageDialog**(Component *parentComponent*, Object *message*, String *title*,
int *messageType*, Icon *icon*);
public static int **showInternalOptionDialog**(Component *parentComponent*, Object *message*, String *title*,
int *optionType*, int *messageType*, Icon *icon*, Object[ ] *options*,
Object *initialValue*);
public static void **showMessageDialog**(Component *parentComponent*, Object *message*);
public static void **showMessageDialog**(Component *parentComponent*, Object *message*, String *title*,
int *messageType*);
public static void **showMessageDialog**(Component *parentComponent*, Object *message*, String *title*,
int *messageType*, Icon *icon*);
public static int **showOptionDialog**(Component *parentComponent*, Object *message*, String *title*, int *optionType*,
int *messageType*, Icon *icon*, Object[ ] *options*, Object *initialValue*);

// *Property Accessor Methods (by property name)*

public AccessibleContext **getAccessibleContext**();	*Implements:Accessible default:AccessibleJOptionPane expert*
public Icon **getIcon**();	*default:null*
public void **setIcon**(Icon *newIcon*);	*bound preferred*
public Object **getInitialSelectionValue**();	*default:null*
public void **setInitialSelectionValue**(Object *newValue*);	*bound*
public Object **getInitialValue**();	*default:null*
public void **setInitialValue**(Object *newInitialValue*);	*bound preferred*
public Object **getInputValue**();	
public void **setInputValue**(Object *newValue*);	*bound preferred*
public int **getMaxCharactersPerLineCount**();	*default:2147483647*
public Object **getMessage**();	
public void **setMessage**(Object *newMessage*);	*bound preferred*
public int **getMessageType**();	*default:-1*
public void **setMessageType**(int *newType*);	*bound preferred*
public Object[ ] **getOptions**();	*default:null*
public void **setOptions**(Object[ ] *newOptions*);	*bound*
public int **getOptionType**();	*default:-1*
public void **setOptionType**(int *newType*);	*bound preferred*
public Object[ ] **getSelectionValues**();	*default:null*
public void **setSelectionValues**(Object[ ] *newValues*);	*bound*
public javax.swing.plaf.OptionPaneUI **getUI**();	
public void **setUI**(javax.swing.plaf.OptionPaneUI *ui*);	*bound hidden*
public String **getUIClassID**();	*Overrides:JComponent default:"OptionPaneUI"*
public Object **getValue**();	
public void **setValue**(Object *newValue*);	*bound preferred*
public boolean **getWantsInput**();	*default:false*
public void **setWantsInput**(boolean *newValue*);	

// *Public Instance Methods*

public JDialog **createDialog**(Component *parentComponent*, String *title*);

```
        public JInternalFrame createInternalFrame(Component parentComponent, String title);
        public void selectInitialValue();
// Methods Implementing Accessible
        public AccessibleContext getAccessibleContext();                    default:AccessibleJOptionPane expert
// Public Methods Overriding JComponent
        public void updateUI();
// Protected Methods Overriding JComponent
        protected String paramString();
// Protected Instance Fields
        protected transient Icon icon;
        protected transient Object initialSelectionValue;
        protected transient Object initialValue;
        protected transient Object inputValue;
        protected transient Object message;
        protected int messageType;
        protected transient Object[ ] options;
        protected int optionType;
        protected transient Object[ ] selectionValues;
        protected transient Object value;
        protected boolean wantsInput;
}
```

Hierarchy: Object→ Component(java.awt.image.ImageObserver, java.awt.MenuContainer, Serializable)→ Container→ JComponent(Serializable)→ JOptionPane(Accessible)

Passed To: javax.swing.plaf.OptionPaneUI.{containsCustomComponents(), selectInitialValue()}

JPanel

javax.swing   *serializable accessible swing component*

This component is a lightweight container that is commonly used to group other components within graphical user interfaces. Use setLayout() to specify a java.awt.LayoutManager to control the arrangement of components within the JPanel. Various JPanel() constructors make it easy to set the values of the inherited layout and doubleBuffered properties.

```
pub ic class JPanel extends JComponent implements Accessible {
// Public Constructors
        public JPanel();
        public JPanel(boolean isDoubleBuffered);
        public JPanel(java.awt.LayoutManager layout);
        public JPanel(java.awt.LayoutManager layout, boolean isDoubleBuffered);
// Inner Classes
        protected class AccessibleJPanel extends JComponent.AccessibleJComponent;
// Property Accessor Methods (by property name)
        public AccessibleContext getAccessibleContext();        Implements:Accessible default:AccessibleJPanel
        public String getUIClassID();                           Overrides:JComponent default:"PanelUI" expert
// Methods Implementing Accessible
        public AccessibleContext getAccessibleContext();                        default:AccessibleJPanel
// Public Methods Overriding JComponent
        public void updateUI();
// Protected Methods Overriding JComponent
        protected String paramString();
}
```

Hierarchy: Object→ Component(java.awt.image.ImageObserver, java.awt.MenuContainer, Serializable)→ Container→ JComponent(Serializable)→ JPanel(Accessible)

Subclasses: javax.swing.colorchooser.AbstractColorChooserPanel

JPasswordField

javax.swing   *serializable accessible(text) swing component*

This JTextField subclass is designed for entering passwords and other sensitive data. It does not display the characters of the entered text, preventing it from being read by onlookers. Use setEchoChar() to specify the character that should appear (e.g., an asterisk) in place of the characters entered by the user.

JPasswordField overrides and deprecates the getText() method of JTextField. Instead, use get-Password() to obtain the user's input. This method returns an array of characters instead of an immutable String object. This means that after you use the password, you can set the elements of the array to 0 for additional security.

```
public class JPasswordField extends JTextField {
// Public Constructors
    public JPasswordField();
    public JPasswordField(String text);
    public JPasswordField(int columns);
    public JPasswordField(String text, int columns);
    public JPasswordField(javax.swing.text.Document doc, String txt, int columns);
// Inner Classes
    protected class AccessibleJPasswordField extends JTextField.AccessibleJTextField;
// Property Accessor Methods (by property name)
    public AccessibleContext getAccessibleContext();          Overrides:JTextField default:AccessibleJPasswordField
    public char getEchoChar();                                                               default:*
    public void setEchoChar(char c);
    public char[ ] getPassword();
    public String getUIClassID();                             Overrides:JTextField default:"PasswordFieldUI"
// Public Instance Methods
    public boolean echoCharIsSet();
// Protected Methods Overriding JTextField
    protected String paramString();
// Public Methods Overriding JTextComponent
    public void copy();
    public void cut();
// Deprecated Public Methods
#   public String getText();                                  Overrides:JTextComponent default:""
#   public String getText(int offs, int len) throws javax.swing.text.BadLocationException;   Overrides:JTextComponent
}
```

Hierarchy: Object→ Component(java.awt.image.ImageObserver, java.awt.MenuContainer, Serializable)→ Container→ JComponent(Serializable)→ javax.swing.text.JTextComponent(Accessible, Scrollable)→ JTextField(SwingConstants)→ JPasswordField

JPopupMenu

javax.swing   *serializable accessible swing component*

This component displays a menu of choices in a popup window. It is used both for standalone popup menus that are posted when the user clicks the right mouse button and for the pulldown and pull-right menus that appear when the user selects a JMenu component. JPopupMenu uses a SingleSelectionModel to maintain its selection state.

After you create a JPopupMenu object, you can add items to it with the add() and addSeparator() methods. The java.awt.event.ActionListener of a menu item is notified when that item is selected. After adding items to the menu, you can pop it up at a specified location with the show() method. This is usually done only after calling the isPopupTrigger() method of a java.awt.event.MouseEvent object. The menu automatically pops itself down when the user selects an item or stops interacting with it. Call setLightWeightPopupEnabled() to specify whether the popup should use a lightweight window or a heavyweight native window. Call the static setDefaultLightWeightPopupEnabled() to specify a default behavior for all popup menus.

```
public class JPopupMenu extends JComponent implements Accessible, MenuElement {
// Public Constructors
    public JPopupMenu();
    public JPopupMenu(String label);
// Inner Classes
    protected class AccessibleJPopupMenu extends JComponent.AccessibleJComponent;
    public static class Separator extends JSeparator;
// Public Class Methods
    public static boolean getDefaultLightWeightPopupEnabled();
    public static void setDefaultLightWeightPopupEnabled(boolean aFlag);
// Event Registration Methods (by event name)
    public void addPopupMenuListener(javax.swing.event.PopupMenuListener l);
    public void removePopupMenuListener(javax.swing.event.PopupMenuListener l);
// Property Accessor Methods (by property name)
    public AccessibleContext getAccessibleContext();            Implements:Accessible default:AccessibleJPopupMenu
    public boolean isBorderPainted();                                                                default:true
    public void setBorderPainted(boolean b);
    public Component getComponent();                               Implements:MenuElement default:JPopupMenu
    public Component getInvoker();                                                                    default:null
    public void setInvoker(Component invoker);                                                             expert
    public String getLabel();                                                                        default:null
    public void setLabel(String label);                                                                    bound
    public boolean isLightWeightPopupEnabled();                                                      default:true
    public void setLightWeightPopupEnabled(boolean aFlag);                                                 expert
    public java.awt.Insets getMargin();
    public SingleSelectionModel getSelectionModel();                  default:DefaultSingleSelectionModel
    public void setSelectionModel(SingleSelectionModel model);                                            expert
    public MenuElement[ ] getSubElements();                                              Implements:MenuElement
    public javax.swing.plaf.PopupMenuUI getUI();
    public void setUI(javax.swing.plaf.PopupMenuUI ui);                                        bound expert hidden
    public String getUIClassID();                            Overrides:JComponent default:"PopupMenuUI"
    public boolean isVisible();                                         Overrides:Component default:false
    public void setVisible(boolean b);                                              Overrides:JComponent
// Public Instance Methods
    public JMenuItem add(Action a);
    public JMenuItem add(JMenuItem menuItem);
    public JMenuItem add(String s);
    public void addSeparator();
    public Component getComponentAtIndex(int i);
    public int getComponentIndex(Component c);
    public void insert(Action a, int index);
    public void insert(Component component, int index);
    public void pack();
    public void setPopupSize(java.awt.Dimension d);
    public void setPopupSize(int width, int height);
    public void setSelected(Component sel);                                                       expert hidden
    public void show(Component invoker, int x, int y);
// Methods Implementing Accessible
    public AccessibleContext getAccessibleContext();                        default:AccessibleJPopupMenu
// Methods Implementing MenuElement
    public Component getComponent();                                                   default:JPopupMenu
    public MenuElement[ ] getSubElements();
    public void menuSelectionChanged(boolean isIncluded);
    public void processKeyEvent(java.awt.event.KeyEvent e, MenuElement[ ] path,                         empty
                                MenuSelectionManager manager);
    public void processMouseEvent(java.awt.event.MouseEvent event, MenuElement[ ] path,                empty
                                  MenuSelectionManager manager);
```

```
// Public Methods Overriding JComponent
    public void updateUI();
// Protected Methods Overriding JComponent
    protected void paintBorder(java.awt.Graphics g);
    protected String paramString();
// Public Methods Overriding Container
    public void remove(Component comp);
    public void remove(int pos);
// Public Methods Overriding Component
    public void setLocation(int x, int y);
// Protected Instance Methods
    protected java.beans.PropertyChangeListener createActionChangeListener(JMenuItem b);
    protected void firePopupMenuCanceled();
    protected void firePopupMenuWillBecomeInvisible();
    protected void firePopupMenuWillBecomeVisible();
}
```

Hierarchy: Object→ Component(java.awt.image.ImageObserver, java.awt.MenuContainer, Serializable)→ Container→ JComponent(Serializable)→ JPopupMenu(Accessible, MenuElement)

Passed To: JMenu.createWinListener(), JMenu.WinListener.WinListener()

Returned By: JMenu.getPopupMenu()

JPopupMenu.Separator

Java 1.2

javax.swing

serializable accessible swing component

This inner class is a JSeparator component customized for use in JPopupMenu components. The addSeparator() method of JPopupMenu returns an instance of this class. This class is a trivial subclass of JSeparator that does nothing except to override the UI delegate class name and ensure that the separator is never vertical. Application-level code never needs to use this class.

```
public static class JPopupMenu.Separator extends JSeparator {
// Public Constructors
    public Separator();
// Property Accessor Methods (by property name)
    public String getUIClassID();                                    Overrides:JSeparator
}
```

JProgressBar

Java 1.2

javax.swing

serializable accessible(value) swing component

This class implements a progress bar: a component that graphically displays a non-adjustable integer value. It is typically used to display a program's progress on some time consuming task, but can also be used to simulate the display of a graphic equalizer, for example. ProgressMonitor is a useful class that displays a JProgressBar in a dialog box.

Like JScrollBar and JSlider, JProgressBar uses a BoundedRangeModel to maintain its state. The value property is the most important; it specifies the currently displayed value. JProgressBar fires a javax.swing.event.ChangeEvent when its value property changes. value must be between the minimum and maximum values. The orientation property should be one of the HORIZONTAL or VERTICAL constants defined by SwingConstants. Set the borderPainted property to false if you do not want the JProgressBar to display a border around itself.

```
public class JProgressBar extends JComponent implements Accessible, SwingConstants {
// Public Constructors
   public JProgressBar();
   public JProgressBar(BoundedRangeModel newModel);
   public JProgressBar(int orient);
   public JProgressBar(int min, int max);
   public JProgressBar(int orient, int min, int max);
// Inner Classes
   protected class AccessibleJProgressBar extends JComponent.AccessibleJComponent implements
      AccessibleValue;
// Event Registration Methods (by event name)
   public void addChangeListener(javax.swing.event.ChangeListener l);
   public void removeChangeListener(javax.swing.event.ChangeListener l);
// Property Accessor Methods (by property name)
   public AccessibleContext                    Implements:Accessible default:AccessibleJProgressBar expert
      getAccessibleContext();
   public boolean isBorderPainted();                                            default:true
   public void setBorderPainted(boolean b);                                           bound
   public int getMaximum();                                                     default:100
   public void setMaximum(int n);                                               preferred
   public int getMinimum();                                                      default:0
   public void setMinimum(int n);                                               preferred
   public BoundedRangeModel getModel();                       default:DefaultBoundedRangeModel
   public void setModel(BoundedRangeModel newModel);                              expert
   public int getOrientation();                                                  default:0
   public void setOrientation(int newOrientation);                          bound preferred
   public double getPercentComplete();                                         default:0.0
   public String getString();                                                default:"0%"
   public void setString(String s);                                                bound
   public boolean isStringPainted();                                         default:false
   public void setStringPainted(boolean b);                                        bound
   public javax.swing.plaf.ProgressBarUI getUI();
   public void setUI(javax.swing.plaf.ProgressBarUI ui);                          expert
   public String getUIClassID();              Overrides:JComponent default:"ProgressBarUI" expert
   public int getValue();                                                        default:0
   public void setValue(int n);                                                 preferred
// Methods Implementing Accessible
   public AccessibleContext getAccessibleContext();          default:AccessibleJProgressBar expert
// Public Methods Overriding JComponent
   public void updateUI();
// Protected Methods Overriding JComponent
   protected void paintBorder(java.awt.Graphics g);
   protected String paramString();
// Protected Instance Methods
   protected javax.swing.event.ChangeListener createChangeListener();
   protected void fireStateChanged();
// Protected Instance Fields
   protected transient javax.swing.event.ChangeEvent changeEvent;
   protected javax.swing.event.ChangeListener changeListener;
   protected BoundedRangeModel model;
   protected int orientation;
   protected boolean paintBorder;
   protected boolean paintString;
   protected String progressString;
}
```

Hierarchy: Object→ Component(java.awt.image.ImageObserver, java.awt.MenuContainer, Serializable)→ Container→ JComponent(Serializable)→ JProgressBar(Accessible, SwingConstants)

JRadioButton

Java 1.2

javax.swing   *serializable accessible(action,value) swing component*

This class implements a radio button: a toggle button with default graphics that indicate mutually exclusive behavior. Because JRadioButton supplies its own default and selected icons, you typically do not use the constructors that take Icon arguments. The selection state of a JRadioButton is stored in a JToggleButton.ToggleButtonModel object by default. The initial selection state can be specified in the call to the constructor. The current state can be set with setSelected() and queried with isSelected().

The default graphics of the JRadioButton are designed to indicate to the user that the button represents one of a group of mutually exclusive choices. (The name "radio button" refers to the mechanical station-preset buttons on old-style car radios: only one button could be pressed at a time.) JRadioButton does not implement or enforce mutual exclusion; this is done by adding JRadioButton components to a ButtonGroup object.

```
public class JRadioButton extends JToggleButton implements Accessible {
// Public Constructors
    public JRadioButton();
    public JRadioButton(Icon icon);
    public JRadioButton(String text);
    public JRadioButton(String text, Icon icon);
    public JRadioButton(Icon icon, boolean selected);
    public JRadioButton(String text, boolean selected);
    public JRadioButton(String text, Icon icon, boolean selected);
// Inner Classes
    protected class AccessibleJRadioButton extends JToggleButton.AccessibleJToggleButton;
// Property Accessor Methods (by property name)
    public AccessibleContext                 Implements:Accessible default:AccessibleJRadioButton expert
        getAccessibleContext();
    public String getUIClassID();            Overrides:JToggleButton default:"RadioButtonUI" expert
// Methods Implementing Accessible
    public AccessibleContext getAccessibleContext();          default:AccessibleJRadioButton expert
// Public Methods Overriding JToggleButton
    public void updateUI();
// Protected Methods Overriding JToggleButton
    protected String paramString();
}
```

Hierarchy: Object→ Component(java.awt.image.ImageObserver, java.awt.MenuContainer, Serializable)→ Container→ JComponent(Serializable)→ AbstractButton(java.awt.ItemSelectable, SwingConstants)→ JToggleButton(Accessible)→ JRadioButton(Accessible)

JRadioButtonMenuItem

Java 1.2

javax.swing   *serializable accessible(action,value) swing component*

This class implements a radio button that appears within a pulldown or popup menu. Its use is similar to that of JRadioButton. Use isSelected() to query the selection state of the menu item and setSelected() to select or deselect the item. By default, the selection state is stored in a JToggleButton.ToggleButtonModel object. Note that JRadioButtonMenuItem, like JRadioButton, does not implement mutually exclusive selection behavior on its own. Each JRadioButtonMenuItem in a mutually exclusive selection group must be added to a corresponding ButtonGroup object. It is this ButtonGroup that enforces mutual exclusion.

```
public class JRadioButtonMenuItem extends JMenuItem implements Accessible {
// Public Constructors
    public JRadioButtonMenuItem();
    public JRadioButtonMenuItem(Icon icon);
```

```
    public JRadioButtonMenuItem(String text);
    public JRadioButtonMenuItem(String text, Icon icon);
    public JRadioButtonMenuItem(Icon icon, boolean selected);
    public JRadioButtonMenuItem(String text, boolean b);
    public JRadioButtonMenuItem(String text, Icon icon, boolean selected);
// Inner Classes
    protected class AccessibleJRadioButtonMenuItem extends JMenuItem.AccessibleJMenuItem;
// Property Accessor Methods (by property name)
    public AccessibleContext                        Implements:Accessible default:AccessibleJRadioButtonMenuItem
       getAccessibleContext();
    public String getUIClassID();                                                    Overrides:JMenuItem
// Methods Implementing Accessible
    public AccessibleContext getAccessibleContext();              default:AccessibleJRadioButtonMenuItem
// Protected Methods Overriding JMenuItem
    protected String paramString();
// Public Methods Overriding JComponent
    public void requestFocus();                                                            empty
}
```

Hierarchy: Object→ Component(java.awt.image.ImageObserver, java.awt.MenuContainer, Serializable)→ Container→ JComponent(Serializable)→ AbstractButton(java.awt.ItemSelectable, SwingConstants)→ JMenuItem(Accessible, MenuElement)→ JRadioButtonMenuItem(Accessible)

JRootPane   Java 1.2

javax.swing   *serializable accessible swing component*

This component is used internally by all the top-level Swing containers: JWindow, JFrame, JDialog, JApplet, and JInternalFrame. Most applications can simply use these top-level containers; they never need to use JRootPane directly.

JRootPane is a container that manages a fixed hierarchy of children, including a content pane and an optional menubar. You cannot add children directly to a JRootPane; instead, you must add them to the container returned by its getContentPane() method. Each of the top-level Swing containers that uses a JRootPane also provides a getContentPane() method that returns the content pane of its JRootPane. Similarly, to add a menubar to a JRootPane or top-level container that uses JRootPane, you can use the setJMenuBar() method. JRootPane has a custom layout manager that manages its various children. You should not try to set your own layout manager on a JRootPane—instead, set it on the content pane.

The content pane and menubar are not actually direct children of the JRootPane. Instead, they are children of a JLayeredPane that is itself a child of the JRootPane. The JLayeredPane of a JRootPane provides the layering features required for Swing to implement modal dialogs, floating palettes, popup menus, tooltips, and drag-and-drop-style graphical effects. These features are used internally by Swing; only very advanced applications need to use them directly.

In addition to its JLayeredPane, a JRootPane also contains another child, known as the glass pane. This child fills the entire JRootPane and sits on top of the JLayeredPane. The glass pane either must be hidden or must be a transparent component. Otherwise it obscures all other contents of the JRootPane. The glass pane can be used both to intercept mouse events destined for other components within the JRootPane and for the temporary display of graphics on top of the components of a JRootPane. Again, these glass pane features are used internally by Swing, and only advanced applications need to use them directly.

```
public class JRootPane extends JComponent implements Accessible {
// Public Constructors
```

```
    public JRootPane();
// Inner Classes
    protected class AccessibleJRootPane extends JComponent.AccessibleJComponent;
    protected class RootLayout implements java.awt.LayoutManager2, Serializable;
// Property Accessor Methods (by property name)
    public AccessibleContext getAccessibleContext();          Implements:Accessible default:AccessibleJRootPane
    public Container getContentPane();                                               default:JPanel
    public void setContentPane(Container content);
    public JButton getDefaultButton();                                                default:null
    public void setDefaultButton(JButton defaultButton);
    public boolean isFocusCycleRoot();                   Overrides:JComponent constant default:true
    public Component getGlassPane();                                                  default:JPanel
    public void setGlassPane(Component glass);
    public JMenuBar getJMenuBar();                                                    default:null
    public void setJMenuBar(JMenuBar menu);
    public JLayeredPane getLayeredPane();
    public void setLayeredPane(JLayeredPane layered);
    public boolean isValidateRoot();                     Overrides:JComponent constant default:true
// Methods Implementing Accessible
    public AccessibleContext getAccessibleContext();                        default:AccessibleJRootPane
// Public Methods Overriding JComponent
    public void addNotify();
    public void removeNotify();
// Protected Methods Overriding JComponent
    protected String paramString();
// Public Methods Overriding Container
    public Component findComponentAt(int x, int y);
// Protected Methods Overriding Container
    protected void addImpl(Component comp, Object constraints, int index);
// Protected Instance Methods
    protected Container createContentPane();
    protected Component createGlassPane();
    protected JLayeredPane createLayeredPane();
    protected java.awt.LayoutManager createRootLayout();
// Protected Instance Fields
    protected Container contentPane;
    protected JButton defaultButton;
    protected JRootPane.DefaultAction defaultPressAction;
    protected JRootPane.DefaultAction defaultReleaseAction;
    protected Component glassPane;
    protected JLayeredPane layeredPane;
    protected JMenuBar menuBar;
// Deprecated Public Methods
#   public JMenuBar getMenuBar();                                                     default:null
#   public void setMenuBar(JMenuBar menu);
}
```

Hierarchy: Object→ Component(java.awt.image.ImageObserver, java.awt.MenuContainer, Serializable)→ Container→ JComponent(Serializable)→ JRootPane(Accessible)

Passed To: JApplet.setRootPane(), JDialog.setRootPane(), JFrame.setRootPane(), JInternalFrame.setRootPane(), JWindow.setRootPane()

Returned By: JApplet.{createRootPane(), getRootPane()}, JComponent.getRootPane(), JDialog.{createRootPane(), getRootPane()}, JFrame.{createRootPane(), getRootPane()}, JInternalFrame.{createRootPane(), getRootPane()}, JWindow.{createRootPane(), getRootPane()}, RootPaneContainer.getRootPane(), SwingUtilities.getRootPane()

Type Of: JApplet.rootPane, JDialog.rootPane, JFrame.rootPane, JInternalFrame.rootPane, JWindow.rootPane

JRootPane.RootLayout

javax.swing

This protected inner class is a custom java.awt.LayoutManager that is responsible for the layout of the children of a JRootPane. Application-level code never needs to use this class.

```
protected class JRootPane.RootLayout implements java.awt.LayoutManager2, Serializable {
// Protected Constructors
    protected RootLayout();
// Methods Implementing LayoutManager
    public void addLayoutComponent(String name, Component comp);                       empty
    public void layoutContainer(Container parent);
    public java.awt.Dimension minimumLayoutSize(Container parent);
    public java.awt.Dimension preferredLayoutSize(Container parent);
    public void removeLayoutComponent(Component comp);                                 empty
// Methods Implementing LayoutManager2
    public void addLayoutComponent(Component comp, Object constraints);                empty
    public float getLayoutAlignmentX(Container target);                             constant
    public float getLayoutAlignmentY(Container target);                             constant
    public void invalidateLayout(Container target);                                    empty
    public java.awt.Dimension maximumLayoutSize(Container target);
}
```

JScrollBar

javax.swing

This class implements a scrollbar component that can be used to scroll the visible region of some entity, within a maximum and a minimum range. The minimum and maximum properties specify the range within which scrolling takes place. The value property specifies the current value of the scrollbar—the beginning of the visible region. visibleAmount specifies how much of the range is visible at once and also specifies the size of the displayed thumb, or knob, of the scrollbar. The values of these properties are all stored in a BoundedRangeModel object. JScrollBar uses DefaultBoundedRangeModel by default. (The visibleAmount property corresponds to the extent property of BoundedRangeModel.) The orientation property specifies whether the JScrollBar is a horizontal or a vertical scrollbar. Use either the HORIZONTAL or the VERTICAL constant defined by the SwingConstants interface. unitIncrement specifies the amount by which the scrollbar thumb should move when the user clicks on the arrows at either end of the scrollbar. The default is 1. The blockIncrement property specifies the amount that the scrollbar should move when the user scrolls a block at a time (how this is accomplished varies in different look-and-feels).

JScrollBar fires a java.awt.event.AdjustmentEvent when one of the value, minimum, maximum, visibleAmount, or valueIsAdjusting properties changes. Some programs may prefer to instead handle the javax.swing.event.ChangeEvent events generated by the model of the JScrollBar. In either case, if the valueIsAdjusting property of the JScrollBar or its model is true, the change is one in a series of changes. Listeners that prefer not to track these transient changes can ignore events when valueIsAdjusting is true.

```
public class JScrollBar extends JComponent implements Accessible, java.awt.Adjustable {
// Public Constructors
    public JScrollBar();
    public JScrollBar(int orientation);
    public JScrollBar(int orientation, int value, int extent, int min, int max);
// Inner Classes
    protected class AccessibleJScrollBar extends JComponent.AccessibleJComponent implements AccessibleValue;
```

javax.swing

```
// Event Registration Methods (by event name)
    public void addAdjustmentListener(java.awt.event.AdjustmentListener I);              Implements:Adjustable
    public void removeAdjustmentListener(java.awt.event.AdjustmentListener I);           Implements:Adjustable
// Property Accessor Methods (by property name)
    public AccessibleContext getAccessibleContext();              Implements:Accessible default:AccessibleJScrollBar
    public int getBlockIncrement();                                       Implements:Adjustable default:10
    public int getBlockIncrement(int direction);
    public void setBlockIncrement(int blockIncrement);                    Implements:Adjustable bound preferred
    public int getMaximum();                                              Implements:Adjustable default:100
    public void setMaximum(int maximum);                                  Implements:Adjustable preferred
    public java.awt.Dimension getMaximumSize();                                     Overrides:JComponent
    public int getMinimum();                                              Implements:Adjustable default:0
    public void setMinimum(int minimum);                                  Implements:Adjustable preferred
    public java.awt.Dimension getMinimumSize();                                     Overrides:JComponent
    public BoundedRangeModel getModel();                                 default:DefaultBoundedRangeModel
    public void setModel(BoundedRangeModel newModel);                                    bound expert
    public int getOrientation();                                          Implements:Adjustable default:1
    public void setOrientation(int orientation);                                        bound preferred
    public javax.swing.plaf.ScrollBarUI getUI();
    public String getUIClassID();                                Overrides:JComponent default:"ScrollBarUI"
    public int getUnitIncrement();                                        Implements:Adjustable default:1
    public int getUnitIncrement(int direction);
    public void setUnitIncrement(int unitIncrement);                      Implements:Adjustable bound preferred
    public int getValue();                                                Implements:Adjustable default:0
    public void setValue(int value);                                      Implements:Adjustable preferred
    public boolean getValueIsAdjusting();                                             default:false
    public void setValueIsAdjusting(boolean b);                                              expert
    public int getVisibleAmount();                                        Implements:Adjustable default:10
    public void setVisibleAmount(int extent);                             Implements:Adjustable preferred
// Public Instance Methods
    public void setValues(int newValue, int newExtent, int newMin, int newMax);
// Methods Implementing Accessible
    public AccessibleContext getAccessibleContext();                          default:AccessibleJScrollBar
// Public Methods Overriding JComponent
    public void setEnabled(boolean x);
    public void updateUI();
// Protected Methods Overriding JComponent
    protected String paramString();
// Protected Instance Methods
    protected void fireAdjustmentValueChanged(int id, int type, int value);
// Protected Instance Fields
    protected int blockIncrement;
    protected BoundedRangeModel model;
    protected int orientation;
    protected int unitIncrement;
}
```

Hierarchy: Object→ Component(java.awt.image.ImageObserver, java.awt.MenuContainer, Serializable)→ Container→ JComponent(Serializable)→ JScrollBar(Accessible, java.awt.Adjustable)

Subclasses: JScrollPane.ScrollBar

Passed To: JScrollPane.{setHorizontalScrollBar(), setVerticalScrollBar()}

Returned By: JScrollPane.{createHorizontalScrollBar(), createVerticalScrollBar(), getHorizontalScrollBar(), getVerticalScrollBar()}, ScrollPaneLayout.{getHorizontalScrollBar(), getVerticalScrollBar()}

Type Of: JScrollPane.{horizontalScrollBar, verticalScrollBar}, ScrollPaneLayout.{hsb, vsb}

JScrollPane

javax.swing   *serializable accessible swing component bean container*

This class is a container that allows a child component to be scrolled horizontally and vertically. The component to be scrolled is not a direct child of the JScrollPane, so it must not be added directly with the add() method. Instead, it is a child of a JViewport contained within the JScrollPane. You specify the component to be scrolled by passing it to the JScrollPane() constructor or to the setViewportView() method. Any type of component can be used within a JScrollPane, but components that implement the Scrollable interface work best. The horizontalScrollBarPolicy and verticalScrollBarPolicy properties control the policy for displaying scrollbars. The legal values are the various ALWAYS, AS_NEEDED, and NEVER constants defined by the ScrollPaneConstants interface. Another useful property is viewportBorder, which allows you to specify a border to appear around the JViewport that contains the component being scrolled.

In addition to the main scrolled component, JScrollPane supports column header and row header components. The column header appears above the main scrolling component and scrolls horizontally, but not vertically, so that it is always visible at the top of the JScrollPane. Similarly, the row header component scrolls vertically but not horizontally, so it is always visible at the left of the JScrollPane. Specify the row and column header components with setColumnHeaderView() and setRowHeaderView(). The JScrollPane can also display arbitrary components in each of its four corners. Use setCorner() to specify a component for a corner. The ScrollPaneConstants interface defines constants that specify which corner a component should appear in. Note that the space available in the corners of a JScrollPane is determined by the width of the scrollbars and the widths of the column and row headers, if any. The layout management of the scrollable JViewport, the scrollbars, the column and row headers, and the corners is provided by the ScrollPaneLayout class, a specialized java.awt.LayoutManager.

See also the JScrollBar and JViewport components, the ScrollPaneLayout layout manager, and the Scrollable and ScrollPaneConstants interfaces.

```
public class JScrollPane extends JComponent implements Accessible, ScrollPaneConstants {
// Public Constructors
     public JScrollPane();
     public JScrollPane(Component view);
     public JScrollPane(int vsbPolicy, int hsbPolicy);
     public JScrollPane(Component view, int vsbPolicy, int hsbPolicy);
// Inner Classes
     protected class AccessibleJScrollPane extends JComponent.AccessibleJComponent implements
          javax.swing.event.ChangeListener;
     protected class ScrollBar extends JScrollBar implements javax.swing.plaf.UIResource;
// Property Accessor Methods (by property name)
     public AccessibleContext getAccessibleContext();        Implements:Accessible default:AccessibleJScrollPane
     public JViewport getColumnHeader();                                                    default:null
     public void setColumnHeader(JViewport columnHeader);                                         bound
     public JScrollBar getHorizontalScrollBar();                                       default:ScrollBar
     public void setHorizontalScrollBar(JScrollBar horizontalScrollBar);                    bound expert
     public int getHorizontalScrollBarPolicy();                                            default:30
     public void setHorizontalScrollBarPolicy(int policy);                              bound preferred
     public void setLayout(java.awt.LayoutManager layout);                      Overrides:Container hidden
     public boolean isOpaque();                                     Overrides:JComponent default:false
     public JViewport getRowHeader();                                                      default:null
     public void setRowHeader(JViewport rowHeader);                                          bound expert
     public javax.swing.plaf.ScrollPaneUI getUI();
     public void setUI(javax.swing.plaf.ScrollPaneUI ui);
     public String getUIClassID();                      Overrides:JComponent default:"ScrollPaneUI" hidden
     public boolean isValidateRoot();                  Overrides:JComponent constant default:true hidden
```

public JScrollBar **getVerticalScrollBar**();	*default:ScrollBar*
public void **setVerticalScrollBar**(JScrollBar *verticalScrollBar*);	*bound expert*
public int **getVerticalScrollBarPolicy**();	*default:20*
public void **setVerticalScrollBarPolicy**(int *policy*);	*bound preferred*
public JViewport **getViewport**();	
public void **setViewport**(JViewport *viewport*);	*bound expert*
public javax.swing.border.Border **getViewportBorder**();	*default:null*
public void **setViewportBorder**(javax.swing.border.Border *viewportBorder*);	*bound preferred*
public java.awt.Rectangle **getViewportBorderBounds**();	

```
// Public Instance Methods
    public JScrollBar createHorizontalScrollBar();
    public JScrollBar createVerticalScrollBar();
    public Component getCorner(String key);
    public void setColumnHeaderView(Component view);
    public void setCorner(String key, Component corner);
    public void setRowHeaderView(Component view);
    public void setViewportView(Component view);
// Methods Implementing Accessible
    public AccessibleContext getAccessibleContext();                    default:AccessibleJScrollPane
// Public Methods Overriding JComponent
    public void updateUI();
// Protected Methods Overriding JComponent
    protected String paramString();
// Protected Instance Methods
    protected JViewport createViewport();
// Protected Instance Fields
    protected JViewport columnHeader;
    protected JScrollBar horizontalScrollBar;
    protected int horizontalScrollBarPolicy;
    protected Component lowerLeft;
    protected Component lowerRight;
    protected JViewport rowHeader;
    protected Component upperLeft;
    protected Component upperRight;
    protected JScrollBar verticalScrollBar;
    protected int verticalScrollBarPolicy;
    protected JViewport viewport;
}
```

Hierarchy: Object → Component(java.awt.image.ImageObserver, java.awt.MenuContainer, Serializable) → Container → JComponent(Serializable) → JScrollPane(Accessible, ScrollPaneConstants)

Passed To: ScrollPaneLayout.{getViewportBorderBounds(), syncWithScrollPane()}

Returned By: JTable.createScrollPaneForTable()

JScrollPane.ScrollBar

Java 1.2

javax.swing   *serializable accessible(action) swing component*

This protected inner class is a trivial subclass of JScrollBar that is used for the scrollbars of a JScrollPane. This subclass exists for two simple reasons: to implement the javax.swing.plaf.UIResource interface and to make the scrollbars work with the Scrollable interface. Application-level code never needs to use this class.

```
protected class JScrollPane.ScrollBar extends JScrollBar implements javax.swing.plaf.UIResource {
// Public Constructors
    public ScrollBar(int orientation);
// Property Accessor Methods (by property name)
    public void setBlockIncrement(int blockIncrement);                    Overrides:JScrollBar
```

```
    public void setUnitIncrement(int unitIncrement);                    Overrides:JScrollBar
// Public Methods Overriding JScrollBar
    public int getBlockIncrement(int direction);
    public int getUnitIncrement(int direction);
}
```

JSeparator

javax.swing   *serializable accessible swing component*

This simple component draws a horizontal or vertical line that is as wide or as tall as
the component itself. The orientation property is the only property of interest. It should
be SwingConstants.HORIZONTAL or SwingConstants.VERTICAL. There are no properties controlling the thickness, color, or other attributes of the JSeparator. Separator objects are commonly used in JPopupMenu and JToolBar components. Note, however, that these
components define addSeparator() methods and implement custom subclasses of JSeparator. These custom subclasses have their own UI delegate subclasses, which allows them
to provide a visual appearance precisely tailored for menus and toolbars.

```
public class JSeparator extends JComponent implements Accessible, SwingConstants {
// Public Constructors
    public JSeparator();
    public JSeparator(int orientation);
// Inner Classes
    protected class AccessibleJSeparator extends JComponent.AccessibleJComponent;
// Property Accessor Methods (by property name)
    public AccessibleContext getAccessibleContext();       Implements:Accessible default:AccessibleJSeparator
    public boolean isFocusTraversable();                    Overrides:JComponent constant default:false
    public int getOrientation();                                               default:0
    public void setOrientation(int orientation);                               bound preferred
    public javax.swing.plaf.SeparatorUI getUI();
    public void setUI(javax.swing.plaf.SeparatorUI ui);                        bound expert hidden
    public String getUIClassID();                    Overrides:JComponent default:"SeparatorUI"
// Methods Implementing Accessible
    public AccessibleContext getAccessibleContext();           default:AccessibleJSeparator
// Public Methods Overriding JComponent
    public void updateUI();
// Protected Methods Overriding JComponent
    protected String paramString();
}
```

Hierarchy: Object→ Component(java.awt.image.ImageObserver, java.awt.MenuContainer, Serializable)→
Container→ JComponent(Serializable)→ JSeparator(Accessible, SwingConstants)

Subclasses: JPopupMenu.Separator, JToolBar.Separator

JSlider

javax.swing   *serializable accessible(value) swing component*

This class implements a component that allows the user to drag a knob, or pointer, in
order to graphically adjust an integer value. The minimum and maximum properties specify the range of the slider, and the value property specifies the current value. extent specifies the width of the knob and also an adjustment increment. The values of these
properties are maintained by a BoundedRangeModel object. By default, JSlider uses a
DefaultBoundedRangeModel object. orientation specifies the orientation of the slider; it
should be one of the SwingConstants values HORIZONTAL or VERTICAL. If the inverted property
is true, the range is inverted to run from right to left or from top to bottom.

A JSlider can display optional tick marks and labels along its length. The paintTicks and paintLabels properties specify whether they should be displayed. majorTickSpacing and minorTickSpacing specify the spacing of long and short tick marks. Note that these spacings are measured in the coordinate space defined by the JSlider minimum and maximum value; they are not pixel spacings. If the snapToTicks property is set true, the user can only adjust the value property to a value at which a tick mark appears. If you set paintLabels and majorTickSpacing, the JSlider automatically displays a numeric label for each major tick mark. You can call createStandardLabels() to force this behavior, even when tick marks are not displayed. You can also specify custom labels by setting the labelTable property to a java.util.Dictionary that maps Integer coordinates to JComponent labels.

A JSlider fires a javax.swing.event.ChangeEvent when one of its value, maximum, minimum, extent, or valueIsAdjusting properties changes. If valueIsAdjusting is true when an event is fired, it means that the event is one of a series of changes. Listeners that do not want to track these rapid-fire transient changes can ignore them.

```
public class JSlider extends JComponent implements Accessible, SwingConstants {
// Public Constructors
    public JSlider();
    public JSlider(BoundedRangeModel brm);
    public JSlider(int orientation);
    public JSlider(int min, int max);
    public JSlider(int min, int max, int value);
    public JSlider(int orientation, int min, int max, int value);
// Inner Classes
    protected class AccessibleJSlider extends JComponent.AccessibleJComponent implements AccessibleValue;
// Event Registration Methods (by event name)
    public void addChangeListener(javax.swing.event.ChangeListener l);
    public void removeChangeListener(javax.swing.event.ChangeListener l);
// Property Accessor Methods (by property name)
    public AccessibleContext getAccessibleContext();            Implements:Accessible default:AccessibleJSlider
    public int getExtent();                                                              default:0
    public void setExtent(int extent);                                                      expert
    public boolean getInverted();                                                    default:false
    public void setInverted(boolean b);                                                      bound
    public java.util.Dictionary getLabelTable();                                       default:null
    public void setLabelTable(java.util.Dictionary labels);                         bound hidden
    public int getMajorTickSpacing();                                                  default:0
    public void setMajorTickSpacing(int n);                                                  bound
    public int getMaximum();                                                         default:100
    public void setMaximum(int maximum);                                                preferred
    public int getMinimum();                                                           default:0
    public void setMinimum(int minimum);                                                preferred
    public int getMinorTickSpacing();                                                  default:0
    public void setMinorTickSpacing(int n);                                                  bound
    public BoundedRangeModel getModel();                           default:DefaultBoundedRangeModel
    public void setModel(BoundedRangeModel newModel);                                        bound
    public int getOrientation();                                                       default:0
    public void setOrientation(int orientation);                                   bound preferred
    public boolean getPaintLabels();                                                 default:false
    public void setPaintLabels(boolean b);                                                   bound
    public boolean getPaintTicks();                                                  default:false
    public void setPaintTicks(boolean b);                                                    bound
    public boolean getPaintTrack();                                                   default:true
    public void setPaintTrack(boolean b);                                                    bound
    public boolean getSnapToTicks();                                                 default:false
    public void setSnapToTicks(boolean b);                                                   bound
    public javax.swing.plaf.SliderUI getUI();
```

```
    public void setUI(javax.swing.plaf.SliderUI ui);                                    bound hidden
    public String getUIClassID();                               Overrides:JComponent default:"SliderUI"
    public int getValue();                                                                default:50
    public void setValue(int n);                                                           preferred
    public boolean getValueIsAdjusting();                                                default:false
    public void setValueIsAdjusting(boolean b);                                               expert
// Public Instance Methods
    public java.util.Hashtable createStandardLabels(int increment);
    public java.util.Hashtable createStandardLabels(int increment, int start);
// Methods Implementing Accessible
    public AccessibleContext getAccessibleContext();                          default:AccessibleJSlider
// Public Methods Overriding JComponent
    public void updateUI();
// Protected Methods Overriding JComponent
    protected String paramString();
// Protected Instance Methods
    protected javax.swing.event.ChangeListener createChangeListener();
    protected void fireStateChanged();
    protected void updateLabelUIs();
// Protected Instance Fields
    protected transient javax.swing.event.ChangeEvent changeEvent;
    protected javax.swing.event.ChangeListener changeListener;
    protected int majorTickSpacing;
    protected int minorTickSpacing;
    protected int orientation;
    protected BoundedRangeModel sliderModel;
    protected boolean snapToTicks;
}
```

Hierarchy: Object→ Component(java.awt.image.ImageObserver, java.awt.MenuContainer, Serializable)→ Container→ JComponent(Serializable)→ JSlider(Accessible, SwingConstants)

JSplitPane   Java 1.2

javax.swing   *serializable accessible(value) swing component*

This class is a container that splits itself horizontally or vertically to display two children. The orientation of the pane is specified by the orientation property, which should be set to either the HORIZONTAL_SPLIT or VERTICAL_SPLIT constant. The two children are specified by a pair of properties that depend on the orientation of the JSplitPane. If the orientation is HORIZONTAL_SPLIT, the children are specified with setLeftComponent() and setRightComponent(). For a VERTICAL_SPLIT JSplitPane, the children are specified with setTopComponent() and setBottomComponent(). The position of the divider between the two panes of a JSplitPane can be set with setDividerLocation(). The argument can be an integer that specifies a pixel position or a double between 0.0 and 1.0 that specifies a percentage of the size of the JSplitPane.

JSplitPane allows the user to adjust the relative sizes of the two children by dragging the divider that appears between the children. The adjustment is constrained, however, so that a child is never made smaller than its specified minimum size. If the continuousLayout property is set to true, the children are resized continuously while the user drags the divider. If this property is false, however, the child components are not resized until the user finishes the drag. Although the divider location of a JSplitPane can be thought of in terms of the BoundedRangeModel, the JSplitPane implementation does not use a separate model object.

javax.swing

```
public class JSplitPane extends JComponent implements Accessible {
// Public Constructors
    public JSplitPane();
    public JSplitPane(int newOrientation);
    public JSplitPane(int newOrientation, boolean newContinuousLayout);
    public JSplitPane(int newOrientation, Component newLeftComponent, Component newRightComponent);
    public JSplitPane(int newOrientation, boolean newContinuousLayout, Component newLeftComponent,
                      Component newRightComponent);
// Public Constants
    public static final String BOTTOM;                                                  ="bcttom"
    public static final String CONTINUOUS_LAYOUT_PROPERTY;                              ="continuousLayout"
    public static final String DIVIDER;                                                 ="divider"
    public static final String DIVIDER_SIZE_PROPERTY;                                   ="dividerSize"
    public static final int HORIZONTAL_SPLIT;                                              =1
    public static final String LAST_DIVIDER_LOCATION_PROPERTY;                          ="lastDividerLocation"
    public static final String LEFT;                                                    ="left"
    public static final String ONE_TOUCH_EXPANDABLE_PROPERTY;                           ="oneTouchExpandable"
    public static final String ORIENTATION_PROPERTY;                                    ="orientation"
    public static final String RIGHT;                                                   ="right"
    public static final String TOP;                                                     ="top"
    public static final int VERTICAL_SPLIT;                                                =0
// Inner Classes
    protected class AccessibleJSplitPane extends JComponent.AccessibleJComponent implements AccessibleValue;
// Property Accessor Methods (by property name)
    public AccessibleContext getAccessibleContext();       Implements:Accessible default:AccessibleJSplitPane expert
    public Component getBottomComponent();                                              default:JButton
    public void setBottomComponent(Component comp);
    public boolean isContinuousLayout();                                                default:false
    public void setContinuousLayout(boolean newContinuousLayout);                       bound
    public int getDividerLocation();                                                    default:0
    public void setDividerLocation(int location);
    public void setDividerLocation(double proportionalLocation);
    public int getDividerSize();                                                        default:8
    public void setDividerSize(int newSize);                                            bound
    public int getLastDividerLocation();                                                default:0
    public void setLastDividerLocation(int newLastLocation);                            bound
    public Component getLeftComponent();                                                default:JButton preferred
    public void setLeftComponent(Component comp);
    public int getMaximumDividerLocation();                                             default:93
    public int getMinimumDividerLocation();                                             default:93
    public boolean isOneTouchExpandable();                                              default:false
    public void setOneTouchExpandable(boolean newValue);                                bound
    public int getOrientation();                                                        default:1
    public void setOrientation(int orientation);                                        bound
    public Component getRightComponent();                                               default:JButton
    public void setRightComponent(Component comp);                                      preferred
    public Component getTopComponent();                                                 default:JButton
    public void setTopComponent(Component comp);
    public javax.swing.plaf.SplitPaneUI getUI();                                        expert
    public void setUI(javax.swing.plaf.SplitPaneUI ui);
    public String getUIClassID();                              Overrides:JComponent default:"SplitPaneUI" expert
    public boolean isValidateRoot();                     Overrides:JComponent constant default:true hidden
// Public Instance Methods
    public void resetToPreferredSizes();
// Methods Implementing Accessible
    public AccessibleContext getAccessibleContext();                        default:AccessibleJSplitPane expert
// Public Methods Overriding JComponent
    public void updateUI();
```

```
// Protected Methods Overriding JComponent
    protected void paintChildren(java.awt.Graphics g);
    protected String paramString();
// Public Methods Overriding Container
    public void remove(Component component);
    public void remove(int index);
    public void removeAll();
// Protected Methods Overriding Container
    protected void addImpl(Component comp, Object constraints, int index);
// Protected Instance Fields
    protected boolean continuousLayout;
    protected int dividerSize;
    protected int lastDividerLocation;
    protected Component leftComponent;
    protected boolean oneTouchExpandable;
    protected int orientation;
    protected Component rightComponent;
}
```

Hierarchy: Object→ Component(java.awt.image.ImageObserver, java.awt.MenuContainer, Serializable)→ Container→ JComponent(Serializable)→ JSplitPane(Accessible)

Passed To: javax.swing.plaf.SplitPaneUI.{finishedPaintingChildren(), getDividerLocation(), getMaximumDividerLocation(), getMinimumDividerLocation(), resetToPreferredSizes(), setDividerLocation()}

JTabbedPane   Java 1.2

javax.swing   *serializable accessible(selection) swing component bean container*

JTabbedPane is a container that can contain any number of children. It displays one child at a time, but displays a tab for each child. The user can click on these tabs to adjust the currently displayed child. JTabbedPane uses a SingleSelectionModel to keep track of the currently selected and displayed child. By default, the tabs appear at the top of the JTabbedPane. You can override this default, however, with setTabPlacement(). The argument to this method should be one of the TOP, BOTTOM, LEFT, or RIGHT constants defined by the SwingConstants interface.

Although you can add children to a JTabbedPane with the standard add() methods, this does not give you much flexibility in specifying the contents of the tab for that child. Instead, JTabbedPane provides several addTab() methods that allow you to specify the child along with the String, Icon, and tooltip text to use for its tab. A corresponding insertTab() method allows you to specify a child, the contents of its tab, and the position of the tab within the list of tabs. Use setSelectedComponent() or setSelectedIndex() to specify which child is currently displayed. setEnabledAt() allows you to enable or disable a tab, specified by its position within the list of tabs. setDisabledIconAt() allows you to specify an icon to display when a tab is disabled. Various other methods whose names end with "At" allow you to alter properties of individual tabs, specified by position.

```
public class JTabbedPane extends JComponent implements Accessible, Serializable, SwingConstants {
// Public Constructors
    public JTabbedPane();
    public JTabbedPane(int tabPlacement);
// Inner Classes
    protected class AccessibleJTabbedPane extends JComponent.AccessibleJComponent implements
        AccessibleSelection, javax.swing.event.ChangeListener;
    protected class ModelListener implements javax.swing.event.ChangeListener, Serializable;
// Event Registration Methods (by event name)
    public void addChangeListener(javax.swing.event.ChangeListener l);
```

```
    public void removeChangeListener(javax.swing.event.ChangeListener l);
// Property Accessor Methods (by property name)
    public AccessibleContext getAccessibleContext();              Implements:Accessible default:AccessibleJTabbedPane
    public SingleSelectionModel getModel();                                    default:DefaultSingleSelectionModel
    public void setModel(SingleSelectionModel model);                                                        bound
    public Component getSelectedComponent();                                                          default:null
    public void setSelectedComponent(Component c);                                                      preferred
    public int getSelectedIndex();                                                                     default:-1
    public void setSelectedIndex(int index);                                                            preferred
    public int getTabCount();                                                                           default:0
    public int getTabPlacement();                                                                       default:1
    public void setTabPlacement(int tabPlacement);                                               bound preferred
    public int getTabRunCount();                                                                        default:0
    public javax.swing.plaf.TabbedPaneUI getUI();
    public void setUI(javax.swing.plaf.TabbedPaneUI ui);                                            bound hidden
    public String getUIClassID();                                 Overrides:JComponent default:"TabbedPaneUI"
// Public Instance Methods
    public void addTab(String title, Component component);
    public void addTab(String title, Icon icon, Component component);
    public void addTab(String title, Icon icon, Component component, String tip);
    public java.awt.Color getBackgroundAt(int index);
    public java.awt.Rectangle getBoundsAt(int index);
    public Component getComponentAt(int index);
    public Icon getDisabledIconAt(int index);
    public java.awt.Color getForegroundAt(int index);
    public Icon getIconAt(int index);
    public String getTitleAt(int index);
    public int indexOfComponent(Component component);
    public int indexOfTab(Icon icon);
    public int indexOfTab(String title);
    public void insertTab(String title, Icon icon, Component component, String tip, int index);
    public boolean isEnabledAt(int index);
    public void removeTabAt(int index);
    public void setBackgroundAt(int index, java.awt.Color background);                                  preferred
    public void setComponentAt(int index, Component component);
    public void setDisabledIconAt(int index, Icon disabledIcon);                                        preferred
    public void setEnabledAt(int index, boolean enabled);
    public void setForegroundAt(int index, java.awt.Color foreground);                                  preferred
    public void setIconAt(int index, Icon icon);                                                        preferred
    public void setTitleAt(int index, String title);                                                    preferred
// Methods Implementing Accessible
    public AccessibleContext getAccessibleContext();                               default:AccessibleJTabbedPane
// Public Methods Overriding JComponent
    public String getToolTipText(java.awt.event.MouseEvent event);
    public void updateUI();
// Protected Methods Overriding JComponent
    protected String paramString();
// Public Methods Overriding Container
    public Component add(Component component);
    public void add(Component component, Object constraints);
    public Component add(Component component, int index);
    public Component add(String title, Component component);
    public void add(Component component, Object constraints, int index);
    public void remove(Component component);
    public void removeAll();
// Protected Instance Methods
    protected javax.swing.event.ChangeListener createChangeListener();
    protected void fireStateChanged();
```

```
// Protected Instance Fields
    protected transient javax.swing.event.ChangeEvent changeEvent;
    protected javax.swing.event.ChangeListener changeListener;
    protected SingleSelectionModel model;
    protected int tabPlacement;
}
```

Hierarchy: Object→ Component(java.awt.image.ImageObserver, java.awt.MenuContainer, Serializable)→
Container→ JComponent(Serializable)→ JTabbedPane(Accessible, Serializable, SwingConstants)

Passed To: javax.swing.plaf.TabbedPaneUI.{getTabBounds(), getTabRunCount(), tabForCoordinate()}

JTabbedPane.ModelListener   Java 1.2
javax.swing   *serializable*

This protected inner class is a trivial ChangeListener implementation used internally by
JTabbedPane to listen for changes from its SingleSelectionModel. Applications never need to
use this class, and it probably should not have been made part of the public API. If you
want to use a different listener implementation, override the createChangeListener()
method of JTabbedPane.

```
protected class JTabbedPane.ModelListener implements javax.swing.event.ChangeListener, Serializable {
// Protected Constructors
    protected ModelListener();
// Methods Implementing ChangeListener
    public void stateChanged(javax.swing.event.ChangeEvent e);
}
```

JTable   Java 1.2
javax.swing   *serializable accessible(selection) swing component*

JTable is a powerful and complex Swing component for displaying and editing tabular
data. JTable relies on the auxiliary classes and interfaces in the javax.swing.table package.
Two JTable constructors exist that make it easy to display tabular data that is stored in
an Object[][] or in a Vector of rows, where each row is a Vector of cell values. These convenience constructors take an additional array or Vector of objects to be used as column
headers for the table. If your data is not already in one of these pure tabular forms, you
must provide a javax.swing.table.TableModel object that enables the JTable to find the value
for each cell. You typically do this by subclassing javax.swing.table.AbstractTableModel.

When displaying a JTable that contains more than a few rows or columns, it is common
to place the JTable within a JScrollPane. JTable components created with the convenience
constructors or with a simple default subclass of AbstractTableModel are not editable.
However, you can enable editing on a cell-by-cell basis by overriding the isCellEditable()
and setValueAt() methods of the AbstractTableModel.

Unlike most Swing components, JTable relies on more than one associated model object.
In addition to the TableModel object that contains table data, a JTable also uses a
TableColumnModel object to keep track of the columns of the table and their ordering and
selection state and a ListSelectionModel used to keep track of selected rows in the table.

The cell values returned by the TableModel are generic objects. By default, JTable knows
how to display and edit String, Boolean, and Number values. If you want to display
another type of objects, you can create a custom javax.swing.table.TableCellRenderer object
and pass it to setDefaultRenderer(). If you want to allow users to edit values of this type,
you can create a custom javax.swing.table.TableCellEditor and pass it to setDefaultEditor().

```
public class JTable extends JComponent implements Accessible, javax.swing.event.CellEditorListener,
    javax.swing.event.ListSelectionListener, Scrollable, javax.swing.event.TableColumnModelListener,
```

```
        javax.swing.event.TableModelListener {
// Public Constructors
    public JTable();
    public JTable(javax.swing.table.TableModel dm);
    public JTable(int numRows, int numColumns);
    public JTable(Object[ ][ ] rowData, Object[ ] columnNames);
    public JTable(javax.swing.table.TableModel dm, javax.swing.table.TableColumnModel cm);
    public JTable(java.util.Vector rowData, java.util.Vector columnNames);
    public JTable(javax.swing.table.TableModel dm, javax.swing.table.TableColumnModel cm, ListSelectionModel sm);
// Public Constants
    public static final int AUTO_RESIZE_ALL_COLUMNS;                                            =4
    public static final int AUTO_RESIZE_LAST_COLUMN;                                            =3
    public static final int AUTO_RESIZE_NEXT_COLUMN;                                            =1
    public static final int AUTO_RESIZE_OFF;                                                    =0
    public static final int AUTO_RESIZE_SUBSEQUENT_COLUMNS;                                     =2
// Inner Classes
    protected class AccessibleJTable extends JComponent.AccessibleJComponent implements AccessibleSelection,
        javax.swing.event.CellEditorListener, javax.swing.event.ListSelectionListener, java.beans.PropertyChangeListener,
        javax.swing.event.TableColumnModelListener, javax.swing.event.TableModelListener;
// Property Accessor Methods (by property name)
    public AccessibleContext getAccessibleContext();                    Implements:Accessible default:AccessibleJTable
    public boolean getAutoCreateColumnsFromModel();                                      default:true
    public void setAutoCreateColumnsFromModel(boolean createColumns);
    public int getAutoResizeMode();                                                      default:2
    public void setAutoResizeMode(int mode);
    public javax.swing.table.TableCellEditor getCellEditor();                            default:null
    public javax.swing.table.TableCellEditor getCellEditor(int row, int column);
    public void setCellEditor(javax.swing.table.TableCellEditor anEditor);
    public boolean getCellSelectionEnabled();                                            default:false
    public void setCellSelectionEnabled(boolean flag);
    public int getColumnCount();                                                         default:0
    public javax.swing.table.TableColumnModel getColumnModel();             default:DefaultTableColumnModel
    public void setColumnModel(javax.swing.table.TableColumnModel newModel);
    public boolean getColumnSelectionAllowed();                                          default:false
    public void setColumnSelectionAllowed(boolean flag);
    public boolean isEditing();                                                          default:false
    public int getEditingColumn();                                                       default:-1
    public void setEditingColumn(int aColumn);
    public int getEditingRow();                                                          default:-1
    public void setEditingRow(int aRow);
    public Component getEditorComponent();                                               default:null
    public java.awt.Color getGridColor();                                          default:ColorUIResource
    public void setGridColor(java.awt.Color newColor);
    public java.awt.Dimension getIntercellSpacing();
    public void setIntercellSpacing(java.awt.Dimension newSpacing);
    public boolean isManagingFocus();                           Overrides:JComponent constant default:true
    public javax.swing.table.TableModel getModel();                        default:DefaultTableModel
    public void setModel(javax.swing.table.TableModel newModel);
    public java.awt.Dimension getPreferredScrollableViewportSize();             Implements:Scrollable
    public void setPreferredScrollableViewportSize(java.awt.Dimension size);
    public int getRowCount();                                                            default:0
    public int getRowHeight();                                                           default:16
    public void setRowHeight(int newHeight);
    public int getRowMargin();                                                           default:1
    public void setRowMargin(int rowMargin);
    public boolean getRowSelectionAllowed();                                             default:true
    public void setRowSelectionAllowed(boolean flag);
    public boolean getScrollableTracksViewportHeight();         Implements:Scrollable constant default:false
    public boolean getScrollableTracksViewportWidth();          Implements:Scrollable default:true
```

public int **getSelectedColumn**( );	*default:-1*
public int **getSelectedColumnCount**( );	*default:0*
public int[ ] **getSelectedColumns**( );	
public int **getSelectedRow**( );	*default:-1*
public int **getSelectedRowCount**( );	*default:0*
public int[ ] **getSelectedRows**( );	
public java.awt.Color **getSelectionBackground**( );	*default:ColorUIResource*
public void **setSelectionBackground**(java.awt.Color *selectionBackground*);	*bound*
public java.awt.Color **getSelectionForeground**( );	*default:ColorUIResource*
public void **setSelectionForeground**(java.awt.Color *selectionForeground*);	*bound*
public ListSelectionModel **getSelectionModel**( );	*default:DefaultListSelectionModel*
public void **setSelectionModel**(ListSelectionModel *newModel*);	
public boolean **getShowHorizontalLines**( );	*default:true*
public void **setShowHorizontalLines**(boolean *b*);	
public boolean **getShowVerticalLines**( );	*default:true*
public void **setShowVerticalLines**(boolean *b*);	
public javax.swing.table.JTableHeader **getTableHeader**( );	
public void **setTableHeader**(javax.swing.table.JTableHeader *newHeader*);	
public javax.swing.plaf.TableUI **getUI**( );	
public void **setUI**(javax.swing.plaf.TableUI *ui*);	
public String **getUIClassID**( );	*Overrides:JComponent default:"TableUI"*

// Public Instance Methods
```
public void addColumn(javax.swing.table.TableColumn aColumn);
public void addColumnSelectionInterval(int index0, int index1);
public void addRowSelectionInterval(int index0, int index1);
public void clearSelection( );
public int columnAtPoint(java.awt.Point point);
public int convertColumnIndexToModel(int viewColumnIndex);
public int convertColumnIndexToView(int modelColumnIndex);
public void createDefaultColumnsFromModel( );
public boolean editCellAt(int row, int column);
public boolean editCellAt(int row, int column, java.util.EventObject e);
public java.awt.Rectangle getCellRect(int row, int column, boolean includeSpacing);
public javax.swing.table.TableCellRenderer getCellRenderer(int row, int column);
public javax.swing.table.TableColumn getColumn(Object identifier);
public Class getColumnClass(int column);
public String getColumnName(int column);
public javax.swing.table.TableCellEditor getDefaultEditor(Class columnClass);
public javax.swing.table.TableCellRenderer getDefaultRenderer(Class columnClass);
public Object getValueAt(int row, int column);
public boolean isCellEditable(int row, int column);
public boolean isCellSelected(int row, int column);
public boolean isColumnSelected(int column);
public boolean isRowSelected(int row);
public void moveColumn(int column, int targetColumn);
public Component prepareEditor(javax.swing.table.TableCellEditor editor, int row, int column);
public Component prepareRenderer(javax.swing.table.TableCellRenderer renderer, int row, int column);
public void removeColumn(javax.swing.table.TableColumn aColumn);
public void removeColumnSelectionInterval(int index0, int index1);
public void removeEditor( );
public void removeRowSelectionInterval(int index0, int index1);
public int rowAtPoint(java.awt.Point point);
public void selectAll( );
public void setColumnSelectionInterval(int index0, int index1);
public void setDefaultEditor(Class columnClass, javax.swing.table.TableCellEditor editor);
public void setDefaultRenderer(Class columnClass, javax.swing.table.TableCellRenderer renderer);
public void setRowSelectionInterval(int index0, int index1);
public void setSelectionMode(int selectionMode);
```

javax.swing

```
      public void setShowGrid(boolean b);
      public void setValueAt(Object aValue, int row, int column);
      public void sizeColumnsToFit(int resizingColumn);
// Methods Implementing Accessible
      public AccessibleContext getAccessibleContext();                              default:AccessibleJTable
// Methods Implementing CellEditorListener
      public void editingCanceled(javax.swing.event.ChangeEvent e);
      public void editingStopped(javax.swing.event.ChangeEvent e);
// Methods Implementing ListSelectionListener
      public void valueChanged(javax.swing.event.ListSelectionEvent e);
// Methods Implementing Scrollable
      public java.awt.Dimension getPreferredScrollableViewportSize();
      public int getScrollableBlockIncrement(java.awt.Rectangle visibleRect, int orientation, int direction);
      public boolean getScrollableTracksViewportHeight();                          constant default:false
      public boolean getScrollableTracksViewportWidth();                                  default:true
      public int getScrollableUnitIncrement(java.awt.Rectangle visibleRect, int orientation, int direction);
// Methods Implementing TableColumnModelListener
      public void columnAdded(javax.swing.event.TableColumnModelEvent e);
      public void columnMarginChanged(javax.swing.event.ChangeEvent e);
      public void columnMoved(javax.swing.event.TableColumnModelEvent e);
      public void columnRemoved(javax.swing.event.TableColumnModelEvent e);
      public void columnSelectionChanged(javax.swing.event.ListSelectionEvent e);
// Methods Implementing TableModelListener
      public void tableChanged(javax.swing.event.TableModelEvent e);
// Public Methods Overriding JComponent
      public void addNotify();
      public String getToolTipText(java.awt.event.MouseEvent event);
      public void reshape(int x, int y, int width, int height);
      public void updateUI();
// Protected Methods Overriding JComponent
      protected String paramString();
// Protected Instance Methods
      protected void configureEnclosingScrollPane();
      protected javax.swing.table.TableColumnModel createDefaultColumnModel();
      protected javax.swing.table.TableModel createDefaultDataModel();
      protected void createDefaultEditors();
      protected void createDefaultRenderers();
      protected ListSelectionModel createDefaultSelectionModel();
      protected javax.swing.table.JTableHeader createDefaultTableHeader();
      protected void initializeLocalVars();
      protected void resizeAndRepaint();
// Protected Instance Fields
      protected boolean autoCreateColumnsFromModel;
      protected int autoResizeMode;
      protected transient javax.swing.table.TableCellEditor cellEditor;
      protected boolean cellSelectionEnabled;
      protected javax.swing.table.TableColumnModel columnModel;
      protected javax.swing.table.TableModel dataModel;
      protected transient java.util.Hashtable defaultEditorsByColumnClass;
      protected transient java.util.Hashtable defaultRenderersByColumnClass;
      protected transient int editingColumn;
      protected transient int editingRow;
      protected transient Component editorComp;
      protected java.awt.Color gridColor;
      protected java.awt.Dimension preferredViewportSize;
      protected int rowHeight;
      protected int rowMargin;
      protected boolean rowSelectionAllowed;
```

```
      protected java.awt.Color selectionBackground;
      protected java.awt.Color selectionForeground;
      protected ListSelectionModel selectionModel;
      protected boolean showHorizontalLines;
      protected boolean showVerticalLines;
      protected javax.swing.table.JTableHeader tableHeader;
// Deprecated Public Methods
#     public static JScrollPane createScrollPaneForTable(JTable aTable);
#     public void sizeColumnsToFit(boolean lastColumnOnly);
}
```

Hierarchy: Object→ Component(java.awt.image.ImageObserver, java.awt.MenuContainer, Serializable)→ Container→ JComponent(Serializable)→ JTable(Accessible, javax.swing.event.CellEditorListener(java.util.EventListener), javax.swing.event.ListSelectionListener(java.util.EventListener), Scrollable, javax.swing.event.TableColumnModelListener(java.util.EventListener), javax.swing.event.TableModelListener(java.util.EventListener))

Passed To: DefaultCellEditor.getTableCellEditorComponent(), JTable.createScrollPaneForTable(), JTable.AccessibleJTable.AccessibleJTableCell.AccessibleJTableCell(), javax.swing.table.DefaultTableCellRenderer.getTableCellRendererComponent(), javax.swing.table.JTableHeader.setTable(), javax.swing.table.JTableHeader.AccessibleJTableHeader.AccessibleJTableHeaderEntry.AccessibleJTableHeaderEntry(), javax.swing.table.TableCellEditor.getTableCellEditorComponent(), javax.swing.table.TableCellRenderer.getTableCellRendererComponent()

Returned By: javax.swing.table.JTableHeader.getTable()

Type Of: javax.swing.table.JTableHeader.table

JTextArea   Java 1.2

javax.swing   *serializable accessible(text) swing component*

JTextArea displays multiple lines of plain, unformatted text and allows the user to edit the text. The JTextArea API is designed to be similar to the java.awt.TextArea API.

You can specify the text to be displayed by passing a String to the JTextArea constructor or by using the setText() and getText() methods inherited from the superclass. Specify the number of rows and columns to be displayed by the JTextArea by passing these values to the constructor or by using the setRows() and setColumns() methods. The lineWrap property specifies whether long lines should wrap. The wrapStyleWord property specifies whether lines should wrap at word boundaries or at character boundaries. If you are displaying more than a few lines of text, you probably want to place your JTextArea within a JScrollPane to enable scrolling as needed.

JTextArea is a subclass of javax.swing.text.JTextComponent and inherits many features of that powerful text editor. Many of the most commonly used JTextArea methods are actually inherited from its superclass. They include the getText() and setText() methods already mentioned, as well as setEditable(), getCaretPosition(), and setCaretPosition(). Like its superclass, JTextArea uses a javax.swing.text.Document object as its model. Since a JTextArea displays only plain text, however, you can typically use a simple String object instead.

```
public class JTextArea extends javax.swing.text.JTextComponent {
// Public Constructors
      public JTextArea();
      public JTextArea(javax.swing.text.Document doc);
      public JTextArea(String text);
      public JTextArea(int rows, int columns);
```

```
    public JTextArea(String text, int rows, int columns);
    public JTextArea(javax.swing.text.Document doc, String text, int rows, int columns);
// Inner Classes
    protected class AccessibleJTextArea extends javax.swing.text.JTextComponent.AccessibleJTextComponent;
// Property Accessor Methods (by property name)
    public AccessibleContext getAccessibleContext();                Overrides:JTextComponent default:AccessibleJTextArea
    public int getColumns();                                                                      default:0
    public void setColumns(int columns);
    public int getLineCount();                                                                    default:0
    public boolean getLineWrap();                                                             default:false
    public void setLineWrap(boolean wrap);                                                  bound preferred
    public boolean isManagingFocus();                          Overrides:JComponent constant default:true
    public java.awt.Dimension getPreferredScrollableViewportSize();            Overrides:JTextComponent
    public java.awt.Dimension getPreferredSize();                             Overrides:JComponent
    public int getRows();                                                                         default:0
    public void setRows(int rows);
    public boolean getScrollableTracksViewportWidth();         Overrides:JTextComponent default.false
    public int getTabSize();                                                                      default:8
    public void setTabSize(int size);                                                     bound preferred
    public String getUIClassID();                             Overrides:JComponent default:"TextAreaUI"
    public boolean getWrapStyleWord();                                                        default:false
    public void setWrapStyleWord(boolean word);                                                    bound
// Public Instance Methods
    public void append(String str);
    public int getLineEndOffset(int line) throws javax.swing.text.BadLocationException;
    public int getLineOfOffset(int offset) throws javax.swing.text.BadLocationException;
    public int getLineStartOffset(int line) throws javax.swing.text.BadLocationException;
    public void insert(String str, int pos);
    public void replaceRange(String str, int start, int end);
// Public Methods Overriding JTextComponent
    public int getScrollableUnitIncrement(java.awt.Rectangle visibleRect, int orientation, int direction);
// Protected Methods Overriding JTextComponent
    protected String paramString();
    protected void processComponentKeyEvent(java.awt.event.KeyEvent e);
// Public Methods Overriding JComponent
    public void setFont(java.awt.Font f);
// Protected Instance Methods
    protected javax.swing.text.Document createDefaultModel();
    protected int getColumnWidth();
    protected int getRowHeight();
}
```

Hierarchy: Object→ Component(java.awt.image.ImageObserver, java.awt.MenuContainer, Serializable)→ Container→ JComponent(Serializable)→ javax.swing.text.JTextComponent(Accessible, Scrollable)→ JTextArea

JTextField   Java 1.2

javax.swing   *serializable accessible(text) swing component*

JTextField allows the user to enter and edit a single line of plain text. JTextField is designed to supersede java.awt.TextField, so it has a similar API. You can set and query the text with the setText() and getText() methods inherited from the superclass. Use setFont() to specify the font in which the text is displayed. Use setColumns() to set the number of characters in the field. Note that the specified number of columns is approximate unless you are using a monospaced font. Note that JTextField inherits a number of useful properties from its superclass. These include enabled, editable, caretPosition, and selectedText.

JTextField fires an ActionEvent to any registered ActionListener objects when the user types Enter. You can specify the action command text sent with the ActionEvent by calling setActionCommand().

```
public class JTextField extends javax.swing.text.JTextComponent implements SwingConstants {
// Public Constructors
    public JTextField();
    public JTextField(String text);
    public JTextField(int columns);
    public JTextField(String text, int columns);
    public JTextField(javax.swing.text.Document doc, String text, int columns);
// Public Constants
    public static final String notifyAction;                                              ="notify-field-accept"
// Inner Classes
    protected class AccessibleJTextField extends javax.swing.text.JTextComponent.AccessibleJTextComponent;
// Event Registration Methods (by event name)
    public void addActionListener(java.awt.event.ActionListener l);                                synchronized
    public void removeActionListener(java.awt.event.ActionListener l);                             synchronized
// Property Accessor Methods (by property name)
    public AccessibleContext getAccessibleContext();         Overrides:JTextComponent default:AccessibleJTextField
    public Action[] getActions();                                            Overrides:JTextComponent
    public int getColumns();                                                          default:0
    public void setColumns(int columns);
    public int getHorizontalAlignment();                                                default:2
    public void setHorizontalAlignment(int alignment);                                bound preferred
    public BoundedRangeModel getHorizontalVisibility();           default:DefaultBoundedRangeModel
    public java.awt.Dimension getPreferredSize();                              Overrides:JComponent
    public int getScrollOffset();                                                       default:0
    public void setScrollOffset(int scrollOffset);
    public String getUIClassID();                          Overrides:JComponent default:"TextFieldUI"
    public boolean isValidateRoot();                   Overrides:JComponent constant default:true
// Public Instance Methods
    public void postActionEvent();
    public void setActionCommand(String command);
// Protected Methods Overriding JTextComponent
    protected String paramString();
// Public Methods Overriding JComponent
    public void scrollRectToVisible(java.awt.Rectangle r);
    public void setFont(java.awt.Font f);
// Protected Instance Methods
    protected javax.swing.text.Document createDefaultModel();
    protected void fireActionPerformed();
    protected int getColumnWidth();
}
```

Hierarchy: Object→ Component(java.awt.image.ImageObserver, java.awt.MenuContainer, Serializable)→ Container→ JComponent(Serializable)→ javax.swing.text.JTextComponent(Accessible, Scrollable)→ JTextField(SwingConstants)

Subclasses: JPasswordField, javax.swing.tree.DefaultTreeCellEditor.DefaultTextField

Passed To: DefaultCellEditor.DefaultCellEditor()

JTextPane   Java 1.2

javax.swing   *serializable accessible(text) swing component*

JTextPane is a component for displaying and editing multiline formatted text. When combined with a GUI that allows the user to select fonts, colors, paragraph styles, and so forth, it provides substantial word-processing functionality for any Java application. JTextPane works with documents that implement the javax.swing.text.StyledDocument interface, typically a DefaultStyledDocument. JTextPane also relies on javax.swing.text.StyledEditorKit to provide auxiliary configuration information.

JTextPane does not directly define methods for inserting styled text into the document. You must work directly with the StyledDocument to do that. JTextPane allows the user to edit text but does not provide any means for the user to specify or change the style of that text. Your application must provide additional GUI components (e.g., a menu of available styles or a dialog box for selecting a font) in order to allow the user to select styles.

Call setCharacterAttributes() to specify attributes, such as font size and style, that apply to individual characters. This method either sets the attributes of the currently selected text, or, if there is no selection, specifies attributes to be applied to text inserted in the future. The boolean *replace* argument indicates whether these attributes should replace the previous attributes or should augment them. setParagraphAttributes() is a similar method, but it sets attributes, such as margins and justification, that apply to entire paragraphs of text.

In addition to displaying formatted text, JTextPane can also display images and arbitrary components. JTextPane provides the insertComponent() and insertIcon() methods to make it easy to insert objects of these types without having to manipulate the StyledDocument object.

```
public class JTextPane extends JEditorPane {
// Public Constructors
     public JTextPane();
     public JTextPane(javax.swing.text.StyledDocument doc);
// Property Accessor Methods (by property name)
     public javax.swing.text.AttributeSet getCharacterAttributes();                         default:LeafElement
     public void setDocument(javax.swing.text.Document doc);                          Overrides:JTextComponent
     public final void setEditorKit(javax.swing.text.EditorKit kit);                       Overrides:JEditorPane
     public javax.swing.text.MutableAttributeSet getInputAttributes();
     public javax.swing.text.Style getLogicalStyle();                                    default:NamedStyle
     public void setLogicalStyle(javax.swing.text.Style s);
     public javax.swing.text.AttributeSet getParagraphAttributes();                       default:BranchElement
     public boolean getScrollableTracksViewportWidth();             Overrides:JEditorPane constant default:true
     public javax.swing.text.StyledDocument getStyledDocument();             default:DefaultStyledDocument
     public void setStyledDocument(javax.swing.text.StyledDocument doc);
     public String getUIClassID();                            Overrides:JEditorPane default:"TextPaneUI"
// Public Instance Methods
     public javax.swing.text.Style addStyle(String nm, javax.swing.text.Style parent);
     public javax.swing.text.Style getStyle(String nm);
     public void insertComponent(Component c);
     public void insertIcon(Icon g);
     public void removeStyle(String nm);
     public void setCharacterAttributes(javax.swing.text.AttributeSet attr, boolean replace);
     public void setParagraphAttributes(javax.swing.text.AttributeSet attr, boolean replace);
// Public Methods Overriding JEditorPane
     public void replaceSelection(String content);
// Protected Methods Overriding JEditorPane
     protected javax.swing.text.EditorKit createDefaultEditorKit();
     protected String paramString();
// Protected Instance Methods
     protected final javax.swing.text.StyledEditorKit getStyledEditorKit();
}
```

Hierarchy: Object→ Component(java.awt.image.ImageObserver, java.awt.MenuContainer, Serializable)→ Container→ JComponent(Serializable)→ javax.swing.text.JTextComponent(Accessible, Scrollable)→ JEditorPane→ JTextPane

JToggleButton   Java 1.2

javax.swing   *serializable accessible(action,value) swing component*

This class implements a toggle button: a button that can be selected or deselected. The user can toggle between the selected and deselected states by clicking the button. Like all Swing buttons, a JToggleButton can display text and an icon. The selection state is typically indicated by the button border and background color. You can also call setIcon() and setSelectedIcon() to specify different icons for the default and selected states. By default, JToggleButton keeps track of its selection state with a JToggleButton.ToggleButtonModel object. JToggleButton is less commonly used than its subclasses JCheckBox and JRadioButton.

```
public class JToggleButton extends AbstractButton implements Accessible {
// Public Constructors
    public JToggleButton();
    public JToggleButton(Icon icon);
    public JToggleButton(String text);
    public JToggleButton(String text, Icon icon);
    public JToggleButton(Icon icon, boolean selected);
    public JToggleButton(String text, boolean selected);
    public JToggleButton(String text, Icon icon, boolean selected);
// Inner Classes
    protected class AccessibleJToggleButton extends AbstractButton.AccessibleAbstractButton implements
        java.awt.event.ItemListener;
    public static class ToggleButtonModel extends DefaultButtonModel;
// Property Accessor Methods (by property name)
    public AccessibleContext                  Implements:Accessible default:AccessibleJToggleButton expert
        getAccessibleContext();
    public String getUIClassID();                    Overrides:JComponent default:"ToggleButtonUI"
// Methods Implementing Accessible
    public AccessibleContext getAccessibleContext();              default:AccessibleJToggleButton expert
// Public Methods Overriding AbstractButton
    public void updateUI();
// Protected Methods Overriding AbstractButton
    protected String paramString();
}
```

Hierarchy: Object→ Component(java.awt.image.ImageObserver, java.awt.MenuContainer, Serializable)→ Container→ JComponent(Serializable)→ AbstractButton(java.awt.ItemSelectable, SwingConstants)→ JToggleButton(Accessible)

Subclasses: JCheckBox, JRadioButton

JToggleButton.ToggleButtonModel   Java 1.2

javax.swing   *serializable model*

This class is the ButtonModel used by default by JToggleButton, JCheckBox, and JRadioButton components. It overrides several methods of DefaultButtonModel in order to delegate button selection state information to a ButtonGroup object. Applications typically never need to instantiate this class.

```
public static class JToggleButton.ToggleButtonModel extends DefaultButtonModel {
// Public Constructors
    public ToggleButtonModel();
```

```
// Public Methods Overriding DefaultButtonModel
    public boolean isSelected();                                                    default:false
    public void setPressed(boolean b);
    public void setSelected(boolean b);
}
```

JToolBar   Java 1.2

javax.swing   *serializable accessible swing component*

JToolBar is a container that displays a row or column of children, typically JButton children, that represent application tools or actions. JToolBar has two special features that make it useful in applications. First, it has a special add() method that allows you to add an Action object, rather than a Component, to it. When you do this, an appropriate JButton is automatically created. This created button tracks the enabled state of the action, so if the action is disabled, the button becomes disabled as well. The JMenu class has this same ability to accept Action objects as children; the commonly used actions of an application frequently appear in both JMenu and JToolBar components of the application. A JToolBar can contain special separator components that serve to group related tools and separate unrelated tools. You can add a separator to a JToolBar with the special addSeparator() method.

The second special feature of JToolBar is that it is draggable. Unless this feature has been disabled with setFloatable(), a JToolBar displays a special grip that the user can use to drag the toolbar. If the user drags the toolbar out of the window in which it appears, it becomes a floating palette in a window of its own. Additionally, if the JToolBar is positioned against one edge of a container that uses a java.awt.BorderLayout layout manager and if there are no other components positioned against the edges, the user can drag the JToolBar to any other edge of the container. The conventional orientation and position for a JToolBar is a horizontal row of controls positioned just below the menubar at the top of a window. By dragging the JToolBar, however, a user can automatically convert it to a vertical toolbar positioned against the left edge of the window, for example.

JToolBar defines only a few interesting properties. As mentioned earlier, floatable specifies whether the user can drag the JToolBar. orientation specifies whether the JToolBar arranges its children into a horizontal or vertical bar. The value of this property should be one of the SwingConstants constants HORIZONTAL or VERTICAL. The default is HORIZONTAL. Finally, the margin property specifies the amount of space between the border of the toolbar and its children.

```
public class JToolBar extends JComponent implements Accessible, SwingConstants {
// Public Constructors
    public JToolBar();
    public JToolBar(int orientation);
// Inner Classes
    protected class AccessibleJToolBar extends JComponent.AccessibleJComponent;
    public static class Separator extends JSeparator;
// Property Accessor Methods (by property name)
    public AccessibleContext getAccessibleContext();       Implements:Accessible default:AccessibleJToolBar
    public boolean isBorderPainted();                                              default:true
    public void setBorderPainted(boolean b);                                     bound expert
    public boolean isFloatable();                                                default:true
    public void setFloatable(boolean b);                                       bound preferred
    public java.awt.Insets getMargin();
    public void setMargin(java.awt.Insets m);                                    bound expert
    public int getOrientation();                                                    default:0
    public void setOrientation(int o);                                         bound preferred
```

```
    public javax.swing.plaf.ToolBarUI getUI();
    public void setUI(javax.swing.plaf.ToolBarUI ui);                          bound expert hidden
    public String getUIClassID();                               Overrides:JComponent default:"ToolBarUI"
// Public Instance Methods
    public JButton add(Action a);
    public void addSeparator();
    public void addSeparator(java.awt.Dimension size);
    public Component getComponentAtIndex(int i);
    public int getComponentIndex(Component c);
// Methods Implementing Accessible
    public AccessibleContext getAccessibleContext();                         default:AccessibleJToolBar
// Public Methods Overriding JComponent
    public void updateUI();
// Protected Methods Overriding JComponent
    protected void paintBorder(java.awt.Graphics g);
    protected String paramString();
// Public Methods Overriding Container
    public void remove(Component comp);
// Protected Methods Overriding Container
    protected void addImpl(Component comp, Object constraints, int index);
// Protected Instance Methods
    protected java.beans.PropertyChangeListener createActionChangeListener(JButton b);
}
```

Hierarchy: Object→ Component(java.awt.image.ImageObserver, java.awt.MenuContainer, Serializable)→ Container→ JComponent(Serializable)→ JToolBar(Accessible, SwingConstants)

JToolBar.Separator   Java 1.2
javax.swing   *serializable accessible swing component*

This subclass of JSeparator defines a visual separator component specially tuned for use within a JToolBar. Practically speaking, this class is no different than JSeparator. You should rarely need to explicitly create or work with a JToolBar.Separator. Just call JTool-Bar.addSeparator() as needed to create separators and add them to a JToolBar.

```
public static class JToolBar.Separator extends JSeparator {
// Public Constructors
    public Separator();
    public Separator(java.awt.Dimension size);
// Property Accessor Methods (by property name)
    public java.awt.Dimension getMaximumSize();                           Overrides:JComponent
    public java.awt.Dimension getMinimumSize();                           Overrides:JComponent
    public java.awt.Dimension getPreferredSize();                         Overrides:JComponent
    public java.awt.Dimension getSeparatorSize();                    default:DimensionUIResource
    public void setSeparatorSize(java.awt.Dimension size);
    public String getUIClassID();                                         Overrides:JSeparator
}
```

JToolTip   Java 1.2
javax.swing   *serializable accessible swing component*

JToolTip is the component used to display tooltips in Swing applications. To display a tooltip over a component, simply call setToolTipText() over that component. You rarely or never need to work with the JToolTip class itself. If you want to customize the appearance of the tooltip displayed by a component, you can override the createToolTip() method of that component, to return your own JToolTip object.

```
public class JToolTip extends JComponent implements Accessible {
// Public Constructors
    public JToolTip();
// Inner Classes
    protected class AccessibleJToolTip extends JComponent.AccessibleJComponent;
// Property Accessor Methods (by property name)
    public AccessibleContext getAccessibleContext();           Implements:Accessible default:AccessibleJToolTip
    public JComponent getComponent();                                                           default:null
    public void setComponent(JComponent c);
    public String getTipText();                                                                 default:null
    public void setTipText(String tipText);                                               bound preferred
    public javax.swing.plaf.ToolTipUI getUI();
    public String getUIClassID();                            Overrides:JComponent default:"ToolTipUI"
// Methods Implementing Accessible
    public AccessibleContext getAccessibleContext();                         default:AccessibleJToolTip
// Public Methods Overriding JComponent
    public void updateUI();
// Protected Methods Overriding JComponent
    protected String paramString();
}
```

Hierarchy: Object→ Component(java.awt.image.ImageObserver, java.awt.MenuContainer, Serializable)→ Container→ JComponent(Serializable)→ JToolTip(Accessible)

Returned By: JComponent.createToolTip()

JTree   Java 1.2

javax.swing   *serializable accessible(selection) swing component*

JTree is a powerful Swing component for displaying hierarchical, tree-structured data in outline form. The user can expand and collapse the outline to show or hide the children of any node in the tree. The user can also select and optionally edit the values displayed in the tree.

JTree relies on the classes and interfaces in the javax.swing.tree package. Most importantly, it uses a TreeModel object to encapsulate the tree data it displays. If your data already has a hierarchical structure, you should implement a TreeModel class to serve as an intermediary between your data structures and the JTree component. If your data is not implicitly hierarchical, you can arrange it into a hierarchy by implementing the TreeNode or MutableTreeNode interface or by encapsulating your objects within DefaultMutableTreeNode objects that implement these interfaces for you. Once you have done this, you can rely on the default JTree model, DefaultTreeModel.

JTree also defines constructors that accept tree data in the form of an Object[], a Vector, or a Hashtable. If your data is relatively simple and you can express it in one of these forms, it is easy to use one of these constructors to display your data. If you specify a vector or object array, the elements of the vector or array become the nodes of the tree. If any of those elements are a vector, array, or hashtable, the contents of that element become the children of that node. If you specify a Hashtable, the keys of the hashtable become the nodes of the tree and the values of the hashtable become the children of those nodes. This is particularly useful, of course, if the hashtable values are arrays or vectors.

By default, tree nodes are not editable. You can change this, however, with the setEditable() method. The selection state and selection mode of a JTree is maintained by a javax.swing.tree.TreeSelectionModel object. By default, JTree uses a DefaultTreeSelectionModel object. You can set your own object with setSelectionModel(). Use the setSelectionMode()

method of the TreeSelectionModel to specify the type of selection that is supported by the JTree. To disable selection in a JTree altogether, pass null to setSelectionModel().

JTree defines a number of methods for setting and querying the current selection state of the tree. It also defines methods for collapsing and expanding nodes and for querying nodes to determine whether they are expanded. These methods use two different techniques for referring to a particular node in the tree. One technique is to specify the integer row number at which the item appears. While this is a convenient way to refer to an item that the user has selected, for example, it does not map naturally to an item in the TreeModel. The other way to refer to an item in a JTree is with a javax.swing.tree.TreePath object. A TreePath is essentially an array of objects that contains the node itself and all of its ancestors up to the root of the tree. The first element in the array is the root, and the last element is the tree node that is being referred to. The methods getPathForRow() and getRowForPath() allow you to convert from one node representation to another. Related methods convert between X, Y coordinates (such as the coordinates contained in a MouseEvent) and the nearest TreePath or tree row.

JTree displays its nodes using a javax.swing.tree.TreeCellRenderer object. By default, it uses DefaultTreeCellRenderer, which displays any object in the tree in text form by calling its toString() method. If you want to display custom objects in a tree, you can implement your own TreeCellRenderer and pass an instance to setCellRenderer(). JTree does not allow its nodes to be edited by default, but when editing is enabled, it is done with a TreeCellEditor object. The DefaultTreeCellEditor allows editing of String and Boolean nodes. You can implement your own TreeCellEditor if you want to allow the user to edit other node types.

JTree defines quite a few methods for querying and setting the state of the tree. The purpose of most of these methods is fairly obvious. One thing to note is that different methods use the word visible to mean different things. The methods isVisible() and makeVisible() use visible to refer to a node that is displayed under an expanded parent. Under this definition, a node may be visible even if it is currently scrolled off the screen. All other methods, such as scrollPathToVisible(), use visible to mean that a node is actually on the screen and currently visible to the user.

JTree implements the Scrollable interface, and, unless you are displaying a very small, fixed-size tree, you should almost always place a JTree within a JScrollPane container. If you are using JTree to view a large amount of data, if all the nodes are of the same type, and if the TreeModel has an efficient implementation, you may get better performance by passing true to setLargeModel().

```
public class JTree extends JComponent implements Accessible, Scrollable {
// Public Constructors
     public JTree();
     public JTree(java.util.Vector value);
     public JTree(javax.swing.tree.TreeNode root);
     public JTree(java.util.Hashtable value);
     public JTree(Object[ ] value);
     public JTree(javax.swing.tree.TreeModel newModel);
     public JTree(javax.swing.tree.TreeNode root, boolean asksAllowsChildren);
// Public Constants
     public static final String CELL_EDITOR_PROPERTY;                           ="cellEditor"
     public static final String CELL_RENDERER_PROPERTY;                         ="cellRenderer"
     public static final String EDITABLE_PROPERTY;                              ="editable"
     public static final String INVOKES_STOP_CELL_EDITING_PROPERTY;   ="messagesStopCellEditing"
     public static final String LARGE_MODEL_PROPERTY;                           ="largeModel"
     public static final String ROOT_VISIBLE_PROPERTY;                          ="rootVisible"
     public static final String ROW_HEIGHT_PROPERTY;                            ="rowHeight"
     public static final String SCROLLS_ON_EXPAND_PROPERTY;                     ="scrollsOnExpand"
```

public static final String **SELECTION_MODEL_PROPERTY**;	*="selectionModel"*
public static final String **SHOWS_ROOT_HANDLES_PROPERTY**;	*="showsRootHandles"*
public static final String **TREE_MODEL_PROPERTY**;	*="treeModel"*
public static final String **VISIBLE_ROW_COUNT_PROPERTY**;	*="visibleRowCount"*

// Inner Classes

protected class **AccessibleJTree** extends JComponent.AccessibleJComponent implements AccessibleSelection,
      javax.swing.event.TreeExpansionListener, javax.swing.event.TreeModelListener,
      javax.swing.event.TreeSelectionListener;

public static class **DynamicUtilTreeNode** extends javax.swing.tree.DefaultMutableTreeNode;

protected static class **EmptySelectionModel** extends javax.swing.tree.DefaultTreeSelectionModel;

protected class **TreeModelHandler** implements javax.swing.event.TreeModelListener;

protected class **TreeSelectionRedirector** implements Serializable, javax.swing.event.TreeSelectionListener;

// Protected Class Methods

protected static javax.swing.tree.TreeModel **createTreeModel**(Object *value*);

protected static javax.swing.tree.TreeModel **getDefaultTreeModel**();

// Event Registration Methods (by event name)

public void **addTreeExpansionListener**(javax.swing.event.TreeExpansionListener *tel*);

public void **removeTreeExpansionListener**(javax.swing.event.TreeExpansionListener *tel*);

public void **addTreeSelectionListener**(javax.swing.event.TreeSelectionListener *tsl*);

public void **removeTreeSelectionListener**(javax.swing.event.TreeSelectionListener *tsl*);

public void **addTreeWillExpandListener**(javax.swing.event.TreeWillExpandListener *tel*);

public void **removeTreeWillExpandListener**(javax.swing.event.TreeWillExpandListener *tel*);

// Property Accessor Methods (by property name)

public AccessibleContext **getAccessibleContext**();	*Implements:Accessible default:AccessibleJTree*
public javax.swing.tree.TreeCellEditor **getCellEditor**();	*default:null*
public void **setCellEditor**(javax.swing.tree.TreeCellEditor *cellEditor*);	*bound*
public javax.swing.tree.TreeCellRenderer **getCellRenderer**();	*default:DefaultTreeCellRenderer*
public void **setCellRenderer**(javax.swing.tree.TreeCellRenderer *x*);	*bound*
public boolean **isEditable**();	*default:false*
public void **setEditable**(boolean *flag*);	*bound*
public boolean **isEditing**();	*default:false*
public javax.swing.tree.TreePath **getEditingPath**();	*default:null*
public boolean **isFixedRowHeight**();	*default:false*
public boolean **getInvokesStopCellEditing**();	*default:false*
public void **setInvokesStopCellEditing**(boolean *newValue*);	*bound*
public boolean **isLargeModel**();	*default:false*
public void **setLargeModel**(boolean *newValue*);	*bound*
public Object **getLastSelectedPathComponent**();	*default:null*
public javax.swing.tree.TreePath **getLeadSelectionPath**();	*default:null*
public int **getLeadSelectionRow**();	*default:-1*
public int **getMaxSelectionRow**();	*default:-1*
public int **getMinSelectionRow**();	*default:-1*
public javax.swing.tree.TreeModel **getModel**();	*default:DefaultTreeModel*
public void **setModel**(javax.swing.tree.TreeModel *newModel*);	*bound*
public java.awt.Dimension **getPreferredScrollableViewportSize**();	*Implements:Scrollable*
public boolean **isRootVisible**();	*default:true*
public void **setRootVisible**(boolean *rootVisible*);	*bound*
public int **getRowCount**();	*default:4*
public int **getRowHeight**();	*default:0*
public void **setRowHeight**(int *rowHeight*);	*bound*
public boolean **getScrollableTracksViewportHeight**();	*Implements:Scrollable default:false*
public boolean **getScrollableTracksViewportWidth**();	*Implements:Scrollable default:false*
public boolean **getScrollsOnExpand**();	*default:true*
public void **setScrollsOnExpand**(boolean *newValue*);	
public int **getSelectionCount**();	*default:0*
public boolean **isSelectionEmpty**();	*default:true*
public javax.swing.tree.TreeSelectionModel **getSelectionModel**();	*default:DefaultTreeSelectionModel*
public void **setSelectionModel**(javax.swing.tree.TreeSelectionModel *selectionModel*);	*bound*

```
    public javax.swing.tree.TreePath getSelectionPath();                                       default:null
    public void setSelectionPath(javax.swing.tree.TreePath path);
    public javax.swing.tree.TreePath[ ] getSelectionPaths();                                   default:null
    public void setSelectionPaths(javax.swing.tree.TreePath[ ] paths);
    public int[ ] getSelectionRows();                                                          default:null
    public void setSelectionRows(int[ ] rows);
    public boolean getShowsRootHandles();                                                      default:false
    public void setShowsRootHandles(boolean newValue);                                         bound
    public javax.swing.plaf.TreeUI getUI();
    public void setUI(javax.swing.plaf.TreeUI ui);
    public String getUIClassID();                                   Overrides:JComponent default:"TreeUI"
    public int getVisibleRowCount();                                                           default:20
    public void setVisibleRowCount(int newCount);                                              bound
// Public Instance Methods
    public void addSelectionInterval(int index0, int index1);
    public void addSelectionPath(javax.swing.tree.TreePath path);
    public void addSelectionPaths(javax.swing.tree.TreePath[ ] paths);
    public void addSelectionRow(int row);
    public void addSelectionRows(int[ ] rows);
    public void cancelEditing();
    public void clearSelection();
    public void collapsePath(javax.swing.tree.TreePath path);
    public void collapseRow(int row);
    public String convertValueToText(Object value, boolean selected, boolean expanded, boolean leaf, int row,
                            boolean hasFocus);
    public void expandPath(javax.swing.tree.TreePath path);
    public void expandRow(int row);
    public void fireTreeCollapsed(javax.swing.tree.TreePath path);
    public void fireTreeExpanded(javax.swing.tree.TreePath path);
    public void fireTreeWillCollapse(javax.swing.tree.TreePath path) throws javax.swing.tree.ExpandVetoException;
    public void fireTreeWillExpand(javax.swing.tree.TreePath path) throws javax.swing.tree.ExpandVetoException;
    public javax.swing.tree.TreePath getClosestPathForLocation(int x, int y);
    public int getClosestRowForLocation(int x, int y);
    public java.util.Enumeration getExpandedDescendants(javax.swing.tree.TreePath parent);
    public java.awt.Rectangle getPathBounds(javax.swing.tree.TreePath path);
    public javax.swing.tree.TreePath getPathForLocation(int x, int y);
    public javax.swing.tree.TreePath getPathForRow(int row);
    public java.awt.Rectangle getRowBounds(int row);
    public int getRowForLocation(int x, int y);
    public int getRowForPath(javax.swing.tree.TreePath path);
    public boolean hasBeenExpanded(javax.swing.tree.TreePath path);
    public boolean isCollapsed(int row);
    public boolean isCollapsed(javax.swing.tree.TreePath path);
    public boolean isExpanded(int row);
    public boolean isExpanded(javax.swing.tree.TreePath path);
    public boolean isPathEditable(javax.swing.tree.TreePath path);
    public boolean isPathSelected(javax.swing.tree.TreePath path);
    public boolean isRowSelected(int row);
    public boolean isVisible(javax.swing.tree.TreePath path);
    public void makeVisible(javax.swing.tree.TreePath path);
    public void removeSelectionInterval(int index0, int index1);
    public void removeSelectionPath(javax.swing.tree.TreePath path);
    public void removeSelectionPaths(javax.swing.tree.TreePath[ ] paths);
    public void removeSelectionRow(int row);
    public void removeSelectionRows(int[ ] rows);
    public void scrollPathToVisible(javax.swing.tree.TreePath path);
    public void scrollRowToVisible(int row);
    public void setSelectionInterval(int index0, int index1);
```

```
      public void setSelectionRow(int row);
      public void startEditingAtPath(javax.swing.tree.TreePath path);
      public boolean stopEditing();
      public void treeDidChange();
// Methods Implementing Accessible
      public AccessibleContext getAccessibleContext();                                    default:AccessibleJTree
// Methods Implementing Scrollable
      public java.awt.Dimension getPreferredScrollableViewportSize();
      public int getScrollableBlockIncrement(java.awt.Rectangle visibleRect, int orientation, int direction);
      public boolean getScrollableTracksViewportHeight();                                 default:false
      public boolean getScrollableTracksViewportWidth();                                  default:false
      public int getScrollableUnitIncrement(java.awt.Rectangle visibleRect, int orientation, int direction);
// Public Methods Overriding JComponent
      public String getToolTipText(java.awt.event.MouseEvent event);
      public void updateUI();
// Protected Methods Overriding JComponent
      protected String paramString();
// Protected Instance Methods
      protected void clearToggledPaths();
      protected javax.swing.event.TreeModelListener createTreeModelListener();
      protected void fireValueChanged(javax.swing.event.TreeSelectionEvent e);
      protected java.util.Enumeration getDescendantToggledPaths(javax.swing.tree.TreePath parent);
      protected javax.swing.tree.TreePath[] getPathBetweenRows(int index0, int index1);
      protected void removeDescendantToggledPaths(java.util.Enumeration toRemove);
      protected void setExpandedState(javax.swing.tree.TreePath path, boolean state);
// Protected Instance Fields
      protected transient javax.swing.tree.TreeCellEditor cellEditor;
      protected transient javax.swing.tree.TreeCellRenderer cellRenderer;
      protected boolean editable;
      protected boolean invokesStopCellEditing;
      protected boolean largeModel;
      protected boolean rootVisible;
      protected int rowHeight;
      protected boolean scrollsOnExpand;
      protected transient javax.swing.tree.TreeSelectionModel selectionModel;
      protected transient JTree.TreeSelectionRedirector selectionRedirector;
      protected boolean showsRootHandles;
      protected int toggleClickCount;
      protected transient javax.swing.tree.TreeModel treeModel;
      protected transient javax.swing.event.TreeModelListener treeModelListener;
      protected int visibleRowCount;
}
```

Hierarchy: Object→ Component(java.awt.image.ImageObserver, java.awt.MenuContainer, Serializable)→ Container→ JComponent(Serializable)→ JTree(Accessible, Scrollable)

Passed To: Too many methods to list.

Type Of: javax.swing.tree.DefaultTreeCellEditor.tree

JTree.DynamicUtilTreeNode   Java 1.2

javax.swing   *cloneable serializable*

This subclass of javax.swing.tree.DefaultMutableTreeNode is used by the JTree constructors that accept tree data in the form of a Vector, Hashtable, or Object[]. The static createChildren() method is used to populate a node with the children contained in a specified Vector, Hashtable, or array. DynamicUtilTreeNode is dynamic in the sense that it dynamically creates children nodes when those nodes are requested for the first time.

```
public static class JTree.DynamicUtilTreeNode extends javax.swing.tree.DefaultMutableTreeNode {
// Public Constructors
    public DynamicUtilTreeNode(Object value, Object children);
// Public Class Methods
    public static void createChildren(javax.swing.tree.DefaultMutableTreeNode parent, Object children);
// Public Methods Overriding DefaultMutableTreeNode
    public java.util.Enumeration children();
    public javax.swing.tree.TreeNode getChildAt(int index);
    public int getChildCount();
    public boolean isLeaf();
// Protected Instance Methods
    protected void loadChildren();
// Protected Instance Fields
    protected Object childValue;
    protected boolean hasChildren;
    protected boolean loadedChildren;
}
```

JTree.EmptySelectionModel

Java 1.2

javax.swing

cloneable serializable model

This subclass of javax.swing.tree.DefaultTreeSelectionModel defines empty selection methods and is used to disable selection in a JTree. You never need to instantiate this class explicitly; simply pass null to the setSelectionModel() method of JTree.

```
protected static class JTree.EmptySelectionModel extends javax.swing.tree.DefaultTreeSelectionModel {
// Protected Constructors
    protected EmptySelectionModel();
// Protected Constants
    protected static final JTree.EmptySelectionModel sharedInstance;
// Public Class Methods
    public static JTree.EmptySelectionModel sharedInstance();
// Public Methods Overriding DefaultTreeSelectionModel
    public void addSelectionPaths(javax.swing.tree.TreePath[ ] paths);                    empty
    public void removeSelectionPaths(javax.swing.tree.TreePath[ ] paths);                 empty
    public void setSelectionPaths(javax.swing.tree.TreePath[ ] pPaths);                   empty
}
```

Returned By: JTree.EmptySelectionModel.sharedInstance()

Type Of: JTree.EmptySelectionModel.sharedInstance

JTree.TreeModelHandler

Java 1.2

javax.swing

This class is a javax.swing.event.TreeModelListener used internally by JTree to track changes made to the tree data contained in the TreeModel. Applications never need to use this class.

```
protected class JTree.TreeModelHandler implements javax.swing.event.TreeModelListener {
// Protected Constructors
    protected TreeModelHandler();
// Methods Implementing TreeModelListener
    public void treeNodesChanged(javax.swing.event.TreeModelEvent e);                     empty
    public void treeNodesInserted(javax.swing.event.TreeModelEvent e);                    empty
    public void treeNodesRemoved(javax.swing.event.TreeModelEvent e);
    public void treeStructureChanged(javax.swing.event.TreeModelEvent e);
}
```

javax.swing

JTree.TreeSelectionRedirector

Java 1.2

javax.swing

serializable

This javax.swing.event.TreeSelectionListener class is used internally by JTree to redirect javax.swing.tree.TreeSelectionEvent objects so that they appear to come from the JTree, rather than the TreeSelectionModel object. Applications never need to use this class.

```
protected class JTree.TreeSelectionRedirector implements Serializable, javax.swing.event.TreeSelectionListener {
// Protected Constructors
   protected TreeSelectionRedirector();
// Methods Implementing TreeSelectionListener
   public void valueChanged(javax.swing.event.TreeSelectionEvent e);
}
```

Type Of: JTree.selectionRedirector

JViewport

Java 1.2

javax.swing

serializable accessible swing component

This component displays a portion of the larger child component it contains. It defines methods for efficiently scrolling the child component within the viewable area. Pass true to setBackingStoreEnabled() to use an off-screen image to increase the efficiency of small scrolls. JViewport is used by JScrollPane, and most applications use JScrollPane instead of using JViewport directly.

```
public class JViewport extends JComponent implements Accessible {
// Public Constructors
   public JViewport();
// Inner Classes
   protected class AccessibleJViewport extends JComponent.AccessibleJComponent;
   protected class ViewListener extends java.awt.event.ComponentAdapter implements Serializable;
// Event Registration Methods (by event name)
   public void addChangeListener(javax.swing.event.ChangeListener l);
   public void removeChangeListener(javax.swing.event.ChangeListener l);
// Property Accessor Methods (by property name)
   public AccessibleContext getAccessibleContext();              Implements:Accessible default:AccessibleJViewport
   public boolean isBackingStoreEnabled();                                                         default:false
   public void setBackingStoreEnabled(boolean x);
   public final void setBorder(javax.swing.border.Border border);                            Overrides:JComponent
   public java.awt.Dimension getExtentSize();
   public void setExtentSize(java.awt.Dimension newExtent);
   public final java.awt.Insets getInsets();                                                 Overrides:JComponent
   public final java.awt.Insets getInsets(java.awt.Insets insets);                    Overrides:JComponent expert
   public boolean isOptimizedDrawingEnabled();                      Overrides:JComponent constant default:false
   public Component getView();                                                                      default:null
   public void setView(Component view);
   public java.awt.Point getViewPosition();
   public void setViewPosition(java.awt.Point p);
   public java.awt.Rectangle getViewRect();
   public java.awt.Dimension getViewSize();
   public void setViewSize(java.awt.Dimension newSize);
// Public Instance Methods
   public java.awt.Dimension toViewCoordinates(java.awt.Dimension size);
   public java.awt.Point toViewCoordinates(java.awt.Point p);
// Methods Implementing Accessible
   public AccessibleContext getAccessibleContext();                                 default:AccessibleJViewport
// Public Methods Overriding JComponent
   public void paint(java.awt.Graphics g);
   public void repaint(long tm, int x, int y, int w, int h);
```

```
    public void reshape(int x, int y, int w, int h);
    public void scrollRectToVisible(java.awt.Rectangle contentRect);
// Protected Methods Overriding JComponent
    protected void firePropertyChange(String propertyName, Object oldValue, Object newValue);
    protected String paramString();
// Public Methods Overriding Container
    public void remove(Component child);
// Protected Methods Overriding Container
    protected void addImpl(Component child, Object constraints, int index);
// Protected Instance Methods
    protected boolean computeBlit(int dx, int dy, java.awt.Point blitFrom, java.awt.Point blitTo,
                     java.awt.Dimension blitSize, java.awt.Rectangle blitPaint);
    protected java.awt.LayoutManager createLayoutManager();
    protected JViewport.ViewListener createViewListener();
    protected void fireStateChanged();
// Protected Instance Fields
    protected boolean backingStore;
    protected transient java.awt.Image backingStoreImage;
    protected boolean isViewSizeSet;
    protected java.awt.Point lastPaintPosition;
    protected boolean scrollUnderway;
}
```

Hierarchy: Object→ Component(java.awt.image.ImageObserver, java.awt.MenuContainer, Serializable)→ Container→ JComponent(Serializable)→ JViewport(Accessible)

Passed To: JScrollPane.{setColumnHeader(), setRowHeader(), setViewport()}

Returned By: JScrollPane.{createViewport(), getColumnHeader(), getRowHeader(), getViewport()}, ScrollPaneLayout.{getColumnHeader(), getRowHeader(), getViewport()}

Type Of: JScrollPane.{columnHeader, rowHeader, viewport}, JScrollPane.AccessibleJScrollPane.viewPort, ScrollPaneLayout.{colHead, rowHead, viewport}

JViewport.ViewListener   Java 1.2

javax.swing   *serializable*

This ComponentListener is used internally by JViewport to detect changes to the child component. Applications never use this class directly.

```
protected class JViewport.ViewListener extends java.awt.event.ComponentAdapter implements Serializable {
// Protected Constructors
    protected ViewListener();
// Public Methods Overriding ComponentAdapter
    public void componentResized(java.awt.event.ComponentEvent e);
}
```

Returned By: JViewport.createViewListener()

JWindow   Java 1.2

javax.swing   *serializable accessible swing component bean container*

This class is the Swing analog of the java.awt.Window class. It is a basic heavyweight top-level window with no titlebar or other frame decorations. Most applications use JFrame and JDialog in preference to JWindow. Like JFrame and JDialog, JWindow is a RootPaneContainer, which means that it has an automatically created JRootPane as its single child. You are not allowed to add children or set a layout manager on the JWindow itself. Instead, you must use the container returned by the getContentPane().

```
public class JWindow extends java.awt.Window implements Accessible, RootPaneContainer {
```
// *Public Constructors*
```
    public JWindow();
    public JWindow(java.awt.Window owner);
    public JWindow(java.awt.Frame owner);
```
// *Inner Classes*
```
        protected class AccessibleJWindow extends AccessibleContext implements AccessibleComponent, Serializable;
```
// *Property Accessor Methods (by property name)*

public AccessibleContext **getAccessibleContext**();	*Implements:Accessible default:AccessibleJWindow*
public Container **getContentPane**();	*Implements:RootPaneContainer default:JPanel*
public void **setContentPane**(Container contentPane);	*Implements:RootPaneContainer hidden*
public Component **getGlassPane**();	*Implements:RootPaneContainer default:JPanel*
public void **setGlassPane**(Component glassPane);	*Implements:RootPaneContainer hidden*
public JLayeredPane **getLayeredPane**();	*Implements:RootPaneContainer*
public void **setLayeredPane**(JLayeredPane layeredPane);	*Implements:RootPaneContainer hidden*
public void **setLayout**(java.awt.LayoutManager manager);	*Overrides:Container*
public JRootPane **getRootPane**();	*Implements:RootPaneContainer*

// *Methods Implementing Accessible*

public AccessibleContext **getAccessibleContext**();	*default:AccessibleJWindow*

// *Methods Implementing RootPaneContainer*

public Container **getContentPane**();	*default:JPanel*
public Component **getGlassPane**();	*default:JPanel*
public JLayeredPane **getLayeredPane**();	
public JRootPane **getRootPane**();	
public void **setContentPane**(Container contentPane);	*hidden*
public void **setGlassPane**(Component glassPane);	*hidden*
public void **setLayeredPane**(JLayeredPane layeredPane);	*hidden*

// *Public Methods Overriding Container*
```
    public void remove(Component comp);
```
// *Protected Methods Overriding Container*
```
    protected void addImpl(Component comp, Object constraints, int index);
    protected String paramString();
```
// *Protected Instance Methods*

protected JRootPane **createRootPane**();	
protected boolean **isRootPaneCheckingEnabled**();	
protected void **setRootPane**(JRootPane root);	*hidden*
protected void **setRootPaneCheckingEnabled**(boolean enabled);	*hidden*
protected void **windowInit**();	

// *Protected Instance Fields*
```
    protected AccessibleContext accessibleContext;
    protected JRootPane rootPane;
    protected boolean rootPaneCheckingEnabled;
}
```

Hierarchy: Object→ Component(java.awt.image.ImageObserver, java.awt.MenuContainer, Serializable)→ Container→ java.awt.Window→ JWindow(Accessible, RootPaneContainer)

KeyStroke

javax.swing *serializable*

Java 1.2

This class represents a single keystroke, specified either as a character or, more flexibly, as a keycode plus a set of keyboard modifiers. KeyStroke objects are immutable, and the KeyStroke class maintains a cache of the objects. There is no public KeyStroke constructor. Instead, call one of the static getKeyStroke() methods to obtain a reference to a KeyStroke object that represents the desired keystroke. Note that some versions of getKeyStroke() take a boolean argument that specifies whether the KeyStroke represents a key release event instead of a key press event. The *keyCode* argument to getKeyStroke() should be one of the VK_ virtual key constants defined by java.awt.event.KeyEvent. The *modifiers* argument should be a bitmask composed of the ALT_MASK, CTRL_MASK, META_MASK, and SHIFT_MASK constants defined by java.awt.Event.

See also the registerKeyboardAction() method of JComponent, the setAccelerator() method of JMenuItem, and javax.awt.swing.text.Keymap.

```
public class KeyStroke implements Serializable {
// No Constructor
// Public Class Methods
    public static KeyStroke getKeyStroke(char keyChar);
    public static KeyStroke getKeyStroke(String s);
    public static KeyStroke getKeyStroke(int keyCode, int modifiers);
    public static KeyStroke getKeyStroke(int keyCode, int modifiers, boolean onKeyRelease);
    public static KeyStroke getKeyStrokeForEvent(java.awt.event.KeyEvent anEvent);
// Property Accessor Methods (by property name)
    public char getKeyChar();
    public int getKeyCode();
    public int getModifiers();
    public boolean isOnKeyRelease();
// Public Methods Overriding Object
    public boolean equals(Object anObject);
    public int hashCode();
    public String toString();
// Deprecated Public Methods
#   public static KeyStroke getKeyStroke(char keyChar, boolean onKeyRelease);
}
```

Hierarchy: Object → KeyStroke(Serializable)

Passed To: JComponent.{getActionForKeyStroke(), getConditionForKeyStroke(), registerKeyboardAction(), unregisterKeyboardAction()}, JMenu.setAccelerator(), JMenuItem.setAccelerator(), javax.swing.text.JTextComponent.KeyBinding.KeyBinding(), javax.swing.text.Keymap.{addActionForKeyStroke(), getAction(), isLocallyDefined(), removeKeyStrokeBinding()}

Returned By: JComponent.getRegisteredKeyStrokes(), JMenuItem.getAccelerator(), KeyStroke.{getKeyStroke(), getKeyStrokeForEvent()}, javax.swing.text.Keymap.{getBoundKeyStrokes(), getKeyStrokesForAction()}

Type Of: javax.swing.text.JTextComponent.KeyBinding.key

ListCellRenderer   Java 1.2

javax.swing

This interface defines the method that must be implemented by any object that wants to be able to render items in a JList component. Most applications can rely on the default behavior of JList (to use a DefaultListCellRenderer) and never need to implement or use this interface. getListCellRendererComponent() is passed information about the list item that is to be rendered; it should return a lightweight java.awt.Component capable of rendering the list item. The JList object first positions this component at the desired location by calling its setBounds() method and then asks the component to draw itself by calling paint(). Note, however, that the component is never actually added to the component hierarchy.

```
public abstract interface ListCellRenderer {
// Public Instance Methods
    public abstract Component getListCellRendererComponent(JList list, Object value, int index,
                                    boolean isSelected, boolean cellHasFocus);
}
```

Implementations: DefaultListCellRenderer

Passed To: JComboBox.setRenderer(), JList.setCellRenderer()

Returned By: JComboBox.getRenderer(), JList.getCellRenderer()

Type Of: JComboBox.renderer

ListModel

Java 1.2

javax.swing

model

This interface defines the methods that must be implemented by any object that wants to maintain a list of values for display in a JList or similar component. A ListModel must be able to return the size of the list, return any numbered element of the list, and fire a ListDataEvent event to any registered ListDataListener objects whenever the contents of the list changes. ListModel implementations that represent immutable lists can provide dummy no-op implementations of the event registration methods. Most applications do not need to implement this interface; they can work with JList directly or use the Default-ListModel class.

```
public abstract interface ListModel {
// Event Registration Methods (by event name)
    public abstract void addListDataListener(javax.swing.event.ListDataListener l);
    public abstract void removeListDataListener(javax.swing.event.ListDataListener l);
// Public Instance Methods
    public abstract Object getElementAt(int index);
    public abstract int getSize();
}
```

Implementations: AbstractListModel, ComboBoxModel

Passed To: JList.{JList(), setModel()}

Returned By: JList.getModel()

ListSelectionModel

Java 1.2

javax.swing

model

This interface defines the methods that an object must implement if it wants to keep track of the selection state for a JList, JTable, or similar component. Most applications use DefaultListSelectionModel and never have to implement this interface.

```
public abstract interface ListSelectionModel {
// Public Constants
    public static final int MULTIPLE_INTERVAL_SELECTION;                              =2
    public static final int SINGLE_INTERVAL_SELECTION;                               =1
    public static final int SINGLE_SELECTION;                                        =0
// Event Registration Methods (by event name)
    public abstract void addListSelectionListener(javax.swing.event.ListSelectionListener x);
    public abstract void removeListSelectionListener(javax.swing.event.ListSelectionListener x);
// Property Accessor Methods (by property name)
    public abstract int getAnchorSelectionIndex();
    public abstract void setAnchorSelectionIndex(int index);
    public abstract int getLeadSelectionIndex();
    public abstract void setLeadSelectionIndex(int index);
    public abstract int getMaxSelectionIndex();
    public abstract int getMinSelectionIndex();
    public abstract boolean isSelectionEmpty();
    public abstract int getSelectionMode();
    public abstract void setSelectionMode(int selectionMode);
    public abstract boolean getValueIsAdjusting();
    public abstract void setValueIsAdjusting(boolean valueIsAdjusting);
```

```
// Public Instance Methods
    public abstract void addSelectionInterval(int index0, int index1);
    public abstract void clearSelection();
    public abstract void insertIndexInterval(int index, int length, boolean before);
    public abstract boolean isSelectedIndex(int index);
    public abstract void removeIndexInterval(int index0, int index1);
    public abstract void removeSelectionInterval(int index0, int index1);
    public abstract void setSelectionInterval(int index0, int index1);
}
```

Implementations: DefaultListSelectionModel

Passed To: JList.setSelectionModel(), JTable.{JTable(), setSelectionModel()},
javax.swing.table.DefaultTableColumnModel.setSelectionModel(),
javax.swing.table.TableColumnModel.setSelectionModel()

Returned By: JList.{createSelectionModel(), getSelectionModel()}, JTable.{createDefaultSelectionModel(),
getSelectionModel()}, javax.swing.table.DefaultTableColumnModel.{createSelectionModel(),
getSelectionModel()}, javax.swing.table.TableColumnModel.getSelectionModel()

Type Of: JTable.selectionModel, javax.swing.table.DefaultTableColumnModel.selectionModel

LookAndFeel   Java 1.2

javax.swing

This abstract class defines the methods that a pluggable look-and-feel must implement.
It also defines some useful static convenience methods. Application programmers
should never have to use or subclass this class. If you are implementing a look-and-
feel, you have to subclass this class and define the abstract methods, of course. You
probably also want to override the default no-op initialize() and getDefaults() methods.
Finally, you have to provide implementations of all the abstract classes in javax.swing.plaf.

```
public abstract class LookAndFeel {
// Public Constructors
    public LookAndFeel();
// Public Class Methods
    public static void installBorder(JComponent c, String defaultBorderName);
    public static void installColors(JComponent c, String defaultBgName, String defaultFgName);
    public static void installColorsAndFont(JComponent c, String defaultBgName, String defaultFgName,
                                String defaultFontName);
    public static Object makeIcon(Class baseClass, String gifFile);
    public static javax.swing.text.JTextComponent.KeyBinding[ ] makeKeyBindings(Object[ ] keyBindingList);
    public static void uninstallBorder(JComponent c);
// Property Accessor Methods (by property name)
    public UIDefaults getDefaults();                                                  constant
    public abstract String getDescription();
    public abstract String getID();
    public abstract String getName();
    public abstract boolean isNativeLookAndFeel();
    public abstract boolean isSupportedLookAndFeel();
// Public Instance Methods
    public void initialize();                                                            empty
    public void uninitialize();                                                          empty
// Public Methods Overriding Object
    public String toString();
}
```

Passed To: UIManager.{addAuxiliaryLookAndFeel(), removeAuxiliaryLookAndFeel(), setLookAndFeel()}

Returned By: UIManager.{getAuxiliaryLookAndFeels(), getLookAndFeel()}

MenuElement

Java 1.2

javax.swing

This interface defines methods that all menu components must implement. The methods allow menu navigation and event handling to be performed in a standard way. Application programmers should never have to implement this interface or use the methods it defines, unless they want to place components other than JMenuItem and its subclasses into menus. See also MenuSelectionManager.

```
public abstract interface MenuElement {
// Public Instance Methods
    public abstract Component getComponent();
    public abstract MenuElement[ ] getSubElements();
    public abstract void menuSelectionChanged(boolean isIncluded);
    public abstract void processKeyEvent(java.awt.event.KeyEvent event, MenuElement[ ] path,
                                         MenuSelectionManager manager);
    public abstract void processMouseEvent(java.awt.event.MouseEvent event, MenuElement[ ] path,
                                           MenuSelectionManager manager);
}
```

Implementations: JMenu, JMenuBar, JMenuItem, JPopupMenu

Passed To: JMenuBar.{processKeyEvent(), processMouseEvent()}, JMenuItem.{processKeyEvent(), processMouseEvent()}, JPopupMenu.{processKeyEvent(), processMouseEvent()}, MenuElement.{processKeyEvent(), processMouseEvent()}, MenuSelectionManager.setSelectedPath(), javax.swing.event.MenuDragMouseEvent.MenuDragMouseEvent(), javax.swing.event.MenuKeyEvent.MenuKeyEvent()

Returned By: JMenu.getSubElements(), JMenuBar.getSubElements(), JMenuItem.getSubElements(), JPopupMenu.getSubElements(), MenuElement.getSubElements(), MenuSelectionManager.getSelectedPath(), javax.swing.event.MenuDragMouseEvent.getPath(), javax.swing.event.MenuKeyEvent.getPath()

MenuSelectionManager

Java 1.2

javax.swing

This class defines methods that manipulate hierarchies of menus. Application programmers do not need to use this class. There is only one instance of MenuSelectionManager, returned by the static defaultManager() method. Menu items rely on MenuSelectionManager for implementations of MenuElement methods, and MenuSelectionManager relies on the methods of the MenuElement interface to allow it to traverse menu hierarchies.

```
public class MenuSelectionManager {
// Public Constructors
    public MenuSelectionManager();
// Public Class Methods
    public static MenuSelectionManager defaultManager();
// Event Registration Methods (by event name)
    public void addChangeListener(javax.swing.event.ChangeListener l);
    public void removeChangeListener(javax.swing.event.ChangeListener l);
// Public Instance Methods
    public void clearSelectedPath();
    public Component componentForPoint(Component source, java.awt.Point sourcePoint);
    public MenuElement[ ] getSelectedPath();
    public boolean isComponentPartOfCurrentMenu(Component c);
    public void processKeyEvent(java.awt.event.KeyEvent e);
```

```
        public void processMouseEvent(java.awt.event.MouseEvent event);
        public void setSelectedPath(MenuElement[ ] path);
   // Protected Instance Methods
        protected void fireStateChanged();
   // Protected Instance Fields
        protected transient javax.swing.event.ChangeEvent changeEvent;
        protected javax.swing.event.EventListenerList listenerList;
   }
```

Passed To: JMenuBar.{processKeyEvent(), processMouseEvent()}, JMenuItem.{processKeyEvent(), processMouseEvent()}, JPopupMenu.{processKeyEvent(), processMouseEvent()}, MenuElement.{processKeyEvent(), processMouseEvent()}, javax.swing.event.MenuDragMouseEvent.MenuDragMouseEvent(), javax.swing.event.MenuKeyEvent.MenuKeyEvent()

Returned By: MenuSelectionManager.defaultManager(), javax.swing.event.MenuDragMouseEvent.getMenuSelectionManager(), javax.swing.event.MenuKeyEvent.getMenuSelectionManager()

MutableComboBoxModel   Java 1.2
javax.swing   *model*

This interface extends ComboBoxModel to add support for adding and removing elements from the list of choices displayed by a JComboBox. See also ComboBoxModel and Default-ComboBoxModel.

```
public abstract interface MutableComboBoxModel extends ComboBoxModel {
   // Public Instance Methods
        public abstract void addElement(Object obj);
        public abstract void insertElementAt(Object obj, int index);
        public abstract void removeElement(Object obj);
        public abstract void removeElementAt(int index);
   }
```

Hierarchy: (MutableComboBoxModel(ComboBoxModel(ListModel)))

Implementations: DefaultComboBoxModel

OverlayLayout   Java 1.2
javax.swing   *serializable layout manager*

This layout manager arranges the children of the container it manages so that the alignment points (specified with the setAlignmentX() and setAlignmentY() methods of JComponent) are on top of each other. This usually means that the children overlap. AbstractButton relies on this layout manager, but applications rarely use it.

```
public class OverlayLayout implements java.awt.LayoutManager2, Serializable {
   // Public Constructors
        public OverlayLayout(Container target);
   // Methods Implementing LayoutManager
        public void addLayoutComponent(String name, Component comp);              empty
        public void layoutContainer(Container target);
        public java.awt.Dimension minimumLayoutSize(Container target);
        public java.awt.Dimension preferredLayoutSize(Container target);
        public void removeLayoutComponent(Component comp);                        empty
   // Methods Implementing LayoutManager2
        public void addLayoutComponent(Component comp, Object constraints);       empty
        public float getLayoutAlignmentX(Container target);
```

```
    public float getLayoutAlignmentY(Container target);
    public void invalidateLayout(Container target);
    public java.awt.Dimension maximumLayoutSize(Container target);
}
```

Hierarchy: Object→ OverlayLayout(java.awt.LayoutManager2(java.awt.LayoutManager), Serializable)

ProgressMonitor   Java 1.2

javax.swing

This class implements a progress monitor. After creating a ProgressMonitor, a program periodically calls setProgress() to indicate its progress toward the completion of a task. Unless progress is quite rapid, the ProgressMonitor displays a dialog box that uses a JProgressBar to display progress to the user. Call setNote() to set the text to display in the dialog box. You can also specify a permanent title or heading for the dialog box with the second argument to the constructor. The ProgressMonitor dialog box automatically closes when the progress property reaches the value of the maximum property. If you want to close it before the task completes, call close().

ProgressMonitor suffers from an important flaw: if the user clicks the **Cancel** buttons in the dialog box, the dialog is dismissed. Unfortunately, the dialog does not fire any event to indicate that this has happened, so your program must call isCancelled() each time it calls setProgress(), to determine whether the user has requested that the operation be cancelled. A related flaw is that the dialog box contains an extraneous **Okay** button that behaves just like the **Cancel** button.

```
public class ProgressMonitor {
// Public Constructors
    public ProgressMonitor(Component parentComponent, Object message, String note, int min, int max);
// Property Accessor Methods (by property name)
    public boolean isCanceled();
    public int getMaximum();
    public void setMaximum(int m);
    public int getMillisToDecideToPopup();
    public void setMillisToDecideToPopup(int millisToDecideToPopup);
    public int getMillisToPopup();
    public void setMillisToPopup(int millisToPopup);
    public int getMinimum();
    public void setMinimum(int m);
    public String getNote();
    public void setNote(String note);
// Public Instance Methods
    public void close();
    public void setProgress(int nv);
}
```

Returned By: ProgressMonitorInputStream.getProgressMonitor()

ProgressMonitorInputStream   Java 1.2

javax.swing

This class combines a java.io.InputStream with a ProgressMonitor to display a program's progress in reading a stream. It is useful when reading a long file or when doing time-consuming processing on data from a shorter file. If the user clicks the **Cancel** button in the dialog, the next call to read data from the stream results in an InterruptedIOException. A ProgressMonitorInputStream can only be wrapped around a stream whose available() method returns the total remaining number of bytes in the stream, such as a java.io.FileInputStream. It does not work with java.io.PipedInputStream, for example.

```
public class ProgressMonitorInputStream extends java.io.FilterInputStream {
// Public Constructors
    public ProgressMonitorInputStream(Component parentComponent, Object message, java.io.InputStream in);
// Public Instance Methods
    public ProgressMonitor getProgressMonitor();
// Public Methods Overriding FilterInputStream
    public void close() throws java.io.IOException;
    public int read() throws java.io.IOException;
    public int read(byte[] b) throws java.io.IOException;
    public int read(byte[] b, int off, int len) throws java.io.IOException;
    public void reset() throws java.io.IOException;                                    synchronized
    public long skip(long n) throws java.io.IOException;
}
```

Hierarchy: Object→ java.io.InputStream→ java.io.FilterInputStream → ProgressMonitorInputStream

Renderer   Java 1.2

javax.swing

This interface defines the basic methods that must be implemented by any class that wants to render a value of some specified type on behalf of a general-purpose component, such as a JList. In practice, the setValue() method defined by this interface is underconstrained, and this interface is unused in the Swing API. Three interfaces, with more specialized methods, are used in its place: ListCellRenderer, javax.swing.table.TableCellRenderer and javax.swing.tree.TreeCellRenderer.

```
public abstract interface Renderer {
// Public Instance Methods
    public abstract Component getComponent();
    public abstract void setValue(Object aValue, boolean isSelected);
}
```

RepaintManager   Java 1.2

javax.swing

This class manages the repaint and relayout process for all Swing components in an application. It also provides a shared off-screen image for Swing components that perform double-buffering. RepaintManager is an integral part of the Swing GUI framework and is used extensively by JComponent internals. Applications rarely need to use it directly. If yours does, you can obtain the current RepaintManager with the static current-Manager() method.

```
public class RepaintManager {
// Public Constructors
    public RepaintManager();
// Public Class Methods
    public static RepaintManager currentManager(JComponent c);
    public static RepaintManager currentManager(Component c);
    public static void setCurrentManager(RepaintManager aRepaintManager);
// Property Accessor Methods (by property name)
    public boolean isDoubleBufferingEnabled();                                          default:true
    public void setDoubleBufferingEnabled(boolean aFlag);
    public java.awt.Dimension getDoubleBufferMaximumSize();
    public void setDoubleBufferMaximumSize(java.awt.Dimension d);
// Public Instance Methods
    public void addDirtyRegion(JComponent c, int x, int y, int w, int h);              synchronized
    public void addInvalidComponent(JComponent invalidComponent);                      synchronized
```

javax.swing

```
    public java.awt.Rectangle getDirtyRegion(JComponent aComponent);
    public java.awt.Image getOffscreenBuffer(Component c, int proposedWidth, int proposedHeight);
    public boolean isCompletelyDirty(JComponent aComponent);
    public void markCompletelyClean(JComponent aComponent);
    public void markCompletelyDirty(JComponent aComponent);
    public void paintDirtyRegions();
    public void removeInvalidComponent(JComponent component);                     synchronized
    public void validateInvalidComponents();
// Public Methods Overriding Object
    public String toString();                                                     synchronized
}
```

Passed To: RepaintManager.setCurrentManager()

Returned By: RepaintManager.currentManager()

RootPaneContainer   Java 1.2

javax.swing

This interface is implemented by all Swing window and applet classes that have a JRoot-Pane as their single child. It defines getRootPane() to return that JRootPane. It also defines other methods to return the various children of the JRootPane. getContentPane() is the most frequently used method of this interface: it returns the container to which children are added.

```
public abstract interface RootPaneContainer {
// Property Accessor Methods (by property name)
    public abstract Container getContentPane();
    public abstract void setContentPane(Container contentPane);
    public abstract Component getGlassPane();
    public abstract void setGlassPane(Component glassPane);
    public abstract JLayeredPane getLayeredPane();
    public abstract void setLayeredPane(JLayeredPane layeredPane);
    public abstract JRootPane getRootPane();
}
```

Implementations: JApplet, JDialog, JFrame, JInternalFrame, JWindow

Scrollable   Java 1.2

javax.swing

This interface defines methods that should be implemented by any component that is likely to be placed within a JScrollPane or similar scrolling container. A JScrollPane can provide more intelligent scrolling services for a Scrollable component than for a non-Scrollable component.

```
public abstract interface Scrollable {
// Public Instance Methods
    public abstract java.awt.Dimension getPreferredScrollableViewportSize();
    public abstract int getScrollableBlockIncrement(java.awt.Rectangle visibleRect, int orientation, int direction);
    public abstract boolean getScrollableTracksViewportHeight();
    public abstract boolean getScrollableTracksViewportWidth();
    public abstract int getScrollableUnitIncrement(java.awt.Rectangle visibleRect, int orientation, int direction);
}
```

Implementations: JList, JTable, JTree, javax.swing.text.JTextComponent

ScrollPaneConstants
Java 1.2

javax.swing

This interface defines constants used by JScrollPane and ScrollPaneLayout. The int constants are the most interesting ones. They are the legal values for the setHorizontalScrollBarPolicy() and setVerticalScrollBarPolicy() methods of JScrollPane.

```
public abstract interface ScrollPaneConstants {
// Public Constants
   public static final String COLUMN_HEADER;                      ="COLUMN_HEADER"
   public static final String HORIZONTAL_SCROLLBAR;          ="HORIZONTAL_SCROLLBAR"
   public static final int HORIZONTAL_SCROLLBAR_ALWAYS;                       =32
   public static final int HORIZONTAL_SCROLLBAR_AS_NEEDED;                    =30
   public static final int HORIZONTAL_SCROLLBAR_NEVER;                        =31
   public static final String HORIZONTAL_SCROLLBAR_POLICY;  ="HORIZONTAL_SCROLLBAR_POLICY"
   public static final String LOWER_LEFT_CORNER;              ="LOWER_LEFT_CORNER"
   public static final String LOWER_RIGHT_CORNER;            ="LOWER_RIGHT_CORNER"
   public static final String ROW_HEADER;                            ="ROW_HEADER"
   public static final String UPPER_LEFT_CORNER;              ="UPPER_LEFT_CORNER"
   public static final String UPPER_RIGHT_CORNER;            ="UPPER_RIGHT_CORNER"
   public static final String VERTICAL_SCROLLBAR;              ="VERTICAL_SCROLLBAR"
   public static final int VERTICAL_SCROLLBAR_ALWAYS;                         =22
   public static final int VERTICAL_SCROLLBAR_AS_NEEDED;                      =20
   public static final int VERTICAL_SCROLLBAR_NEVER;                          =21
   public static final String VERTICAL_SCROLLBAR_POLICY;    ="VERTICAL_SCROLLBAR_POLICY"
   public static final String VIEWPORT;                                ="VIEWPORT"
}
```

Implementations: JScrollPane, ScrollPaneLayout

ScrollPaneLayout
Java 1.2

javax.swing
serializable layout manager

This class is the layout manager used by JScrollPane. It arranges up to nine components: the JViewport that contains the component being scrolled, the horizontal and vertical scrollbars, the column and row header components, and up to four small corner components. Applications typically use JScrollPane directly and do not have to use this class.

```
public class ScrollPaneLayout implements java.awt.LayoutManager, ScrollPaneConstants, Serializable {
// Public Constructors
   public ScrollPaneLayout();
// Inner Classes
   public static class UIResource extends ScrollPaneLayout implements javax.swing.plaf.UIResource;
// Property Accessor Methods (by property name)
   public JViewport getColumnHeader();                                  default:null
   public JScrollBar getHorizontalScrollBar();                          default:null
   public int getHorizontalScrollBarPolicy();                           default:30
   public void setHorizontalScrollBarPolicy(int x);
   public JViewport getRowHeader();                                     default:null
   public JScrollBar getVerticalScrollBar();                            default:null
   public int getVerticalScrollBarPolicy();                             default:20
   public void setVerticalScrollBarPolicy(int x);
   public JViewport getViewport();                                      default:null
// Public Instance Methods
   public Component getCorner(String key);
   public void syncWithScrollPane(JScrollPane sp);
// Methods Implementing LayoutManager
   public void addLayoutComponent(String s, Component c);
   public void layoutContainer(Container parent);
```

javax.swing

```
        public java.awt.Dimension minimumLayoutSize(Container parent);
        public java.awt.Dimension preferredLayoutSize(Container parent);
        public void removeLayoutComponent(Component c);
// Protected Instance Methods
        protected Component addSingletonComponent(Component oldC, Component newC);
// Protected Instance Fields
        protected JViewport colHead;
        protected JScrollBar hsb;
        protected int hsbPolicy;
        protected Component lowerLeft;
        protected Component lowerRight;
        protected JViewport rowHead;
        protected Component upperLeft;
        protected Component upperRight;
        protected JViewport viewport;
        protected JScrollBar vsb;
        protected int vsbPolicy;
// Deprecated Public Methods
#       public java.awt.Rectangle getViewportBorderBounds(JScrollPane scrollpane);
}
```

Hierarchy: Object→ ScrollPaneLayout(java.awt.LayoutManager, ScrollPaneConstants, Serializable)

Subclasses: ScrollPaneLayout.UIResource

ScrollPaneLayout.UIResource   Java 1.2

javax.swing   *serializable layout manager*

This class is a trivial subclass of ScrollPaneLayout that implements the UIResource marker
interface. It is used only by look-and-feel implementations.

```
public static class ScrollPaneLayout.UIResource extends ScrollPaneLayout
        implements javax.swing.plaf.UIResource {
// Public Constructors
    public UIResource();
}
```

SingleSelectionModel   Java 1.2

javax.swing   *model*

This interface defines the methods that must be implemented by a class that wants to
keep track of a single selected item for a JTabbedPane, JMenuBar, JPopupMenu, or similar
component. Applications do not often implement this interface. Instead, they rely on
the DefaultSingleSelectionModel class, which is the default model for components that
allow a single selected item.

```
public abstract interface SingleSelectionModel {
// Event Registration Methods (by event name)
    public abstract void addChangeListener(javax.swing.event.ChangeListener listener);
    public abstract void removeChangeListener(javax.swing.event.ChangeListener listener);
// Public Instance Methods
    public abstract void clearSelection();
    public abstract int getSelectedIndex();
    public abstract boolean isSelected();
    public abstract void setSelectedIndex(int index);
}
```

Implementations: DefaultSingleSelectionModel

Passed To: JMenuBar.setSelectionModel(), JPopupMenu.setSelectionModel(), JTabbedPane.setModel()

Returned By: JMenuBar.getSelectionModel(), JPopupMenu.getSelectionModel(), JTabbedPane.getModel()

Type Of: JTabbedPane.model

SizeRequirements

Java 1.2

javax.swing

serializable

This class exists for the convenience of layout managers. It is used internally by BoxLayout and OverlayLayout. Application programmers should not need to use it. Component developers writing custom layout managers may find it useful.

```
public class SizeRequirements implements Serializable {
// Public Constructors
    public SizeRequirements();
    public SizeRequirements(int min, int pref, int max, float a);
// Public Class Methods
    public static int[ ] adjustSizes(int delta, SizeRequirements[ ] children);
    public static void calculateAlignedPositions(int allocated, SizeRequirements total, SizeRequirements[ ] children,
                                    int[ ] offsets, int[ ] spans);
    public static void calculateTiledPositions(int allocated, SizeRequirements total, SizeRequirements[ ] children,
                                    int[ ] offsets, int[ ] spans);
    public static SizeRequirements getAlignedSizeRequirements(SizeRequirements[ ] children);
    public static SizeRequirements getTiledSizeRequirements(SizeRequirements[ ] children);
// Public Methods Overriding Object
    public String toString();
// Public Instance Fields
    public float alignment;
    public int maximum;
    public int minimum;
    public int preferred;
}
```

Hierarchy: Object→ SizeRequirements(Serializable)

Passed To: Too many methods to list.

Returned By: SizeRequirements.{getAlignedSizeRequirements(), getTiledSizeRequirements()}, javax.swing.text.BoxView.{baselineRequirements(), calculateMajorAxisRequirements(), calculateMinorAxisRequirements()}, javax.swing.text.ParagraphView.calculateMinorAxisRequirements(), javax.swing.text.TableView.calculateMinorAxisRequirements(), javax.swing.text.html.BlockView.{calculateMajorAxisRequirements(), calculateMinorAxisRequirements()}, javax.swing.text.html.ParagraphView.calculateMinorAxisRequirements()

SwingConstants

Java 1.2

javax.swing

This interface defines a number of constants used throughout the Swing API to specify component positions and orientations.

```
public abstract interface SwingConstants {
// Public Constants
    public static final int BOTTOM;                                                      =3
    public static final int CENTER;                                                      =0
    public static final int EAST;                                                        =3
    public static final int HORIZONTAL;                                                  =0
    public static final int LEADING;                                                     =10
    public static final int LEFT;                                                        =2
    public static final int NORTH;                                                       =1
```

javax.swing

```
    public static final int NORTH_EAST;                                           =2
    public static final int NORTH_WEST;                                           =8
    public static final int RIGHT;                                                =4
    public static final int SOUTH;                                                =5
    public static final int SOUTH_EAST;                                           =4
    public static final int SOUTH_WEST;                                           =6
    public static final int TOP;                                                  =1
    public static final int TRAILING;                                            =11
    public static final int VERTICAL;                                             =1
    public static final int WEST;                                                 =7
}
```

Implementations: AbstractButton, JCheckBoxMenuItem, JLabel, JProgressBar, JSeparator, JSlider, JTabbedPane, JTextField, JToolBar, SwingUtilities, javax.swing.text.View

SwingUtilities   Java 1.2

javax.swing

This class defines a variety of static methods that are useful in Swing applications. Highlights include:

invokeLater(), invokeAndWait()

Place the specified Runnable object on the event queue, so that its run() method is invoked (later) from the event dispatch thread. invokeLater() returns immediately; invokeAndWait() blocks until the run() method has run. Since Swing is not generally thread safe, these methods are useful when you need to update the GUI from a thread that is not the event dispatch thread.

isEventDispatchThread()

Determines whether the current thread is the event dispatch thread.

updateComponentTreeUI()

Traverses the entire component tree rooted at the specified component and asks each component to update its UI delegate. This method is useful after you have changed the pluggable look-and-feel of a running application.

isLeftMouseButton(), isMiddleMouseButton(), isRightMouseButton()

Determine whether a specified MouseEvent involves the left, middle, or right mouse button. For portability reasons, this information is encoded in the modifiers property that the MouseEvent inherits. These methods simplify access to it.

getAncestorOfClass()

Given a component and a component class, this method searches the ancestors of the component until it finds one of the specified class. getRoot(), getRootPane(), windowForComponent(), and getAncestorNamed() are related methods.

```
public class SwingUtilities implements SwingConstants {
// No Constructor
// Public Class Methods
    public static java.awt.Rectangle[ ] computeDifference(java.awt.Rectangle rectA, java.awt.Rectangle rectB);
    public static java.awt.Rectangle computeIntersection(int x, int y, int width, int height, java.awt.Rectangle dest);
    public static int computeStringWidth(java.awt.FontMetrics fm, String str);
    public static java.awt.Rectangle computeUnion(int x, int y, int width, int height, java.awt.Rectangle dest);
    public static java.awt.event.MouseEvent convertMouseEvent(Component source,
                                        java.awt.event.MouseEvent sourceEvent,
                                        Component destination);
```

```
    public static java.awt.Point convertPoint(Component source, java.awt.Point aPoint, Component destination);
    public static java.awt.Point convertPoint(Component source, int x, int y, Component destination);
    public static void convertPointFromScreen(java.awt.Point p, Component c);
    public static void convertPointToScreen(java.awt.Point p, Component c);
    public static java.awt.Rectangle convertRectangle(Component source, java.awt.Rectangle aRectangle,
                                                     Component destination);
    public static Component findFocusOwner(Component c);
    public static Accessible getAccessibleAt(Component c, java.awt.Point p);
    public static Accessible getAccessibleChild(Component c, int i);
    public static int getAccessibleChildrenCount(Component c);
    public static int getAccessibleIndexInParent(Component c);
    public static AccessibleStateSet getAccessibleStateSet(Component c);
    public static Container getAncestorNamed(String name, Component comp);
    public static Container getAncestorOfClass(Class c, Component comp);
    public static Component getDeepestComponentAt(Component parent, int x, int y);
    public static java.awt.Rectangle getLocalBounds(Component aComponent);
    public static Component getRoot(Component c);
    public static JRootPane getRootPane(Component c);
    public static void invokeAndWait(Runnable doRun) throws InterruptedException,
        java.lang.reflect.InvocationTargetException;
    public static void invokeLater(Runnable doRun);
    public static boolean isDescendingFrom(Component a, Component b);
    public static boolean isEventDispatchThread();
    public static boolean isLeftMouseButton(java.awt.event.MouseEvent anEvent);
    public static boolean isMiddleMouseButton(java.awt.event.MouseEvent anEvent);
    public static final boolean isRectangleContainingRectangle(java.awt.Rectangle a, java.awt.Rectangle b);
    public static boolean isRightMouseButton(java.awt.event.MouseEvent anEvent);
    public static String layoutCompoundLabel(java.awt.FontMetrics fm, String text, Icon icon, int verticalAlignment,
                                int horizontalAlignment, int verticalTextPosition,
                                int horizontalTextPosition, java.awt.Rectangle viewR,
                                java.awt.Rectangle iconR, java.awt.Rectangle textR, int textIconGap);
    public static String layoutCompoundLabel(JComponent c, java.awt.FontMetrics fm, String text, Icon icon,
                                int verticalAlignment, int horizontalAlignment, int verticalTextPosition,
                                int horizontalTextPosition, java.awt.Rectangle viewR,
                                java.awt.Rectangle iconR, java.awt.Rectangle textR, int textIconGap);
    public static void paintComponent(java.awt.Graphics g, Component c, Container p, java.awt.Rectangle r);
    public static void paintComponent(java.awt.Graphics g, Component c, Container p, int x, int y, int w, int h);
    public static void updateComponentTreeUI(Component c);
    public static java.awt.Window windowForComponent(Component aComponent);
}
```

Hierarchy: Object→ SwingUtilities(SwingConstants)

Timer   Java 1.2
javax.swing   *serializable*

This utility class fires an ActionEvent to a list of registered ActionListener objects after a specified period of time has elapsed. Optionally, it may continue to fire action events at specified time intervals. This class is useful for triggering delayed or repeated actions, such as animations. After creating a Timer object, adding one or more ActionListener objects, and setting any necessary properties, call start() to make the Timer object start timing and firing events. If you have configured the Timer to fire events repeatedly, use the stop() method when you want the events to stop.

The initialDelay property specifies the time in milliseconds between the invocation of the start() method and the firing of the first ActionEvent. The repeats property specifies whether the Timer fires events repeatedly. If repeats is true, the delay property specifies the interval (in milliseconds) between repeated events. If the delay property is set to a short interval or if the ActionEvent triggers a complex action, the Timer may sometimes get behind and develop a backlog of events. Set the coalesce property to true if the Timer is allowed to coalesce multiple pending events into a single ActionEvent in this situation. The Timer constructor sets the repeats and coalesce properties to true, so be sure to change these properties if you don't want that behavior. The constructor also sets both the delay and initialDelay properties to the specified interval. The static setLogTimers() method is useful when debugging code that uses the Timer class. Passing true to this method causes Timer to print a debugging message to standard output each time it fires an event.

```
public class Timer implements Serializable {
// Public Constructors
    public Timer(int delay, java.awt.event.ActionListener listener);
// Public Class Methods
    public static boolean getLogTimers();
    public static void setLogTimers(boolean flag);
// Event Registration Methods (by event name)
    public void addActionListener(java.awt.event.ActionListener listener);
    public void removeActionListener(java.awt.event.ActionListener listener);
// Property Accessor Methods (by property name)
    public boolean isCoalesce();
    public void setCoalesce(boolean flag);
    public int getDelay();
    public void setDelay(int delay);
    public int getInitialDelay();
    public void setInitialDelay(int initialDelay);
    public boolean isRepeats();
    public void setRepeats(boolean flag);
    public boolean isRunning();
// Public Instance Methods
    public void restart();
    public void start();
    public void stop();
// Protected Instance Methods
    protected void fireActionPerformed(java.awt.event.ActionEvent e);
// Protected Instance Fields
    protected javax.swing.event.EventListenerList listenerList;
}
```

Hierarchy: Object→ Timer(Serializable)

Type Of: javax.swing.tree.DefaultTreeCellEditor.timer

ToolTipManager   Java 1.2

javax.swing

This class manages tooltips for a Swing application. There is only one ToolTipManager per application; you can obtain a reference to it with the static sharedInstance() method. Any Swing component that has a tooltip set on it (with setToolTipText()) is automatically registered with the ToolTipManager, so applications do not usually have to work with this class explicitly. If you want to explicitly register or unregister a component without setting its tooltip text, you can do so with registerComponent() and unregisterComponent(), respectively.

To disable all tooltips in an application (at the request of an advanced user, for example), set the enabled property to false. The other ToolTipManager properties are various delays that affect the behavior of tooltips. These values are user preferences, and an application should not modify them except in response to an explicit user request made through some kind of preferences dialog or control panel.

```
public class ToolTipManager extends java.awt.event.MouseAdapter implements java.awt.event.MouseMotionListener {
// No Constructor
// Inner Classes
    protected class insideTimerAction implements java.awt.event.ActionListener;
    protected class outsideTimerAction implements java.awt.event.ActionListener;
    protected class stillInsideTimerAction implements java.awt.event.ActionListener;
// Public Class Methods
    public static ToolTipManager sharedInstance();
// Property Accessor Methods (by property name)
    public int getDismissDelay();
    public void setDismissDelay(int microSeconds);
    public boolean isEnabled();
    public void setEnabled(boolean flag);
    public int getInitialDelay();
    public void setInitialDelay(int microSeconds);
    public boolean isLightWeightPopupEnabled();
    public int getReshowDelay();
    public void setReshowDelay(int microSeconds);
// Public Instance Methods
    public void registerComponent(JComponent component);
    public void unregisterComponent(JComponent component);
// Methods Implementing MouseMotionListener
    public void mouseDragged(java.awt.event.MouseEvent event);                              empty
    public void mouseMoved(java.awt.event.MouseEvent event);
// Public Methods Overriding MouseAdapter
    public void mouseEntered(java.awt.event.MouseEvent event);
    public void mouseExited(java.awt.event.MouseEvent event);
    public void mousePressed(java.awt.event.MouseEvent event);
// Protected Instance Fields
    protected boolean heavyWeightPopupEnabled;
    protected boolean lightWeightPopupEnabled;
// Deprecated Public Methods
#   public void setLightWeightPopupEnabled(boolean aFlag);
}
```

Hierarchy: Object → java.awt.event.MouseAdapter(java.awt.event.MouseListener(java.util.EventListener)) → ToolTipManager(java.awt.event.MouseMotionListener(java.util.EventListener))

Returned By: ToolTipManager.sharedInstance()

ToolTipManager.insideTimerAction

Java 1.2

javax.swing

This protected inner class is used internally by ToolTipManager. Applications never need to use it, and it probably should not be part of the public API.

```
protected class ToolTipManager.insideTimerAction implements java.awt.event.ActionListener {
// Protected Constructors
    protected insideTimerAction();
// Methods Implementing ActionListener
    public void actionPerformed(java.awt.event.ActionEvent e);
}
```

ToolTipManager.outsideTimerAction

Java 1.2

javax.swing

This protected inner class is used internally by ToolTipManager. Applications never need to use it, and it probably should not be part of the public API.

```
protected class ToolTipManager.outsideTimerAction implements java.awt.event.ActionListener {
// Protected Constructors
    protected outsideTimerAction();
// Methods Implementing ActionListener
    public void actionPerformed(java.awt.event.ActionEvent e);
}
```

ToolTipManager.stillInsideTimerAction   Java 1.2

javax.swing

This protected inner class is used internally by ToolTipManager. Applications never need
to use it, and it probably should not be part of the public API.

```
protected class ToolTipManager.stillInsideTimerAction implements java.awt.event.ActionListener {
// Protected Constructors
    protected stillInsideTimerAction();
// Methods Implementing ActionListener
    public void actionPerformed(java.awt.event.ActionEvent e);
}
```

UIDefaults   Java 1.2

javax.swing   *cloneable serializable collection*

UIDefaults is a Hashtable subclass used to maintain a table of named resources for use by
a look-and-feel implementation. Like any hashtable, UIDefaults defines a get() and a put()
method. In addition, it defines numerous more specific getXXX() *methods that are used to look up
resources of specific types. Unless you are defining a custom look-and-feel, you probably do not have to use this class
explicitly.*

The generic get() method and all the more specific methods that use it have a special
behavior if the returned resource value implements either of the inner interfaces
defined by UIDefaults. If the returned object is a UIDefaults.ActiveValue, the value returned
by the get() method is computed by calling the createValue() method of the ActiveValue
object. Similarly, if the returned value is a LazyValue, the final return value of the get()
method is computed by calling the createValue() method of the LazyValue object. Once
this computation is done the first time, however, the LazyValue is replaced in the UIDefaults table with the computed value it yielded. This is a useful technique for resources
such as icons that have to be read in from external files. It prevents them from being
created unless they are actually needed.

```
public class UIDefaults extends java.util.Hashtable {
// Public Constructors
    public UIDefaults();
    public UIDefaults(Object[ ] keyValueList);
// Inner Classes
    public abstract static interface ActiveValue;
    public abstract static interface LazyValue;
// Event Registration Methods (by event name)
    public void addPropertyChangeListener(java.beans.PropertyChangeListener listener);          synchronized
    public void removePropertyChangeListener(java.beans.PropertyChangeListener listener);       synchronized
// Public Instance Methods
    public javax.swing.border.Border getBorder(Object key);
    public java.awt.Color getColor(Object key);
    public java.awt.Dimension getDimension(Object key);
    public java.awt.Font getFont(Object key);
    public Icon getIcon(Object key);
    public java.awt.Insets getInsets(Object key);
```

```
    public int getInt(Object key);
    public String getString(Object key);
    public javax.swing.plaf.ComponentUI getUI(JComponent target);
    public Class getUIClass(String uiClassID);
    public Class getUIClass(String uiClassID, ClassLoader uiClassLoader);
    public void putDefaults(Object[ ] keyValueList);
// Public Methods Overriding Hashtable
    public Object get(Object key);
    public Object put(Object key, Object value);
// Protected Instance Methods
    protected void firePropertyChange(String propertyName, Object oldValue, Object newValue);
    protected void getUIError(String msg);
}
```

Hierarchy: Object→ java.util.Dictionary→ java.util.Hashtable(Cloneable, java.util.Map, Serializable)→ UIDefaults

Passed To: UIDefaults.ActiveValue.createValue(), UIDefaults.LazyValue.createValue()

Returned By: LookAndFeel.getDefaults(), UIManager.{getDefaults(), getLookAndFeelDefaults()}

UIDefaults.ActiveValue   Java 1.2

javax.swing

This interface defines a special kind of resource that can be stored in a UIDefaults hashtable. When the get() method of UIDefaults finds a ActiveValue in the table, it does not return the ActiveValue object. Instead, it invokes its createValue() method and returns the object returned by that method.

```
public abstract static interface UIDefaults.ActiveValue {
// Public Instance Methods
    public abstract Object createValue(UIDefaults table);
}
```

UIDefaults.LazyValue   Java 1.2

javax.swing

This interface defines a special kind of resource that can be stored in a UIDefaults hashtable. When the get() method of UIDefaults finds an LazyValue in the table, it does not return the LazyValue object. Instead, it invokes its createValue() method. The object returned by createValue() is used to replace the LazyValue in the UIDefaults table and is then returned by the get() method.

```
public abstract static interface UIDefaults.LazyValue {
// Public Instance Methods
    public abstract Object createValue(UIDefaults table);
}
```

UIManager   Java 1.2

javax.swing   *serializable*

The static methods of this class perform a number of look-and-feel related functions. setLookAndFeel() is the most important. It takes a LookAndFeel object or the class name of the desired look-and-feel and makes it the current look-and-feel. getLookAndFeel() returns the LookAndFeel object that represents the current look-and-feel. getCrossPlatformLookAnd-FeelClassName() and getSystemLookAndFeelClassName() return class names for the default Java look-and-feel and for the look-and-feel that mimics the native platform look-and-feel, if one exists. getInstalledLookAndFeels() returns information about all look-and-feels that are installed on the system.

The UIManager also manages user interface defaults specified both by the current look-and-feel and by the application. The get() method looks up a value for the named key, checking the table of application defaults first and then checking the defaults specified by the look-and-feel. The put() method inserts a new key/value binding into the application defaults table; it does not modify the look-and-feel defaults. UIManager defines various other type-specific getXXX() *methods that can be used to look up default UI resources of various types.*

Although all the methods of UIManager are static, they are implemented in such a way that each separate application context can independently set its own look-and-feel defaults. This means, for example, that multiple applets running in the same Java VM can install and use different look-and-feel implementations.

```
public class UIManager implements Serializable {
// Public Constructors
    public UIManager();
// Inner Classes
    public static class LookAndFeelInfo;
// Public Class Methods
    public static void addAuxiliaryLookAndFeel(LookAndFeel laf);
    public static void addPropertyChangeListener(java.beans.PropertyChangeListener listener);
    public static Object get(Object key);
    public static LookAndFeel[ ] getAuxiliaryLookAndFeels();
    public static javax.swing.border.Border getBorder(Object key);
    public static java.awt.Color getColor(Object key);
    public static String getCrossPlatformLookAndFeelClassName();
    public static UIDefaults getDefaults();
    public static java.awt.Dimension getDimension(Object key);
    public static java.awt.Font getFont(Object key);
    public static Icon getIcon(Object key);
    public static java.awt.Insets getInsets(Object key);
    public static UIManager.LookAndFeelInfo[ ] getInstalledLookAndFeels();
    public static int getInt(Object key);
    public static LookAndFeel getLookAndFeel();
    public static UIDefaults getLookAndFeelDefaults();
    public static String getString(Object key);
    public static String getSystemLookAndFeelClassName();
    public static javax.swing.plaf.ComponentUI getUI(JComponent target);
    public static void installLookAndFeel(UIManager.LookAndFeelInfo info);
    public static void installLookAndFeel(String name, String className);
    public static Object put(Object key, Object value);
    public static boolean removeAuxiliaryLookAndFeel(LookAndFeel laf);
    public static void removePropertyChangeListener(java.beans.PropertyChangeListener listener);
    public static void setInstalledLookAndFeels(UIManager.LookAndFeelInfo[ ] infos) throws SecurityException;
    public static void setLookAndFeel(LookAndFeel newLookAndFeel) throws UnsupportedLookAndFeelException;
    public static void setLookAndFeel(String className) throws ClassNotFoundException, InstantiationException,
        IllegalAccessException;
}
```

Hierarchy: Object → UIManager(Serializable)

UIManager.LookAndFeelInfo   Java 1.2

javax.swing

Instances of this class are returned by the getInstalledLookAndFeels() method of UIManager. The getName() method of each LookAndFeelInfo provides a simple human-presentable name that can be displayed to the user in a list or menu that allows the user to choose a look-and-feel.

```
public static class UIManager.LookAndFeelInfo {
// Public Constructors
    public LookAndFeelInfo(String name, String className);
// Public Instance Methods
    public String getClassName();
    public String getName();
// Public Methods Overriding Object
    public String toString();
}
```

Passed To: UIManager.{installLookAndFeel(), setInstalledLookAndFeels()}

Returned By: UIManager.getInstalledLookAndFeels()

UnsupportedLookAndFeelException   Java 1.2

javax.swing   *serializable checked*

Thrown by the setLookAndFeel() method of the UIManager class to indicate that the requested look-and-feel is not installed, not supported, or not licensed on the current system.

```
public class UnsupportedLookAndFeelException extends Exception {
// Public Constructors
    public UnsupportedLookAndFeelException(String s);
}
```

Hierarchy: Object→ Throwable(Serializable)→ Exception→ UnsupportedLookAndFeelException

Thrown By: UIManager.setLookAndFeel()

ViewportLayout   Java 1.2

javax.swing   *serializable layout manager*

This class is the default LayoutManager for the JViewport component. Applications should never need to use this class explicitly.

```
public class ViewportLayout implements java.awt.LayoutManager, Serializable {
// Public Constructors
    public ViewportLayout();
// Methods Implementing LayoutManager
    public void addLayoutComponent(String name, Component c);                    empty
    public void layoutContainer(Container parent);
    public java.awt.Dimension minimumLayoutSize(Container parent);
    public java.awt.Dimension preferredLayoutSize(Container parent);
    public void removeLayoutComponent(Component c);                             empty
}
```

Hierarchy: Object→ ViewportLayout(java.awt.LayoutManager, Serializable)

WindowConstants   Java 1.2

javax.swing

This interface defines three constants that describe possible actions that can be taken when the user requests that a window be closed. These three constants are the legal arguments to the setDefaultCloseOperation() methods of JFrame, JInternalFrame, and JDialog. Note that setDefaultCloseOperation() specifies only the default action when the user tries to close the window. An application that registers a WindowListener object can augment this default operation with one of its own.

```
public abstract interface WindowConstants {
// Public Constants
   public static final int DISPOSE_ON_CLOSE;                                =2
   public static final int DO_NOTHING_ON_CLOSE;                             =0
   public static final int HIDE_ON_CLOSE;                                   =1
}
```

Implementations: JDialog, JFrame, JInternalFrame

CHAPTER 24

The javax.swing.border Package

The javax.swing.border package is a simple package that defines the Border interface, which specifies how to draw a border around an arbitrary Swing component. The various classes in this package implement commonly used border styles. Applications can easily define custom border styles by creating custom implementations of Border. Figure 24-1 shows the class hierarchy of this package.

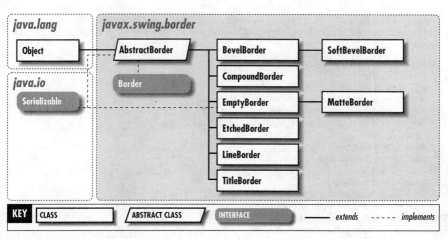

Figure 24-1: The javax.swing.border package

AbstractBorder   Java 1.2

javax.swing.border   *serializable*

This abstract class implements a zero-width, nonopaque border. AbstractBorder implements the Border interface. To create a custom border type, subclass AbstractBorder, reimplementing at least the getBorderInsets() and paintBorder() methods. getInteriorRectangle() in its static and nonstatic versions is a convenience method that returns a rectangle that represents the region of the component inside the border.

AbstractBorder provides a two-argument version of getBorderInsets(), in addition to the one-argument version required by Border. The two-argument version should place the insets in the supplied Insets object. Doing so does not require a new Insets object to be created, so it is more efficient than the one-argument version. Swing components use this more efficient method whenever possible.

```
public abstract class AbstractBorder implements Border, Serializable {
// Public Constructors
    public AbstractBorder();
// Public Class Methods
    public static java.awt.Rectangle getInteriorRectangle(Component c, Border b, int x, int y, int width, int height);
// Public Instance Methods
    public java.awt.Insets getBorderInsets(Component c, java.awt.Insets insets);
    public java.awt.Rectangle getInteriorRectangle(Component c, int x, int y, int width, int height);
// Methods Implementing Border
    public java.awt.Insets getBorderInsets(Component c);
    public boolean isBorderOpaque();                                                    constant
    public void paintBorder(Component c, java.awt.Graphics g, int x, int y, int width, int height);   empty
}
```

Hierarchy: Object→ AbstractBorder(Border, Serializable)

Subclasses: BevelBorder, CompoundBorder, EmptyBorder, EtchedBorder, LineBorder, TitledBorder

BevelBorder   Java 1.2

javax.swing.border   *serializable*

This class displays a two-pixel-wide beveled edge around a Swing component, giving the appearance of a raised or lowered surface. The RAISED and LOWERED constants specify the type of bevel. It usually is not necessary to specify bevel colors, as appropriate defaults are derived from the component background color. See also the createBevelBorder(), createLoweredBevelBorder(), and createRaisedBevelBorder() methods of javax.swing.BorderFactory.

```
public class BevelBorder extends AbstractBorder {
// Public Constructors
    public BevelBorder(int bevelType);
    public BevelBorder(int bevelType, java.awt.Color highlight, java.awt.Color shadow);
    public BevelBorder(int bevelType, java.awt.Color highlightOuter, java.awt.Color highlightInner,
                       java.awt.Color shadowOuter, java.awt.Color shadowInner);
// Public Constants
    public static final int LOWERED;                                                   =1
    public static final int RAISED;                                                    =0
// Public Instance Methods
    public int getBevelType();
    public java.awt.Color getHighlightInnerColor(Component c);
    public java.awt.Color getHighlightOuterColor(Component c);
    public java.awt.Color getShadowInnerColor(Component c);
    public java.awt.Color getShadowOuterColor(Component c);
// Public Methods Overriding AbstractBorder
    public java.awt.Insets getBorderInsets(Component c);
    public java.awt.Insets getBorderInsets(Component c, java.awt.Insets insets);
    public boolean isBorderOpaque();                                                   constant
    public void paintBorder(Component c, java.awt.Graphics g, int x, int y, int width, int height);
```

```
// Protected Instance Methods
    protected void paintLoweredBevel(Component c, java.awt.Graphics g, int x, int y, int width, int height);
    protected void paintRaisedBevel(Component c, java.awt.Graphics g, int x, int y, int width, int height);
// Protected Instance Fields
    protected int bevelType;
    protected java.awt.Color highlightInner;
    protected java.awt.Color highlightOuter;
    protected java.awt.Color shadowInner;
    protected java.awt.Color shadowOuter;
}
```

Hierarchy: Object→ AbstractBorder(Border, Serializable)→ BevelBorder

Subclasses: SoftBevelBorder, javax.swing.plaf.BorderUIResource.BevelBorderUIResource

Border
javax.swing.border

Java 1.2

This simple interface defines the methods that must be implemented by any object that wants to display a border around a Swing component. getBorderInsets() returns a java.awt.Insets object that specifies the size of each edge of the border. isBorderOpaque() indicates either that the border is opaque or that it allows the container background to show through. Opaque borders are required to paint all pixels in the border region. Finally, paintBorder() is the method that is responsible for drawing the border around the specified component at the specified location, using the specified java.awt.Graphics object.

The javax.swing.border package contains a number of Border implementations that are useful with Swing classes. Note, however, that Border instances are intended to be shared among components. This means that you typically should obtain references to shared Border objects by calling the static factory methods of javax.swing.BorderFactory. To define your own custom type of border, you can subclass AbstractBorder.

```
public abstract interface Border {
// Public Instance Methods
    public abstract java.awt.Insets getBorderInsets(Component c);
    public abstract boolean isBorderOpaque();
    public abstract void paintBorder(Component c, java.awt.Graphics g, int x, int y, int width, int height);
}
```

Implementations: AbstractBorder, javax.swing.plaf.BorderUIResource

Passed To: Too many methods to list.

Returned By: Too many methods to list.

Type Of: DefaultListCellRenderer.noFocusBorder, CompoundBorder.{insideBorder, outsideBorder}, TitledBorder.border, javax.swing.table.DefaultTableCellRenderer.noFocusBorder, javax.swing.tree.DefaultTreeCellEditor.DefaultTextField.border

CompoundBorder
javax.swing.border

Java 1.2

serializable

This class combines two borders and displays the result around a Swing component. For example, you can use CompoundBorder to combine a beveled outer border and an etched inner border. Or you can use CompoundBorder to combine a MatteBorder and an EmptyBorder, to create an additional margin within the MatteBorder. See also the createCompoundBorder() method of javax.swing.BorderFactory.

```
public class CompoundBorder extends AbstractBorder {
// Public Constructors
    public CompoundBorder( );
    public CompoundBorder(Border outsideBorder, Border insideBorder);
// Property Accessor Methods (by property name)
    public boolean isBorderOpaque( );                                    Overrides:AbstractBorder default:false
    public Border getInsideBorder( );                                                           default:null
    public Border getOutsideBorder( );                                                          default:null
// Public Methods Overriding AbstractBorder
    public java.awt.Insets getBorderInsets(Component c);
    public java.awt.Insets getBorderInsets(Component c, java.awt.Insets insets);
    public void paintBorder(Component c, java.awt.Graphics g, int x, int y, int width, int height);
// Protected Instance Fields
    protected Border insideBorder;
    protected Border outsideBorder;
}
```

Hierarchy: Object→ AbstractBorder(Border, Serializable)→ CompoundBorder

Subclasses: javax.swing.plaf.BorderUIResource.CompoundBorderUIResource

Returned By: BorderFactory.createCompoundBorder()

EmptyBorder   Java 1.2

javax.swing.border   *serializable*

This class implements a transparent, empty border. It is used to place a blank margin around a Swing component. The arguments to the constructor specify the number of pixels of blank space to appear on each edge of the component. See also the createEmptyBorder() method of javax.swing.BorderFactory.

```
public class EmptyBorder extends AbstractBorder implements Serializable {
// Public Constructors
    public EmptyBorder(java.awt.Insets insets);
    public EmptyBorder(int top, int left, int bottom, int right);
// Public Methods Overriding AbstractBorder
    public java.awt.Insets getBorderInsets(Component c);
    public java.awt.Insets getBorderInsets(Component c, java.awt.Insets insets);
    public boolean isBorderOpaque( );                                                             constant
    public void paintBorder(Component c, java.awt.Graphics g, int x, int y, int width, int height);   empty
// Protected Instance Fields
    protected int bottom;
    protected int left;
    protected int right;
    protected int top;
}
```

Hierarchy: Object→ AbstractBorder(Border, Serializable)→ EmptyBorder(Serializable)

Subclasses: MatteBorder, javax.swing.plaf.BorderUIResource.EmptyBorderUIResource

EtchedBorder   Java 1.2

javax.swing.border   *serializable*

This class displays an etched border around a Swing component. By default, the border appears etched into the screen. You can create a border that appears etched out by passing the RAISED constant to the EtchedBorder() constructor. It usually is not necessary to specify colors for the border, since EtchedBorder automatically chooses correct defaults based on the component's background color. See also the createEtchedBorder() method of javax.swing.BorderFactory.

```
public class EtchedBorder extends AbstractBorder {
// Public Constructors
    public EtchedBorder();
    public EtchedBorder(int etchType);
    public EtchedBorder(java.awt.Color highlight, java.awt.Color shadow);
    public EtchedBorder(int etchType, java.awt.Color highlight, java.awt.Color shadow);
// Public Constants
    public static final int LOWERED;                                                              =1
    public static final int RAISED;                                                               =0
// Public Instance Methods
    public int getEtchType();                                                              default:1
    public java.awt.Color getHighlightColor(Component c);
    public java.awt.Color getShadowColor(Component c);
// Public Methods Overriding AbstractBorder
    public java.awt.Insets getBorderInsets(Component c);
    public java.awt.Insets getBorderInsets(Component c, java.awt.Insets insets);
    public boolean isBorderOpaque();                                      constant default:true
    public void paintBorder(Component c, java.awt.Graphics g, int x, int y, int width, int height);
// Protected Instance Fields
    protected int etchType;
    protected java.awt.Color highlight;
    protected java.awt.Color shadow;
}
```

Hierarchy: Object→ AbstractBorder(Border, Serializable)→ EtchedBorder

Subclasses: javax.swing.plaf.BorderUIResource.EtchedBorderUIResource

LineBorder   Java 1.2

javax.swing.border   *serializable*

This class draws a solid line of the specified color and thickness around a Swing component. The default thickness is one pixel. The two static methods return shared LineBorder instances that draw black and gray lines that are one-pixel wide. See also the createLineBorder() method of javax.swing.BorderFactory.

```
public class LineBorder extends AbstractBorder {
// Public Constructors
    public LineBorder(java.awt.Color color);
    public LineBorder(java.awt.Color color, int thickness);
// Public Class Methods
    public static Border createBlackLineBorder();
    public static Border createGrayLineBorder();
// Public Instance Methods
    public java.awt.Color getLineColor();
    public int getThickness();
// Public Methods Overriding AbstractBorder
    public java.awt.Insets getBorderInsets(Component c);
    public java.awt.Insets getBorderInsets(Component c, java.awt.Insets insets);
    public boolean isBorderOpaque();                                          constant
    public void paintBorder(Component c, java.awt.Graphics g, int x, int y, int width, int height);
// Protected Instance Fields
    protected java.awt.Color lineColor;
    protected boolean roundedCorners;
    protected int thickness;
}
```

Hierarchy: Object→ AbstractBorder(Border, Serializable)→ LineBorder

Subclasses: javax.swing.plaf.BorderUIResource.LineBorderUIResource

MatteBorder

Java 1.2

javax.swing.border

serializable

This class uses a solid color or tiled icon to paint a border around a Swing component. The sizes of each edge of the border can be independently specified. If an icon is specified and border sizes are not, the top and bottom insets of the border equal the icon height, and the left and right insets equal the icon width. See also the createMatteBorder() method of javax.swing.BorderFactory.

```
public class MatteBorder extends EmptyBorder {
// Public Constructors
    public MatteBorder(Icon tileIcon);
    public MatteBorder(int top, int left, int bottom, int right, Icon tileIcon);
    public MatteBorder(int top, int left, int bottom, int right, java.awt.Color color);
// Public Methods Overriding EmptyBorder
    public java.awt.Insets getBorderInsets(Component c);
    public java.awt.Insets getBorderInsets(Component c, java.awt.Insets insets);
    public boolean isBorderOpaque();
    public void paintBorder(Component c, java.awt.Graphics g, int x, int y, int width, int height);
// Protected Instance Fields
    protected java.awt.Color color;
    protected Icon tileIcon;
}
```

Hierarchy: Object→ AbstractBorder(Border, Serializable)→ EmptyBorder(Serializable)→ MatteBorder

Subclasses: javax.swing.plaf.BorderUIResource.MatteBorderUIResource

Returned By: BorderFactory.createMatteBorder()

SoftBevelBorder

Java 1.2

javax.swing.border

serializable

This class displays a two-pixel-wide raised or lowered beveled border around a Swing component. SoftBevelBorder differs from its superclass BevelBorder in that it draws a softer bevel (i.e., a bevel whose corners do not appear as sharp). Unlike the other border types, shared SoftBevelBorder instances cannot be created through the javax.swing.BorderFactory class.

```
public class SoftBevelBorder extends BevelBorder {
// Public Constructors
    public SoftBevelBorder(int bevelType);
    public SoftBevelBorder(int bevelType, java.awt.Color highlight, java.awt.Color shadow);
    public SoftBevelBorder(int bevelType, java.awt.Color highlightOuter, java.awt.Color highlightInner,
                           java.awt.Color shadowOuter, java.awt.Color shadowInner);
// Public Methods Overriding BevelBorder
    public java.awt.Insets getBorderInsets(Component c);
    public boolean isBorderOpaque();                                                       constant
    public void paintBorder(Component c, java.awt.Graphics g, int x, int y, int width, int height);
}
```

Hierarchy: Object→ AbstractBorder(Border, Serializable)→ BevelBorder→ SoftBevelBorder

TitledBorder

javax.swing.border

serializable

This class combines a textual title with another border. This can be a useful effect when, for example, you want to group and title several components, such as a group of JRadioButton objects. By default, TitledBorder draws an EtchedBorder and displays the title left justified on the top edge of that border. Arguments to the constructor and property-setting methods allow you to specify the Border to be drawn, the position of the title relative to the top or bottom of that border, the justification of the title, the title font, and the title color. The title can be positioned above, on top of, or below the top or bottom edge of the border, and it can be left, center, or right justified. The positioning is specified by the titlePosition and titleJustification properties. TitledBorder constants define the legal values of these properties.

TitledBorder instances are not typically shared among components because different components do not typically have the same title. Since the TitledBorder instances are not shared, they need not be immutable. TitledBorder is unique among the classes in javax.swing.border in that it has properties that can be set after the instance is created. You can still use the createTitledBorder() method of javax.swing.BorderFactory to create TitledBorder instances, but since they are unlikely to be shared, this is typically not very useful.

```java
public class TitledBorder extends AbstractBorder {
// Public Constructors
    public TitledBorder(Border border);
    public TitledBorder(String title);
    public TitledBorder(Border border, String title);
    public TitledBorder(Border border, String title, int titleJustification, int titlePosition);
    public TitledBorder(Border border, String title, int titleJustification, int titlePosition, java.awt.Font titleFont);
    public TitledBorder(Border border, String title, int titleJustification, int titlePosition, java.awt.Font titleFont,
                java.awt.Color titleColor);
// Public Constants
    public static final int ABOVE_BOTTOM;                                                        =4
    public static final int ABOVE_TOP;                                                           =1
    public static final int BELOW_BOTTOM;                                                        =6
    public static final int BELOW_TOP;                                                           =3
    public static final int BOTTOM;                                                              =5
    public static final int CENTER;                                                              =2
    public static final int DEFAULT_JUSTIFICATION;                                               =0
    public static final int DEFAULT_POSITION;                                                    =0
    public static final int LEFT;                                                                =1
    public static final int RIGHT;                                                               =3
    public static final int TOP;                                                                 =2
// Protected Constants
    protected static final int EDGE_SPACING;                                                     =2
    protected static final int TEXT_INSET_H;                                                     =5
    protected static final int TEXT_SPACING;                                                     =2
// Property Accessor Methods (by property name)
    public Border getBorder();
    public void setBorder(Border border);
    public boolean isBorderOpaque();                                    Overrides:AbstractBorder constant
    public String getTitle();
    public void setTitle(String title);
    public java.awt.Color getTitleColor();
    public void setTitleColor(java.awt.Color titleColor);
    public java.awt.Font getTitleFont();
    public void setTitleFont(java.awt.Font titleFont);
    public int getTitleJustification();
    public void setTitleJustification(int titleJustification);
```

```
        public int getTitlePosition();
        public void setTitlePosition(int titlePosition);
// Public Instance Methods
        public java.awt.Dimension getMinimumSize(Component c);
// Public Methods Overriding AbstractBorder
        public java.awt.Insets getBorderInsets(Component c);
        public java.awt.Insets getBorderInsets(Component c, java.awt.Insets insets);
        public void paintBorder(Component c, java.awt.Graphics g, int x, int y, int width, int height);
// Protected Instance Methods
        protected java.awt.Font getFont(Component c);
// Protected Instance Fields
        protected Border border;
        protected String title;
        protected java.awt.Color titleColor;
        protected java.awt.Font titleFont;
        protected int titleJustification;
        protected int titlePosition;
}
```

Hierarchy: Object → AbstractBorder(Border, Serializable) → TitledBorder

Subclasses: javax.swing.plaf.BorderUIResource.TitledBorderUIResource

Returned By: BorderFactory.createTitledBorder()

CHAPTER 25

The javax.swing.colorchooser Package

The classes and interfaces of the javax.swing.colorchooser package support the JColor-Chooser component of the javax.swing package and allow customization of that component. Figure 25-1 shows the class hierarchy of this package.

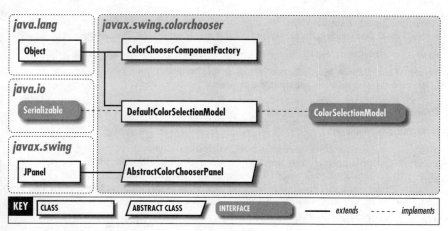

Figure 25–1: The javax.swing.colorchooser package

AbstractColorChooserPanel
javax.swing.colorchooser

Java 1.2

serializable accessible swing component

This abstract subclass of JPanel provides the basic framework for creating new color selection panels for the JColorChooser component. The default color selection panels provided by the JColorChooser are adequate for most applications. If you want to add a custom panel, you must subclass this class and provide implementations for the abstract methods. The buildChooser() method should create the GUI components that your color selection panel uses. getDisplayName(), getLargeDisplayIcon(), and getSmallDisplayIcon() should return a name and icons for your custom panel, respectively. These are displayed in the JTabbedPane tab for your color selection panel.

The most important task for your AbstractColorChooserPanel, however, is communicating with the ColorSelectionModel object of the JColorChooser. Call the getColorSelectionModel() method to obtain the model. When the user selects a color in your panel, you must change the selected color in the model, so that the JColorChooser knows of your selection. Conversely. if the user selects a color in some other panel, the abstract update-Chooser() method is called to notify your panel of the change. Your panel should update itself to reflect the new color selection.

```
public abstract class AbstractColorChooserPanel extends JPanel {
// Public Constructors
    public AbstractColorChooserPanel();
// Property Accessor Methods (by property name)
    public ColorSelectionModel getColorSelectionModel();
    public abstract String getDisplayName();
    public abstract Icon getLargeDisplayIcon();
    public abstract Icon getSmallDisplayIcon();
// Public Instance Methods
    public void installChooserPanel(JColorChooser enclosingChooser);
    public void uninstallChooserPanel(JColorChooser enclosingChooser);
    public abstract void updateChooser();
// Public Methods Overriding JComponent
    public void paint(java.awt.Graphics g);
// Protected Instance Methods
    protected abstract void buildChooser();
    protected java.awt.Color getColorFromModel();
}
```

Hierarchy: Object→ Component(java.awt.image.ImageObserver, java.awt.MenuContainer, Serializable)→ Container→ JComponent(Serializable)→ JPanel(Accessible)→ AbstractColorChooserPanel

Passed To: JColorChooser.{addChooserPanel(), removeChooserPanel(), setChooserPanels()}

Returned By: JColorChooser.{getChooserPanels(), removeChooserPanel()},
ColorChooserComponentFactory.getDefaultChooserPanels()

ColorChooserComponentFactory   Java 1.2

javax.swing.colorchooser

This class consists of static methods that return the individual color selection and color preview components that are used to create a default JColorChooser component. This class is used by the JColorChooser UI delegate object and normally is not used by applications. However, you may find it useful if you want to arrange standard color chooser components in a custom custom dialog box of your own.

```
public class ColorChooserComponentFactory {
// No Constructor
// Public Class Methods
    public static AbstractColorChooserPanel[ ] getDefaultChooserPanels();
    public static JComponent getPreviewPanel();
}
```

ColorSelectionModel   Java 1.2

javax.swing.colorchooser   *model*

This interface defines the methods that must be implemented by an object that wants to keep track of a selected color for a JColorChooser. The interface is a simple one, consisting only of a pair of property accessor methods for the selected color and a pair of event registration methods for listeners that are interested in knowing when the selection changes. DefaultColorSelectionModel provides a simple implementation of this interface.

```
public abstract interface ColorSelectionModel {
// Event Registration Methods (by event name)
    public abstract void addChangeListener(javax.swing.event.ChangeListener listener);
    public abstract void removeChangeListener(javax.swing.event.ChangeListener listener);
// Public Instance Methods
    public abstract java.awt.Color getSelectedColor();
    public abstract void setSelectedColor(java.awt.Color color);
}
```

Implementations: DefaultColorSelectionModel

Passed To: JColorChooser.{JColorChooser(), setSelectionModel()}

Returned By: JColorChooser.getSelectionModel(), AbstractColorChooserPanel.getColorSelectionModel()

DefaultColorSelectionModel   Java 1.2

javax.swing.colorchooser   *serializable model*

This class is a simple default implementation of the ColorSelectionModel interface.

```
public class DefaultColorSelectionModel implements ColorSelectionModel, Serializable {
// Public Constructors
    public DefaultColorSelectionModel();
    public DefaultColorSelectionModel(java.awt.Color color);
// Event Registration Methods (by event name)
    public void addChangeListener(javax.swing.event.ChangeListener l);          Implements:ColorSelectionModel
    public void removeChangeListener(javax.swing.event.ChangeListener l);       Implements:ColorSelectionModel
// Methods Implementing ColorSelectionModel
    public void addChangeListener(javax.swing.event.ChangeListener l);
    public java.awt.Color getSelectedColor();
    public void removeChangeListener(javax.swing.event.ChangeListener l);
    public void setSelectedColor(java.awt.Color color);
// Protected Instance Methods
    protected void fireStateChanged();
// Protected Instance Fields
    protected transient javax.swing.event.ChangeEvent changeEvent;
    protected javax.swing.event.EventListenerList listenerList;
}
```

Hierarchy: Object→ DefaultColorSelectionModel(ColorSelectionModel, Serializable)

CHAPTER 26

The javax.swing.event Package

The javax.swing.event package augments the java.awt.event package and defines event objects, listeners, and adapters that are specific to Swing components. Classes with names ending in "Event" define event types; their fields and methods provide details about the event that occurred. Interfaces with names ending in "Listener" are event listeners. The methods of these interfaces are invoked to notify interested objects when specific events occur. Classes with names ending in "Adapter" are convenient no-op implementations of listener interfaces. Typically, it is easier to subclass an adapter class than implement the corresponding listener interface from scratch. Figure 26-1 shows the event classes of this package, while Figure 26-2 shows the event listeners.

AncestorEvent
Java 1.2

javax.swing.event
serializable event

An event of this type is generated by a JComponent when it is moved, becomes visible, or becomes invisible. Often, the event is generated when one of the component's ancestors is moved, becomes visible, or becomes invisible. The inherited getID() method returns the type of the event, which is one of the constants defined by the class. ANCESTOR_ADDED is used when the component becomes visible, and ANCESTOR_REMOVED is used when the component becomes invisible. getAncestor() returns the ancestor component that was modified, and, as a convenience, getAncestorParent() returns the parent of that ancestor. getComponent() is a synonym for the inherited getSource() method, except that it casts its return value to a JComponent.

```
public class AncestorEvent extends java.awt.AWTEvent {
// Public Constructors
    public AncestorEvent(JComponent source, int id, Container ancestor, Container ancestorParent);
// Public Constants
    public static final int ANCESTOR_ADDED;                                          =1
    public static final int ANCESTOR_MOVED;                                          =3
    public static final int ANCESTOR_REMOVED;                                        =2
```

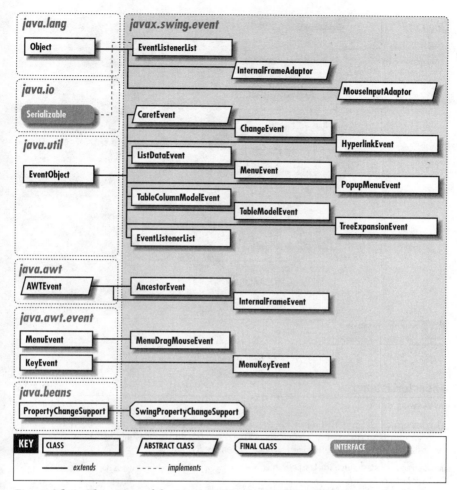

Figure 26-1: The events of the javax.swing.event package

```
// Public Instance Methods
    public Container getAncestor();
    public Container getAncestorParent();
    public JComponent getComponent();
}
```

Hierarchy: Object→ java.util.EventObject(Serializable)→ java.awt.AWTEvent→ AncestorEvent

Passed To: AncestorListener.{ancestorAdded(), ancestorMoved(), ancestorRemoved()}

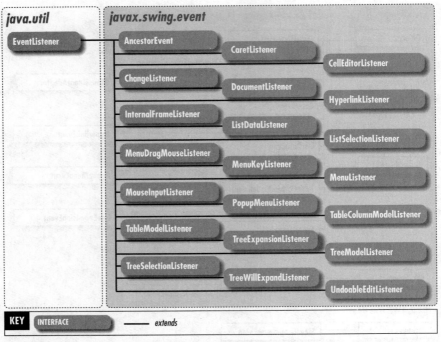

Figure 26-2: The event listeners of the javax.swing.event package

AncestorListener

Java 1.2

javax.swing.event

event listener

This interface defines the methods that must be implemented by an object that wants to receive notification when a JComponent is moved (with ancestorMoved()), made visible (ancestorAdded()),or made invisible (ancestorRemoved()).

```
public abstract interface AncestorListener extends java.util.EventListener {
// Public Instance Methods
    public abstract void ancestorAdded(AncestorEvent event);
    public abstract void ancestorMoved(AncestorEvent event);
    public abstract void ancestorRemoved(AncestorEvent event);
}
```

Hierarchy: (AncestorListener(java.util.EventListener))

Passed To: JComponent.{addAncestorListener(), removeAncestorListener()}

CaretEvent

Java 1.2

javax.swing.event

serializable event

This event is generated by JTextComponent and its subclasses JTextField, JTextArea, JTextPane, and JEditorPane when the caret position changes. The text caret maintains both the current insertion position (the dot) and a marker position (the mark). A CaretEvent is generated when either position changes. The changed values can be obtained with getDot() and getMark(), respectively. The text component that contains the caret can be queried with the inherited getSource() method.

```
public abstract class CaretEvent extends java.util.EventObject {
// Public Constructors
    public CaretEvent(Object source);
// Public Instance Methods
    public abstract int getDot();
    public abstract int getMark();
}
```

Hierarchy: Object→ java.util.EventObject(Serializable)→ CaretEvent

Passed To: CaretListener.caretUpdate(), javax.swing.text.JTextComponent.fireCaretUpdate(), javax.swing.text.JTextComponent.AccessibleJTextComponent.caretUpdate()

CaretListener

javax.swing.event

Java 1.2

event listener

This interface defines a method that an object must implement if it wants to receive notification when the caret position changes in a JTextComponent or one of its subclasses.

```
public abstract interface CaretListener extends java.util.EventListener {
// Public Instance Methods
    public abstract void caretUpdate(CaretEvent e);
}
```

Hierarchy: (CaretListener(java.util.EventListener))

Implementations: javax.swing.text.JTextComponent.AccessibleJTextComponent

Passed To: javax.swing.text.JTextComponent.{addCaretListener(), removeCaretListener()}

CellEditorListener

javax.swing.event

Java 1.2

event listener

This interface defines the methods that must be implemented by an object that wants to receive notification of state changes in a javax.swing.CellEditor. Note that these methods are passed a ChangeEvent; there is no special CellEditorEvent type.

```
public abstract interface CellEditorListener extends java.util.EventListener {
// Public Instance Methods
    public abstract void editingCanceled(ChangeEvent e);
    public abstract void editingStopped(ChangeEvent e);
}
```

Hierarchy: (CellEditorListener(java.util.EventListener))

Implementations: JTable, JTable.AccessibleJTable

Passed To: CellEditor.{addCellEditorListener(), removeCellEditorListener()}, DefaultCellEditor.{addCellEditorListener(), removeCellEditorListener()}, javax.swing.tree.DefaultTreeCellEditor.{addCellEditorListener(), removeCellEditorListener()}

ChangeEvent

javax.swing.event

Java 1.2

serializable event

This class is a generic event type that is generated by many Swing components to indicate that something has changed within the component. ChangeEvent does not contain any fields to indicate the type of the change; the type of state change should be implicit in the event listener to which the ChangeEvent object is passed. The only state maintained by ChangeEvent is the component that generated the event (returned by the inherited getSource() method). Because ChangeEvent is immutable and effectively stateless,

Swing components can reuse a single shared ChangeEvent object for all their state changes, instead of allocating an event object for every change.

```
public class ChangeEvent extends java.util.EventObject {
// Public Constructors
    public ChangeEvent(Object source);
}
```

Hierarchy: Object→ java.util.EventObject(Serializable) → ChangeEvent

Passed To: Too many methods to list.

Type Of: AbstractButton.changeEvent, DefaultBoundedRangeModel.changeEvent, DefaultButtonModel.changeEvent, DefaultCellEditor.changeEvent, DefaultSingleSelectionModel.changeEvent, JProgressBar.changeEvent, JSlider.changeEvent, JTabbedPane.changeEvent, MenuSelectionManager.changeEvent, javax.swing.colorchooser.DefaultColorSelectionModel.changeEvent, javax.swing.table.DefaultTableColumnModel.changeEvent, javax.swing.text.DefaultCaret.changeEvent, javax.swing.text.StyleContext.NamedStyle.changeEvent

ChangeListener   Java 1.2

javax.swing.event   *event listener*

This interface defines the method that an object must implement to receive notifications of state change events in Swing components.

```
public abstract interface ChangeListener extends java.util.EventListener {
// Public Instance Methods
    public abstract void stateChanged(ChangeEvent e);
}
```

Hierarchy: (ChangeListener(java.util.EventListener))

Implementations: AbstractButton.ButtonChangeListener, JMenuItem.AccessibleJMenuItem, JScrollPane.AccessibleJScrollPane, JTabbedPane.AccessibleJTabbedPane, JTabbedPane.ModelListener

Passed To: Too many methods to list.

Returned By: AbstractButton.createChangeListener(), JProgressBar.createChangeListener(), JSlider.createChangeListener(), JTabbedPane.createChangeListener()

Type Of: AbstractButton.changeListener, JProgressBar.changeListener, JSlider.changeListener, JTabbedPane.changeListener

DocumentEvent   Java 1.2

javax.swing.event

Events of this type are generated by a javax.swing.text.Document object when the document it represents changes. getDocument() returns the Document that was modified. getType() returns the type of the changes; its return value is one of the three constants defined by the DocumentEvent.EventType inner class. getOffset() returns the document coordinate of the start of the change, and getLength() returns the length of the change. getChange() returns a DocumentEvent.ElementChange object that describes the change in terms of its effect on the specified javax.swing.text.Element of the document.

```
public abstract interface DocumentEvent {
// Inner Classes
    public abstract static interface ElementChange;
    public static final class EventType;
// Property Accessor Methods (by property name)
    public abstract javax.swing.text.Document getDocument();
    public abstract int getLength();
```

```
    public abstract int getOffset();
    public abstract DocumentEvent.EventType getType();
// Public Instance Methods
    public abstract DocumentEvent.ElementChange getChange(javax.swing.text.Element elem);
}
```

Implementations: javax.swing.text.AbstractDocument.DefaultDocumentEvent

Passed To: Too many methods to list.

DocumentEvent.ElementChange

javax.swing.event

This interface defines methods that provide information about changes to an javax.swing.text.Element object within a javax.swing.text.Document.

```
public abstract static interface DocumentEvent.ElementChange {
// Property Accessor Methods (by property name)
    public abstract javax.swing.text.Element[ ] getChildrenAdded();
    public abstract javax.swing.text.Element[ ] getChildrenRemoved();
    public abstract javax.swing.text.Element getElement();
    public abstract int getIndex();
}
```

Implementations: javax.swing.text.AbstractDocument.ElementEdit

Returned By: DocumentEvent.getChange(),
javax.swing.text.AbstractDocument.DefaultDocumentEvent.getChange()

DocumentEvent.EventType

javax.swing.event

This class defines three type-safe object constants that are used to specify the type of a DocumentEvent.

```
public static final class DocumentEvent.EventType {
// No Constructor
// Public Constants
    public static final DocumentEvent.EventType CHANGE;
    public static final DocumentEvent.EventType INSERT;
    public static final DocumentEvent.EventType REMOVE;
// Public Methods Overriding Object
    public String toString();
}
```

Passed To: javax.swing.text.AbstractDocument.DefaultDocumentEvent.DefaultDocumentEvent()

Returned By: DocumentEvent.getType(),
javax.swing.text.AbstractDocument.DefaultDocumentEvent.getType()

Type Of: DocumentEvent.EventType.{CHANGE, INSERT, REMOVE}

DocumentListener

javax.swing.event
event listener

This interface defines the method that an object must implement in order to register for notifications of changes to a javax.swing.text.Document object.

```
public abstract interface DocumentListener extends java.util.EventListener {
// Public Instance Methods
```

```
    public abstract void changedUpdate(DocumentEvent e);
    public abstract void insertUpdate(DocumentEvent e);
    public abstract void removeUpdate(DocumentEvent e);
}
```

Hierarchy: (DocumentListener(java.util.EventListener))

Implementations: javax.swing.text.JTextComponent.AccessibleJTextComponent

Passed To: javax.swing.text.AbstractDocument.{addDocumentListener(), removeDocumentListener()},
javax.swing.text.DefaultStyledDocument.{addDocumentListener(), removeDocumentListener()},
javax.swing.text.Document.{addDocumentListener(), removeDocumentListener()}

EventListenerList
Java 1.2

javax.swing.event
serializable

This utility class is used by many Swing classes to maintain lists of event listeners. An
EventListenerList maintains a list of event listener objects, possibly of several different
types. In order to allow the type of each listener to be determined efficiently, EventListenerList also maintains the java.lang.Class object for each EventListener.

The add() and remove() methods add and remove an event listener and its Class object to
and from the list. When a component needs to send an event to all registered listeners
of a given type, it calls getListenerList(). This method returns an array of objects, where
the elements of this array are grouped in pairs. Each even-numbered element is a Class
object that specifies the type of the event listener stored in the following odd-numbered
element. Thus, you can quickly loop through the list of event listeners, comparing Class
objects to find any registered listeners of the desired type. Objects that make use of
EventListenerList must be careful not to modify the contents of the array returned by
getListenerList().

```
public class EventListenerList implements Serializable {
// Public Constructors
    public EventListenerList();
// Property Accessor Methods (by property name)
    public int getListenerCount();                                                    default:0
    public int getListenerCount(Class t);
    public Object[] getListenerList();
// Public Instance Methods
    public void add(Class t, java.util.EventListener l);                          synchronized
    public void remove(Class t, java.util.EventListener l);                       synchronized
// Public Methods Overriding Object
    public String toString();
// Protected Instance Fields
    protected transient Object[] listenerList;
}
```

Hierarchy: Object→ EventListenerList(Serializable)

Type Of: Too many fields to list.

HyperlinkEvent
Java 1.2

javax.swing.event
serializable event

An event of this type is generated by JEditorPane when the user moves the mouse over,
clicks on, or moves the mouse off a hypertext link. getURL() returns the URL of the
hyperlink. getEventType() returns an object constant indicating what was done to the
hyperlink. The inherited getSource() method returns the JEditorPane that contains the
hyperlink.

```
public class HyperlinkEvent extends java.util.EventObject {
// Public Constructors
    public HyperlinkEvent(Object source, HyperlinkEvent.EventType type, java.net.URL u);
    public HyperlinkEvent(Object source, HyperlinkEvent.EventType type, java.net.URL u, String desc);
// Inner Classes
    public static final class EventType;
// Public Instance Methods
    public String getDescription();
    public HyperlinkEvent.EventType getEventType();
    public java.net.URL getURL();
}
```

Hierarchy: Object → java.util.EventObject(Serializable) → HyperlinkEvent

Subclasses: javax.swing.text.html.HTMLFrameHyperlinkEvent

Passed To: JEditorPane.fireHyperlinkUpdate(), HyperlinkListener.hyperlinkUpdate()

HyperlinkEvent.EventType

Java 1.2

javax.swing.event

This class defines three type-safe object constants that are used to specify the type of a HyperlinkEvent.

```
public static final class HyperlinkEvent.EventType {
// No Constructor
// Public Constants
    public static final HyperlinkEvent.EventType ACTIVATED;
    public static final HyperlinkEvent.EventType ENTERED;
    public static final HyperlinkEvent.EventType EXITED;
// Public Methods Overriding Object
    public String toString();
}
```

Passed To: HyperlinkEvent.HyperlinkEvent(),
javax.swing.text.html.HTMLFrameHyperlinkEvent.HTMLFrameHyperlinkEvent()

Returned By: HyperlinkEvent.getEventType()

Type Of: HyperlinkEvent.EventType.{ACTIVATED, ENTERED, EXITED}

HyperlinkListener

Java 1.2

javax.swing.event

event listener

This interface defines the method that an object must implement in order to register for notifications about hyperlink activity in a JEditorPane component.

```
public abstract interface HyperlinkListener extends java.util.EventListener {
// Public Instance Methods
    public abstract void hyperlinkUpdate(HyperlinkEvent e);
}
```

Hierarchy: (HyperlinkListener(java.util.EventListener))

Passed To: JEditorPane.{addHyperlinkListener(), removeHyperlinkListener()}

InternalFrameAdapter

Java 1.2

javax.swing.event

event adapter

This class is an empty implementation of InternalFrameListener. It is usually easier to extend this class than it is to implement InternalFrameListener from scratch.

```
public abstract class InternalFrameAdapter implements InternalFrameListener {
// Public Constructors
    public InternalFrameAdapter();
// Methods Implementing InternalFrameListener
    public void internalFrameActivated(InternalFrameEvent e);                      empty
    public void internalFrameClosed(InternalFrameEvent e);                         empty
    public void internalFrameClosing(InternalFrameEvent e);                        empty
    public void internalFrameDeactivated(InternalFrameEvent e);                    empty
    public void internalFrameDeiconified(InternalFrameEvent e);                    empty
    public void internalFrameIconified(InternalFrameEvent e);                      empty
    public void internalFrameOpened(InternalFrameEvent e);                         empty
}
```

Hierarchy: Object→ InternalFrameAdapter(InternalFrameListener(java.util.EventListener))

InternalFrameEvent
Java 1.2

javax.swing.event
serializable event

Events of this type are generated when a JInternalFrame component changes state. An InternalFrameEvent is very similar to the java.awt.event.WindowEvent generated when a native window (such as a JFrame or JDialog) changes state. The inherited getSource() method returns the JInternalFrame object that generated the event. The inherited getID() method returns the type of the event; this return value is one of the constants defined by this class. The meanings of these constants are mostly straightforward. Note the distinction between INTERNAL_FRAME_CLOSING and INTERNAL_FRAME_CLOSED, however. The first type of event is generated when the user requests that the JInternalFrame be closed. The program may respond by hiding or destroying the window (it is poor style to ignore this type of event). The second type of event is generated only after the internal frame is actually hidden or destroyed.

```
public class InternalFrameEvent extends java.awt.AWTEvent {
// Public Constructors
    public InternalFrameEvent(JInternalFrame source, int id);
// Public Constants
    public static final int INTERNAL_FRAME_ACTIVATED;                              =25554
    public static final int INTERNAL_FRAME_CLOSED;                                 =25551
    public static final int INTERNAL_FRAME_CLOSING;                                =25550
    public static final int INTERNAL_FRAME_DEACTIVATED;                            =25555
    public static final int INTERNAL_FRAME_DEICONIFIED;                            =25553
    public static final int INTERNAL_FRAME_FIRST;                                  =25549
    public static final int INTERNAL_FRAME_ICONIFIED;                              =25552
    public static final int INTERNAL_FRAME_LAST;                                   =25555
    public static final int INTERNAL_FRAME_OPENED;                                 =25549
// Public Methods Overriding AWTEvent
    public String paramString();
}
```

Hierarchy: Object→ java.util.EventObject(Serializable)→ java.awt.AWTEvent→ InternalFrameEvent

Passed To: InternalFrameAdapter.{internalFrameActivated(), internalFrameClosed(), internalFrameClosing(), internalFrameDeactivated(), internalFrameDeiconified(), internalFrameIconified(), internalFrameOpened()}, InternalFrameListener.{internalFrameActivated(), internalFrameClosed(), internalFrameClosing(), internalFrameDeactivated(), internalFrameDeiconified(), internalFrameIconified(), internalFrameOpened()}

InternalFrameListener

javax.swing.event
event listener

This class defines the methods that an object must implement to receive notifications about state changes in a JInternalFrame. See InternalFrameEvent for a discussion of the difference between internalFrameClosed() and internalFrameClosing(). It is usually easier to subclass InternalFrameAdapter than to implement this interface from scratch.

```
public abstract interface InternalFrameListener extends java.util.EventListener {
// Public Instance Methods
    public abstract void internalFrameActivated(InternalFrameEvent e);
    public abstract void internalFrameClosed(InternalFrameEvent e);
    public abstract void internalFrameClosing(InternalFrameEvent e);
    public abstract void internalFrameDeactivated(InternalFrameEvent e);
    public abstract void internalFrameDeiconified(InternalFrameEvent e);
    public abstract void internalFrameIconified(InternalFrameEvent e);
    public abstract void internalFrameOpened(InternalFrameEvent e);
}
```

Hierarchy: (InternalFrameListener(java.util.EventListener))

Implementations: InternalFrameAdapter

Passed To: JInternalFrame.{addInternalFrameListener(), removeInternalFrameListener()}

ListDataEvent

javax.swing.event
serializable event

An event of this type is generated by a javax.swing.ListModel when the contents of the model changes. getType() returns one of the three constants defined by the class, to indicate the type of change that occurred. The inherited getSource() method returns the ListModel object that changed. getIndex0() and getIndex1() return the end points of the modified interval.

```
public class ListDataEvent extends java.util.EventObject {
// Public Constructors
    public ListDataEvent(Object source, int type, int index0, int index1);
// Public Constants
    public static final int CONTENTS_CHANGED;                              =0
    public static final int INTERVAL_ADDED;                                =1
    public static final int INTERVAL_REMOVED;                              =2
// Public Instance Methods
    public int getIndex0();
    public int getIndex1();
    public int getType();
}
```

Hierarchy: Object → java.util.EventObject(Serializable) → ListDataEvent

Passed To: JComboBox.{contentsChanged(), intervalAdded(), intervalRemoved()},
JList.AccessibleJList.{contentsChanged(), intervalAdded(), intervalRemoved()},
ListDataListener.{contentsChanged(), intervalAdded(), intervalRemoved()}

ListDataListener

javax.swing.event
event listener

This interface defines the methods that must be implemented by an object to receive notifications of changes to the contents of a javax.swing.ListModel.

javax.swing.
event

```
public abstract interface ListDataListener extends java.util.EventListener {
// Public Instance Methods
    public abstract void contentsChanged(ListDataEvent e);
    public abstract void intervalAdded(ListDataEvent e);
    public abstract void intervalRemoved(ListDataEvent e);
}
```

Hierarchy: (ListDataListener(java.util.EventListener))

Implementations: JComboBox, JList.AccessibleJList

Passed To: AbstractListModel.{addListDataListener(), removeListDataListener()}, ListModel.{addListDataListener(), removeListDataListener()}

ListSelectionEvent
Java 1.2

javax.swing.event
serializable event

An event of this type is generated by a JList component or its underlying ListSelection-Model object to indicate a change in the current list selection. getFirstIndex() and getLastIndex() return the first and last elements in the list that may have had their selection state changed. The ListSelectionEvent does not contain the new selection state; you must query the JList or ListSelectionModel for that information. (Use the inherited getSource() method to obtain the source of the event). getValueIsAdjusting() returns true if the event is one in a series of rapid-fire events, such as those that are generated when the user drags the mouse through a JList. Some programs may choose to ignore these rapid-fire events and wait for an event for which getValueIsAdjusting() returns false.

```
public class ListSelectionEvent extends java.util.EventObject {
// Public Constructors
    public ListSelectionEvent(Object source, int firstIndex, int lastIndex, boolean isAdjusting);
// Public Instance Methods
    public int getFirstIndex();
    public int getLastIndex();
    public boolean getValueIsAdjusting();
// Public Methods Overriding EventObject
    public String toString();
}
```

Hierarchy: Object → java.util.EventObject(Serializable) → ListSelectionEvent

Passed To: JList.AccessibleJList.valueChanged(), JTable.{columnSelectionChanged(), valueChanged()}, JTable.AccessibleJTable.{columnSelectionChanged(), valueChanged()}, ListSelectionListener.valueChanged(), TableColumnModelListener.columnSelectionChanged(), javax.swing.table.DefaultTableColumnModel.{fireColumnSelectionChanged(), valueChanged()}, javax.swing.table.JTableHeader.columnSelectionChanged()

ListSelectionListener
Java 1.2

javax.swing.event
event listener

This interface defines the method that an object must implement in order to receive notifications of changes in the selection state of a JList or ListSelectionModel.

```
public abstract interface ListSelectionListener extends java.util.EventListener {
// Public Instance Methods
    public abstract void valueChanged(ListSelectionEvent e);
}
```

Hierarchy: (ListSelectionListener(java.util.EventListener))

Implementations: JList.AccessibleJList, JTable, JTable.AccessibleJTable, javax.swing.table.DefaultTableColumnModel

Passed To: DefaultListSelectionModel.{addListSelectionListener(), removeListSelectionListener()}, JList.{addListSelectionListener(), removeListSelectionListener()}, ListSelectionModel.{addListSelectionListener(), removeListSelectionListener()}

MenuDragMouseEvent
javax.swing.event

Java 1.2

serializable event

JMenuItem sends events of this type to registered MenuDragMouseListener objects to signal that the mouse has entered or exited the menu item, that it is moving over the menu item, or that the user has released the mouse button over the menu item.

```
public class MenuDragMouseEvent extends java.awt.event.MouseEvent {
// Public Constructors
    public MenuDragMouseEvent(Component source, int id, long when, int modifiers, int x, int y, int clickCount,
                              boolean popupTrigger, MenuElement[ ] p, MenuSelectionManager m);
// Public Instance Methods
    public MenuSelectionManager getMenuSelectionManager();
    public MenuElement[ ] getPath();
}
```

Hierarchy: Object→ java.util.EventObject(Serializable) → java.awt.AWTEvent→ java.awt.event.ComponentEvent→ java.awt.event.InputEvent→ java.awt.event.MouseEvent→ MenuDragMouseEvent

Passed To: JMenuItem.{fireMenuDragMouseDragged(), fireMenuDragMouseEntered(), fireMenuDragMouseExited(), fireMenuDragMouseReleased(), processMenuDragMouseEvent()}, MenuDragMouseListener.{menuDragMouseDragged(), menuDragMouseEntered(), menuDragMouseExited(), menuDragMouseReleased()}

MenuDragMouseListener
javax.swing.event

Java 1.2

event listener

This interface defines the methods that JMenuItem invokes on registered objects when the user drags the mouse into, over, or out of the menu item or releases the mouse button over the item.

```
public abstract interface MenuDragMouseListener extends java.util.EventListener {
// Public Instance Methods
    public abstract void menuDragMouseDragged(MenuDragMouseEvent e);
    public abstract void menuDragMouseEntered(MenuDragMouseEvent e);
    public abstract void menuDragMouseExited(MenuDragMouseEvent e);
    public abstract void menuDragMouseReleased(MenuDragMouseEvent e);
}
```

Hierarchy: (MenuDragMouseListener(java.util.EventListener))

Passed To: JMenuItem.{addMenuDragMouseListener(), removeMenuDragMouseListener()}

MenuEvent
javax.swing.event

Java 1.2

serializable event

Events of this type are generated by a JMenu component to indicate that the menu button has been selected or deselected. (When the menu attached to that button actually pops up or down, the JPopupMenu component generates a PopupMenuEvent.) The inherited getSource() method returns the JMenu object that generated the event. The type of the MenuEvent depends on which MenuListener method it is passed to.

```
public class MenuEvent extends java.util.EventObject {
// Public Constructors
    public MenuEvent(Object source);
}
```

Hierarchy: Object→ java.util.EventObject(Serializable) → MenuEvent

Passed To: MenuListener.{menuCanceled(), menuDeselected(), menuSelected()}

MenuKeyEvent   Java 1.2

javax.swing.event   *serializable event*

JMenuItem sends events of this type to registered MenuKeyListener objects when the user types a key over the menu item.

```
public class MenuKeyEvent extends java.awt.event.KeyEvent {
// Public Constructors
    public MenuKeyEvent(Component source, int id, long when, int modifiers, int keyCode, char keyChar,
                        MenuElement[ ] p, MenuSelectionManager m);
// Public Instance Methods
    public MenuSelectionManager getMenuSelectionManager();
    public MenuElement[ ] getPath();
}
```

Hierarchy: Object→ java.util.EventObject(Serializable)→ java.awt.AWTEvent→
java.awt.event.ComponentEvent→ java.awt.event.InputEvent→ java.awt.event.KeyEvent→ MenuKeyEvent

Passed To: JMenuItem.{fireMenuKeyPressed(), fireMenuKeyReleased(), fireMenuKeyTyped(),
processMenuKeyEvent()}, MenuKeyListener.{menuKeyPressed(), menuKeyReleased(), menuKeyTyped()}

MenuKeyListener   Java 1.2

javax.swing.event   *event listener*

This interface defines the method that a JMenuItem invokes on registered listeners when the user types a key in the menu item.

```
public abstract interface MenuKeyListener extends java.util.EventListener {
// Public Instance Methods
    public abstract void menuKeyPressed(MenuKeyEvent e);
    public abstract void menuKeyReleased(MenuKeyEvent e);
    public abstract void menuKeyTyped(MenuKeyEvent e);
}
```

Hierarchy: (MenuKeyListener(java.util.EventListener))

Passed To: JMenuItem.{addMenuKeyListener(), removeMenuKeyListener()}

MenuListener   Java 1.2

javax.swing.event   *event listener*

This interface defines the methods that an object must implement in order to be notified when a JMenu button is selected or deselected or when a menu selection is canceled.

```
public abstract interface MenuListener extends java.util.EventListener {
// Public Instance Methods
    public abstract void menuCanceled(MenuEvent e);
    public abstract void menuDeselected(MenuEvent e);
    public abstract void menuSelected(MenuEvent e);
}
```

Hierarchy: (MenuListener(java.util.EventListener))

Passed To: JMenu.{addMenuListener(), removeMenuListener()}

MouseInputAdapter   Java 1.2

javax.swing.event   *event adapter*

This class is an empty implementation of MouseInputListener. It often is easier to subclass this class, overriding only the methods you are interested in, than it is to implement all the methods of java.awt.event.MouseMotionListener from scratch.

```
public abstract class MouseInputAdapter implements MouseInputListener {
// Public Constructors
    public MouseInputAdapter();
// Methods Implementing MouseListener
    public void mouseClicked(java.awt.event.MouseEvent e);              empty
    public void mouseEntered(java.awt.event.MouseEvent e);             empty
    public void mouseExited(java.awt.event.MouseEvent e);             empty
    public void mousePressed(java.awt.event.MouseEvent e);            empty
    public void mouseReleased(java.awt.event.MouseEvent e);           empty
// Methods Implementing MouseMotionListener
    public void mouseDragged(java.awt.event.MouseEvent e);            empty
    public void mouseMoved(java.awt.event.MouseEvent e);              empty
}
```

Hierarchy: Object→
MouseInputAdapter(MouseInputListener(java.awt.event.MouseListener(java.util.EventListener),
java.awt.event.MouseMotionListener(java.util.EventListener)))

MouseInputListener   Java 1.2

javax.swing.event   *event listener*

MouseInputListener combines into a single interface the methods of the closely related MouseListener and MouseMotionListener interfaces of the java.awt.event package. This interface is a simple utility that makes it easier to implement both MouseEvent listener interfaces at once.

```
public abstract interface MouseInputListener extends java.awt.event.MouseListener,
        java.awt.event.MouseMotionListener {
}
```

Hierarchy: (MouseInputListener(java.awt.event.MouseListener(java.util.EventListener),
java.awt.event.MouseMotionListener(java.util.EventListener)))

Implementations: MouseInputAdapter

PopupMenuEvent   Java 1.2

javax.swing.event   *serializable event*

An event of this type is generated just before a JPopupMenu is popped up or popped down or when a JPopupMenu is canceled (i.e., when it is popped down without the user making a selection). The inherited getSource() method returns the JPopupMenu, but Popup-MenuEvent contains no other state. The type of the event is determined by the Popup-MenuListener method to which it is passed.

```
public class PopupMenuEvent extends java.util.EventObject {
// Public Constructors
    public PopupMenuEvent(Object source);
}
```

Hierarchy: Object→ java.util.EventObject(Serializable) → PopupMenuEvent

Passed To: PopupMenuListener.{popupMenuCanceled(), popupMenuWillBecomeInvisible(),
popupMenuWillBecomeVisible()}

PopupMenuListener

Java 1.2

javax.swing.event

event listener

This interface defines the methods that an object must implement to receive notifications that a JPopupMenu is about to pop up or pop down or that a JPopupMenu was canceled without a user selection.

```
public abstract interface PopupMenuListener extends java.util.EventListener {
// Public Instance Methods
    public abstract void popupMenuCanceled(PopupMenuEvent e);
    public abstract void popupMenuWillBecomeInvisible(PopupMenuEvent e);
    public abstract void popupMenuWillBecomeVisible(PopupMenuEvent e);
}
```

Hierarchy: (PopupMenuListener(java.util.EventListener))

Passed To: JPopupMenu.{addPopupMenuListener(), removePopupMenuListener()}

SwingPropertyChangeSupport

Java 1.2

javax.swing.event

serializable

This utility class is useful when you are defining a Swing component that has bound properties and must fire java.beans.PropertyChangeEvent events when the value of various properties change. This class is a subclass of java.beans.PropertyChangeSupport and provides the same features as that class. This Swing-specific version is somewhat more memory efficient than the JavaBeans version and does not use synchronized methods.

```
public final class SwingPropertyChangeSupport extends java.beans.PropertyChangeSupport {
// Public Constructors
    public SwingPropertyChangeSupport(Object sourceBean);
// Event Registration Methods (by event name)
    public void addPropertyChangeListener(                    Overrides:PropertyChangeSupport synchronized
                            java.beans.PropertyChangeListener listener);
    public void removePropertyChangeListener(                 Overrides:PropertyChangeSupport synchronized
                            java.beans.PropertyChangeListener listener);
// Public Methods Overriding PropertyChangeSupport
    public void addPropertyChangeListener(String propertyName,                        synchronized
                            java.beans.PropertyChangeListener listener);
    public void firePropertyChange(java.beans.PropertyChangeEvent evt);
    public void firePropertyChange(String propertyName, Object oldValue, Object newValue);
    public boolean hasListeners(String propertyName);                                 synchronized
    public void removePropertyChangeListener(String propertyName,                     synchronized
                            java.beans.PropertyChangeListener listener);
}
```

Hierarchy: Object→ java.beans.PropertyChangeSupport(Serializable) → SwingPropertyChangeSupport

Type Of: AbstractAction.changeSupport, javax.swing.tree.DefaultTreeSelectionModel.changeSupport

TableColumnModelEvent

Java 1.2

javax.swing.event

serializable event

An event of this type is generated when a column is added, deleted, or moved from a javax.swing.table.TableColumnModel. The inherited getSource() method returns the TableColumnModel object that was changed. When a column is added, getToIndex() specifies the index of the column. When a column is removed, getFromIndex() specifies the index that it used to occupy. When a column is moved, getFromIndex() returns the column's old position and getToIndex() returns the column's new position.

```
public class TableColumnModelEvent extends java.util.EventObject {
// Public Constructors
     public TableColumnModelEvent(javax.swing.table.TableColumnModel source, int from, int to);
// Public Instance Methods
     public int getFromIndex();
     public int getToIndex();
// Protected Instance Fields
     protected int fromIndex;
     protected int toIndex;
}
```

Hierarchy: Object→ java.util.EventObject(Serializable)→ TableColumnModelEvent

Passed To: JTable.{columnAdded(), columnMoved(), columnRemoved()},
JTable.AccessibleJTable.{columnAdded(), columnMoved(), columnRemoved()},
TableColumnModelListener.{columnAdded(), columnMoved(), columnRemoved()},
javax.swing.table.DefaultTableColumnModel.{fireColumnAdded(), fireColumnMoved(), fireColumnRemoved()},
javax.swing.table.JTableHeader.{columnAdded(), columnMoved(), columnRemoved()}

TableColumnModelListener

Java 1.2

javax.swing.event

event listener

This interface defines the methods that an object must implement to receive notifications of changes in a javax.swing.table.TableColumnModel. Note that unlike most event listeners, the methods of this object are passed different types of event objects.

```
public abstract interface TableColumnModelListener extends java.util.EventListener {
// Public Instance Methods
     public abstract void columnAdded(TableColumnModelEvent e);
     public abstract void columnMarginChanged(ChangeEvent e);
     public abstract void columnMoved(TableColumnModelEvent e);
     public abstract void columnRemoved(TableColumnModelEvent e);
     public abstract void columnSelectionChanged(ListSelectionEvent e);
}
```

Hierarchy: (TableColumnModelListener(java.util.EventListener))

Implementations: JTable, JTable.AccessibleJTable, javax.swing.table.JTableHeader

Passed To: javax.swing.table.DefaultTableColumnModel.{addColumnModelListener(),
removeColumnModelListener()}, javax.swing.table.TableColumnModel.{addColumnModelListener(),
removeColumnModelListener()}

TableModelEvent

Java 1.2

javax.swing.event

serializable event

An event of this type is generated by a javax.swing.table.TableModel when the data it contains changes. getColumn() indicates the column that changed; it may return the constant ALL_COLUMNS. getFirstRow() and getLastRow() get the range of modified rows. If either returns the constant HEADER_ROW, that indicates that the entire structure of the table has changed along with the table data. getType() specifies the type of the change; it returns one of the constants DELETE, INSERT, or UPDATE. The inherited getSource() method returns the modified TableModel object.

```
public class TableModelEvent extends java.util.EventObject {
// Public Constructors
```

```
      public TableModelEvent(javax.swing.table.TableModel source);
      public TableModelEvent(javax.swing.table.TableModel source, int row);
      public TableModelEvent(javax.swing.table.TableModel source, int firstRow, int lastRow);
      public TableModelEvent(javax.swing.table.TableModel source, int firstRow, int lastRow, int column);
      public TableModelEvent(javax.swing.table.TableModel source, int firstRow, int lastRow, int column, int type);
  // Public Constants
      public static final int ALL_COLUMNS;                                                        =-1
      public static final int DELETE;                                                             =-1
      public static final int HEADER_ROW;                                                         =-1
      public static final int INSERT;                                                             =1
      public static final int UPDATE;                                                             =0
  // Property Accessor Methods (by property name)
      public int getColumn();
      public int getFirstRow();
      public int getLastRow();
      public int getType();
  // Protected Instance Fields
      protected int column;
      protected int firstRow;
      protected int lastRow;
      protected int type;
  }
```

Hierarchy: Object→ java.util.EventObject(Serializable)→ TableModelEvent

Passed To: JTable.tableChanged(), JTable.AccessibleJTable.{tableChanged(), tableRowsDeleted(), tableRowsInserted()}, TableModelListener.tableChanged(), javax.swing.table.AbstractTableModel.fireTableChanged(), javax.swing.table.DefaultTableModel.{newDataAvailable(), newRowsAdded(), rowsRemoved()}

TableModelListener   Java 1.2

javax.swing.event   *event listener*

This interface defines the method that an object must implement to receive notifications about changes to the state of a javax.swing.table.TableModel.

```
public abstract interface TableModelListener extends java.util.EventListener {
  // Public Instance Methods
      public abstract void tableChanged(TableModelEvent e);
  }
```

Hierarchy: (TableModelListener(java.util.EventListener))

Implementations: JTable, JTable.AccessibleJTable

Passed To: javax.swing.table.AbstractTableModel.{addTableModelListener(), removeTableModelListener()}, javax.swing.table.TableModel.{addTableModelListener(), removeTableModelListener()}

TreeExpansionEvent   Java 1.2

javax.swing.event   *serializable event*

An event of this type is generated by a JTree component when a node in the tree is expanded or collapsed. The inherited getSource() method returns the JTree component, and getPath() returns a TreePath that specifies which node was expanded or collapsed.

```
public class TreeExpansionEvent extends java.util.EventObject {
  // Public Constructors
      public TreeExpansionEvent(Object source, javax.swing.tree.TreePath path);
  // Public Instance Methods
```

```
    public javax.swing.tree.TreePath getPath();
// Protected Instance Fields
    protected javax.swing.tree.TreePath path;
}
```

Hierarchy: Object→ java.util.EventObject(Serializable)→ TreeExpansionEvent

Passed To: JTree.AccessibleJTree.{treeCollapsed(), treeExpanded()}, TreeExpansionListener.{treeCollapsed(), treeExpanded()}, TreeWillExpandListener.{treeWillCollapse(), treeWillExpand()}, javax.swing.tree.ExpandVetoException.ExpandVetoException()

Type Of: javax.swing.tree.ExpandVetoException.event

TreeExpansionListener

javax.swing.event   Java 1.2

event listener

This interface defines the methods that an object must implement to be notified when a JTree component expands or collapses a node.

```
public abstract interface TreeExpansionListener extends java.util.EventListener {
// Public Instance Methods
    public abstract void treeCollapsed(TreeExpansionEvent event);
    public abstract void treeExpanded(TreeExpansionEvent event);
}
```

Hierarchy: (TreeExpansionListener(java.util.EventListener))

Implementations: JTree.AccessibleJTree

Passed To: JTree.{addTreeExpansionListener(), removeTreeExpansionListener()}

TreeModelEvent

javax.swing.event   Java 1.2

serializable event

An event of this type is generated when the contents of a java.awt.event.tree.TreeModel change. The inherited getSource() method returns the TreeModel object that was changed. getPath() and getTreePath() specify the path to the parent of the changed nodes. getChildIndices() returns an array of integers that specifies which children of that parent node have changed. Alternatively, getChildren() returns the modified children directly. TreeModelEvent does not directly indicate what type of change has occurred; that is determined by the TreeModelListener method to which the TreeModelEvent is passed.

```
public class TreeModelEvent extends java.util.EventObject {
// Public Constructors
    public TreeModelEvent(Object source, Object[ ] path);
    public TreeModelEvent(Object source, javax.swing.tree.TreePath path);
    public TreeModelEvent(Object source, javax.swing.tree.TreePath path, int[ ] childIndices, Object[ ] children);
    public TreeModelEvent(Object source, Object[ ] path, int[ ] childIndices, Object[ ] children);
// Property Accessor Methods (by property name)
    public int[ ] getChildIndices();
    public Object[ ] getChildren();
    public Object[ ] getPath();
    public javax.swing.tree.TreePath getTreePath();
// Public Methods Overriding EventObject
    public String toString();
// Protected Instance Fields
    protected int[ ] childIndices;
    protected Object[ ] children;
```

```
    protected javax.swing.tree.TreePath path;
}
```

Hierarchy: Object→ java.util.EventObject(Serializable)→ TreeModelEvent

Passed To: Too many methods to list.

TreeModelListener

Java 1.2

javax.swing.event

event listener

This interface defines the methods that an object must implement to receive notifications of changes to a javax.swing.tree.TreeModel.

```
public abstract interface TreeModelListener extends java.util.EventListener {
// Public Instance Methods
    public abstract void treeNodesChanged(TreeModelEvent e);
    public abstract void treeNodesInserted(TreeModelEvent e);
    public abstract void treeNodesRemoved(TreeModelEvent e);
    public abstract void treeStructureChanged(TreeModelEvent e);
}
```

Hierarchy: (TreeModelListener(java.util.EventListener))

Implementations: JTree.AccessibleJTree, JTree.TreeModelHandler

Passed To: javax.swing.tree.DefaultTreeModel.{addTreeModelListener(), removeTreeModelListener()}, javax.swing.tree.TreeModel.{addTreeModelListener(), removeTreeModelListener()}

Returned By: JTree.createTreeModelListener()

Type Of: JTree.treeModelListener

TreeSelectionEvent

Java 1.2

javax.swing.event

serializable event

An event of this type is generated by a javax.swing.tree.TreeSelectionModel or by the JTree component that uses that model when the selection state of the tree changes. getPaths() returns the array of javax.swing.tree.TreePath objects that were added to or removed from the selection. getPath() returns the first element of this array. The one-argument version of isAddedPath() tests whether a specified TreePath (it must be one of the ones returned by getPaths()) was added to the selection (true) or removed from it (false). The no-argument version of this method tests whether the value returned by getPath() was selected or deselected.

```
public class TreeSelectionEvent extends java.util.EventObject {
// Public Constructors
    public TreeSelectionEvent(Object source, javax.swing.tree.TreePath[] paths, boolean[] areNew,
                              javax.swing.tree.TreePath oldLeadSelectionPath,
                              javax.swing.tree.TreePath newLeadSelectionPath);
    public TreeSelectionEvent(Object source, javax.swing.tree.TreePath path, boolean isNew,
                              javax.swing.tree.TreePath oldLeadSelectionPath,
                              javax.swing.tree.TreePath newLeadSelectionPath);
// Property Accessor Methods (by property name)
    public boolean isAddedPath();
    public boolean isAddedPath(javax.swing.tree.TreePath path);
    public javax.swing.tree.TreePath getNewLeadSelectionPath();
    public javax.swing.tree.TreePath getOldLeadSelectionPath();
    public javax.swing.tree.TreePath getPath();
    public javax.swing.tree.TreePath[] getPaths();
// Public Instance Methods
```

```
    public Object cloneWithSource(Object newSource);
// Protected Instance Fields
    protected boolean[ ] areNew;
    protected javax.swing.tree.TreePath newLeadSelectionPath;
    protected javax.swing.tree.TreePath oldLeadSelectionPath;
    protected javax.swing.tree.TreePath[ ] paths;
}
```

Hierarchy: Object→ java.util.EventObject(Serializable)→ TreeSelectionEvent

Passed To: JTree.fireValueChanged(), JTree.AccessibleJTree.valueChanged(),
JTree.TreeSelectionRedirector.valueChanged(), TreeSelectionListener.valueChanged(),
javax.swing.tree.DefaultTreeCellEditor.valueChanged(),
javax.swing.tree.DefaultTreeSelectionModel.fireValueChanged()

TreeSelectionListener   Java 1.2

javax.swing.event   *event listener*

This interface defines the method that an object must implement to receive notifications
about changes to the selection state of a javax.swing.tree.TreeSelectionModel object or JTree
component.

```
public abstract interface TreeSelectionListener extends java.util.EventListener {
// Public Instance Methods
    public abstract void valueChanged(TreeSelectionEvent e);
}
```

Hierarchy: (TreeSelectionListener(java.util.EventListener))

Implementations: JTree.AccessibleJTree, JTree.TreeSelectionRedirector,
javax.swing.tree.DefaultTreeCellEditor

Passed To: JTree.{addTreeSelectionListener(), removeTreeSelectionListener()},
javax.swing.tree.DefaultTreeSelectionModel.{addTreeSelectionListener(), removeTreeSelectionListener()},
javax.swing.tree.TreeSelectionModel.{addTreeSelectionListener(), removeTreeSelectionListener()}

TreeWillExpandListener   Java 1.2

javax.swing.event   *event listener*

This interface defines the methods that JTree invokes on registered listeners immediately
before it expands or collapses a node. Do not confuse this interface with TreeExpansion-
Listener, which is notified immediately after a node is expanded or collapsed. Both listeners share the same TreeExpansionEvent event type, however. Note that the methods of
this interface can throw an ExpandVetoException to veto the proposed expansion or collapse of the node.

```
public abstract interface TreeWillExpandListener extends java.util.EventListener {
// Public Instance Methods
    public abstract void treeWillCollapse(TreeExpansionEvent event) throws javax.swing.tree.ExpandVetoException;
    public abstract void treeWillExpand(TreeExpansionEvent event) throws javax.swing.tree.ExpandVetoException;
}
```

Hierarchy: (TreeWillExpandListener(java.util.EventListener))

Passed To: JTree.{addTreeWillExpandListener(), removeTreeWillExpandListener()}

UndoableEditEvent

javax.swing.event

serializable event

An event of this type is generated by a javax.swing.text.Document when an undoable edit has occurred. The inherited getSource() method returns the Document object on which the edit occurred, and getEdit() returns a description of the edit itself.

```
public class UndoableEditEvent extends java.util.EventObject {
// Public Constructors
    public UndoableEditEvent(Object source, javax.swing.undo.UndoableEdit edit);
// Public Instance Methods
    public javax.swing.undo.UndoableEdit getEdit();
}
```

Hierarchy: Object→ java.util.EventObject(Serializable)→ UndoableEditEvent

Passed To: UndoableEditListener.undoableEditHappened(),
javax.swing.text.AbstractDocument.fireUndoableEditUpdate(),
javax.swing.text.html.HTMLDocument.fireUndoableEditUpdate(),
javax.swing.undo.UndoManager.undoableEditHappened()

UndoableEditListener

javax.swing.event

event listener

This interface defines the method that an object must implement in order to receive notifications when an undoable edit occurs in a javax.swing.text.Document.

```
public abstract interface UndoableEditListener extends java.util.EventListener {
// Public Instance Methods
    public abstract void undoableEditHappened(UndoableEditEvent e);
}
```

Hierarchy: (UndoableEditListener(java.util.EventListener))

Implementations: javax.swing.undo.UndoManager

Passed To: javax.swing.text.AbstractDocument.{addUndoableEditListener(), removeUndoableEditListener()},
javax.swing.text.Document.{addUndoableEditListener(), removeUndoableEditListener()},
javax.swing.undo.UndoableEditSupport.{addUndoableEditListener(), removeUndoableEditListener()}

CHAPTER 27

The javax.swing.filechooser Package

The javax.swing.filechooser package defines auxiliary classes used by the javax.-swing.JFileChooser component. You can customize the behavior of a JFileChooser by defining concrete subclasses of these abstract classes. Define a FileFilter to specify what files should be displayed by the JFileChooser. Define a FileView to specify how it should display those classes. And define a FileSystemView to specify how it should traverse the file system. Figure 27-1 shows the class hierarchy of this package.

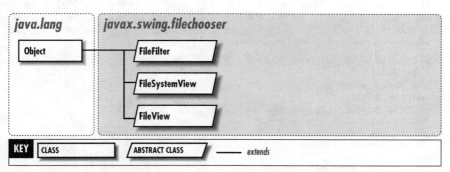

Figure 27-1: The javax.swing.filechooser package

FileFilter   Java 1.2

javax.swing.filechooser

This abstract class defines the methods used by the JFileChooser component to select a subset of files for display. When the accept() method is passed a File object, it should return true if that file should be displayed by the JFileChooser and false otherwise. accept() often makes its determination based on the filename extension, but it can also take other factors into account, such as the readability and writability of the file. The getDe-scription() method must return a human-readable description (preferably localized for the current locale) of the filtering operation performed by the filter. For example, if a

FileFilter accepts files that end with extensions *.gif*, *.jpg*, and *.png*, the getDescription() method might return the string Image files.

Once you have created a FileFilter, you can tell a JFileChooser to use it by passing the filter to the setFileFilter() method. If you want to allow the user to choose among a set of file filters, pass the FileFilter objects to the addChooseableFileFilter() method of JFileChooser. Do not confuse javax.swing.filechooser.FileFilter with its less-powerful relative, java.io.FilenameFilter.

```
public abstract class FileFilter {
// Public Constructors
    public FileFilter();
// Public Instance Methods
    public abstract boolean accept(java.io.File f);
    public abstract String getDescription();
}
```

Passed To: JFileChooser.{addChoosableFileFilter(), removeChoosableFileFilter(), setFileFilter()}

Returned By: JFileChooser.{getAcceptAllFileFilter(), getChoosableFileFilters(), getFileFilter()}, javax.swing.plaf.FileChooserUI.getAcceptAllFileFilter()

FileSystemView   Java 1.2

javax.swing.filechooser

FileSystemView abstracts the system dependencies of the native filesystem and provides a platform-independent view of the filesystem for the JFileChooser component. As of Java 1.2, the features of FileSystemView are provided directly by the java.io.File class, so this class exists for portability to Java 1.1 systems.

You can obtain the FileSystemView object for the current platform by calling the static getFileSystemView() method. The getRoots() method returns a list of root directories for the system. For Unix systems, there is only one, the / directory. On Windows systems, however, there is a root directory for each active drive letter. Use getHomeDirectory() to obtain a user's home directory on systems that have such a concept. Use isHiddenFile() to determine if a file is a hidden file according to the conventions of the native platform. Use getFiles() to list the contents of a directory, optionally omitting hidden files.

```
public abstract class FileSystemView {
// Public Constructors
    public FileSystemView();
// Public Class Methods
    public static FileSystemView getFileSystemView();
// Property Accessor Methods (by property name)
    public java.io.File getHomeDirectory();
    public abstract java.io.File[ ] getRoots();
// Public Instance Methods
    public java.io.File createFileObject(String path);
    public java.io.File createFileObject(java.io.File dir, String filename);
    public abstract java.io.File createNewFolder(java.io.File containingDir) throws java.io.IOException;
    public java.io.File[ ] getFiles(java.io.File dir, boolean useFileHiding);
    public java.io.File getParentDirectory(java.io.File dir);
    public abstract boolean isHiddenFile(java.io.File f);
    public abstract boolean isRoot(java.io.File f);
}
```

Passed To: JFileChooser.{JFileChooser(), setFileSystemView(), setup()}

Returned By: JFileChooser.getFileSystemView(), FileSystemView.getFileSystemView()

FileView

javax.swing.filechooser

This abstract class defines methods that the JFileChooser component uses to obtain information about how it should display a file. JFileChooser uses a FileView object provided by the current look-and-feel implementation to provide such things as the default icons for files and directories. You can implement your own FileView object to override some or all of the default behavior of the FileView provided by a look-and-feel. To do so, pass your FileView to the setFileView() method of the JFileChooser. The JFileChooser always queries your FileView object first, but when any of your methods return null, it calls the corresponding method of the look-and-feel FileView. By far, the most common reason to create a custom FileView class is to implement the getIcon() method to return custom icons for specific types of files. The other methods of FileView are not so commonly used.

```
public abstract class FileView {
// Public Constructors
    public FileView();
// Public Instance Methods
    public abstract String getDescription(java.io.File f);
    public abstract Icon getIcon(java.io.File f);
    public abstract String getName(java.io.File f);
    public abstract String getTypeDescription(java.io.File f);
    public abstract Boolean isTraversable(java.io.File f);
}
```

Passed To: JFileChooser.setFileView()

Returned By: JFileChooser.getFileView(), javax.swing.plaf.FileChooserUI.getFileView()

CHAPTER 28

The javax.swing.plaf Package

This package contains classes and interfaces used in the definition of a pluggable look-and-feel (hence the acronym "plaf"). It defines abstract UI delegate classes for Swing components. Typically, only look-and-feel developers and advanced component developers need to use this package. Figure 28-1 shows the class hierarchy of this package. See Chapter 3, *Swing Programming Topics*, for further discussion of Swing's pluggable look-and-feel architecture.

The javax.swing.plaf.basic package contains classes that extend the UI delegate classes of this package to create a basic pluggable look-and-feel UI framework. The classes in javax.swing.plaf.metal extend the classes of javax.swing.plaf.basic to implement the default Java look-and-feel. The classes in javax.swing.plaf.multi also extend the abstract classes of javax.swing.plaf to produce a multiplexing look-and-feel that combines a primary look-and-feel with one or more auxiliary look-and-feel implementations. These various subpackages of javax.swing.plaf are not documented in this book because they are very infrequently used and because they are straightforward implementations of the classes in this package that do not define any new public APIs.

BorderUIResource

javax.swing.plaf
serializable

This class implements the UIResource marker interface and serves as a wrapper around an existing javax.swing.border.Border object. It differs from other UIResource implementations in this package, in that it does not subclass an existing resource type. In addition, this class includes inner classes that provide UIResource versions of the standard Swing border classes. Several static methods exist for obtaining shared instances of commonly used UIResource borders.

```
public class BorderUIResource implements javax.swing.border.Border, Serializable, UIResource {
// Public Constructors
    public BorderUIResource(javax.swing.border.Border delegate);
// Inner Classes
    public static class BevelBorderUIResource extends javax.swing.border.BevelBorder implements UIResource;
```

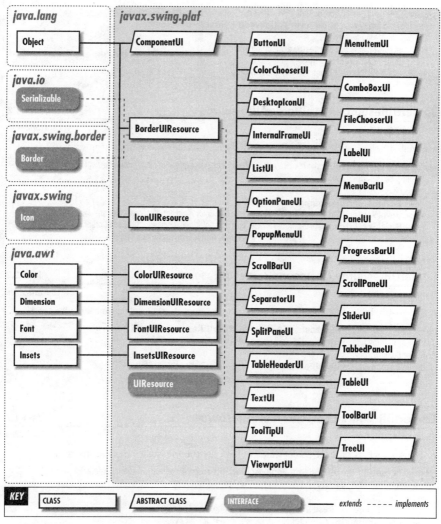

Figure 28–1: The javax.swing.plaf package

public static class **CompoundBorderUIResource** extends javax.swing.border.CompoundBorder
    implements UIResource;
public static class **EmptyBorderUIResource** extends javax.swing.border.EmptyBorder implements UIResource;
public static class **EtchedBorderUIResource** extends javax.swing.border.EtchedBorder implements UIResource;
public static class **LineBorderUIResource** extends javax.swing.border.LineBorder implements UIResource;
public static class **MatteBorderUIResource** extends javax.swing.border.MatteBorder implements UIResource;
public static class **TitledBorderUIResource** extends javax.swing.border.TitledBorder implements UIResource;
// Public Class Methods
public static javax.swing.border.Border **getBlackLineBorderUIResource**();
public static javax.swing.border.Border **getEtchedBorderUIResource**();

```
   public static javax.swing.border.Border getLoweredBevelBorderUIResource();
   public static javax.swing.border.Border getRaisedBevelBorderUIResource();
// Methods Implementing Border
   public java.awt.Insets getBorderInsets(Component c);
   public boolean isBorderOpaque();
   public void paintBorder(Component c, java.awt.Graphics g, int x, int y, int width, int height);
}
```

BorderUIResource.BevelBorderUIResource   Java 1.2

javax.swing.plaf   *serializable*

A trivial subclass of BevelBorder that implements the UIResource marker interface.

```
public static class BorderUIResource.BevelBorderUIResource extends javax.swing.border.BevelBorder
      implements UIResource {
// Public Constructors
   public BevelBorderUIResource(int bevelType);
   public BevelBorderUIResource(int bevelType, java.awt.Color highlight, java.awt.Color shadow);
   public BevelBorderUIResource(int bevelType, java.awt.Color highlightOuter, java.awt.Color highlightInner,
                  java.awt.Color shadowOuter, java.awt.Color shadowInner);
}
```

BorderUIResource.CompoundBorderUIResource   Java 1.2

javax.swing.plaf   *serializable*

A trivial subclass of CompoundBorder that implements the UIResource marker interface.

```
public static class BorderUIResource.CompoundBorderUIResource extends
      javax.swing.border.CompoundBorder implements UIResource {
// Public Constructors
   public CompoundBorderUIResource(javax.swing.border.Border outsideBorder,
                  javax.swing.border.Border insideBorder);
}
```

BorderUIResource.EmptyBorderUIResource   Java 1.2

javax.swing.plaf   *serializable*

A trivial subclass of EmptyBorder that implements the UIResource marker interface.

```
public static class BorderUIResource.EmptyBorderUIResource extends javax.swing.border.EmptyBorder
      implements UIResource {
// Public Constructors
   public EmptyBorderUIResource(java.awt.Insets insets);
   public EmptyBorderUIResource(int top, int left, int bottom, int right);
}
```

BorderUIResource.EtchedBorderUIResource   Java 1.2

javax.swing.plaf   *serializable*

A trivial subclass of EtchedBorder that implements the UIResource marker interface.

```
public static class BorderUIResource.EtchedBorderUIResource extends javax.swing.border.EtchedBorder
      implements UIResource {
// Public Constructors
   public EtchedBorderUIResource();
   public EtchedBorderUIResource(int etchType);
   public EtchedBorderUIResource(java.awt.Color highlight, java.awt.Color shadow);
```

public **EtchedBorderUIResource**(int *etchType*, java.awt.Color *highlight*, java.awt.Color *shadow*);
}

BorderUIResource.LineBorderUIResource

javax.swing.plaf *serializable*

A trivial subclass of LineBorder that implements the UIResource marker interface.

public static class **BorderUIResource.LineBorderUIResource** extends javax.swing.border.LineBorder
    implements UIResource {
// *Public Constructors*
    public **LineBorderUIResource**(java.awt.Color *color*);
    public **LineBorderUIResource**(java.awt.Color *color*, int *thickness*);
}

BorderUIResource.MatteBorderUIResource

javax.swing.plaf *serializable*

A trivial subclass of MatteBorder that implements the UIResource marker interface.

public static class **BorderUIResource.MatteBorderUIResource** extends javax.swing.border.MatteBorder
    implements UIResource {
// *Public Constructors*
    public **MatteBorderUIResource**(Icon *tileIcon*);
    public **MatteBorderUIResource**(int *top*, int *left*, int *bottom*, int *right*, Icon *tileIcon*);
    public **MatteBorderUIResource**(int *top*, int *left*, int *bottom*, int *right*, java.awt.Color *color*);
}

BorderUIResource.TitledBorderUIResource

javax.swing.plaf *serializable*

A trivial subclass of TitledBorder that implements the UIResource marker interface.

public static class **BorderUIResource.TitledBorderUIResource** extends javax.swing.border.TitledBorder
    implements UIResource {
// *Public Constructors*
    public **TitledBorderUIResource**(javax.swing.border.Border *border*);
    public **TitledBorderUIResource**(String *title*);
    public **TitledBorderUIResource**(javax.swing.border.Border *border*, String *title*);
    public **TitledBorderUIResource**(javax.swing.border.Border *border*, String *title*, int *titleJustification*,
            int *titlePosition*);
    public **TitledBorderUIResource**(javax.swing.border.Border *border*, String *title*, int *titleJustification*,
            int *titlePosition*, java.awt.Font *titleFont*);
    public **TitledBorderUIResource**(javax.swing.border.Border *border*, String *title*, int *titleJustification*,
            int *titlePosition*, java.awt.Font *titleFont*, java.awt.Color *titleColor*);
}

ButtonUI

javax.swing.plaf

This abstract class defines the methods that must be implemented by a pluggable look-and-feel delegate for JButton.

public abstract class **ButtonUI** extends ComponentUI {
// *Public Constructors*
    public **ButtonUI**();
}

Subclasses: MenuItemUI

Passed To: AbstractButton.setUI()

Returned By: AbstractButton.getUI()

ColorChooserUI
Java 1.2

javax.swing.plaf

This abstract class defines the methods that must be implemented by a pluggable look-and-feel delegate for JColorChooser.

```
public abstract class ColorChooserUI extends ComponentUI {
// Public Constructors
    public ColorChooserUI();
}
```

Passed To: JColorChooser.setUI()

Returned By: JColorChooser.getUI()

ColorUIResource
Java 1.2

javax.swing.plaf
serializable

A trivial subclass of java.awt.Color that implements the UIResource marker interface.

```
public class ColorUIResource extends java.awt.Color implements UIResource {
// Public Constructors
    public ColorUIResource(java.awt.Color c);
    public ColorUIResource(int rgb);
    public ColorUIResource(float r, float g, float b);
    public ColorUIResource(int r, int g, int b);
}
```

ComboBoxUI
Java 1.2

javax.swing.plaf

This abstract class defines the methods that must be implemented by a pluggable look-and-feel delegate for JComboBox.

```
public abstract class ComboBoxUI extends ComponentUI {
// Public Constructors
    public ComboBoxUI();
// Public Instance Methods
    public abstract boolean isFocusTraversable(JComboBox c);
    public abstract boolean isPopupVisible(JComboBox c);
    public abstract void setPopupVisible(JComboBox c, boolean v);
}
```

Passed To: JComboBox.setUI()

Returned By: JComboBox.getUI()

ComponentUI
Java 1.2

javax.swing.plaf

This abstract class defines the methods that must be implemented by a pluggable look-and-feel delegate for JComponent.

```
public abstract class ComponentUI {
// Public Constructors
    public ComponentUI();
// Public Class Methods
    public static ComponentUI createUI(JComponent c);
// Public Instance Methods
    public boolean contains(JComponent c, int x, int y);
    public Accessible getAccessibleChild(JComponent c, int i);
    public int getAccessibleChildrenCount(JComponent c);
    public java.awt.Dimension getMaximumSize(JComponent c);
    public java.awt.Dimension getMinimumSize(JComponent c);
    public java.awt.Dimension getPreferredSize(JComponent c);                   constant
    public void installUI(JComponent c);                                        empty
    public void paint(java.awt.Graphics g, JComponent c);                       empty
    public void uninstallUI(JComponent c);                                      empty
    public void update(java.awt.Graphics g, JComponent c);
}
```

Subclasses: Too many classes to list.

Passed To: JComponent.setUI()

Returned By: UIDefaults.getUI(), UIManager.getUI(), ComponentUI.createUI()

Type Of: JComponent.ui

DesktopIconUI   Java 1.2

javax.swing.plaf

This abstract class defines the methods that must be implemented by a pluggable look-and-feel delegate for JDesktopIcon.

```
public abstract class DesktopIconUI extends ComponentUI {
// Public Constructors
    public DesktopIconUI();
}
```

Passed To: JInternalFrame.JDesktopIcon.setUI()

Returned By: JInternalFrame.JDesktopIcon.getUI()

DesktopPaneUI   Java 1.2

javax.swing.plaf

This abstract class defines the methods that must be implemented by a pluggable look-and-feel delegate for JDesktopPane.

```
public abstract class DesktopPaneUI extends ComponentUI {
// Public Constructors
    public DesktopPaneUI();
}
```

Passed To: JDesktopPane.setUI()

Returned By: JDesktopPane.getUI()

DimensionUIResource   Java 1.2

javax.swing.plaf   *cloneable serializable*

A trivial subclass of java.awt.Dimension that implements the UIResource marker interface.

```
public class DimensionUIResource extends java.awt.Dimension implements UIResource {
// Public Constructors
    public DimensionUIResource(int width, int height);
}
```

FileChooserUI

Java 1.2

javax.swing.plaf

This abstract class defines the methods that must be implemented by a pluggable look-and-feel delegate for JFileChooser.

```
public abstract class FileChooserUI extends ComponentUI {
// Public Constructors
    public FileChooserUI();
// Public Instance Methods
    public abstract void ensureFileIsVisible(JFileChooser fc, java.io.File f);
    public abstract javax.swing.filechooser.FileFilter getAcceptAllFileFilter(JFileChooser fc);
    public abstract String getApproveButtonText(JFileChooser fc);
    public abstract String getDialogTitle(JFileChooser fc);
    public abstract javax.swing.filechooser.FileView getFileView(JFileChooser fc);
    public abstract void rescanCurrentDirectory(JFileChooser fc);
}
```

Returned By: JFileChooser.getUI()

FontUIResource

Java 1.2

javax.swing.plaf

serializable

A trivial subclass of java.awt.Font that implements the UIResource marker interface.

```
public class FontUIResource extends java.awt.Font implements UIResource {
// Public Constructors
    public FontUIResource(java.awt.Font font);
    public FontUIResource(String name, int style, int size);
}
```

IconUIResource

Java 1.2

javax.swing.plaf

serializable

A trivial subclass of javax.swing.Icon that implements the UIResource marker interface.

```
public class IconUIResource implements Icon, Serializable, UIResource {
// Public Constructors
    public IconUIResource(Icon delegate);
// Methods Implementing Icon
    public int getIconHeight();
    public int getIconWidth();
    public void paintIcon(Component c, java.awt.Graphics g, int x, int y);
}
```

InsetsUIResource

Java 1.2

javax.swing.plaf

cloneable serializable

A trivial subclass of java.awt.Insets that implements the UIResource marker interface.

```
public class InsetsUIResource extends java.awt.Insets implements UIResource {
// Public Constructors
    public InsetsUIResource(int top, int left, int bottom, int right);
}
```

InternalFrameUI

Java 1.2

javax.swing.plaf

This abstract class defines the methods that must be implemented by a pluggable look-and-feel delegate for JInternalFrame.

```
public abstract class InternalFrameUI extends ComponentUI {
// Public Constructors
    public InternalFrameUI();
}
```

Passed To: JInternalFrame.setUI()

Returned By: JInternalFrame.getUI()

LabelUI

Java 1.2

javax.swing.plaf

This abstract class defines the methods that must be implemented by a pluggable look-and-feel delegate for JLabel.

```
public abstract class LabelUI extends ComponentUI {
// Public Constructors
    public LabelUI();
}
```

Passed To: JLabel.setUI()

Returned By: JLabel.getUI()

ListUI

Java 1.2

javax.swing.plaf

This abstract class defines the methods that must be implemented by a pluggable look-and-feel delegate for JList.

```
public abstract class ListUI extends ComponentUI {
// Public Constructors
    public ListUI();
// Public Instance Methods
    public abstract java.awt.Rectangle getCellBounds(JList list, int index1, int index2);
    public abstract java.awt.Point indexToLocation(JList list, int index);
    public abstract int locationToIndex(JList list, java.awt.Point location);
}
```

Passed To: JList.setUI()

Returned By: JList.getUI()

MenuBarUI

Java 1.2

javax.swing.plaf

This abstract class defines the methods that must be implemented by a pluggable look-and-feel delegate for JMenuBar.

```
public abstract class MenuBarUI extends ComponentUI {
// Public Constructors
   public MenuBarUI();
}
```

Passed To: JMenuBar.setUI()

Returned By: JMenuBar.getUI()

MenuItemUI

javax.swing.plaf

This abstract class defines the methods that must be implemented by a pluggable look-and-feel delegate for JMenuItem.

```
public abstract class MenuItemUI extends ButtonUI {
// Public Constructors
   public MenuItemUI();
}
```

Passed To: JMenuItem.setUI()

OptionPaneUI

javax.swing.plaf

This abstract class defines the methods that must be implemented by a pluggable look-and-feel delegate for JOptionPane.

```
public abstract class OptionPaneUI extends ComponentUI {
// Public Constructors
   public OptionPaneUI();
// Public Instance Methods
   public abstract boolean containsCustomComponents(JOptionPane op);
   public abstract void selectInitialValue(JOptionPane op);
}
```

Passed To: JOptionPane.setUI()

Returned By: JOptionPane.getUI()

PanelUI

javax.swing.plaf

This abstract class defines the methods that must be implemented by a pluggable look-and-feel delegate for JPanel.

```
public abstract class PanelUI extends ComponentUI {
// Public Constructors
   public PanelUI();
}
```

PopupMenuUI

javax.swing.plaf

This abstract class defines the methods that must be implemented by a pluggable look-and-feel delegate for JPopupMenu.

```
public abstract class PopupMenuUI extends ComponentUI {
// Public Constructors
    public PopupMenuUI();
}
```

Passed To: JPopupMenu.setUI()

Returned By: JPopupMenu.getUI()

ProgressBarUI

javax.swing.plaf

This abstract class defines the methods that must be implemented by a pluggable look-and-feel delegate for JProgressBar.

```
public abstract class ProgressBarUI extends ComponentUI {
// Public Constructors
    public ProgressBarUI();
}
```

Passed To: JProgressBar.setUI()

Returned By: JProgressBar.getUI()

ScrollBarUI

javax.swing.plaf

This abstract class defines the methods that must be implemented by a pluggable look-and-feel delegate for JScrollBar.

```
public abstract class ScrollBarUI extends ComponentUI {
// Public Constructors
    public ScrollBarUI();
}
```

Returned By: JScrollBar.getUI()

ScrollPaneUI

javax.swing.plaf

This abstract class defines the methods that must be implemented by a pluggable look-and-feel delegate for JScrollPane.

```
public abstract class ScrollPaneUI extends ComponentUI {
// Public Constructors
    public ScrollPaneUI();
}
```

Passed To: JScrollPane.setUI()

Returned By: JScrollPane.getUI()

SeparatorUI

javax.swing.plaf

This abstract class defines the methods that must be implemented by a pluggable look-and-feel delegate for JSeparator.

```
public abstract class SeparatorUI extends ComponentUI {
// Public Constructors
   public SeparatorUI();
}
```

Passed To: JSeparator.setUI()

Returned By: JSeparator.getUI()

SliderUI   Java 1.2

javax.swing.plaf

This abstract class defines the methods that must be implemented by a pluggable look-and-feel delegate for JSlider.

```
public abstract class SliderUI extends ComponentUI {
// Public Constructors
   public SliderUI();
}
```

Passed To: JSlider.setUI()

Returned By: JSlider.getUI()

SplitPaneUI   Java 1.2

javax.swing.plaf

This abstract class defines the methods that must be implemented by a pluggable look-and-feel delegate for JSplitPane.

```
public abstract class SplitPaneUI extends ComponentUI {
// Public Constructors
   public SplitPaneUI();
// Public Instance Methods
   public abstract void finishedPaintingChildren(JSplitPane jc, java.awt.Graphics g);
   public abstract int getDividerLocation(JSplitPane jc);
   public abstract int getMaximumDividerLocation(JSplitPane jc);
   public abstract int getMinimumDividerLocation(JSplitPane jc);
   public abstract void resetToPreferredSizes(JSplitPane jc);
   public abstract void setDividerLocation(JSplitPane jc, int location);
}
```

Passed To: JSplitPane.setUI()

Returned By: JSplitPane.getUI()

TabbedPaneUI   Java 1.2

javax.swing.plaf

This abstract class defines the methods that must be implemented by a pluggable look-and-feel delegate for JTabbedPane.

```
public abstract class TabbedPaneUI extends ComponentUI {
// Public Constructors
   public TabbedPaneUI();
// Public Instance Methods
   public abstract java.awt.Rectangle getTabBounds(JTabbedPane pane, int index);
   public abstract int getTabRunCount(JTabbedPane pane);
   public abstract int tabForCoordinate(JTabbedPane pane, int x, int y);
}
```

Passed To: JTabbedPane.setUI()

Returned By: JTabbedPane.getUI()

TableHeaderUI

javax.swing.plaf

This abstract class defines the methods that must be implemented by a pluggable look-and-feel delegate for JTableHeader.

```
public abstract class TableHeaderUI extends ComponentUI {
// Public Constructors
    public TableHeaderUI();
}
```

Passed To: javax.swing.table.JTableHeader.setUI()

Returned By: javax.swing.table.JTableHeader.getUI()

TableUI

javax.swing.plaf

This abstract class defines the methods that must be implemented by a pluggable look-and-feel delegate for JTable.

```
public abstract class TableUI extends ComponentUI {
// Public Constructors
    public TableUI();
}
```

Passed To: JTable.setUI()

Returned By: JTable.getUI()

TextUI

javax.swing.plaf

This abstract class defines the methods that must be implemented by a pluggable look-and-feel delegate for JTextComponent.

```
public abstract class TextUI extends ComponentUI {
// Public Constructors
    public TextUI();
// Public Instance Methods
    public abstract void damageRange(javax.swing.text.JTextComponent t, int p0, int p1);
    public abstract void damageRange(javax.swing.text.JTextComponent t, int p0, int p1,
                            javax.swing.text.Position.Bias firstBias,
                            javax.swing.text.Position.Bias secondBias);
    public abstract javax.swing.text.EditorKit getEditorKit(javax.swing.text.JTextComponent t);
    public abstract int getNextVisualPositionFrom(javax.swing.text.JTextComponent t, int pos,
                                javax.swing.text.Position.Bias b, int direction,
                                javax.swing.text.Position.Bias[] biasRet)
        throws javax.swing.text.BadLocationException;
    public abstract javax.swing.text.View getRootView(javax.swing.text.JTextComponent t);
    public abstract java.awt.Rectangle modelToView(javax.swing.text.JTextComponent t, int pos)
        throws javax.swing.text.BadLocationException;
    public abstract java.awt.Rectangle modelToView(javax.swing.text.JTextComponent t, int pos,
                                javax.swing.text.Position.Bias bias)
        throws javax.swing.text.BadLocationException;
    public abstract int viewToModel(javax.swing.text.JTextComponent t, java.awt.Point pt);
```

```
    public abstract int viewToModel(javax.swing.text.JTextComponent t, java.awt.Point pt,
                                    javax.swing.text.Position.Bias[ ] biasReturn);
}
```

Passed To: javax.swing.text.JTextComponent.setUI()

Returned By: javax.swing.text.JTextComponent.getUI()

ToolBarUI   Java 1.2

javax.swing.plaf

This abstract class defines the methods that must be implemented by a pluggable look-and-feel delegate for JToolBar.

```
public abstract class ToolBarUI extends ComponentUI {
// Public Constructors
    public ToolBarUI();
}
```

Passed To: JToolBar.setUI()

Returned By: JToolBar.getUI()

ToolTipUI   Java 1.2

javax.swing.plaf

This abstract class defines the methods that must be implemented by a pluggable look-and-feel delegate for JToolTip.

```
public abstract class ToolTipUI extends ComponentUI {
// Public Constructors
    public ToolTipUI();
}
```

Returned By: JToolTip.getUI()

TreeUI   Java 1.2

javax.swing.plaf

This abstract class defines the methods that must be implemented by a pluggable look-and-feel delegate for JTree.

```
public abstract class TreeUI extends ComponentUI {
// Public Constructors
    public TreeUI();
// Public Instance Methods
    public abstract void cancelEditing(JTree tree);
    public abstract javax.swing.tree.TreePath getClosestPathForLocation(JTree tree, int x, int y);
    public abstract javax.swing.tree.TreePath getEditingPath(JTree tree);
    public abstract java.awt.Rectangle getPathBounds(JTree tree, javax.swing.tree.TreePath path);
    public abstract javax.swing.tree.TreePath getPathForRow(JTree tree, int row);
    public abstract int getRowCount(JTree tree);
    public abstract int getRowForPath(JTree tree, javax.swing.tree.TreePath path);
    public abstract boolean isEditing(JTree tree);
    public abstract void startEditingAtPath(JTree tree, javax.swing.tree.TreePath path);
    public abstract boolean stopEditing(JTree tree);
}
```

Passed To: JTree.setUI()

Returned By: JTree.getUI()

UIResource
javax.swing.plaf

This marker interface defines no methods; it is used to distinguish user-interface property values specified by a UI delegate from property values specified explicitly by an application. Only programmers writing custom look-and-feels or custom UI delegate objects need to use this interface. Application-level code never uses it.

Any component properties set by the installUI() method of a UI delegate object should be set to objects that implement the UIResource interface. This allows the uninstallUI() method to determine which properties were explicitly set by the application and leave these properties unchanged.

The requirement for property values that implement UIResource means that the javax.swing.plaf package contains a number of trivial wrapper classes that extend common resource types such as java.awt.Color, java.awt.Font, and so on. These wrapper classes add no new functionality but exist simply to implement UIResource.

```
public abstract interface UIResource {
}
```

Implementations: DefaultListCellRenderer.UIResource, JScrollPane.ScrollBar, ScrollPaneLayout.UIResource, BorderUIResource, BorderUIResource.BevelBorderUIResource, BorderUIResource.CompoundBorderUIResource, BorderUIResource.EmptyBorderUIResource, BorderUIResource.EtchedBorderUIResource, BorderUIResource.LineBorderUIResource, BorderUIResource.MatteBorderUIResource, BorderUIResource.TitledBorderUIResource, ColorUIResource, DimensionUIResource, FontUIResource, IconUIResource, InsetsUIResource, javax.swing.table.DefaultTableCellRenderer.UIResource

ViewportUI
javax.swing.plaf

This abstract class defines the methods that must be implemented by a pluggable look-and-feel delegate for JViewport.

```
public abstract class ViewportUI extends ComponentUI {
// Public Constructors
    public ViewportUI();
}
```

CHAPTER 29

The javax.swing.table Package

The javax.swing.table package contains classes and interfaces that are used with the powerful JTable component of the javax.swing package. TableModel is the central interface in this package; it provides access to the data to be displayed in the table. TableColumn represents the attributes of a column in the table. TableColumnModel represents a set of columns in the table. JTableHeader is a component that displays the resizable and draggable column headers of a table. The TableCellRenderer interface defines how individual cells are drawn using a GUI component as a template. Figure 29-1 shows the class hierarchy of this package. See Chapter 3, *Swing Programming Topics*, for a discussion of and example using JTable and the javax.swing.table package.

AbstractTableModel
Java 1.2

javax.swing.table
serializable model

This abstract class is a convenient partial implementation of the TableModel interface. An application that needs a noneditable TableModel needs only to provide implementations for the abstract methods getColumnCount(), getRowCount(), and getValueAt(). An application that wants to allow the table data to be edited must additionally override the default implementations of isCellEditable() and setValueAt(). AbstractTableModel provides default implementations of the event listener registration methods. Additionally, it defines a number of methods for sending various types of TableModelEvent objects to the registered TableModelListener objects. This is useful because of the fairly complex way that TableModelEvent is used to describe different types of changes to the table data. If the data underlying the table model ever changes, the application can call one of these methods to notify the JTable, and any other interested listeners, of the change.

```
public abstract class AbstractTableModel implements Serializable, TableModel {
// Public Constructors
    public AbstractTableModel();
// Event Registration Methods (by event name)
    public void addTableModelListener(javax.swing.event.TableModelListener l);          Implements:TableModel
                                                                                        Implements:TableModel
```

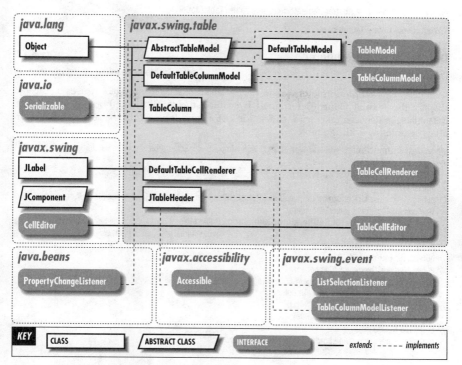

Figure 29–1: The javax.swing.table package

```
    public void removeTableModelListener(javax.swing.event.TableModelListener l);
// Public Instance Methods
    public int findColumn(String columnName);
    public void fireTableCellUpdated(int row, int column);
    public void fireTableChanged(javax.swing.event.TableModelEvent e);
    public void fireTableDataChanged();
    public void fireTableRowsDeleted(int firstRow, int lastRow);
    public void fireTableRowsInserted(int firstRow, int lastRow);
    public void fireTableRowsUpdated(int firstRow, int lastRow);
    public void fireTableStructureChanged();
// Methods Implementing TableModel
    public void addTableModelListener(javax.swing.event.TableModelListener l);
    public Class getColumnClass(int columnIndex);
    public abstract int getColumnCount();
    public String getColumnName(int column);
    public abstract int getRowCount();
    public abstract Object getValueAt(int rowIndex, int columnIndex);
    public boolean isCellEditable(int rowIndex, int columnIndex);                    constant
    public void removeTableModelListener(javax.swing.event.TableModelListener l);
    public void setValueAt(Object aValue, int rowIndex, int columnIndex);           empty
// Protected Instance Fields
    protected javax.swing.event.EventListenerList listenerList;
}
```

Hierarchy: Object→ AbstractTableModel(Serializable, TableModel)

Subclasses: DefaultTableModel

DefaultTableCellRenderer

Java 1.2

javax.swing.table

serializable accessible swing component

This class is a simple implementation of the TableCellRenderer interface. It uses a JLabel to display the textual value (determined by calling the toString() method) of any object. DefaultTableCellRenderer takes care to use the colors and fonts of the JTable, so that it interfaces seamlessly with the table.

```
public class DefaultTableCellRenderer extends JLabel implements Serializable, TableCellRenderer {
// Public Constructors
    public DefaultTableCellRenderer();
// Inner Classes
    public static class UIResource extends DefaultTableCellRenderer implements javax.swing.plaf.UIResource;
// Methods Implementing TableCellRenderer
    public Component getTableCellRendererComponent(JTable table, Object value, boolean isSelected,
                                                  boolean hasFocus, int row, int column);
// Public Methods Overriding JLabel
    public void updateUI();
// Public Methods Overriding JComponent
    public void setBackground(java.awt.Color c);
    public void setForeground(java.awt.Color c);
// Protected Instance Methods
    protected void setValue(Object value);
// Protected Class Fields
    protected static javax.swing.border.Border noFocusBorder;
}
```

Hierarchy: Object→ Component(java.awt.image.ImageObserver, java.awt.MenuContainer, Serializable)→ Container→ JComponent(Serializable)→ JLabel(Accessible, SwingConstants)→ DefaultTableCellRenderer(Serializable, TableCellRenderer)

Subclasses: DefaultTableCellRenderer.UIResource

DefaultTableCellRenderer.UIResource

Java 1.2

javax.swing.table

serializable accessible swing component

This class is a trivial subclass of DefaultTableCellRenderer that exists only to implement the javax.swing.plaf.UIResource marker interface.

```
public static class DefaultTableCellRenderer.UIResource extends DefaultTableCellRenderer
        implements javax.swing.plaf.UIResource {
// Public Constructors
    public UIResource();
}
```

DefaultTableColumnModel

Java 1.2

javax.swing.table

serializable model

This class implements the TableColumnModel and keeps track of the number, order, size, and selection state of the columns in a JTable component. The JTable uses this class by default; few applications have any reason to use anything else.

```
public class DefaultTableColumnModel implements javax.swing.event.ListSelectionListener,
        java.beans.PropertyChangeListener, Serializable, TableColumnModel {
// Public Constructors
    public DefaultTableColumnModel();
// Methods Implementing ListSelectionListener
    public void valueChanged(javax.swing.event.ListSelectionEvent e);
// Methods Implementing PropertyChangeListener
    public void propertyChange(java.beans.PropertyChangeEvent evt);
// Methods Implementing TableColumnModel
    public void addColumn(TableColumn aColumn);
    public void addColumnModelListener(javax.swing.event.TableColumnModelListener x);
    public TableColumn getColumn(int columnIndex);
    public int getColumnCount();                                                    default:0
    public int getColumnIndex(Object identifier);
    public int getColumnIndexAtX(int xPosition);
    public int getColumnMargin();                                                   default:1
    public java.util.Enumeration getColumns();
    public boolean getColumnSelectionAllowed();                                 default:false
    public int getSelectedColumnCount();                                            default:0
    public int[ ] getSelectedColumns();
    public ListSelectionModel getSelectionModel();                 default:DefaultListSelectionModel
    public int getTotalColumnWidth();                                               default:0
    public void moveColumn(int columnIndex, int newIndex);
    public void removeColumn(TableColumn column);
    public void removeColumnModelListener(javax.swing.event.TableColumnModelListener x);
    public void setColumnMargin(int newMargin);
    public void setColumnSelectionAllowed(boolean flag);
    public void setSelectionModel(ListSelectionModel newModel);
// Protected Instance Methods
    protected ListSelectionModel createSelectionModel();
    protected void fireColumnAdded(javax.swing.event.TableColumnModelEvent e);
    protected void fireColumnMarginChanged();
    protected void fireColumnMoved(javax.swing.event.TableColumnModelEvent e);
    protected void fireColumnRemoved(javax.swing.event.TableColumnModelEvent e);
    protected void fireColumnSelectionChanged(javax.swing.event.ListSelectionEvent e);
    protected void recalcWidthCache();
// Protected Instance Fields
    protected transient javax.swing.event.ChangeEvent changeEvent;
    protected int columnMargin;
    protected boolean columnSelectionAllowed;
    protected javax.swing.event.EventListenerList listenerList;
    protected ListSelectionModel selectionModel;
    protected java.util.Vector tableColumns;
    protected int totalColumnWidth;
}
```

javax.swing. table

Hierarchy: Object→
DefaultTableColumnModel(javax.swing.event.ListSelectionListener(java.util.EventListener),
java.beans.PropertyChangeListener(java.util.EventListener), Serializable, TableColumnModel)

DefaultTableModel   Java 1.2

javax.swing.table   *serializable model*

This class is a relatively simple implementation of TableModel that works with table data
that is expressed either as an array of rows, where each row is an array of objects, or as
a vector of rows, where each row is a vector of objects. In addition to the table cell
data, DefaultTableModel also allows you to specify the column header values in an array
or vector. DefaultTableModel is the only concrete TableModel implementation in Swing.

Several of the JTable constructors initialize and use a DefaultTableModel object as the component's model. In addition to its TableModel methods, DefaultTableModel also defines methods for changing the table data, adding and removing columns, and so on.

```
public class DefaultTableModel extends AbstractTableModel implements Serializable {
// Public Constructors
    public DefaultTableModel();
    public DefaultTableModel(Object[ ] columnNames, int numRows);
    public DefaultTableModel(java.util.Vector data, java.util.Vector columnNames);
    public DefaultTableModel(Object[ ][ ] data, Object[ ] columnNames);
    public DefaultTableModel(int numRows, int numColumns);
    public DefaultTableModel(java.util.Vector columnNames, int numRows);
// Protected Class Methods
    protected static java.util.Vector convertToVector(Object[ ][ ] anArray);
    protected static java.util.Vector convertToVector(Object[ ] anArray);
// Property Accessor Methods (by property name)
    public int getColumnCount();                                   Overrides:AbstractTableModel default:0
    public java.util.Vector getDataVector();
    public int getRowCount();                                      Overrides:AbstractTableModel default:0
// Public Instance Methods
    public void addColumn(Object columnName);
    public void addColumn(Object columnName, java.util.Vector columnData);
    public void addColumn(Object columnName, Object[ ] columnData);
    public void addRow(Object[ ] rowData);
    public void addRow(java.util.Vector rowData);
    public void insertRow(int row, Object[ ] rowData);
    public void insertRow(int row, java.util.Vector rowData);
    public void moveRow(int startIndex, int endIndex, int toIndex);
    public void newDataAvailable(javax.swing.event.TableModelEvent event);
    public void newRowsAdded(javax.swing.event.TableModelEvent event);
    public void removeRow(int row);
    public void rowsRemoved(javax.swing.event.TableModelEvent event);
    public void setColumnIdentifiers(Object[ ] newIdentifiers);
    public void setColumnIdentifiers(java.util.Vector newIdentifiers);
    public void setDataVector(Object[ ][ ] newData, Object[ ] columnNames);
    public void setDataVector(java.util.Vector newData, java.util.Vector columnNames);
    public void setNumRows(int newSize);
// Public Methods Overriding AbstractTableModel
    public String getColumnName(int column);
    public Object getValueAt(int row, int column);
    public boolean isCellEditable(int row, int column);                            constant
    public void setValueAt(Object aValue, int row, int column);
// Protected Instance Fields
    protected java.util.Vector columnIdentifiers;
    protected java.util.Vector dataVector;
}
```

Hierarchy: Object → AbstractTableModel(Serializable, TableModel) → DefaultTableModel(Serializable)

JTableHeader   Java 1.2

javax.swing.table   *serializable accessible swing component*

This class is a Swing component that displays the header of a JTable. This header component displays the name of each column and, optionally, allows the user to resize and reorder the columns by dragging them. JTableHeader uses the TableColumnModel of its JTable to obtain information about the column headers it must display.

A JTable component automatically creates a suitable JTableHeader component; an application should not have to create one of its own. Nevertheless, JTableHeader does define some interesting methods that applications may want to use. Obtain the JTableHeader of a JTable with the getTableHeader() method of JTable. Once you have the JTableHeader object, use its resizingAllowed and reorderingAllowed properties to specify how the user is allowed to manipulate the columns. Also, set the updateTableInRealTime property to specify if the entire JTable should be updated as the user drags a column or if the update should be postponed until the user completes the drag.

```
public class JTableHeader extends JComponent implements Accessible, javax.swing.event.TableColumnModelListener {
// Public Constructors
    public JTableHeader();
    public JTableHeader(TableColumnModel cm);
// Inner Classes
    protected class AccessibleJTableHeader extends JComponent.AccessibleJComponent;
// Property Accessor Methods (by property name)
    public AccessibleContext getAccessibleContext();          Implements:Accessible default:AccessibleJTableHeader
    public TableColumnModel getColumnModel();                             default:DefaultTableColumnModel
    public void setColumnModel(TableColumnModel newModel);
    public TableColumn getDraggedColumn();                                             default:null
    public void setDraggedColumn(TableColumn aColumn);
    public int getDraggedDistance();                                                    default:0
    public void setDraggedDistance(int distance);
    public boolean getReorderingAllowed();                                            default:true
    public void setReorderingAllowed(boolean b);
    public boolean getResizingAllowed();                                              default:true
    public void setResizingAllowed(boolean b);
    public TableColumn getResizingColumn();                                            default:null
    public void setResizingColumn(TableColumn aColumn);
    public JTable getTable();                                                          default:null
    public void setTable(JTable aTable);
    public javax.swing.plaf.TableHeaderUI getUI();
    public void setUI(javax.swing.plaf.TableHeaderUI ui);
    public String getUIClassID();                         Overrides:JComponent default:"TableHeaderUI"
    public boolean getUpdateTableInRealTime();                                        default:true
    public void setUpdateTableInRealTime(boolean flag);
// Public Instance Methods
    public int columnAtPoint(java.awt.Point point);
    public java.awt.Rectangle getHeaderRect(int columnIndex);
    public void resizeAndRepaint();
// Methods Implementing Accessible
    public AccessibleContext getAccessibleContext();                  default:AccessibleJTableHeader
// Methods Implementing TableColumnModelListener
    public void columnAdded(javax.swing.event.TableColumnModelEvent e);
    public void columnMarginChanged(javax.swing.event.ChangeEvent e);
    public void columnMoved(javax.swing.event.TableColumnModelEvent e);
    public void columnRemoved(javax.swing.event.TableColumnModelEvent e);
    public void columnSelectionChanged(javax.swing.event.ListSelectionEvent e);                empty
// Public Methods Overriding JComponent
    public String getToolTipText(java.awt.event.MouseEvent event);
    public void updateUI();
// Protected Methods Overriding JComponent
    protected String paramString();
// Protected Instance Methods
    protected TableColumnModel createDefaultColumnModel();
    protected void initializeLocalVars();
// Protected Instance Fields
    protected TableColumnModel columnModel;
    protected transient TableColumn draggedColumn;
    protected transient int draggedDistance;
    protected boolean reorderingAllowed;
    protected boolean resizingAllowed;
```

```
    protected transient TableColumn resizingColumn;
    protected JTable table;
    protected boolean updateTableInRealTime;
}
```

Hierarchy: Object→ Component(java.awt.image.ImageObserver, java.awt.MenuContainer, Serializable)→ Container→ JComponent(Serializable)→ JTableHeader(Accessible, javax.swing.event.TableColumnModelListener(java.util.EventListener))

Passed To: JTable.setTableHeader(), JTableHeader.AccessibleJTableHeader.AccessibleJTableHeaderEntry.AccessibleJTableHeaderEntry()

Returned By: JTable.{createDefaultTableHeader(), getTableHeader()}

Type Of: JTable.tableHeader

TableCellEditor   Java 1.2

javax.swing.table

This interface extends CellEditor and adds an additional method that must be implemented by classes that want to serve as editors for table cells displayed by a JTable. Most applications can rely on the default set of table-cell-editing capabilities of javax.-swing.DefaultCellEditor and do not have to implement this interface. If you do need to implement this interface, see javax.swing.CellEditor and javax.swing.tree.TreeCellEditor for further details.

```
public abstract interface TableCellEditor extends CellEditor {
// Public Instance Methods
    public abstract Component getTableCellEditorComponent(JTable table, Object value, boolean isSelected,
                                                 int row, int column);
}
```

Hierarchy: (TableCellEditor(CellEditor))

Implementations: DefaultCellEditor

Passed To: JTable.{prepareEditor(), setCellEditor(), setDefaultEditor()}, TableColumn.{setCellEditor(), TableColumn()}

Returned By: JTable.{getCellEditor(), getDefaultEditor()}, TableColumn.getCellEditor()

Type Of: JTable.cellEditor, TableColumn.cellEditor

TableCellRenderer   Java 1.2

javax.swing.table

This interface defines the method that must be implemented by any class wishing to display data within a JTable component. getTableCellRendererComponent() is passed the value that appears in a specified table cell; it must return a Component object capable of displaying that value in some fashion. Other arguments to the method specify whether the cell is selected and whether it has the keyboard focus. A renderer should take these factors into account when deciding how to display the value. The JTable is responsible for positioning the returned Component properly and causing it to draw itself. The Table-CellRenderer simply has to configure the appearance and content of the component before returning it. Most applications can rely on the DefaultTableCellRenderer class to display a textual representation of any object and do not have to implement this interface themselves.

public abstract interface **TableCellRenderer** {
// Public Instance Methods
    public abstract Component **getTableCellRendererComponent**(JTable *table*, Object *value*, boolean *isSelected*,
                                    boolean *hasFocus*, int *row*, int *column*);
}

Implementations: DefaultTableCellRenderer

Passed To: JTable.{prepareRenderer(), setDefaultRenderer()}, TableColumn.{setCellRenderer(),
setHeaderRenderer(), TableColumn()}

Returned By: JTable.{getCellRenderer(), getDefaultRenderer()},
TableColumn.{createDefaultHeaderRenderer(), getCellRenderer(), getHeaderRenderer()}

Type Of: TableColumn.{cellRenderer, headerRenderer}

TableColumn

Java 1.2

javax.swing.table

serializable

This class contains information about a single column displayed within a JTable. The
JTable component creates TableColumn objects automatically, and applications rarely need
to create their own. To obtain the TableColumn objects automatically created by a JTable,
first obtain the TableColumnModel of the table and then use its methods to query the individual columns.

TableColumn exposes a number of useful properties. width, preferredWidth, minWidth, and
maxWidth specify the current, preferred, minimum, and maximum sizes for the column.
The resizable property specifies whether the user is allowed to resize the column. The
identifier property allows you to attach a name to a column, which can sometimes be
useful when working with columns that may be reordered. The identifier is never displayed. On the other hand, the headerValue property specifies the object (usually a String)
that is displayed in the column header. The headerValue is displayed by the TableCellRenderer specified with the headerRenderer property. Do not confuse the headerRenderer with
the cellRenderer and cellEditor properties. If these properties are not null, they specify a
custom renderer object and a custom editor object to be used for the cells in this column. Finally, the modelIndex property specifies the column number to be used when
extracting data for this column from the TableModel. Since JTable allows its columns to be
rearranged by the user, there are two different coordinate systems for referring to
columns. The first is the index of the TableColumn object within the TableColumnModel.
This is the visual order of columns as displayed by the JTable. The other coordinate system is the more fundamental index of the column data within the underlying TableModel.
The modelIndex property uses the latter coordinate system and specifies where to obtain
data for the column.

public class **TableColumn** implements Serializable {
// Public Constructors
    public **TableColumn**();
    public **TableColumn**(int *modelIndex*);
    public **TableColumn**(int *modelIndex*, int *width*);
    public **TableColumn**(int *modelIndex*, int *width*, TableCellRenderer *cellRenderer*, TableCellEditor *cellEditor*);
// Public Constants
    public static final String **CELL_RENDERER_PROPERTY**;   =*"cellRenderer"*
    public static final String **COLUMN_WIDTH_PROPERTY**;   =*"columWidth"*
    public static final String **HEADER_RENDERER_PROPERTY**;   =*"headerRenderer"*
    public static final String **HEADER_VALUE_PROPERTY**;   =*"headerValue"*
// Event Registration Methods (by event name)
    public void **addPropertyChangeListener**(java.beans.PropertyChangeListener *listener*);   *synchronized*
    public void **removePropertyChangeListener**(java.beans.PropertyChangeListener *listener*);   *synchronized*

```
// Property Accessor Methods (by property name)
    public TableCellEditor getCellEditor();                                     default:null
    public void setCellEditor(TableCellEditor anEditor);
    public TableCellRenderer getCellRenderer();                                 default:null
    public void setCellRenderer(TableCellRenderer aRenderer);
    public TableCellRenderer getHeaderRenderer();
    public void setHeaderRenderer(TableCellRenderer aRenderer);
    public Object getHeaderValue();                                             default:null
    public void setHeaderValue(Object aValue);
    public Object getIdentifier();                                              default:null
    public void setIdentifier(Object anIdentifier);
    public int getMaxWidth();                                            default:2147483647
    public void setMaxWidth(int maxWidth);
    public int getMinWidth();                                                    default:15
    public void setMinWidth(int minWidth);
    public int getModelIndex();                                                   default:0
    public void setModelIndex(int anIndex);
    public int getPreferredWidth();                                              default:75
    public void setPreferredWidth(int preferredWidth);
    public boolean getResizable();                                             default:true
    public void setResizable(boolean flag);
    public int getWidth();                                                       default:75
    public void setWidth(int width);
// Public Instance Methods
    public void disableResizedPosting();
    public void enableResizedPosting();
    public void sizeWidthToFit();
// Protected Instance Methods
    protected TableCellRenderer createDefaultHeaderRenderer();
// Protected Instance Fields
    protected TableCellEditor cellEditor;
    protected TableCellRenderer cellRenderer;
    protected TableCellRenderer headerRenderer;
    protected Object headerValue;
    protected Object identifier;
    protected boolean isResizable;
    protected int maxWidth;
    protected int minWidth;
    protected int modelIndex;
    protected transient int resizedPostingDisableCount;
    protected int width;
}
```

Hierarchy: Object → TableColumn(Serializable)

Passed To: JTable.{addColumn(), removeColumn()}, DefaultTableColumnModel.{addColumn(), removeColumn()}, JTableHeader.{setDraggedColumn(), setResizingColumn()}, TableColumnModel.{addColumn(), removeColumn()}

Returned By: JTable.getColumn(), DefaultTableColumnModel.getColumn(), JTableHeader.{getDraggedColumn(), getResizingColumn()}, TableColumnModel.getColumn()

Type Of: JTableHeader.{draggedColumn, resizingColumn}

TableColumnModel

Java 1.2

javax.swing.table

model

A JTable component uses a TableColumnModel object to keep track of the columns it displays, the order they are in, and their selection state. In essence, a TableColumnModel maintains a list of TableColumn objects and remembers which are selected. Most applications rely on the DefaultTableColumnModel implementation and rarely need to implement this interface themselves.

```
public abstract interface TableColumnModel {
// Property Accessor Methods (by property name)
    public abstract int getColumnCount();
    public abstract int getColumnMargin();
    public abstract void setColumnMargin(int newMargin);
    public abstract java.util.Enumeration getColumns();
    public abstract boolean getColumnSelectionAllowed();
    public abstract void setColumnSelectionAllowed(boolean flag);
    public abstract int getSelectedColumnCount();
    public abstract int[ ] getSelectedColumns();
    public abstract ListSelectionModel getSelectionModel();
    public abstract void setSelectionModel(ListSelectionModel newModel);
    public abstract int getTotalColumnWidth();
// Public Instance Methods
    public abstract void addColumn(TableColumn aColumn);
    public abstract void addColumnModelListener(javax.swing.event.TableColumnModelListener x);
    public abstract TableColumn getColumn(int columnIndex);
    public abstract int getColumnIndex(Object columnIdentifier);
    public abstract int getColumnIndexAtX(int xPosition);
    public abstract void moveColumn(int columnIndex, int newIndex);
    public abstract void removeColumn(TableColumn column);
    public abstract void removeColumnModelListener(javax.swing.event.TableColumnModelListener x);
}
```

Implementations: DefaultTableColumnModel

Passed To: JTable.{JTable(), setColumnModel()},
javax.swing.event.TableColumnModelEvent.TableColumnModelEvent(), JTableHeader.{JTableHeader(),
setColumnModel()}

Returned By: JTable.{createDefaultColumnModel(), getColumnModel()},
JTableHeader.{createDefaultColumnModel(), getColumnModel()}

Type Of: JTable.columnModel, JTableHeader.columnModel

TableModel   Java 1.2

javax.swing.table   *model*

This interface is the intermediary between a JTable component and the data it displays. Every JTable uses a TableModel to encapsulate its data. getColumnCount() and getRowCount() return the size of the table. getColumnName() returns the header text for a given column number. getColumnClass() returns the Class object for a numbered column. (If you want to display different types of objects in a column, this method should return values of type Object.) The most important method of the interface, however, is getValueAt(), which, given a column number and a row number, returns the cell value. The JTable class can be configured to allow the user to reorder columns by dragging them. Note that this visual reordering does not change the underlying column numbers used to access data from the TableModel.

If you are allowing users to edit data in your TableModel, you must also provide meaningful implementations of isCellEditable() and setValueAt(). If the model can be edited or if the data it contains can otherwise change (e.g., if rows are added), you must also implement addTableModelListener() and removeTableModelListener() and send a TableModelEvent when the contents of the table change.

Applications with simple table display needs can rely on the DefaultTableModel. Because tabular data can come from an wide variety of sources, in a wide variety of formats, however, many applications need a custom TableModel implementation. Most applications find it easer to subclass AbstractTableModel than to implement TableModel from scratch.

```
public abstract interface TableModel {
// Event Registration Methods (by event name)
    public abstract void addTableModelListener(javax.swing.event.TableModelListener l);
    public abstract void removeTableModelListener(javax.swing.event.TableModelListener l);
// Public Instance Methods
    public abstract Class getColumnClass(int columnIndex);
    public abstract int getColumnCount();
    public abstract String getColumnName(int columnIndex);
    public abstract int getRowCount();
    public abstract Object getValueAt(int rowIndex, int columnIndex);
    public abstract boolean isCellEditable(int rowIndex, int columnIndex);
    public abstract void setValueAt(Object aValue, int rowIndex, int columnIndex);
}
```

Implementations: AbstractTableModel

Passed To: JTable.{JTable(), setModel()}, javax.swing.event.TableModelEvent.TableModelEvent()

Returned By: JTable.{createDefaultDataModel(), getModel()}

Type Of: JTable.dataModel

CHAPTER 30

The javax.swing.text Package

This large and complex package contains the powerful JTextComponent text editor and all of its supporting infrastructure. The JTextField, JTextArea, JEditorPane, and other text input components of the javax.swing package all subclass JTextComponent and rely on the other classes and interfaces of this package.

The Document interface defines the data model for the JTextComponent. It is the basic abstraction for documents that can be displayed and edited. The AbstractDocument class implements this interface and provides a number of useful features and extensions. StyledDocument extends Document to define support for documents that have styles associated with their content. DefaultStyledDocument is a concrete implementation based on AbstractDocument. Other important classes and interfaces in this package include: EditorKit, Element, View, AbstractDocument.Content, Caret, and Highlighter. Figure 30-1 shows the class hierarchy of this package.

AbstractDocument   Java 1.2

javax.swing.text   *serializable*

This class is a partial, abstract implementation of the Document interface, which also defines several important inner classes and interfaces. Typical applications do not have to use or subclass this class. Instead, they can rely on predefined concrete implementations such as PlainDocument, DefaultStyledDocument, and javax.swing.text.html.HTMLDocument.

```
public abstract class AbstractDocument implements Document, Serializable {
// Protected Constructors
    protected AbstractDocument(AbstractDocument.Content data);
    protected AbstractDocument(AbstractDocument.Content data, AbstractDocument.AttributeContext context);
// Public Constants
    public static final String BidiElementName;                          ="bidi level"
    public static final String ContentElementName;                        ="content"
    public static final String ElementNameAttribute;                      ="$ename"
    public static final String ParagraphElementName;                    ="paragraph"
    public static final String SectionElementName;                        ="section"
```

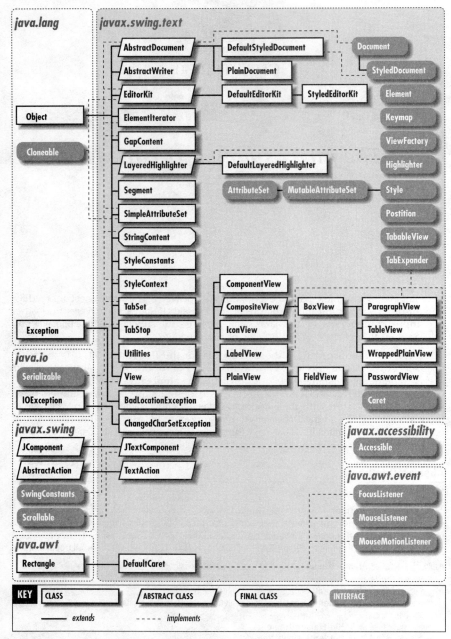

Figure 30–1: The javax.swing.text package

```
// Protected Constants
    protected static final String BAD_LOCATION;                          ="document location failure"
// Inner Classes
    public abstract class AbstractElement implements javax.swing.text.Element, MutableAttributeSet, Serializable,
        javax.swing.tree.TreeNode;
    public abstract static interface AttributeContext;
    public class BranchElement extends AbstractDocument.AbstractElement;
    public abstract static interface Content;
    public class DefaultDocumentEvent extends javax.swing.undo.CompoundEdit
        implements javax.swing.event.DocumentEvent;
    public static class ElementEdit extends javax.swing.undo.AbstractUndoableEdit
        implements javax.swing.event.DocumentEvent.ElementChange;
    public class LeafElement extends AbstractDocument.AbstractElement;
// Event Registration Methods (by event name)
    public void addDocumentListener(javax.swing.event.DocumentListener listener);      Implements:Document
    public void removeDocumentListener(javax.swing.event.DocumentListener listener);    Implements:Document
    public void addUndoableEditListener(javax.swing.event.UndoableEditListener listener);  Implements:Document
    public void removeUndoableEditListener(                                          Implements:Document
        javax.swing.event.UndoableEditListener listener);
// Public Instance Methods
    public void dump(java.io.PrintStream out);
    public int getAsynchronousLoadPriority();
    public javax.swing.text.Element getBidiRootElement();
    public java.util.Dictionary getDocumentProperties();
    public abstract javax.swing.text.Element getParagraphElement(int pos);
    public final void readLock();                                                   synchronized
    public final void readUnlock();                                                 synchronized
    public void setAsynchronousLoadPriority(int p);
    public void setDocumentProperties(java.util.Dictionary x);
// Methods Implementing Document
    public void addDocumentListener(javax.swing.event.DocumentListener listener);
    public void addUndoableEditListener(javax.swing.event.UndoableEditListener listener);
    public Position createPosition(int offs) throws BadLocationException;            synchronized
    public abstract javax.swing.text.Element getDefaultRootElement();
    public final Position getEndPosition();
    public int getLength();
    public final Object getProperty(Object key);
    public javax.swing.text.Element[ ] getRootElements();
    public final Position getStartPosition();
    public String getText(int offset, int length) throws BadLocationException;
    public void getText(int offset, int length, Segment txt) throws BadLocationException;
    public void insertString(int offs, String str, AttributeSet a) throws BadLocationException;
    public final void putProperty(Object key, Object value);
    public void remove(int offs, int len) throws BadLocationException;
    public void removeDocumentListener(javax.swing.event.DocumentListener listener);
    public void removeUndoableEditListener(javax.swing.event.UndoableEditListener listener);
    public void render(Runnable r);
// Protected Instance Methods
    protected javax.swing.text.Element createBranchElement(javax.swing.text.Element parent, AttributeSet a);
    protected javax.swing.text.Element createLeafElement(javax.swing.text.Element parent, AttributeSet a, int p0,
        int p1);
    protected void fireChangedUpdate(javax.swing.event.DocumentEvent e);
    protected void fireInsertUpdate(javax.swing.event.DocumentEvent e);
    protected void fireRemoveUpdate(javax.swing.event.DocumentEvent e);
    protected void fireUndoableEditUpdate(javax.swing.event.UndoableEditEvent e);
    protected final AbstractDocument.AttributeContext getAttributeContext();
    protected final AbstractDocument.Content getContent();
    protected final Thread getCurrentWriter();                                       synchronized
```

```
    protected void insertUpdate(AbstractDocument.DefaultDocumentEvent chng, AttributeSet attr);
    protected void postRemoveUpdate(AbstractDocument.DefaultDocumentEvent chng);
    protected void removeUpdate(AbstractDocument.DefaultDocumentEvent chng);                    empty
    protected final void writeLock();                                                    synchronized
    protected final void writeUnlock();                                                  synchronized
// Protected Instance Fields
    protected javax.swing.event.EventListenerList listenerList;
}
```

Hierarchy: Object→ AbstractDocument(Document, Serializable)

Subclasses: DefaultStyledDocument, PlainDocument

AbstractDocument.AbstractElement   Java 1.2

javax.swing.text   *serializable*

This abstract class is a partial implementation of the Element interface. Document objects derived from AbstractDocument are composed of Element objects derived from AbstractDocument.AbstractElement. In addition to implementing Element, this class also implements the MutableAttributeSet interface, so it can serve as its own attribute set. And it implements the TreeNode interface, which can make it easy to display the element structure of an AbstractDocument using the JTree component (a useful debugging technique). Applications typically do not use or subclass this class. See also the BranchElement and LeafElement subclasses, both of which are also inner classes of AbstractDocument.

```
public abstract class AbstractDocument.AbstractElement implements javax.swing.text.Element,
      MutableAttributeSet, Serializable, javax.swing.tree.TreeNode {
// Public Constructors
    public AbstractElement(javax.swing.text.Element parent, AttributeSet a);
// Public Instance Methods
    public void dump(java.io.PrintStream psOut, int indentAmount);
// Methods Implementing AttributeSet
    public boolean containsAttribute(Object name, Object value);
    public boolean containsAttributes(AttributeSet attrs);
    public AttributeSet copyAttributes();
    public Object getAttribute(Object attrName);
    public int getAttributeCount();
    public java.util.Enumeration getAttributeNames();
    public AttributeSet getResolveParent();
    public boolean isDefined(Object attrName);
    public boolean isEqual(AttributeSet attr);
// Methods Implementing Element
    public AttributeSet getAttributes();
    public Document getDocument();
    public abstract javax.swing.text.Element getElement(int index);
    public abstract int getElementCount();
    public abstract int getElementIndex(int offset);
    public abstract int getEndOffset();
    public String getName();
    public javax.swing.text.Element getParentElement();
    public abstract int getStartOffset();
    public abstract boolean isLeaf();
// Methods Implementing MutableAttributeSet
    public void addAttribute(Object name, Object value);
    public void addAttributes(AttributeSet attr);
    public void removeAttribute(Object name);
    public void removeAttributes(AttributeSet attrs);
    public void removeAttributes(java.util.Enumeration names);
```

```
    public void setResolveParent(AttributeSet parent);
// Methods Implementing TreeNode
    public abstract java.util.Enumeration children();
    public abstract boolean getAllowsChildren();
    public abstract javax.swing.tree.TreeNode getChildAt(int childIndex);
    public int getChildCount();
    public int getIndex(javax.swing.tree.TreeNode node);
    public javax.swing.tree.TreeNode getParent();
// Protected Methods Overriding Object
    protected void finalize() throws Throwable;
}
```

Subclasses: AbstractDocument.BranchElement, AbstractDocument.LeafElement

Returned By: DefaultStyledDocument.createDefaultRoot(), PlainDocument.createDefaultRoot(), javax.swing.text.html.HTMLDocument.createDefaultRoot()

AbstractDocument.AttributeContext   Java 1.2

javax.swing.text

This interface defines methods that accept an immutable AttributeSet argument and return another immutable AttributeSet object. These methods can be used to implement the MutableAttributeSet interface entirely in terms of immutable AttributeSet objects. Most documents frequently reuse a small set of common attribute sets. The use of immutable AttributeSet objects is desirable because they may be cached and shared, resulting in substantial memory savings. JTextComponent uses the attribute set caching technique by default, and typical applications never need to use or implement this interface. See StyleContext for a concrete implementation of this interface.

```
public abstract static interface AbstractDocument.AttributeContext {
// Public Instance Methods
    public abstract AttributeSet addAttribute(AttributeSet old, Object name, Object value);
    public abstract AttributeSet addAttributes(AttributeSet old, AttributeSet attr);
    public abstract AttributeSet getEmptySet();
    public abstract void reclaim(AttributeSet a);
    public abstract AttributeSet removeAttribute(AttributeSet old, Object name);
    public abstract AttributeSet removeAttributes(AttributeSet old, AttributeSet attrs);
    public abstract AttributeSet removeAttributes(AttributeSet old, java.util.Enumeration names);
}
```

Implementations: StyleContext

Passed To: AbstractDocument.AbstractDocument()

Returned By: AbstractDocument.getAttributeContext()

AbstractDocument.BranchElement   Java 1.2

javax.swing.text   *serializable*

This class is an Element implementation suitable for Document elements that contain other elements (e.g., paragraph elements).

```
public class AbstractDocument.BranchElement extends AbstractDocument.AbstractElement {
// Public Constructors
    public BranchElement(javax.swing.text.Element parent, AttributeSet a);
// Public Instance Methods
    public javax.swing.text.Element positionToElement(int pos);
    public void replace(int offset, int length, javax.swing.text.Element[ ] elems);
```

```
// Public Methods Overriding AbstractDocument.AbstractElement
    public java.util.Enumeration children();
    public boolean getAllowsChildren();                                                          constant
    public javax.swing.text.Element getElement(int index);
    public int getElementCount();
    public int getElementIndex(int offset);
    public int getEndOffset();
    public String getName();
    public int getStartOffset();
    public boolean isLeaf();                                                                      constant
// Public Methods Overriding Object
    public String toString();
}
```

Subclasses: DefaultStyledDocument.SectionElement, javax.swing.text.html.HTMLDocument.BlockElement

AbstractDocument.Content   Java 1.2

javax.swing.text

This interface defines an abstract representation of an editable piece of text. An Abstract-
Document.Content object is used to represent the contents of any Document derived from
AbstractDocument. A Content implementation must be able to return arbitrary text segments, insert and delete text, and return Position objects that mark positions within the
content. If the Content implementation allows undo operations, the insertString() method
should return an UndoableEdit object; otherwise it should return null. Applications typically do not use or implement this interface. See StringContent and GapContent for two
implementations.

```
public abstract static interface AbstractDocument.Content {
// Public Instance Methods
    public abstract Position createPosition(int offset) throws BadLocationException;
    public abstract void getChars(int where, int len, Segment txt) throws BadLocationException;
    public abstract String getString(int where, int len) throws BadLocationException;
    public abstract javax.swing.undo.UndoableEdit insertString(int where, String str) throws BadLocationException;
    public abstract int length();
    public abstract javax.swing.undo.UndoableEdit remove(int where, int nitems) throws BadLocationException;
}
```

Implementations: GapContent, StringContent

Passed To: AbstractDocument.AbstractDocument(), DefaultStyledDocument.DefaultStyledDocument(),
PlainDocument.PlainDocument(), javax.swing.text.html.HTMLDocument.HTMLDocument()

Returned By: AbstractDocument.getContent()

AbstractDocument.DefaultDocumentEvent   Java 1.2

javax.swing.text   *serializable*

This class is the javax.swing.event.DocumentEvent implementation used by documents
derived from AbstractDocument. It is also an UndoableEdit and therefore can be used with
the undo architecture of javax.swing.undo.

```
public class AbstractDocument.DefaultDocumentEvent extends javax.swing.undo.CompoundEdit
        implements javax.swing.event.DocumentEvent {
// Public Constructors
    public DefaultDocumentEvent(int offs, int len, javax.swing.event.DocumentEvent.EventType type);
// Methods Implementing DocumentEvent
    public javax.swing.event.DocumentEvent.ElementChange getChange(javax.swing.text.Element elem);
```

```
     public Document getDocument();
     public int getLength();
     public int getOffset();
     public javax.swing.event.DocumentEvent.EventType getType();
// Public Methods Overriding CompoundEdit
     public boolean addEdit(javax.swing.undo.UndoableEdit anEdit);
     public String getPresentationName();
     public String getRedoPresentationName();
     public String getUndoPresentationName();
     public boolean isSignificant();                                              constant
     public void redo() throws javax.swing.undo.CannotRedoException;
     public String toString();
     public void undo() throws javax.swing.undo.CannotUndoException;
}
```

Passed To: AbstractDocument.{insertUpdate(), postRemoveUpdate(), removeUpdate()},
DefaultStyledDocument.{insertUpdate(), removeUpdate()}, DefaultStyledDocument.ElementBuffer.{change(),
insert(), remove()}, PlainDocument.{insertUpdate(), removeUpdate()},
javax.swing.text.html.HTMLDocument.insertUpdate()

AbstractDocument.ElementEdit   Java 1.2

javax.swing.text   *serializable*

This class is the implementation of DocumentEvent.ElementEdit used by AbstractDocument.

```
public static class AbstractDocument.ElementEdit extends javax.swing.undo.AbstractUndoableEdit
        implements javax.swing.event.DocumentEvent.ElementChange {
// Public Constructors
     public ElementEdit(javax.swing.text.Element e, int index, javax.swing.text.Element[ ] removed,
                        javax.swing.text.Element[ ] added);
// Methods Implementing DocumentEvent.ElementChange
     public javax.swing.text.Element[ ] getChildrenAdded();
     public javax.swing.text.Element[ ] getChildrenRemoved();
     public javax.swing.text.Element getElement();
     public int getIndex();
// Public Methods Overriding AbstractUndoableEdit
     public void redo() throws javax.swing.undo.CannotRedoException;
     public void undo() throws javax.swing.undo.CannotUndoException;
}
```

AbstractDocument.LeafElement   Java 1.2

javax.swing.text   *serializable*

This class is an Element implementation suitable for Document elements that do not contain children elements (e.g., runs of styled text).

```
public class AbstractDocument.LeafElement extends AbstractDocument.AbstractElement {
// Public Constructors
     public LeafElement(javax.swing.text.Element parent, AttributeSet a, int offs0, int offs1);
// Public Methods Overriding AbstractDocument.AbstractElement
     public java.util.Enumeration children();                                     constant
     public boolean getAllowsChildren();                                          constant
     public javax.swing.text.Element getElement(int index);                       constant
     public int getElementCount();                                                constant
     public int getElementIndex(int pos);                                         constant
     public int getEndOffset();
     public String getName();
     public int getStartOffset();
```

```
    public boolean isLeaf();                                                                    constant
// Public Methods Overriding Object
    public String toString();
}
```

Subclasses: javax.swing.text.html.HTMLDocument.RunElement

AbstractWriter   Java 1.2

javax.swing.text

This abstract class provides a simple but convenient starting place for applications that
want to write a textual representation of a Document or Element tree. The abstract write()
method must be implemented by a subclass. This method must iterate over the Document or Element tree (using the ElementIterator provided by getElementIterator()) and write
out a textual description of the Element objects using the other methods of the class.
Applications do not typically use or subclass this class.

```
public abstract class AbstractWriter {
// Protected Constructors
    protected AbstractWriter(java.io.Writer w, javax.swing.text.Element root);
    protected AbstractWriter(java.io.Writer w, Document doc);
    protected AbstractWriter(java.io.Writer w, javax.swing.text.Element root, int pos, int len);
    protected AbstractWriter(java.io.Writer w, Document doc, int pos, int len);
// Protected Constants
    protected static final char NEWLINE;                                                        ='\12'
// Protected Instance Methods
    protected void decrIndent();
    protected Document getDocument();
    protected ElementIterator getElementIterator();
    protected String getText(javax.swing.text.Element elem) throws BadLocationException;
    protected void incrIndent();
    protected void indent() throws java.io.IOException;
    protected boolean inRange(javax.swing.text.Element next);
    protected void setIndentSpace(int space);
    protected void setLineLength(int l);
    protected void text(javax.swing.text.Element elem) throws BadLocationException, java.io.IOException;
    protected abstract void write() throws java.io.IOException, BadLocationException;
    protected void write(String str) throws java.io.IOException;
    protected void write(char ch) throws java.io.IOException;
    protected void writeAttributes(AttributeSet attr) throws java.io.IOException;
}
```

Subclasses: javax.swing.text.html.HTMLWriter, javax.swing.text.html.MinimalHTMLWriter

AttributeSet   Java 1.2

javax.swing.text

This interface defines the basic methods required for a set of attributes. It defines a
mapping from attribute names, or keys, to attribute values. Both keys and values can
be arbitrary objects. The StyleConstants class defines a number of commonly used
attribute keys. The AttributeSet interface defines four inner interfaces. These empty interfaces serve as marker interfaces and should be implemented by an attribute key object
to specify the general category of the key.

An AttributeSet can have another AttributeSet as its parent. When you look up a value
with getAttribute(), the local mappings are searched first. If no matching attribute is found
locally, however, the search continues (recursively) on the parent AttributeSet. The
parent attribute set is itself stored as an attribute, using the key defined by the

ResolveAttribute constant. Call getResolveParent() to query the parent AttributeSet. The isDefined() and getAttributeNames() methods operate only on the local attribute mappings and do not use the parent AttributeSet.

See also MutableAttributeSet, SimpleAttributeSet, Style, and StyleConstants.

```
public abstract interface AttributeSet {
// Public Constants
    public static final Object NameAttribute;
    public static final Object ResolveAttribute;
// Inner Classes
    public abstract static interface CharacterAttribute;
    public abstract static interface ColorAttribute;
    public abstract static interface FontAttribute;
    public abstract static interface ParagraphAttribute;
// Public Instance Methods
    public abstract boolean containsAttribute(Object name, Object value);
    public abstract boolean containsAttributes(AttributeSet attributes);
    public abstract AttributeSet copyAttributes();
    public abstract Object getAttribute(Object key);
    public abstract int getAttributeCount();
    public abstract java.util.Enumeration getAttributeNames();
    public abstract AttributeSet getResolveParent();
    public abstract boolean isDefined(Object attrName);
    public abstract boolean isEqual(AttributeSet attr);
}
```

Implementations: MutableAttributeSet, StyleContext.SmallAttributeSet

Passed To: Too many methods to list.

Returned By: Too many methods to list.

Type Of: DefaultStyledDocument.AttributeUndoableEdit.{copy, newAttributes}, SimpleAttributeSet.EMPTY

AttributeSet.CharacterAttribute   Java 1.2

javax.swing.text

This marker interface should be implemented by any object that serves as the key for a character attribute.

```
public abstract static interface AttributeSet.CharacterAttribute {
}
```

Implementations: StyleConstants.CharacterConstants, StyleConstants.ColorConstants, StyleConstants.FontConstants

AttributeSet.ColorAttribute   Java 1.2

javax.swing.text

This marker interface should be implemented by any object that serves as the key for a color attribute.

```
public abstract static interface AttributeSet.ColorAttribute {
}
```

Implementations: StyleConstants.ColorConstants

AttributeSet.FontAttribute

Java 1.2

javax.swing.text

This marker interface should be implemented by any object that serves as the key for a font attribute.

```
public abstract static interface AttributeSet.FontAttribute {
}
```

Implementations: StyleConstants.FontConstants

AttributeSet.ParagraphAttribute

Java 1.2

javax.swing.text

This marker interface should be implemented by any object that serves as the key for a paragraph attribute.

```
public abstract static interface AttributeSet.ParagraphAttribute {
}
```

Implementations: StyleConstants.ParagraphConstants

BadLocationException

Java 1.2

javax.swing.text

serializable checked

Thrown by methods throughout javax.swing.text when they are passed a document position that does not exist.

```
public class BadLocationException extends Exception {
// Public Constructors
    public BadLocationException(String s, int offs);
// Public Instance Methods
    public int offsetRequested();
}
```

Hierarchy: Object → Throwable(Serializable) → Exception → BadLocationException

Thrown By: Too many methods to list.

BoxView

Java 1.2

javax.swing.text

This class is a CompositeView that arranges its children into a row or a column.

```
public class BoxView extends CompositeView {
// Public Constructors
    public BoxView(javax.swing.text.Element elem, int axis);
// Public Instance Methods
    public final int getHeight();
    public final int getWidth();
// Public Methods Overriding CompositeView
    public java.awt.Shape getChildAllocation(int index, java.awt.Shape a);
    public java.awt.Shape modelToView(int pos, java.awt.Shape a, Position.Bias b) throws BadLocationException;
    public void replace(int offset, int length, View[] elems);
    public int viewToModel(float x, float y, java.awt.Shape a, Position.Bias[] bias);
// Protected Methods Overriding CompositeView
    protected void childAllocation(int index, java.awt.Rectangle alloc);
    protected boolean flipEastAndWestAtEnds(int position, Position.Bias bias);
    protected View getViewAtPoint(int x, int y, java.awt.Rectangle alloc);
    protected boolean isAfter(int x, int y, java.awt.Rectangle innerAlloc);
```

```
    protected boolean isBefore(int x, int y, java.awt.Rectangle innerAlloc);
// Public Methods Overriding View
    public float getAlignment(int axis);
    public float getMaximumSpan(int axis);
    public float getMinimumSpan(int axis);
    public float getPreferredSpan(int axis);
    public int getResizeWeight(int axis);
    public void paint(java.awt.Graphics g, java.awt.Shape allocation);
    public void preferenceChanged(View child, boolean width, boolean height);
    public void setSize(float width, float height);
// Protected Instance Methods
    protected void baselineLayout(int targetSpan, int axis, int[ ] offsets, int[ ] spans);
    protected SizeRequirements baselineRequirements(int axis, SizeRequirements r);
    protected SizeRequirements calculateMajorAxisRequirements(int axis, SizeRequirements r);
    protected SizeRequirements calculateMinorAxisRequirements(int axis, SizeRequirements r);
    protected final int getOffset(int axis, int childIndex);
    protected final int getSpan(int axis, int childIndex);
    protected boolean isAllocationValid( );
    protected void layout(int width, int height);
    protected void layoutMajorAxis(int targetSpan, int axis, int[ ] offsets, int[ ] spans);
    protected void layoutMinorAxis(int targetSpan, int axis, int[ ] offsets, int[ ] spans);
    protected void paintChild(java.awt.Graphics g, java.awt.Rectangle alloc, int index);
}
```

Hierarchy: Object→ View(SwingConstants)→ CompositeView→ BoxView

Subclasses: javax.swing.text.ParagraphView, TableView, TableView.TableCell, TableView.TableRow, WrappedPlainView, javax.swing.text.html.BlockView

Caret

Java 1.2

javax.swing.text

This interface defines the methods that must be implemented by a class that wants to keep track of the insertion cursor position and draw the insertion cursor for a JTextComponent. In the nomenclature of text editing, the *dot* is the current insertion position, and the *mark* is some other position in the text. The text between the dot and the mark is implicitly selected, and certain editing commands operate on this text. The setDot() method sets the position of both the dot and the mark, while moveDot() sets the position of the dot, leaving the mark where it is. The paint() method is called when the insertion cursor needs to be drawn or redrawn. setBlinkRate() specifies how often the cursor should blink. If the cursor does blink, Caret is responsible for causing this blinking; paint() is not automatically called to implement blinking. The Caret should notify any registered ChangeListener objects when the position of the cursor changes.

Although the Caret interface allows the appearance and behavior of the JTextComponent cursor to be customized, it is uncommon to do this. Most applications are perfectly content to use DefaultCaret, which is the Caret implementation installed by all the standard look-and-feels.

```
public abstract interface Caret {
// Event Registration Methods (by event name)
    public abstract void addChangeListener(javax.swing.event.ChangeListener l);
    public abstract void removeChangeListener(javax.swing.event.ChangeListener l);
// Property Accessor Methods (by property name)
    public abstract int getBlinkRate( );
    public abstract void setBlinkRate(int rate);
    public abstract int getDot( );
    public abstract void setDot(int dot);
```

```
    public abstract java.awt.Point getMagicCaretPosition();
    public abstract void setMagicCaretPosition(java.awt.Point p);
    public abstract int getMark();
    public abstract boolean isSelectionVisible();
    public abstract voic setSelectionVisible(boolean v);
    public abstract boolean isVisible();
    public abstract void setVisible(boolean v);
// Public Instance Methods
    public abstract void deinstall(JTextComponent c);
    public abstract void install(JTextComponent c);
    public abstract void moveDot(int dot);
    public abstract void paint(java.awt.Graphics g);
}
```

Implementations: DefaultCaret

Passed To: JTextComponent.setCaret()

Returned By: DefaultEditorKit.createCaret(), EditorKit.createCaret(), JTextComponent.getCaret()

ChangedCharSetException   Java 1.2

javax.swing.text   *serializable checked*

This subclass of IOException is thrown by the read() method of an EditorKit when it reads a document that it expects to be encoded in a given character set and finds that the document specifies that it is encoded using some other character set. Typically, this happens when reading HTML documents that specify their encoding using a <META> tag.

```
public class ChangedCharSetException extends java.io.IOException {
// Public Constructors
    public ChangedCharSetException(String charSetSpec, boolean charSetKey);
// Public Instance Methods
    public String getCharSetSpec();
    public boolean keyEqualsCharSet();
}
```

Hierarchy: Object → Throwable(Serializable) → Exception → java.io.IOException → ChangedCharSetException

Thrown By: javax.swing.text.html.parser.DocumentParser.handleEmptyTag(), javax.swing.text.html.parser.Parser.{handleEmptyTag(), startTag()}

ComponentView   Java 1.2

javax.swing.text

This class is a View that encapsulates a Component and allows it to be displayed within a Document.

```
public class ComponentView extends View {
// Public Constructors
    public ComponentView(javax.swing.text.Element elem);
// Public Instance Methods
    public final Component getComponent();
// Public Methods Overriding View
    public float getAlignment(int axis);
    public float getMaximumSpan(int axis);
    public float getMinimumSpan(int axis);
    public float getPreferredSpan(int axis);
    public java.awt.Shape modelToView(int pos, java.awt.Shape a, Position.Bias b) throws BadLocationException;
```

```
    public void paint(java.awt.Graphics g, java.awt.Shape a);
    public void setParent(View p);
    public void setSize(float width, float height);
    public int viewToModel(float x, float y, java.awt.Shape a, Position.Bias[ ] bias);
// Protected Instance Methods
    protected Component createComponent();
}
```

Hierarchy: Object→ View(SwingConstants)→ ComponentView

Subclasses: javax.swing.text.html.FormView, javax.swing.text.html.ObjectView

CompositeView

javax.swing.text

This abstract class is a View that can have children.

```
public abstract class CompositeView extends View {
// Public Constructors
    public CompositeView(javax.swing.text.Element elem);
// Public Instance Methods
    public void append(View v);
    public void insert(int offs, View v);
    public void removeAll();
    public void replace(int offset, int length, View[ ] views);
// Public Methods Overriding View
    public void changedUpdate(javax.swing.event.DocumentEvent e, java.awt.Shape a, ViewFactory f);
    public java.awt.Shape getChildAllocation(int index, java.awt.Shape a);
    public int getNextVisualPositionFrom(int pos, Position.Bias b, java.awt.Shape a, int direction,
                              Position.Bias[ ] biasRet) throws BadLocationException;
    public View getView(int n);
    public int getViewCount();
    public void insertUpdate(javax.swing.event.DocumentEvent e, java.awt.Shape a, ViewFactory f);
    public java.awt.Shape modelToView(int pos, java.awt.Shape a, Position.Bias b) throws BadLocationException;
    public java.awt.Shape modelToView(int p0, Position.Bias b0, int p1, Position.Bias b1, java.awt.Shape a)
        throws BadLocationException;
    public void removeUpdate(javax.swing.event.DocumentEvent e, java.awt.Shape a, ViewFactory f);
    public void setParent(View parent);
    public int viewToModel(float x, float y, java.awt.Shape a, Position.Bias[ ] bias);
// Protected Instance Methods
    protected abstract void childAllocation(int index, java.awt.Rectangle a);
    protected boolean flipEastAndWestAtEnds(int position, Position.Bias bias);                    constant
    protected final short getBottomInset();
    protected java.awt.Rectangle getInsideAllocation(java.awt.Shape a);
    protected final short getLeftInset();
    protected int getNextEastWestVisualPositionFrom(int pos, Position.Bias b, java.awt.Shape a, int direction,
                                  Position.Bias[ ] biasRet) throws BadLocationException;
    protected int getNextNorthSouthVisualPositionFrom(int pos, Position.Bias b, java.awt.Shape a, int direction,
                                  Position.Bias[ ] biasRet) throws BadLocationException;
    protected final short getRightInset();
    protected final short getTopInset();
    protected abstract View getViewAtPoint(int x, int y, java.awt.Rectangle alloc);
    protected View getViewAtPosition(int pos, java.awt.Rectangle a);
    protected int getViewIndexAtPosition(int pos);
    protected abstract boolean isAfter(int x, int y, java.awt.Rectangle alloc);
    protected abstract boolean isBefore(int x, int y, java.awt.Rectangle alloc);
    protected void loadChildren(ViewFactory f);
    protected final void setInsets(short top, short left, short bottom, short right);
```

```
      protected final void setParagraphInsets(AttributeSet attr);
}
```

Hierarchy: Object→ View(SwingConstants)→ CompositeView

Subclasses: BoxView

DefaultCaret   Java 1.2

javax.swing.text   *cloneable serializable shape*

This is the default Caret implementation installed on all JTextComponent components by all
of the standard look-and-feel implementations. It displays the caret as a thin vertical
line between characters. Most applications do not have to use this class directly and
can simply rely on its automatic use by JTextComponent.

```
public class DefaultCaret extends java.awt.Rectangle implements Caret, java.awt.event.FocusListener,
        java.awt.event.MouseListener, java.awt.event.MouseMotionListener {
// Public Constructors
   public DefaultCaret();
// Event Registration Methods (by event name)
   public void addChangeListener(javax.swing.event.ChangeListener l);          Implements:Caret
   public void removeChangeListener(javax.swing.event.ChangeListener l);       Implements:Caret
// Methods Implementing Caret
   public void addChangeListener(javax.swing.event.ChangeListener l);
   public void deinstall(JTextComponent c);
   public int getBlinkRate();                                                        default:0
   public int getDot();                                                              default:0
   public java.awt.Point getMagicCaretPosition();                                 default:null
   public int getMark();                                                            default:0
   public void install(JTextComponent c);
   public boolean isSelectionVisible();                                          default:false
   public boolean isVisible();                                                   default:false
   public void moveDot(int dot);
   public void paint(java.awt.Graphics g);
   public void removeChangeListener(javax.swing.event.ChangeListener l);
   public void setBlinkRate(int rate);
   public void setDot(int dot);
   public void setMagicCaretPosition(java.awt.Point p);
   public void setSelectionVisible(boolean vis);
   public void setVisible(boolean e);
// Methods Implementing FocusListener
   public void focusGained(java.awt.event.FocusEvent e);
   public void focusLost(java.awt.event.FocusEvent e);
// Methods Implementing MouseListener
   public void mouseClicked(java.awt.event.MouseEvent e);
   public void mouseEntered(java.awt.event.MouseEvent e);                              empty
   public void mouseExited(java.awt.event.MouseEvent e);                               empty
   public void mousePressed(java.awt.event.MouseEvent e);
   public void mouseReleased(java.awt.event.MouseEvent e);                             empty
// Methods Implementing MouseMotionListener
   public void mouseDragged(java.awt.event.MouseEvent e);
   public void mouseMoved(java.awt.event.MouseEvent e);                                empty
// Public Methods Overriding Rectangle
   public boolean equals(Object obj);
   public String toString();
// Protected Instance Methods
   protected void adjustVisibility(java.awt.Rectangle nloc);
   protected void damage(java.awt.Rectangle r);                                  synchronized
```

```
   protected void fireStateChanged();
   protected final JTextComponent getComponent();
   protected Highlighter.HighlightPainter getSelectionPainter();
   protected void moveCaret(java.awt.event.MouseEvent e);
   protected void positionCaret(java.awt.event.MouseEvent e);
   protected final void repaint();                                              synchronized
// Protected Instance Fields
   protected transient javax.swing.event.ChangeEvent changeEvent;
   protected javax.swing.event.EventListenerList listenerList;
}
```

Hierarchy: Object→ java.awt.geom.RectangularShape(Cloneable, java.awt.Shape)→
java.awt.geom.Rectangle2D→ java.awt.Rectangle(Serializable, java.awt.Shape)→ DefaultCaret(Caret,
java.awt.event.FocusListener(java.util.EventListener), java.awt.event.MouseListener(java.util.EventListener),
java.awt.event.MouseMotionListener(java.util.EventListener))

DefaultEditorKit   Java 1.2

javax.swing.text   *cloneable serializable*

This class is an EditorKit for plain text. You can configure a JEditorPane to display plain,
unformatted text using an instance of this class. The actions defined by this class are
used by default by JTextComponent. DefaultEditorKit defines a number of String constants,
which it uses as the names of the various Action objects it returns from its getActions()
method.

```
public class DefaultEditorKit extends EditorKit {
// Public Constructors
   public DefaultEditorKit();
// Public Constants
   public static final String backwardAction;                        ="caret-backward"
   public static final String beepAction;                                     ="beep"
   public static final String beginAction;                              ="caret-begin"
   public static final String beginLineAction;                     ="caret-begin-line"
   public static final String beginParagraphAction;          ="caret-begin-paragraph"
   public static final String beginWordAction;                   ="caret-begin-word"
   public static final String copyAction;                        ="copy-to-clipboard"
   public static final String cutAction;                          ="cut-to-clipboard"
   public static final String defaultKeyTypedAction;               ="default-typed"
   public static final String deleteNextCharAction;                  ="delete-next"
   public static final String deletePrevCharAction;              ="delete-previous"
   public static final String downAction;                            ="caret-down"
   public static final String endAction;                              ="caret-end"
   public static final String endLineAction;                     ="caret-end-line"
   public static final String EndOfLineStringProperty;            ="__EndOfLine__"
   public static final String endParagraphAction;              ="caret-end-paragraph"
   public static final String endWordAction;                     ="caret-end-word"
   public static final String forwardAction;                       ="caret-forward"
   public static final String insertBreakAction;                   ="insert-break"
   public static final String insertContentAction;               ="insert-content"
   public static final String insertTabAction;                       ="insert-tab"
   public static final String nextWordAction;                    ="caret-next-word"
   public static final String pageDownAction;                        ="page-down"
   public static final String pageUpAction;                            ="page-up"
   public static final String pasteAction;                     ="paste-from-clipboard"
   public static final String previousWordAction;            ="caret-previous-word"
   public static final String readOnlyAction;                      ="set-read-only"
   public static final String selectAllAction;                        ="select-all"
   public static final String selectionBackwardAction;         ="selection-backward"
```

public static final String **selectionBeginAction**;	=*"selection-begin"*
public static final String **selectionBeginLineAction**;	=*"selection-begin-line"*
public static final String **selectionBeginParagraphAction**;	=*"selection-begin-paragraph"*
public static final String **selectionBeginWordAction**;	=*"selection-begin-word"*
public static final String **selectionDownAction**;	=*"selection-down"*
public static final String **selectionEndAction**;	=*"selection-end"*
public static final String **selectionEndLineAction**;	=*"selection-end-line"*
public static final String **selectionEndParagraphAction**;	=*"selection-end-paragraph"*
public static final String **selectionEndWordAction**;	=*"selection-end-word"*
public static final String **selectionForwardAction**;	=*"selection-forward"*
public static final String **selectionNextWordAction**;	=*"selection-next-word"*
public static final String **selectionPreviousWordAction**;	=*"selection-previous-word"*
public static final String **selectionUpAction**;	=*"selection-up"*
public static final String **selectLineAction**;	=*"select-line"*
public static final String **selectParagraphAction**;	=*"select-paragraph"*
public static final String **selectWordAction**;	=*"select-word"*
public static final String **upAction**;	=*"caret-up"*
public static final String **writableAction**;	=*"set-writable"*

// Inner Classes
    public static class **BeepAction** extends TextAction;
    public static class **CopyAction** extends TextAction;
    public static class **CutAction** extends TextAction;
    public static class **DefaultKeyTypedAction** extends TextAction;
    public static class **InsertBreakAction** extends TextAction;
    public static class **InsertContentAction** extends TextAction;
    public static class **InsertTabAction** extends TextAction;
    public static class **PasteAction** extends TextAction;

// Public Methods Overriding EditorKit

public Object **clone**();	
public Caret **createCaret**();	*constant*
public Document **createDefaultDocument**();	
public Action[ ] **getActions**();	
public String **getContentType**();	*default:"text/plain"*
public ViewFactory **getViewFactory**();	*constant default:null*

    public void **read**(java.io.Reader *in*, Document *doc*, int *pos*) throws java.io.IOException, BadLocationException;
    public void **read**(java.io.InputStream *in*, Document *doc*, int *pos*) throws java.io.IOException, BadLocationException;
    public void **write**(java.io.Writer *out*, Document *doc*, int *pos*, int *len*) throws java.io.IOException,
        BadLocationException;
    public void **write**(java.io.OutputStream *out*, Document *doc*, int *pos*, int *len*) throws java.io.IOException,
        BadLocationException;
}

Hierarchy: Object→ EditorKit(Cloneable, Serializable)→ DefaultEditorKit

Subclasses: StyledEditorKit

DefaultEditorKit.BeepAction   Java 1.2

javax.swing.text   *cloneable serializable*

This Action causes a beep.

public static class **DefaultEditorKit.BeepAction** extends TextAction {
// Public Constructors
    public **BeepAction**();
// Public Methods Overriding AbstractAction
    public void **actionPerformed**(java.awt.event.ActionEvent *e*);
}

DefaultEditorKit.CopyAction

javax.swing.text

cloneable serializable

This action causes the selected region of the JTextComponent to be placed on the system clipboard and made available for pasting.

```
public static class DefaultEditorKit.CopyAction extends TextAction {
// Public Constructors
    public CopyAction();
// Public Methods Overriding AbstractAction
    public void actionPerformed(java.awt.event.ActionEvent e);
}
```

DefaultEditorKit.CutAction

javax.swing.text

cloneable serializable

This Action deletes the selected region of the JTextComponent and makes its contents available for pasting on the system clipboard.

```
public static class DefaultEditorKit.CutAction extends TextAction {
// Public Constructors
    public CutAction();
// Public Methods Overriding AbstractAction
    public void actionPerformed(java.awt.event.ActionEvent e);
}
```

DefaultEditorKit.DefaultKeyTypedAction

javax.swing.text

cloneable serializable

This Action is invoked when no other action is registered for a keystroke. It inserts the action command string (which is usually the key that triggered the action) at the current cursor position. Or, if there is currently a selection, it replaces the selected text with this text. This is the most commonly used action in a JTextComponent, since it is used to insert all characters the user types.

```
public static class DefaultEditorKit.DefaultKeyTypedAction extends TextAction {
// Public Constructors
    public DefaultKeyTypedAction();
// Public Methods Overriding AbstractAction
    public void actionPerformed(java.awt.event.ActionEvent e);
}
```

DefaultEditorKit.InsertBreakAction

javax.swing.text

cloneable serializable

This Action inserts a new line break into the document and deletes any currently selected text.

```
public static class DefaultEditorKit.InsertBreakAction extends TextAction {
// Public Constructors
    public InsertBreakAction();
// Public Methods Overriding AbstractAction
    public void actionPerformed(java.awt.event.ActionEvent e);
}
```

DefaultEditorKit.InsertContentAction

Java 1.2

javax.swing.text

cloneable serializable

This Action inserts the ActionEvent command string into the document at the current position, deleting any current selection in the process.

```
public static class DefaultEditorKit.InsertContentAction extends TextAction {
// Public Constructors
    public InsertContentAction();  .
// Public Methods Overriding AbstractAction
    public void actionPerformed(java.awt.event.ActionEvent e);
}
```

DefaultEditorKit.InsertTabAction

Java 1.2

javax.swing.text

cloneable serializable

This Action inserts a horizontal tab into the document, replacing the selected text, if any.

```
public static class DefaultEditorKit.InsertTabAction extends TextAction {
// Public Constructors
    public InsertTabAction();
// Public Methods Overriding AbstractAction
    public void actionPerformed(java.awt.event.ActionEvent e);
}
```

DefaultEditorKit.PasteAction

Java 1.2

javax.swing.text

cloneable serializable

This Action gets the current text selection from the system clipboard and pastes it into the current document at the current insertion position, replacing any selected text.

```
public static class DefaultEditorKit.PasteAction extends TextAction {
// Public Constructors
    public PasteAction();  .
// Public Methods Overriding AbstractAction
    public void actionPerformed(java.awt.event.ActionEvent e);
}
```

DefaultHighlighter

Java 1.2

javax.swing.text

This class is the default highlighter object used by JTextComponent to keep track of highlighted regions within the Document.

```
public class DefaultHighlighter extends LayeredHighlighter {
// Public Constructors
    public DefaultHighlighter();
// Inner Classes
    public static class DefaultHighlightPainter extends LayeredHighlighter.LayerPainter;
// Public Instance Methods
    public boolean getDrawsLayeredHighlights();                                          default:true
    public void setDrawsLayeredHighlights(boolean newValue);
// Public Methods Overriding LayeredHighlighter
    public Object addHighlight(int p0, int p1, Highlighter.HighlightPainter p) throws BadLocationException;
    public void changeHighlight(Object tag, int p0, int p1) throws BadLocationException;
    public void deinstall(JTextComponent c);
    public Highlighter.Highlight[ ] getHighlights();
    public void install(JTextComponent c);
```

```
    public void paint(java.awt.Graphics g);
    public void paintLayeredHighlights(java.awt.Graphics g, int p0, int p1, java.awt.Shape viewBounds,
                                       JTextComponent editor, View view);
    public void removeAllHighlights();
    public void removeHighlight(Object tag);
// Public Class Fields
    public static LayeredHighlighter.LayerPainter DefaultPainter;
}
```

Hierarchy: Object → LayeredHighlighter(Highlighter) → DefaultHighlighter

DefaultHighlighter.DefaultHighlightPainter

Java 1.2

javax.swing.text

This class is the default highlight painter object used by JTextComponent to draw its high-lighted regions. It fills the highlighted area with a solid color. By default, the color is obtained with the getSelectionColor() method of the associated JTextComponent.

```
public static class DefaultHighlighter.DefaultHighlightPainter extends LayeredHighlighter.LayerPainter {
// Public Constructors
    public DefaultHighlightPainter(java.awt.Color c);
// Public Instance Methods
    public java.awt.Color getColor();
// Public Methods Overriding LayeredHighlighter.LayerPainter
    public void paint(java.awt.Graphics g, int offs0, int offs1, java.awt.Shape bounds, JTextComponent c);
    public java.awt.Shape paintLayer(java.awt.Graphics g, int offs0, int offs1, java.awt.Shape bounds,
                                     JTextComponent c, View view);
}
```

DefaultStyledDocument

Java 1.2

javax.swing.text

serializable

This class extends AbstractDocument and implements StyledDocument. It represents format-ted text annotated with character and paragraph attributes. To insert text into a Default-StyledDocument, use the inherited insertString() method, specifying a document position, the string to insert, and the AttributeSet of attributes that should be applied to the inserted string. You can display the contents of a DefaultStyledDocument using a JTextPane component.

```
public class DefaultStyledDocument extends AbstractDocument implements StyledDocument {
// Public Constructors
    public DefaultStyledDocument();
    public DefaultStyledDocument(StyleContext styles);
    public DefaultStyledDocument(AbstractDocument.Content c, StyleContext styles);
// Public Constants
    public static final int BUFFER_SIZE_DEFAULT;                                              =4096
// Inner Classes
    public static class AttributeUndoableEdit extends javax.swing.undo.AbstractUndoableEdit;
    public class ElementBuffer implements Serializable;
    public static class ElementSpec;
    protected class SectionElement extends AbstractDocument.BranchElement;
// Event Registration Methods (by event name)
    public void addDocumentListener(javax.swing.event.DocumentListener listener);     Implements:Document
    public void removeDocumentListener(javax.swing.event.DocumentListener listener);  Implements:Document
// Public Instance Methods
    public java.util.Enumeration getStyleNames();
```

```
// Methods Implementing Document
    public void addDocumentListener(javax.swing.event.DocumentListener listener);
    public javax.swing.text.Element getDefaultRootElement();                               default:SectionElement
    public void removeDocumentListener(javax.swing.event.DocumentListener listener);
// Methods Implementing StyledDocument
    public Style addStyle(String nm, Style parent);
    public java.awt.Color getBackground(AttributeSet attr);
    public javax.swing.text.Element getCharacterElement(int pos);
    public java.awt.Font getFont(AttributeSet attr);
    public java.awt.Color getForeground(AttributeSet attr);
    public Style getLogicalStyle(int p);
    public javax.swing.text.Element getParagraphElement(int pos);
    public Style getStyle(String nm);
    public void removeStyle(String nm);
    public void setCharacterAttributes(int offset, int length, AttributeSet s, boolean replace);
    public void setLogicalStyle(int pos, Style s);
    public void setParagraphAttributes(int offset, int length, AttributeSet s, boolean replace);
// Protected Methods Overriding AbstractDocument
    protected void insertUpdate(AbstractDocument.DefaultDocumentEvent chng, AttributeSet attr);
    protected void removeUpdate(AbstractDocument.DefaultDocumentEvent chng);
// Protected Instance Methods
    protected void create(DefaultStyledDocument.ElementSpec[ ] data);
    protected AbstractDocument.AbstractElement createDefaultRoot();
    protected void insert(int offset, DefaultStyledDocument.ElementSpec[ ] data) throws BadLocationException;
    protected void styleChanged(Style style);
// Protected Instance Fields
    protected DefaultStyledDocument.ElementBuffer buffer;
}
```

Hierarchy: Object → AbstractDocument(Document, Serializable) →
DefaultStyledDocument(StyledDocument(Document))

Subclasses: javax.swing.text.html.HTMLDocument

DefaultStyledDocument.AttributeUndoableEdit   Java 1.2

javax.swing.text   *serializable*

This UndoableEdit implementation is used internally by DefaultStyledDocument to remember
(and undo) changes to the AttributeSet of an Element.

```
public static class DefaultStyledDocument.AttributeUndoableEdit extends
        javax.swing.undo.AbstractUndoableEdit {
// Public Constructors
    public AttributeUndoableEdit(javax.swing.text.Element element, AttributeSet newAttributes,
                                 boolean isReplacing);
// Public Methods Overriding AbstractUndoableEdit
    public void redo() throws javax.swing.undo.CannotRedoException;
    public void undo() throws javax.swing.undo.CannotUndoException;
// Protected Instance Fields
    protected AttributeSet copy;
    protected javax.swing.text.Element element;
    protected boolean isReplacing;
    protected AttributeSet newAttributes;
}
```

DefaultStyledDocument.ElementBuffer

javax.swing.text

This class allows insertions into an Element tree in the form of an array of DefaultStyled-Document.ElementSpec objects. This is useful because a linear array of ElementSpec objects is often easier to work with than a tree of Element objects.

```
public class DefaultStyledDocument.ElementBuffer implements Serializable {
// Public Constructors
    public ElementBuffer(javax.swing.text.Element root);
// Public Instance Methods
    public void change(int offset, int length, AbstractDocument.DefaultDocumentEvent de);
    public javax.swing.text.Element clone(javax.swing.text.Element parent, javax.swing.text.Element clonee);
    public javax.swing.text.Element getRootElement();
    public void insert(int offset, int length, DefaultStyledDocument.ElementSpec[ ] data,
                AbstractDocument.DefaultDocumentEvent de);
    public void remove(int offset, int length, AbstractDocument.DefaultDocumentEvent de);
// Protected Instance Methods
    protected void changeUpdate();
    protected void insertUpdate(DefaultStyledDocument.ElementSpec[ ] data);
    protected void removeUpdate();
}
```

Type Of: DefaultStyledDocument.buffer

DefaultStyledDocument.ElementSpec

javax.swing.text

This class is used to represent the elements of a document in a flat structure, instead of a tree. An ElementSpec object represent a start tag, an end tag, or document content. Arrays of ElementSpec objects can be used to represent a document or a portion of a document, and these ElementSpec objects can later be converted into a tree of Element objects. This class can be useful because it is often easier to work with an array of ElementSpec objects than with a tree of Element objects.

```
public static class DefaultStyledDocument.ElementSpec {
// Public Constructors
    public ElementSpec(AttributeSet a, short type);
    public ElementSpec(AttributeSet a, short type, int len);
    public ElementSpec(AttributeSet a, short type, char[ ] txt, int offs, int len);
// Public Constants
    public static final short ContentType;                                          =3
    public static final short EndTagType;                                           =2
    public static final short JoinFractureDirection;                                =7
    public static final short JoinNextDirection;                                    =5
    public static final short JoinPreviousDirection;                                =4
    public static final short OriginateDirection;                                   =6
    public static final short StartTagType;                                         =1
// Property Accessor Methods (by property name)
    public char[ ] getArray();
    public AttributeSet getAttributes();
    public short getDirection();
    public void setDirection(short direction);
    public int getLength();
    public int getOffset();
    public short getType();
    public void setType(short type);
```

```
// Public Methods Overriding Object
    public String toString();
}
```

Passed To: DefaultStyledDocument.{create(), insert()}, DefaultStyledDocument.ElementBuffer.{insert(),
insertUpdate()}, javax.swing.text.html.HTMLDocument.{create(), insert()}

DefaultStyledDocument.SectionElement   Java 1.2

javax.swing.text   *serializable*

This protected inner class is the default root element used by DefaultStyledDocument.
Applications do not need to use or subclass this class.

```
protected class DefaultStyledDocument.SectionElement extends AbstractDocument.BranchElement {
// Public Constructors
    public SectionElement();
// Public Methods Overriding AbstractDocument.BranchElement
    public String getName();
}
```

DefaultTextUI   Java 1.2; Deprecated in Java 1.2

javax.swing.text

This class is deprecated and should not be used. As a text component UI delegate
class, it never should have been part of this package.

```
public abstract class DefaultTextUI extends javax.swing.plaf.basic.BasicTextUI {
// Public Constructors
    public DefaultTextUI();
}
```

Hierarchy: javax.swing.plaf.basic.BasicTextUI → DefaultTextUI

Document   Java 1.2

javax.swing.text

This interface defines the fundamental methods required in a class that stores document
text to be displayed and edited by a JTextComponent. The methods of this interface
require that a Document object be able to represent document content both as a linear
sequence of characters and as a tree of hierarchical Element objects. Element objects
model the document structure and are used to represent things like paragraphs, lines,
and runs of styled text. When a JTree component displays a Document, the Element tree is
used to create a tree of View objects that display the individual elements.

The getText() methods return text from the document, either as a String or in a supplied
Segment object. insertString() inserts a run of text associated with the specified attributes.
remove() deletes text from the Document. The Document object must fire appropriate DocumentEvent and UndoableEditEvent events when edits like these are performed. createPosi-
tion() returns a Position object that represents a relative position in the document. The
Position reference remains valid even if text is inserted or deleted from the document.
The putProperty() and getProperty() methods allow arbitrary key/value pairs to be associated with a Document. These properties can be used to hold metainformation, such as
the author and title of the document. The TitleProperty and StreamDescriptionProperty constants are two predefined property keys. Finally, the render() method must run the specified Runnable object while guaranteeing that there will not be any changes to the
document. This method is used to perform the potentially time-consuming document-
rendering process in a thread-safe way.

See also Element, AttributeSet, Position, and Segment.

```
public abstract interface Document {
// Public Constants
    public static final String StreamDescriptionProperty;                        ="stream"
    public static final String TitleProperty;                                    ="title"
// Event Registration Methods (by event name)
    public abstract void addDocumentListener(javax.swing.event.DocumentListener listener);
    public abstract void removeDocumentListener(javax.swing.event.DocumentListener listener);
    public abstract void addUndoableEditListener(javax.swing.event.UndoableEditListener listener);
    public abstract void removeUndoableEditListener(javax.swing.event.UndoableEditListener listener);
// Property Accessor Methods (by property name)
    public abstract javax.swing.text.Element getDefaultRootElement();
    public abstract Position getEndPosition();
    public abstract int getLength();
    public abstract javax.swing.text.Element[ ] getRootElements();
    public abstract Position getStartPosition();
// Public Instance Methods
    public abstract Position createPosition(int offs) throws BadLocationException;
    public abstract Object getProperty(Object key);
    public abstract String getText(int offset, int length) throws BadLocationException;
    public abstract void getText(int offset, int length, Segment txt) throws BadLocationException;
    public abstract void insertString(int offset, String str, AttributeSet a) throws BadLocationException;
    public abstract void putProperty(Object key, Object value);
    public abstract void remove(int offs, int len) throws BadLocationException;
    public abstract void render(Runnable r);
}
```

Implementations: AbstractDocument, StyledDocument

Passed To: Too many methods to list.

Returned By: JTextArea.createDefaultModel(), JTextField.createDefaultModel(),
javax.swing.event.DocumentEvent.getDocument(), AbstractDocument.AbstractElement.getDocument(),
AbstractDocument.DefaultDocumentEvent.getDocument(), AbstractWriter.getDocument(),
DefaultEditorKit.createDefaultDocument(), EditorKit.createDefaultDocument(),
javax.swing.text.Element.getDocument(), JTextComponent.getDocument(),
StyledEditorKit.createDefaultDocument(), View.getDocument(),
javax.swing.text.html.HTMLEditorKit.createDefaultDocument()

EditorKit   Java 1.2

javax.swing.text   *cloneable serializable*

This abstract class defines the methods that are used to configure a JEditorPane to display
and edit a particular type of document. Swing contains concrete subclasses for plain
text, as well as HTML and RTF documents. To configure a JEditorPane, instantiate an EditorKit object and pass it to the setEditorKit() method of your JEditorPane.

The getContentType() method of an EditorKit returns the MIME type supported by the kit.
createDefaultDocument() creates an appropriate type of empty Document object to hold the
document. The read() and write() methods read and write document content from and to
streams. getViewFactory() returns a ViewFactory object for this document type. The ViewFactory is used to convert the Element objects of the document into View objects that display
the document on the screen. createCaret() returns a Caret object that the JEditorPane can
use to navigate the document, and getActions() returns an array of Action objects that the
JEditorPane can bind to keystrokes. EditorKit implementations typically define a number of
Action implementations as inner classes.

```
public abstract class EditorKit implements Cloneable, Serializable {
// Public Constructors
    public EditorKit();
// Property Accessor Methods (by property name)
    public abstract Action[ ] getActions();
    public abstract String getContentType();
    public abstract ViewFactory getViewFactory();
// Public Instance Methods
    public abstract Caret createCaret();
    public abstract Document createDefaultDocument();
    public void deinstall(JEditorPane c);                                                        empty
    public void install(JEditorPane c);                                                          empty
    public abstract void read(java.io.Reader in, Document doc, int pos) throws java.io.IOException,
        BadLocationException;
    public abstract void read(java.io.InputStream in, Document doc, int pos) throws java.io.IOException,
        BadLocationException;
    public abstract void write(java.io.Writer out, Document doc, int pos, int len) throws java.io.IOException,
        BadLocationException;
    public abstract void write(java.io.OutputStream out, Document doc, int pos, int len) throws java.io.IOException,
        BadLocationException;
// Public Methods Overriding Object
    public abstract Object clone();
}
```

Hierarchy: Object → EditorKit(Cloneable, Serializable)

Subclasses: DefaultEditorKit

Passed To: JEditorPane.{setEditorKit(), setEditorKitForContentType()}, JTextPane.setEditorKit()

Returned By: JEditorPane.{createDefaultEditorKit(), createEditorKitForContentType(), getEditorKit(), getEditorKitForContentType()}, JTextPane.createDefaultEditorKit(), javax.swing.plaf.TextUI.getEditorKit()

Element   Java 1.2

javax.swing.text

This interface defines the methods required for objects that want to be part of a Document object's element tree. An Element object must keep track of its parent and its children. It must also know its position and the position of its children within the linear sequence of characters that comprise the Document. Finally, an Element must be able to return the set of attributes that have been applied it it. getParentElement() returns the parent. getElementCount() and getElement() return the number of child elements and the specified child element, respectively. getStartOffset() and getEndOffset() return the start and end positions of this element. getElementIndex() returns the index of the child element that contains the specified position. getAttributes() returns the AttributeSet for this element.

```
public abstract interface Element {
// Property Accessor Methods (by property name)
    public abstract AttributeSet getAttributes();
    public abstract Document getDocument();
    public abstract int getElementCount();
    public abstract int getEndOffset();
    public abstract boolean isLeaf();
    public abstract String getName();
    public abstract javax.swing.text.Element getParentElement();
    public abstract int getStartOffset();
```

// Public Instance Methods
```
    public abstract javax.swing.text.Element getElement(int index);
    public abstract int getElementIndex(int offset);
}
```

Implementations: AbstractDocument.AbstractElement

Passed To: Too many methods to list.

Returned By: Too many methods to list.

Type Of: DefaultStyledDocument.AttributeUndoableEdit.element

ElementIterator   Java 1.2

javax.swing.text   *cloneable*

This class is used to perform a depth-first traversal, or iteration, through a tree of Element objects. The Element tree structure should not be changed while the iteration is in progress. Note that despite its name, this class does not implement java.util.Iterator.

```
public class ElementIterator implements Cloneable {
// Public Constructors
    public ElementIterator(javax.swing.text.Element root);
    public ElementIterator(Document document);
// Public Instance Methods
    public javax.swing.text.Element current();
    public int depth();
    public javax.swing.text.Element first();
    public javax.swing.text.Element next();
    public javax.swing.text.Element previous();
// Public Methods Overriding Object
    public Object clone();                                               synchronized
}
```

Hierarchy: Object → ElementIterator(Cloneable)

Returned By: AbstractWriter.getElementIterator()

FieldView   Java 1.2

javax.swing.text

This View class displays a single line of plain text. It is used, for example, by JTextField.

```
public class FieldView extends PlainView {
// Public Constructors
    public FieldView(javax.swing.text.Element elem);
// Public Methods Overriding PlainView
    public float getPreferredSpan(int axis);
    public void insertUpdate(javax.swing.event.DocumentEvent changes, java.awt.Shape a, ViewFactory f);
    public java.awt.Shape modelToView(int pos, java.awt.Shape a, Position.Bias b) throws BadLocationException;
    public void paint(java.awt.Graphics g, java.awt.Shape a);
    public void removeUpdate(javax.swing.event.DocumentEvent changes, java.awt.Shape a, ViewFactory f);
    public int viewToModel(float fx, float fy, java.awt.Shape a, Position.Bias[ ] bias);
// Public Methods Overriding View
    public int getResizeWeight(int axis);
// Protected Instance Methods
    protected java.awt.Shape adjustAllocation(java.awt.Shape a);
```

```
    protected java.awt.FontMetrics getFontMetrics();
}
```

Hierarchy: Object→ View(SwingConstants)→ PlainView(TabExpander)→ FieldView

Subclasses: PasswordView

GapContent — Java 1.2

javax.swing.text — *serializable*

This class is an implementation of the AbstractDocument.Content interface that uses an array of characters with a gap of unused characters in it. This gap is positioned near the current insertion position so that subsequent insertions require fewer characters to be shifted in the array. This implementation is more complicated than StringContent, but it works efficiently with documents of any size. This is the default Content implementation for all documents derived from AbstractDocument. This class inherits from a private superclass, GapVector, which is not covered in this book because it is private.

```
public class GapContent extends GapVector implements AbstractDocument.Content, Serializable {
// Public Constructors
    public GapContent();
    public GapContent(int initialLength);
// Methods Implementing AbstractDocument.Content
    public Position createPosition(int offset) throws BadLocationException;
    public void getChars(int where, int len, Segment chars) throws BadLocationException;
    public String getString(int where, int len) throws BadLocationException;
    public javax.swing.undo.UndoableEdit insertString(int where, String str) throws BadLocationException;
    public int length();
    public javax.swing.undo.UndoableEdit remove(int where, int nitems) throws BadLocationException;
// Protected Instance Methods
    protected Object allocateArray(int len);
    protected int getArrayLength();
    protected java.util.Vector getPositionsInRange(java.util.Vector v, int offset, int length);
    protected void resetMarksAtZero();
    protected void shiftEnd(int newSize);
    protected void shiftGap(int newGapStart);
    protected void shiftGapEndUp(int newGapEnd);
    protected void shiftGapStartDown(int newGapStart);
    protected void updateUndoPositions(java.util.Vector positions, int offset, int length);
}
```

Hierarchy: Object→ GapVector(Serializable)→ GapContent(AbstractDocument.Content, Serializable)

Highlighter — Java 1.2

javax.swing.text

This interface defines the methods that must be implemented by an object that wants to maintain and draw the list of selected regions within a JTextComponent. The methods of Highlighter allow selected regions to be added, changed, and removed for the set of highlighted regions. Each region is specified as a start and end position within the Document and a Highlighter.HighlightPainter object that is used to draw the highlight. The getHighlights() method returns an array of Highlighter.Highlight objects that describe the individual highlighted regions and their painter objects. Most applications can rely on the DefaultHighlighter class that is used by default by JTextComponent and never have to implement this interface.

```
public abstract interface Highlighter {
// Inner Classes
    public abstract static interface Highlight;
    public abstract static interface HighlightPainter;
// Public Instance Methods
    public abstract Object addHighlight(int p0, int p1, Highlighter.HighlightPainter p) throws BadLocationException;
    public abstract void changeHighlight(Object tag, int p0, int p1) throws BadLocationException;
    public abstract void deinstall(JTextComponent c);
    public abstract Highlighter.Highlight[ ] getHighlights();
    public abstract void install(JTextComponent c);
    public abstract void paint(java.awt.Graphics g);
    public abstract void removeAllHighlights();
    public abstract void removeHighlight(Object tag);
}
```

Implementations: LayeredHighlighter

Passed To: JTextComponent.setHighlighter()

Returned By: JTextComponent.getHighlighter()

Highlighter.Highlight   Java 1.2

javax.swing.text

The methods of this interface describe a highlighted region in a Document by specifying the start and end positions of the region and the Highlighter.HighlightPainter object that is used to draw the highlighted region.

```
public abstract static interface Highlighter.Highlight {
// Public Instance Methods
    public abstract int getEndOffset();
    public abstract Highlighter.HighlightPainter getPainter();
    public abstract int getStartOffset();
}
```

Returned By: DefaultHighlighter.getHighlights(), Highlighter.getHighlights(),
LayeredHighlighter.getHighlights()

Highlighter.HighlightPainter   Java 1.2

javax.swing.text

This interface defines the paint() method used to draw a highlighted region.

```
public abstract static interface Highlighter.HighlightPainter {
// Public Instance Methods
    public abstract void paint(java.awt.Graphics g, int p0, int p1, java.awt.Shape bounds, JTextComponent c);
}
```

Implementations: LayeredHighlighter.LayerPainter

Passed To: DefaultHighlighter.addHighlight(), Highlighter.addHighlight(), LayeredHighlighter.addHighlight()

Returned By: DefaultCaret.getSelectionPainter(), Highlighter.Highlight.getPainter()

IconView   Java 1.2

javax.swing.text

This View class encapsulates a javax.swing.Icon and allows icons and images to be displayed within a Document.

```
public class IconView extends View {
// Public Constructors
    public IconView(javax.swing.text.Element elem);
// Public Methods Overriding View
    public float getAlignment(int axis);
    public float getPreferredSpan(int axis);
    public java.awt.Shape modelToView(int pos, java.awt.Shape a, Position.Bias b) throws BadLocationException;
    public void paint(java.awt.Graphics g, java.awt.Shape a);
    public void setSize(float width, float height);                                              empty
    public int viewToModel(float x, float y, java.awt.Shape a, Position.Bias[ ] bias);
}
```

Hierarchy: Object → View(SwingConstants) → IconView

JTextComponent   Java 1.2

javax.swing.text   *serializable accessible(text) swing component*

This is the base class for all Swing text-editing components. Applications do not use this class directly, but instead use one of its subclasses in the javax.swing package: JTextField, JTextArea, JPasswordField, JEditorPane, or JTextPane. A JTextComponent displays the text contained in its model object, an object of type Document. Other important classes and interfaces used by JTextComponent are Caret, Highlighter, Keymap, Style, EditorKit, TextAction, and View.

```
public abstract class JTextComponent extends JComponent implements Accessible, Scrollable {
// Public Constructors
    public JTextComponent();
// Public Constants
    public static final String DEFAULT_KEYMAP;                                        ="default"
    public static final String FOCUS_ACCELERATOR_KEY;                          ="focusAcceleratorKey"
// Inner Classes
    public class AccessibleJTextComponent extends JComponent.AccessibleJComponent implements AccessibleText,
        javax.swing.event.CaretListener, javax.swing.event.DocumentListener;
    public static class KeyBinding;
// Public Class Methods
    public static Keymap addKeymap(String nm, Keymap parent);
    public static Keymap getKeymap(String nm);
    public static void loadKeymap(Keymap map, JTextComponent.KeyBinding[ ] bindings, Action[ ] actions);
    public static Keymap removeKeymap(String nm);
// Event Registration Methods (by event name)
    public void addCaretListener(javax.swing.event.CaretListener listener);
    public void removeCaretListener(javax.swing.event.CaretListener listener);
    public void addInputMethodListener(java.awt.event.InputMethodListener l);          Overrides:Component
// Property Accessor Methods (by property name)
    public AccessibleContext getAccessibleContext();                                Implements:Accessible
    public Action[ ] getActions();
    public Caret getCaret();
    public void setCaret(Caret c);                                                      bound expert
    public java.awt.Color getCaretColor();
    public void setCaretColor(java.awt.Color c);                                        bound preferred
    public int getCaretPosition();
    public void setCaretPosition(int position);
    public java.awt.Color getDisabledTextColor();
    public void setDisabledTextColor(java.awt.Color c);                                 bound preferred
    public Document getDocument();
    public void setDocument(Document doc);                                              bound expert
    public boolean isEditable();
    public void setEditable(boolean b);
```

```
      public char getFocusAccelerator();
      public void setFocusAccelerator(char aKey);                                       bound
      public boolean isFocusTraversable();                               Overrides:JComponent
      public Highlighter getHighlighter();
      public void setHighlighter(Highlighter h);                                 bound expert
      public java.awt.im.InputMethodRequests getInputMethodRequests();    Overrides:Component
      public Keymap getKeymap();
      public void setKeymap(Keymap map);                                              bound
      public java.awt.Insets getMargin();
      public void setMargin(java.awt.Insets m);                                       bound
      public boolean isOpaque();                                         Overrides:JComponent
      public void setOpaque(boolean o);                                  Overrides:JComponent
      public java.awt.Dimension getPreferredScrollableViewportSize();    Implements:Scrollable
      public boolean getScrollableTracksViewportHeight();                Implements:Scrollable
      public boolean getScrollableTracksViewportWidth();                 Implements:Scrollable
      public String getSelectedText();
      public java.awt.Color getSelectedTextColor();
      public void setSelectedTextColor(java.awt.Color c);                    bound preferred
      public java.awt.Color getSelectionColor();
      public void setSelectionColor(java.awt.Color c);                       bound preferred
      public int getSelectionEnd();
      public void setSelectionEnd(int selectionEnd);
      public int getSelectionStart();
      public void setSelectionStart(int selectionStart);
      public String getText();
      public String getText(int offs, int len) throws BadLocationException;
      public void setText(String t);
      public javax.swing.plaf.TextUI getUI();
      public void setUI(javax.swing.plaf.TextUI ui);
// Public Instance Methods
      public void copy();
      public void cut();
      public java.awt.Rectangle modelToView(int pos) throws BadLocationException;
      public void moveCaretPosition(int pos);
      public void paste();
      public void read(java.io.Reader in, Object desc) throws java.io.IOException;
      public void replaceSelection(String content);
      public void select(int selectionStart, int selectionEnd);
      public void selectAll();
      public int viewToModel(java.awt.Point pt);
      public void write(java.io.Writer out) throws java.io.IOException;
// Methods Implementing Accessible
      public AccessibleContext getAccessibleContext();
// Methods Implementing Scrollable
      public java.awt.Dimension getPreferredScrollableViewportSize();
      public int getScrollableBlockIncrement(java.awt.Rectangle visibleRect, int orientation, int direction);
      public boolean getScrollableTracksViewportHeight();
      public boolean getScrollableTracksViewportWidth();
      public int getScrollableUnitIncrement(java.awt.Rectangle visibleRect, int orientation, int direction);
// Public Methods Overriding JComponent
      public void removeNotify();
      public void setEnabled(boolean b);
      public void updateUI();
// Protected Methods Overriding JComponent
      protected String paramString();
      protected void processComponentKeyEvent(java.awt.event.KeyEvent e);
// Protected Methods Overriding Component
      protected void processInputMethodEvent(java.awt.event.InputMethodEvent e);
```

*javax.swing.
text*

```
// Protected Instance Methods
    protected void fireCaretUpdate(javax.swing.event.CaretEvent e);
}
```

Hierarchy: Object→ Component(java.awt.image.ImageObserver, java.awt.MenuContainer, Serializable)→ Container→ JComponent(Serializable)→ JTextComponent(Accessible, Scrollable)

Subclasses: JEditorPane, JTextArea, JTextField

Passed To: Too many methods to list.

Returned By: DefaultCaret.getComponent(), TextAction.{getFocusedComponent(), getTextComponent()}

JTextComponent.KeyBinding   Java 1.2

javax.swing.text

This class encapsulates a KeyStroke and the name of an Action object. The JTextComponent.KeyBinding class is used primarily for communication between the JTextComponent and its UI delegate object.

```
public static class JTextComponent.KeyBinding {
// Public Constructors
    public KeyBinding(KeyStroke key, String actionName);
// Public Instance Fields
    public String actionName;
    public KeyStroke key;
}
```

Passed To: JTextComponent.loadKeymap()

Returned By: LookAndFeel.makeKeyBindings()

Keymap   Java 1.2

javax.swing.text

This interface defines the methods of an object that can map javax.swing.KeyStroke objects to javax.swing.Action objects. A Keymap object is used to maintain the set of key bindings for a JTextComponent. Key-to-action bindings are added to a Keymap with addAction-ForKeyStroke(). The action bound to a given keystroke is queried with getAction(). Every Keymap can refer to another Keymap as its parent. If getAction() cannot find a specified KeyStroke mapping locally, it searches (recursively) in the parent Keymap.

There are no public implementations of the Keymap interface, so you cannot create a Keymap simply by calling a constructor. JTextComponent relies on a private implementation of Keymap, however, and you can obtain an instance by calling the static addKeymap() method of that class. Once you have initialized this Keymap with any desired bindings, you can pass it to the setKeymap() method of any JTextComponent instance.

```
public abstract interface Keymap {
// Property Accessor Methods (by property name)
    public abstract Action[] getBoundActions();
    public abstract KeyStroke[] getBoundKeyStrokes();
    public abstract Action getDefaultAction();
    public abstract void setDefaultAction(Action a);
    public abstract String getName();
    public abstract Keymap getResolveParent();
    public abstract void setResolveParent(Keymap parent);
// Public Instance Methods
    public abstract void addActionForKeyStroke(KeyStroke key, Action a);
    public abstract Action getAction(KeyStroke key);
```

```
    public abstract KeyStroke[ ] getKeyStrokesForAction(Action a);
    public abstract boolean isLocallyDefined(KeyStroke key);
    public abstract void removeBindings( );
    public abstract void removeKeyStrokeBinding(KeyStroke keys);
}
```

Passed To: JTextComponent.{addKeymap(), loadKeymap(), setKeymap()}, Keymap.setResolveParent()

Returned By: JTextComponent.{addKeymap(), getKeymap(), removeKeymap()}, Keymap.getResolveParent()

LabelView   Java 1.2

javax.swing.text

This View class displays a run of text that has a single set of character attributes, such as colors and fonts, associated with it. It supports line breaking and tab expansion.

```
public class LabelView extends View {
// Public Constructors
    public LabelView(javax.swing.text.Element elem);
// Public Methods Overriding View
    public View breakView(int axis, int p0, float pos, float len);
    public void changedUpdate(javax.swing.event.DocumentEvent e, java.awt.Shape a, ViewFactory f);
    public View createFragment(int p0, int p1);
    public float getAlignment(int axis);
    public int getBreakWeight(int axis, float pos, float len);
    public int getNextVisualPositionFrom(int pos, Position.Bias b, java.awt.Shape a, int direction,
                                       Position.Bias[ ] biasRet) throws BadLocationException;
    public float getPreferredSpan(int axis);
    public void insertUpdate(javax.swing.event.DocumentEvent e, java.awt.Shape a, ViewFactory f);
    public java.awt.Shape modelToView(int pos, java.awt.Shape a, Position.Bias b) throws BadLocationException;
    public void paint(java.awt.Graphics g, java.awt.Shape a);
    public void removeUpdate(javax.swing.event.DocumentEvent changes, java.awt.Shape a, ViewFactory f);
    public int viewToModel(float x, float y, java.awt.Shape a, Position.Bias[ ] biasReturn);
// Public Methods Overriding Object
    public String toString( );
// Protected Instance Methods
    protected java.awt.Font getFont( );
    protected java.awt.FontMetrics getFontMetrics( );
    protected void setPropertiesFromAttributes( );
    protected void setStrikeThrough(boolean s);
    protected void setSubscript(boolean s);
    protected void setSuperscript(boolean s);
    protected void setUnderline(boolean u);
}
```

Hierarchy: Object→ View(SwingConstants)→ LabelView

Subclasses: javax.swing.text.html.InlineView

LayeredHighlighter   Java 1.2

javax.swing.text

This abstract class is a Highlighter. Instead of implementing the abstract methods of the Highlighter interface, however, it adds another abstract method of its own. This new method, paintLayeredHighlights(), is called to draw a portion of the highlight that appears within the region defined by a single View object. Typical applications can rely on the DefaultHighlighter class that is automatically used by JTextComponent and never have to use or implement this class.

```
public abstract class LayeredHighlighter implements Highlighter {
// Public Constructors
   public LayeredHighlighter();
// Inner Classes
   public abstract static class LayerPainter implements Highlighter.HighlightPainter;
// Public Instance Methods
   public abstract void paintLayeredHighlights(java.awt.Graphics g, int p0, int p1, java.awt.Shape viewBounds,
                                               JTextComponent editor, View view);
// Methods Implementing Highlighter
   public abstract Object addHighlight(int p0, int p1, Highlighter.HighlightPainter p) throws BadLocationException;
   public abstract void changeHighlight(Object tag, int p0, int p1) throws BadLocationException;
   public abstract void deinstall(JTextComponent c);
   public abstract Highlighter.Highlight[ ] getHighlights();
   public abstract void install(JTextComponent c);
   public abstract void paint(java.awt.Graphics g);
   public abstract void removeAllHighlights();
   public abstract void removeHighlight(Object tag);
}
```

Hierarchy: Object→ LayeredHighlighter(Highlighter)

Subclasses: DefaultHighlighter

LayeredHighlighter.LayerPainter   Java 1.2

javax.swing.text

This abstract inner class implements Highlighter.HighlightPainter and adds another abstract method. Typical applications do not need to use or implement this class and can rely on the DefaultHighlighter.DefaultHighlightPainter implementation.

```
public abstract static class LayeredHighlighter.LayerPainter implements Highlighter.HighlightPainter {
// Public Constructors
   public LayerPainter();
// Public Instance Methods
   public abstract java.awt.Shape paintLayer(java.awt.Graphics g, int p0, int p1, java.awt.Shape viewBounds,
                                             JTextComponent editor, View view);
// Methods Implementing Highlighter.HighlightPainter
   public abstract void paint(java.awt.Graphics g, int p0, int p1, java.awt.Shape bounds, JTextComponent c);
}
```

Subclasses: DefaultHighlighter.DefaultHighlightPainter

Type Of: DefaultHighlighter.DefaultPainter

MutableAttributeSet   Java 1.2

javax.swing.text

This interface extends AttributeSet to add methods that allow the set of attributes and parent attributes to be modified. See also AttributeSet and Style.

```
public abstract interface MutableAttributeSet extends AttributeSet {
// Public Instance Methods
   public abstract void addAttribute(Object name, Object value);
   public abstract void addAttributes(AttributeSet attributes);
   public abstract void removeAttribute(Object name);
   public abstract void removeAttributes(AttributeSet attributes);
   public abstract void removeAttributes(java.util.Enumeration names);
   public abstract void setResolveParent(AttributeSet parent);
}
```

Hierarchy: (MutableAttributeSet(AttributeSet))

Implementations: AbstractDocument.AbstractElement, SimpleAttributeSet, Style

Passed To: Too many methods to list.

Returned By: JTextPane.getInputAttributes(), StyleContext.createLargeAttributeSet(), StyledEditorKit.getInputAttributes(), javax.swing.text.html.HTMLEditorKit.getInputAttributes(), javax.swing.text.html.StyleSheet.createLargeAttributeSet()

Type Of: javax.swing.text.html.HTMLDocument.HTMLReader.charAttr

ParagraphView   Java 1.2

javax.swing.text

This BoxView subclass displays a column of subviews, one for each row or line in the paragraph. These rows are implemented by a private internal BoxView class. ParagraphView handles word wrapping by breaking its views as necessary to fit them into the row views it creates. ParagraphView supports various paragraph-level attributes such as margins, line spacing, and first-line indent.

```
public class ParagraphView extends BoxView implements TabExpander {
// Public Constructors
   public ParagraphView(javax.swing.text.Element elem);
// Public Instance Methods
   public View breakView(int axis, float len, java.awt.Shape a);
   public int getBreakWeight(int axis, float len);
// Methods Implementing TabExpander
   public float nextTabStop(float x, int tabOffset);
// Public Methods Overriding BoxView
   public float getAlignment(int axis);
   public void paint(java.awt.Graphics g, java.awt.Shape a);
// Protected Methods Overriding BoxView
   protected SizeRequirements calculateMinorAxisRequirements(int axis, SizeRequirements r);
   protected boolean flipEastAndWestAtEnds(int position, Position.Bias bias);
   protected void layout(int width, int height);
// Public Methods Overriding CompositeView
   public void changedUpdate(javax.swing.event.DocumentEvent changes, java.awt.Shape a, ViewFactory f);
   public void insertUpdate(javax.swing.event.DocumentEvent changes, java.awt.Shape a, ViewFactory f);
   public void removeUpdate(javax.swing.event.DocumentEvent changes, java.awt.Shape a, ViewFactory f);
// Protected Methods Overriding CompositeView
   protected int getNextNorthSouthVisualPositionFrom(int pos, Position.Bias b, java.awt.Shape a, int direction,
                                    Position.Bias[ ] biasRet) throws BadLocationException;
   protected View getViewAtPosition(int pos, java.awt.Rectangle a);
   protected int getViewIndexAtPosition(int pos);
   protected void loadChildren(ViewFactory f);
// Protected Instance Methods
   protected void adjustRow(ParagraphView.Row r, int desiredSpan, int x);
   protected int findOffsetToCharactersInString(char[ ] string, int start);
   protected int getClosestPositionTo(int pos, Position.Bias b, java.awt.Shape a, int direction,
                                    Position.Bias[ ] biasRet, int rowIndex, int x) throws BadLocationException;
   protected View getLayoutView(int index);
   protected int getLayoutViewCount();
   protected float getPartialSize(int startOffset, int endOffset);
   protected float getTabBase();
   protected TabSet getTabSet();
   protected void setFirstLineIndent(float fi);
   protected void setJustification(int j);
   protected void setLineSpacing(float ls);
   protected void setPropertiesFromAttributes();
```

```
// Protected Instance Fields
    protected int firstLineIndent;
}
```

Hierarchy: Object→ View(SwingConstants)→ CompositeView→ BoxView→
javax.swing.text.ParagraphView(TabExpander)

Subclasses: javax.swing.text.html.ParagraphView

PasswordView
Java 1.2

javax.swing.text

This view displays a single line of text in a way that is suitable for the JPasswordField
component.

```
public class PasswordView extends FieldView {
// Public Constructors
    public PasswordView(javax.swing.text.Element elem);
// Public Methods Overriding FieldView
    public java.awt.Shape modelToView(int pos, java.awt.Shape a, Position.Bias b) throws BadLocationException;
    public int viewToModel(float fx, float fy, java.awt.Shape a, Position.Bias[ ] bias);
// Protected Methods Overriding PlainView
    protected int drawSelectedText(java.awt.Graphics g, int x, int y, int p0, int p1) throws BadLocationException;
    protected int drawUnselectedText(java.awt.Graphics g, int x, int y, int p0, int p1) throws BadLocationException;
// Protected Instance Methods
    protected int drawEchoCharacter(java.awt.Graphics g, int x, int y, char c);
}
```

Hierarchy: Object→ View(SwingConstants)→ PlainView(TabExpander)→ FieldView→ PasswordView

PlainDocument
Java 1.2

javax.swing.text
serializable

This concrete AbstractDocument subclass defines a plain-text document with no character
attributes. The root element of the document has one child element for each line in the
document. By default, PlainDocument uses a GapContent object to hold its textual content.
Applications rarely need to work with a PlainDocument class directly. Typically, they can
simply use the JTextArea or JTextField components for displaying and editing text.

```
public class PlainDocument extends AbstractDocument {
// Public Constructors
    public PlainDocument();
// Protected Constructors
    protected PlainDocument(AbstractDocument.Content c);
// Public Constants
    public static final String lineLimitAttribute;                              ="lineLimit"
    public static final String tabSizeAttribute;                                ="tabSize"
// Public Methods Overriding AbstractDocument
    public javax.swing.text.Element getDefaultRootElement();                    default:BranchElement
    public javax.swing.text.Element getParagraphElement(int pos);
// Protected Methods Overriding AbstractDocument
    protected void insertUpdate(AbstractDocument.DefaultDocumentEvent chng, AttributeSet attr);
    protected void removeUpdate(AbstractDocument.DefaultDocumentEvent chng);
// Protected Instance Methods
    protected AbstractDocument.AbstractElement createDefaultRoot();
}
```

Hierarchy: Object→ AbstractDocument(Document, Serializable)→ PlainDocument

PlainView

javax.swing.text

This View class is used to display multiple lines of plain text. It can perform tab expansion, but it does not perform line wrapping. See also WrappedPlainView.

```
public class PlainView extends View implements TabExpander {
// Public Constructors
    public PlainView(javax.swing.text.Element elem);
// Methods Implementing TabExpander
    public float nextTabStop(float x, int tabOffset);
// Public Methods Overriding View
    public void changedUpdate(javax.swing.event.DocumentEvent changes, java.awt.Shape a, ViewFactory f);
    public float getPreferredSpan(int axis);
    public void insertUpdate(javax.swing.event.DocumentEvent changes, java.awt.Shape a, ViewFactory f);
    public java.awt.Shape modelToView(int pos, java.awt.Shape a, Position.Bias b) throws BadLocationException;
    public void paint(java.awt.Graphics g, java.awt.Shape a);
    public void preferenceChanged(View child, boolean width, boolean height);
    public void removeUpdate(javax.swing.event.DocumentEvent changes, java.awt.Shape a, ViewFactory f);
    public int viewToModel(float fx, float fy, java.awt.Shape a, Position.Bias[ ] bias);
// Protected Instance Methods
    protected void drawLine(int lineIndex, java.awt.Graphics g, int x, int y);
    protected int drawSelectedText(java.awt.Graphics g, int x, int y, int p0, int p1) throws BadLocationException;
    protected int drawUnselectedText(java.awt.Graphics g, int x, int y, int p0, int p1) throws BadLocationException;
    protected final Segment getLineBuffer();
    protected int getTabSize();
// Protected Instance Fields
    protected java.awt.FontMetrics metrics;
}
```

Hierarchy: Object→ View(SwingConstants)→ PlainView(TabExpander)

Subclasses: FieldView

Position

javax.swing.text

This interface describes a position within a Document in a way that is insensitive to insertions and deletions within the document. The getOffset() method returns the character offset of that position. For editable documents, a Position object must keep track of edits and adjust the character offset as necessary.

```
public abstract interface Position {
// Inner Classes
    public static final class Bias;
// Public Instance Methods
    public abstract int getOffset();
}
```

Returned By: AbstractDocument.{createPosition(), getEndPosition(), getStartPosition()}, AbstractDocument.Content.createPosition(), Document.{createPosition(), getEndPosition(), getStartPosition()}, GapContent.createPosition(), StringContent.createPosition()

Position.Bias

javax.swing.text

The Document interface describes positions within the document using integer offsets. These numbers refer not to the actual characters of the document, but to the spaces between the characters. This means that, in some cases, a simple integer position might refer to either the character before it or the character after it. In ambiguous cases, therefore, the position must be augmented with a bias value. This inner class defines the two legal bias values: Position.Bias.Backward and Position.Bias.Forward. A number of methods in the javax.swing.text package require one or the other of these constants as an argument.

```
public static final class Position.Bias {
// No Constructor
// Public Constants
    public static final Position.Bias Backward;
    public static final Position.Bias Forward;
// Public Methods Overriding Object
    public String toString();
}
```

Passed To: Too many methods to list.

Type Of: Position.Bias.{Backward, Forward}

Segment   Java 1.2

javax.swing.text

The Segment class represents a segment of text through three public fields. These are a reference to a character array, the array offset of the first character in the array, and the number of characters in the segment. This is an efficient way to pass references to text segments, since it does not require new String objects to be created. However, it is dangerous because it exposes the character array directly and makes it vulnerable to changes. Users of a Segment object must treat the text segment as if it were immutable, using it for read-only access to the text.

```
public class Segment {
// Public Constructors
    public Segment();
    public Segment(char[ ] array, int offset, int count);
// Public Methods Overriding Object
    public String toString();
// Public Instance Fields
    public char[ ] array;
    public int count;
    public int offset;
}
```

Passed To: AbstractDocument.getText(), AbstractDocument.Content.getChars(), Document.getText(), GapContent.getChars(), StringContent.getChars(), Utilities.{drawTabbedText(), getBreakLocation(), getTabbedTextOffset(), getTabbedTextWidth()}

Returned By: PlainView.getLineBuffer(), WrappedPlainView.getLineBuffer()

SimpleAttributeSet   Java 1.2

javax.swing.text   *cloneable serializable*

This class is a simple implementation of the MutableAttributeSet interface that uses an internal hashtable. See AttributeSet and MutableAttributeSet for details. When working with many attribute sets, it may be more efficient to define styles using a StyleContext object.

```
public class SimpleAttributeSet implements Cloneable, MutableAttributeSet, Serializable {
// Public Constructors
    public SimpleAttributeSet();
    public SimpleAttributeSet(AttributeSet source);
// Public Constants
    public static final AttributeSet EMPTY;
```

```
// Public Instance Methods
    public boolean isEmpty();                                                      default:true
// Methods Implementing AttributeSet
    public boolean containsAttribute(Object name, Object value);
    public boolean containsAttributes(AttributeSet attributes);
    public AttributeSet copyAttributes();
    public Object getAttribute(Object name);
    public int getAttributeCount();                                                default:0
    public java.util.Enumeration getAttributeNames();
    public AttributeSet getResolveParent();                                        default:null
    public boolean isDefined(Object attrName);
    public boolean isEqual(AttributeSet attr);
// Methods Implementing MutableAttributeSet
    public void addAttribute(Object name, Object value);
    public void addAttributes(AttributeSet attributes);
    public void removeAttribute(Object name);
    public void removeAttributes(java.util.Enumeration names);
    public void removeAttributes(AttributeSet attributes);
    public void setResolveParent(AttributeSet parent);
// Public Methods Overriding Object
    public Object clone();
    public boolean equals(Object obj);
    public int hashCode();
    public String toString();
}
```

Hierarchy: Object→ SimpleAttributeSet(Cloneable, MutableAttributeSet(AttributeSet), Serializable)

Returned By: javax.swing.text.html.parser.Parser.getAttributes()

StringContent   Java 1.2

javax.swing.text   *serializable*

This class is a simple implementation of the AbstractDocument.Content interface based on
simple String manipulation. It is suitable only for short documents. By default, all documents derived from AbstractDocument use the GapContent implementation instead of String-
Content.

```
public final class StringContent implements AbstractDocument.Content, Serializable {
// Public Constructors
    public StringContent();
    public StringContent(int initialLength);
// Methods Implementing AbstractDocument.Content
    public Position createPosition(int offset) throws BadLocationException;
    public void getChars(int where, int len, Segment chars) throws BadLocationException;
    public String getString(int where, int len) throws BadLocationException;
    public javax.swing.undo.UndoableEdit insertString(int where, String str) throws BadLocationException;
    public int length();
    public javax.swing.undo.UndoableEdit remove(int where, int nitems) throws BadLocationException;
// Protected Instance Methods
    protected java.util.Vector getPositionsInRange(java.util.Vector v, int offset, int length);
    protected void updateUndoPositions(java.util.Vector positions);
}
```

Hierarchy: Object→ StringContent(AbstractDocument.Content, Serializable)

Style Java 1.2

javax.swing.text

This interface extends MutableAttributeSet by adding both a convenience method for retrieving the name of the attribute set and ChangeListener registration methods. A Style object is typically used to represent a named set of attributes. The style name is usually stored as an attribute. Because a Style is a kind of MutableAttributeSet, objects that use the style may want to know when the attributes of the Style change. Interested listeners can register with the addChangeListener() method. They are notified with a ChangeEvent when attributes are added to or removed from the Style.

```
public abstract interface Style extends MutableAttributeSet {
// Event Registration Methods (by event name)
    public abstract void addChangeListener(javax.swing.event.ChangeListener l);
    public abstract void removeChangeListener(javax.swing.event.ChangeListener l);
// Public Instance Methods
    public abstract String getName();
}
```

Hierarchy: (Style(MutableAttributeSet(AttributeSet)))

Implementations: StyleContext.NamedStyle

Passed To: JTextPane.{addStyle(), setLogicalStyle()}, DefaultStyledDocument.{addStyle(), setLogicalStyle(), styleChanged()}, StyleContext.addStyle(), StyleContext.NamedStyle.NamedStyle(), StyledDocument.{addStyle(), setLogicalStyle()}

Returned By: JTextPane.{addStyle(), getLogicalStyle(), getStyle()}, DefaultStyledDocument.{addStyle(), getLogicalStyle(), getStyle()}, StyleContext.{addStyle(), getStyle()}, StyledDocument.{addStyle(), getLogicalStyle(), getStyle()}, javax.swing.text.html.StyleSheet.getRule()

StyleConstants Java 1.2

javax.swing.text

This class defines a number of standard attribute keys for commonly used character and paragraph attributes. It also defines a number of static convenience methods that use these attributes to query the value of an attribute from an AttributeSet or to set the value of an attribute in a MutableAttributeSet.

Usually, the type of the value to be associated with an attribute key is obvious from the context. The method signatures for the static get and set methods make the value explicit. The value associated with the Alignment key should be one of the four ALIGN_ constants defined by the class. Any length values associated with attributes such as Left-Indent and LineSpacing should be float values expressed in printer's points (there are 72 printer's points in one inch).

StyleConstants defines four inner subclasses, each of which implements a different marker interface that serves to group attribute keys into broad categories. These inner classes define attribute key constants as well, but these constants are also available directly from the StyleConstants class.

```
public class StyleConstants {
// No Constructor
// Public Constants
    public static final int ALIGN_CENTER;                                       =1
    public static final int ALIGN_JUSTIFIED;                                    =3
    public static final int ALIGN_LEFT;                                         =0
    public static final int ALIGN_RIGHT;                                        =2
    public static final Object Alignment;
    public static final Object Background;
```

```
    public static final Object BidiLevel;
    public static final Object Bold;
    public static final Object ComponentAttribute;
    public static final String ComponentElementName;                    ="component"
    public static final Object ComposedTextAttribute;
    public static final Object FirstLineIndent;
    public static final Object FontFamily;
    public static final Object FontSize;
    public static final Object Foreground;
    public static final Object IconAttribute;
    public static final String IconElementName;                         ="icon"
    public static final Object Italic;
    public static final Object LeftIndent;
    public static final Object LineSpacing;
    public static final Object ModelAttribute;
    public static final Object NameAttribute;
    public static final Object Orientation;
    public static final Object ResolveAttribute;
    public static final Object RightIndent;
    public static final Object SpaceAbove;
    public static final Object SpaceBelow;
    public static final Object StrikeThrough;
    public static final Object Subscript;
    public static final Object Superscript;
    public static final Object TabSet;
    public static final Object Underline;
// Inner Classes
    public static class CharacterConstants extends StyleConstants implements AttributeSet.CharacterAttribute;
    public static class ColorConstants extends StyleConstants implements AttributeSet.CharacterAttribute,
        AttributeSet.ColorAttribute;
    public static class FontConstants extends StyleConstants implements AttributeSet.CharacterAttribute,
        AttributeSet.FontAttribute;
    public static class ParagraphConstants extends StyleConstants implements AttributeSet.ParagraphAttribute;
// Public Class Methods
    public static int getAlignment(AttributeSet a);
    public static java.awt.Color getBackground(AttributeSet a);
    public static int getBidiLevel(AttributeSet a);
    public static Component getComponent(AttributeSet a);
    public static float getFirstLineIndent(AttributeSet a);
    public static String getFontFamily(AttributeSet a);
    public static int getFontSize(AttributeSet a);
    public static java.awt.Color getForeground(AttributeSet a);
    public static Icon getIcon(AttributeSet a);
    public static float getLeftIndent(AttributeSet a);
    public static float getLineSpacing(AttributeSet a);
    public static float getRightIndent(AttributeSet a);
    public static float getSpaceAbove(AttributeSet a);
    public static float getSpaceBelow(AttributeSet a);
    public static TabSet getTabSet(AttributeSet a);
    public static boolean isBold(AttributeSet a);
    public static boolean isItalic(AttributeSet a);
    public static boolean isStrikeThrough(AttributeSet a);
    public static boolean isSubscript(AttributeSet a);
    public static boolean isSuperscript(AttributeSet a);
    public static boolean isUnderline(AttributeSet a);
    public static void setAlignment(MutableAttributeSet a, int align);
    public static void setBackground(MutableAttributeSet a, java.awt.Color fg);
    public static void setBidiLevel(MutableAttributeSet a, int o);
```

```
    public static void setBold(MutableAttributeSet a, boolean b);
    public static void setComponent(MutableAttributeSet a, Component c);
    public static void setFirstLineIndent(MutableAttributeSet a, float i);
    public static void setFontFamily(MutableAttributeSet a, String fam);
    public static void setFontSize(MutableAttributeSet a, int s);
    public static void setForeground(MutableAttributeSet a, java.awt.Color fg);
    public static void setIcon(MutableAttributeSet a, Icon c);
    public static void setItalic(MutableAttributeSet a, boolean b);
    public static void setLeftIndent(MutableAttributeSet a, float i);
    public static void setLineSpacing(MutableAttributeSet a, float i);
    public static void setRightIndent(MutableAttributeSet a, float i);
    public static void setSpaceAbove(MutableAttributeSet a, float i);
    public static void setSpaceBelow(MutableAttributeSet a, float i);
    public static void setStrikeThrough(MutableAttributeSet a, boolean b);
    public static void setSubscript(MutableAttributeSet a, boolean b);
    public static void setSuperscript(MutableAttributeSet a, boolean b);
    public static void setTabSet(MutableAttributeSet a, TabSet tabs);
    public static void setUnderline(MutableAttributeSet a, boolean b);
// Public Methods Overriding Object
    public String toString();
}
```

Subclasses: StyleConstants.CharacterConstants, StyleConstants.ColorConstants,
StyleConstants.FontConstants, StyleConstants.ParagraphConstants

StyleConstants.CharacterConstants   Java 1.2

javax.swing.text

This inner subclass of StyleConstants implements the AttributeSet.CharacterAttribute marker interface and defines various standard attribute key constants for character attributes. Copies of these constants are also defined by StyleConstants itself.

```
public static class StyleConstants.CharacterConstants extends StyleConstants
        implements AttributeSet.CharacterAttribute {
// No Constructor
// Public Constants
    public static final Object Background;
    public static final Object BidiLevel;
    public static final Object Bold;
    public static final Object ComponentAttribute;
    public static final Object Family;
    public static final Object Foreground;
    public static final Object IconAttribute;
    public static final Object Italic;
    public static final Object Size;
    public static final Object StrikeThrough;
    public static final Object Subscript;
    public static final Object Superscript;
    public static final Object Underline;
}
```

StyleConstants.ColorConstants   Java 1.2

javax.swing.text

This inner subclass of StyleConstants implements the AttributeSet.FontAttribute and Attribute-Set.CharacterAttribute marker interfaces and defines standard attribute key constants for color attributes. Copies of these constants are also defined by StyleConstants itself.

```
public static class StyleConstants.ColorConstants extends StyleConstants
        implements AttributeSet.CharacterAttribute, AttributeSet.ColorAttribute {
// No Constructor
// Public Constants
    public static final Object Background;
    public static final Object Foreground;
}
```

StyleConstants.FontConstants   Java 1.2

javax.swing.text

This inner subclass of StyleConstants implements the AttributeSet.FontAttribute and Attribute-Set.CharacterAttribute marker interfaces and defines standard attribute key constants for font attributes. Copies of these constants are also defined by StyleConstants itself.

```
public static class StyleConstants.FontConstants extends StyleConstants
        implements AttributeSet.CharacterAttribute, AttributeSet.FontAttribute {
// No Constructor
// Public Constants
    public static final Object Bold;
    public static final Object Family;
    public static final Object Italic;
    public static final Object Size;
}
```

StyleConstants.ParagraphConstants   Java 1.2

javax.swing.text

This inner subclass of StyleConstants implements the AttributeSet.ParagraphAttribute marker interface and defines various standard attribute key constants for paragraph attributes. Copies of these constants are also defined by StyleConstants itself.

```
public static class StyleConstants.ParagraphConstants extends StyleConstants
        implements AttributeSet.ParagraphAttribute {
// No Constructor
// Public Constants
    public static final Object Alignment;
    public static final Object FirstLineIndent;
    public static final Object LeftIndent;
    public static final Object LineSpacing;
    public static final Object Orientation;
    public static final Object RightIndent;
    public static final Object SpaceAbove;
    public static final Object SpaceBelow;
    public static final Object TabSet;
}
```

StyleContext   Java 1.2

javax.swing.text   *serializable*

This class is a collection of and a factory for Style objects. It is implemented in a way that allows caching and reuse of common attribute sets. Use addStyle() to create a new Style object and add it to the collection. Use the methods of the returned Style object to specify the attributes of the Style. Use getStyle() to look up a Style by name and removeStyle() to delete a Style from the collection. The static getDefaultStyleContext() method returns a default StyleContext object suitable for shared use by multiple documents. Style-

Context also includes a simple Font cache. You can access shared Font instances with the getFont() method.

StyleContext also implements the AbstractDocument.AttributeContext interface, which means that it implements various methods for creating new AttributeSet objects by copying existing AttributeSet objects and adding or removing individual attributes. These methods make it possible to implement the MutableAttributeSet or Style interfaces in terms of immutable AttributeSet objects that can be cached and shared. The Style objects returned by addStyle() are instances of StyleContext.NamedStyle, which is implemented in this way. Styles that contain only a small number of attributes are implemented as immutable StyleContext.SmallAttributeSet objects that are cached and reused, resulting in significant memory savings.

```
public class StyleContext implements AbstractDocument.AttributeContext, Serializable {
// Public Constructors
     public StyleContext();
// Public Constants
     public static final String DEFAULT_STYLE;                                                    ="default"
// Inner Classes
     public class NamedStyle implements Serializable, Style;
     public class SmallAttributeSet implements AttributeSet;
// Public Class Methods
     public static final StyleContext getDefaultStyleContext();
     public static Object getStaticAttribute(Object key);
     public static Object getStaticAttributeKey(Object key);
     public static void readAttributeSet(java.io.ObjectInputStream in, MutableAttributeSet a)
          throws ClassNotFoundException, java.io.IOException;
     public static void registerStaticAttributeKey(Object key);
     public static void writeAttributeSet(java.io.ObjectOutputStream out, AttributeSet a) throws java.io.IOException;
// Event Registration Methods (by event name)
     public void addChangeListener(javax.swing.event.ChangeListener l);
     public void removeChangeListener(javax.swing.event.ChangeListener l);
// Public Instance Methods
     public Style addStyle(String nm, Style parent);
     public java.awt.Color getBackground(AttributeSet attr);
     public java.awt.Font getFont(AttributeSet attr);
     public java.awt.Font getFont(String family, int style, int size);
     public java.awt.FontMetrics getFontMetrics(java.awt.Font f);
     public java.awt.Color getForeground(AttributeSet attr);
     public Style getStyle(String nm);
     public java.util.Enumeration getStyleNames();
     public void readAttributes(java.io.ObjectInputStream in, MutableAttributeSet a) throws ClassNotFoundException,
          java.io.IOException;
     public void removeStyle(String nm);
     public void writeAttributes(java.io.ObjectOutputStream out, AttributeSet a) throws java.io.IOException;
// Methods Implementing AbstractDocument.AttributeContext
     public AttributeSet addAttribute(AttributeSet old, Object name, Object value);              synchronized
     public AttributeSet addAttributes(AttributeSet old, AttributeSet attr);                     synchronized
     public AttributeSet getEmptySet();
     public void reclaim(AttributeSet a);
     public AttributeSet removeAttribute(AttributeSet old, Object name);                         synchronized
     public AttributeSet removeAttributes(AttributeSet old, AttributeSet attrs);                 synchronized
     public AttributeSet removeAttributes(AttributeSet old, java.util.Enumeration names);        synchronized
// Public Methods Overriding Object
     public String toString();
// Protected Instance Methods
     protected MutableAttributeSet createLargeAttributeSet(AttributeSet a);
     protected StyleContext.SmallAttributeSet createSmallAttributeSet(AttributeSet a);
```

```
    protected int getCompressionThreshold();
}
```

Hierarchy: Object→ StyleContext(AbstractDocument.AttributeContext, Serializable)

Subclasses: javax.swing.text.html.StyleSheet

Passed To: DefaultStyledDocument.DefaultStyledDocument()

Returned By: StyleContext.getDefaultStyleContext()

StyleContext.NamedStyle   Java 1.2

javax.swing.text   *serializable*

This class is a Style implementation that uses the StyleContext to implement its MutableAttributeSet methods in terms of immutable, possibly shared, AttributeSet objects.

```
public class StyleContext.NamedStyle implements Serializable, Style {
// Public Constructors
    public NamedStyle();
    public NamedStyle(Style parent);
    public NamedStyle(String name, Style parent);
// Event Registration Methods (by event name)
    public void addChangeListener(javax.swing.event.ChangeListener l);        Implements:Style
    public void removeChangeListener(javax.swing.event.ChangeListener l);     Implements:Style
// Public Instance Methods
    public void setName(String name);
// Methods Implementing AttributeSet
    public boolean containsAttribute(Object name, Object value);
    public boolean containsAttributes(AttributeSet attrs);
    public AttributeSet copyAttributes();
    public Object getAttribute(Object attrName);
    public int getAttributeCount();
    public java.util.Enumeration getAttributeNames();
    public AttributeSet getResolveParent();
    public boolean isDefined(Object attrName);
    public boolean isEqual(AttributeSet attr);
// Methods Implementing MutableAttributeSet
    public void addAttribute(Object name, Object value);
    public void addAttributes(AttributeSet attr);
    public void removeAttribute(Object name);
    public void removeAttributes(AttributeSet attrs);
    public void removeAttributes(java.util.Enumeration names);
    public void setResolveParent(AttributeSet parent);
// Methods Implementing Style
    public void addChangeListener(javax.swing.event.ChangeListener l);
    public String getName();
    public void removeChangeListener(javax.swing.event.ChangeListener l);
// Public Methods Overriding Object
    public String toString();
// Protected Instance Methods
    protected void fireStateChanged();
// Protected Instance Fields
    protected transient javax.swing.event.ChangeEvent changeEvent;
    protected javax.swing.event.EventListenerList listenerList;
}
```

StyleContext.SmallAttributeSet

javax.swing.text

This immutable class implements the AttributeSet interface using a simple Object array, rather than a hashtable. This implementation is memory efficient and time efficient for small attribute sets.

```
public class StyleContext.SmallAttributeSet implements AttributeSet {
// Public Constructors
    public SmallAttributeSet(Object[ ] attributes);
    public SmallAttributeSet(AttributeSet attrs);
// Methods Implementing AttributeSet
    public boolean containsAttribute(Object name, Object value);
    public boolean containsAttributes(AttributeSet attrs);
    public AttributeSet copyAttributes();
    public Object getAttribute(Object key);
    public int getAttributeCount();
    public java.util.Enumeration getAttributeNames();
    public AttributeSet getResolveParent();
    public boolean isDefined(Object key);
    public boolean isEqual(AttributeSet attr);
// Public Methods Overriding Object
    public Object clone();
    public boolean equals(Object obj);
    public int hashCode();
    public String toString();
}
```

Returned By: StyleContext.createSmallAttributeSet(),
javax.swing.text.html.StyleSheet.createSmallAttributeSet()

StyledDocument

javax.swing.text

This interface extends Document with the methods required for styled documents. A styled document allows attributes such as colors and font sizes to be applied to characters and runs of characters in the document. It also allows attributes such as margin sizes and line spacings to be applied to paragraphs. setCharacterAttributes() and setParagraphAttributes() apply a specified set of attributes to the specified region of the document. They can be used to augment or replace the existing attributes of that region. getCharacterElement() and getParagraphElement() return the Element object that most directly represents or contains the character or paragraph at the specified position.

The StyledDocument interface also defines methods for managing styles. A Style object is a named set of attributes, with an optional parent attribute set that is used to look up attributes that are not specified directly in the Style object. addStyle() creates a new Style object and registers it by name with the StyledDocument. getStyle() looks up a Style object by name. The intent of Style objects is to represent named paragraph types such as "heading," "blockquote," and so forth. The setLogicalStyle() method applies one of these named paragraph styles to the paragraph at the specified position. This is the default style for that paragraph, unless it is overridden by attributes specified with setCharacterAttributes() or setParagraphAttributes().

See also DefaultStyledDocument, Element, Style, and AttributeSet.

```
public abstract interface StyledDocument extends Document {
// Public Instance Methods
    public abstract Style addStyle(String nm, Style parent);
    public abstract java.awt.Color getBackground(AttributeSet attr);
```

```
    public abstract javax.swing.text.Element getCharacterElement(int pos);
    public abstract java.awt.Font getFont(AttributeSet attr);
    public abstract java.awt.Color getForeground(AttributeSet attr);
    public abstract Style getLogicalStyle(int p);
    public abstract javax.swing.text.Element getParagraphElement(int pos);
    public abstract Style getStyle(String nm);
    public abstract void removeStyle(String nm);
    public abstract void setCharacterAttributes(int offset, int length, AttributeSet s, boolean replace);
    public abstract void setLogicalStyle(int pos, Style s);
    public abstract void setParagraphAttributes(int offset, int length, AttributeSet s, boolean replace);
}
```

Hierarchy: (StyledDocument(Document))

Implementations: DefaultStyledDocument

Passed To: JTextPane.{JTextPane(), setStyledDocument()},
javax.swing.text.html.MinimalHTMLWriter.MinimalHTMLWriter()

Returned By: JTextPane.getStyledDocument(), StyledEditorKit.StyledTextAction.getStyledDocument()

StyledEditorKit

Java 1.2

javax.swing.text

cloneable serializable

This class is an EditorKit for generic styled text. It is the default EditorKit used to configure the JTextPane component. In addition to the standard EditorKit methods, StyledEditorKit defines getInputAttributes() and getCharacterAttributeRun() as conveniences for the various Action implementations it defines.

```
public class StyledEditorKit extends DefaultEditorKit {
// Public Constructors
    public StyledEditorKit();
// Inner Classes
    public static class AlignmentAction extends StyledEditorKit.StyledTextAction;
    public static class BoldAction extends StyledEditorKit.StyledTextAction;
    public static class FontFamilyAction extends StyledEditorKit.StyledTextAction;
    public static class FontSizeAction extends StyledEditorKit.StyledTextAction;
    public static class ForegroundAction extends StyledEditorKit.StyledTextAction;
    public static class ItalicAction extends StyledEditorKit.StyledTextAction;
    public abstract static class StyledTextAction extends TextAction;
    public static class UnderlineAction extends StyledEditorKit.StyledTextAction;
// Property Accessor Methods (by property name)
    public Action[ ] getActions();                                          Overrides:DefaultEditorKit
    public javax.swing.text.Element getCharacterAttributeRun();                          default:null
    public MutableAttributeSet getInputAttributes();
    public ViewFactory getViewFactory();                                    Overrides:DefaultEditorKit
// Public Methods Overriding DefaultEditorKit
    public Object clone();
    public Document createDefaultDocument();
// Public Methods Overriding EditorKit
    public void deinstall(JEditorPane c);
    public void install(JEditorPane c);
// Protected Instance Methods
    protected void createInputAttributes(javax.swing.text.Element element, MutableAttributeSet set);
}
```

Hierarchy: Object→ EditorKit(Cloneable, Serializable)→ DefaultEditorKit→ StyledEditorKit

Subclasses: javax.swing.text.html.HTMLEditorKit, javax.swing.text.rtf.RTFEditorKit

Returned By: JTextPane.getStyledEditorKit(), StyledEditorKit.StyledTextAction.getStyledEditorKit()

StyledEditorKit.AlignmentAction

Java 1.2

javax.swing.text

cloneable serializable

This action class sets the alignment paragraph attribute for the currently selected text in a JEditorPane. StyledEditorKit creates three distinct instances of AlignmentAction to handle left, right, and center alignment. If the command string is set in the ActionEvent, it is interpreted as the integer value to use for the alignment attribute.

```
public static class StyledEditorKit.AlignmentAction extends StyledEditorKit.StyledTextAction {
// Public Constructors
    public AlignmentAction(String nm, int a);
// Public Methods Overriding AbstractAction
    public void actionPerformed(java.awt.event.ActionEvent e);
}
```

StyledEditorKit.BoldAction

Java 1.2

javax.swing.text

cloneable serializable

This action toggles the bold text character attribute, either on the selected text or, if there is no selection, on the current set of attributes used for inserted text.

```
public static class StyledEditorKit.BoldAction extends StyledEditorKit.StyledTextAction {
// Public Constructors
    public BoldAction();
// Public Methods Overriding AbstractAction
    public void actionPerformed(java.awt.event.ActionEvent e);
}
```

StyledEditorKit.FontFamilyAction

Java 1.2

javax.swing.text

cloneable serializable

This action sets the font family for the selected text or, if no text is selected, sets the font family that is used for newly inserted text. StyledEditorKit creates several instances of this class, each of which is configured to use a different font family.

```
public static class StyledEditorKit.FontFamilyAction extends StyledEditorKit.StyledTextAction {
// Public Constructors
    public FontFamilyAction(String nm, String family);
// Public Methods Overriding AbstractAction
    public void actionPerformed(java.awt.event.ActionEvent e);
}
```

StyledEditorKit.FontSizeAction

Java 1.2

javax.swing.text

cloneable serializable

This action sets the font size for the selected text or, if no text is selected, sets the font size that is used for newly inserted text. StyledEditorKit creates several instances of this class, each of which is configured to use a different font size.

```
public static class StyledEditorKit.FontSizeAction extends StyledEditorKit.StyledTextAction {
// Public Constructors
    public FontSizeAction(String nm, int size);
```

```
// Public Methods Overriding AbstractAction
    public void actionPerformed(java.awt.event.ActionEvent e);
}
```

StyledEditorKit.ForegroundAction

javax.swing.text   *cloneable serializable*

This action sets the color of the selected text or, if no text is selected, sets the color that is used for newly inserted text. The color to be used is specified when the ForegroundAction constructor is called. Or the color may be specified by the command string of the ActionEvent. In this case, the color string should be in a format that can be interpreted by the decode() method of java.awt.Color. StyledEditorKit does not include any objects of this type in the array of actions returned by its getAction() method.

```
public static class StyledEditorKit.ForegroundAction extends StyledEditorKit.StyledTextAction {
// Public Constructors
    public ForegroundAction(String nm, java.awt.Color fg);
// Public Methods Overriding AbstractAction
    public void actionPerformed(java.awt.event.ActionEvent e);
}
```

StyledEditorKit.ItalicAction

javax.swing.text   *cloneable serializable*

This action toggles the italic text character attribute, either on the selected text or, if there is no selection, on the current set of attributes used for inserted text.

```
public static class StyledEditorKit.ItalicAction extends StyledEditorKit.StyledTextAction {
// Public Constructors
    public ItalicAction();
// Public Methods Overriding AbstractAction
    public void actionPerformed(java.awt.event.ActionEvent e);
}
```

StyledEditorKit.StyledTextAction

javax.swing.text   *cloneable serializable*

This class is the abstract superclass for Action objects that operate on a JEditorPane configured with a StyledEditorKit. This class defines convenience methods that are used by the other inner Action classes defined by StyledEditorKit.

```
public abstract static class StyledEditorKit.StyledTextAction extends TextAction {
// Public Constructors
    public StyledTextAction(String nm);
// Protected Instance Methods
    protected final JEditorPane getEditor(java.awt.event.ActionEvent e);
    protected final StyledDocument getStyledDocument(JEditorPane e);
    protected final StyledEditorKit getStyledEditorKit(JEditorPane e);
    protected final void setCharacterAttributes(JEditorPane editor, AttributeSet attr, boolean replace);
    protected final void setParagraphAttributes(JEditorPane editor, AttributeSet attr, boolean replace);
}
```

Subclasses: StyledEditorKit.AlignmentAction, StyledEditorKit.BoldAction, StyledEditorKit.FontFamilyAction, StyledEditorKit.FontSizeAction, StyledEditorKit.ForegroundAction, StyledEditorKit.ItalicAction, StyledEditorKit.UnderlineAction, javax.swing.text.html.HTMLEditorKit.HTMLTextAction

StyledEditorKit.UnderlineAction

Java 1.2

javax.swing.text

cloneable serializable

This action toggles the underline character attribute, either on the selected text or, if there is no selection, on the set of attributes used for newly inserted text.

```
public static class StyledEditorKit.UnderlineAction extends StyledEditorKit.StyledTextAction {
// Public Constructors
    public UnderlineAction();
// Public Methods Overriding AbstractAction
    public void actionPerformed(java.awt.event.ActionEvent e);
}
```

TabableView

Java 1.2

javax.swing.text

This interface is implemented by View objects whose width may be dependent on the expansion of Tab characters. getTabbedSpan() is passed a horizontal position and a TabExpander object and should return the appropriate width for the View. The getPreferredSpan() method of the View object should return the same width. Applications do not need to use or implement this interface.

```
public abstract interface TabableView {
// Public Instance Methods
    public abstract float getPartialSpan(int p0, int p1);
    public abstract float getTabbedSpan(float x, TabExpander e);
}
```

TabExpander

Java 1.2

javax.swing.text

This interface specifies how horizontal Tab characters in a Document are expanded. Given the position in the document and on the screen of the Tab character, it returns the horizontal position that the Tab character should tab to. Applications do not typically need to use or implement this interface themselves.

```
public abstract interface TabExpander {
// Public Instance Methods
    public abstract float nextTabStop(float x, int tabOffset);
}
```

Implementations: javax.swing.text.ParagraphView, PlainView, WrappedPlainView

Passed To: TabableView.getTabbedSpan(), Utilities.{drawTabbedText(), getBreakLocation(), getTabbedTextOffset(), getTabbedTextWidth()}

TableView

Java 1.2

javax.swing.text

This BoxView class displays a table composed of TableView.TableRow and TableView.TableCell subviews.

```
public abstract class TableView extends BoxView {
// Public Constructors
    public TableView(javax.swing.text.Element elem);
// Inner Classes
    public class TableCell extends BoxView;
    public class TableRow extends BoxView;
```

```
// Public Methods Overriding BoxView
    public void replace(int offset, int length, View[ ] views);
// Protected Methods Overriding BoxView
    protected SizeRequirements calculateMinorAxisRequirements(int axis, SizeRequirements r);
    protected void layoutMinorAxis(int targetSpan, int axis, int[ ] offsets, int[ ] spans);
// Protected Methods Overriding CompositeView
    protected View getViewAtPosition(int pos, java.awt.Rectangle a);
// Protected Instance Methods
    protected TableView.TableCell createTableCell(javax.swing.text.Element elem);
    protected TableView.TableRow createTableRow(javax.swing.text.Element elem);
    protected void layoutColumns(int targetSpan, int[ ] offsets, int[ ] spans, SizeRequirements[ ] reqs);
}
```

Hierarchy: Object→ View(SwingConstants)→ CompositeView→ BoxView→ TableView

TableView.TableCell   Java 1.2

javax.swing.text

This BoxView class displays the contents of a table cell. It may contain any type of child views.

```
public class TableView.TableCell extends BoxView {
// Public Constructors
    public TableCell(javax.swing.text.Element elem);
// Property Accessor Methods (by property name)
    public int getColumnCount();                                            constant
    public int getGridColumn();
    public int getGridRow();
    public int getRowCount();                                               constant
// Public Instance Methods
    public void setGridLocation(int row, int col);
}
```

Returned By: TableView.createTableCell()

TableView.TableRow   Java 1.2

javax.swing.text

This BoxView displays one row in a table. It should contain TableView.TableCell children.

```
public class TableView.TableRow extends BoxView {
// Public Constructors
    public TableRow(javax.swing.text.Element elem);
// Public Methods Overriding BoxView
    public int getResizeWeight(int axis);                                   constant
    public void replace(int offset, int length, View[ ] views);
// Protected Methods Overriding BoxView
    protected void layoutMajorAxis(int targetSpan, int axis, int[ ] offsets, int[ ] spans);
    protected void layoutMinorAxis(int targetSpan, int axis, int[ ] offsets, int[ ] spans);
// Protected Methods Overriding CompositeView
    protected View getViewAtPosition(int pos, java.awt.Rectangle a);
}
```

Returned By: TableView.createTableRow()

TabSet

javax.swing.text

serializable

This class represents a set of TabStop objects and provides several methods for querying that set of tab stops.

```
public class TabSet implements Serializable {
// Public Constructors
    public TabSet(TabStop[ ] tabs);
// Public Instance Methods
    public TabStop getTab(int index);
    public TabStop getTabAfter(float location);
    public int getTabCount();
    public int getTabIndex(TabStop tab);
    public int getTabIndexAfter(float location);
// Public Methods Overriding Object
    public String toString();
}
```

Hierarchy: Object→ TabSet(Serializable)

Passed To: StyleConstants.setTabSet()

Returned By: javax.swing.text.ParagraphView.getTabSet(), StyleConstants.getTabSet()

TabStop

Java 1.2

javax.swing.text

serializable

This class represents a tab stop in a document. Each tab stop has a horizontal position (measured in points), an alignment, and a leader character that is used to fill in the space between the previous character and the tab stop. The various constants defined by this class represent the legal alignment and leader values. See also TabSet.

```
public class TabStop implements Serializable {
// Public Constructors
    public TabStop(float pos);
    public TabStop(float pos, int align, int leader);
// Public Constants
    public static final int ALIGN_BAR;                 =5
    public static final int ALIGN_CENTER;              =2
    public static final int ALIGN_DECIMAL;             =4
    public static final int ALIGN_LEFT;                =0
    public static final int ALIGN_RIGHT;               =1
    public static final int LEAD_DOTS;                 =1
    public static final int LEAD_EQUALS;               =5
    public static final int LEAD_HYPHENS;              =2
    public static final int LEAD_NONE;                 =0
    public static final int LEAD_THICKLINE;            =4
    public static final int LEAD_UNDERLINE;            =3
// Public Instance Methods
    public int getAlignment();
    public int getLeader();
    public float getPosition();
// Public Methods Overriding Object
    public boolean equals(Object other);
    public int hashCode();
    public String toString();
}
```

Hierarchy: Object→ TabStop(Serializable)

Passed To: TabSet.{getTabIndex(), TabSet()}

Returned By: TabSet.{getTab(), getTabAfter()}

TextAction

javax.swing.text

This abstract class is an Action that extends AbstractAction. It does not implement any of the abstract methods of AbstractAction but merely adds new protected methods that subclasses can use to figure out on what JTextComponent they are supposed to operate. These methods allow subclasses to define generic actions that are not specific to a particular JTextComponent but that can be used on any text component. Applications may subclass this interface to define custom actions, but they do not often need to do so. DefaultEditorKit and StyledEditorKit define a number of inner classes that subclass TextAction.

```
public abstract class TextAction extends AbstractAction {
// Public Constructors
    public TextAction(String name);
// Public Class Methods
    public static final Action[ ] augmentList(Action[ ] list1, Action[ ] list2);
// Protected Instance Methods
    protected final JTextComponent getFocusedComponent();
    protected final JTextComponent getTextComponent(java.awt.event.ActionEvent e);
}
```

Hierarchy: Object→ AbstractAction(Action(java.awt.event.ActionListener(java.util.EventListener)), Cloneable, Serializable)→ TextAction

Subclasses: DefaultEditorKit.BeepAction, DefaultEditorKit.CopyAction, DefaultEditorKit.CutAction, DefaultEditorKit.DefaultKeyTypedAction, DefaultEditorKit.InsertBreakAction, DefaultEditorKit.InsertContentAction, DefaultEditorKit.InsertTabAction, DefaultEditorKit.PasteAction, StyledEditorKit.StyledTextAction

Utilities

javax.swing.text

This class defines various static utility methods that are used internally by the javax.swing.text package. Although applications may occasionally find some of these methods useful, they are intended primarily for internal use and for use by programmers who are subclassing or heavily customizing javax.swing.text classes.

```
public class Utilities {
// Public Constructors
    public Utilities();
// Public Class Methods
    public static final int drawTabbedText(Segment s, int x, int y, java.awt.Graphics g, TabExpander e, int startOffset);
    public static final int getBreakLocation(Segment s, java.awt.FontMetrics metrics, int x0, int x, TabExpander e,
                            int startOffset);
    public static final int getNextWord(JTextComponent c, int offs) throws BadLocationException;
    public static final javax.swing.text.Element getParagraphElement(JTextComponent c, int offs);
    public static final int getPositionAbove(JTextComponent c, int offs, int x) throws BadLocationException;
    public static final int getPositionBelow(JTextComponent c, int offs, int x) throws BadLocationException;
    public static final int getPreviousWord(JTextComponent c, int offs) throws BadLocationException;
    public static final int getRowEnd(JTextComponent c, int offs) throws BadLocationException;
    public static final int getRowStart(JTextComponent c, int offs) throws BadLocationException;
    public static final int getTabbedTextOffset(Segment s, java.awt.FontMetrics metrics, int x0, int x, TabExpander e,
                            int startOffset);
    public static final int getTabbedTextOffset(Segment s, java.awt.FontMetrics metrics, int x0, int x, TabExpander e,
                            int startOffset, boolean round);
```

```
    public static final int getTabbedTextWidth(Segment s, java.awt.FontMetrics metrics, int x, TabExpander e,
                                               int startOffset);
    public static final int getWordEnd(JTextComponent c, int offs) throws BadLocationException;
    public static final int getWordStart(JTextComponent c, int offs) throws BadLocationException;
}
```

View   Java 1.2

javax.swing.text

This class is the abstract superclass of a hierarchy of classes used to display various parts of a text document. Just as java.awt.Component is the root of the component hierarchy and has many subclasses in java.awt and javax.swing, View is the root of the view hierarchy and has many subclasses in javax.swing.text and javax.swing.text.html. Just as the various Component classes are used to display different GUI elements, the various View classes are used to display different types of document elements.

Each type of Document has a ViewFactory object that is used to create an appropriate View object for a given Element of a document. Because a Document consists of a tree of Element objects, the document is displayed using a tree of View objects. Just like GUI components, View objects are nested into a containment hierarchy. Thus, a BoxView might contain a TableView and several ParagraphView objects, each of which contains a number of PlainView objects interspersed with IconView objects.

Like a component, a View implementation must be able to paint itself, return its children, report its preferred size, and so on. In fact, you can think of a View as a kind of extremely lightweight component, with a number of methods analogous to Component methods. These include paint(), getView(), getViewCount(), getParent(), getPreferredSpan(), getMinimumSpan(), getMaximumSpan(), and isVisible().

A View implementation must also be able to convert between the document coordinate system—an integer position within the document—and the on-screen coordinate system in which things like mouse clicks and drags are measured. The viewToModel() and modelToView() methods are called to perform these conversions.

View objects are unlike components in one important aspect, however. They may be subject to word-wrapping and line breaking. The getBreakWeight() method returns an integer that specifies whether a given position is a reasonable place at which to insert a line break. If a View supports line breaking, its breakView() method should break the view into two and return the newly created View.

Programmers defining custom document types or custom document content types may need to create custom View implementations. Applications typically do not need to use or subclass this class directly.

```
public abstract class View implements SwingConstants {
// Public Constructors
    public View(javax.swing.text.Element elem);
// Public Constants
    public static final int BadBreakWeight;                                    =0
    public static final int ExcellentBreakWeight;                           =2000
    public static final int ForcedBreakWeight;                              =3000
    public static final int GoodBreakWeight;                                =1000
    public static final int X_AXIS;                                            =0
    public static final int Y_AXIS;                                            =1
// Property Accessor Methods (by property name)
    public AttributeSet getAttributes();
    public Container getContainer();
    public Document getDocument();
```

```
      public javax.swing.text.Element getElement();
      public int getEndOffset();
      public View getParent();
      public void setParent(View parent);
      public int getStartOffset();
      public int getViewCount();
      public ViewFactory getViewFactory();                                                          constant
      public boolean isVisible();                                                                    constant
// Public Instance Methods
      public View breakView(int axis, int offset, float pos, float len);
      public void changedUpdate(javax.swing.event.DocumentEvent e, java.awt.Shape a, ViewFactory f);    empty
      public View createFragment(int p0, int p1);
      public float getAlignment(int axis);
      public int getBreakWeight(int axis, float pos, float len);
      public java.awt.Shape getChildAllocation(int index, java.awt.Shape a);                          constant
      public float getMaximumSpan(int axis);
      public float getMinimumSpan(int axis);
      public int getNextVisualPositionFrom(int pos, Position.Bias b, java.awt.Shape a, int direction,
                                 Position.Bias[ ] biasRet) throws BadLocationException;
      public abstract float getPreferredSpan(int axis);
      public int getResizeWeight(int axis);                                                           constant
      public View getView(int n);                                                                     constant
      public void insertUpdate(javax.swing.event.DocumentEvent e, java.awt.Shape a, ViewFactory f);     empty
      public abstract java.awt.Shape modelToView(int pos, java.awt.Shape a, Position.Bias b)
          throws BadLocationException;
      public java.awt.Shape modelToView(int p0, Position.Bias b0, int p1, Position.Bias b1, java.awt.Shape a)
          throws BadLocationException;
      public abstract void paint(java.awt.Graphics g, java.awt.Shape allocation);
      public void preferenceChanged(View child, boolean width, boolean height);
      public void removeUpdate(javax.swing.event.DocumentEvent e, java.awt.Shape a, ViewFactory f);     empty
      public void setSize(float width, float height);                                                  empty
      public abstract int viewToModel(float x, float y, java.awt.Shape a, Position.Bias[ ] biasReturn);
// Deprecated Public Methods
#    public java.awt.Shape modelToView(int pos, java.awt.Shape a) throws BadLocationException;
#    public int viewToModel(float x, float y, java.awt.Shape a);
}
```

Hierarchy: Object→ View(SwingConstants)

Subclasses: ComponentView, CompositeView, IconView, LabelView, PlainView

Passed To: Too many methods to list.

Returned By: Too many methods to list.

ViewFactory

Java 1.2

javax.swing.text

The ViewFactory interface defines a basic create() method that creates View objects from the individual Element nodes of a Document. Different types of documents use different ViewFactory implementations to implement a custom Element to View mapping. The get-ViewFactory() method of EditorKit returns a ViewFactory for a particular document type.

```
public abstract interface ViewFactory {
// Public Instance Methods
      public abstract View create(javax.swing.text.Element elem);
}
```

Implementations: javax.swing.text.html.HTMLEditorKit.HTMLFactory

Passed To: Too many methods to list.

Returned By: DefaultEditorKit.getViewFactory(), EditorKit.getViewFactory(), StyledEditorKit.getViewFactory(), View.getViewFactory(). javax.swing.text.html.HTMLEditorKit.getViewFactory()

WrappedPlainView   Java 1.2

javax.swing.text

This class displays multiple lines of plain text. It can perform tab expansion and line wrapping. See also PlainView.

```
public class WrappedPlainView extends BoxView implements TabExpander {
// Public Constructors
    public WrappedPlainView(javax.swing.text.Element elem);
    public WrappedPlainView(javax.swing.text.Element elem, boolean wordWrap);
// Methods Implementing TabExpander
    public float nextTabStop(float x, int tabOffset);
// Public Methods Overriding BoxView
    public float getMaximumSpan(int axis);
    public float getMinimumSpan(int axis);
    public float getPreferredSpan(int axis);
    public void paint(java.awt.Graphics g, java.awt.Shape a);
    public void setSize(float width, float height);
// Public Methods Overriding CompositeView
    public void changedUpdate(javax.swing.event.DocumentEvent e, java.awt.Shape a, ViewFactory f);
    public void insertUpdate(javax.swing.event.DocumentEvent e, java.awt.Shape a, ViewFactory f);
    public void removeUpdate(javax.swing.event.DocumentEvent e, java.awt.Shape a, ViewFactory f);
// Protected Methods Overriding CompositeView
    protected void loadChildren(ViewFactory f);
// Protected Instance Methods
    protected int calculateBreakPosition(int p0, int p1);
    protected void drawLine(int p0, int p1, java.awt.Graphics g, int x, int y);
    protected int drawSelectedText(java.awt.Graphics g, int x, int y, int p0, int p1) throws BadLocationException;
    protected int drawUnselectedText(java.awt.Graphics g, int x, int y, int p0, int p1) throws BadLocationException;
    protected final Segment getLineBuffer();
    protected int getTabSize();
}
```

Hierarchy: Object→ View(SwingConstants)→ CompositeView→ BoxView→ WrappedPlainView(TabExpander)

CHAPTER 31

The javax.swing.text.html Package

The javax.swing.text.html package defines classes to support the display and editing of HTML documents. The key class is **HTMLEditorKit**, which is used to customize a javax.swing.JEditorPane component to work with HTML. Figure 31-1 shows the class hierarchy of this package. See Chapter 3, *Swing Programming Topics*, for a discussion and example of using the **HTMLEditorKit**.

BlockView   Java 1.2

javax.swing.text.html

This View implementation displays HTML block elements and can handle CSS attributes for those elements.

```
public class BlockView extends BoxView {
// Public Constructors
    public BlockView(javax.swing.text.Element elem, int axis);
// Public Methods Overriding BoxView
    public float getAlignment(int axis);
    public int getResizeWeight(int axis);
    public void paint(java.awt.Graphics g, java.awt.Shape allocation);
// Protected Methods Overriding BoxView
    protected SizeRequirements calculateMajorAxisRequirements(int axis, SizeRequirements r);
    protected SizeRequirements calculateMinorAxisRequirements(int axis, SizeRequirements r);
// Public Methods Overriding CompositeView
    public void changedUpdate(javax.swing.event.DocumentEvent changes, java.awt.Shape a, ViewFactory f);
// Public Methods Overriding View
    public AttributeSet getAttributes();
// Protected Instance Methods
    protected StyleSheet getStyleSheet();
    protected void setPropertiesFromAttributes();
}
```

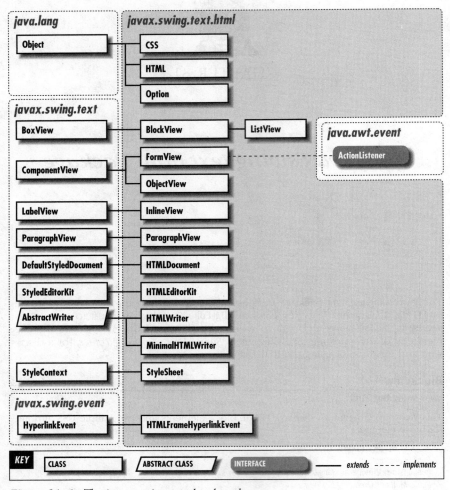

Figure 31–1: *The javax.swing.text.html package*

Hierarchy: Object→ View(SwingConstants)→ CompositeView→ BoxView→ BlockView

Subclasses: ListView

CSS

javax.swing.text.html

This class defines an inner class that is used to represent Cascading Style Sheet (CSS) attributes in an AttributeSet. It also defines static methods that return all defined CSS attribute objects and allow you to look up a CSS attribute object by name.

```
public class CSS {
// Public Constructors
   public CSS();
```

```
// Inner Classes
     public static final class Attribute;
// Public Class Methods
     public static CSS.Attribute[ ] getAllAttributeKeys( );
     public static final CSS.Attribute getAttribute(String name);
}
```

CSS.Attribute   Java 1.2

javax.swing.text.html

Instances of this class are used as key values in an AttributeSet to represent CSS
attributes. Each CSS.Attribute object supports getDefaultValue() and isInherited() methods that
return more information about the attribute. In addition, the toString() method returns
the name of the attribute. The CSS.Attribute class is final and does not have a public constructor, so it cannot be instantiated or subclassed. However, it defines constant object
values for each of the CSS attributes specified by the CSS specification.

```
public static final class CSS.Attribute {
// No Constructor
// Public Constants
     public static final CSS.Attribute BACKGROUND;
     public static final CSS.Attribute BACKGROUND_ATTACHMENT;
     public static final CSS.Attribute BACKGROUND_COLOR;
     public static final CSS.Attribute BACKGROUND_IMAGE;
     public static final CSS.Attribute BACKGROUND_POSITION;
     public static final CSS.Attribute BACKGROUND_REPEAT;
     public static final CSS.Attribute BORDER;
     public static final CSS.Attribute BORDER_BOTTOM;
     public static final CSS.Attribute BORDER_BOTTOM_WIDTH;
     public static final CSS.Attribute BORDER_COLOR;
     public static final CSS.Attribute BORDER_LEFT;
     public static final CSS.Attribute BORDER_LEFT_WIDTH;
     public static final CSS.Attribute BORDER_RIGHT;
     public static final CSS.Attribute BORDER_RIGHT_WIDTH;
     public static final CSS.Attribute BORDER_STYLE;
     public static final CSS.Attribute BORDER_TOP;
     public static final CSS.Attribute BORDER_TOP_WIDTH;
     public static final CSS.Attribute BORDER_WIDTH;
     public static final CSS.Attribute CLEAR;
     public static final CSS.Attribute COLOR;
     public static final CSS.Attribute DISPLAY;
     public static final CSS.Attribute FLOAT;
     public static final CSS.Attribute FONT;
     public static final CSS.Attribute FONT_FAMILY;
     public static final CSS.Attribute FONT_SIZE;
     public static final CSS.Attribute FONT_STYLE;
     public static final CSS.Attribute FONT_VARIANT;
     public static final CSS.Attribute FONT_WEIGHT;
     public static final CSS.Attribute HEIGHT;
     public static final CSS.Attribute LETTER_SPACING;
     public static final CSS.Attribute LINE_HEIGHT;
     public static final CSS.Attribute LIST_STYLE;
     public static final CSS.Attribute LIST_STYLE_IMAGE;
     public static final CSS.Attribute LIST_STYLE_POSITION;
     public static final CSS.Attribute LIST_STYLE_TYPE;
     public static final CSS.Attribute MARGIN;
     public static final CSS.Attribute MARGIN_BOTTOM;
```

```
    public static final CSS.Attribute MARGIN_LEFT;
    public static final CSS.Attribute MARGIN_RIGHT;
    public static final CSS.Attribute MARGIN_TOP;
    public static final CSS.Attribute PADDING;
    public static final CSS.Attribute PADDING_BOTTOM;
    public static final CSS.Attribute PADDING_LEFT;
    public static final CSS.Attribute PADDING_RIGHT;
    public static final CSS.Attribute PADDING_TOP;
    public static final CSS.Attribute TEXT_ALIGN;
    public static final CSS.Attribute TEXT_DECORATION;
    public static final CSS.Attribute TEXT_INDENT;
    public static final CSS.Attribute TEXT_TRANSFORM;
    public static final CSS.Attribute VERTICAL_ALIGN;
    public static final CSS.Attribute WHITE_SPACE;
    public static final CSS.Attribute WIDTH;
    public static final CSS.Attribute WORD_SPACING;
// Public Instance Methods
    public String getDefaultValue();
    public boolean isInherited();
// Public Methods Overriding Object
    public String toString();
}
```

Returned By: CSS.{getAllAttributeKeys(), getAttribute()}

Type Of: Too many fields to list.

FormView   Java 1.2

javax.swing.text.html

This View displays <INPUT>, <SELECT>, and <TEXTAREA> elements within an HTML <FORM>.

```
public class FormView extends ComponentView implements java.awt.event.ActionListener {
// Public Constructors
    public FormView(javax.swing.text.Element elem);
// Public Constants
    public static final String RESET;
    public static final String SUBMIT;
// Inner Classes
    protected class MouseEventListener extends java.awt.event.MouseAdapter;
// Methods Implementing ActionListener
    public void actionPerformed(java.awt.event.ActionEvent evt);
// Protected Methods Overriding ComponentView
    protected Component createComponent();
// Protected Instance Methods
    protected void imageSubmit(String imageData);
    protected void submitData(String data);
}
```

Hierarchy: Object→ View(SwingConstants) → ComponentView→
FormView(java.awt.event.ActionListener(java.util.EventListener))

FormView.MouseEventListener   Java 1.2

javax.swing.text.html

This class is used internally by FormView to handle clicks on HTML <INPUT> tags that have the TYPE=image attribute specified.

```
protected class FormView.MouseEventListener extends java.awt.event.MouseAdapter {
// Protected Constructors
    protected MouseEventListener();
// Public Methods Overriding MouseAdapter
    public void mouseReleased(java.awt.event.MouseEvent evt);
}
```

HTML   Java 1.2

javax.swing.text.html

This class defines inner classes that are used to represent HTML tags and attributes. It
also defines several static convenience methods that are used with the inner classes. In
particular, getAttributeKey() and getTag() look up HTML.Attribute and HTML.Tag values by name.

```
public class HTML {
// Public Constructors
    public HTML();
// Public Constants
    public static final String NULL_ATTRIBUTE_VALUE;                       ="#DEFAULT"
// Inner Classes
    public static final class Attribute;
    public static class Tag;
    public static class UnknownTag extends HTML.Tag implements Serializable;
// Public Class Methods
    public static HTML.Attribute[ ] getAllAttributeKeys();
    public static HTML.Tag[ ] getAllTags();
    public static HTML.Attribute getAttributeKey(String attName);
    public static int getIntegerAttributeValue(AttributeSet attr, HTML.Attribute key, int def);
    public static HTML.Tag getTag(String tagName);
}
```

HTML.Attribute   Java 1.2

javax.swing.text.html

This class defines a number of constant instances of itself to represent HTML attributes.
The class has no public constructor and is final, so new attribute objects cannot be created by instantiation or subclassing.

```
public static final class HTML.Attribute {
// No Constructor
// Public Constants
    public static final HTML.Attribute ACTION;
    public static final HTML.Attribute ALIGN;
    public static final HTML.Attribute ALINK;
    public static final HTML.Attribute ALT;
    public static final HTML.Attribute ARCHIVE;
    public static final HTML.Attribute BACKGROUND;
    public static final HTML.Attribute BGCOLOR;
    public static final HTML.Attribute BORDER;
    public static final HTML.Attribute CELLPADDING;
    public static final HTML.Attribute CELLSPACING;
    public static final HTML.Attribute CHECKED;
    public static final HTML.Attribute CLASS;
    public static final HTML.Attribute CLASSID;
    public static final HTML.Attribute CLEAR;
    public static final HTML.Attribute CODE;
    public static final HTML.Attribute CODEBASE;
```

```
public static final HTML.Attribute CODETYPE;
public static final HTML.Attribute COLOR;
public static final HTML.Attribute COLS;
public static final HTML.Attribute COLSPAN;
public static final HTML.Attribute COMMENT;
public static final HTML.Attribute COMPACT;
public static final HTML.Attribute CONTENT;
public static final HTML.Attribute COORDS;
public static final HTML.Attribute DATA;
public static final HTML.Attribute DECLARE;
public static final HTML.Attribute DIR;
public static final HTML.Attribute DUMMY;
public static final HTML.Attribute ENCTYPE;
public static final HTML.Attribute ENDTAG;
public static final HTML.Attribute FACE;
public static final HTML.Attribute FRAMEBORDER;
public static final HTML.Attribute HALIGN;
public static final HTML.Attribute HEIGHT;
public static final HTML.Attribute HREF;
public static final HTML.Attribute HSPACE;
public static final HTML.Attribute HTTPEQUIV;
public static final HTML.Attribute ID;
public static final HTML.Attribute ISMAP;
public static final HTML.Attribute LANG;
public static final HTML.Attribute LANGUAGE;
public static final HTML.Attribute LINK;
public static final HTML.Attribute LOWSRC;
public static final HTML.Attribute MARGINHEIGHT;
public static final HTML.Attribute MARGINWIDTH;
public static final HTML.Attribute MAXLENGTH;
public static final HTML.Attribute METHOD;
public static final HTML.Attribute MULTIPLE;
public static final HTML.Attribute N;
public static final HTML.Attribute NAME;
public static final HTML.Attribute NOHREF;
public static final HTML.Attribute NORESIZE;
public static final HTML.Attribute NOSHADE;
public static final HTML.Attribute NOWRAP;
public static final HTML.Attribute PROMPT;
public static final HTML.Attribute REL;
public static final HTML.Attribute REV;
public static final HTML.Attribute ROWS;
public static final HTML.Attribute ROWSPAN;
public static final HTML.Attribute SCROLLING;
public static final HTML.Attribute SELECTED;
public static final HTML.Attribute SHAPE;
public static final HTML.Attribute SHAPES;
public static final HTML.Attribute SIZE;
public static final HTML.Attribute SRC;
public static final HTML.Attribute STANDBY;
public static final HTML.Attribute START;
public static final HTML.Attribute STYLE;
public static final HTML.Attribute TARGET;
public static final HTML.Attribute TEXT;
public static final HTML.Attribute TITLE;
public static final HTML.Attribute TYPE;
public static final HTML.Attribute USEMAP;
public static final HTML.Attribute VALIGN;
```

```
     public static final HTML.Attribute VALUE;
     public static final HTML.Attribute VALUETYPE;
     public static final HTML.Attribute VERSION;
     public static final HTML.Attribute VLINK;
     public static final HTML.Attribute VSPACE;
     public static final HTML.Attribute WIDTH;
// Public Methods Overriding Object
     public String toString();
}
```

Passed To: HTML.getIntegerAttributeValue()

Returned By: HTML.{getAllAttributeKeys(), getAttributeKey()}

Type Of: Too many fields to list.

HTML.Tag

javax.swing.text.html

This class defines constant instances of itself that represent HTML tags. The breaksFlow(), isBlock(), and isPreformatted() methods return additional information about the basic behav-iorbehavior of each tag. HTML.Tag defines constants for all of the standard HTML tags. It can be subclassed to add support for custom tags used with a customized HTML parser.

```
public static class HTML.Tag {
// Protected Constructors
     protected Tag(String id);
     protected Tag(String id, boolean causesBreak, boolean isBlock);
// Public Constants
     public static final HTML.Tag A;
     public static final HTML.Tag ADDRESS;
     public static final HTML.Tag APPLET;
     public static final HTML.Tag AREA;
     public static final HTML.Tag B;
     public static final HTML.Tag BASE;
     public static final HTML.Tag BASEFONT;
     public static final HTML.Tag BIG;
     public static final HTML.Tag BLOCKQUOTE;
     public static final HTML.Tag BODY;
     public static final HTML.Tag BR;
     public static final HTML.Tag CAPTION;
     public static final HTML.Tag CENTER;
     public static final HTML.Tag CITE;
     public static final HTML.Tag CODE;
     public static final HTML.Tag COMMENT;
     public static final HTML.Tag CONTENT;
     public static final HTML.Tag DD;
     public static final HTML.Tag DFN;
     public static final HTML.Tag DIR;
     public static final HTML.Tag DIV;
     public static final HTML.Tag DL;
     public static final HTML.Tag DT;
     public static final HTML.Tag EM;
     public static final HTML.Tag FONT;
     public static final HTML.Tag FORM;
     public static final HTML.Tag FRAME;
     public static final HTML.Tag FRAMESET;
     public static final HTML.Tag H1;
```

```
    public static final HTML.Tag H2;
    public static final HTML.Tag H3;
    public static final HTML.Tag H4;
    public static final HTML.Tag H5;
    public static final HTML.Tag H6;
    public static final HTML.Tag HEAD;
    public static final HTML.Tag HR;
    public static final HTML.Tag HTML;
    public static final HTML.Tag I;
    public static final HTML.Tag IMG;
    public static final HTML.Tag IMPLIED;
    public static final HTML.Tag INPUT;
    public static final HTML.Tag ISINDEX;
    public static final HTML.Tag KBD;
    public static final HTML.Tag LI;
    public static final HTML.Tag LINK;
    public static final HTML.Tag MAP;
    public static final HTML.Tag MENU;
    public static final HTML.Tag META;
    public static final HTML.Tag NOFRAMES;
    public static final HTML.Tag OBJECT;
    public static final HTML.Tag OL;
    public static final HTML.Tag OPTION;
    public static final HTML.Tag P;
    public static final HTML.Tag PARAM;
    public static final HTML.Tag PRE;
    public static final HTML.Tag S;
    public static final HTML.Tag SAMP;
    public static final HTML.Tag SCRIPT;
    public static final HTML.Tag SELECT;
    public static final HTML.Tag SMALL;
    public static final HTML.Tag STRIKE;
    public static final HTML.Tag STRONG;
    public static final HTML.Tag STYLE;
    public static final HTML.Tag SUB;
    public static final HTML.Tag SUP;
    public static final HTML.Tag TABLE;
    public static final HTML.Tag TD;
    public static final HTML.Tag TEXTAREA;
    public static final HTML.Tag TH;
    public static final HTML.Tag TITLE;
    public static final HTML.Tag TR;
    public static final HTML.Tag TT;
    public static final HTML.Tag U;
    public static final HTML.Tag UL;
    public static final HTML.Tag VAR;
// Public Instance Methods
    public boolean breaksFlow();
    public boolean isBlock();
    public boolean isPreformatted();
// Public Methods Overriding Object
    public String toString();
}
```

Subclasses: HTML.UnknownTag

Passed To: Too many methods to list.

Returned By: HTML.{getAllTags(), getTag()}, HTMLDocument.Iterator.getTag(), javax.swing.text.html.parser.TagElement.getHTMLTag()

Type Of: Too many fields to list.

HTML.UnknownTag   Java 1.2

javax.swing.text.html   *serializable*

This HTML.Tag subclass is used to represent nonstandard tags that the HTML parser does not recognize.

```
public static class HTML.UnknownTag extends HTML.Tag implements Serializable {
// Public Constructors
    public UnknownTag(String id);
// Public Methods Overriding Object
    public boolean equals(Object obj);
    public int hashCode();
}
```

HTMLDocument   Java 1.2

javax.swing.text.html   *serializable*

This class represents an HTML document, optionally augmented with CSS style sheets. The document is composed of a tree of BlockElement and RunElement objects, each of which has an HTML.Tag object specified as the value of its StyleContext.NameAttribute attribute. setBase() specifies a base URL relative to which hyperlinks in the document are interpreted. setTokenThreshold() specifies how many parsed tokens should be parsed before they are inserted into the document. setPreservesUnknownTags() specifies whether unknown tags in a document should be saved in the document structure or discarded. If you are not writing the document back out, they usually can be discarded. getStyle-Sheet() returns a StyleSheet object that represents any CSS style sheet that appeared in the document itself. getIterator() returns an HTMLDocument.Iterator object that can be used to find all tags of a given type in the document. The getReader() methods return an HTML-Document.HTMLReader object that converts method calls from the HTML parser into document elements. Subclasses that want to perform customized HTML parsing should override these methods to return an appropriately customized subclass of HTMLReader.

```
public class HTMLDocument extends DefaultStyledDocument {
// Public Constructors
    public HTMLDocument();
    public HTMLDocument(StyleSheet styles);
    public HTMLDocument(AbstractDocument.Content c, StyleSheet styles);
// Public Constants
    public static final String AdditionalComments;                  ="AdditionalComments"
// Inner Classes
    public class BlockElement extends AbstractDocument.BranchElement;
    public class HTMLReader extends HTMLEditorKit.ParserCallback;
    public abstract static class Iterator;
    public class RunElement extends AbstractDocument.LeafElement;
// Property Accessor Methods (by property name)
    public java.net.URL getBase();                                            default:null
    public void setBase(java.net.URL u);
    public boolean getPreservesUnknownTags();                                default:true
    public void setPreservesUnknownTags(boolean preservesTags);
    public StyleSheet getStyleSheet();
    public int getTokenThreshold();                                    default:2147483647
    public void setTokenThreshold(int n);
```

```
// Public Instance Methods
    public HTMLDocument.Iterator getIterator(HTML.Tag t);
    public HTMLEditorKit.ParserCallback getReader(int pos);
    public HTMLEditorKit.ParserCallback getReader(int pos, int popDepth, int pushDepth, HTML.Tag insertTag);
    public void processHTMLFrameHyperlinkEvent(HTMLFrameHyperlinkEvent e);
// Public Methods Overriding DefaultStyledDocument
    public void setParagraphAttributes(int offset, int length, AttributeSet s, boolean replace);
// Protected Methods Overriding DefaultStyledDocument
    protected void create(DefaultStyledDocument.ElementSpec[] data);
    protected AbstractDocument.AbstractElement createDefaultRoot();
    protected void insert(int offset, DefaultStyledDocument.ElementSpec[] data) throws BadLocationException;
    protected void insertUpdate(AbstractDocument.DefaultDocumentEvent chng, AttributeSet attr);
// Protected Methods Overriding AbstractDocument
    protected javax.swing.text.Element createBranchElement(javax.swing.text.Element parent, AttributeSet a);
    protected javax.swing.text.Element createLeafElement(javax.swing.text.Element parent, AttributeSet a, int p0,
                                                         int p1);
    protected void fireChangedUpdate(javax.swing.event.DocumentEvent e);
    protected void fireUndoableEditUpdate(javax.swing.event.UndoableEditEvent e);
}
```

Hierarchy: Object→ AbstractDocument(Document, Serializable) →
DefaultStyledDocument(StyledDocument(Document)) → HTMLDocument

Passed To: HTMLEditorKit.insertHTML(), HTMLEditorKit.HTMLTextAction.{elementCountToTag(),
findElementMatchingTag(), getElementsAt()}, HTMLEditorKit.InsertHTMLTextAction.{insertAtBoundry(),
insertHTML()}, HTMLWriter.HTMLWriter()

Returned By: HTMLEditorKit.HTMLTextAction.getHTMLDocument()

HTMLDocument.BlockElement   Java 1.2

javax.swing.text.html   *serializable*

This class is used to represent block elements (i.e., elements that contain other elements) of an HTML document.

```
public class HTMLDocument.BlockElement extends AbstractDocument.BranchElement {
// Public Constructors
    public BlockElement(javax.swing.text.Element parent, AttributeSet a);
// Public Methods Overriding AbstractDocument.BranchElement
    public String getName();
// Public Methods Overriding AbstractDocument.AbstractElement
    public AttributeSet getResolveParent();                                        constant
}
```

HTMLDocument.HTMLReader   Java 1.2

javax.swing.text.html

This class implements the HTMLEditorKit.ParserCallback interface and serves as an adapter between the HTML parser of the javax.swing.text.html.parser package and the HTMLDocument class. The parser invokes methods of the HTMLReader object, and the HTMLReader is responsible for converting those methods into content in the HTMLDocument. This class defines a number of inner classes of type HTMLDocument.HTMLReader.TagAction. These classes define special code to be executed when the parser encounters particular start and end tags. HTMLDocument.HTMLReader subclasses can perform customized HTML parsing by defining new TagAction subclasses and associating them with specific HTML tags by calling registerTag().

```
public class HTMLDocument.HTMLReader extends HTMLEditorKit.ParserCallback {
// Public Constructors
   public HTMLReader(int offset);
   public HTMLReader(int offset, int popDepth, int pushDepth, HTML.Tag insertTag);
// Inner Classes
   public class BlockAction extends HTMLDocument.HTMLReader.TagAction;
   public class CharacterAction extends HTMLDocument.HTMLReader.TagAction;
   public class FormAction extends HTMLDocument.HTMLReader.SpecialAction;
   public class HiddenAction extends HTMLDocument.HTMLReader.TagAction;
   public class IsindexAction extends HTMLDocument.HTMLReader.TagAction;
   public class ParagraphAction extends HTMLDocument.HTMLReader.BlockAction;
   public class PreAction extends HTMLDocument.HTMLReader.BlockAction;
   public class SpecialAction extends HTMLDocument.HTMLReader.TagAction;
   public class TagAction;
// Public Methods Overriding HTMLEditorKit.ParserCallback
   public void flush() throws BadLocationException;
   public void handleComment(char[ ] data, int pos);
   public void handleEndTag(HTML.Tag t, int pos);
   public void handleSimpleTag(HTML.Tag t, MutableAttributeSet a, int pos);
   public void handleStartTag(HTML.Tag t, MutableAttributeSet a, int pos);
   public void handleText(char[ ] data, int pos);
// Protected Instance Methods
   protected void addContent(char[ ] data, int offs, int length);
   protected void addContent(char[ ] data, int offs, int length, boolean generateImpliedPIfNecessary);
   protected void addSpecialElement(HTML.Tag t, MutableAttributeSet a);
   protected void blockClose(HTML.Tag t);
   protected void blockOpen(HTML.Tag t, MutableAttributeSet attr);
   protected void popCharacterStyle();
   protected void preContent(char[ ] data);
   protected void pushCharacterStyle();
   protected void registerTag(HTML.Tag t, HTMLDocument.HTMLReader.TagAction a);
   protected void textAreaContent(char[ ] data);
// Protected Instance Fields
   protected MutableAttributeSet charAttr;
   protected java.util.Vector parseBuffer;
}
```

HTMLDocument.HTMLReader.BlockAction   Java 1.2

javax.swing.text.html

This TagAction handles blocks, such as <TD> and <DIV> tags.

```
public class HTMLDocument.HTMLReader.BlockAction extends HTMLDocument.HTMLReader.TagAction {
// Public Constructors
   public BlockAction();
// Public Methods Overriding HTMLDocument.HTMLReader.TagAction
   public void end(HTML.Tag t);
   public void start(HTML.Tag t, MutableAttributeSet attr);
}
```

Subclasses: HTMLDocument.HTMLReader.ParagraphAction, HTMLDocument.HTMLReader.PreAction

HTMLDocument.HTMLReader.CharacterAction   Java 1.2

javax.swing.text.html

This TagAction handles character elements, such as <B> and <FONT> tags.

```
public class HTMLDocument.HTMLReader.CharacterAction extends HTMLDocument.HTMLReader.TagAction {
// Public Constructors
    public CharacterAction();
// Public Methods Overriding HTMLDocument.HTMLReader.TagAction
    public void end(HTML.Tag t);
    public void start(HTML.Tag t, MutableAttributeSet attr);
}
```

HTMLDocument.HTMLReader.FormAction

Java 1.2

javax.swing.text.html

This TagAction handles form elements, such as <INPUT> and <SELECT> tags.

```
public class HTMLDocument.HTMLReader.FormAction extends HTMLDocument.HTMLReader.SpecialAction {
// Public Constructors
    public FormAction();
// Public Methods Overriding HTMLDocument.HTMLReader.SpecialAction
    public void start(HTML.Tag t, MutableAttributeSet attr);
// Public Methods Overriding HTMLDocument.HTMLReader.TagAction
    public void end(HTML.Tag t);
}
```

HTMLDocument.HTMLReader.HiddenAction

Java 1.2

javax.swing.text.html

This TagAction handles elements that have no visual appearance, such as <LINK> and <MAP> tags.

```
public class HTMLDocument.HTMLReader.HiddenAction extends HTMLDocument.HTMLReader.TagAction {
// Public Constructors
    public HiddenAction();
// Public Methods Overriding HTMLDocument.HTMLReader.TagAction
    public void end(HTML.Tag t);
    public void start(HTML.Tag t, MutableAttributeSet a);
}
```

HTMLDocument.HTMLReader.IsindexAction

Java 1.2

javax.swing.text.html

This TagAction handles the <ISINDEX> tag.

```
public class HTMLDocument.HTMLReader.IsindexAction extends HTMLDocument.HTMLReader.TagAction {
// Public Constructors
    public IsindexAction();
// Public Methods Overriding HTMLDocument.HTMLReader.TagAction
    public void start(HTML.Tag t, MutableAttributeSet a);
}
```

HTMLDocument.HTMLReader.ParagraphAction

Java 1.2

javax.swing.text.html

This TagAction handles paragraph elements, such as <P> and <H1> tags.

```
public class HTMLDocument.HTMLReader.ParagraphAction extends HTMLDocument.HTMLReader.BlockAction {
// Public Constructors
    public ParagraphAction();
```

```
// Public Methods Overriding HTMLDocument.HTMLReader.BlockAction
    public void end(HTML.Tag t);
    public void start(HTML.Tag t, MutableAttributeSet a);
}
```

HTMLDocument.HTMLReader.PreAction   Java 1.2

javax.swing.text.html

This TagAction handles the <PRE> tag.

```
public class HTMLDocument.HTMLReader.PreAction extends HTMLDocument.HTMLReader.BlockAction {
// Public Constructors
    public PreAction();
// Public Methods Overriding HTMLDocument.HTMLReader.BlockAction
    public void end(HTML.Tag t);
    public void start(HTML.Tag t, MutableAttributeSet attr);
}
```

HTMLDocument.HTMLReader.SpecialAction   Java 1.2

javax.swing.text.html

This TagAction handles elements that require special handling, such as <OBJECT> and <FRAME> tags.

```
public class HTMLDocument.HTMLReader.SpecialAction extends HTMLDocument.HTMLReader.TagAction {
// Public Constructors
    public SpecialAction();
// Public Methods Overriding HTMLDocument.HTMLReader.TagAction
    public void start(HTML.Tag t, MutableAttributeSet a);
}
```

Subclasses: HTMLDocument.HTMLReader.FormAction

HTMLDocument.HTMLReader.TagAction   Java 1.2

javax.swing.text.html

This class defines methods that are called when the HTML parser encounters start and end tags of a particular type. To customize HTML parsing, implement a subclass of Tag-Action, create an instance, and register it with an HTMLReader subclass by calling registerTag().

```
public class HTMLDocument.HTMLReader.TagAction {
// Public Constructors
    public TagAction();
// Public Instance Methods
    public void end(HTML.Tag t);                                              empty
    public void start(HTML.Tag t, MutableAttributeSet a);                     empty
}
```

Subclasses: HTMLDocument.HTMLReader.BlockAction, HTMLDocument.HTMLReader.CharacterAction,
HTMLDocument.HTMLReader.HiddenAction, HTMLDocument.HTMLReader.IsindexAction,
HTMLDocument.HTMLReader.SpecialAction

Passed To: HTMLDocument.HTMLReader.registerTag()

HTMLDocument.Iterator

javax.swing.text.html

This class is used to iterate through an HTMLDocument, returning only tags of a specified type. This class is abstract and cannot be instantiated. Call the getIterator() method of HTMLDocument to obtain an instance that returns all instances of a specified HTML.Tag. getAttributes(), getStartOffset(), and getEndOffset() return information about the current tag. next() moves the iterator to the next tag, and isValid() returns true if there is a current tag or false if there are no more tags.

```
public abstract static class HTMLDocument.Iterator {
// Public Constructors
    public Iterator();
// Property Accessor Methods (by property name)
    public abstract AttributeSet getAttributes();
    public abstract int getEndOffset();
    public abstract int getStartOffset();
    public abstract HTML.Tag getTag();
    public abstract boolean isValid();
// Public Instance Methods
    public abstract void next();
}
```

Returned By: HTMLDocument.getIterator()

HTMLDocument.RunElement

javax.swing.text.html *serializable*

This class is used to represent content elements of an HTML document.

```
public class HTMLDocument.RunElement extends AbstractDocument.LeafElement {
// Public Constructors
    public RunElement(javax.swing.text.Element parent, AttributeSet a, int offs0, int offs1);
// Public Methods Overriding AbstractDocument.LeafElement
    public String getName();
// Public Methods Overriding AbstractDocument.AbstractElement
    public AttributeSet getResolveParent();                                       constant
}
```

HTMLEditorKit

javax.swing.text.html *cloneable serializable*

This class is used to customize a JEditorPane component to display and edit HTML documents. Most applications need do nothing more than instantiate an HTMLEditorKit and pass it to the setEditorKit() method of a JEditorPane. The write() method converts the contents of an HTMLDocument into HTML text and writes it to the specified stream. The read() method parses HTML text from a stream and creates a corresponding element structure in the specified HTMLDocument. insertHTML() parses HTML text from a string and inserts it into the specified HTMLDocument.

You can customize the appearance of HTML text displayed using an HTMLEditorKit by passing a StyleSheet object to setStyleSheet(). Other customizations require you to subclass HTMLEditorKit and override some of its methods. Override getViewFactory() if you want to use customized View subclasses to display certain HTML document elements. Override createDefaultDocument() if you want to change the properties of the default HTMLDocument or if you want to return a subclass of HTMLDocument. Override getParser() if you want to use a custom HTML parser implementation, instead of the default parser implemented in javax.swing.text.html.parser.

```
public class HTMLEditorKit extends StyledEditorKit {
// Public Constructors
     public HTMLEditorKit( );
// Public Constants
     public static final String BOLD_ACTION;                              ="html-bold-action"
     public static final String COLOR_ACTION;                             ="html-color-action"
     public static final String DEFAULT_CSS;                                  ="default.css"
     public static final String FONT_CHANGE_BIGGER;                        ="html-font-bigger"
     public static final String FONT_CHANGE_SMALLER;                      ="html-font-smaller"
     public static final String IMG_ALIGN_BOTTOM;                   ="html-image-align-bottom"
     public static final String IMG_ALIGN_MIDDLE;                  ="html-image-align-middle"
     public static final String IMG_ALIGN_TOP;                        ="html-image-align-top"
     public static final String IMG_BORDER;                              ="html-image-border"
     public static final String ITALIC_ACTION;                          ="html-italic-action"
     public static final String LOGICAL_STYLE_ACTION;            ="html-logical-style-action"
     public static final String PARA_INDENT_LEFT;                   ="html-para-indent-left"
     public static final String PARA_INDENT_RIGHT;                 ="html-para-indent-right"
// Inner Classes
     public static class HTMLFactory implements ViewFactory;
     public abstract static class HTMLTextAction extends StyledEditorKit.StyledTextAction;
     public static class InsertHTMLTextAction extends HTMLEditorKit.HTMLTextAction;
     public static class LinkController extends java.awt.event.MouseAdapter implements Serializable;
     public abstract static class Parser;
     public static class ParserCallback;
// Public Instance Methods
     public StyleSheet getStyleSheet( );
     public void insertHTML(HTMLDocument doc, int offset, String html, int popDepth, int pushDepth,
                          HTML.Tag insertTag) throws BadLocationException, java.io.IOException;
     public void setStyleSheet(StyleSheet s);
// Public Methods Overriding StyledEditorKit
     public Object clone( );
     public Document createDefaultDocument( );
     public void deinstall(JEditorPane c);
     public Action[ ] getActions( );
     public MutableAttributeSet getInputAttributes( );                    default:NamedStyle
     public ViewFactory getViewFactory( );                               default:HTMLFactory
     public void install(JEditorPane c);
// Protected Methods Overriding StyledEditorKit
     protected void createInputAttributes(javax.swing.text.Element element, MutableAttributeSet set);
// Public Methods Overriding DefaultEditorKit
     public String getContentType( );                                    default:"text/html"
     public void read(java.io.Reader in, Document doc, int pos) throws java.io.IOException, BadLocationException;
     public void write(java.io.Writer out, Document doc, int pos, int len) throws java.io.IOException,
         BadLocationException;
// Protected Instance Methods
     protected HTMLEditorKit.Parser getParser( );
}
```

Hierarchy: Object→ EditorKit(Cloneable, Serializable)→ DefaultEditorKit→ StyledEditorKit→ HTMLEditorKit

Returned By: HTMLEditorKit.HTMLTextAction.getHTMLEditorKit()

HTMLEditorKit.HTMLFactory   Java 1.2

javax.swing.text.html

This class is a ViewFactory for HTML documents. Its create() method returns a View object that is appropriate for the display of a given Element object. The View object is an instance of one of the View subclasses defined in this package.

```
public static class HTMLEditorKit.HTMLFactory implements ViewFactory {
// Public Constructors
    public HTMLFactory();
// Methods Implementing ViewFactory
    public View create(javax.swing.text.Element elem);
}
```

HTMLEditorKit.HTMLTextAction

Java 1.2

javax.swing.text.html

cloneable serializable

This class is an abstract Action implementation that provides protected convenience methods that may be helpful to Action implementations that manipulate or edit an HTML-Document.

```
public abstract static class HTMLEditorKit.HTMLTextAction extends StyledEditorKit.StyledTextAction {
// Public Constructors
    public HTMLTextAction(String name);
// Protected Instance Methods
    protected int elementCountToTag(HTMLDocument doc, int offset, HTML.Tag tag);
    protected javax.swing.text.Element findElementMatchingTag(HTMLDocument doc, int offset, HTML.Tag tag);
    protected javax.swing.text.Element[ ] getElementsAt(HTMLDocument doc, int offset);
    protected HTMLDocument getHTMLDocument(JEditorPane e);
    protected HTMLEditorKit getHTMLEditorKit(JEditorPane e);
}
```

Subclasses: HTMLEditorKit.InsertHTMLTextAction

HTMLEditorKit.InsertHTMLTextAction

Java 1.2

javax.swing.text.html

cloneable serializable

This Action implementation can be used to insert HTML text into an HTML document at the current location. You can create custom instances of this class and bind them to KeyStroke objects to provide custom editing actions for your users. When you create an InsertHTMLTextAction instance, you must specify the string of HTML text to be inserted and two HTML.Tag objects. The first HTML.Tag specifies the parent tag of the inserted text. For example, if the text you are inserting belongs in a paragraph element, you specify HTML.Tag.P. If the text you are inserting is a <DIV> or a <TABLE>, you specify HTML.Tag.BODY. The second HTML.Tag you must specify is the first tag of the parsed HTML string that is actually being inserted. For example, you may want to insert only a <TD> tag but may have to specify an HTML string that contains <TABLE> and <TR> tags so that the parser can correctly parse the HTML text. In this case, your second HTML.Tag argument is HTML.Tag.TD.

```
public static class HTMLEditorKit.InsertHTMLTextAction extends HTMLEditorKit.HTMLTextAction {
// Public Constructors
    public InsertHTMLTextAction(String name, String html, HTML.Tag parentTag, HTML.Tag addTag);
    public InsertHTMLTextAction(String name, String html, HTML.Tag parentTag, HTML.Tag addTag,
                                HTML.Tag alternateParentTag, HTML.Tag alternateAddTag);
// Public Methods Overriding AbstractAction
    public void actionPerformed(java.awt.event.ActionEvent ae);
// Protected Instance Methods
    protected void insertAtBoundry(JEditorPane editor, HTMLDocument doc, int offset,
                                javax.swing.text.Element insertElement, String html, HTML.Tag parentTag,
                                HTML.Tag addTag);
    protected void insertHTML(JEditorPane editor, HTMLDocument doc, int offset, String html, int popDepth,
                                int pushDepth, HTML.Tag addTag);
```

```
// Protected Instance Fields
    protected HTML.Tag addTag;
    protected HTML.Tag alternateAddTag;
    protected HTML.Tag alternateParentTag;
    protected String html;
    protected HTML.Tag parentTag;
}
```

HTMLEditorKit.LinkController

javax.swing.text.html   *serializable*

This class is a MouseAdapter that listens for mouse clicks and responds when the user clicks the mouse on a hyperlink. An instance of this class is installed on a JEditorPane by the install() method of the HTMLEditorKit.

```
public static class HTMLEditorKit.LinkController extends java.awt.event.MouseAdapter implements Serializable {
// Public Constructors
    public LinkController();
// Public Methods Overriding MouseAdapter
    public void mouseClicked(java.awt.event.MouseEvent e);
// Protected Instance Methods
    protected void activateLink(int pos, JEditorPane editor);
}
```

HTMLEditorKit.Parser

javax.swing.text.html

This is the abstract superclass of any class that wants to serve as an HTML parser for an HTMLEditorKit. The parse() method must read HTML text from the specified stream and convert the structure of the HTML text into a sequence of calls to the appropriate methods of the specified HTMLEditorKit.ParserCallback object. It is the responsibility of the Parser-Callback object to initialize the HTMLDocument as appropriate in response to those method calls. If the *ignoreCharSet* argument is true, the parser ignores any HTML <META> tags that specify the document encoding. If this argument is false and the parser encounters such a tag, it should compare the document-specified encoding to the encoding used by the Reader stream from which it is reading. If the encodings do not match, it should throw a javax.swing.text.ChangedCharSetException.

Most applications can rely on the full-featured HTML parser provided by the javax.swing.text.html.parser package and do not need to subclass this class. The default parser is DTD-driven and can also be customized by providing a custom DTD. If you implement your own Parser subclass or customize the default parser, you must subclass HTMLEditorKit and override the getParser() method.

```
public abstract static class HTMLEditorKit.Parser {
// Public Constructors
    public Parser();
// Public Instance Methods
    public abstract void parse(java.io.Reader r, HTMLEditorKit.ParserCallback cb, boolean ignoreCharSet)
        throws java.io.IOException;
}
```

Subclasses: javax.swing.text.html.parser.ParserDelegator

Returned By: HTMLEditorKit.getParser()

HTMLEditorKit.ParserCallback   Java 1.2

javax.swing.text.html

This class defines the methods that are invoked by an HTMLEditorKit.Parser to describe the structure of an HTML document. The methods should be implemented to add appropriate content to an HTMLDocument. HTMLEditorKit uses an HTMLDocument.HTMLReader object as its default implementation of ParserCallback.

```
public static class HTMLEditorKit.ParserCallback {
// Public Constructors
    public ParserCallback();
// Public Instance Methods
    public void flush() throws BadLocationException;                                empty
    public void handleComment(char[ ] data, int pos);                               empty
    public void handleEndTag(HTML.Tag t, int pos);                                  empty
    public void handleError(String errorMsg, int pos);                             empty
    public void handleSimpleTag(HTML.Tag t, MutableAttributeSet a, int pos);       empty
    public void handleStartTag(HTML.Tag t, MutableAttributeSet a, int pos);        empty
    public void handleText(char[ ] data, int pos);                                 empty
}
```

Subclasses: HTMLDocument.HTMLReader

Passed To: HTMLEditorKit.Parser.parse(), javax.swing.text.html.parser.DocumentParser.parse(), javax.swing.text.html.parser.ParserDelegator.parse()

Returned By: HTMLDocument.getReader()

HTMLFrameHyperlinkEvent   Java 1.2

javax.swing.text.html   *serializable event*

This class is an extension of HyperlinkEvent that is used when a hyperlink in one frame refers to another frame with an HTML TARGET attribute. getSourceElement() returns the Element object in the HTMLDocument that corresponds to the <FRAME> tag of the source frame. getTarget() returns a string that specifies the target frame. This may be a frame name or one of the standard special target names, "_self", "_parent", or "_top". The processHTMLFrameHyperlinkEvent() method of HTMLDocument can handle events of this type.

```
public class HTMLFrameHyperlinkEvent extends javax.swing.event.HyperlinkEvent {
// Public Constructors
    public HTMLFrameHyperlinkEvent(Object source, javax.swing.event.HyperlinkEvent.EventType type,
                                   java.net.URL targetURL, String targetFrame);
    public HTMLFrameHyperlinkEvent(Object source, javax.swing.event.HyperlinkEvent.EventType type,
                                   java.net.URL targetURL, javax.swing.text.Element sourceElement,
                                   String targetFrame);
    public HTMLFrameHyperlinkEvent(Object source, javax.swing.event.HyperlinkEvent.EventType type,
                                   java.net.URL targetURL, String desc, String targetFrame);
    public HTMLFrameHyperlinkEvent(Object source, javax.swing.event.HyperlinkEvent.EventType type,
                                   java.net.URL targetURL, String desc, javax.swing.text.Element sourceElement,
                                   String targetFrame);
// Public Instance Methods
    public javax.swing.text.Element getSourceElement();
    public String getTarget();
}
```

Hierarchy: Object→ java.util.EventObject(Serializable)→ javax.swing.event.HyperlinkEvent→ HTMLFrameHyperlinkEvent

Passed To: HTMLDocument.processHTMLFrameHyperlinkEvent()

HTMLWriter

javax.swing.text.html

This class knows how to convert an HTMLDocument to textual form and write it to a specified stream. To use an HTMLWriter, simply pass an HTMLDocument and a Writer stream to the constructor, then call the public write() method. The various protected methods are used internally to output the document and can be overridden in a subclass to customize the HTML output process.

```
public class HTMLWriter extends AbstractWriter {
// Public Constructors
    public HTMLWriter(java.io.Writer w, HTMLDocument doc);
    public HTMLWriter(java.io.Writer w, HTMLDocument doc, int pos, int len);
// Public Methods Overriding AbstractWriter
    public void write() throws java.io.IOException, BadLocationException;
// Protected Methods Overriding AbstractWriter
    protected void decrIndent();
    protected void incrIndent();
    protected void indent() throws java.io.IOException;
    protected void setIndentSpace(int space);
    protected void setLineLength(int l);
    protected void text(javax.swing.text.Element elem) throws BadLocationException, java.io.IOException;
    protected void write(String content) throws java.io.IOException;
    protected void write(char ch) throws java.io.IOException;
    protected void writeAttributes(AttributeSet attr) throws java.io.IOException;
// Protected Instance Methods
    protected void closeOutUnwantedEmbeddedTags(AttributeSet attr) throws java.io.IOException;
    protected void comment(javax.swing.text.Element elem) throws BadLocationException, java.io.IOException;
    protected void emptyTag(javax.swing.text.Element elem) throws BadLocationException, java.io.IOException;
    protected void endTag(javax.swing.text.Element elem) throws java.io.IOException;
    protected boolean isBlockTag(AttributeSet attr);
    protected boolean matchNameAttribute(AttributeSet attr, HTML.Tag tag);
    protected void selectContent(AttributeSet attr) throws java.io.IOException;
    protected void startTag(javax.swing.text.Element elem) throws java.io.IOException, BadLocationException;
    protected boolean synthesizedElement(javax.swing.text.Element elem);
    protected void textAreaContent(AttributeSet attr) throws BadLocationException, java.io.IOException;
    protected void writeEmbeddedTags(AttributeSet attr) throws java.io.IOException;
    protected void writeOption(Option option) throws java.io.IOException;
}
```

Hierarchy: Object→ AbstractWriter→ HTMLWriter

InlineView

javax.swing.text.html

This View class displays styled text that appears in an HTML document. It extends javax.swing.text.LabelView to add support for CSS attributes.

```
public class InlineView extends LabelView {
// Public Constructors
    public InlineView(javax.swing.text.Element elem);
// Public Methods Overriding LabelView
    public void changedUpdate(javax.swing.event.DocumentEvent e, java.awt.Shape a, ViewFactory f);
// Protected Methods Overriding LabelView
    protected void setPropertiesFromAttributes();
// Public Methods Overriding View
    public AttributeSet getAttributes();
```

```
// Protected Instance Methods
    protected StyleSheet getStyleSheet();
}
```

Hierarchy: Object→ View(SwingConstants)→ LabelView→ InlineView

ListView   Java 1.2

javax.swing.text.html

This View class displays HTML list elements.

```
public class ListView extends BlockView {
// Public Constructors
    public ListView(javax.swing.text.Element elem);
// Public Methods Overriding BlockView
    public float getAlignment(int axis);
    public void paint(java.awt.Graphics g, java.awt.Shape allocation);
// Protected Methods Overriding BlockView
    protected void setPropertiesFromAttributes();
// Protected Methods Overriding BoxView
    protected void paintChild(java.awt.Graphics g, java.awt.Rectangle alloc, int index);
}
```

Hierarchy: Object→ View(SwingConstants)→ CompositeView→ BoxView→ BlockView→ ListView

MinimalHTMLWriter   Java 1.2

javax.swing.text.html

This class knows how to convert an arbitrary StyledDocument to simple HTML text. Its use is similar to the use of HTMLWriter. Because there is not an exact mapping between the character and paragraph attributes supported by StyledDocument objects and those defined by standard HTML tags and attributes, MinimalHTMLWriter relies heavily on CSS attributes in the HTML text it outputs.

```
public class MinimalHTMLWriter extends AbstractWriter {
// Public Constructors
    public MinimalHTMLWriter(java.io.Writer w, StyledDocument doc);
    public MinimalHTMLWriter(java.io.Writer w, StyledDocument doc, int pos, int len);
// Public Methods Overriding AbstractWriter
    public void write() throws java.io.IOException, BadLocationException;
// Protected Methods Overriding AbstractWriter
    protected void text(javax.swing.text.Element elem) throws java.io.IOException, BadLocationException;
    protected void writeAttributes(AttributeSet attr) throws java.io.IOException;
// Protected Instance Methods
    protected void endFontTag() throws java.io.IOException;
    protected boolean inFontTag();
    protected boolean isText(javax.swing.text.Element elem);
    protected void startFontTag(String style) throws java.io.IOException;
    protected void writeBody() throws java.io.IOException, BadLocationException;
    protected void writeComponent(javax.swing.text.Element elem) throws java.io.IOException;         empty
    protected void writeContent(javax.swing.text.Element elem, boolean reedsIndenting) throws java.io.IOException,
        BadLocationException;
    protected void writeEndParagraph() throws java.io.IOException;
    protected void writeEndTag(String endTag) throws java.io.IOException;
    protected void writeHeader() throws java.io.IOException;
    protected void writeHTMLTags(AttributeSet attr) throws java.io.IOException;
    protected void writeImage(javax.swing.text.Element elem) throws java io.IOException;              empty
    protected void writeLeaf(javax.swing.text.Element elem) throws java.io.IOException;
```

```
    protected void writeNonHTMLAttributes(AttributeSet attr) throws java.io.IOException;
    protected void writeStartParagraph(javax.swing.text.Element elem) throws java.io.IOException;
    protected void writeStartTag(String tag) throws java.io.IOException;
    protected void writeStyles() throws java.io.IOException;
}
```

Hierarchy: Object→ AbstractWriter→ MinimalHTMLWriter

ObjectView
Java 1.2

javax.swing.text.html

This View subclass dynamically loads, instantiates, and displays an arbitrary java.awt.Component object specified by the CLASSID attribute of an HTML <OBJECT> tag.

```
public class ObjectView extends ComponentView {
// Public Constructors
    public ObjectView(javax.swing.text.Element elem);
// Protected Methods Overriding ComponentView
    protected Component createComponent();
}
```

Hierarchy: Object→ View(SwingConstants)→ ComponentView→ ObjectView

Option
Java 1.2

javax.swing.text.html

This class is used internally by HTMLDocument to represent <OPTION> tags within a <SELECT> tag.

```
public class Option {
// Public Constructors
    public Option(AttributeSet attr);
// Property Accessor Methods (by property name)
    public AttributeSet getAttributes();
    public String getLabel();
    public void setLabel(String label);
    public boolean isSelected();
    public String getValue();
// Public Methods Overriding Object
    public String toString();
// Protected Instance Methods
    protected void setSelection(boolean state);
}
```

Passed To: HTMLWriter.writeOption()

ParagraphView
Java 1.2

javax.swing.text.html

This class displays HTML paragraph elements. It extends the javax.swing.text.ParagraphView class to add support for CSS attributes.

```
public class ParagraphView extends javax.swing.text.ParagraphView {
// Public Constructors
    public ParagraphView(javax.swing.text.Element elem);
// Public Methods Overriding ParagraphView
    public void changedUpdate(javax.swing.event.DocumentEvent e, java.awt.Shape a, ViewFactory f);
    public void paint(java.awt.Graphics g, java.awt.Shape a);
```

```
// Protected Methods Overriding ParagraphView
    protected SizeRequirements calculateMinorAxisRequirements(int axis, SizeRequirements r);
    protected void setPropertiesFromAttributes();
// Public Methods Overriding BoxView
    public float getMaximumSpan(int axis);
    public float getMinimumSpan(int axis);
    public float getPreferredSpan(int axis);
// Public Methods Overriding CompositeView
    public void setParent(View parent);
// Public Methods Overriding View
    public AttributeSet getAttributes();
    public boolean isVisible();
// Protected Instance Methods
    protected StyleSheet getStyleSheet();
}
```

Hierarchy: Object → View(SwingConstants) → CompositeView → BoxView → javax.swing.text.ParagraphView(TabExpander) → javax.swing.text.html.ParagraphView

StyleSheet

Java 1.2

javax.swing.text.html

serializable

This class is a StyleContext subclass that represents a CSS style sheet. In Java 1.2, it is only partially implemented. However, it can parse CSS style sheets with the loadRules() method. View objects are the primary user of this class. A View object calls getViewAttributes() to obtain an appropriate AttributeSet that takes all cascading styles into account to use when displaying itself.

StyleSheet also defines two inner classes that perform certain common drawing tasks for HTML View classes. The getBoxPainter() and getListPainter() methods return immutable (possibly shared and cached) instances of these inner classes that are suitable for drawing text boxes and list items for a given AttributeSet. Various View implementations use this cache for efficiency.

```
public class StyleSheet extends StyleContext {
// Public Constructors
    public StyleSheet();
// Inner Classes
    public static class BoxPainter implements Serializable;
    public static class ListPainter implements Serializable;
// Public Class Methods
    public static int getIndexOfSize(float pt);
// Public Instance Methods
    public void addRule(String rule);
    public StyleSheet.BoxPainter getBoxPainter(AttributeSet a);
    public AttributeSet getDeclaration(String decl);
    public StyleSheet.ListPainter getListPainter(AttributeSet a);
    public float getPointSize(String size);
    public float getPointSize(int index);
    public Style getRule(String selector);
    public Style getRule(HTML.Tag t, javax.swing.text.Element e);
    public AttributeSet getViewAttributes(View v);
    public void loadRules(java.io.Reader in, java.net.URL ref) throws java.io.IOException;
    public void setBaseFontSize(String size);
    public void setBaseFontSize(int sz);
    public java.awt.Color stringToColor(String string);
    public AttributeSet translateHTMLToCSS(AttributeSet htmlAttrSet);
```

```
// Public Methods Overriding StyleContext
    public AttributeSet addAttribute(AttributeSet old, Object key, Object value);
    public AttributeSet addAttributes(AttributeSet old, AttributeSet attr);
    public java.awt.Color getBackground(AttributeSet a);
    public java.awt.Font getFont(AttributeSet a);
    public java.awt.Color getForeground(AttributeSet a);
    public AttributeSet removeAttribute(AttributeSet old, Object key);
    public AttributeSet removeAttributes(AttributeSet old, AttributeSet attrs);
    public AttributeSet removeAttributes(AttributeSet old, java.util.Enumeration names);
    public void removeStyle(String nm);
// Protected Methods Overriding StyleContext
    protected MutableAttributeSet createLargeAttributeSet(AttributeSet a);
    protected StyleContext.SmallAttributeSet createSmallAttributeSet(AttributeSet a);
}
```

Hierarchy: Object→ StyleContext(AbstractDocument.AttributeContext, Serializable)→ StyleSheet

Passed To: HTMLDocument.HTMLDocument(), HTMLEditorKit.setStyleSheet()

Returned By: BlockView.getStyleSheet(), HTMLDocument.getStyleSheet(), HTMLEditorKit.getStyleSheet(), InlineView.getStyleSheet(), javax.swing.text.html.ParagraphView.getStyleSheet()

StyleSheet.BoxPainter

Java 1.2

javax.swing.text.html

serializable

This class knows how to display the CSS border and background box attributes of an HTML element. Various HTML View objects use this object to perform this drawing.

```
public static class StyleSheet.BoxPainter implements Serializable {
// No Constructor
// Public Instance Methods
    public float getInset(int side, View v);
    public void paint(java.awt.Graphics g, float x, float y, float w, float h, View v);
}
```

Returned By: StyleSheet.getBoxPainter()

StyleSheet.ListPainter

Java 1.2

javax.swing.text.html

serializable

This class knows how to display list bullets and numbers as specified by the various list-related CSS attributes. View objects responsible for displaying HTML lists delegate to this class to perform this drawing.

```
public static class StyleSheet.ListPainter implements Serializable {
// No Constructor
// Public Instance Methods
    public void paint(java.awt.Graphics g, float x, float y, float w, float h, View v, int item);
}
```

Returned By: StyleSheet.getListPainter()

CHAPTER 32

The javax.swing.text.html.parser Package

This package includes classes and interfaces for parsing HTML text. The parser is configured by a DTD (document type definition) and is therefore customizable. The parser conforms to the HTMLEditorKit.Parser and HTMLEditorKit.ParserCallback interfaces defined in the javax.swing.text.html package. Most applications can ignore this package and simply use javax.swing.JEditorPane and javax.swing.text.html.HTMLEditorKit to handle their HTML parsing and display needs. Figure 32-1 shows the class hierarchy of this package.

AttributeList   Java 1.2

javax.swing.text.html.parser   *serializable*

This class is an element in a linked list of attribute specifications. The complete list of attribute specifications represents an ATTLIST element of a DTD. Each AttributeList object represents the name, type, and values of a single attribute. Use the getNext() method to obtain the next AttributeList object in the linked list.

```
public final class AttributeList implements DTDConstants, Serializable {
// Public Constructors
    public AttributeList(String name);
    public AttributeList(String name, int type, int modifier, String value, java.util.Vector values, AttributeList next);
// Public Class Methods
    public static int name2type(String nm);
    public static String type2name(int tp);
// Property Accessor Methods (by property name)
    public int getModifier();
    public String getName();
    public AttributeList getNext();
    public int getType();
    public String getValue();
    public java.util.Enumeration getValues();
// Public Methods Overriding Object
    public String toString();
```

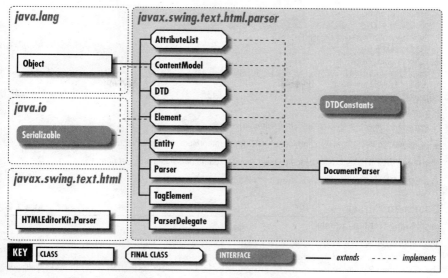

Figure 32-1: The javax.swing.text.html.parser package

```
// Public Instance Fields
    public int modifier;
    public String name;
    public AttributeList next;
    public int type;
    public String value;
    public java.util.Vector values;
}
```

Hierarchy: Object → AttributeList(DTDConstants, Serializable)

Passed To: AttributeList.AttributeList(), DTD.{defAttributeList(), defElement(), defineAttributes(), defineElement()}

Returned By: AttributeList.getNext(), DTD.defAttributeList(), javax.swing.text.html.parser.Element.{getAttribute(), getAttributeByValue(), getAttributes()}

Type Of: AttributeList.next, javax.swing.text.html.parser.Element.atts

ContentModel   Java 1.2

javax.swing.text.html.parser   *serializable model*

This class represents a content model of an element in a DTD.

```
public final class ContentModel implements Serializable {
// Public Constructors
    public ContentModel();
    public ContentModel(javax.swing.text.html.parser.Element content);
    public ContentModel(int type, ContentModel content);
    public ContentModel(int type, Object content, ContentModel next);
// Public Instance Methods
    public boolean empty();
    public javax.swing.text.html.parser.Element first();
```

```
    public boolean first(Object token);
    public void getElements(java.util.Vector elemVec);
// Public Methods Overriding Object
    public String toString();
// Public Instance Fields
    public Object content;
    public ContentModel next;
    public int type;
}
```

Hierarchy: Object→ ContentModel(Serializable)

Passed To: ContentModel.ContentModel(), DTD.{defContentModel(), defElement(), defineElement()}

Returned By: DTD.defContentModel(), javax.swing.text.html.parser.Element.getContent()

Type Of: ContentModel.next, javax.swing.text.html.parser.Element.content

DocumentParser   Java 1.2

javax.swing.text.html.parser

This Parser subclass is the delegate of the ParserDelegator class. The parse() method reads a document from the specified Reader stream, parses it using the DTD specified when the DocumentParser was created, and notifies the specified HTMLEditorKit.ParserCallback object of the document structure by calling its various methods.

```
public class DocumentParser extends Parser {
// Public Constructors
    public DocumentParser(DTD dtd);
// Public Instance Methods
    public void parse(java.io.Reader in, HTMLEditorKit.ParserCallback callback, boolean ignoreCharSet)
        throws java.io.IOException;
// Protected Methods Overriding Parser
    protected void handleComment(char[ ] text);
    protected void handleEmptyTag(TagElement tag) throws ChangedCharSetException;
    protected void handleEndTag(TagElement tag);
    protected void handleError(int ln, String errorMsg);
    protected void handleStartTag(TagElement tag);
    protected void handleText(char[ ] data);
}
```

Hierarchy: Object→ Parser(DTDConstants)→ DocumentParser

DTD   Java 1.2

javax.swing.text.html.parser

This class represents a document type definition (DTD). A DTD specifies the grammar of the document to be parsed. The methods of this class allow you to define the elements and entities of the grammar and look those elements and entities up by name. It also defines a read() method that can read a DTD stored in a binary format. ParserDelegator reads the default HTML 3.2 DTD from the file *html32.bdtd*, which is stored in the same directory or ZIP archive as the *DTD.class* class file.

```
public class DTD implements DTDConstants {
// Protected Constructors
    protected DTD(String name);
// Public Class Methods
    public static DTD getDTD(String name) throws java.io.IOException;
    public static void putDTDHash(String name, DTD dtd);
```

```
// Public Instance Methods
    public Entity defEntity(String name, int type, int ch);
    public void defineAttributes(String name, AttributeList atts);
    public javax.swing.text.html.parser.Element defineElement(String name, int type, boolean omitStart,
                                                boolean omitEnd, ContentModel content,
                                                java.util.BitSet exclusions, java.util.BitSet inclusions,
                                                AttributeList atts);
    public Entity defineEntity(String name, int type, char[ ] data);
    public javax.swing.text.html.parser.Element getElement(String name);
    public javax.swing.text.html.parser.Element getElement(int index);
    public Entity getEntity(String name);
    public Entity getEntity(int ch);
    public String getName();
    public void read(java.io.DataInputStream in) throws java.io.IOException;
// Public Methods Overriding Object
    public String toString();
// Protected Instance Methods
    protected AttributeList defAttributeList(String name, int type, int modifier, String value, String values,
                                                AttributeList atts);
    protected ContentModel defContentModel(int type, Object obj, ContentModel next);
    protected javax.swing.text.html.parser.Element defElement(String name, int type, boolean omitStart,
                                                boolean omitEnd, ContentModel content,
                                                String[ ] exclusions, String[ ] inclusions,
                                                AttributeList atts);
    protected Entity defEntity(String name, int type, String str);
// Public Class Fields
    public static int FILE_VERSION;
// Public Instance Fields
    public final javax.swing.text.html.parser.Element applet;
    public final javax.swing.text.html.parser.Element base;
    public final javax.swing.text.html.parser.Element body;
    public java.util.Hashtable elementHash;
    public java.util.Vector elements;
    public java.util.Hashtable entityHash;
    public final javax.swing.text.html.parser.Element head;
    public final javax.swing.text.html.parser.Element html;
    public final javax.swing.text.html.parser.Element isindex;
    public final javax.swing.text.html.parser.Element meta;
    public String name;
    public final javax.swing.text.html.parser.Element p;
    public final javax.swing.text.html.parser.Element param;
    public final javax.swing.text.html.parser.Element pcdata;
    public final javax.swing.text.html.parser.Element title;
}
```

Hierarchy: Object→ DTD(DTDConstants)

Passed To: DocumentParser.DocumentParser(), DTD.putDTDHash(), Parser.Parser(),
ParserDelegator.createDTD()

Returned By: DTD.getDTD(), ParserDelegator.createDTD()

Type Of: Parser.dtd

DTDConstants   Java 1.2

javax.swing.text.html.parser

This interface defines various integer constants used in a DTD.

```
public abstract interface DTDConstants {
// Public Constants
    public static final int ANY;                                             =19
    public static final int CDATA;                                           =1
    public static final int CONREF;                                          =4
    public static final int CURRENT;                                         =3
    public static final int DEFAULT;                                    =131072
    public static final int EMPTY;                                          =17
    public static final int ENDTAG;                                         =14
    public static final int ENTITIES;                                        =3
    public static final int ENTITY;                                          =2
    public static final int FIXED;                                           =1
    public static final int GENERAL;                                     =65536
    public static final int ID;                                              =4
    public static final int IDREF;                                           =5
    public static final int IDREFS;                                          =6
    public static final int IMPLIED;                                         =5
    public static final int MD;                                             =16
    public static final int MODEL;                                          =18
    public static final int MS;                                             =15
    public static final int NAME;                                            =7
    public static final int NAMES;                                           =8
    public static final int NMTOKEN;                                         =9
    public static final int NMTOKENS;                                       =10
    public static final int NOTATION;                                       =11
    public static final int NUMBER;                                         =12
    public static final int NUMBERS;                                        =13
    public static final int NUTOKEN;                                        =14
    public static final int NUTOKENS;                                       =15
    public static final int PARAMETER;                                  =262144
    public static final int PI;                                             =12
    public static final int PUBLIC;                                         =10
    public static final int RCDATA;                                         =16
    public static final int REQUIRED;                                        =2
    public static final int SDATA;                                          =11
    public static final int STARTTAG;                                       =13
    public static final int SYSTEM;                                         =17
}
```

Implementations: AttributeList, DTD, javax.swing.text.html.parser.Element, Entity, Parser

Element   Java 1.2

javax.swing.text.html.parser   *serializable*

This class encapsulates all of the details of a single ELEMENT of a DTD. It describes the
type of a tag, its allowed attributes and their types, and the content model of the tag.

```
public final class Element implements DTDConstants, Serializable {
// No Constructor
// Public Class Methods
    public static int name2type(String nm);
// Property Accessor Methods (by property name)
    public AttributeList getAttributes();
    public ContentModel getContent();
    public boolean isEmpty();
    public int getIndex();
    public String getName();
    public int getType();
```

```
// Public Instance Methods
    public AttributeList getAttribute(String name);
    public AttributeList getAttributeByValue(String name);
    public boolean omitEnd();
    public boolean omitStart();
// Public Methods Overriding Object
    public String toString();
// Public Instance Fields
    public AttributeList atts;
    public ContentModel content;
    public Object data;
    public java.util.BitSet exclusions;
    public java.util.BitSet inclusions;
    public int index;
    public String name;
    public boolean oEnd;
    public boolean oStart;
    public int type;
}
```

Hierarchy: Object→ javax.swing.text.html.parser.Element(DTDConstants, Serializable)

Passed To: ContentModel.ContentModel(), Parser.{makeTag(), markFirstTime()}, TagElement.TagElement()

Returned By: ContentModel.first(), DTD.{defElement(), defineElement(), getElement()}, TagElement.getElement()

Type Of: DTD.{applet, base, body, head, html, isindex, meta, p, param, pcdata, title}

Entity

javax.swing.text.html.parser

This class represents an ENTITY specification in a DTD. It specifies the name, type, and value of the entity.

```
public final class Entity implements DTDConstants {
// Public Constructors
    public Entity(String name, int type, char[ ] data);
// Public Class Methods
    public static int name2type(String nm);
// Property Accessor Methods (by property name)
    public char[ ] getData();
    public boolean isGeneral();
    public String getName();
    public boolean isParameter();
    public String getString();
    public int getType();
// Public Instance Fields
    public char[ ] data;
    public String name;
    public int type;
}
```

Hierarchy: Object→ Entity(DTDConstants)

Returned By: DTD.{defEntity(), defineEntity(), getEntity()}

Parser

javax.swing.text.html.parser

This class is an HTML parser that uses a DTD object to specify the specific HTML grammar it should parse. The parse() method reads HTML text from a stream and parses it.
Parser calls its various protected methods at appropriate points during the parsing process. In order to do anything useful, a subclass must provide non-empty implementations for these methods. See also DocumentParser.

```
public class Parser implements DTDConstants {
// Public Constructors
    public Parser(DTD dtd);
// Public Instance Methods
    public void parse(java.io.Reader in) throws java.io.IOException;                       synchronized
    public String parseDTDMarkup() throws java.io.IOException;
// Protected Instance Methods
    protected void endTag(boolean omitted);
    protected void error(String err);
    protected void error(String err, String arg1);
    protected void error(String err, String arg1, String arg2);
    protected void error(String err, String arg1, String arg2, String arg3);
    protected void flushAttributes();
    protected SimpleAttributeSet getAttributes();
    protected int getCurrentLine();
    protected int getCurrentPos();
    protected void handleComment(char[ ] text);                                                   empty
    protected void handleEmptyTag(TagElement tag) throws ChangedCharSetException;                  empty
    protected void handleEndTag(TagElement tag);                                                   empty
    protected void handleEOFInComment();
    protected void handleError(int ln, String msg);
    protected void handleStartTag(TagElement tag);                                                 empty
    protected void handleText(char[ ] text);                                                       empty
    protected void handleTitle(char[ ] text);
    protected TagElement makeTag(javax.swing.text.html.parser.Element elem);
    protected TagElement makeTag(javax.swing.text.html.parser.Element elem, boolean fictional);
    protected void markFirstTime(javax.swing.text.html.parser.Element elem);
    protected boolean parseMarkupDeclarations(StringBuffer strBuff) throws java.io.IOException;
    protected void startTag(TagElement tag) throws ChangedCharSetException;
// Protected Instance Fields
    protected DTD dtd;
    protected boolean strict;
}
```

Hierarchy: Object → Parser(DTDConstants)

Subclasses: DocumentParser

ParserDelegator

javax.swing.text.html.parser

This class extends the HTMLEditorKit.Parser class and provides a definition of the parse()
method, which reads HTML text from a stream and parses it into a sequence of calls to
the methods of the specified HTMLEditorKit.ParserCallback object. Each time parse() is called,
the ParserDelegator class creates a new instance of DocumentParser to perform the parsing
and maintain state for the parsing process.

```
public class ParserDelegator extends HTMLEditorKit.Parser {
// Public Constructors
    public ParserDelegator();
```

```
// Protected Class Methods
    protected static DTD createDTD(DTD dtd, String name);
    protected static void setDefaultDTD();
// Public Methods Overriding HTMLEditorKit.Parser
    public void parse(java.io.Reader r, HTMLEditorKit.ParserCallback cb, boolean ignoreCharSet)
        throws java.io.IOException;
}
```

Hierarchy: Object→ HTMLEditorKit.Parser→ ParserDelegator

TagElement

javax.swing.text.html.parser

This class is used internally by DocumentParser and its superclass Parser to describe the type and behavior of an HTML tag that has been parsed.

```
public class TagElement {
// Public Constructors
    public TagElement(javax.swing.text.html.parser.Element elem);
    public TagElement(javax.swing.text.html.parser.Element elem, boolean fictional);
// Public Instance Methods
    public boolean breaksFlow();
    public boolean fictional();
    public javax.swing.text.html.parser.Element getElement();
    public HTML.Tag getHTMLTag();
    public boolean isPreformatted();
}
```

Passed To: DocumentParser.{handleEmptyTag(), handleEndTag(), handleStartTag()}, Parser.{handleEmptyTag(), handleEndTag(), handleStartTag(), startTag()}

Returned By: Parser.makeTag()

## CHAPTER 33

The javax.swing.text.rtf Package

This simple package defines an RTFEditorKit that enables the javax.swing.JEditorPane component to display and edit Rich Text Format (RTF) documents. Figure 33-1 shows the class hierarchy of this package.

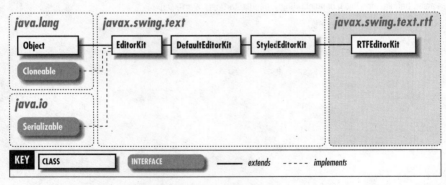

Figure 33-1: The javax.swing.text.rtf package

RTFEditorKit   Java 1.2

javax.swing.text.rtf   *cloneable serializable*

This EditorKit subclass provides support to a JEditorPane component for displaying and editing text stored in Microsoft's Rich Text Format (RTF). The getContentType() method returns "text/rtf". The read() and write() methods know how to translate between the RTF file format and the Element tree structure of a DefaultStyledDocument.

```
public class RTFEditorKit extends StyledEditorKit {
// Public Constructors
   public RTFEditorKit();
```

```
// Public Methods Overriding StyledEditorKit
    public Object clone();
// Public Methods Overriding DefaultEditorKit
    public String getContentType();                                          default:"text/rtf"
    public void read(java.io.Reader in, Document doc, int pos) throws java.io.IOException, BadLocationException;
    public void read(java.io.InputStream in, Document doc, int pos) throws java.io.IOException, BadLocationException;
    public void write(java.io.Writer out, Document doc, int pos, int len) throws java.io.IOException,
       BadLocationException;
    public void write(java.io.OutputStream out, Document doc, int pos, int len) throws java.io.IOException,
       BadLocationException;
}
```

Hierarchy: Object→ EditorKit(Cloneable, Serializable)→ DefaultEditorKit→ StyledEditorKit→ RTFEditorKit

CHAPTER 34

The javax.swing.tree Package

The javax.swing.tree package defines classes and interfaces used with the javax.swing.JTree component. The TreeModel interface defines the data to be displayed by a JTree component. DefaultTreeModel provides a commonly used implementation of this interface; it is implemented in terms of the TreeNode and MutableTreeNode interfaces. The TreeCellRenderer and TreeCellEditor interfaces are implemented by objects that can display or edit cells in the tree, using a Swing component as a template. Figure 34-1 shows the class hierarchy of this package. See Chapter 3, *Swing Programming Topics*, for a discussion of and example using JTree and the javax.swing.tree package.

AbstractLayoutCache   Java 1.2

javax.swing.tree

This abstract class defines the methods that must be implemented by a class that wants to cache a JTree layout. This class is used by the JTree UI delegate. Applications never need to use or subclass this class.

```
public abstract class AbstractLayoutCache implements RowMapper {
// Public Constructors
    public AbstractLayoutCache();
// Inner Classes
    public abstract static class NodeDimensions;
// Property Accessor Methods (by property name)
    public TreeModel getModel();
    public void setModel(TreeModel newModel);
    public AbstractLayoutCache.NodeDimensions getNodeDimensions();
    public void setNodeDimensions(AbstractLayoutCache.NodeDimensions nd);
    public int getPreferredHeight();
    public boolean isRootVisible();
    public void setRootVisible(boolean rootVisible);                             bound
    public abstract int getRowCount();
    public int getRowHeight();
```

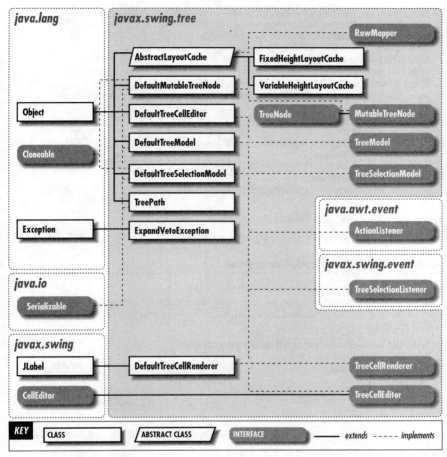

Figure 34–1: The javax.swing.tree package

```
    public void setRowHeight(int rowHeight);                                                              bound
    public TreeSelectionModel getSelectionModel( );
    public void setSelectionModel(TreeSelectionModel newLSM);
// Public Instance Methods
    public abstract java.awt.Rectangle getBounds(TreePath path, java.awt.Rectangle placeIn);
    public abstract boolean getExpandedState(TreePath path);
    public abstract TreePath getPathClosestTo(int x, int y);
    public abstract TreePath getPathForRow(int row);
    public int getPreferredWidth(java.awt.Rectangle bounds);
    public abstract int getRowForPath(TreePath path);
    public abstract int getVisibleChildCount(TreePath path);
    public abstract java.util.Enumeration getVisiblePathsFrom(TreePath path);
    public abstract void invalidatePathBounds(TreePath path);
    public abstract void invalidateSizes( );
    public abstract boolean isExpanded(TreePath path);
    public abstract void setExpandedState(TreePath path, boolean isExpanded);
```

```
    public abstract void treeNodesChanged(javax.swing.event.TreeModelEvent e);
    public abstract void treeNodesInserted(javax.swing.event.TreeModelEvent e);
    public abstract void treeNodesRemoved(javax.swing.event.TreeModelEvent e);
    public abstract void treeStructureChanged(javax.swing.event.TreeModelEvent e);
// Methods Implementing RowMapper
    public int[ ] getRowsForPaths(TreePath[ ] paths);
// Protected Instance Methods
    protected java.awt.Rectangle getNodeDimensions(Object value, int row, int depth, boolean expanded,
                                        java.awt.Rectange placeIn);
    protected boolean isFixedRowHeight( );
// Protected Instance Fields
    protected AbstractLayoutCache.NodeDimensions nodeDimensions;
    protected boolean rootVisible;
    protected int rowHeight;
    protected TreeModel treeModel;
    protected TreeSelectionModel treeSelectionModel;
}
```

Hierarchy: Object→ AbstractLayoutCache(RowMapper)

Subclasses: FixedHeightLayoutCache, VariableHeightLayoutCache

AbstractLayoutCache.NodeDimensions   Java 1.2

javax.swing.tree

This class defines a method that can compute the dimensions of a node in a JTree. It is used internally by AbstractLayoutCache and its subclasses and by the JTree UI delegate. Applications never need to use it.

```
public abstract static class AbstractLayoutCache.NodeDimensions {
// Public Constructors
    public NodeDimensions( );
// Public Instance Methods
    public abstract java.awt.Rectangle getNodeDimensions(Object value, int row, int depth, boolean expanded,
                                        java.awt.Rectangle bounds);
}
```

Passed To: AbstractLayoutCache.setNodeDimensions(), VariableHeightLayoutCache.setNodeDimensions()

Returned By: AbstractLayoutCache.getNodeDimensions()

Type Of: AbstractLayoutCache.nodeDimensions

DefaultMutableTreeNode   Java 1.2

javax.swing.tree   *cloneable serializable*

This class implements the MutableTreeNode interface and adds a number of useful tree-manipulation methods. When you create a DefaultMutableTreeNode, you can optionally specify a user object—the data associated with the node—and a boolean value that specifies whether the node is allowed to have children. DefaultMutableTreeNode implements the MutableTreeNode methods that allow the parent and children of the node to be set and the TreeNode methods that allow the parent and children to be queried. In addition to these basic methods, DefaultMutableTreeNode includes a number of useful tree-manipulation methods, such as breadthFirstEnumeration() and depthFirstEnumeration(), which recursively enumerate the children of a node in breadth-first or depth-first order, respectively. See also DefaultTreeModel, the class with which DefaultMutableTreeNode is designed to work.

```
public class DefaultMutableTreeNode implements Cloneable, MutableTreeNode, Serializable {
// Public Constructors
    public DefaultMutableTreeNode();
    public DefaultMutableTreeNode(Object userObject);
    public DefaultMutableTreeNode(Object userObject, boolean allowsChildren);
// Public Constants
    public static final java.util.Enumeration EMPTY_ENUMERATION;
// Property Accessor Methods (by property name)
    public boolean getAllowsChildren();                                           Implements:TreeNode default:true
    public void setAllowsChildren(boolean allows);
    public int getChildCount();                                                   Implements:TreeNode default:0
    public int getDepth();                                                                           default:0
    public TreeNode getFirstChild();
    public DefaultMutableTreeNode getFirstLeaf();
    public TreeNode getLastChild();
    public DefaultMutableTreeNode getLastLeaf();
    public boolean isLeaf();                                                       Implements:TreeNode default:true
    public int getLeafCount();                                                                       default:1
    public int getLevel();                                                                           default:0
    public DefaultMutableTreeNode getNextLeaf();                                                      default:null
    public DefaultMutableTreeNode getNextNode();                                                      default:null
    public DefaultMutableTreeNode getNextSibling();                                                   default:null
    public TreeNode getParent();                                                  Implements:TreeNode default:null
    public void setParent(MutableTreeNode newParent);                                    Implements:MutableTreeNode
    public TreeNode[ ] getPath();
    public DefaultMutableTreeNode getPreviousLeaf();                                                  default:null
    public DefaultMutableTreeNode getPreviousNode();                                                  default:null
    public DefaultMutableTreeNode getPreviousSibling();                                               default:null
    public TreeNode getRoot();                                          default:DefaultMutableTreeNode
    public boolean isRoot();                                                                         default:true
    public int getSiblingCount();                                                                    default:1
    public Object getUserObject();                                                                   default:null
    public void setUserObject(Object userObject);                                        Implements:MutableTreeNode
    public Object[ ] getUserObjectPath();
// Public Instance Methods
    public void add(MutableTreeNode newChild);
    public java.util.Enumeration breadthFirstEnumeration();
    public java.util.Enumeration depthFirstEnumeration();
    public TreeNode getChildAfter(TreeNode aChild);
    public TreeNode getChildBefore(TreeNode aChild);
    public TreeNode getSharedAncestor(DefaultMutableTreeNode aNode);
    public boolean isNodeAncestor(TreeNode anotherNode);
    public boolean isNodeChild(TreeNode aNode);
    public boolean isNodeDescendant(DefaultMutableTreeNode anotherNode);
    public boolean isNodeRelated(DefaultMutableTreeNode aNode);
    public boolean isNodeSibling(TreeNode anotherNode);
    public java.util.Enumeration pathFromAncestorEnumeration(TreeNode ancestor);
    public java.util.Enumeration postorderEnumeration();
    public java.util.Enumeration preorderEnumeration();
    public void removeAllChildren();
// Methods Implementing MutableTreeNode
    public void insert(MutableTreeNode newChild, int childIndex);
    public void remove(MutableTreeNode aChild);
    public void remove(int childIndex);
    public void removeFromParent();
    public void setParent(MutableTreeNode newParent);
    public void setUserObject(Object userObject);
```

```
// Methods Implementing TreeNode
    public java.util.Enumeration children( );
    public boolean getAllowsChildren( );                                                    default:true
    public TreeNode getChildAt(int index);
    public int getChildCount( );                                                            default:0
    public int getIndex(TreeNode aChild);
    public TreeNode getParent( );                                                           default:null
    public boolean isLeaf( );                                                               default:true
// Public Methods Overriding Object
    public Object clone( );
    public String toString( );
// Protected Instance Methods
    protected TreeNode[ ] getPathToRoot(TreeNode aNode, int depth);
// Protected Instance Fields
    protected boolean allowsChildren;
    protected java.util.Vector children;
    protected MutableTreeNode parent;
    protected transient Object userObject;
}
```

Hierarchy: Object→ DefaultMutableTreeNode(Cloneable, MutableTreeNode(TreeNode), Serializable)

Subclasses: JTree.DynamicUtilTreeNode

Passed To: JTree.DynamicUtilTreeNode.createChildren(), DefaultMutableTreeNode.{getSharedAncestor(), isNodeDescendant(), isNodeRelated()}

Returned By: DefaultMutableTreeNode.{getFirstLeaf(), getLastLeaf(), getNextLeaf(), getNextNode(), getNextSibling(), getPreviousLeaf(), getPreviousNode(), getPreviousSibling()}

DefaultTreeCellEditor   Java 1.2

javax.swing.tree

This TreeCellEditor implementation is the default editor for editing simple tree node values. By default, it displays the standard icons for the tree node and allows the user to edit the node using a JTextField. When you create a DefaultTreeCellEditor, you supply a DefaultTreeCellRenderer and a TreeCellEditor. The DefaultTreeCellEditor combines the icon display capability of the renderer with the editing capability of the TreeCellEditor into a single functional TreeCellEditor. Often, you can use a javax.swing.DefaultCellEditor as the internal TreeCellEditor. Or, if you do not specify a TreeCellEditor, a default one that allows the user to edit text values is used. DefaultTreeCellEditor allows the user to edit a cell by triple-clicking on the node. You can change this behavior by subclassing and overriding the canEditImmediately() method.

```
public class DefaultTreeCellEditor implements java.awt.event.ActionListener, TreeCellEditor,
        javax.swing.event.TreeSelectionListener {
// Public Constructors
    public DefaultTreeCellEditor(JTree tree, DefaultTreeCellRenderer renderer);
    public DefaultTreeCellEditor(JTree tree, DefaultTreeCellRenderer renderer, TreeCellEditor editor);
// Inner Classes
    public class DefaultTextField extends JTextField;
    public class EditorContainer extends Container;
// Event Registration Methods (by event name)
    public void addCellEditorListener(javax.swing.event.CellEditorListener l);              Implements:CellEditor
    public void removeCellEditorListener(javax.swing.event.CellEditorListener l);           Implements:CellEditor
// Public Instance Methods
    public java.awt.Color getBorderSelectionColor();
    public java.awt.Font getFont();
```

```
    public void setBorderSelectionColor(java.awt.Color newColor);
    public void setFont(java.awt.Font font);
// Methods Implementing ActionListener
    public void actionPerformed(java.awt.event.ActionEvent e);
// Methods Implementing CellEditor
    public void addCellEditorListener(javax.swing.event.CellEditorListener l);
    public void cancelCellEditing();
    public Object getCellEditorValue();
    public boolean isCellEditable(java.util.EventObject event);
    public void removeCellEditorListener(javax.swing.event.CellEditorListener l);
    public boolean shouldSelectCell(java.util.EventObject event);
    public boolean stopCellEditing();
// Methods Implementing TreeCellEditor
    public Component getTreeCellEditorComponent(JTree tree, Object value, boolean isSelected,
                                    boolean expanded, boolean leaf, int row);
// Methods Implementing TreeSelectionListener
    public void valueChanged(javax.swing.event.TreeSelectionEvent e);
// Protected Instance Methods
    protected boolean canEditImmediately(java.util.EventObject event);
    protected Container createContainer();
    protected TreeCellEditor createTreeCellEditor();
    protected void determineOffset(JTree tree, Object value, boolean isSelected, boolean expanded, boolean leaf,
                                    int row);
    protected boolean inHitRegion(int x, int y);
    protected void prepareForEditing();
    protected void setTree(JTree newTree);
    protected boolean shouldStartEditingTimer(java.util.EventObject event);
    protected void startEditingTimer();
// Protected Instance Fields
    protected java.awt.Color borderSelectionColor;
    protected boolean canEdit;
    protected transient Component editingComponent;
    protected Container editingContainer;
    protected transient Icon editingIcon;
    protected java.awt.Font font;
    protected transient TreePath lastPath;
    protected transient int lastRow;
    protected transient int offset;
    protected TreeCellEditor realEditor;
    protected DefaultTreeCellRenderer renderer;
    protected transient Timer timer;
    protected transient JTree tree;
}
```

Hierarchy: Object→ DefaultTreeCellEditor(java.awt.event.ActionListener(java.util.EventListener),
TreeCellEditor(CellEditor), javax.swing.event.TreeSelectionListener(java.util.EventListener))

DefaultTreeCellEditor.DefaultTextField   Java 1.2

javax.swing.tree   *serializable accessible(text) swing component*

This class is a customized version of JTextField used by DefaultTreeCellEditor if no custom
TreeCellEditor is supplied. Applications never need to use it.

```
public class DefaultTreeCellEditor.DefaultTextField extends JTextField {
// Public Constructors
    public DefaultTextField(javax.swing.border.Border border);
// Property Accessor Methods (by property name)
    public javax.swing.border.Border getBorder();                        Overrides:JComponent
```

```
    public java.awt.Font getFont();                                                   Overrides:Component
    public java.awt.Dimension getPreferredSize();                                      Overrides:JTextField
// Protected Instance Fields
    protected javax.swing.border.Border border;
}
```

DefaultTreeCellEditor.EditorContainer   Java 1.2

javax.swing.tree   *serializable swing component*

This simple container implementation is used internally by DefaultTreeCellEditor to combine the icons of its DefaultTreeCellRenderer with the editing component of the supplied TreeCellRenderer or the default text field. Applications never need to use this class.

```
public class DefaultTreeCellEditor.EditorContainer extends Container {
// Public Constructors
    public EditorContainer();
// Property Accessor Methods (by property name)
    public java.awt.Dimension getPreferredSize();                                      Overrides:Container
// Public Instance Methods
    public void EditorContainer();
// Public Methods Overriding Container
    public void doLayout();
    public void paint(java.awt.Graphics g);
}
```

DefaultTreeCellRenderer   Java 1.2

javax.swing.tree   *serializable accessible swing component*

This JLabel subclass implements the TreeCellRenderer methods and is the default cell renderer used by JTree. It displays an icon for the node and the string that results from calling the toString() method of the node value. The various properties of this class exist primarily to allow customization of node colors and icons.

```
public class DefaultTreeCellRenderer extends JLabel implements TreeCellRenderer {
// Public Constructors
    public DefaultTreeCellRenderer();
// Property Accessor Methods (by property name)
    public java.awt.Color getBackgroundNonSelectionColor();                            default:ColorUIResource
    public void setBackgroundNonSelectionColor(java.awt.Color newColor);
    public java.awt.Color getBackgroundSelectionColor();                               default:ColorUIResource
    public void setBackgroundSelectionColor(java.awt.Color newColor);
    public java.awt.Color getBorderSelectionColor();                                   default:ColorUIResource
    public void setBorderSelectionColor(java.awt.Color newColor);
    public Icon getClosedIcon();
    public void setClosedIcon(Icon newIcon);
    public Icon getDefaultClosedIcon();
    public Icon getDefaultLeafIcon();
    public Icon getDefaultOpenIcon();
    public Icon getLeafIcon();
    public void setLeafIcon(Icon newIcon);
    public Icon getOpenIcon();
    public void setOpenIcon(Icon newIcon);
    public java.awt.Dimension getPreferredSize();                                      Overrides:JComponent
    public java.awt.Color getTextNonSelectionColor();                                  default:ColorUIResource
    public void setTextNonSelectionColor(java.awt.Color newColor);
    public java.awt.Color getTextSelectionColor();                                     default:ColorUIResource
    public void setTextSelectionColor(java.awt.Color newColor);
```

```
// Methods Implementing TreeCellRenderer
    public Component getTreeCellRendererComponent(JTree tree, Object value, boolean sel, boolean expanded,
                                                  boolean leaf, int row, boolean hasFocus);
// Public Methods Overriding JComponent
    public void paint(java.awt.Graphics g);
    public void setBackground(java.awt.Color color);
    public void setFont(java.awt.Font font);
// Protected Instance Fields
    protected java.awt.Color backgroundNonSelectionColor;
    protected java.awt.Color backgroundSelectionColor;
    protected java.awt.Color borderSelectionColor;
    protected transient Icon closedIcon;
    protected transient Icon leafIcon;
    protected transient Icon openIcon;
    protected boolean selected;
    protected java.awt.Color textNonSelectionColor;
    protected java.awt.Color textSelectionColor;
}
```

Hierarchy: Object→ Component(java.awt.image.ImageObserver, java.awt.MenuContainer, Serializable)→ Container→ JComponent(Serializable)→ JLabel(Accessible, SwingConstants)→ DefaultTreeCellRenderer(TreeCellRenderer)

Passed To: DefaultTreeCellEditor.DefaultTreeCellEditor()

Type Of: DefaultTreeCellEditor.renderer

DefaultTreeModel

Java 1.2

javax.swing.tree *serializable model*

This class implements the TreeModel interface for TreeNode or MutableTreeNode objects. When you create a DefaultTreeModel, you specify the TreeNode at the root of the tree. You also can specify how the tree distinguishes leaf nodes from nonleaf nodes. Usually, DefaultTreeModel calls the isLeaf() method of a TreeNode to determine whether it is a leaf. For the commonly used DefaultMutableTreeNode class, isLeaf() returns true if the node has no children. On the other hand, if the asksAllowsChildren property is set to true, Default-TreeModel calls the getAllowsChildren() method of a TreeNode instead.

The TreeModel interface allows registration of javax.swing.event.TreeModelListener objects that are notified when the tree data or structure is changed. DefaultTreeModel provides a number of methods that make this notification simple. If you modify any of the TreeNode objects contained within a DefaultTreeModel after that model is in use, call one of the methods beginning with node or nodes. These methods send out the appropriate javax.swing.event.TreeModelEvent notifications. If your modifications consist solely of inserting and removing nodes, you can use insertNodeInto() and removeNodeFromParent(). These methods make the appropriate modifications to the specified MutableTreeNode objects and also send out notification events.

```
public class DefaultTreeModel implements Serializable, TreeModel {
// Public Constructors
    public DefaultTreeModel(TreeNode root);
    public DefaultTreeModel(TreeNode root, boolean asksAllowsChildren);
// Event Registration Methods (by event name)
    public void addTreeModelListener(javax.swing.event.TreeModelListener l);        Implements:TreeModel
    public void removeTreeModelListener(javax.swing.event.TreeModelListener l);     Implements:TreeModel
// Public Instance Methods
    public boolean asksAllowsChildren();
    public TreeNode[] getPathToRoot(TreeNode aNode);
```

```
    public void insertNodeInto(MutableTreeNode newChild, MutableTreeNode parent, int index);
    public void nodeChanged(TreeNode node);
    public void nodesChanged(TreeNode node, int[ ] childIndices);
    public void nodeStructureChanged(TreeNode node);
    public void nodesWereInserted(TreeNode node, int[ ] childIndices);
    public void nodesWereRemoved(TreeNode node, int[ ] childIndices, Object[ ] removedChildren);
    public void reload( );
    public void reload(TreeNode node);
    public void removeNodeFromParent(MutableTreeNode node);
    public void setAsksAllowsChildren(boolean newValue);
    public void setRoot(TreeNode root);
// Methods Implementing TreeModel
    public void addTreeModelListener(javax.swing.event.TreeModelListener l);
    public Object getChild(Object parent, int index);
    public int getChildCount(Object parent);
    public int getIndexOfChild(Object parent, Object child);
    public Object getRoot( );
    public boolean isLeaf(Object node);
    public void removeTreeModelListener(javax.swing.event.TreeModelListener l);
    public void valueForPathChanged(TreePath path, Object newValue);
// Protected Instance Methods
    protected void fireTreeNodesChanged(Object source, Object[ ] path, int[ ] childIndices, Object[ ] children);
    protected void fireTreeNodesInserted(Object source, Object[ ] path, int[ ] childIndices, Object[ ] children);
    protected void fireTreeNodesRemoved(Object source, Object[ ] path, int[ ] childIndices, Object[ ] children);
    protected void fireTreeStructureChanged(Object source, Object[ ] path, int[ ] childIndices, Object[ ] children);
    protected TreeNode[ ] getPathToRoot(TreeNode aNode, int depth);
// Protected Instance Fields
    protected boolean asksAllowsChildren;
    protected javax.swing.event.EventListenerList listenerList;
    protected TreeNode root;
}
```

Hierarchy: Object → DefaultTreeModel(Serializable, TreeModel)

DefaultTreeSelectionModel

Java 1.2

javax.swing.tree

cloneable serializable model

This class is used by default to maintain the selection state for the JTree component. Methods such as addSelectionPaths(), removeSelectionPaths(), setSelectionPaths(), getSelection-Paths(), clearSelection(), isPathSelected(), and isSelectionEmpty() can be used to manipulate and query the selection state. However, application programmers generally call similarly named methods of JTree, rather than interacting with the DefaultTreeSelectionModel directly. setSelectionMode() is an important method that does not have a JTree analog. Its argument should be one of the three constants defined by the TreeSelectionModel interface. These three constants allow a single item to be selected, a single contiguous range of items to be selected, or any number of possibly discontiguous items to be selected. DefaultTreeSelectionModel has methods for setting and querying the selection in terms of rows. These methods are intended for internal use by JTree and its UI delegate object. They typically are not useful to application programmers.

```
public class DefaultTreeSelectionModel implements Cloneable, Serializable, TreeSelectionModel {
// Public Constructors
    public DefaultTreeSelectionModel( );
// Public Constants
    public static final String SELECTION_MODE_PROPERTY;                          ="selectionMode"
// Event Registration Methods (by event name)
    public void addPropertyChangeListener(                        Implements:TreeSelectionModel synchronized
                              java.beans.PropertyChangeListener listener);
```

```
    public void removePropertyChangeListener(                        Implements:TreeSelectionModel synchronized
                                    java.beans.PropertyChangeListener listener);
    public void addTreeSelectionListener(                                    Implements:TreeSelectionModel
                            javax.swing.event.TreeSelectionListener x);
    public void removeTreeSelectionListener(                                 Implements:TreeSelectionModel
                            javax.swing.event.TreeSelectionListener x);
// Methods Implementing TreeSelectionModel
    public void addPropertyChangeListener(java.beans.PropertyChangeListener listener);              synchronized
    public void addSelectionPath(TreePath path);
    public void addSelectionPaths(TreePath[ ] paths);
    public void addTreeSelectionListener(javax.swing.event.TreeSelectionListener x);
    public void clearSelection();
    public TreePath getLeadSelectionPath();                                              default:null
    public int getLeadSelectionRow();                                                    default:-1
    public int getMaxSelectionRow();                                                     default:-1
    public int getMinSelectionRow();                                                     default:-1
    public RowMapper getRowMapper();                                                     default:null
    public int getSelectionCount();                                                      default:0
    public int getSelectionMode();                                                       default:4
    public TreePath getSelectionPath();                                                  default:null
    public TreePath[ ] getSelectionPaths();                                              default:null
    public int[ ] getSelectionRows();                                                    default:null
    public boolean isPathSelected(TreePath path);
    public boolean isRowSelected(int row);
    public boolean isSelectionEmpty();                                                   default:true
    public void removePropertyChangeListener(java.beans.PropertyChangeListener listener);         synchronized
    public void removeSelectionPath(TreePath path);
    public void removeSelectionPaths(TreePath[ ] paths);
    public void removeTreeSelectionListener(javax.swing.event.TreeSelectionListener x);
    public void resetRowSelection();
    public void setRowMapper(RowMapper newMapper);
    public void setSelectionMode(int mode);
    public void setSelectionPath(TreePath path);
    public void setSelectionPaths(TreePath[ ] pPaths);
// Public Methods Overriding Object
    public Object clone() throws CloneNotSupportedException;
    public String toString();
// Protected Instance Methods
    protected boolean arePathsContiguous(TreePath[ ] paths);
    protected boolean canPathsBeAdded(TreePath[ ] paths);
    protected boolean canPathsBeRemoved(TreePath[ ] paths);
    protected void fireValueChanged(javax.swing.event.TreeSelectionEvent e);
    protected void insureRowContinuity();
    protected void insureUniqueness();
    protected void notifyPathChange(java.util.Vector changedPaths, TreePath oldLeadSelection);
    protected void updateLeadIndex();
// Protected Instance Fields
    protected javax.swing.event.SwingPropertyChangeSupport changeSupport;
    protected int leadIndex;
    protected TreePath leadPath;
    protected int leadRow;
    protected javax.swing.event.EventListenerList listenerList;
    protected DefaultListSelectionModel listSelectionModel;
    protected transient RowMapper rowMapper;
    protected TreePath[ ] selection;
    protected int selectionMode;
}
```

Hierarchy: Object→ DefaultTreeSelectionModel(Cloneable, Serializable, TreeSelectionModel)

Subclasses: JTree.EmptySelectionModel

ExpandVetoException

Java 1.2

javax.swing.tree

serializable checked

Thrown by one of the methods of a TreeWillExpandListener object to veto a proposed expansion or collapse of a node.

```
public class ExpandVetoException extends Exception {
// Public Constructors
    public ExpandVetoException(javax.swing.event.TreeExpansionEvent event);
    public ExpandVetoException(javax.swing.event.TreeExpansionEvent event, String message);
// Protected Instance Fields
    protected javax.swing.event.TreeExpansionEvent event;
}
```

Hierarchy: Object→ Throwable(Serializable)→ Exception→ ExpandVetoException

Thrown By: JTree.{fireTreeWillCollapse(), fireTreeWillExpand()},
javax.swing.event.TreeWillExpandListener.{treeWillCollapse(), treeWillExpand()}

FixedHeightLayoutCache

Java 1.2

javax.swing.tree

This class caches the layout of nodes in a JTree. It makes the simplifying assumption that all nodes in the tree have the same height. This class is used by the JTree UI delegate; applications never need to use it.

```
public class FixedHeightLayoutCache extends AbstractLayoutCache {
// Public Constructors
    public FixedHeightLayoutCache();
// Public Methods Overriding AbstractLayoutCache
    public java.awt.Rectangle getBounds(TreePath path, java.awt.Rectangle placeIn);
    public boolean getExpandedState(TreePath path);
    public int getRowCount();                                                            default:0
    public TreePath getPathClosestTo(int x, int y);
    public TreePath getPathForRow(int row);
    public int getRowForPath(TreePath path);
    public int getVisibleChildCount(TreePath path);
    public java.util.Enumeration getVisiblePathsFrom(TreePath path);
    public void invalidatePathBounds(TreePath path);                                      empty
    public void invalidateSizes();
    public boolean isExpanded(TreePath path);
    public void setExpandedState(TreePath path, boolean isExpanded);
    public void setModel(TreeModel newModel);
    public void setRootVisible(boolean rootVisible);
    public void setRowHeight(int rowHeight);
    public void treeNodesChanged(javax.swing.event.TreeModelEvent e);
    public void treeNodesInserted(javax.swing.event.TreeModelEvent e);
    public void treeNodesRemoved(javax.swing.event.TreeModelEvent e);
    public void treeStructureChanged(javax.swing.event.TreeModelEvent e);
}
```

Hierarchy: Object→ AbstractLayoutCache(RowMapper)→ FixedHeightLayoutCache

MutableTreeNode
Java 1.2

javax.swing.tree

This interface extends TreeNode and adds methods for inserting and removing children of a node and for setting the parent of a node. Additionally, it defines a method for associating an arbitrary object with a node. This user object is the data associated with the node, data that is displayed in some way by the JTree component.

```
public abstract interface MutableTreeNode extends TreeNode {
// Public Instance Methods
    public abstract void insert(MutableTreeNode child, int index);
    public abstract void remove(MutableTreeNode node);
    public abstract void remove(int index);
    public abstract void removeFromParent();
    public abstract void setParent(MutableTreeNode newParent);
    public abstract void setUserObject(Object object);
}
```

Hierarchy: (MutableTreeNode(TreeNode))

Implementations: DefaultMutableTreeNode

Passed To: DefaultMutableTreeNode.{add(), insert(), remove(), setParent()}, DefaultTreeModel.{insertNodeInto(), removeNodeFromParent()}, MutableTreeNode.{insert(), remove(), setParent()}

Type Of: DefaultMutableTreeNode.parent

RowMapper
Java 1.2

javax.swing.tree

This interface defines a method that maps from TreePath nodes in a JTree to numerical rows in the tree presentation. Because the arrangement of items in a tree is specific to the look-and-feel, RowMapper implementations are private to the look-and-feel. Application programmers never have to use or implement this interface.

```
public abstract interface RowMapper {
// Public Instance Methods
    public abstract int[ ] getRowsForPaths(TreePath[ ] path);
}
```

Implementations: AbstractLayoutCache

Passed To: DefaultTreeSelectionModel.setRowMapper(), TreeSelectionModel.setRowMapper()

Returned By: DefaultTreeSelectionModel.getRowMapper(), TreeSelectionModel.getRowMapper()

Type Of: DefaultTreeSelectionModel.rowMapper

TreeCellEditor
Java 1.2

javax.swing.tree

This interface extends the javax.swing.CellEditor interface to make it specific to the JTree component. getTreeCellEditorComponent() should initialize and return a shared component or container (typically a JComponent) that is to be used for editing the value of a tree node. The second argument to getTreeCellEditorComponent() is the tree node that is to be edited. If you use the DefaultTreeModel, this argument is a TreeNode. Note that this argument is the node itself, *not* the user object associated with the TreeNode. The additional arguments passed to getTreeCellEditorComponent() can be used to further configure the cell editor component, as desired. A TreeCellEditor must also implement all the methods defined by CellEditor, and it must correctly implement the protocol for communication between a JComponent and its cell editor. Most importantly, it must generate a javax.swing.event.ChangeEvent when editing is done.

```
public abstract interface TreeCellEditor extends CellEditor {
// Public Instance Methods
    public abstract Component getTreeCellEditorComponent(JTree tree, Object value, boolean isSelected,
                                                          boolean expanded, boolean leaf, int row);
}
```

Hierarchy: (TreeCellEditor(CellEditor))

Implementations: DefaultCellEditor, DefaultTreeCellEditor

Passed To: JTree.setCellEditor(), DefaultTreeCellEditor.DefaultTreeCellEditor()

Returned By: JTree.getCellEditor(), DefaultTreeCellEditor.createTreeCellEditor()

Type Of: JTree.cellEditor, DefaultTreeCellEditor.realEditor

TreeCellRenderer
Java 1.2

javax.swing.tree

This interface defines the getTreeCellRendererComponent() method, which is responsible for returning a component (typically a JComponent) that is fully configured to render a node of a JTree. JTree uses a default TreeCellRenderer that is suitable in most situations. If you want custom rendering of tree nodes, however, you must implement this interface. The second argument to getTreeCellRendererComponent() is the node to be rendered. If you use the DefaultTreeModel, this argument is a TreeNode object. Note that it is *not* the user object associated with a TreeNode. The remaining arguments specify other information about the node. The renderer may choose to use this information in its rendering of the cell or not. The renderer is responsible for highlighting any selected nodes and for drawing any icons or other desired graphics that distinguish leaf nodes from branch nodes.

```
public abstract interface TreeCellRenderer {
// Public Instance Methods
    public abstract Component getTreeCellRendererComponent(JTree tree, Object value, boolean selected,
                                                            boolean expanded, boolean leaf, int row,
                                                            boolean hasFocus);
}
```

Implementations: DefaultTreeCellRenderer

Passed To: JTree.setCellRenderer()

Returned By: JTree.getCellRenderer()

Type Of: JTree.cellRenderer

TreeModel
Java 1.2

javax.swing.tree
model

This interface defines the methods necessary to represent a tree of objects for display in a JTree component. getRoot() returns the object at the root of the tree. getChildCount() returns the number of children a tree node has. getChild() returns a specified child of a node. The poorly named valueForPathChanged() method sets the data value associated with a node identified by a TreePath object. When this method is called, a TreeModel should generate a javax.swing.event.TreeModelEvent and notify all registered javax.swing.event.TreeModelListener objects by invoking their treeNodesChanged() methods.

When working with objects that have an implicit tree hierarchy, such as java.io.File objects, you can directly implement TreeModel to encapsulate the details of that tree hierarchy. In other cases, it is usually easier to use the DefaultTreeModel class, which implements the TreeModel interface for TreeNode objects.

```
public abstract interface TreeModel {
// Event Registration Methods (by event name)
    public abstract void addTreeModelListener(javax.swing.event.TreeModelListener l);
    public abstract void removeTreeModelListener(javax.swing.event.TreeModelListener l);
// Public Instance Methods
    public abstract Object getChild(Object parent, int index);
    public abstract int getChildCount(Object parent);
    public abstract int getIndexOfChild(Object parent, Object child);
    public abstract Object getRoot();
    public abstract boolean isLeaf(Object node);
    public abstract void valueForPathChanged(TreePath path, Object newValue);
}
```

Implementations: DefaultTreeModel

Passed To: JTree.{JTree(), setModel()}, AbstractLayoutCache.setModel(), FixedHeightLayoutCache.setModel(), VariableHeightLayoutCache.setModel()

Returned By: JTree.{createTreeModel(), getDefaultTreeModel(), getModel()}, AbstractLayoutCache.getModel()

Type Of: JTree.treeModel, AbstractLayoutCache.treeModel

TreeNode   Java 1.2
javax.swing.tree

This interface is used by DefaultTreeModel to represent one node in a tree. Implementations must be able both to return the parent and the children, if any, of a node, and to distinguish between leaf nodes and branch nodes in the tree. Any useful implementation must also associate some kind of data with each node. Note that the TreeNode interface is used by DefaultTreeModel, not by TreeModel or by the JTree component. If you write your own implementation of TreeModel, you do not have to use the TreeNode interface. See also MutableTreeNode and DefaultMutableTreeNode.

```
public abstract interface TreeNode {
// Property Accessor Methods (by property name)
    public abstract boolean getAllowsChildren();
    public abstract int getChildCount();
    public abstract boolean isLeaf();
    public abstract TreeNode getParent();
// Public Instance Methods
    public abstract java.util.Enumeration children();
    public abstract TreeNode getChildAt(int childIndex);
    public abstract int getIndex(TreeNode node);
}
```

Implementations: javax.swing.text.AbstractDocument.AbstractElement, MutableTreeNode

Passed To: Too many methods to list.

Returned By: Too many methods to list.

Type Of: DefaultTreeModel.root

TreePath   Java 1.2
javax.swing.tree   *serializable*

This class represents a node in a tree and the path of nodes between that node and the root of the tree. The TreeModel interface does not contain methods for querying the parent of a given node. Therefore, the JTree component and its related classes rely on TreePath to encapsulate the list of ancestors of a node. getLastPathComponent() returns the node represented by the path. getPath() returns an array of objects that represents the complete path. The first element in the array is the root of the tree, and the last element is the node returned by getLastPathComponent(). isDescendant() tests whether a TreePath is a descendant of this one.

```
public class TreePath implements Serializable {
// Public Constructors
    public TreePath(Object singlePath);
    public TreePath(Object[ ] path);
// Protected Constructors
    protected TreePath();
    protected TreePath(Object[ ] path, int length);
    protected TreePath(TreePath parent, Object lastElement);
// Property Accessor Methods (by property name)
    public Object getLastPathComponent();
    public TreePath getParentPath();
    public Object[ ] getPath();
    public int getPathCount();
// Public Instance Methods
    public Object getPathComponent(int element);
    public boolean isDescendant(TreePath aTreePath);
    public TreePath pathByAddingChild(Object child);
// Public Methods Overriding Object
    public boolean equals(Object o);
    public int hashCode();
    public String toString();
}
```

Hierarchy: Object→ TreePath(Serializable)

Passed To: Too many methods to list.

Returned By: Too many methods to list.

Type Of: javax.swing.event.TreeExpansionEvent.path, javax.swing.event.TreeModelEvent.path, javax.swing.event.TreeSelectionEvent.{newLeadSelectionPath, oldLeadSelectionPath, paths}, DefaultTreeCellEditor.lastPath, DefaultTreeSelectionModel.{leadPath, selection}

TreeSelectionModel   Java 1.2

javax.swing.tree   *model*

This interface defines the methods that must be implemented for an object to maintain the selection state of a JTree component. See the DefaultTreeSelectionModel implementation for details.

```
public abstract interface TreeSelectionModel {
// Public Constants
    public static final int CONTIGUOUS_TREE_SELECTION;                        =2
    public static final int DISCONTIGUOUS_TREE_SELECTION;                     =4
    public static final int SINGLE_TREE_SELECTION;                            =1
// Event Registration Methods (by event name)
    public abstract void addPropertyChangeListener(java.beans.PropertyChangeListener listener);
    public abstract void removePropertyChangeListener(java.beans.PropertyChangeListener listener);
    public abstract void addTreeSelectionListener(javax.swing.event.TreeSelectionListener x);
    public abstract void removeTreeSelectionListener(javax.swing.event.TreeSelectionListener x);
// Property Accessor Methods (by property name)
    public abstract TreePath getLeadSelectionPath();
    public abstract int getLeadSelectionRow();
```

```
    public abstract int getMaxSelectionRow();
    public abstract int getMinSelectionRow();
    public abstract RowMapper getRowMapper();
    public abstract void setRowMapper(RowMapper newMapper);
    public abstract int getSelectionCount();
    public abstract boolean isSelectionEmpty();
    public abstract int getSelectionMode();
    public abstract void setSelectionMode(int mode);
    public abstract TreePath getSelectionPath();
    public abstract void setSelectionPath(TreePath path);
    public abstract TreePath[ ] getSelectionPaths();
    public abstract void setSelectionPaths(TreePath[ ] paths);
    public abstract int[ ] getSelectionRows();
// Public Instance Methods
    public abstract void addSelectionPath(TreePath path);
    public abstract void addSelectionPaths(TreePath[ ] paths);
    public abstract void clearSelection();
    public abstract boolean isPathSelected(TreePath path);
    public abstract boolean isRowSelected(int row);
    public abstract void removeSelectionPath(TreePath path);
    public abstract void removeSelectionPaths(TreePath[ ] paths);
    public abstract void resetRowSelection();
}
```

Implementations: DefaultTreeSelectionModel

Passed To: JTree.setSelectionModel(), AbstractLayoutCache.setSelectionModel()

Returned By: JTree.getSelectionModel(), AbstractLayoutCache.getSelectionModel()

Type Of: JTree.selectionModel, AbstractLayoutCache.treeSelectionModel

VariableHeightLayoutCache   Java 1.2

javax.swing.tree

This class caches the layout of nodes in a JTree. It allows tree nodes to have variable heights. This class is used by the JTree UI delegate; applications never need to use it.

```
public class VariableHeightLayoutCache extends AbstractLayoutCache {
// Public Constructors
    public VariableHeightLayoutCache();
// Public Methods Overriding AbstractLayoutCache
    public java.awt.Rectangle getBounds(TreePath path, java.awt.Rectangle placeIn);
    public boolean getExpandedState(TreePath path);
    public TreePath getPathClosestTo(int x, int y);
    public TreePath getPathForRow(int row);
    public int getPreferredWidth(java.awt.Rectangle bounds);
    public int getRowCount();                                                    default:0
    public int getRowForPath(TreePath path);
    public int getVisibleChildCount(TreePath path);
    public java.util.Enumeration getVisiblePathsFrom(TreePath path);
    public void invalidatePathBounds(TreePath path);
    public void invalidateSizes();
    public boolean isExpanded(TreePath path);
    public void setExpandedState(TreePath path, boolean isExpanded);
    public void setModel(TreeModel newModel);                                       bound
    public void setNodeDimensions(AbstractLayoutCache.NodeDimensions nd);
    public void setRootVisible(boolean rootVisible);                                bound
    public void setRowHeight(int rowHeight);                                        bound
    public void treeNodesChanged(javax.swing.event.TreeModelEvent e);
```

javax.swing.tree

```
    public void treeNodesInserted(javax.swing.event.TreeModelEvent e);
    public void treeNodesRemoved(javax.swing.event.TreeModelEvent e);
    public void treeStructureChanged(javax.swing.event.TreeModelEvent e);
}
```

Hierarchy: Object→ AbstractLayoutCache(RowMapper)→ VariableHeightLayoutCache

CHAPTER 35

The javax.swing.undo Package

The classes and interfaces in this package form the undo framework for Swing applications. The **UndoManager** manages a list of **UndoableEdit** objects, each of which can be individually undone or redone. Any Swing application that wants to provide an undo capability will find this package useful. Figure 35-1 shows the class hierarchy of this package.

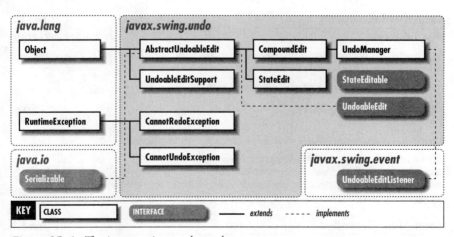

Figure 35-1: The javax.swing.undo package

AbstractUndoableEdit

Java 1.2

javax.swing.undo

serializable

This class is a simple implementation of **UndoableEdit**. It enforces the restriction that an edit cannot be undone twice or redone without first being undone. Although the undo() and redo() methods do not actually undo or redo anything, subclasses should still call super.undo() and super.redo() in order to retain these restrictions. addEdit() and replaceEdit() return false; this implementation makes no attempt to merge events. getUndoPresentation-Name() and getRedoPresentationName() return the strings "Undo" and "Redo", followed by the string returned from getPresentationName(). Therefore, typical subclasses only need to override getPresentationName().

```
public class AbstractUndoableEdit implements Serializable, UndoableEdit {
// Public Constructors
    public AbstractUndoableEdit();
// Protected Constants
    protected static final String RedoName;                                        ="Redo"
    protected static final String UndoName;                                        ="Undo"
// Methods Implementing UndoableEdit
    public boolean addEdit(UndoableEdit anEdit);                                   constant
    public boolean canRedo();
    public boolean canUndo();
    public void die();
    public String getPresentationName();                                       default:""
    public String getRedoPresentationName();                               default:"Redo"
    public String getUndoPresentationName();                               default:"Undo"
    public boolean isSignificant();                                constant default:true
    public void redo() throws CannotRedoException;
    public boolean replaceEdit(UndoableEdit anEdit);                              constant
    public void undo() throws CannotUndoException;
// Public Methods Overriding Object
    public String toString();
}
```

Hierarchy: Object→ AbstractUndoableEdit(Serializable, UndoableEdit)

Subclasses: javax.swing.text.AbstractDocument.ElementEdit,
javax.swing.text.DefaultStyledDocument.AttributeUndoableEdit, CompoundEdit, StateEdit

CannotRedoException   Java 1.2

javax.swing.undo   *serializable unchecked*

Signals that an UndoableEdit cannot be redone, perhaps because it has not been undone yet or because it has already been redone.

```
public class CannotRedoException extends RuntimeException {
// Public Constructors
    public CannotRedoException();
}
```

Hierarchy: Object→ Throwable(Serializable)→ Exception→ RuntimeException→ CannotRedoException

Thrown By: javax.swing.text.AbstractDocument.DefaultDocumentEvent.redo(),
javax.swing.text.AbstractDocument.ElementEdit.redo(),
javax.swing.text.DefaultStyledDocument.AttributeUndoableEdit.redo(), AbstractUndoableEdit.redo(),
CompoundEdit.redo(), UndoableEdit.redo(), UndoManager.{redo(), redoTo(), undoOrRedo()}

CannotUndoException   Java 1.2

javax.swing.undo   *serializable unchecked*

Signals that an UndoableEdit cannot be undone, perhaps because it has already been undone.

```
public class CannotUndoException extends RuntimeException {
// Public Constructors
    public CannotUndoException();
}
```

Hierarchy: Object→ Throwable(Serializable)→ Exception→ RuntimeException→ CannotUndoException

Thrown By: javax.swing.text.AbstractDocument.DefaultDocumentEvent.undo(),
javax.swing.text.AbstractDocument.ElementEdit.undo(),
javax.swing.text.DefaultStyledDocument.AttributeUndoableEdit.undo(), AbstractUndoableEdit.undo(),
CompoundEdit.undo(), UndoableEdit.undo(), UndoManager.{undo(), undoOrRedo(), undoTo()}

CompoundEdit

Java 1.2

javax.swing.undo   *serializable*

This class is a compound UndoableEdit that collects a group of UndoableEdit objects into a
single object and allows them to be undone and redone as a group. After creating a
CompoundEdit object, you use addEdit() to add UndoableEdit objects to it. When you are
done adding edits, call end(). Once end() has been called, you can freely use the undo()
and redo() methods. The isInProgress() method returns true if end() has not been called yet
and edits are still being added. While CompoundEdit maintains a list of UndoableEdit
objects to undo and redo, the addEdit() method does not simply add edits to this list.
When a new edit is added, CompoundEdit first attempts to merge it with the previously
added edit by calling the addEdit() and replaceEdit() methods of the individual UndoableEdit
objects. If these methods fail to merge the two edits into one, the new edit is added to
the list of edits. The isSignificant() method returns true if any of the edits on the list of
edits is significant and returns false otherwise. getPresentationName() returns the name of
the last edit on the list, if it has one.

```
public class CompoundEdit extends AbstractUndoableEdit {
// Public Constructors
    public CompoundEdit();
// Public Instance Methods
    public void end();
    public boolean isInProgress();                                              default:true
// Public Methods Overriding AbstractUndoableEdit
    public boolean addEdit(UndoableEdit anEdit);
    public boolean canRedo();
    public boolean canUndo();
    public void die();
    public String getPresentationName();                                        default:""
    public String getRedoPresentationName();                                    default:"Redo"
    public String getUndoPresentationName();                                    default:"Undo"
    public boolean isSignificant();                                             default:false
    public void redo() throws CannotRedoException;
    public String toString();
    public void undo() throws CannotUndoException;
// Protected Instance Methods
    protected UndoableEdit lastEdit();
// Protected Instance Fields
    protected java.util.Vector edits;
}
```

Hierarchy: Object→ AbstractUndoableEdit(Serializable, UndoableEdit)→ CompoundEdit

Subclasses: javax.swing.text.AbstractDocument.DefaultDocumentEvent, UndoManager

Returned By: UndoableEditSupport.createCompoundEdit()

Type Of: UndoableEditSupport.compoundEdit

StateEdit
javax.swing.undo

This class is an UndoableEdit implementation that works with StateEditable objects. First, create a StateEcit object, passing the StateEditable object to be edited to the constructor (and optionally specifying a presentation name for the StateEdit). The constructor queries the initial state of the StateEditable object and saves it. Next, make your edits to the StateEditable object and then call the end() method on your StateEdit object. This method queries the edited state of the object and saves that state. StateEdit implements the undo() method by restoring the saved preedit state and implements the redo() method by restoring the saved postedit state. For efficiency, StateEdit removes duplicate state entries from the preedit and postedit hashtables, so only the state that changes is saved.

```
public class StateEdit extends AbstractUndoableEdit {
// Public Constructors
    public StateEdit(StateEditable anObject);
    public StateEdit(StateEditable anObject, String name);
// Protected Constants
    protected static final String RCSID;
// Public Instance Methods
    public void end();
// Public Methods Overriding AbstractUndoableEdit
    public String getPresentationName();
    public void redo();
    public void undo();
// Protected Instance Methods
    protected void init(StateEditable anObject, String name);
    protected void removeRedundantState();
// Protected Instance Fields
    protected StateEditable object;
    protected java.util.Hashtable postState;
    protected java.util.Hashtable preState;
    protected String undoRedoName;
}
```

Hierarchy: Object→ AbstractUndoableEdit(Serializable, UndoableEdit)→ StateEdit

StateEditable
javax.swing.undo

This interface defines methods that allow an object to save and restore its state to and from a java.util.Hashtable. Objects that are able to implement this interface can easily support undo management with the StateEdit class.

```
public abstract interface StateEditable {
// Public Constants
    public static final String RCSID;
// Public Instance Methods
    public abstract void restoreState(java.util.Hashtable state);
    public abstract void storeState(java.util.Hashtable state);
}
```

Passed To: StateEdit.{init(), StateEdit()}

Type Of: StateEdit.object

UndoableEdit

javax.swing.undo

This interface defines methods that encapsulate an undoable and redoable change to the state of an application or component. The undo() and redo() methods are the most important: they must actually undo and redo the edit. They throw exceptions if an edit is undone twice or redone twice or if for some other reason an edit cannot be undone or redone. canUndo() and canRedo() specify whether an UndoableEdit can currently be undone or redone. die() tells an edit that it is no longer needed, so it can release any resources it is holding. Neither undo() nor redo() should be called once die() has been called.

getPresentationName() returns a human-readable description of the edit. getUndoPresentationName() and getRedoPresentationName() return human-readable descriptions of undoing and redoing the edit. These two methods are usually implemented in terms of getPresentationName() and might return strings like Undo typing or Redo deletion. isSignificant() specifies whether the edit is a significant one. Typically, significant edits are presented to the user in a user interface, while insignificant edits are simply undone and redone in conjunction with adjacent significant edits. The UndoManager class treats insignificant edits in this way, for example.

addEdit() and replaceEdit() are used for merging two UndoableEdit objects into one. addEdit() is called to see if an existing UndoableEdit is willing to merge or absorb another edit into itself. For example, if the user strikes the **Backspace** key twice in a row, the UndoableEdit object generated by the first keystroke might absorb the UndoableEdit object generated by the second keystroke, changing itself from a backspace 1 edit to a backspace 2 edit. addEdit() should return true if it adds the edit and false otherwise. replaceEdit() has a similar purpose but operates in the other direction. It gives a new UndoableEdit object the opportunity to absorb and replace an existing UndoableEdit. For example, if the user of a text editor selects a paragraph of text and then deletes that paragraph, the delete-paragraph edit might simply subsume and replace the select-paragraph edit. replaceEdit() should return true if it replaces the specified UndoableEdit object.

```
public abstract interface UndoableEdit {
// Property Accessor Methods (by property name)
    public abstract String getPresentationName();
    public abstract String getRedoPresentationName();
    public abstract boolean isSignificant();
    public abstract String getUndoPresentationName();
// Public Instance Methods
    public abstract boolean addEdit(UndoableEdit anEdit);
    public abstract boolean canRedo();
    public abstract boolean canUndo();
    public abstract void die();
    public abstract void redo() throws CannotRedoException;
    public abstract boolean replaceEdit(UndoableEdit anEdit);
    public abstract void undo() throws CannotUndoException;
}
```

Implementations: AbstractUndoableEdit

Passed To: javax.swing.event.UndoableEditEvent.UndoableEditEvent(), javax.swing.text.AbstractDocument.DefaultDocumentEvent.addEdit(), AbstractUndoableEdit.{addEdit(), replaceEdit()}, CompoundEdit.addEdit(), UndoableEdit.{addEdit(), replaceEdit()}, UndoableEditSupport.{_postEdit(), postEdit()}, UndoManager.{addEdit(), redoTo(), undoTo()}

Returned By: javax.swing.event.UndoableEditEvent.getEdit(),
javax.swing.text.AbstractDocument.Content.{insertString(), remove()},
javax.swing.text.GapContent.{insertString(), remove()}, javax.swing.text.StringContent.{insertString(), remove()},
CompoundEdit.lastEdit(), UndoManager.{editToBeRedone(), editToBeUndone()}

UndoableEditSupport   Java 1.2

javax.swing.undo

This utility class is useful for classes that support undoable edits and send
javax.swing.event.UndoableEditEvent events to javax.swing.event.UndoableEditListener objects. An
object that generates undoable events must allow the registration and deregistration of
event listeners for those events. Such an object can simply create an UndoableEditSupport
object and delegate to its addUndoableEditListener() and removeUndoableEditListener() methods.

UndoableEditSupport normally sends an UndoableEditEvent to all registered listeners when
the postEdit() method is invoked. It also allows batching of edits into a CompoundEdit,
however. If beginUpdate() is called, all UndoableEdit objects passed to postEdit() are batched
into a CompoundEdit until endUpdate() is called. In this case, the UndoableEditEvent that contains the CompoundEdit is not sent to the registered UndoableEditListener objects until endUp-
date() is invoked. If beginUpdate() is called more than once, endUpdate() must be called a
matching number of times.

```
public class UndoableEditSupport {
// Public Constructors
    public UndoableEditSupport();
    public UndoableEditSupport(Object r);
// Event Registration Methods (by event name)
    public void addUndoableEditListener(javax.swing.event.UndoableEditListener l);      synchronized
    public void removeUndoableEditListener(javax.swing.event.UndoableEditListener l);   synchronized
// Public Instance Methods
    public void beginUpdate();                                                          synchronized
    public void endUpdate();                                                            synchronized
    public int getUpdateLevel();                                                          default:0
    public void postEdit(UndoableEdit e);                                               synchronized
// Public Methods Overriding Object
    public String toString();
// Protected Instance Methods
    protected void _postEdit(UndoableEdit e);
    protected CompoundEdit createCompoundEdit();
// Protected Instance Fields
    protected CompoundEdit compoundEdit;
    protected java.util.Vector listeners;
    protected Object realSource;
    protected int updateLevel;
}
```

UndoManager   Java 1.2

javax.swing.undo   *serializable*

This class maintains a list of UndoableEdit objects and allows them to be undone and
redone one significant edit at a time. Edits can be added explicitly by calling addEdit().
UndoManager implements the javax.swing.event.UndoableEditListener interface and automatically calls addEdit() to add an edit to its list when it receives a javax.swing.event.UndoableEd-
itEvent. The addEdit() method works like the addEdit() method of CompoundEdit: it first
attempts to merge the new edit with the last edit on the list by calling the addEdit() and
replaceEdit() methods of those edits. The edit is added as a separate edit only if it could
not be merged.

After an edit is made and added to the UndoManager, the undo() method undoes it. After it is undone, the redo() method redoes it. However, if a new edit is made after the first is undone, that first undone edit is removed from the list and is no longer redoable. This is the normal and expected behavior for an undo system. UndoManager distinguishes between significant and insignificant edits. When you call undo(), it undoes all edits up to the last significant edit that occurred. When you call redo(), it redoes the next significant edit and all insignificant edits that follow it. A significant UndoableEdit is one whose isSignificant() method returns true. getUndoPresentationName() returns the undo presentation name of the significant UndoableEdit that is undone by undo(). getRedoPresentationName() returns the redo presentation name of the significant UndoableEdit that is performed by the redo() action. setLimit() and getLimit() set and query the maximum number of UndoableEdit objects that the UndoManager tracks. The default is 100.

UndoManager is a subclass of CompoundEdit. If you call the end() method on an UndoManager, its behavior becomes that of a CompoundEdit and the list of edits is undone and redone all at once. This can occasionally be useful when doing nested edits.

```
public class UndoManager extends CompoundEdit implements javax.swing.event.UndoableEditListener {
// Public Constructors
    public UndoManager();
// Property Accessor Methods (by property name)
    public int getLimit();                                           synchronized default:100
    public void setLimit(int l);                                            synchronized
    public String getRedoPresentationName();          Overrides:CompoundEdit synchronized default:"Redo"
    public String getUndoOrRedoPresentationName();            synchronized default:"Undo"
    public String getUndoPresentationName();          Overrides:CompoundEdit synchronized default:"Undo"
// Public Instance Methods
    public boolean canUndoOrRedo();                                        synchronized
    public void discardAllEdits();                                         synchronized
    public void undoOrRedo() throws CannotRedoException, CannotUndoException;   synchronized
// Methods Implementing UndoableEditListener
    public void undoableEditHappened(javax.swing.event.UndoableEditEvent e);
// Public Methods Overriding CompoundEdit
    public boolean addEdit(UndoableEdit anEdit);                            synchronized
    public boolean canRedo();                                              synchronized
    public boolean canUndo();                                              synchronized
    public void end();                                                     synchronized
    public void redo() throws CannotRedoException;                         synchronized
    public String toString();
    public void undo() throws CannotUndoException;                         synchronized
// Protected Instance Methods
    protected UndoableEdit editToBeRedone();
    protected UndoableEdit editToBeUndone();
    protected void redoTo(UndoableEdit edit) throws CannotRedoException;
    protected void trimEdits(int from, int to);
    protected void trimForLimit();
    protected void undoTo(UndoableEdit edit) throws CannotUndoException;
}
```

Hierarchy: Object→ AbstractUndoableEdit(Serializable, UndoableEdit)→ CompoundEdit→ UndoManager(javax.swing.event.UndoableEditListener(java.util.EventListener))

CHAPTER 36

Class Index

The following index allows you to look up a class of interface and find what package it is defined in. Use it when you want to look up a class but don't know its package.

AccessibleJEditorPane: javax.swing.JEditorPane
AccessibleJEditorPaneHTML: javax.swing.JEditorPane
AccessibleJFileChooser: javax.swing.JFileChooser
AccessibleJFrame: javax.swing.JFrame
AccessibleJInternalFrame: javax.swing.JInternalFrame
AccessibleJLabel: javax.swing.JLabel
AccessibleJLayeredPane: javax.swing.JLayeredPane
AccessibleJList: javax.swing.JList
AccessibleJListChild: javax.swing.JList.AccessibleJList
AccessibleJMenu: javax.swing.JMenu
AccessibleJMenuBar: javax.swing.JMenuBar
AccessibleJMenuItem: javax.swing.JMenuItem
AccessibleJOptionPane: javax.swing.JOptionPane
AccessibleJPanel: javax.swing.JPanel
AccessibleJPasswordField: javax.swing.JPassword-
Field
AccessibleJPopupMenu: javax.swing.JPopupMenu
AccessibleJProgressBar: javax.swing.JProgressBar
AccessibleJRadioButton: javax.swing.JRadioButton
AccessibleJRadioButtonMenuItem: javax.swing.JRa-
dioButtonMenuItem
AccessibleJRootPane: javax.swing.JRootPane
AccessibleJScrollBar: javax.swing.JScrollBar
AccessibleJScrollPane: javax.swing.JScrollPane
AccessibleJSeparator: javax.swing.JSeparator
AccessibleJSlider: javax.swing.JSlider
AccessibleJSplitPane: javax.swing.JSplitPane
AccessibleJTabbedPane: javax.swing.JTabbedPane
AccessibleJTable: javax.swing.JTable
AccessibleJTableCell: javax.swing.JTable.Accessible-
JTable
AccessibleJTableHeader: javax.swing.table.JTable-
Header
AccessibleJTableHeaderEntry:
javax.swing.table.JTableHeader.AccessibleJTable-
Header
AccessibleJTextArea: javax.swing.JTextArea
AccessibleJTextComponent:
javax.swing.text.JTextComponent
AccessibleJTextField: javax.swing.JTextField
AccessibleJToggleButton: javax.swing.JToggleButton
AccessibleJToolBar: javax.swing.JToolBar
AccessibleJToolTip: javax.swing.JToolTip
AccessibleJTree: javax.swing.JTree
AccessibleJTreeNode: javax.swing.JTree.Accessible-
JTree
AccessibleJViewport: javax.swing.JViewport
AccessibleJWindow: javax.swing.JWindow
AccessibleResourceBundle: javax.accessibility
AccessibleRole: javax.accessibility

AccessibleSelection: javax.accessibility
AccessibleState: javax.accessibility
AccessibleStateSet: javax.accessibility
AccessibleText: javax.accessibility
AccessibleValue: javax.accessibility
AccessibleWindowPopup: javax.swing.JPopup-
Menu.WindowPopup
Action: javax.swing
ActionEvent: java.awt.event
ActionListener: java.awt.event
ActiveEvent: java.awt
ActiveValue: javax.swing.UIDefaults
Adjustable: java.awt
AdjustmentEvent: java.awt.event
AdjustmentListener: java.awt.event
AffineTransform: java.awt.geom
AffineTransformOp: java.awt.image
AlignmentAction: javax.swing.text.StyledEditorKit
AlphaComposite: java.awt
AncestorEvent: javax.swing.event
AncestorListener: javax.swing.event
Applet: java.applet
AppletContext: java.applet
AppletStub: java.applet
Arc2D: java.awt.geom
Arc2D.Double: java.awt.geom
Arc2D.Float: java.awt.geom
Area: java.awt.geom
AreaAveragingScaleFilter: java.awt.image
Attribute: javax.swing.text.html.CSS,
javax.swing.text.html.HTML
AttributeContext: javax.swing.text.AbstractDocument
AttributeList: javax.swing.text.html.parser
AttributeSet: javax.swing.text
AttributeSet.CharacterAttribute: javax.swing.text
AttributeSet.ColorAttribute: javax.swing.text
AttributeSet.FontAttribute: javax.swing.text
AttributeSet.ParagraphAttribute: javax.swing.text
AttributeUndoableEdit: javax.swing.text.DefaultStyled-
Document
AudioClip: java.applet
Autoscroll: java.awt.dnd
AWTError: java.awt
AWTEvent: java.awt
AWTEventListener: java.awt.event
AWTEventMulticaster: java.awt
AWTException: java.awt
AWTPermission: java.awt

B

BadLocationException: javax.swing.text
BandCombineOp: java.awt.image
BandedSampleModel: java.awt.image
BasicStroke: java.awt
BeepAction: javax.swing.text.DefaultEditorKit
BevelBorder: javax.swing.border
BevelBorderUIResource: javax.swing.plaf.BorderUIResource
Bias: javax.swing.text.Position
BlockAction: javax.swing.text.html.HTMLDocument.HTMLReader
BlockElement: javax.swing.text.html.HTMLDocument
BlockView: javax.swing.text.html
BoldAction: javax.swing.text.StyledEditorKit
Book: java.awt.print
Border: javax.swing.border
BorderFactory: javax.swing
BorderLayout: java.awt
BorderUIResource: javax.swing.plaf
BorderUIResource.BevelBorderUIResource:
javax.swing.plaf
BorderUIResource.CompoundBorderUIResource:
javax.swing.plaf
BorderUIResource.EmptyBorderUIResource:
javax.swing.plaf
BorderUIResource.EtchedBorderUIResource:
javax.swing.plaf
BorderUIResource.LineBorderUIResource:
javax.swing.plaf
BorderUIResource.MatteBorderUIResource:
javax.swing.plaf
BorderUIResource.TitledBorderUIResource:
javax.swing.plaf
BoundedRangeModel: javax.swing
Box: javax.swing
Box.AccessibleBox: javax.swing
Box.Filler: javax.swing
Box.Filler.AccessibleBoxFiller: javax.swing
BoxLayout: javax.swing
BoxPainter: javax.swing.text.html.StyleSheet
BoxView: javax.swing.text
BranchElement: javax.swing.text.AbstractDocument
BufferedImage: java.awt.image
BufferedImageFilter: java.awt.image
BufferedImageOp: java.awt.image
Button: java.awt
ButtonChangeListener: javax.swing.AbstractButton
ButtonGroup: javax.swing

ButtonModel: javax.swing
ButtonPeer: java.awt.peer
ButtonUI: javax.swing.plaf
ByteLookupTable: java.awt.image

C

CannotRedoException: javax.swing.undo
CannotUndoException: javax.swing.undo
Canvas: java.awt
CanvasPeer: java.awt.peer
CardLayout: java.awt
Caret: javax.swing.text
CaretEvent: javax.swing.event
CaretListener: javax.swing.event
CaretPolicy: java.awt.font.TextLayout
CellEditor: javax.swing
CellEditorListener: javax.swing.event
CellRendererPane: javax.swing
CellRendererPane.AccessibleCellRendererPane:
javax.swing
ChangedCharSetException: javax.swing.text
ChangeEvent: javax.swing.event
ChangeListener: javax.swing.event
CharacterAction: javax.swing.text.html.HTMLDocument.HTMLReader
CharacterAttribute: javax.swing.text.AttributeSet
CharacterConstants: javax.swing.text.StyleConstants
Checkbox: java.awt
CheckboxGroup: java.awt
CheckboxMenuItem: java.awt
CheckboxMenuItemPeer: java.awt.peer
CheckboxPeer: java.awt.peer
Choice: java.awt
ChoicePeer: java.awt.peer
Clipboard: java.awt.datatransfer
ClipboardOwner: java.awt.datatransfer
CMMException: java.awt.color
Color: java.awt
ColorAttribute: javax.swing.text.AttributeSet
ColorChooserComponentFactory: javax.swing.colorchooser
ColorChooserUI: javax.swing.plaf
ColorConstants: javax.swing.text.StyleConstants
ColorConvertOp: java.awt.image
ColorModel: java.awt.image
ColorSelectionModel: javax.swing.colorchooser
ColorSpace: java.awt.color
ColorUIResource: javax.swing.plaf
ComboBoxEditor: javax.swing

Class Index

DefaultTextUI: javax.swing.text
DefaultTreeCellEditor: javax.swing.tree
DefaultTreeCellEditor.DefaultTextField:
  javax.swing.tree
DefaultTreeCellEditor.EditorContainer:
  javax.swing.tree
DefaultTreeCellRenderer: javax.swing.tree
DefaultTreeModel: javax.swing.tree
DefaultTreeSelectionModel: javax.swing.tree
DesktopIconUI: javax.swing.plaf
DesktopManager: javax.swing
DesktopPaneUI: javax.swing.plaf
Dialog: java.awt
DialogPeer: java.awt.peer
Dimension: java.awt
Dimension2D: java.awt.geom
DimensionUIResource: javax.swing.plaf
DirectColorModel: java.awt.image
DnDConstants: java.awt.dnd
Document: javax.swing.text
DocumentEvent: javax.swing.event
DocumentEvent.ElementChange: javax.swing.event
DocumentEvent.EventType: javax.swing.event
DocumentListener: javax.swing.event
DocumentParser: javax.swing.text.html.parser
Double: java.awt.geom.Arc2D, java.awt.geom.Cubic-
  Curve2D, java.awt.geom.Ellipse2D,
  java.awt.geom.Line2D, java.awt.geom.Point2D,
  java.awt.geom.QuadCurve2D, java.awt.geom.Rect-
  angle2D, java.awt.geom.RoundRectangle2D
DragGestureEvent: java.awt.dnd
DragGestureListener: java.awt.dnd
DragGestureRecognizer: java.awt.dnd
DragSource: java.awt.dnd
DragSourceContext: java.awt.dnd
DragSourceContextPeer: java.awt.dnd.peer
DragSourceDragEvent: java.awt.dnd
DragSourceDropEvent: java.awt.dnd
DragSourceEvent: java.awt.dnd
DragSourceListener: java.awt.dnd
DropTarget: java.awt.dnd
DropTarget.DropTargetAutoScroller: java.awt.dnd
DropTargetAutoScroller: java.awt.dnd.DropTarget
DropTargetContext: java.awt.dnd
DropTargetContext.TransferableProxy: java.awt.dnd
DropTargetContextPeer: java.awt.dnd.peer
DropTargetDragEvent: java.awt.dnd
DropTargetDropEvent: java.awt.dnd
DropTargetEvent: java.awt.dnd
DropTargetListener: java.awt.dnd

DropTargetPeer: java.awt.dnd.peer
DTD: javax.swing.text.html.parser
DTDConstants: javax.swing.text.html.parser
DynamicUtilTreeNode: javax.swing.JTree

E

EditorContainer: javax.swing.tree.DefaultTreeCellEdi-
  tor
EditorDelegate: javax.swing.DefaultCellEditor
EditorKit: javax.swing.text
Element: javax.swing.text, javax.swing.text.html.parser
ElementBuffer: javax.swing.text.DefaultStyledDocu-
  ment
ElementChange: javax.swing.event.DocumentEvent
ElementEdit: javax.swing.text.AbstractDocument
ElementIterator: javax.swing.text
ElementSpec: javax.swing.text.DefaultStyledDocument
Ellipse2D: java.awt.geom
Ellipse2D.Double: java.awt.geom
Ellipse2D.Float: java.awt.geom
EmptyBorder: javax.swing.border
EmptyBorderUIResource: javax.swing.plaf.Bor-
  derUIResource
EmptySelectionModel: javax.swing.JTree
Entity: javax.swing.text.html.parser
EtchedBorder: javax.swing.border
EtchedBorderUIResource: javax.swing.plaf.Bor-
  derUIResource
Event: java.awt
EventListenerList: javax.swing.event
EventQueue: java.awt
EventType: javax.swing.event.DocumentEvent,
  javax.swing.event.HyperlinkEvent
ExpandVetoException: javax.swing.tree

F

FieldView: javax.swing.text
FileChooserUI: javax.swing.plaf
FileDialog: java.awt
FileDialogPeer: java.awt.peer
FileFilter: javax.swing.filechooser
FileSystemView: javax.swing.filechooser
FileView: javax.swing.filechooser
Filler: javax.swing.Box
FilteredImageSource: java.awt.image
FixedHeightLayoutCache: javax.swing.tree
FlatteningPathIterator: java.awt.geom
FlavorMap: java.awt.datatransfer

HTMLWriter: javax.swing.text.html
HyperlinkEvent: javax.swing.event
HyperlinkEvent.EventType: javax.swing.event
HyperlinkListener: javax.swing.event

I

ICC_ColorSpace: java.awt.color
ICC_Profile: java.awt.color
ICC_ProfileGray: java.awt.color
ICC_ProfileRGB: java.awt.color
Icon: javax.swing
IconUIResource: javax.swing.plaf
IconView: javax.swing.text
IllegalComponentStateException: java.awt
IllegalPathStateException: java.awt.geom
Image: java.awt
ImageConsumer: java.awt.image
ImageFilter: java.awt.image
ImageGraphicAttribute: java.awt.font
ImageIcon: javax.swing
ImageObserver: java.awt.image
ImageProducer: java.awt.image
ImagingOpException: java.awt.image
IndexColorModel: java.awt.image
InlineView: javax.swing.text.html
InputContext: java.awt.im
InputEvent: java.awt.event
InputMethodEvent: java.awt.event
InputMethodHighlight: java.awt.im
InputMethodListener: java.awt.event
InputMethodRequests: java.awt.im
InputSubset: java.awt.im
InsertBreakAction: javax.swing.text.DefaultEditorKit
InsertContentAction: javax.swing.text.DefaultEditorKit
InsertHTMLTextAction: javax.swing.text.html.HTMLEditorKit
InsertTabAction: javax.swing.text.DefaultEditorKit
Insets: java.awt
InsetsUIResource: javax.swing.plaf
insideTimerAction: javax.swing.ToolTipManager
InternalFrameAdapter: javax.swing.event
InternalFrameEvent: javax.swing.event
InternalFrameListener: javax.swing.event
InternalFrameUI: javax.swing.plaf
InvalidDnDOperationException: java.awt.dnd
InvocationEvent: java.awt.event
IsindexAction: javax.swing.text.html.HTMLDocument.HTMLReader
ItalicAction: javax.swing.text.StyledEditorKit

ItemEvent: java.awt.event
ItemListener: java.awt.event
ItemSelectable: java.awt
Iterator: javax.swing.text.html.HTMLDocument

J

JApplet: javax.swing
JApplet.AccessibleJApplet: javax.swing
JButton: javax.swing
JButton.AccessibleJButton: javax.swing
JCheckBox: javax.swing
JCheckBox.AccessibleJCheckBox: javax.swing
JCheckBoxMenuItem: javax.swing
JCheckBoxMenuItem.AccessibleJCheckBoxMenuItem: javax.swing
JColorChooser: javax.swing
JColorChooser.AccessibleJColorChooser: javax.swing
JComboBox: javax.swing
JComboBox.AccessibleJComboBox: javax.swing
JComboBox.KeySelectionManager: javax.swing
JComponent: javax.swing
JComponent.AccessibleJComponent: javax.swing
JComponent.AccessibleJComponent.AccessibleContainerHandler: javax.swing
JDesktopIcon: javax.swing.JInternalFrame
JDesktopPane: javax.swing
JDesktopPane.AccessibleJDesktopPane: javax.swing
JDialog: javax.swing
JDialog.AccessibleJDialog: javax.swing
JEditorPane: javax.swing
JEditorPane.AccessibleJEditorPane: javax.swing
JEditorPane.AccessibleJEditorPaneHTML: javax.swing
JEditorPane.JEditorPaneAccessibleHypertextSupport: javax.swing
JEditorPane.JEditorPaneAccessibleHypertextSupport.HTMLLink: javax.swing
JEditorPaneAccessibleHypertextSupport: javax.swing.JEditorPane
JFileChooser: javax.swing
JFileChooser.AccessibleJFileChooser: javax.swing
JFrame: javax.swing
JFrame.AccessibleJFrame: javax.swing
JInternalFrame: javax.swing
JInternalFrame.AccessibleJInternalFrame: javax.swing
JInternalFrame.JDesktopIcon: javax.swing
JInternalFrame.JDesktopIcon.AccessibleJDesktopIcon: javax.swing
JLabel: javax.swing

JLabel.AccessibleJLabel: javax.swing
JLayeredPane: javax.swing
JLayeredPane.AccessibleJLayeredPane: javax.swing
JList: javax.swing
JList.AccessibleJList: javax.swing
JList.AccessibleJList.AccessibleJListChild:
    javax.swing
JMenu: javax.swing
JMenu.AccessibleJMenu: javax.swing
JMenu.WinListener: javax.swing
JMenuBar: javax.swing
JMenuBar.AccessibleJMenuBar: javax.swing
JMenuItem: javax.swing
JMenuItem.AccessibleJMenuItem: javax.swing
JOptionPane: javax.swing
JOptionPane.AccessibleJOptionPane: javax.swing
JPanel: javax.swing
JPanel.AccessibleJPanel: javax.swing
JPasswordField: javax.swing
JPasswordField.AccessibleJPasswordField:
    javax.swing
JPopupMenu: javax.swing
JPopupMenu.AccessibleJPopupMenu: javax.swing
JPopupMenu.Separator: javax.swing
JPopupMenu.WindowPopup.AccessibleWindow-
    Popup: javax.swing
JProgressBar: javax.swing
JProgressBar.AccessibleJProgressBar: javax.swing
JRadioButton: javax.swing
JRadioButton.AccessibleJRadioButton: javax.swing
JRadioButtonMenuItem: javax.swing
JRadioButtonMenuItem.AccessibleJRadioButton-
    MenuItem: javax.swing
JRootPane: javax.swing
JRootPane.AccessibleJRootPane: javax.swing
JRootPane.RootLayout: javax.swing
JScrollBar: javax.swing
JScrollBar.AccessibleJScrollBar: javax.swing
JScrollPane: javax.swing
JScrollPane.AccessibleJScrollPane: javax.swing
JScrollPane.ScrollBar: javax.swing
JSeparator: javax.swing
JSeparator.AccessibleJSeparator: javax.swing
JSlider: javax.swing
JSlider.AccessibleJSlider: javax.swing
JSplitPane: javax.swing
JSplitPane.AccessibleJSplitPane: javax.swing
JTabbedPane: javax.swing
JTabbedPane.AccessibleJTabbedPane: javax.swing
JTabbedPane.ModelListener: javax.swing

JTable: javax.swing
JTable.AccessibleJTable: javax.swing
JTable.AccessibleJTable.AccessibleJTableCell:
    javax.swing
JTableHeader: javax.swing.table
JTableHeader.AccessibleJTableHeader:
    javax.swing.table
JTableHeader.AccessibleJTableHeader.Accessible-
    JTableHeaderEntry: javax.swing.table
JTextArea: javax.swing
JTextArea.AccessibleJTextArea: javax.swing
JTextComponent: javax.swing.text
JTextComponent.AccessibleJTextComponent:
    javax.swing.text
JTextComponent.KeyBinding: javax.swing.text
JTextField: javax.swing
JTextField.AccessibleJTextField: javax.swing
JTextPane: javax.swing
JToggleButton: javax.swing
JToggleButton.AccessibleJToggleButton: javax.swing
JToggleButton.ToggleButtonModel: javax.swing
JToolBar: javax.swing
JToolBar.AccessibleJToolBar: javax.swing
JToolBar.Separator: javax.swing
JToolTip: javax.swing
JToolTip.AccessibleJToolTip: javax.swing
JTree: javax.swing
JTree.AccessibleJTree: javax.swing
JTree.AccessibleJTree.AccessibleJTreeNode:
    javax.swing
JTree.DynamicUtilTreeNode: javax.swing
JTree.EmptySelectionModel: javax.swing
JTree.TreeModelHandler: javax.swing
JTree.TreeSelectionRedirector: javax.swing
JViewport: javax.swing
JViewport.AccessibleJViewport: javax.swing
JViewport.ViewListener: javax.swing
JWindow: javax.swing
JWindow.AccessibleJWindow: javax.swing

K

Kernel: java.awt.image
Key: java.awt.RenderingHints
KeyAdapter: java.awt.event
KeyBinding: javax.swing.text.JTextComponent
KeyEvent: java.awt.event
KeyListener: java.awt.event
Keymap: javax.swing.text

KeySelectionManager: javax.swing.JComboBox
KeyStroke: javax.swing

L

Label: java.awt
LabelPeer: java.awt.peer
LabelUI: javax.swing.plaf
LabelView: javax.swing.text
LayeredHighlighter: javax.swing.text
LayeredHighlighter.LayerPainter: javax.swing.text
LayerPainter: javax.swing.text.LayeredHighlighter
LayoutManager: java.awt
LayoutManager2: java.awt
LazyValue: javax.swing.UIDefaults
LeafElement: javax.swing.text.AbstractDocument
LightweightPeer: java.awt.peer
Line2D: java.awt.geom
Line2D.Double: java.awt.geom
Line2D.Float: java.awt.geom
LineBorder: javax.swing.border
LineBorderUIResource: javax.swing.plaf.BorderUIResource
LineBreakMeasurer: java.awt.font
LineMetrics: java.awt.font
LinkController: javax.swing.text.html.HTMLEditorKit
List: java.awt
ListCellRenderer: javax.swing
ListDataEvent: javax.swing.event
ListDataListener: javax.swing.event
ListModel: javax.swing
ListPainter: javax.swing.text.html.StyleSheet
ListPeer: java.awt.peer
ListSelectionEvent: javax.swing.event
ListSelectionListener: javax.swing.event
ListSelectionModel: javax.swing
ListUI: javax.swing.plaf
ListView: javax.swing.text.html
LookAndFeel: javax.swing
LookAndFeelInfo: javax.swing.UIManager
LookupOp: java.awt.image
LookupTable: java.awt.image

M

MatteBorder: javax.swing.border
MatteBorderUIResource: javax.swing.plaf.BorderUIResource
MediaTracker: java.awt
MemoryImageSource: java.awt.image

Menu: java.awt
MenuBar: java.awt
MenuBarPeer: java.awt.peer
MenuBarUI: javax.swing.plaf
MenuComponent: java.awt
MenuComponentPeer: java.awt.peer
MenuContainer: java.awt
MenuDragMouseEvent: javax.swing.event
MenuDragMouseListener: javax.swing.event
MenuElement: javax.swing
MenuEvent: javax.swing.event
MenuItem: java.awt
MenuItemPeer: java.awt.peer
MenuItemUI: javax.swing.plaf
MenuKeyEvent: javax.swing.event
MenuKeyListener: javax.swing.event
MenuListener: javax.swing.event
MenuPeer: java.awt.peer
MenuSelectionManager: javax.swing
MenuShortcut: java.awt
MinimalHTMLWriter: javax.swing.text.html
ModelListener: javax.swing.JTabbedPane
MouseAdapter: java.awt.event
MouseDragGestureRecognizer: java.awt.dnd
MouseEvent: java.awt.event
MouseEventListener: javax.swing.text.html.FormView
MouseInputAdapter: javax.swing.event
MouseInputListener: javax.swing.event
MouseListener: java.awt.event
MouseMotionAdapter: java.awt.event
MouseMotionListener: java.awt.event
MultiPixelPackedSampleModel: java.awt.image
MultipleMaster: java.awt.font
MutableAttributeSet: javax.swing.text
MutableComboBoxModel: javax.swing
MutableTreeNode: javax.swing.tree

N

NamedStyle: javax.swing.text.StyleContext
NodeDimensions: javax.swing.tree.AbstractLayoutCache
NoninvertibleTransformException: java.awt.geom

O

ObjectView: javax.swing.text.html
OpenType: java.awt.font
Option: javax.swing.text.html
OptionPaneUI: javax.swing.plaf

Class
Index

S

SampleModel: java.awt.image
Scrollable: javax.swing
ScrollBar: javax.swing.JScrollPane
Scrollbar: java.awt
ScrollbarPeer: java.awt.peer
ScrollBarUI: javax.swing.plaf
ScrollPane: java.awt
ScrollPaneConstants: javax.swing
ScrollPaneLayout: javax.swing
ScrollPaneLayout.UIResource: javax.swing
ScrollPanePeer: java.awt.peer
ScrollPaneUI: javax.swing.plaf
SectionElement: javax.swing.text.DefaultStyledDocument
Segment: javax.swing.text
Separator: javax.swing.JPopupMenu,
   javax.swing.JToolBar
SeparatorUI: javax.swing.plaf
Shape: java.awt
ShapeGraphicAttribute: java.awt.font
ShortLookupTable: java.awt.image
SimpleAttributeSet: javax.swing.text
SinglePixelPackedSampleModel: java.awt.image
SingleSelectionModel: javax.swing
SizeRequirements: javax.swing
SliderUI: javax.swing.plaf
SmallAttributeSet: javax.swing.text.StyleContext
SoftBevelBorder: javax.swing.border
SpecialAction: javax.swing.text.html.HTMLDocument.HTMLReader
SplitPaneUI: javax.swing.plaf
StateEdit: javax.swing.undo
StateEditable: javax.swing.undo
stillInsideTimerAction: javax.swing.ToolTipManager
StringContent: javax.swing.text
StringSelection: java.awt.datatransfer
Stroke: java.awt
Style: javax.swing.text
StyleConstants: javax.swing.text
StyleConstants.CharacterConstants: javax.swing.text
StyleConstants.ColorConstants: javax.swing.text
StyleConstants.FontConstants: javax.swing.text
StyleConstants.ParagraphConstants: javax.swing.text
StyleContext: javax.swing.text
StyleContext.NamedStyle: javax.swing.text
StyleContext.SmallAttributeSet: javax.swing.text
StyledDocument: javax.swing.text
StyledEditorKit: javax.swing.text

StyledEditorKit.AlignmentAction: javax.swing.text
StyledEditorKit.BoldAction: javax.swing.text
StyledEditorKit.FontFamilyAction: javax.swing.text
StyledEditorKit.FontSizeAction: javax.swing.text
StyledEditorKit.ForegroundAction: javax.swing.text
StyledEditorKit.ItalicAction: javax.swing.text
StyledEditorKit.StyledTextAction: javax.swing.text
StyledEditorKit.UnderlineAction: javax.swing.text
StyledTextAction: javax.swing.text.StyledEditorKit
StyleSheet: javax.swing.text.html
StyleSheet.BoxPainter: javax.swing.text.html
StyleSheet.ListPainter: javax.swing.text.html
SwingConstants: javax.swing
SwingPropertyChangeSupport: javax.swing.event
SwingUtilities: javax.swing
SystemColor: java.awt
SystemFlavorMap: java.awt.datatransfer

T

TabableView: javax.swing.text
TabbedPaneUI: javax.swing.plaf
TabExpander: javax.swing.text
TableCell: javax.swing.text.TableView
TableCellEditor: javax.swing.table
TableCellRenderer: javax.swing.table
TableColumn: javax.swing.table
TableColumnModel: javax.swing.table
TableColumnModelEvent: javax.swing.event
TableColumnModelListener: javax.swing.event
TableHeaderUI: javax.swing.plaf
TableModel: javax.swing.table
TableModelEvent: javax.swing.event
TableModelListener: javax.swing.event
TableRow: javax.swing.text.TableView
TableUI: javax.swing.plaf
TableView: javax.swing.text
TableView.TableCell: javax.swing.text
TableView.TableRow: javax.swing.text
TabSet: javax.swing.text
TabStop: javax.swing.text
Tag: javax.swing.text.html.HTML
TagAction: javax.swing.text.html.HTMLDocument.HTMLReader
TagElement: javax.swing.text.html.parser
TextAction: javax.swing.text
TextArea: java.awt
TextAreaPeer: java.awt.peer
TextAttribute: java.awt.font
TextComponent: java.awt

TextComponentPeer: java.awt.peer
TextEvent: java.awt.event
TextField: java.awt
TextFieldPeer: java.awt.peer
TextHitInfo: java.awt.font
TextLayout: java.awt.font
TextLayout.CaretPolicy: java.awt.font
TextLine.TextLineMetrics: java.awt.font
TextLineMetrics: java.awt.font.TextLine
TextListener: java.awt.event
TextUI: javax.swing.plaf
TexturePaint: java.awt
TileObserver: java.awt.image
Timer: javax.swing
TitledBorder: javax.swing.border
TitledBorderUIResource: javax.swing.plaf.BorderUIResource
ToggleButtonModel: javax.swing.JToggleButton
ToolBarUI: javax.swing.plaf
Toolkit: java.awt
ToolTipManager: javax.swing
ToolTipManager.insideTimerAction: javax.swing
ToolTipManager.outsideTimerAction: javax.swing
ToolTipManager.stillInsideTimerAction: javax.swing
ToolTipUI: javax.swing.plaf
Transferable: java.awt.datatransfer
TransferableProxy: java.awt.dnd.DropTargetContext
TransformAttribute: java.awt.font
Transparency: java.awt
TreeCellEditor: javax.swing.tree
TreeCellRenderer: javax.swing.tree
TreeExpansionEvent: javax.swing.event
TreeExpansionListener: javax.swing.event
TreeModel: javax.swing.tree
TreeModelEvent: javax.swing.event
TreeModelHandler: javax.swing.JTree
TreeModelListener: javax.swing.event
TreeNode: javax.swing.tree
TreePath: javax.swing.tree
TreeSelectionEvent: javax.swing.event
TreeSelectionListener: javax.swing.event
TreeSelectionModel: javax.swing.tree
TreeSelectionRedirector: javax.swing.JTree
TreeUI: javax.swing.plaf
TreeWillExpandListener: javax.swing.event

U

UIDefaults: javax.swing
UIDefaults.ActiveValue: javax.swing
UIDefaults.LazyValue: javax.swing
UIManager: javax.swing
UIManager.LookAndFeelInfo: javax.swing
UIResource: javax.swing.DefaultListCellRenderer,
    javax.swing.plaf, javax.swing.ScrollPaneLayout,
    javax.swing.table.DefaultTableCellRenderer
UnderlineAction: javax.swing.text.StyledEditorKit
UndoableEdit: javax.swing.undo
UndoableEditEvent: javax.swing.event
UndoableEditListener: javax.swing.event
UndoableEditSupport: javax.swing.undo
UndoManager: javax.swing.undo
UnknownTag: javax.swing.text.html.HTML
UnsupportedFlavorException: java.awt.datatransfer
UnsupportedLookAndFeelException: javax.swing
Utilities: javax.swing.text

V

VariableHeightLayoutCache: javax.swing.tree
View: javax.swing.text
ViewFactory: javax.swing.text
ViewListener: javax.swing.JViewport
ViewportLayout: javax.swing
ViewportUI: javax.swing.plaf

W

Window: java.awt
WindowAdapter: java.awt.event
WindowConstants: javax.swing
WindowEvent: java.awt.event
WindowListener: java.awt.event
WindowPeer: java.awt.peer
WinListener: javax.swing.JMenu
WrappedPlainView: javax.swing.text
WritableRaster: java.awt.image
WritableRenderedImage: java.awt.image

Index

C

About the Author

David Flanagan is the author of the bestselling *Java in a Nutshell*. When David isn't busy writing about Java, he is a consulting computer programmer, user interface designer, and trainer. His other books with O'Reilly include *JavaScript: The Definitive Guide, Netscape IFC in a Nutshell, X Toolkit Intrinsics Reference Manual*, and *Motif Tools: Streamlined GUI Design and Programming with the Xmt Library*. David has a degree in computer science and engineering from the Massachusetts Institute of Technology.

Colophon

Our look is the result of reader comments, our own experimentation, and feedback from distribution channels. Distinctive covers complement our distinctive approach to technical topics, breathing personality and life into potentially dry subjects.

The animal appearing on the cover of *Java Foundation Classes in a Nutshell* is a Florida panther (*Felis concolor coryi*), one of the rarest mammals on the globe.

These large cats feature a long slender tail, and are anywhere from pale to dark brown on the top of their bodies, and white to tan on the underside. Their ears, nose, and tip of their tail are almost black. Males range from 100–150 pounds and are seven feet long, while females range from 50–100 pounds and are six feet long. A female can produce one to four kittens every two years, and they become fertile just over the age of two.

Florida panthers used to be found in several southeastern states in the U.S., but urbanization and agriculture have caused their habitat to drastically shrink to the point where these animals can now be found only in Florida. They require some forestation and underbrush, for hunting and nesting, though they can be found in swamplands, as well. They prey primarily on deer, wild hogs, raccoons, and birds.

Florida panthers are highly endangered, with reports of only fifty remaining in the world. The biggest threat is loss of habitat. A few organizations are working to keep this animal from becoming extinct. There is a Florida Panther National Wildlife Refuge in the Big Cypress Watershed on which some female panthers have given birth to and raised their kittens.

Nicole Arigo was the production editor for *Java Foundation Classes in a Nutshell*. Nancy Crumpton provided production services and wrote the index. Nicole Arigo and Jane Ellin provided quality control.

Edie Freedman designed the cover of this book, using an original drawing by Lorrie LeJeune. Kathleen Wilson produced the cover layout with Quark XPress 3.3 using Adobe's ITC Garamond font.

Alicia Cech designed the interior layout based on a series design by Nancy Priest. The text was written in DocBook SGML with extensions developed by Chris Maden and David Flanagan for Java code; the design was implemented in *gtroff* by Lenny Muellner. Interior fonts are Adobe ITC Garamond and Adobe ITC Franklin Gothic. The illustrations that appear in the book were produced by Robert Romano and Rhon Porter using Macromedia Free-Hand 8 and Adobe Photoshop 5. This colophon was written by Nicole Arigo.

Java

Java Servlet Programming

By Jason Hunter with William Crawford
1st Edition November 1998
528 pages, ISBN 1-56592-391-X

Java servlets offer a fast, powerful, portable replacement for CGI scripts. *Java Servlet Programming* covers everything you need to know to write effective servlets. Topics include: serving dynamic Web content, maintaining state information, session tracking, database connectivity using JDBC, and applet-servlet communication.

JavaServer Pages

By Hans Bergsten
1st Edition November 2000 (est.)
450 pages (est.), ISBN 1-56592-746-X

JavaServer Pages shows how to develop Java-based web applications without having to be a hardcore programmer. The author provides an overview of JSP concepts and illuminates how JSP fits into the larger picture of web applications. There are chapters for web authors on generating dynamic content, handling session information, and accessing databases, as well as material for Java programmers on creating Java components and custom JSP tags for web authors to use in JSP pages.

Enterprise JavaBeans, 2nd Edition

By Richard Monson-Haefel
2nd Edition March 2000
492 pages, ISBN 1-56592-869-5

Enterprise JavaBeans, 2nd Edition provides a thorough introduction to EJB 1.1 and 1.0 for the enterprise software developer. It shows you how to develop enterprise Beans to model your business objects and processes. The EJB architecture provides a highly flexible system in which components can easily be reused, and which can be changed to suit your needs without upsetting other parts of the system. *Enterprise JavaBeans* teaches you how to take advantage of the flexibility and simplicity that this powerful new architecture provides.

Java and XML

By Brett McLaughlin
1st Edition June 2000
498 pages, ISBN 0-596-00016-2

Java revolutionized the programming world by providing a platform-independent programming language. XML takes the revolution a step further with a platform-independent language for interchanging data. *Java and XML* shows how to put the two together, building real-world applications in which both the code and the data are truly portable.

Developing Java Beans

By Robert Englander
1st Edition June 1997
316 pages, ISBN 1-56592-289-1

Developing Java Beans is a complete introduction to Java's component architecture. It describes how to write Beans, which are software components that can be used in visual programming environments. This book discusses event adapters, serialization, introspection, property editors, and customizers, and shows how to use Beans within ActiveX controls.

In a Nutshell Quick References

Java in a Nutshell, 3rd Edition

By David Flanagan
3rd Edition November 1999
668 pages, ISBN 1-56592-487-8

The third edition of this bestselling book covers Java 1.2 and 1.3. It contains an advanced introduction to Java and its key APIs and provides quick-reference material on all the classes and interfaces in the following APIs: java.lang, java.io, java.beans, java.math, java.net, java.security, java.text, java.util, and javax.crypto.

In a Nutshell Quick References

Java Enterprise in a Nutshell

By David Flanagan, Jim Farley,
William Crawford & Kris Magnusson
1st Edition September 1999
622 pages, ISBN 1-56592-483-5

The Java Enterprise APIs are essential
building blocks for creating enterprise-
wide distributed applications in Java.
Java Enterprise in a Nutshell covers the
RMI, Java IDL, JDBC, JNDI, Java Servlet,
and Enterprise JavaBeans APIs, providing
a fast-paced tutorial and compact reference material on each of
the technologies. Covers Java 2.

Jini in a Nutshell

By Scott Oaks & Henry Wong
1st Edition March 2000
416 pages, ISBN 1-56592-759-1

Jini is a simple set of Java classes
and services that allows devices (i.e.,
printers) and services (i.e., printing)
to seamlessly interact with each other.
Jini in a Nutshell is an O'Reilly-style
quick reference guide to developing
these services and clients using Jini.
It covers everything an experienced Java programmer needs
to know about Jini, including tutorial chapters to get you up to
speed quickly and reference chapters that analyze and explain
every Java package related to Jini.

Java Examples in a Nutshell, 2nd Edition

By David Flanagan
2nd Edition September 2000
584 pages, ISBN 0-596-00039-1

In *Java Examples in a Nutshell*,
the author of *Java in a Nutshell* has
created an entire book of example
programs that not only serve as great
learning tools, but can also be modified
for individual use. The second edition
of this bestselling book covers Java 1.3,
and includes new chapters on JSP and servlets, XML, Swing,
and Java 2D. This is the book for those who learn best "by
example."

How to stay in touch with O'Reilly

1. Visit Our Award-Winning Site

http://www.oreilly.com/

★ "Top 100 Sites on the Web" —*PC Magazine*
★ "Top 5% Web sites" —*Point Communications*
★ "3-Star site" —*The McKinley Group*

Our web site contains a library of comprehensive product information (including book excerpts and tables of contents), downloadable software, background articles, interviews with technology leaders, links to relevant sites, book cover art, and more. File us in your Bookmarks or Hotlist!

2. Join Our Email Mailing Lists

New Product Releases

To receive automatic email with brief descriptions of all new O'Reilly products as they are released, send email to:
listproc@online.oreilly.com
Put the following information in the first line of your message (*not* in the Subject field):
subscribe oreilly-news

O'Reilly Events

If you'd also like us to send information about trade show events, special promotions, and other O'Reilly events, send email to:
listproc@online.oreilly.com
Put the following information in the first line of your message (*not* in the Subject field):
subscribe oreilly-events

3. Get Examples from Our Books via FTP

There are two ways to access an archive of example files from our books:

Regular FTP

- ftp to:
  ftp.oreilly.com
  (login: anonymous
  password: your email address)
- Point your web browser to:
  ftp://ftp.oreilly.com/

FTPMAIL

- Send an email message to:
  ftpmail@online.oreilly.com
  (Write "help" in the message body)

4. Contact Us via Email

order@oreilly.com
To place a book or software order online. Good for North American and international customers.

subscriptions@oreilly.com
To place an order for any of our newsletters or periodicals.

books@oreilly.com
General questions about any of our books.

software@oreilly.com
For general questions and product information about our software. Check out O'Reilly Software Online at **http://software.oreilly.com/** for software and technical support information. Registered O'Reilly software users send your questions to:
website-support@oreilly.com

cs@oreilly.com
For answers to problems regarding your order or our products.

booktech@oreilly.com
For book content technical questions or corrections.

proposals@oreilly.com
To submit new book or software proposals to our editors and product managers.

international@oreilly.com
For information about our international distributors or translation queries. For a list of our distributors outside of North America check out:
http://www.oreilly.com/www/order/country.html

5. Work with Us

Check out our website for current employment opportunites:
www.jobs@oreilly.com
Click on "Work with Us"

O'Reilly & Associates, Inc.
101 Morris Street, Sebastopol, CA 95472 USA
TEL   707-829-0515 or 800-998-9938
       (6am to 5pm PST)
FAX   707-829-0104

O'REILLY®